The Road Taken

The Road Taken

China's Incorporation Process into the
Capitalist World System and Its Capitalist Transition

SUNG HEE RU

Cover credit: Where "east and west meet" a modern thoroughfare in picturesque Hong Kong. Hong Kong China, ca. 1913. https://www.loc.gov/item/97506047

Published by State University of New York Press, Albany

© 2025 State University of New York

All rights reserved

Printed in the United States of America

No part of this book may be used or reproduced in any manner whatsoever without written permission. No part of this book may be stored in a retrieval system or transmitted in any form or by any means including electronic, electrostatic, magnetic tape, mechanical, photocopying, recording, or otherwise without the prior permission in writing of the publisher.

Links to third-party websites are provided as a convenience and for informational purposes only. They do not constitute an endorsement or an approval of any of the products, services, or opinions of the organization, companies, or individuals. SUNY Press bears no responsibility for the accuracy, legality, or content of a URL, the external website, or for that of subsequent websites.

EU GPSR Authorised Representative:
Logos Europe, 9 rue Nicolas Poussin, 17000, La Rochelle, France
contact@logoseurope.eu

For information, contact State University of New York Press, Albany, NY
www.sunypress.edu

Library of Congress Cataloging-in-Publication Data

Name: Ru, Sung Hee, author.
Title: The road taken : China's incorporation process into the capitalist world system and its capitalist transition / Sung Hee Ru.
Description: Albany : State University of New York Press, [2025] | Includes bibliographical references and index.
Identifiers: ISBN 9798855803075 (hardcover : alk. paper) | ISBN 9798855803051 (ebook) | ISBN 9798855803068 (pbk. : alk. paper)
Further information is available at the Library of Congress.

The historians neither make nor guide history. Their share in such is usually so small as to be almost negligible. But if they do not learn something from history, their activities would then be cultural decoration, or a pleasant pastime, equally useless in these troubled times.

—Eric Williams, *Capitalism and Slavery*

Contents

List of Illustrations	ix
Acknowledgments	xi
Introduction: Nineteenth-Century China, World-Systems Analysis, and China's Incorporation Process	1
Chapter 1. Past Incorporation Studies and an Alternative Approach to China's Incorporation Process	37
Chapter 2. China's Incorporation Process: Production, New Classes, and Geography	63
Chapter 3. China's Incorporation Process: The Interstate System	113
Chapter 4. Global Geopolitics: The Rise of Pacific Powers and Their Impact on China's Incorporation Process	159
Chapter 5. China's Backlash Against the Penetration of the Capitalist World-Economy	193
Conclusion: The Development and Outcomes of China's Incorporation Process	217
Appendix	241
Notes	253
Bibliography	343
Index	389

Illustrations

Figures

I.1	Estimated annual revenue of the central government in the early 1890s	17
I.2	The diagrammatic representation of an analytical framework	33
1.1	Commodities brought from China by the British East India Company	58
2.1	Shipments of Indian opium to China, 1795–1840	66
2.2	Silver holdings by the central government, 1777–1843	69
2.3	China's bullion shipments to India, 1801–1858	71
2.4	The export of Taiwanese tea, 1866–1885	74
2.5	Tea exports from China, India, Ceylon, and Japan to the world, 1890–1920	76
2.6	Statistics of China's tea-exporting countries, 1862–1920	77
2.7	China's major port cities' export volume of tea, 1843–1920	78
2.8	A rise of new economic classes within the logic of the capitalist world-economy	89
2.9	Distribution of the Chinese by US state (1860, 1870, and 1880).	91
2.10	*Qing Yiming Dayunhe Detu* (Map of the Grand Canal)	95
2.11	Interconnections among inland cities through waterways	97
2.12	*Shanghai xian cheng xiang zu jie quan tu* (Complete map of Shanghai County), 1884	99

2.13	Waterfront of the Central District in Hong Kong, 1867	102
2.14	*The Canton Bund, 1915*	104
2.15	Customs revenues from 1841 to 1872	105
2.16	*Coolies unloading tea at Hankow, 1900*	106
2.17	Port city–hinterland relationships during the incorporation process	108
3.1	Diagrammatic representation of an analytical framework of the West's modern state transition	117
4.1	Comparison of British and Japanese interests in China, 1899–1931	178–179
4.2	Soybeans and related products: Export statistics from Yingkou, 1872–1901	181
5.1	The death rate of coolies on ships at sea, 1847–1873	211

Tables

I.1	Qing's Estimated Tax Revenue, 1766–1903	18
I.2	Comparison of the Three Major World-Systems Methodologies	32
2.1	The Export Trade of Canton, 1818 Season	70
2.2	Qing Regime's Opium Prohibition, 1729–1836	72
2.3	Indentured Laborers in Suriname	86
3.1	Projects of the Self-Strengthening Movement, 1860–1870	134–135
3.2	Seven Diplomatic Affairs of the Zongliyamen	141
3.3	Foreign Concessions in China, 1911	154
4.1	Total Population of the European and Pacific Powers, 1890–1938	160
4.2	Energy Consumption of the European and Pacific Powers, 1890–1938	160
4.3	Total Industrial Potential of the European and Pacific Powers in Relative Perspective, 1880–1938	161
5.1	Typology of Three Resistance Movements to the Colonial Powers	215

Acknowledgments

This book analyzes China's integration into the capitalist world-system in the long nineteenth century. It is a revised version of my doctoral dissertation, "China's Incorporation Process into the Capitalist World-Economy, 1780s–1890s." While turning my PhD dissertation into a publishable book, I owe a debt to those who have studied incorporation along with world-systems analysis including Terence K. Hopkins, Immanuel Wallerstein, Peter D. Philips, William G. Martin, Reşat Kasaba, and Wilma A. Dunaway. Just as Isaac Newton (1675) stated that "If I have seen further it is by standing on the shoulders of Giants" (*nanos gigantitum humeris insidentes*), I was able to conduct China's incorporation study by following previous incorporation research.

Most of all, I am indebted to Professor Ravi Palat who set the path for my book project and generously provided a meticulous review and productive and valuable comments and resources to improve my book. Thanks to him, I was able to complete the book project journey. Professor William G. Martin and Professor Frederic Deyo (Department of Sociology, SUNY Binghamton) gave me good advice on the incorporation study for world-systems analysis and East Asian studies, respectively. Their comments inspired me with confidence. Professor Ana Maria Candela (Department of Sociology, SUNY Binghamton) guided me to a deeper understanding of Chinese history, in particular the overseas Chinese experience. Thanks to her kind guidance, I found my own way in the convoluted Ming and Qing history. I also thank Professor Fa-ti Fan (Department of History, SUNY Binghamton) for his productive comments on the dynamic of Inner Asia and the importance of the new Qing historical approach.

Professor P. McMichael of the Department of Development Sociology at Cornell University reviewed an earlier version of my article, "The Critical Appraisal of Existing Comparison Methods: Bringing the Connected Histories into Chinese Stagnation Studies." His kind and generous guidance enabled me to invent and develop the idea of "incorporating dynamics." Professor Robert Gardella (Department of Humanities, US Merchant Marine Academy) provided productive comments on tea cultivation in nineteenth-century China, enabling me to talk about the roles of Chinese tea in the world-economy. Productive communication with Professor Dennis O. Flynn (Professor of Economics, University of the Pacific) provided in-depth knowledge of the global silver trade. Lee Chang Wook (Researcher at the Northeast Asian History Foundation) has been a kind guide to me through readings on the socioeconomic history of the Qing Empire. I am deeply grateful for their historical insight and support.

I am also thankful to Professor Chung Il-Joon (Department of Sociology, Korea University) and Professor Baek Seung-wook (Department of Sociology, Chung-Ang University). Their unstinting support helped me to finish this book project. Professor Kim Hyung Jong (Department of History, Seoul National University) and Yoo Ha Young (Researcher at the Northeast Asian History Foundation) provided me with valuable archival data on the formation of the borders of nineteenth-century China. My gratitude also goes to my colleagues, Huahsuan Chu, Kai Wen Yang, Changling Cai, Jung Sungshin, Jung Chungse, Lee Yeon-Hwa, and Kevin D. Revier, who encouraged me whenever I doubted I was up to the challenge of completing this project.

The staff at the Center for East Asian Studies at Stanford University, Seoul National University Libraries, Kyujanggak Institute for Korean Studies, and Korea University Library gave me a warm welcome whenever I needed to work in the Korean and Chinese archives. The library staff at Stanford University, Seoul National University, and Korea University were very helpful in providing advice and explaining how to access the materials. My research work would be fundamentally rudderless without their unsparing help.

Finally, this book could not have been finished without the support of my family, first and foremost my mother, Hong Jung Sun. It was her dedication to supporting me and her endless love that helped me to finish this book project. Without her support and determination, I could not have started or completed this research.

Part of chapter 1 is based on "The Critical Appraisal of Existing Comparison Methods: Bringing the Connected Histories into Chinese Stagnation Studies," *Journal of Asian Sociology* 48, no. 2 (2019): 231–61. Another part of chapter 1 is based on "A Comparison of Weber's and Wallerstein's Historical Methods: The Contribution of Weber's Methods in Developing Existing World-Systems Methods," *Journal of Asian Sociology* 52, no. 1 (2023): 33–64. Parts of chapter 3 are based on "Conceptualizing China's Tea History in the 19th Century: Incorporation into the Capitalist World-Economy," *Journal of Agrarian Change* 22, no. 4 (2022): 812–30. Another part of chapter 3 appeared in "Mapping Transformation of Nineteenth-Century Chinese Cities Within China's Incorporation Process," *Comparative Sociology* 18 (2019): 822–48. Parts of chapter 5 appeared in "The State Formation of Late Qing China Within Global Geopolitical Dynamics," *Sungkyun Journal of East Asian Studies* 22, no. 1 (2022): 87–111. Another part of chapter 5 appeared in "The Rise of Pacific Powers in the 19th Century Capitalist World-System and China's Incorporation Process," *Korean Journal of Sociology* 56, no. 2 (2022): 119–61. In all cases, I have revised the original articles or papers for this book. I thank the *Journal of Asian Sociology, Journal of Agrarian Change, Comparative*

Sociology, *Sungkyun Journal of East Asian Studies*, and the *Korean Journal of Sociology* for permission to reprint here.

I have received permission to reprint figure 3.12, "Waterfront of Central District in Hong Kong," 1867, and figure 3.13, "The Canton Bund, 1915," from the University of Hong Kong and the Presbyterian Research Centre, respectively. I express my deepest gratitude to Chen Weixin for his support and consideration.

Introduction

Nineteenth-Century China, World-Systems Analysis, and China's Incorporation Process

> In the first part of the nineteenth century, China began a series of transformations that would change the country forever.
>
> —Odd Arne Westad, *Restless Empire: China and the World Since 1750*

Theoretical Frameworks for an Unprecedented Juncture in Nineteenth-Century China

The nineteenth century was a great turning point in global history. The reason I use global history rather than world history is that there are important differences between the two. World history often excludes national history from its own research project. On the contrary, a global historical perspective is not likely to distinguish between national history and global history, but to place its own national history on the global geopolitical stage.[1] Based on the global history concept, the nineteenth century was the first time the Malthusian trap, or material life based on survival, which had lasted from ancient times to the eighteenth century, had been overcome.[2] It was also a period when the world was physically connected as one world thanks to the development of the scientific idea and the rapid technological advance of navigation technology.[3] This approach to the great divergence of the nineteenth century does not end here. As Kenneth Pomeranz pointed out, the nineteenth century was the first time that the West surpassed China in economic development and material abundance, and, as Jack A. Goldstone asserted, it was a time when advanced European countries caught up with Asian countries' technology and moved toward economic-military monopolization.[4]

As these changes occurred in the nineteenth century, many countries in non-European regions also had to undergo changes to keep pace with the global dynamics. China was no exception. The global transformation in the nineteenth century pushed China into the whirlpool of change as well. As they encountered unprecedented changes, often marked by challenges and opportunities, a small number of countries used this external pressure as a driving force for their own internal development and reform plans (e.g., Meiji Japan), whereas many other countries experienced great socioeconomic and political turmoil and the collapse of the ancien régime. The Chinese empire was closer to the latter than the former.[5] When Sun I-yen's plaintive lyric about the fall of a seemingly impregnable Chinese fortress to the barbarians during the First Opium War echoed across China's coastal areas,[6] China encountered an unprecedented crisis. During the nineteenth century, China went into prolonged economic decline, encountered explosive social upheavals, and suffered from the encroachment of foreign powers. This ended in undermining the Qing regime's political authority and socioeconomic system, while rendering Chinese society defenseless against foreign aggression.

Nevertheless, China's great transformation in the nineteenth century was not caused by external pressure alone. I argue rather that, in each important phase of the nineteenth century, external pressure that the Chinese civilization had never experienced before induced and often forced the Chinese empire to make crucial choices. In a situation where the Chinese empire had to make a choice, China either took a path that was considered optimal in its own way or sometimes pioneered a new one; nonetheless, these could not stop the fall of the ancien régime. To borrow the metaphor of Max Weber's idea of "switchmen" (*Weichensteller*),[7] it can be said that in the nineteenth century, on the railroad tracks of the global dynamics and unprecedented external pressure created by these global dynamics, China decided to go in its own direction. Of course, that does not mean that China had taken a wrong or improper choice or path. The Chinese empire took the one less traveled by, and that has made all the difference, if I may borrow Robert Frost's wording.[8]

Yet, from an outside point of view, it seems difficult to dispute that China in the nineteenth century was facing a great crisis. For many decades of the nineteenth century, the Qing Empire just muddled through. Late Qing society got into difficulties from the combined pressures of massive rebellions from below, fiscal crisis, explosive population growth, famine, ecological crisis, and separation and hostility among elites (e.g., the rise of local elites and their anti-Manchu sentiments). Added to this mix, colonial powers infiltrated China on an unprecedented scale. Suddenly the Qing regime, which seemed so strong and solid until the eighteenth century, began to look very frail.

The gloomy and bleak reality of nineteenth-century China, which was distinguished from China's splendid economic prosperity prior to the nineteenth century,[9] has often perplexed historians and comparative historical sociologists because their praise for imperial China's remarkable achievements was suddenly transformed into disparagement and ignorance when they interpreted nineteenth-century China. Comparative or global studies undertaken by historical sociologists since the 1960s have also considered it a Chinese dark age, or the period of the sleeping giant (or the sick man of Asia).[10] Among Chinese researchers, Nan Bingwen and Zhang Xianqing dedicated themselves to finding the Ming's civilization to be a prime example of one that equaled or surpassed Europe's productivity, economic growth, and scientific technology. Nan's high praise of the Ming dynasty, however, contrasted with his derogation of the Qing's civilization and state capabilities. He insisted that China's national power was diminished during the Qing era and that China finally became a semicolony in the mid-nineteenth century or did not transform into a capitalist state.[11]

How should China's decline in the nineteenth century be analyzed? And how much did outside influence accelerate China's decline? To some extent, I believe that external influences changed Chinese society in a more positive way. Andrew Gordon has pointed out, in regard to modern Japanese history, the inevitability of contact with the outside world and ambivalence as positive and negative aspects of external influence in tracing unprecedented changes.[12] Connections with a larger history of the modern world and positive and negative aspects of external impacts are indispensable in studying modern Chinese history. I also believe that Chinese society promoted entry into the modernized and industrialized world by foreign forces on the one hand and accelerated the decline of the ancien régime on the other hand. Thus, different interpretations may be possible depending on which aspects are more emphasized or what position researchers take.

Furthermore, in analyzing changes in Chinese society in the nineteenth century, what are the main points and limitations of past studies discussed in the history and comparative historical sociology? And compared to these past studies, what are the theoretical or methodological advantages of interpreting nineteenth-century Chinee society through the methodological lens of incorporation? The methodological tool of incorporation that I propose here was originally devised in world-systems analysis. Regions located in the external arena of the capitalist world-economy are not directly affected by the logics of the capitalist world-system. However, a zone that was once located in the external arena of the capitalist system becomes part of the capitalist system at a later point in time. This transition process is called the "external arena's incorporation process into the capitalist world-system." In this way, the so-called incorporated areas experience political, economic, sociocultural, and geopolitical changes in tune with the logics of capitalist world-systems. Incorporation studies aim to closely track these processes of transformation. The following section attempts to cover these questions.

China's Decline in the Field of Comparative Historical Sociology

Since Émile Durkheim pointed out that comparative sociology is the essence of sociology,[13] and Charles Tilly formulated his three types of the comparative method—"individualizing comparison," "universalizing comparison," and "variation-finding comparison"[14]—

the comparative approach has become a methodological commonplace in Chinese stagnation studies.[15]

To explore the causes of China's eventual decline in the nineteenth century, comparative historical sociologists have presented several failure factors. First, the Chinese stagnation conception has been developed by a self-generative disparity. Such a dichotomous comparison between the West and the non-West, which is well known throughout the comparative sociology field, originates with Karl Marx and Max Weber. Both share the concept of Europe's exceptionalism: Marx and Weber strongly argue that the genesis of capitalist modernity was in Europe, whereas non-Western regions did not invent it autonomously. According to Weber, in contrast to China, the West developed formal rationality, which contained features of calculability, efficiency, predictability, impersonality, and quantitative calculation. Therefore, Western societies avoided the "magic garden" (*Zaubergarten*).[16] Weber argued that Europe had turned into a "disenchanting world" since the advent of modern society, but that non-European regions, including China, were still strongly influenced by tradition and magic, and thus referred to them as "magic gardens." Western society, in achieving "disenchantment (*Entzauberung*) of the world," invented a distinctive form of socioeconomic order that swept across the globe. Although Weber emphasized the fact that the sociological method (i.e., "ideal type") should be used as a heuristic instrument for understanding historical or time-developmental events or social phenomenon,[17] use of his ideal type to evaluate Chinese society was not liberated from a preconceived and value-laden, Europe-centered epistemology. Marx is no exception. Although Marx contended that China's stagnation was partially connected to the coercive and predatory invasion of colonial powers,[18] the root of his comparative view originates from a Europe-centered epistemology. For Marx, Asian society did not have its own landed property because all private property was controlled by communes or the central government. Marx, therefore, considered that Asian society had not arrived "at landed property, not even in its feudal from."[19] Under such traditional rules, Marx believed that without landed property Asian society could not create the historical energy of capitalism.[20] Preoccupied with the ideas of Western-centered evolution and unitary historical development, he tended to assign a specific developmental stage or mode of production to non-Western societies. In the *Grundrisse*, Marx described Asian society as being in the "Asiatic mode" of production. In his theoretical frame, Asian societies, which were not only controlled by despotic rulers but also had agrarian-centered socioeconomic orders, were static and passive as compared to European ones.

One commonality in Marx's and Weber's arguments is that Europe's giant leap was produced by its societies' immanent dynamics and distinctive developmental trajectory. This idea reinforces the belief that modernity and modern capitalism only developed within the "hermetically sealed and socio-culturally coherent geographical confines of Europe."[21] By defining Western development as a self-generative rise, Europe's exceptionalism is conceptualized as an endogenous or self-propelling path.

On the contrary, China, which did not follow the same developmental course as the West, did not have the chance to attain this advancement. Therefore, China stifled its own socioeconomic evolution.

Marx and Weber gave subsequent researchers considerable room to examine the fruitful question of why only early modern England made great progress, while late imperial China did not;[22] however, the issue of connected history between the West and China has received scant attention. The peculiar trajectory of the nineteenth century in human history, featuring the West's expansion into the rest of the world, including China, offers global connected history; therefore, analytically combining the massive transformations of Chinese society caused by Western expansion with nineteenth-century Chinese history is necessary. However, Marx's and Weber's comparative idea has been reproduced without in-depth discussion of the expansion of Western civilization and its impacts on China.

For instance, Robert Brenner and Christopher Isett, influenced by Marx's idea of European exceptionalism, contended that a strong tie between Chinese peasants and landlords did not need to heavily rely on the necessary items that were traded on the market.[23] These ties were instead based on traditional and personal relationships, not contract-based relationships. This consequently led to the underdevelopment of the market. Plus, according to them, the rapid population increase from 1650 to 1850 was an essential factor in Chinese stagnation in that the amount of arable land did not catch up to the increase of population. Their analysis provides us with informative and insightful ideas in examining late imperial China's sudden decline; nonetheless, they paid little attention to China's stagnation caused by outside impacts. A major problem with this approach to China's stagnation is the lack of connected histories between the West and China.

Influenced by Weber's idea that Western cities are critical resources for the development of capitalism and rationality,[24] Peter Saunders, Brian Elliott, and David McCrone relied on his primary dichotomy of the West's modern rationality and China's enchantment.[25] Such comparative approaches, nonetheless, overshadowed any understanding of the decline of China's inland cities caused by the colonial powers' penetration.

The second methodological lens used by historical sociologists is comparison through agreement and difference. Kenneth Pomeranz used this method to present England and China (in particular, the Yangtze River valley) as having similar socioeconomic developmental patterns until the nineteenth century and to analyze England's great divergence from China after 1800. First, Pomeranz used comparison through agreement to elicit similar traits between Europe and China. For Pomeranz, there is little evidence to support "a quantitative advantage in Western Europe's capital stock before 1800" or "a set of durable circumstances—demographic or otherwise—that gave Europe a significant edge in capital accumulation."[26] Therefore, he reveals a similar developmental pattern in terms of measures like life expectancy, wage levels, and patterns of consumption. By adopting reciprocal comparisons between "parts of Europe" and "parts of China, India, and so on," Pomeranz asserts that China's internally driven growth and economic patterns were comparable to Europe's until 1800. Thus, his basic aim, based on comparison through agreements between Europe and China, was to express doubts about the earlier European victory that had been widely accepted by past Eurocentric scholars. Simultaneously, Pomeranz used comparison through difference to separate England's exceptionalism from China's stagnation. To show how England greatly diverged after 1800, he emphasized two fortuitous factors. The first is the coal deposits in England that contributed to the production of iron and steam engines. The second is the resources from the New World, such as precious metals, large workforces, and massive profits from increased sugar and cotton trading. On the contrary, a sharp population increase in China brought about ecological degradation, such as deforestation and soil depletion caused by the development of farmlands. Unlike England, China did not make a significant breakthrough from its "exceptional resource bonanzas."[27] Faced with an ecological cul de sac, China began to plateau and finally encountered socioeconomic stagnation. This strongly indicates that Pomeranz conducted his analysis of England's great divergence and China's stagnation under the principle of comparison through difference.

Of the new explanations, Ho-Fung Hung's actor-based approach offers us valuable insights about the limited success of the urban entrepreneurial class in seventeenth- and eighteenth-century China, which led to a failed capitalist takeoff. According to him, the Confucian state could not continue developing unlimited opportunities for profiteering, even though the Qing regime had a favorable disposition toward commercial development.[28] The urban entrepreneurial class, compelled to pursue economic interests but not to contradict the country's dominant Confucian ideology, was forced to make every effort to appear favorable to government authorities and to forge strong ties with those from the same hometown to maintain (or expand) their commercial networks. This resulted, on the one hand, in a fairly closed social-economic circle and, on the other hand, in a failure to produce entrepreneurs who were free from government control.

The numerous large-scale social revolts during the late Qing dynasty also directly or indirectly prevented the reproduction of China's entrepreneurial elite. The social rebels who wreaked havoc on Chinese society had strong egalitarian motives and hated, and sometimes executed, China's entrepreneurial elite, who had amassed enormous wealth. For example, the Huizhou merchant class fell during the Taiping Rebellion when rebels massacred Huizhou merchant families in the cities they captured. Furthermore, the emerging military elites of the nineteenth century, even if they had considerable wealth, used it to maintain or develop their military capabilities rather than invest in the further reproduction of capital.[29] In turn, the golden age of late imperial China, which lasted until the nineteenth century, enabled commercial development, urban growth, and rapid the population increase; nonetheless, late imperial China did not enter a new phase in its capitalist transition.[30]

However, these comparative historical studies have also been criticized because of an inattention to connected histories between the West and China in China's stagnation (or radical changes). In fact, these studies contain an implicit or explicit assumption: Each society (or nation-state) being compared is autonomous, self-generating, and self-justifying. There is little consideration of larger forces or external influences from larger entities. The exclusive emphasis on the comparative historical method, in turn, has precluded comparative historical researchers from writing connected historical narratives between the West and China in fostering China's stagnation (or massive transformation). These narratives often compel us to ignore Europe's role in China's stagnation. The insufficient attention to interconnections between the West and non-West has consequently led to omitting the concrete practices of the West in facilitating non-European areas' underdevelopment, while reproducing "methodological internalism."[31]

Some historical sociologists, including Theda Skocpol, Charles Tilly, Jeffery M. Paige, and Eric Wolf, have addressed the international and global-historical context in analyzing China's massive social upheavals or China's decline. Nonetheless, Skocpol tended to emphasize the relative autonomy of the state, which pushed her into paying little attention to the relationships between the outside impacts and China's decline.[32] Tilly insisted that Western Europe had over time evolved a competitive, aggressive, and violent interstate system.[33] Given that each European state was aggressive and violent and its interstate competition went beyond the bounds of European territory, Tilly believed that the global expansion of European interstate competition at least partially influenced the decline of China.[34] However, unlike his interest in the expansion of Europe's interstate system, he was little concerned with the decline of China. Put differently, he did not provide a systematic and detailed explanation for China's decline or the relationship between the Western impacts and the decline of China.[35]

Transformation of China in the Nineteenth Century Through Historians' Eyes

I suggested a couple of approaches that have been widely used by comparative historical sociologists; however, most failed to provide an analysis of outside impacts on China's decline at a critical juncture of nineteenth-century Chinese history. In contrast to the dominant view in the field of comparative historical sociology, a spate of recent historical studies have begun to look at the connected histories. For instance, methodologically, Gurminder K. Bhambra has strongly insisted that the connected histories between Europe and non-European areas give a profound insight into what the modern world is and how it is shaped by these dynamics.[36] Theoretically, Stephen Platt reminded us of the importance of the Opium Wars in China's stagnation.[37] Carl A. Trocki pointed out that opium, one of the important commodities that made up the global political economy of the nineteenth century, caused China's "social decay."[38]

Tansen Sen examined how European powers' reliance on coercive force to achieve their political and economic interests turned the peaceful and mutual relationships in Asia, including China, into imperial connections.[39] This favorable disposition toward interconnected histories contributes to new insights into China's abrupt stagnation or transformation in the nineteenth century.

Even if we exclude recent historical studies of the link between Western influence and the massive transformations of Chinese society in the nineteenth century, historians have extensively discussed this connection.

China and the West in the Nineteenth Century

Researchers in modern Chinese history have viewed the nineteenth century as a century of great divergence for China. By interpreting nineteenth-century China's massive changes, John K. Fairbank, Edwin O. Reischauer, Albert M. Craig, Paul H. Clyde, and Burton F. Beers, in particular, stressed Western effects on China and China's response to Western penetration. Ssu-yū Teng and Fairbank described the unprecedented changes made by contact with the West as follows: "In every sphere of social activity, the old order was challenged, attacked, undermined, or overwhelmed by a complex series of processes—political, economic, social, ideological, cultural—which were set in motion within China as a result of this penetration of an alien and more powerful society."[40] These scholars had a common idea ("the impact-response approach") that the accumulation of Western pressure in the nineteenth century, unlike the earlier history of Sino-Western contacts, brought about a serious threat and a new opportunity (e.g., its contribution to the modernization of China) to Chinese society. Moreover, Chinese society did not simply change to imitate the West. As Fairbank pointed out, changes in Chinese society have progressed only to the extent that China could accept them.[41]

Yet the so-called impact-response approach, which stresses the West's unprecedented effects on nineteenth-century China and China's passive responses, tends to overshadow China's active and effective use of westernized rules in reformulating international relations with neighboring countries. When China signed treaties with neighboring countries, China capitalized on modernized and westernized international rules learned from the Sino-Western treaties during the early and mid-nineteenth century; in doing so, China often held an advantageous position.

For instance, the fisheries agreement between the Qing government and Korea, as a part of the China-Korea Treaty of 1882, showed how the Qing was at an advantage in the Sino-Korean relationship. By defining sea trade and fisheries between China and Korea, the Qing used modernized and westernized protocols to secure its advantage. It consequently signed an agreement guaranteeing favorable terms for itself. Korea was in a disadvantaged position after signing the treaty: "Many fishermen of Shandong flock to the Sochŏngdo and Daechŏngdo of the Hwanghae Province because many fishes migrated to the Korean shores. The annual number of Chinese fishermen who have fishing activities at the Sochŏngdo and Daechŏngdo of Korean territory exceeds 1,000."[42] As seen in the results of the fisheries agreement between the Qing and Korea, the Chinese government skillfully applied westernized and modernized international rules to Korea to maximize its national interest. Kirk Wyne Larsen, in this sense, insisted that it was not Sinocentrism that was used to reestablish the suzerainty of China's Chosŏn policy during and after the port opening period. It rather can be regarded as an "informal imperialism" highlighting a policy to maximize the economic interests of the Qing Empire.[43]

Taking matters one step further, the Qing government played a significant role in helping Chinese merchants enter Korea. Tamgŏlsaeng 譚傑生 (1853–1929) is a representative Chinese merchant who entered the Korean market in the late nineteenth century. In 1885, he opened Tongsunt'ae 同順泰, a store in Seoul that focused on import-export and the wholesale-retail business. From the beginning, Tongsunt'ae had a large share of the Korean market. And when he came to enter the Korean market, Tamgŏlsaeng had a strong relationship with the major Qing officials including Yuan Shikai who was dispatched by the Qing government to Chosŏn. Tongsunt'ae, indeed, achieved rapid growth through transactions with the Chosŏn government.[44]

As an example of Tongsunt'ae's usefulness in transactions with the Chosŏn and Qing government, Tongsunt'ae's name was included in a loan transaction between the two governments. In 1887, the Chosŏn government had to borrow 100,000 *liang* 兩 from the Qing to repay a debt on a ship (i.e., *Ch'angnyongho* 蒼龍號) purchased through Sech'angyanghaeng 世昌洋行.[45] To that end, the Qing government provided a loan to the Chosŏn government in the name of Tongsunt'ae to avoid conflicts related to anti-Chinese opinion in the Chosŏn government (August 19, 1893). On October 6, the Chosŏn government again requested a loan of 100,000 *liang* from the Qing to repay interest on a loan borrowed from the Japan-owned First Bank and past debts borrowed from Walter D. Townsend, an American merchant. No different than the past loan agreement between the Qing and the Chosŏn government, the nominal name lending money in the contract was Tongsunt'ae, not the Qing government.[46] Thanks to being directly involved in the economic transactions between the Chosŏn and Qing governments, Tongsunt'ae enabled China to obtain the Han River navigation rights from the Chosŏn government.[47] Indeed, Tongsunt'ae distributed Chinese lottery tickets[48] to the Korean market and even jumped into the transportation business.[49]

Not only that, with the goal of putting its own political interests first, the Qing government also sometimes broke down the framework of the tributary relationship. To maintain a premodern ideological system centered on Neo-Confucianism and the ancien régime and to keep the traditional framework of international relations, Qing and Chosŏn agreed on the Chosŏn government's isolation policy.[50] Yet, when European colonial powers contacted the Qing government to advance into Korea, the Qing government did not inform the Chosŏn government. For instance, at the end of October 1865, Thomas Francis Wade, one of the British diplomats dispatched to China, relayed a message from the British government to the Chinese government, telling them that British warships were planning to explore the northern coast of China and the area off the coast of Korea and advising the Qing government not to interfere with such British exploration. In addition, Wade mentioned that the Qing government had informed the Korean government of the British warships' expedition plans.[51] In response, the Qing bureaucracy ordered local officials in their coastal areas to cooperate with the British exploration.[52] However, the Qing government did not notify the Korean government of the British government's exploration plan for the Korean coast.[53] To prevent conflicts with Britain and avoid responsibility for the problems between Korea and the Western colonial powers, the Qing regime made most diplomatic and political decisions in its own national interest.

As Mary Wright notes, the Qing government's ambivalent attitude toward Chosŏn after the 1860s was partly inevitable.[54] On the one hand, the Qing regime was reluctant to enter into disputes with European powers over Chosŏn, and on the other hand, it had no moral justification for opening up to Chosŏn without denying the tributary relationship between the Qing and Chosŏn or encouraging Chosŏn to abandon the Confucian traditions on which Chosŏn (and the Qing regime) depended.[55] Even considering the Qing regime's difficult situation with Chosŏn from the 1860s through the 1890s, it cannot be denied that the Qing prioritized its own political interests within the traditional East Asian order and also considered coexistence with the Western international order as a vital interest. The Qing pursued "Chinezation through Western rules" in its economic and diplomatic relations with Chosŏn. Therefore, the Qing regime had to make an ironic claim to the European powers that the isolation policy of Chosŏn had nothing to do with the Qing Empire, while acknowledging the traditional tribute system with Chosŏn and Qing influence over Chosŏn. On these grounds, scholars defining nineteenth-century China as going through a period of "all-out Westernization" render "Chinezation through Western rules" less viable.[56]

Unlike the "impact-response" approach to China's encounter with the West, Marxist historians like Harold Isaacs and Mao Zedong investigated the Qing Empire's rural poverty, economic decline, and governmental weakness from a slightly different angle.[57] They insisted that the violence and coercion of the colonial powers, along with British-led free-trade imperialism, meant that China's underdevelopment was coupled with the colonial powers' rabid exploitation of Chinese resources. As Mao noted, the colonial powers' "purpose is to transform China into their own semi-colony or colony."[58] China's autonomous developmental path was derailed by a predatory invasion of colonial powers. Mao's view of Western imperialism is basically the same as that of Vladimir Lenin, who viewed colonial exploitation as an important factor in capitalist development. Harold Isaacs echoed this point and noted that China's underdevelopment was interdigitated with the colonial powers' political, economic, and social domination.[59] They shared a common belief that China was a colony. They struggled to show the destructive powers of the colonial powers, while marginalizing the existence of a trans-societal entity and conceptual and practical differences between a colony of imperialism and an incorporated area of the capitalist world-economy. Under their intellectual influence some scholars popularized a version of China under the rule of imperialism that called for historical traces of exploitation during the late Qing and the Republic of China. This version was also welcomed by the Chinese Communist Party, which considered Western imperialism a main cause of the underdevelopment of the Chinese economy. By presenting China as a victim of Western imperialism, they kept characterizing imperialism as an optimal extortion mechanism. Clearly, Mao's and Issacs's attempts to provide a fundamental reason for China's underdevelopment found an answer in the coercive and destructive invasions of the colonial powers. China remained weak because Chinese resources and laborers had been exploited by relatively strong colonial powers as well as by China's political system, and government officials had been subordinated by the pressures of the colonial powers. From this perspective, China could be described as a colony or semicolony.

I do not play down the impact of Western colonial powers. Nonetheless, the exclusive emphasis on bilateral relations between the colonial powers and China tends to stigmatize China as a political and economic scapegoat of imperialism, while omitting the benefits China experienced after the colonial powers' penetration into China.[60] In fact, their arguments can best be refuted by noting the rise of a new Chinese class (i.e., compradors, the petit bourgeoisie in port cities, and bankers) that benefited from a turbulent modern China since the nineteenth century. This meant that China experienced both positive and negative results during the colonial powers' penetration, even though the latter was much stronger than the former.

Can the New Qing History Be a Panacea?

In the above discussion I have attributed the intellectual lineage of the global-connected analysis of late Qing history to the impact-response and colonial approaches. In fact, both approaches have investigated how Western-related aspects of nineteenth-century China brought about unprecedented socioeconomic changes. But the growing problem of Ming-Qing China as a part of Chinese history, above all the need for Qing history, has gone unheeded. In fact, the term "Ming-Qing China," foregrounding a Ming-Qing continuum or a similarity between the Ming and Qing historical paths, is inclined to stress common patterns of the Ming and Qing that transcend the narrative of specific events of the Qing.[61]

While the impact-response approach emphasizes the two-sided aspects of Western aggressive penetration and China's response to it, the colonial approach tends to focus more on the unilateral aspect of Western ruthlessness and unprecedented penetration into China. Nevertheless, the two theoretical approaches have common aspects in that social and economic instability increased in late Qing China along with Western development, and traditional ideologies and the old regime's political system fell into decline. Although the late Qing period embraced westernized ideas and institutions and carried out reforms, it did not prevent the decline of the Qing Empire. Furthermore, both of these approaches basically assume that the Ming and Qing dynasties were part of the same long-standing Chinese empire. However, the new Qing history, which questions the fundamental notion that the Ming and Qing are part of the single and continuous long-standing Chinese empire, emphasizes that the Qing empire should be qualitatively distinguished from the Ming. Veering from the new Qing historical view, the erroneous assumption of Ming-Qing China cannot offer valuable explanations of Qing history. Unlike the past two approaches (the impact-response and colonial approach), which explicitly or implicitly agree with the idea of a Ming-Qing continuum, new Qing historians have stressed the uniqueness of the Qing as distinguished from the Ming.[62] In support of the new Qing historical view, Wiliam T. Rowe contended that the Qing historical path occurred not as a part of Chinese history but as a substratum of Manchu history.[63] This strongly implies that the Qing Empire did not emulate the Ming's ruling principles; instead, the Aisin Gioro established its identify as a ruling race and was dedicated to maintaining its own Manchu identity by drawing a racial distinction between Manchu and Han Chinese. Although part of the Manchu identity, like the idea of "Manchu origin," may be subverted for political ends—it evolved from justifying Manchu dominance in the early Qing period to justifying the ruling powers' dominance in the mid-Qing period[64]—the fundamental roots of Manchu identity were distinguished from the Han Chinese. In this sense, Mark C. Elliott called it "Manchu apartheid," or segregation between Manchu and Han Chinese.[65] For these scholars, furthermore, the early nineteenth century is characterized by full-blown Qing imperial expansion and a multiracial society. The Qing Empire extended its territory to the north, west, and south around the early 1800s. After incorporating new frontiers (Xinjiang, Tibet, and Burma), the Qing Empire turned itself into a new type of empire comprising five independent ethnic, linguistic, and cultural units (Manchu, Han Chinese, Mongolian, Tibetan, and Muslim) under the governance of the Aisin Gioro. Patricia Berger developed the idea of a "plurality" of Qing governance by showing how each ethnic group referred to the Qing emperor differently.[66] For Tibetans, the Qing emperor was recognized as the Wheel-King or "chakravatin"; for Manchu people and Mongolians, he was considered "Khan" or "Chinggis Khan"; lastly, for Han Chinese, the Qing emperor was generally accepted as *Huangdi*. In this sense, "the Manchus disseminated different images of rulership to the different subject peoples of their empire."[67] This indicates that early nineteenth-century Qing history is not a mere history of China but also a history of a larger part of Eurasia.

In this sense, when speaking of the Western impact, it needs to be identified as the contact between the West and the Eurasian or Qing Empire (not China). For instance, according to Kim Kwang Min, a new Qing historian, the Qing Empire's political instability after the Opium War undermined its intrinsic development, such as through the fall of the state-sponsored oasis market in Xinjiang. Specifically, he argued that pro-Qing Muslims in the Xinjiang area, supported economically by the Qing regime through silver transfer from China to Central Asia, developed a China-centered eastern market at the border. However, after the Opium War (1839–1842), the Qing regime blocked the silver outflow to Xinjiang, which led to the decline of the oasis market.[68]

These scholars have made an important theoretical contribution in excavating the Qing's distinctive history. However, their epistemological turn, unduly emphasizing the Eurasian context and cultural or political aspects, tends to develop Manchu or Eurasia-centrism, while discounting the connected histories between the West and China. For example, Peter Perdue pointed out the similarities between the interstate competition between European countries that developed after the sixteenth century and geopolitical competition between the Zunghar Mongols, the Russians, and the Qing Empire over the Eurasian continent after the fifteenth century. Driven by geopolitical competition, the Qing Empire, the Zunghar Mongols, and Russia valued war, trade, and diplomacy, and to achieve this, each country developed *stateness*. Based on Charles Maier's assertion that the establishment of borders against external invasions was accomplished by a new concept of the country's social and political territory (and this is not a phenomenon confined to Western Europe),[69] Perdue insisted that the Qing Empire also created its own new border concept. Furthermore, after bringing down the Zunghar regime, the Qing government eliminated the autonomy of pastoralists within the border.[70] Perdue in this sense criticized the logical limitations of the discussion of the European state system: "In sum, the models that argue for distinctive features of a European state system, marked by pluralism, competition, or special core-periphery structures, draw an oversimplified contrast between western Europe and the rest of the Eurasian world. They ignore analogous features found in Eastern Eurasia until 1750, and they fail to assess accurately the interactions between commercial exchange and military force across the continent."[71]

To recapitulate his arguments briefly, a theoretical model that claims the distinctive features of the European state system or Europe's interstate system, namely represented by pluralism and competition-based governance systems, relies on oversimplified contrasts between the West and the rest of the Eurasian world. Thus, if this model is taken uncritically, we may ignore similar features of the European state system found in eastern Eurasia until 1750 and fail to provide accurate explanations of the large-scale interaction of transcontinental and commercial exchange and military competition that happened in eastern Eurasia.

Perdue's argument seems persuasive and convincing. Contrary to the perspectives of some historical sociologists or world history scholars who have attempted to differentiate between the formation of states and geopolitical competition between early modern Europe and late imperial China, he tried to reveal similarities between Western Europe and the Qing Empire. Nonetheless, I am inclined to disagree with Perdue's idea that geopolitical competition in Eurasia including the Qing Empire was similar to competition in Western Europe. This is because Western Europe's interstate competition, which began in the sixteenth century, changed non-European geopolitical environments as well as the European geopolitical environment. This European advantage in turn had grown to a global standard that determined geopolitical characteristics around the world, while Eurasia's interstate competition had consequently failed to achieve geopolitical expansion beyond Eurasia. Indeed, the geopolitical struggle for about one hundred years, in which the Qing Empire struggled for supremacy in the Eurasian region, resulted in the Qing being incorporated into the interstate system of Europe in the nineteenth century. Although it is important to note that some historians focus on "process" itself rather than "outcome," if taken uncritically, the discontinuity of the legacy of interstate competition in the Qing Empire and Eurasia could be ignored. Not only did the Qing Empire lose hegemony in Eurasia to Russia after the nineteenth century, but also, from a larger perspective, ocean-based geopolitical struggles became as important as land-based geopolitical struggles in East Asia after the nineteenth century.

Perdue's research on the rivalry between the Qing Empire, Russia, and the Zunghar regime over supremacy on the Eurasian continent is informative and insightful. Yet, if Eurasia's interstate competition had driven the geopolitical dynamics of the Qing Empire and its march to the west at least until the middle of the eighteenth century, we might well ask this question again: Why did the Qing Empire, which followed a development path similar to Western Europe until the eighteenth century, decline quickly as soon as it entered the nineteenth century? Perdue said that the Qing Empire began to lose dynamism at the national level after the mid-eighteenth century when the empire's western expansion ended. Indeed, he believed that "there is a connection between the completion of frontier expansion in the northwest and China's numerous troubles with social order in the nineteenth century."[72] To be specific, he noted that the decline of the Qing Empire began in earnest with four factors: "Four interacting processes opened the Qing to western European penetration in the nineteenth century: new challengers appeared on the south coast shortly after the defeat of the Mongols; policies that were effective against steppe nomads failed in the maritime environment of the south; the negotiated settlements that balanced Qing central interests with local powerholders began to shift toward decentralization; and commercialization under way since the sixteenth century undermined loyalties to the center."[73] In this context, he concluded that the decline of China and the rise of Europe in the nineteenth century were heavily dependent on "contingent timing."[74] For instance, after the 1780s, British power happened to arrive on the southern coast of China with a desire to expand the opium trade. This, however, was soon after the Qing army won a great victory in the northwest and welcomed the return of the Torghuts.[75] The Qing did not regard Britain's penetration as a significant threat compared to the Mongols they had just defeated. At the same time, socioeconomic tensions within the empire, led by the depletion of arable land in the frontier peripheries, left the Qing regime unable to respond immediately to the threat from the coast.⁷⁶ According to Perdue, these fortuitous circumstances for the British consequently brought China into an unexpected decline.

But was it really accidental that Britain opened up the Chinese market in the 1780s to expand its opium trade? And was it due to accidental timing that the invasion of European maritime powers and the lack of interest in the growth of Qing maritime power led to the sudden decline of the Qing Empire? The advance of European maritime powers into non-European areas including the South China Sea and Indian Ocean (e.g., Taiwan, Batavia, Malacca, and Siam) had continued and even developed over a long period of time coterminous with the Qing's western expansion. As William Atwell shows, starting in the sixteenth and seventeenth centuries global economic trade networks connected the West with Asia through the ocean including intercontinental trade and "regional or country trade within Asia."⁷⁷

The Asian economic system did not change or become incorporated into the Europe-led capitalist world-system at least until the eighteenth century. European maritime powers, in fact, did not impose their will on Asia; on the contrary, they sometimes had to adapt to Asian economic systems.⁷⁸ Indeed, can the importance of the Chinese market in the establishment and maintenance of the triangular India-China-Britain trade in opium, tea, and cotton, which began in earnest around the mid-eighteenth century, be dismissed as a historical coincidence or accidental event? If the expansion of the British opium trade in China can be undervalued as a contingent event, then, on an equal footing, could the western advance of the Qing Empire be interpreted as an accidental historical developmental path of Chinese history rather than as a result of the inevitable developmental path of the Manchu? As can be inferred from Perdue's point of view, prominent accounts of Qing history have a far too limited understanding of the Chinese economy's unprecedented changes caused by these global dynamics.

Unit of Analysis: The Extent of Western Influence

Unlike the new Qing historical studies, a series of Chinese studies have focused on the unit of analysis in analyzing the link between Western influence and socioeconomic changes; the unit of analysis is significant in determining an analytical framework for the Western impact and China's responses to it. By selecting the boundary of the incorporating area or Chinese space influenced by colonial powers, a number of Chinese historians have continued to adhere to a Chinese region or city as a unit of analysis since William G. Skinner's study of urbanization in the nineteenth century.⁷⁹ Based on the idea that "in China, the various city systems were never integrated into a single national system,"⁸⁰ Chinese historians have tackled the uniqueness of the Chinese city. Under their intellectual influence, city identity and everyday life were rediscovered in opposition to the dynastic-focused histories. By doing so, vivid and detailed pictures that cannot be captured by the dynasty-based approach can be obtained in a long-term historical context. Historians continuously applied small-size analysis (e.g., region or city) even in the case of the massive transformations of China created by the West because many rural and inland areas in China were insulated from Western impacts.[81] Elizabeth Perry added that with the lower level of commerce, there were few socioeconomic changes in Huaibei caused by contact with the outside.[82] Rhoads Murphey, hence, argued for the conceptualization of an "urban-rural split"[83] and Lin Man-houng called the urban-rural split of the mid-nineteenth century China's "dual economy."[84] For them, the capitalist mode of production did not spill into the inland areas. Thus, taking the whole of China as an object of study is inapt at describing detailed pictures of colonial powers' impacts: instead, a smaller unit, such as a (port) city-based analysis, may be much more effective at recognizing Western effects.[85]

Nonetheless, a (port) city, as a unit of analysis, makes it difficult to comprehend nineteenth-century China. First, the (port) city-based analysis prevents long-term and large-scale analysis of the multifaceted and sometimes uneven aspects of the Chinese transformation, making it especially difficult to cover unprecedented changes in Chinese society in the nineteenth century. China's transition to a capitalist society, as a quantum leap during and after China's incorporation process, generated a dual but contrary socioeconomic system: one part was ruled by the precapitalist mode of production and the other by the capitalist mode of production. Obviously, in most inland areas of China a traditional and agricultural economy still prospered. The condition of the coastal areas of China—in particular port cities—was contingent upon the sea trade led by Western merchants. Under this circumstance, a certain exclusive emphasis on the (port) city without consideration of other areas is apt to override a whole picture of social changes. Given that structural changes in China's politics, economy, and social system during China's incorporation process progressed ceaselessly and sometimes moved at a glacial pace, the parochial approach consequently makes it difficult for us to comprehend integral parts or critical moments of China's massive transformation.[86]

Second, an increasing concern with the spatial division between city (or town) and country and a relatively narrow focus on cities ingrained a parochial idea that developmental paths between city and countryside were so different that they should be treated separately, without consideration of the relationships between city and countryside. By considering the city category as a distinct and coherent entity, researchers tended to assume that a city was a self-contained and discrete social unit and thus comparable to others. Those who are predisposed to reify Chinese city boundaries, however, often omitted relationships between city and hinterland. The relationships (or network) between the city and the hinterlands should not be ignored because the basic and main elements of the urban form overlapped significantly with the hinterlands.[87]

The immoderate increase in these Chinese urban histories went a long way toward illuminating all the specialized and distinctive cities of China, but their limited scope makes it quite difficult to provide a relational context between city and hinterlands. The predominant view of Chinese historians makes it difficult to explore the relationships between city and hinterlands because it is prone to fix the boundary of the city and ignore factors extraneous to city-related issues.

Third, because Chinese historians have focused on the (port) city as a place of penetration by the colonial powers, they were prone to analytically liberate port cities (e.g., Canton and Shanghai) from the influence of China's central government. Although these cities were relatively freed from the central government's control after the 1840s, port cities were not autonomous political and economic places totally liberated from the influences of the central government. Conversely, in China these cities played a centripetal role in ensuring a regular source of revenue to relieve the government's severe financial hardship (see figure I.1 and table I.1).

Figure I.1. and table I.1. illustrate the profound significance of foreign maritime customs for the central government's fiscal revenue and can help elaborate on the interrelationship between the Qing's central government and port cities. This insight is also supported by Donna Brunero's study of the Chinese Maritime Customs Service.[88] She revealed that the service, which was located in port cities, was an important source of revenue for the Qing government. Because an invaluable source of revenue and financial security originated from the international trade of Chinese port cities, the Qing government (and later Republican governments) was dedicated to connecting with port cities. In this sense, without consideration of the inseparable relationship between city and government, sole emphasis on the relationships between cities and the world-economy will reintroduce another problem. Therefore, despite the tangible

Figure I.1. Estimated annual revenue of the central government in the early 1890s. *Source*: Created by the author, based on George Jamieson, "Report on the Revenue and Expenditure of the Chinese Empire," Foreign Office, Miscellaneous Series, No. 415 (London: H. M. Stationery Office, 1897), 33.

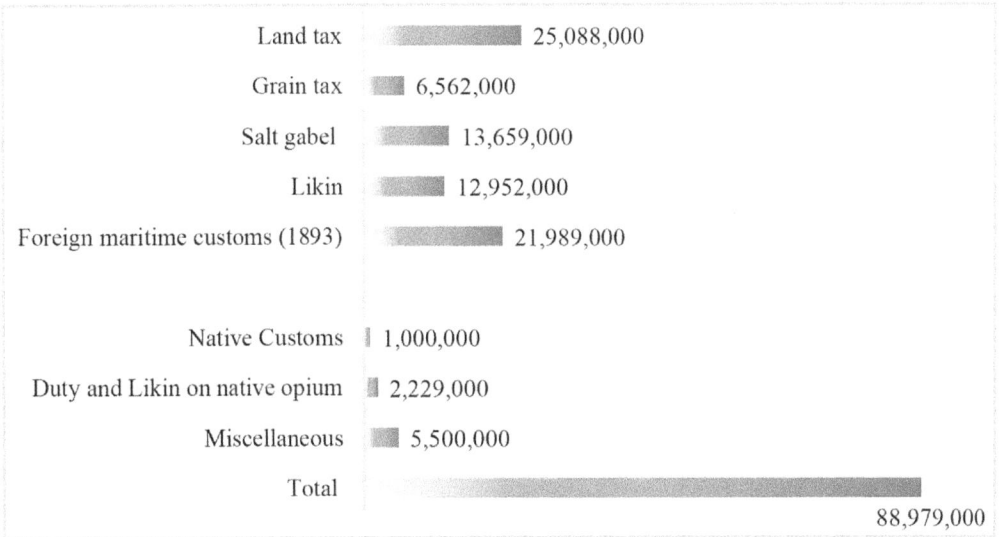

Land tax	25,088,000
Grain tax	6,562,000
Salt gabel	13,659,000
Likin	12,952,000
Foreign maritime customs (1893)	21,989,000
Native Customs	1,000,000
Duty and Likin on native opium	2,229,000
Miscellaneous	5,500,000
Total	88,979,000

Table I.1. Qing's Estimated Tax Revenue, 1766–1903 (in 1,000 taels)*

Year	Land tax	Salt tax	Customs (native and foreign maritime customs)	Miscellaneous taxes	Total
1766	54,214	8,768	5,405	5,405	73,702
1885	32,450	7,390	30,180	7,140	77,160
1903	35,460	12,500	53,400	3,560	104,920

*Yeh-chien Wang, *Land Taxation in Imperial China, 1750–1911* (Harvard University Press, 1973), 72; Yumin Zhou 周育民, *Wan Qing caizheng yu shehui bianqian* 晚清财政与社会变迁 [Financial and social changes in the late Qing] (Shanghai renmin chubanshe, 2000), 239; Zhichu Zhou 周志初, *Wan Qing caizheng jingji yanjiu* 晚清財政經濟研究 [Research into fiscal policy and economy during the late Qing] (Qirushushe, 2002), 187.

rewards of the city-based approach, I will consider both city and China as a whole as a unit of analysis in illustrating China's transformations.

In addition, a state-centered approach also tends to present us with analytical difficulties in looking at Chinese history and global history together. State-centered studies, although not all of them, trapped by the narrow scope of China's reality, have often missed the important connections between China and trans-societal entities. In terms of studies based on archival data, state-centered studies have adhered to the narrow question of whether China's fiscal conditions, social class arrangements, or antigovernment rebellions were related to nineteenth-century China's decline and, if so, to what extent each was a factor. For example, Philip Kuhn concluded that the Chinese crisis in the late eighteenth century originated from accumulated tensions between a strong and effective centralized government and independent and uncontrollable local communities, and included chronic abuses embedded in the tax system.[89] The Qing regime brought "the authority of the throne, the discipline of the bureaucracy, and the efficiency of imperial communication to a level previously unknown in Chinese history,"[90] based on the idea that "governing a huge society with a small bureaucracy"[91] was effective, at least until the eighteenth century. Nonetheless, after the late eighteenth century, when the population surged, the instability of the governance system increased, caused by the disparity between a small but well-organized central bureaucratic system and weakened governance over the local areas. As control over the local community became increasingly tenuous, local administration and local tax collections were left at the mercy of low-status men like "clerks and runners including tax-collectors and process-servers."[92] In addition, due mainly to the requirement for timely payment of tax to be sent to the central government, most county magistrates had to rely heavily on clerks' capabilities in collecting taxes. Under this circumstance, "every magistrate found himself a co-conspirator with his clerks,"[93] which in turn kept the taxpayers "in a condition of debt peonage."[94] This brought about the rise of local moneylenders and induced local elites to engage in tax evasion and embezzlement like "hiding defalcations under the general heading of 'taxpayer deficits.'"[95] Certain historians, including Kuhn, however, focus on a limited research topic, while discounting the connections among various Chinese socioeconomic-political-international circumstances. This epistemic restriction of historians may induce us to use global historical narratives, especially world-system analysis. As discussion of global historical context has proceeded, it has—given its macrohistorical narratives and transnational approach—persuasively led to a reevaluation of China's historical path and its unprecedented transformations in global history. This sheds light beyond the borders of China, while avoiding ongoing monolithic explanations rooted in narrow historical research.

Synthesis Discussion: Sociological and Historical Epistemology and Historical Juncture in Nineteenth-Century China

In the previous section, I reviewed the different approaches for analyzing socioeconomic and spatial changes in late imperial China. Comparative historical sociologists present two types of comparison methods. One is comparison through self-generative disparity (Marx and Weber), which emphasizes a self-fulfilling or self-congratulatory view of Europe's developmental path and draws a boundary line between Europe and China. The other is comparison through agreement and difference (Pomeranz), which stresses both similar traits between England and China (a similar economic development until the nineteenth century) and different traits between England and China (exceptional development of England during the nineteenth century). These types of comparison, however, contain an implicit or explicit assumption: each society (or nation-state) being compared is autonomous, self-generating, and self-justifying. There is little consideration of external influences or connected histories between Europe and China in analyzing nineteenth-century China's decline or transformations.

Compared with comparative historical sociology, historical studies have done a lot to illuminate the outside impact that led to massive changes in Chinese society during the nineteenth century. The impact-response approach helps us to grasp the powerful influences of the West and China's response to the West and how these affected the ancien régime's decline. Also, a series of historians drawing upon the colonial perspective strongly argue that China's failure to become a capitalist state is related to the forceful invasions and resource exploitation of China by Western Europe. They attribute China's underdevelopment and the collapse of the Qing Empire to European exploitation.

Other historical approaches (i.e., city-based studies, the state-centered approach, and the new Qing history) play an important role in developing detailed narratives of individual cities or a more accurate account of Qing dynamics or decline. They help offset stubborn theoretical weakness in comparative historical sociology, stemming from its original purposes. The fundamental aim of comparative historical sociology is to seek "an historically-grounded causal analysis,"[96] or the universal principle of causality. Comparative historical sociologists often, but not always, fail to offer in-depth explanations of the subject of study or historical cases. This may lead to a decoupling between concrete but important historical facts and a causality of historical generalization or an ignorance of historical specificities. These historical approaches will be welcomed in the field of comparative historical sociology, as these are expected to contribute to the development of a more sophisticated causality.

Despite the theoretical merits of the first two approaches in the field of history (i.e., the impact and response approach and the colonial approach), these historians share a common ground in that their approach accentuates the aggressive penetrations of the colonial powers. Late imperial China is often described as a victim of the expansion of colonial powers, and its transformation as unavoidable changes based on compulsion. The existence of a predominant view—the colonial powers' involvement in the exploitation of China's resources—is not the real problem. More concerning is that the uniformity of this view has led to an unconditional acceptance of the negative impact of the colonial presence on China's massive transformations. As a result, these approaches have given a negative and passive portrayal of China's transformations without the historical facts of the positive impacts of the colonial powers and China's active response to the West. It is difficult to deny that the encroachment of colonial powers brought about social turmoil, political insecurity for the ancien régime, financial difficulty, and a number of casualties; however, both the impact-response approach and the colonial perspective look at only one aspect while ignoring the other.

The city-based approach, the state-centered approach, and the new Qing historical view also have theoretical problems. Given that city-based historical studies usually stay at a far less general level of analysis, their intellectual boundary remains consistently within delimited themes. However, the exclusive emphasis on the micro-level units of analysis (e.g., city) make it impossible for researchers to grasp city-hinterland relationships or large-scale social changes. For example, in her study of Shanghai, Emily Honig notes that the "foreign development of industry in Shanghai had a profound effect on the Jiangsu rural economy. It intensified the division of the province at the Yangtze River, such that southern and northern Jiangsu came to represent, respectively, wealth and poverty."[97] Due mainly to Western effects, Shanghai paved the way for an international commercial center, while the Subei economy of northern Jiangsu Province remained poor. The intraregional disparities between Shanghai, in a booming region, and Subei, in a languishing region—though the two cities are geographically close to each other—prompted an exodus of Subei residents. Many of Subei's poor moved to Shanghai and became unskilled laborers as the economic gap between Shanghai and Subei grew. As seen from this account, measuring Shanghai simply as an isolated port city and defining it as an autonomous and independent unit of analysis is a very poor guide to a study of China's incorporation into capitalism. The evolving path of Shanghai in China's incorporation process was interlocked with its neighboring areas.

In this sense, investigating such a relationship between a port city and its surrounding areas in the evolution of China's incorporation process requires us to not do spatially delimited research but to conduct a more far-reaching spatial study.

The state-centered approach is not much different from city-based studies. The state-centered approach often prioritizes internal dynamics or internal factors in examining China's transformation. Making the state a unit of analysis while simultaneously viewing it as insulated from the outside world is ineffective, at least in analyzing the unprecedented transformation of China in the nineteenth century.

The new Qing historical perspective fails to explain how China made unprecedented contact with the West in the nineteenth century. Making histories of the Qing Empire the main research theme without detailed narratives of global connections make nineteenth-century Chinese histories very unrealistic because they seem to arise out of the flat Manchu (or Eurasian) history. Thus, any narrow assessment of how the Qing Empire came into being and then evolved will explicitly or implicitly rest on a whole raft of ideas that can be shown to be profoundly mistaken about many of the important features of the Western impact on Qing history and Chinese modern history.

These criticisms of comparative methods of historical sociology and the historical approach, however, do not mean that all of them are ineffective or unfruitful. Insofar as historical sociology tries to find causal linkages among historical events and the systemic significance of historical processes, it enables us to place China's long-term social, political, and economic changes within a systematic and structured perspective. In addition, the historical framework shows us the multidimensional distinctiveness of nineteenth-century Chinese society's changes and allows us to escape from an invisible trap that is prone to marginalize an abstract, intangible, but important cataclysm of Chinese society.

The impact-response framework, colonial perspective, city-based approach, state-centered approach, and new Qing history have not given a fuller picture of the relationships between China and global dynamics. However, I cannot rule out their theoretical contributions; they have uncovered historical evidence in which China's distinctive experiences along with Western-influenced change does matter. The impact-response approach and colonial perspective assume in common that late imperial China's general changes, caused by coercive Western impacts, fostered the westernization of China. City-based and state-centered approaches help to interpret the massive transformations of each port city or country-level changes during the nineteenth century. The new Qing historical approach offers us valuable insights about long-term Manchu and Eurasian history, which contribute to analyzing the dynamics of northeastern border regions (especially after the penetration of Russia and Japan). On all these grounds, in tracing nineteenth-century China's massive changes, I will partially accept theoretical insights from the five different historical perspectives.

My approach thus intends to strengthen and sharpen the advantages and compensate for the disadvantages in sociological and historical approaches to Chinese studies.

To that end, I will propose a theory that I am calling the "incorporation process" and a new methodological approach that I am calling "incorporating dynamics."

Incorporation Process: A Theoretical Framework for Nineteenth-Century Chinese History

In this book, I aim to examine nineteenth-century China's massive transformation by using a world-systems perspective, in particular the incorporation process. Within the literature of world-systems research, the incorporation theme has attracted much attention because it contains the essential idea of the self-expansion process of the capitalist world-economy.[98] Since the capitalist world-economy constitutes a set of ongoing international divisions of labor networks and globalized production systems over time, one of the main themes of world-systems studies is the incorporation process.[99] The entire process is characterized as a coercive expansion of the European-led capitalist mode of production and the responses of external arenas to the capitalist world-economy in the *longue-durée*. It has often been called an external arena's incorporation process into the capitalist world-economy.

Why are incorporation studies so important? Simply put, by examining the process of incorporation we can demonstrate the self-fulfilling expansiveness of the capitalist world-system while also tracing the political, economic, social, and cultural changes in the regions that are being incorporated. The capitalist world-system links a myriad of national, regional, racial, gender, and other economic, political, and cultural structures within the logics of capitalism (e.g., networks of inequality). The problem is that, as long as the capitalist world-system exists, these unequal networks are constantly expanded and reproduced, and in order to do so the capitalist world-system, like a juggernaut, incorporates all noncapitalist regions into the system. It is important to analyze how the capitalist world-system has incorporated different cultures, political and economic structures, cultural systems, races, and genders into its networks, and how they have come to internalize the logics of the capitalist world-system. In other words, incorporation studies aim to explain the new or changed political and economic systems, cultural systems, and race, gender, and class relations observed in the incorporated areas and to elaborate the historical development of their roles and functions within the capitalist world-system. Incorporation studies have been considered important because of their explanatory power.

With this in mind, the conception of China's incorporation process differs from Dipesh Chakrabarty's description—"first in the West, and then elsewhere"—as an isomorphic phenomenon of a European model.[100] China's incorporation process is rather understood as a process of subsuming into a trans-societal entity. Assuming that the development of the capitalist world-economy represents the dynamics of a trans-societal system, studying the incorporation process is in itself significant, not only for revealing how capital accumulates through an alliance between capitalists and states[101] but also for showing how incorporated regions are coming to terms with and responding to the transnational system, the global production system, the logics of the international division of labor, and the changing spatial geography of capital accumulation.

In focusing attention on China's incorporation process, my premise is that China's transformations occurred within the boundary of the expansion of the European-led capitalist mode of production rather than within the boundary of the Chinese empire.

Obviously, the rise of European mercantilism marked a new epoch not only in Europe but elsewhere as well. Associated with the geographic exploration of (to them) unknown territories, European merchants were supported by their governments and enlarged the scope of the market and developed the forces that led to capitalism.[102] In general, those who engage in trade, whether long distance or not, aim to be peaceful (*doux commerce*), with the goal of increasing surplus and lowering production costs through the specialization of production. Furthermore, trading in the marketplace, in Adam Smith's view, transforms individual economic greed into social prosperity, leading to an economically prosperous world. Unlike the expectation of Adam Smith—the optimum use of human skills and free and fair trade in an advanced mercantile system[103]—European states instead depended on violent means, monopolies, and exploitation, along with plundering and looting by establishing a globalized market[104] beginning in the sixteenth century. Crucial in this respect is that the zone of European capitalism is mainly composed of "monopoly" and "exploitation: that is, unequal or forced exchange,"[105] "the conquest and plunder of the oceans and continents,"[106] and these extra-European resources were central to the development of European capitalism.[107]

When it comes to Europe's rise, I accept the fact that Europe enjoyed second-mover advantages before the fifteenth century. According to Alexander Anievas and Kerem Nişancioğlu, the expansion of the Mongol Empire enabled Italian city-states to stimulate economic development through international trade and cultural exchange. In addition, Europe, as a latecomer, reaped advantages, such as "mathematics, navigational invention, arts of war, and significant military technologies."[108] Taking matters one step further, Prasannan Parthasarathi contends that the economic dynamics of eighteenth-century Europe, spurred by Indian and Chinese imports, led to its industrialization.[109]

However, the capitalist world-system created by European countries in the late fifteenth or early sixteenth century generated a global capitalism that was qualitatively different from the existing economic systems. The capitalist world-system, having transformed European and non-European networks into a dense web, began to devour the resources of the non-European world. Since these resources were the fuel that allowed the capitalist world-system that originated in Europe to expand throughout the world, all means were used to capture them. Fernand Braudel noted the emergence of monopoly as a new type of exchange relationship created by long-distance trade, which led to the formation of capitalism. Marx argued that the West's expansion into the non-West and its acquisition of non-West resources played an important role in the rise of capitalism.[110] Building on Marx's analysis of the advent of capitalism, Leon Trotsky suggested it was characterized by "the combined and uneven development of capitalism on a global scale."[111] And when the European world-economy made its own distinctive economic path and expanded its boundaries to Asia, China was gradually subsumed into the capitalist world-economy. The outcome of this integration was a set of remarkable transformations of Chinese society. This view emphasizes not only intentional, preplanned, and strategic movements of the capitalist world-economy's expansion but also the violent and coercive effects of the capitalist world-economy. It contrasts with dominant analyses prioritizing China's autonomous changes and self-transforming growth from a precapitalist mode of production to a capitalist mode of production during the late imperial period.

Nonetheless, Wallerstein's concept of incorporation is not necessarily the one that I use in this research. In Wallerstein's view, incorporation is designed to explain the origins and development of the peripheries that were continuously produced in the spatial expansion of the capitalist world-system that emerged in modern Europe.[112] Incorporation refers to the process by which a region outside the capitalist world-system is gradually transformed into a part of the system, and once incorporation is complete, the region is eventually transformed into a periphery. Wallerstein describes this process in three stages: "the mode we are using involves three successive moments for a zone: being in the external arena, being incorporated and being peripheralized. None of these moments is static; all of them involve processes."[113] Hence, for Wallerstein, incorporation is a theoretical tool for tracing the ongoing historical production of the periphery, which is the least powerful entity in the unequal core-semiperiphery-periphery dynamic that underpins the capitalist world-system.

However, in the case of Wallerstein, in analyzing the process of incorporation, he tended to emphasize mainly the political and economic aspects[114] and overly simplified the process of incorporation.[115] Furthermore, he focused on a one-way process. By focusing exclusively on how the incorporated areas accept the logic of the capitalist world-system and what political and economic changes occur in this process, the historical context of the reactions of the incorporated areas (e.g., resistance to the logics of the capitalist world-system) is often omitted. At the same time, there is little consideration of the influence that the incorporated or incorporating areas can exert on the dynamics of the capitalist world-system, even if it is relatively weak compared to the influence of the capitalist world-system on the incorporated areas.

In order to overcome Wallerstein's analytical weaknesses and to trace in detail the complex and diverse ways in which China's incorporation process has taken place, I will cover the (a) socioeconomic changes identified during China's incorporation process, but also the political, cultural, and spatial changes, as well as (b) the changes in frontier and contact zones (e.g., the rise of port cities or geopolitical and geoeconomic demarcation of borders), to further elaborate on the distinctive features identified in

China's incorporation process. Furthermore, I will present (c) the various types of resistance that emerged in China's incorporation process and the impact of China's incorporation process on the capitalist world-system.

Based on this schema, what happened during the incorporation processes of the external arenas, including that of China? One was the reorganization of the production process. Faced with the capitalist world-economy's expansion, an external arena's economic system was reorganized to serve the globalized production networks of capitalism. In the case of China, the development of entrepôts to increase international trade volumes, entry into the international commodity chains, and workers' (e.g., coolies') participation in the axial division of labor were evident during the incorporation process. The second fundamental structural transformation involved a change from an ancien régime to an interstate system, as the society was restructured within a globalized hierarchical frame. In other words, almost all parts of precapitalist political structures declined and were simultaneously reconstituted as part of the interstate system in response to the capitalist world-economy. As was the case in China, during the nineteenth century its political structure and tributary system was debilitated.

In contrast to the methodological approach of historical sociology, this incorporation process stemming from world-systems analysis allows us to include these outside impacts in investigating nineteenth-century China. According to Wallerstein, cross-national comparisons consider a state (or society) as a self-evident and discrete social unit, and thus it can be compared to others. He criticizes cross-national comparisons, however, because to make them is "to reify parts of the totality into such units and then to compare these reified structures."[116] Cross-national comparisons transform a historical and dynamic society (or state) into an ahistorical structure and unchanged society (or state). In contrast, Wallerstein contends that "social change can only be understood as an historical system that operates at a different level from the conventional national society."[117] Unlike cross-national comparisons that "place nations within systemic processes operating at levels 'beneath' and 'above' the nation state,"[118] Wallerstein proposed the modern world-system, with its "transsocietal structures," which has existed for the last five centuries.[119] World-systems do not consider a state (or society) as a "universal" and "discrete" category. Rather, a state (or society) is structured and restructured in the development processes of the world-systems.[120] Wallerstein's analysis is compelled to move away from any assumption of a self-regulating nation-state and toward a description of the process of continual change for nation-states within the larger canvas of the world-economy. The world-systems perspective's maneuver has successfully challenged exclusive state-based comparisons propagated by past (comparative) historical sociologists and it also brings in outside influence and the relational processes between the world-economy and states.

In addition, unlike the theoretical approaches of historians (e.g., the colonial approach), it also enables us to include China's active response and positive impacts during and after the penetration of the foreign powers. Calling China an incorporated area of the capitalist world-economy should not categorize it simply as the prey of imperial plunderers but as a relatively weak member of the hierarchical and competitive world market system. This idea most of all allows us to consider the possibility of China's rise after the nineteenth century.[121] In this regard, Wallerstein argued that the political reconstruction of an incorporated area does not need to be as a colonial state.[122] He also insisted that "we know, by looking backward in history, that among peripheral countries some have changed status."[123] To systematically theorize the cases that experienced upward shifts within the capitalist world-economy, Wallerstein presented three ideal types: "the strategy of seizing the chance, the strategy of promotion by invitation, and the strategy of self-reliance."[124]

Giovanni Arrighi, as a world-systems researcher, looked more into how China's incorporation process into the capitalist world-economy paved the way for the expansion of the network of overseas Chinese and their businesses. In a process begun by the Opium Wars and large-scale uprisings, the Qing government's control of the international movements of commodities and people loosened. The weakening of the Qing government's control may have opened the door to new opportunities for overseas Chinese businesses. Arrighi argued that the opium trade and coolie trade were good opportunities for overseas Chinese businesses to expand and consequently led to their rise.[125] Furthermore, when we view the Chinese defeat in the First Sino-Japanese War (1895) through the prism of economic development, it at least partially paved the way for Pacific powers, including the Russians, Japanese, and Americans, and an expanded group of European powers' direct investment in the Chinese economy.[126]

Such a theoretical frame of the incorporated area of the capitalist world-economy was not initially established to analyze the underdevelopment of a colony, nor is it a theory of the unequal (and international) relationships between colonial powers and colonies.[127] On the contrary, the incorporated area operated by the logic of the capitalist mode of production. It strongly implies that China, defined as an incorporated area, cannot simply be equated to, or confined within, the unequal relationships between Western colonial powers and China. By using a world-systems perspective I can do more; I can dig deeper.

Furthermore, the expansion of the capitalist world-system tended to produce a strong Eurocentric idea and spread it to the incorporated areas. In the process of China's incorporation, certain ideological perspectives were likely to define Chinese society as an underdeveloped and inferior civilization (or semicivilized country) or as an object to be enlightened, while valuing Western knowledge and culture and justifying Europe's entry into China. The more Chinese society experienced the economic and military power of European countries, the more Chinese intellectuals and bureaucrats rushed to accept European ideologies. The internalization of Europe-centered ideas emerged in the process of China's incorporation and infused the Western standard of civilization into Chinese society[128] and stipulated that this is a global standard and value.

Considering these aspects, the idea of a "contact zone" proposed by Mary Louise Pratt may usefully complement world-systems analysis.[129] The contact zone deals mainly with the geoculture of colonial regions created by the mutual relationship between colonies and mother countries.[130] The theoretical idea of the contact zone refers to the dyadic model, thereby featuring a narrower place and relations concept compared to the idea of incorporated areas. However, the contact zone and the incorporated areas have some important common characteristics like asymmetric and unequal relationships between countries with strong economic-diplomatic-military power and countries (regions) with relatively weak economic-diplomatic-military power, and yet, paradoxical as it may seem, these relationships create a situation in which both are influencing each other.

More importantly, the culture and knowledge of the incorporated area are sometimes transformed according to the direction required by global rules. As Lydia Liu points out, the global rules of the capitalist world-system directly or indirectly exert pressure on incorporated areas.[131] For example, the concept of modern sovereignty with capitalist logics urged (or induced) incorporated areas to embrace a new set of socioeconomic and political rules or norms. Liu analyzed how the concept of barbarian came to occupy a special intercultural (and interlingual) status in the course of the military conflict between Britain and the Qing Empire, and then showed how the translation of barbarian/*yi* was reborn and fixed by British intellectuals and bureaucrats. By presenting a fixedly paired translation of barbarian/*yi*, Liu discussed how the European world's desire and legitimacy for colonial expansion were formed at the ideological level. Liu's analysis is an example of the Western-oriented ideological power that can be observed during China's incorporation process.

Lastly, by using the incorporation idea, we could consider not only the port city and China as a whole but also a larger entity (the world-economy) as a unit of analysis in explaining China's incorporation process. Researchers need to look at relationships between the dynamics of the world-economy at a transnational level and the transformations of city, hinterlands, and China as a whole, on the local (or city) and national level. The dynamics generated by these interconnections show detailed historical narratives representing interrelationships between China and the world-economy; thereby, we can observe China's changing process that is harmonized (and sometimes disharmonized) with capitalist development.

Methodological Frameworks for China's Incorporation Process: The Modern World-Systems, Incorporating Comparison, World Region, and Incorporating Dynamics

This book attempts to work through theoretical and methodological issues within world-systems analysis through a close engagement with one of its more controversial—but relatively understudied—incorporation studies, China's incorporation process. Theoretically, the incorporation process of world-systems analysis has many advantages.

Methodologically, however, conventional world-systems analysis has been criticized for its functional and holistic approach to the capitalist world-economy. Stanley Aronowitz and David Washbrook are among those who have expressed negative opinions on this.[132] Wallerstein unduly focuses on examining the dynamics of the modern world-system itself, such as its origins and evolution, the conflicts between core countries, and the relationships between cores and peripherals. This has been critiqued by Marshall Sahlins and Thomas Hall as problematic because it overlooks the influence of peripheries on cores.[133] Wallerstein, in addition, viewed the capitalist world-economy as a preconceived entity, and simplified the relationship between colonial powers (especially Britain) and China as merely a commodity exchange relationship within the system.[134] This perspective disregards non-economic events and momentum of both colonial powers and China, which are essential for understanding the impact of colonial powers on China and China's response to the colonial powers. Wallerstein's methodology was criticized for focusing too much on the "internal logic of its (modern world-systems) function"[135] and failing to provide detailed accounts of the political, cultural, and geopolitical issues surrounding the influence of colonial powers on China, and vice versa.

Philip McMichael proposes a different approach to Wallerstein's methodology that addresses its totalizing or functional problems. Wallerstein focuses solely on the self-determined properties of the modern world-system, overlooking the significance of its individual parts. However, since the modern world-system cannot exist independently without the various components that make it up, McMichael argues that it is crucial to investigate the relationships between the parts and the system itself. This is important because it reveals how these connections brought about historical changes in the modern world-system.[136] McMichael also claims that the role of the parts was important even at the beginning stage of the modern world-system, which shows that the modern world-system is not an a priori conception but rather a historically shaped one.

To some extent, McMichael's incorporating comparison method helps us escape Wallerstein's functional and totalizing trap. However, one methodological problem with McMichael's approach in incorporation studies is that it does not fully address how the parts are interconnected in various ways under the influence of the modern world-system. World-system methodologies have traditionally focused on either the dynamics of the whole (Wallerstein's approach) or the relationships between the parts and the whole (McMichael's approach), while neglecting the relationships among the parts themselves. Drawing on Karel Kosik's dialectical conception of totality, which asserts that the parts not only interact and interconnect with each other but also with the whole, McMichael argued that the parts reveal and realize the changing whole.[137] Nevertheless, his methodology emphasizes the relationships between parts and the whole without providing specific explanations of the dynamics that emerge from interpart relationships.[138] For example, it is difficult to identify connections between preincorporated areas and areas that are in the process of being incorporated. The opium trade led by British traders in India (part 1) played a key role in initiating and developing China's incorporation process into the capitalist world-system in the nineteenth century (part 2). China's incorporation into the capitalist world-system (part 2) also, directly or indirectly, influenced the incorporation of its neighbor, Korea (Chosŏn) (part 3). As a tributary state to the Qing Empire, Chosŏn had no official relations with any other country except the Qing until the mid-nineteenth century. China's incorporation process, which began in the 1780s, left Chosŏn largely defenseless. The country's isolated position in the international political scene, deeply dependent on the Chinese-centered world order, meant that it was unable to respond appropriately and agilely to the foreign invasions that began in the nineteenth century and later, and, as a result, Chosŏn experienced Japanese invasion and Japanese colonization and faced the unprecedented situation of capitalist integration. It is difficult to explain the interconnectedness and relevance of the parts (India-China-Chosŏn) that can be seen in this chain of incorporation processes using McMichael's method alone.

Giovanni Arrighi, Takeshi Hamashita, and Mark Selden have developed the concept of a "world region" to explicate the active and constructive role of the East Asian region within the world-system while avoiding Eurocentric perspectives stemming from a conventional world-systems analysis.[139] They believe that the "uni-directional convergence of the East Asian pattern of social, economic and political interaction" has been overshadowed by the holistic and Eurocentric view of conventional world-systems research.[140] While escaping from the old world-systems idea, they have tried to find an exceptional dynamism in the East Asian region. They believe that the peculiar trajectories of East Asian dynamics, involving three different temporalities (fifty years after the mid-twentieth century, 150 years after the mid-nineteenth century, and five hundred years after the sixteenth century), could offer an opportunity to reilluminate an interdependent, interactive, and culturally homogenous East Asian region, distinguished from the dynamism of the European world-economy. Yet this is not all. Hamashita even argues that the emergence of the multilateral trade network and the Qing's decline in the international order of East Asia that happened in the mid and late nineteenth century (1830s–1890s) should be interpreted as a result of "internal changes in the East Asian region," not as a result of the relentless penetrations of colonial powers.[141] I share with Arrighi, Hamashita, and Selden a methodological critique of the Eurocentric and holistic explanations of the modern world-system. But a key question—have they identified substantial interactions between the capitalist world-economy and East Asian countries—remains. The world-region theory typically focuses on the common ground (e.g., culture) or interdependence of each state (e.g., trade network) of the East Asian region as the primacy loci of regional processes. Yet their analysis often neglects the unique incorporation process of each East Asian state, thereby remaining unable to observe key insights from the incorporation framework. When looking at the

East Asian region from the viewpoint of the incorporation process, Japan, China, and Korea have been incorporated into the capitalist world-economy differently: China was beset by the encroachments of colonial powers and turned into a periphery when its incorporation process was completed; Japan's incorporation process started later than that of China and its incorporation period ended quickly. Furthermore, and contrary to China's trajectory, Japan's status was changed to a semiperiphery at the end of the nineteenth century.[142] As the most unfortunate of the East Asian countries to undergo an incorporation process, Korea was made into a colony of the Japanese Empire when its incorporation process concluded. Yet Arrighi, Hamashita, and Selden focus on the common context of East Asia and do not discuss how the expansion of the capitalist world-economy interacted with each East Asian country differently and therefore caused different consequences for each of them. Not that their analysis is wrong, but it is incomplete, precisely due to the absence of histories of each East Asian state's incorporation process. For this reason, viewed from the incorporation framework, the concept of the world region does not sufficiently elaborate and develop the world-systems analysis but may weaken the explanatory power of incorporation studies. Instead of depending on the existing literature on regional dynamics, I pay more attention to the nature of interactions linking China and the capitalist world-system and China and its neighboring countries within the capitalist world-system.

Unlike McMichael's comparison method, which mainly focuses on the relationships between parts and the whole, and Arrighi, Hamashita, and Selden's idea of world region, which puts undue emphasis on finding a common East Asian context, incorporating dynamics proposes interpart relationships as a methodological strategy for analyzing the connections between parts within a system. The aim of this approach is to trace the formation and reformation processes of interpart relationships and understand how they interact with the whole, thereby affecting the dynamics of the entire system. Interpart relationships are essential as they act as capillaries of the part-whole relationships.[143]

For instance, during and after China's incorporation into the capitalist world-system in the nineteenth century, the dynamic relationship between Hunan and Guangdong merchants (i.e., that they reversed position over the course of the century) can be confirmed by using the incorporating dynamics method. Hunan is an inland province and Guangdong a coastal one that for centuries was involved in trade. Prior to China's incorporation into the capitalist world-system, Hunan Province was renowned as a typical Chinese granary; large amounts of rice from Hunan Province were exported to the lower Yangtze River and the major merchants in Hunan were non-Hunan people like Guangdong merchants.

However, during China's incorporation process, especially after the Opium War, commercialized markets emerged in various places in Hunan, and Hunan merchants' guilds also began to be organized. For example, before China's incorporation process hemp produced in Hunan Province was mainly handled by Guangdong merchants who took the hemp from Hunan Province to the Foshan (佛山) in Guangdong and sold it to Guangdong people. However, during and after China's incorporation process, Guangdong merchants were replaced by Hunan merchants.[144] In relation to the tea industry in Hunan Province, the activities of the Hunan merchants were remarkable: the black tea produced by Hunan Province had mainly been exported abroad since the nineteenth century. At first, the Guangdong merchants monopolized the profits stemming from the export-oriented tea industry. After the early days of the reign of Emperor Guangxu, however, Hunan merchants actively entered the tea industry and achieved a certain degree of economic success.[145] Historical sources show that the commercial activities of local merchants in Hunan Province noticeably increased during and after China's incorporation process, whereas the scope of activities of Guangdong merchants in Hunan decreased. In comprehending such an opposite socioeconomic situation of multiple merchant groups in the incorporated area, combined with the logics of global dynamics, the incorporating dynamics method may be effective.

Moreover, interpart relationships influence the dynamics of the capitalist world-economy. After the discovery of the Americas, for example, silver mines in the New World became functionally interconnected with a global production-distribution network. As a result, the size of the Europe-led capitalist world-economy expanded further. As Adam Smith explicitly noted, the discovery of the Americas influenced the development of agriculture and manufacturing systems in England, the Netherlands, Germany, Sweden, Denmark, and Russia.[146] Furthermore, as the silver market in America emerged and advanced, Europe's oceangoing business also expanded. In fact, European traders gained enormous wealth through the silver trade with China, which consumed enormous amounts of silver.[147] This consequently paved the way for the expansion of the capitalist world-economy. In sum, the interpart relationship at least partially influences the whole in that the connection of the interparts (e.g., the connections between silver mines in America and European merchants) led to the expansion of the capitalist world-system (see table I.2).

Although I introduced the incorporating dynamics to close existing logical loopholes of world-systems methods, that does not mean that my methodological framework is superior to others. Rather, by combining Wallerstein's, McMichael's, and Arrighi, Hamashita, and Selden's approach with incorporating dynamics, we may be able to maximize the methodological advantages of the world-systems method.

In sum, based on a theoretical idea of the incorporation process and a methodological approach of incorporating comparison, world region, and incorporating dynamics, I pose a series of questions to stimulate curiosity in looking for ways to analyze China's incorporation. This leads to the following core questions: What problems did previous Chinese incorporation studies have? How long did China's incorporation

Table I.2. Comparison of the Three Major World-Systems Methodologies

	World-systems analysis	Incorporating comparison	World region	Incorporating dynamics
Main aims	Tracing long-term, large-scale social change in the past, present, and future	Adding the role of parts that enable the dynamism of the capitalist world-system	Unique economic path based on Asian context (e.g., industrious revolution)	Seeking various models formed in the relationships between parts
Method	Considering the capitalist world-system as a "complex, structured, and historical whole"*	The part-whole relationships	Escaping from Eurocentric views	Interpart relationships
Methodological advantages	Historicizing and locating the state(s) in the context of dynamics of the capitalist world-system. (e.g., the roles of the state in the international division of labor system or globalized commodity chains)	Explaining how the capitalist world-system can exist as a single entity and develop as a self-fulfilling form	Finding East Asia's distinctive trajectory of development (including China)	– Discovering the dynamics that take place in the relationships between parts – Presenting relational features between parts created before the incorporation process and tracing the relationships between parts that have been changed after the incorporation process
Methodological disadvantages	Inattention to the role or function of the various types of parts that make the capitalist world-system dynamic	Due mainly to the emphasis on the relationships between parts and the whole, it tends to ignore various types of interpart relationships	– Ignoring the different incorporation path in each East Asian country – Difficult to see how each East Asian country has come to accept the logics of the capitalist world-system during the in-corporation process	By overemphasizing the connections between historical parts (cases) in the whole, the uniqueness of the meaning of the cases themselves may be de-emphasized.

*Richard E. Lee and Dale Tomich, "Method and Practice in World-Systems Analysis: An Introduction to the Collection," Review 39, no. 1 (2016): 8.

Figure I.2. The diagrammatic representation of an analytical framework. *Source*: Created by the author.

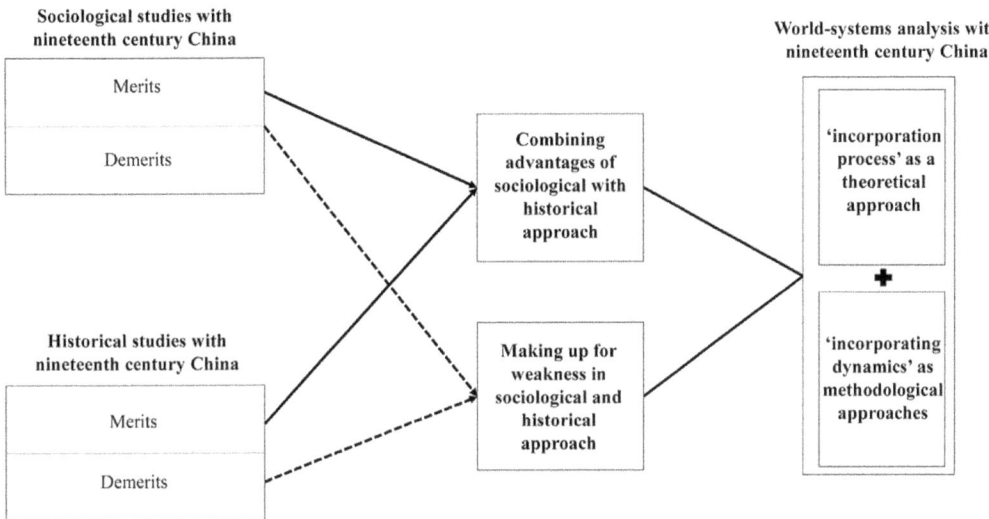

process take from the first sign of incorporation to the end? What distinctiveness will I find when I examine the capitalist world-economy's penetration into China? Equally importantly, what are China's unique movements of resistance against the rules imposed by the capitalist world-economy? These important but thorny questions guide me on where I can further existing research on China's incorporation process.

Structure of the Book

This book seeks to examine how the globalized capitalist mode of production came to incorporate China and how this incorporation process changed over time. Influenced by a layered geopolitical order and an interconnected production network of the capitalist mode of production, Chinese society experienced an unprecedented and massive transformation. Bearing this in mind, this book is divided into two parts. The first focuses not only on interpreting China's incorporation process but also on background knowledge of the nineteenth-century capitalist world-economy. The second part fleshes out China's incorporation process.

Chapter 1 begins with past incorporation studies. Existing incorporation studies have not paid much attention to China's incorporation process. There are a few studies dealing with China's incorporation process, but these have faulty premises or illogical proofs that ironically make it difficult to grasp the relationships between China and the capitalist world-economy. While putting the missing link of China's incorporation process into incorporation studies, this book aims to provide a comprehensive approach to China's incorporation process into the capitalist world-economy. Next, to show a connected history, albeit brief, between the West and China, I will explain the long-term interlinked history between late imperial China (Ming and Qing) and the West before China's incorporation process. Late imperial China implicitly and explicitly is interconnected with the West in many different ways. By disclosing the connected histories between China and the West, I reveal how these connected histories affect nineteenth-century China's incorporation process. After that, I suggest the duration of China's incorporation process—from the 1780s to the 1890s—and explain how this duration militates in favor of connected histories between the capitalist world-economy and China. While conducting research on China's incorporation, an important advantage of archival data is the possibility of inspecting a record of what really happened in Chinese history. In contrast with nineteenth-century Chinese history from the point of view of sociologists, which depends heavily on secondary sources, I will examine archival data to look afresh at nineteenth-century China's transformations. In particular, by drawing on and addressing the hitherto-unexplored archival history data in the sociology field,[148] I will show how China was subsumed into the capitalist world-economy.

Chapters 2 and 3 flesh out China's incorporation process. The encroachment of the capitalist world-economy left its mark on Chinese society in numerous ways, including export-oriented crop cultivation (e.g., tea), the outflow of silver, imports of opium, Chinese coolies' integration into the international division of labor system, the rise of a comprador class that collaborated with Western merchants, the transformations of port cities, changed relationships between port cities and the hinterland, the ancien régime's decline, the Qing's acceptance of the logic of the interstate system, and the rise of a new social classes. To accurately further one of my book's aims—a detailed description of China's incorporation process into the capitalist world-economy—I will also investigate China's political, economic, social, and geographical transformations in chapters 2 and 3.

Chapter 4 explores how changes at the global geopolitical level influenced China's incorporation process. Since the late nineteenth century, the colonial powers that have exerted the greatest influence in East Asia, including China, have not been European powers, but rather three emerging colonial powers centered in the Pacific: the United States, Russia, and Japan. In chapter 4, I will examine how these powers emerged within the capitalist world-system and how they influenced China's incorporation process.

In chapter 5, I analyze China's responses to the pressures of the capitalist world-economy. This research does not pursue a simple unilateral expansion process of the capitalist world-economy; instead, it is by definition bilateral. My purpose is not to study the China that was incorporated by the dynamics of the capitalist world-economy, but to analyze the China formulated by interactions between the powerful driving force of the capitalist world-economy and a variety of types of China's responses. For this, I will engage with various resistance movements against China's incorporation process. This gives rise to multidimensional facets of China's incorporation process, each of which offers particularly rich and distinctive historical moments.

In the concluding chapter, I will recapitulate the book's findings. I will reveal how the new method allows us to analyze the process of China's incorporation into the capitalist world-system and show how the parts came together in this process and how they affected the modern world-system. After that, I briefly discuss the consequences within China of incorporation. This will help to illustrate long-term trends in China's capitalist transition after China's incorporation process.

Chapter 1

Past Incorporation Studies and an Alternative Approach to China's Incorporation Process

Past Incorporation Studies

Over the past several decades, scholars from a wide range of disciplines, including late imperial Chinese history, global history of the early modern period, and even world-systems analysis, have analyzed nineteenth-century China's massive transformations in combination with analyzing the impact of colonial powers. In explaining nineteenth-century China's encounter with colonial powers, they have tended to label everything as "China's incorporation." Despite the widespread use of "China's incorporation process," this term, ironically, has been debased because it was too long overused in different academic fields to the point of near meaninglessness. To delimit a term that has several layers of meaning and provide a lucid explanation of this ambiguous buzzword, I will use it in the context of world-systems analysis. Put differently, my inquiries into China's incorporation process are conceptually and methodologically grounded within a world-systems perspective. From the conceptual point of view, an external arena's incorporation process into the capitalist world-economy was not merely a reorganization of its society or a restructuring of its economic system, which has often been observed from the spontaneous politico-economic transformation of Chinese society. Rather, it can be seen in the pressures of the capitalist world-economy and the responses to them.

I shall examine a few incorporation studies within world-systems analysis and incorporation studies within other analyses. Then I will analyze the limitations of two different approaches. The critical analysis of the two approaches will help to draw up a new guideline for China's incorporation study.[1]

Incorporation Studies within World-Systems Analysis

Since incorporation studies have become notable as a tendency in world-systems analysis, incorporation-related topics have become the object of attention among world-systems researchers. They have been enshrined in the incorporation studies of Peter D. Phillips, Reşat Kasaba, and William G. Martin that highlight a long-established theoretical frame of incorporation characterized as a coercive expansion of a Europe-led capitalist mode of production and the responses of external arenas to the capitalist world-economy.[2]

Borrowing the concept of incorporation from world-systems analysis, Frances V. Moulder and Dilip Basu sketched the colonial powers' encroachment on imperial China after the Opium Wars.[3] They assumed that the opium trade led to China's incorporation (and decline). They did not, however, delve into the specifics of China's incorporation process. They outlined the connections between the world-economy and China. In their attempts to reveal the uniqueness of the European capitalist path, they erased China's distinctive incorporation process somewhat. Moulder and Basu's cursory narratives consequently brought about the relative neglect of China's transformations even though Moulder added a little more to the dynamics of China's incorporation process and discussed this process in a comparative historical context.

To provide a more complete picture Alvin So fleshed out China's nineteenth-century incorporation process.[4] In contrast to the conventional world-systems perspective, he distinguished political incorporation from economic incorporation. So assumes that China's political power was not a whole entity during its incorporation process. He separates South China's violent and continuous opposition to the penetration of the colonial powers (e.g., the Sanyuanli Incident of 1841[5] and the rise of local governance, such as the gentry militia) from the starkly contrasting Qing government's incompetent and passive responses to the colonial powers' penetration.[6] Political incorporation cannot be evaluated solely by the central government's responses. More importantly, So argues that political and economic incorporation were sometimes decoupled, and at other times reunited depending on how local classes within South China, in particular the gentry class and peasants, responded to the penetration of the capitalist world-system. China was gradually incorporated into the capitalist world-system economically when it began importing opium in the 1830s and politically when it lost the Opium War in the early 1840s, but this incorporation process faced strong resistance from South China. In particular, "the strong South Chinese gentry class, together with the nationalistic peasantry, had waged a strong antiforeign movement to force the foreign capitalists to stay out of South China,"[7] which led to South China's decoupling from the capitalist world-system. However, the separation of South China from the capitalist world-system led to a decrease in the volume of South China's exports abroad. As a result, many common people lost their jobs, and the center of international trade shifted from Canton to Shanghai, causing South China's local economy to experience a decline.

In the face of increasing economic hardship in South China, the gentry-led militia, which was organized against the threat of foreigners, did not serve as a vanguard for social reform, but rather, in the eyes of the peasants, only reinforced local governance and economic polarization. In turn, many peasants, whose economic base was weak, became highly involved in the rebellion.[8] For the gentry class, it was hardly possible to fight both external enemies (i.e., colonial powers) and internal enemies (i.e., peasant-centered rebels), and the news that the central government had signed a peace treaty with the colonial powers diluted their reasons for opposing those powers. Added to this, the lack of support for the gentry-led militia from the central government, which had signed treaties with the colonial powers, and the continued failure of the gentry militia's military attacks on foreigners made the gentry class once again seek to link South China to the capitalist world-system. The international silk market also turned in South China's advantage. When silkworm diseases broke out in Europe and silk production plummeted as a result, international demand for Chinese silk increased.[9] After the 1860s, the South China gentry class promoted export-oriented sericulture in South China while maintaining cooperative relationships with foreign merchants. As a result, "foreign trade in Canton revived with silk export rising sharply from 390 piculs in 1848 to 5,571 piculs in 1860, and then to 16,772 piculs in 1871."[10]

In sum, So noted that the politically strong resistance movements of southern China were so unique that these should be distinguished from the economic incorporation process. In addition to this, the relationship of the classes in the South China region to the dynamics of the capitalist world-system drove political or economic incorporation, on the one hand, and opposed it, on the other. So's class-based study presents a distinctive incorporation process and serves as a fascinating case study for examining the historical expansion of the boundaries of the capitalist world-system.

In another study, Alvin So and Stephen Chiu offered additional explanations for China's political and economic incorporation process.[11] Although their historical narrative of China's incorporation process enumerates the rise of South China's silk industry, the impacts of the Opium War, and the penetrations of Western missionaries, they believe that China had not been degraded to the status of a peripheral country in the capitalist world-economy. The economy in the twilight years of imperial China was largely incorporated into the European-led world-economy; yet they insisted that its political and cultural dimensions did not deteriorate nor were they incorporated into the world-economy. To throw into sharp relief a fundamental reason for China's failure to become a peripheral country in the trimodal hierarchy of the capitalist world-economy, they separated political and cultural incorporation from economic incorporation. In their view, China maintained political stability through a tributary system with its neighboring countries, and through a strong Confucian ideology kept ingrained long-term or perpetual shared cultural values. So and Chiu insisted that Qing China did not become a peripheral country even after the 1840s.

There is a sense in which highlighting the striking difference between the economic and political (including cultural) aspects of China's incorporation process is a new perspective. Still, two conundrums remain. First, if So and Chiu wanted to distinguish the economic aspects of the Chinese incorporation process from its political aspects and to support the idea of the restoration of the traditional political regime after the 1840s, they should have explained specifically how China's government officials and political elites or the China-centered tributary system responded to and resisted China's participation in the capitalist world-economy. Without that, their exclusive focus on the China-led tributary system as a proof of its international ascendency and the revitalization of the ancien régime as proof of its political ascendancy after the 1840s becomes untenable.

The second problem lies with So and Chiu's erroneous emphasis on the primacy of the dynastic cycle in Qing decline. Dynastic cycle analysis focuses on internal causes, such as revolts, for dynastic decline, and downplays external factors.[12]

Unlike Moulder's and Basu's studies, So and Chiu's study focuses on China's responses to the world-economy's relentless expansion. They describe how the government of the Qing Empire struggled to recover the traditional world order politically and culturally after the 1840s to resist the penetration of the capitalist world-economy. For example, according to So and Chiu, China's Self-Strengthening Movement was a resistance movement and a rebuilding process that opposed this capitalist expansion.[13] In this regard, So and Chiu argue that the Qing Empire declined because of the dynastic cycle rather than due to the influence of the capitalist world-economy.

So and Chiu try their best to make a convincing case about China's unique incorporation process, but their account is theoretically ambiguous. Although they adopt world-systems perspectives to examine the Qing's economic changes, they place greater emphasis on the dynastic cycle—and exclusive emphasis on internal causes—when they summarize the Qing regime's collapse. Put differently, their study of Chinese incorporation started from a world-systems analysis, but their conclusion did not escape dynastic cycle analysis. Worse, as Victor Nee and James Peck note, the important elements of dynastic decline, like "segments of gentry," divided between the gentry who supported the governance of the Qing regime and those who did not, and "peasant uprisings," were not only unable to bring about a fundamental politico-economic transformation of Chinese society,[14] but they could not lead China to a new historical path.[15] Nevertheless, So and Chiu's attempt to combine the collapse of the ancien régime based on internal causes with the socioeconomic changes in China brought about by the incorporation process is unconvincing. To summarize, So's equivocal and erroneous statements about the Chinese incorporation process come from confusion regarding the dynastic cycle and world-systems analysis and fail to clarify the complicated Chinese incorporation process.

To recap, previous Chinese incorporation studies have been faced with difficulties like the omission of China's distinctive processes (Basu's and Moulder's view) and interpretative problems caused by confusion between the world-systems view and the dynastic cycle (So's view). Such a selective and biased understanding of the underlying dynamics of China's incorporation process contributes little that casts a new light on the Chinese incorporation process or develops it further. Unlike past studies, I will investigate the Chinese incorporation process in empirically more unique and theoretically more cogent ways that may contribute to the development of incorporation studies.

INCORPORATION STUDIES WITHIN OTHER ANALYSES

In Chinese historians' frame of reference, one idea of China's incorporation process into the capitalist world-economy has often been used to identify the economic influence of the West on China.[16] Based on the transnationality of the capital accumulation process, these scholars have focused primarily on the presence of Western merchants and industries in China and their effects on the Chinese economy. They, however, tend to have erroneous conceptions of China's incorporation process in that they do not comprehend the meaning of external arenas' incorporation process into the capitalist world-economy. This has misled researchers about the essence of incorporation.

Hao Yen-P'ing, a Chinese historian, has partially examined China's incorporation process to analyze China's grand exogenous shock and the transformations of Chinese society caused mainly by the penetration of the West. Hao acknowledged that the capitalist world-economy's influence was essential to understanding the massive changes in late imperial China's economic system. By interpreting the rise of what he called the "commercial capitalism" of China during the nineteenth century (1840–1880), he stressed an accelerated Sino-Western commerce. The birthplaces of commercial capitalism were in littoral zones, such as Hong Kong, Shanghai, Canton, and Amoy.

Those cities, which played an important role in the unprecedented growth of imports, exports, and the volume of trade with foreign countries, paved the way for a thriving commercial capitalism not only through the standing centers of international commerce but also by creating new merchant groups (e.g., traders, bankers, and speculators). This attention led Hao to the conclusion that without close relations with the West it was difficult for China to facilitate a commercial revolution toward capitalism.

Although Hao accepted the influence of the capitalist world-economy by analyzing the rise of China's commercial capitalism, his use of world-systems analysis was perfunctory. First, whether intentionally or not, he tended to equate dependency theory with world-systems analysis. His explanation of China's incorporation process depended heavily on dependency theory:

> The dependency theory asserts that the degree of underdevelopment of satellite countries is proportional to their contact with the metropolitan West. The central theme of the dependency theory is that capitalism creates underdevelopment. To what extent is the concept of "capitalistic underdevelopment" applicable to China?" . . . Admittedly, China experienced certain negative consequences of the opening of the country to trade with the industrial nations. And viewed in a larger perspective, the treaty system in

general and the opium trade in particular were in many ways detrimental to China economically, socially, politically, and psychologically.[17]

Hao's explanations of China's change have partially contributed to our understanding of China's politico-economic-social conditions on the macro level. However, he downplayed different points between the concept of capitalistic underdevelopment in dependency theory and the incorporation process within world-systems analysis: A unit of analysis is the most fundamental difference between dependency theory's concept of underdevelopment and an external arena's incorporation process into the capitalist world-economy. Dependency theory's conception, which is based on the unequal relationships between core and peripheral countries, emphasizes enriching core countries at the expense of peripheral countries.[18] This means that dependency theory strongly considers the state or society as an autonomous unit, thereby allowing inequality and exploitation to come between core and periphery countries with little consideration of the trans-societal entity of the capitalist world-economy.[19] In contrast, the incorporation process as considered by world-systems analysis focuses more on the dynamics of a transnational entity. Unlike the cross-national comparison of dependency theory that applies a one-size-fits-all categorization to all peripherical countries as underdeveloped or prey for core countries, the incorporation study of world-systems analysis does not apply processes of capitalistic underdevelopment to all incorporated areas uniformly. For example, the Indian subcontinent and West Africa experienced colonization, whereas Japan did not. These case studies are reflected in world-systems analysis but not in dependency theory.[20] Plus, in contrast to the conception of an external arena's incorporation process into the capitalist world-economy, dependency theory does not look at state deformation in the periphery as a part of incorporation and peripheralization.

Second, I partially acknowledge that China's advanced market economy was achieved by adventurous and risk-taking mercantile activities (e.g., China's junk trade[21]); nonetheless, it is difficult to accept Hao's entire idea of how the main components of capitalism's rise were organized. According to Hao, China's commercial capitalism appeared after it met all the criteria for it, such as free commerce, competition, and private ownership and the use of accumulated wealth for the production and exchange of goods and services with the aim of earning a profit.[22] An important corollary of Hao's argument is the view that China experienced the same (or at least a similar) developmental path toward capitalism as did northwestern European countries.

According to Rebecca Jean Emigh, Hao's work fell into a trap of "European bias of much of the development literature—the assumption of universally applicable models of economic change";[23] for this reason, he failed to distinguish China's international transactions in the nineteenth century from those of advanced Western countries. Northwestern Europe's economic expansion to non-Western areas was characterized by the international division of labor and endless accumulation of capital,[24] featuring an unrelenting exploitation based on unequal exchange.²⁵ The international trade of China in the nineteenth century does not seem analogous to that of northwestern Europe. Late imperial China international trade—even a dramatic shift in China's commercial capitalism in the nineteenth century—did not pursue the privatization of profits or the maximization of commercial profits stemming from rabid exploitation or monopolization. Late imperial China, characterized as a protection-providing enterprise, also did not develop close ties with financiers or merchants in pioneering and exploiting a new market. Furthermore, in contrast with advanced European countries that experienced "low levels of foreign intervention" in their international trade,²⁶ China's international trade was gradually influenced by Western impacts after the beginning of China's incorporation process. Put differently, after the 1780s, such trade ensued in large part from China's entrance into the European world-economy's frame.

The Qing regime's failure to provide various institutional benefits, including protection for Chinese businesses, is a point of contrast when compared to cooperative relationships between government and businesses that emerged in Western Europe, or the government policies of Western Europe that protected and supported overseas businesses. Above all, the institutional benefits of overseas business have greatly contributed to the expansion of Western Europe's own brand of capitalistic system to the outside world.

Consequently, Hao's conception of both a world-systems perspective and dependency theory derailed China's incorporation study, on the one hand, while, on the other hand, his focus on China's commercial activities, which he equated with the rise of Western commercial capitalism, was unable to elicit the fact that the early stage of China's capitalist mode of production was a transplanted capitalism following penetration by the colonial powers.

Hanchao Lu explicates how China was incorporated into the capitalist world-economy, providing a more sophisticated and refined approach toward world-systems analysis. Unlike Hao, Lu explains how the theoretical approach to the modern world-system is differentiated from cross-national comparisons and how it functions for the ongoing process of capital accumulation on a global scale. Within the world-systems context, she also examines how China was situated in the capitalist world-economy. In her account, China has been incorporated into the capitalist world-economy since the 1840s, and thus the defeat of China in the Opium Wars during the mid-nineteenth century was a watershed event of China's incorporation. Her distinctive view separates the peripheralization from the incorporation process. She does not view nineteenth-century China as a peripheral country even though China was incorporated into the capitalist world-economy.

In terms of "a supplier of raw materials and cheap labor of the world commodity chain,"²⁷ China served this role less than fully peripheralized countries such as Latin American colonies. For this reason, Lu contends that China could not be interpreted as a periphery. Assessing the differences of "degree of colonization" between Latin

American countries and China was a meaningful experiment, but one problem remained: it was an insufficient account. Although she distinguishes Latin America from China, Lu does not present detailed narratives on the differences of degree of colonization or the uniqueness of China's incorporation process. As she acknowledges, her study does not map out the entire history of China's incorporation. She focuses more on China's ability to catch up economically after China's incorporation. In this sense, her attempt to examine China's incorporation process tends to shoehorn it into her own fundamental research purpose.

She also contends that, because foreign capital did not destroy China's traditional or precapitalist mode of production completely, the traditional Chinese economic system coexisted with the capitalist system during and after China's incorporation process. This is another reason China is not viewed as a typical periphery in her account. In lieu of this periphery conception, Lu considers late imperial China as a semicolonial, semifeudal society. On first viewing, her advanced study about China's incorporation process seems persuasive because the capitalist world-economy, eager for external markets, could not turn China into a periphery. Yet this is scarcely borne out by an in-depth examination of the incorporation idea as revealed in in the incorporation studies of Wallerstein and others. Her own idea and explanations may be helpful in depicting the panorama of modern Chinese history, but it does not tend to advance a specific definition of the incorporation process. Unlike Lu's distinguishing the incorporation process from the post-incorporation process, being a part of the capitalist world-economy was produced at a critical point or at the end point of its incorporation process. The successive expansion of the capitalist world-economy always treated external arenas (including China) as areas of commercial potential and watched for an opportunity to integrate them. If an external arena entered into the capitalist world-economy, it could not escape from its influence. Once an external arena was incorporated into the capitalist world-economy and then turned into a part of it, its economic and political activities were increasingly coupled with the logic of the capitalist world-economy. Within this framework, each part has had a unique historical trajectory after its incorporation process. Even though each periphery had common characteristics, like their contributions to the "reproduction of the hierarchy of the world-economy,"[28] unilateral transfers of labor and capital between core and periphery,[29] and unequal trades between core and periphery, a greater or lesser degree of each form of incorporation into the capitalist world-economy made a difference.

For example, a given incorporated area's politico-economic power was coupled with its first position in the world-system's three-layer hierarchical network when it was incorporated into the modern world-system. Additionally, the hierarchical position of the incorporated areas (or states) can change, depending on their responses to the capitalist world-economy. Based on the degree of integration into the capitalist world-economy and the responses of the incorporated areas (or states), given their own capability, to the capitalist world-economy, each incorporated area (or state) was shaped and reshaped and thereby made its own historical path. China was no exception. Although China had a different degree of integration into the capitalist world-economy and a variety of responses to it compared with other countries, defining China in a different category, such as a semicolonial or semifeudal society, is inappropriate within world-systems analysis. It can rather be called a distinctive historical path of incorporated China.

Ways to Approach China's Incorporation Process

As mentioned earlier, past incorporation studies do not provide a clear theoretical idea of China's incorporation process or a suitable approach to examine that process. In taking a different approach from past incorporation studies, it is imperative to clarify what I mean by China's incorporation process. To analyze China's incorporation process from a new perspective, I first reassert the importance of China's export-oriented industries in the nineteenth century. Next, I deal with the interlinked history of late imperial China and how its international trade patterns influenced China's incorporation process. For this, I shall explain commercial channels in Ming and Qing times and their impacts on China's incorporation process. After that, I reformulate China's incorporation process and delimit its duration before delving into that process.

THE ROLES OF EXPORTS IN CHINA'S INCORPORATION PROCESS

Given the fact that world-systems analysis has had some theoretical merit in analyzing Chinese society and history and appropriate conceptual usage about the incorporation process is required, our primary task is to find ways that world-systems analysis is useful for analyzing the incorporation process. To that end, I first analyze the roles of exports in incorporating areas.

China's exports are as important as its imports in explaining China's incorporation process; in fact, China's exports provide a clearer picture of on-the-ground reality. The idea that an incorporated area's exports are important is derived from Wallerstein:

> The new pattern of "exports" and "imports" was to be one that replicated the core-peripheral dichotomy that constituted the axial division of labor in the capitalist world-economy. This meant essentially at that time the exchange of peripheral raw materials against core manufactures. In order that the four zones concentrate on raw materials exports, there had to be changes in their productive processes in two directions: in the creation or significant expansion of cash-crop agriculture (and analogous forms of primary sector production) destined for sale on the market of the capitalist world-economy. And, as economic rationality moved toward the creation of hierarchies of work forces, perhaps under the authority of property owners,

still other areas began to specialize in exporting people to work on both the cash-crop land units and the food-crop land units. The emergence of a three-tiered spatial specialization within a zone—"export" cash crops, "local market" food crops, and "crops" of migrant workers—has been a telltale sign of incorporation of an erstwhile arena into the ongoing divisioning of labor of the capitalist world-economy.[30]

Wallerstein contends that an external arena's exports and export-related activities are significant for figuring out its incorporation process. Just as "East Africa was forced into producing cotton for export" or Indonesia was pushed into "the production of sugar, tobacco, and rubber" during its incorporation process,[31] China also became a vehicle for export goods. In effect, tea as an export-oriented crop and coolies as an export of human labor are obviously two important determinants of how China was incorporated into the capitalist world-economy. The historical background to Chinese tea exports directly pertained to China's silver imports, a dramatic increase in British tea consumption, and the opium trade. In order to get a continuous supply of silver from abroad, China needed to trade with Western countries. A Britain highly dependent on Chinese tea imports found an alternative means of exchange instead of silver: opium. By exporting opium both legally and illegally using the Indian-Chinese-British triangular trade route, Britain did not export silver while securing enough quantities of Chinese tea. The sharp increase in tea consumption in Britain also paved the way for China's incorporation process, given the fact that it induced (indeed, forced) China to enlarge tea cultivation areas and produce migrant workers for tea cultivation. In addition, Chinese coolies, as a substitute for slave labor and a cheap labor source, were supplied to the sugar plantations in an already embedded axial division of labor system of the capitalist world-economy. The ongoing division of labor in the capitalist world-economy necessitates endless surplus (and cheap) labor. China's exports (tea and coolies) became telltale signs of the Chinese incorporation process. In this regard, I deal with two exports of China's incorporating features, demonstrating that the capitalist world-economy had embarked on the path toward extending its range for a more effective international commercial network and an axial division of labor system. However, I do not focus exclusively on China's exports when describing China's incorporation process. I also consider China's domestic transformations and imports (e.g., opium and silver), port cities' transformations under the influence of capitalist logic, and the central government's acceptance of interstate system logics for explaining China's incorporation process.

An Interlinked History Between China and the West

An analysis of China's export industry relies on an interpretation of historical facts to develop a picture of China's incorporation, and an idea of the interlinked history between China and the West can be referred to as an intellectual resource for thinking about the historical and geopolitical conditions for China's incorporation. Interlinked histories assume that ideas, products, and people produced or appearing in one region are not created independently of external influences or interactions with other regions but are formulated or reformulated through interconnections and mutual influencing between regions. For example, according to the interlinked historical perspective, modern Europe's rise is not conceptualized as due to self-propelling processes. It rather can be understood as a result of effective utilization of non-European areas' resources.[32] My argument for interlinked histories is directly or indirectly related to China's incorporation process.

However, curiously enough, few have attempted to address the interlinked histories between China and the West before and after China's incorporation process. I use a comparison method to present the unparalleled changes of these interlinked histories. The next section elaborates on this comparison

An Interlinked History Between China and the West Before China's Incorporation Process and Its Implications

As explained in the introduction, the emergence of the capitalist world-economy in Europe was preceded by the creation of a world-economy led by non-European regions (including China); the powerful dynamics of the thirteenth-century world-system had a significant impact on the rise of the European-led capitalist world-economy. This does not mean, however, that Europe's capitalist world-economy is qualitatively equivalent to the past world-economies that originated from non-European areas. The capitalist world-economy is a politico-economic system that prioritizes the nonequivalent exchange system and the accumulation of capital itself, which is accompanied by mechanisms such as violence and exploitation. Indeed, this capitalist world-economy resulted from the progress that was made in overcoming the crisis of European feudalism, which was begun in the fourteenth century. Europeans' exploration of the Americas, most of all, are important in the appearance and rise of the capitalist world-economy during the long sixteenth century of 1450 to 1600.[33] Nonetheless, the full-scale expansion of the European-led commercial network into major non-European areas had to wait until after circa 1800.

During the period from 1733 to 1817, the capitalist world-economy gobbled up the Indian subcontinent, the Ottoman Empire, the Russian Empire, and West Africa. Ultimately, one capitalist world-economy remained by the late nineteenth century or the beginning of the twentieth century. With European expansion into non-Western areas, the nineteenth-century capitalist world-economy was a peculiar watershed in the economic dominance of the planet. From Wallerstein's point of view, the nineteenth century was the period of reexpansion of the world-economy into the Asian region, including China.[34] Although the starting points of the incorporation process varied according to the geographical conditions or political capacities of the Asian regions, most of these regions were part of the capitalist world-economy by around 1900.[35] In this regard, where the world-economy was concerned, the nineteenth century involved an eastward sweep of the European-led capitalist mode of production.

There is little doubt that Chinese society was appalled by the unprecedented penetration of colonial powers in nineteenth century; however, this does not mean that China had no contact with the West beforehand or closed its eyes to the world before the nineteenth century. Prior to China's incorporation process, late imperial China was already interconnected with Western countries in different ways. First, there was the bullion trade between China and Western merchants during the sixteenth century.[36] Due mainly to the silver standard for tax payments in the Ming and Qing regimes and the lack of silver deposits in China, late imperial China had to import silver from outside Chinese territory. European merchants, supported by the expansionist policies of European countries, entered the silver trade. They in turn could obtain goods such as silk,[37] porcelain,[38] and tea in exchange for silver. In particular, Spanish merchants who participated in the Manila galleon (Galeón de Manila) engaged in the silver bullion trade with China despite the risk of shipwrecks.[39] Spanish trading ships made highly profitable round-trip sailing voyages once or twice a year across the Pacific Ocean from the port of Acapulco in Mexico to Manila in the Philippines.[40] Not only did Spanish merchants participate in the international silver trade, but Portuguese and Dutch merchants also entered the silver trade with China even though the Chinese government often described them as pirates.[41]

Due to the growth of China's silver trade, Gemeli Carrei, the Italian globetrotter of the seventeenth century, said "the Emperor of China calls the King of Spain, the King of Silver; because there being no Mine of it in his dominions, all they have there is brought in by the Spaniards in Pieces of Eight."[42] As we can see from Carrei's observation, an enormous quantity of silver passed over the Pacific, especially out of Acapulco and through Manila on its way to China.[43]

Second, China imported food plants like maize, sweet potatoes, Irish potatoes, and peanuts from the New World in the seventeenth and eighteenth centuries, which gave individual smallholders or peasants new crops to supply their daily food.[44] In fact, new crops had to be brought in from the New World to escape a Malthusian crisis.[45] The unprecedentedly rapid growth of the Chinese population between the 1670s and 1800 backfired against Chinese society's long-run economic prosperity by increasing the gap between the amount of arable land and the increase of population. According to Ho Ping-ti, Chinese population in 1750 was 179,538,540 but the population kept growing so that it reached a peak at 429,932,034 in 1850.[46] It pushed China into the Malthusian trap in that the amount of crop cultivation did not catch up to the increase of population.[47] It consequently brought about an economic downturn and a widespread scarcity of food. Thanks in part to new crops from the New World, however, many Chinese people were able to escape from starvation.

Third, China also participated in the international fur trade network. During the fifteenth and sixteenth centuries, fur markets connected fur consumers in China,

Korea, and Japan with the fur-producing regions of the Sungari River, Amur region, and islands of the northwestern Pacific. In the sixteenth and seventeenth centuries, under the rule of the Qing Empire, the international fur network was further expanded to include Russian traders, and the network extended into eastern Siberia.[48] This history of commodity exchange created a transnational network linking China and the West that was not limited to material goods Commodified human beings (migrant workers) also connected China and the West. Fourth, there were Chinese immigrants who moved to the Western colonies (e.g., Malay or Batavia) before the nineteenth century.[49] China's overseas migration began at least two or three centuries before its incorporation process began. As a Fujian gazette put it, "The fields are few, but the sea is vast; so men have made fields from the sea."[50] Many Fujian and Guangdong peasants moved to European colonies. Chinese migration during the sixteenth and seventeenth centuries was more directly related to China's internal problems like (a) social and political disorder between the late Ming and early Qing and (b) the lack of arable land (and population increase) from the seventeenth century until the end of the eighteenth century.[51] This Chinese migration to European colonies connected China with Western powers before China's incorporation process.

Can we identify this mesh of international connections between China and the West with Wallerstein's contention that long-distance trade between China and Europe between the 1500s and 1780s was merely an "exchange of preciosities [luxury goods]"?[52] Unlike Wallerstein's idea of late imperial China's long-distance trade, we need to consider China's need for international trade in staples with Western countries. In the period when late imperial China imported new kinds of crop plants for solving peasants' hunger, the country, via international trade, was linked increasingly to Western merchants. From the evidence of China's import items like silver and crops through long-distance trade, it is misleading to regard exchanging goods as an exchange of preciosities that were consumed mainly by the wealthy.[53]

Why then did Wallerstein fail to include the long-standing nonluxury trade between the West and late imperial China? Wallerstein's inattention to the China's long-distance staple trade may be partially attributed to his Eurocentric ideas. Although Wallerstein conceptualized the modern world-system as trans-societal structures that existed for the last five centuries, his analysis of the world-economy does not escape from an ontologically singular Europe-centered idea that the Western (or a European) world-economy became a watershed of global history.[54]

From the moment the West's rise began, the uneven development of the capitalist world-economy transformed the globe by the international division of labor and spatial relationships within a hierarchical world market. In Wallerstein's theoretical schema, the West is regarded as the pioneering creator of the global economic system, whereas the East is a place that is a shadow of its past glory.[55] Based on such a premise, he believed that a global market, international division of labor system, and a maritime trade system characterized by long-distance and regular trade could only have been developed from modern Europe.⁵⁶ This led Wallerstein two ignore the long-distance staple trade between the West and China and to marginalize the extraordinary achievements of China's foreign trade between the 1500s and 1780s.⁵⁷

A more serious problem arises from the lack of interlinked history between the world-economy and nineteenth-century China. Wallerstein acknowledged that China was eventually incorporated into the Europe-centered world-system in the nineteenth century after the end of the England-led triangle trade.⁵⁸ However, his inattention to late imperial China's international trade betrayed a Eurocentric bias in his picture of the sluggish economic activities in the global commerce network.⁵⁹ Consequently, Wallerstein has not sufficiently addressed China's long-distance trades, and an analysis of China's incorporation process and its implications also have yet to be developed to any significant degree by other world-systems researchers.

The history of late imperial China's international trade often induced European powers to participate in the Chinese market. China's incorporation process was closely connected in late imperial China's long-distance trade. For example, late imperial China's long-distance trade, formed between China's demand for silver and the West's demand for tea, played an important role in promoting the British-led opium trade that spurred British merchants to penetrate China. The stress on the connection between the pre-incorporated history of China and the incorporated history of China requires a rethinking of the conventional world-systems analysis. Put differently, while it is suitable to acknowledge that the Chinese history of long-distance trade is connected with China's integration into the capitalist world-economy, the methodological approach and empirical study of China's incorporation process, liberated from Wallerstein' narrow ideas, has to be sketched out afresh. It is to these issues that I now turn.

Escaping from Eurocentric Perspectives and Understanding the Nineteenth-Century Capitalist World-Economy

Late imperial China's international trade between the 1500s and the 1780s affected China's incorporation process. In contrast with Wallerstein's approach, identifying late imperial China's international trade with Europe as the exchange of preciosities for the wealthy, late imperial China's long-distance trade can be defined as a trade of staples for the needs of commoners.

An important question then arises: What distinctions can be made between late imperial China's international trade and incorporating (or incorporated) China's international trade? What changes occurred in China's trade with the colonial powers during and after China's incorporation process? How was China's overseas migration differently defined and treated by the Qing government during China's incorporation process?

First, the most noticeable difference between late imperial China's international trades and incorporating (or incorporated) China's international trades is the nonexistence of capitalist logics. Late imperial China's international trade did not have (or develop) the essential nature or *mot d'ordre* of capitalism like "Marx analyzing the search for an endless accumulation of capital or [John Maynard] Keynes's references to the 'animal spirits' of ([Joseph] Schumpeter's) entrepreneurs,"[60] accompanied by exploitative, coercive, violent, and monopolistic practices. In fact, the silver trade between late imperial China and the New World was reciprocal and was not dependent on the unilateral aggressive use of force. Indeed, unlike a primary characteristic of modern capitalism—the pursuit of a single unified market system—"the two sides (China and the New World) integrate but remain apart."[61] During and after incorporation, however, China's capitalist nature began to emerge. Overseas Chinese merchants, indirectly or directly supported by the state, became more active (e.g., Tamgŏlsaeng)[62] and a merchant class with a new mindset toward capital accumulation emerged (e.g., compradors' profit-seeking activities).

Second, China's international trade had been influenced by colonial powers since the first sign of China's incorporation process. Before this process began, from the 1500s to the 1780s, China was not a part of the European world-economy, meaning that China was linked to the world market without the intervention or pressure of the colonial powers. In contrast, European merchants were repeatedly denied access to trade with China at a time when Chinese-led international trade was dominant in many overland and maritime trades. For example, after 1600 Dutch merchants visited Guangzhou and requested formal trade relations with the Chinese government, but they were rejected on the grounds that there was no tribute relationship. As access to South Chinese ports was blocked, Dutch merchants tried to obtain Chinese goods from Siam, Cambodia, Annam, and Tonkin, but with little success. In 1622, twelve Dutch ships were dispatched to attack Macau, the Portuguese stronghold, but failed. Instead of entering Chinese territory, the Dutch besieged Fort Zelandia in Taiwan in 1624.[63] After Dutch seizure of Zelandia, Taiwan served as a center of Dutch trade with China, Japan, the Philippines, Southeast Asia, and Batavia. China tacitly authorized its ships to go to Taiwan and trade with the Dutch. Moreover, it was Chinese migrants who made a decisive contribution to Europe's entry into Southeast Asia (e.g., Malaysia, Indonesia, the Philippines) and the formation of colonial governance in the region. As Philip Kuhn points out, although Chinese migrants and merchants were not the founders of the colonial regime in Southeast Asia, they become essential allies of European colonial powers.[64] Without the help or close cooperation of Chinese people, many Europeans who entered Asia would have had difficulty in accomplishing colonial expansion and a seamless web of commercial interactions, especially the interregional trading network. While collaborating with the European colonial regime in Southeast Asia, some Chinese migrants and merchants also gained significant economic profits. This allows us to reach the following conclusion: Until the nineteenth century, when Europe's dominance in Asia was evident, European powers' arbitrariness and unilateral action in Asian trade did not have much success. Rather, the priority of trade was given to European powers that cooperated with local powers in Asia and flexibly responded to their needs.⁶⁵ In this sense, Holden Furber referred to the seventeenth and eighteenth centuries, when European maritime forces were active in the Asian maritime world, as the age of partnership.⁶⁶

After the beginning of China's incorporation process, however, China's international trade was gradually influenced by colonial powers. The rise of late imperial China's international trade occurred through the determination of China, whereas the emergence of incorporating (or incorporated) China's international trade occurred through the will of the capitalist world-economy.⁶⁷ After China was incorporated into the capitalist world-economy, China had to accept and follow the logics of the capitalist world-economy even though these logics resulted in the underdevelopment of China and socioeconomic and ecological problems. For example, in the mid-eighteenth century, China's tea trade with Western countries, especially the Dutch, was one of several options for China to seize the initiative in trading with Western merchants. However, after Britain became China's trading partner China was entrapped in the pressures of the international tea trade. Right after the late eighteenth century or early nineteenth century, Chinese tea producers came under strong pressure to increase production. In line with the increase in tea production, the export volume of Chinese tea soared in proportion to the increase of China's imports of silver and opium and increasing tea consumption in Britain. Chinese tea agriculture became integrally linked to the commercial network of the capitalist world-economy; China had to keep producing tea even though China's tea cultivation areas suffered from economic crises (e.g., Chinese tea producers' economic disaster after Britain diversified the sources of tea imports) and ecological problems (e.g., deforestation, soil erosion, and landslides). These crises were the result of export-oriented tea cultivation.

Third, before China was incorporated into the capitalist world-economy, the state bureaucracy often considered overseas migrants as "abandoned people" (*qimin* 棄民). For instance, in 1727, Emperor Yongzheng warned that "most traders traveling abroad are lawbreakers," while regarding those who returned from abroad as insidious persons who "may have plans to secretly conspire with foreigners."⁶⁸ A conversation between Tan Tingxiang (譚廷襄, ? –1870), a viceroy of Zhili, and Capt. Samuel F. Dupont, a US naval attaché in 1858, also provides a glimpse into how the Qing regime treated overseas immigrants (in this case Chinese immigrants to the United States):

> VICEROY (TAN TINGXIANG): It is not our custom to send officials beyond our own borders.
>
> DUPONT: But your people on the farther shore of the Pacific are very numerous, numbering several tens of thousands.
>
> VICEROY (TAN TINGXIANG): When the emperor rules over so many millions, what does he care for the few waifs that have drifted away to a foreign land?

DUPONT: Those people are, many of them, rich, having gathered gold in our mines. They might be worth looking after on that account.

VICEROY (TAN TINGXIANG): The emperor's wealth is beyond computation; why should he care for those of these subjects who have left their home, or for the sands they have scraped together?[69]

This is because oversea migrants arbitrarily left their homeland, abjuring the state's (or the emperor's) protection. The state bureaucracy did not pay attention to the protection of overseas Chinese; however, after China's incorporation process, the Qing regime had to perceive overseas Chinese differently.

Once the Qing government itself legalized overseas migration in 1860, this migration increased significantly. As the number of foreign migrants increased, so did the number of abuses they suffered abroad. Whenever the issue of overseas Chinese was raised as a problem in Western countries, interest in and protection for them was also increasingly recognized as an important task of the Qing regime. For example, in 1886, Qing government officials investigated the treatment of Chinese coolie laborers working on the plantations of the Dutch East Indies and then reported to the Qing government:

> For many days, we met many Chinese coolies who worked at the plantations of the Dutch East Indies. They said they were mainly brought to Singapore and Penang by Chinese recruitment brokers from various counties near Shantou. . . . They signed a contract in Chinese. According to the contract, each worker had to receive $30 as an advance payment; however, most of the money was often taken by recruitment brokers without prior consent of the coolie workers. In the end, the worker only got three or four dollars.[70]

The Qing regime, when informed of the harsh working conditions of Chinese overseas migrants, looked at them from a different perspective than before. Li Hongzhang 李鴻章 (1823–1901) also viewed the protection of overseas Chinese workers as an essential national obligation: "Even in a country where there is an uncivilized area, we [had to] send envoys from our side. If so, Chinese oversea workers would receive help through our envoys. With the support of envoys, they may be able to avoid fraud and abuse."[71] In sum, the Qing government did not define oversea Chinese as abandoned people any longer.[72] In a changed geopolitical and geoeconomic situation, overseas Chinese are beginning to be seen as beings to be cared for and protected.

Last but not least, from the fifteenth to the eighteenth centuries, the Chinese government and society went in different directions with maritime commerce and business. The Ming and Qing Empires, the powerhouses of Asia, controlled the seas and often blocked maritime trade.[73] In great contrast, Chinese merchants actively participated in maritime trade and even moved to foreign countries near China to do so. Merchants in southern China built a huge maritime trade network from the South China Sea to the Indian Ocean world without the financial, military, and institutional backing of the Chinese government.[74] For this reason, Wang Gungwu called them "merchants without empire."[75] A Chinese maritime map, the Selden Map of China,[76] which was drawn around 1608, is a visual resource that shows the advance of these Chinese merchants into the South China Sea.[77] The Selden map shows the perception of the ocean world of the Chinese maritime merchants and suggests a different image from other existing maps emphasizing the topographical form and visual appearance of land. In addition, the contradictory perception of the sea shaped by the state-led sea ban policy and merchant-led vigorous maritime trade is also a major example confirming how the state and society came to be separated surrounding maritime trade.[78]

However, beginning in the nineteenth century, government (*guan* 官) and society (*min* 民) began to share the same voice in maritime-related business and its activities. This is because the paradigm of state management of the Qing Empire changed to include maritime activities after the defeats in the Opium Wars and the First Sino-Japanese War. In a situation in which China could no longer continue the sea ban policy, the Qing regime had to establish new relationships with maritime colonial powers while complying with their politico-economic and diplomatic rules. Indeed, from this time on, the Qing regime began to take an interest in Chinese merchants and migrants who moved overseas.

The Long Nineteenth Century (1780s–1890s): The Duration of China's Incorporation Process

In this setting, we now need to seek China's pathway toward the incorporation process. China was incorporated into the capitalist world-economy in the nineteenth century, as its international trade started to be affected by colonial powers. When did China's incorporation process begin and end? It is an important question, and the answer will illuminate the overall duration of China's incorporation process.

A statistical, mathematical, data-oriented mindset about time can be inappropriate when analyzing unprecedented change in a society such as an incorporation process. This is because a neutral, linear, predictable, and objectified representation of time may reduce lumpy, unpredictable, and uneven social events to a single, standardized way of thinking about temporality. To assume that humanity has experienced the same temporality across all time periods is to exclude from temporality the contingencies and fluctuations of human histories. For example, the temporality of a low-level laborer in the port of Guangzhou in the mid-nineteenth century would have been very different from that of his grandfather—even if they were born and lived in the same place—because the historical background and social structure in which he lived was different from the one in which his grandfather lived, and, as a result, an unexpected temporality was implanted in his life. People who lived in a time of unexpected events probably lived in a different time frame than the generations before them. To understand and explain these temporalities, we need to consider a different temporality than that of previous eras, and to build on this new concept of temporality. As William H. Sewell Jr. points out, "temporal heterogeneity" can lead to "causal heterogeneity."[79] Understanding or explaining radical change at a particular point in time requires an appropriate historical contextualization and concept of temporality.

In this study, I will use a temporality of world-systems analysis, which I do not believe will suffer from the deficiencies and fallacies of "teleological temporality" that Sewell is concerned about. According to Sewell, Wallerstein's world-systems methodology sought to fit history into the workings of the modern world-system rather than to provide a "correct description of history"; Wallerstein's purpose was to discover the laws of the capitalist world-system rather than to provide detailed and reasonable histories.[80] Furthermore, in Sewell's view Wallerstein stressed that the fate of a particular region or state is determined by exogenous variables created by the modern world-system rather than by endogenous dynamics expressed in that region or state, and thus most contingent events that might be found in a particular history are replaced by the purpose of generating, maintaining, and expanding the modern world-system.

At first glance, Sewell's critical approach to Wallerstein seems reasonable. However, what Sewell overlooks is that Wallerstein did not postulate his world-system view as a law or theory. Wallerstein aimed to place the capitalist world-system in global history while defining the capitalist world-system as a unit of analysis and an object of study. Given that the capitalist world-system is also assumed to be an independent organism with a beginning and an end, for him the advent of the global system of capitalism in the context of a long human history is considered as a self-contained history of its own to emerge, develop, and decline. In short, Wallerstein's modern world-system is a sort of historical system. To understand this historical capitalist system, Wallerstein called it a perspective or analysis rather than a theory because the modern world-system shows historical properties and world-systems analysis cannot produce generalized historical rules or propositions.[81] Wallerstein thought that his methodology merely provided clues for interpreting the history of capitalism, while avoiding a reification where concepts or theories judge and overwhelm historical reality.[82] Furthermore, under the assumption that it is difficult to present a theory of a single static world-system, Wallerstein proposed "world-systems." Here, the idea of the world-systems is qualitatively different from the "world system" suggested by Andre Gunder Frank. Frank used the world system to encompass "all of historical time and space";[83] on the contrary, Wallerstein provided plural world-systems that have appeared in human history. The modern capitalist world-system, considered as one of these world-systems, emerged after the sixteenth century. Wallerstein's conception of the modern world-system therefore is wary of a unified theoretical narrative or teleological implications.[84]

In addition, other recent world-systems researchers have proposed a methodologically new world-systems perspective.[85] According to them, the capitalist world-system is a constantly changing entity that interacts with various types of parts (nations, regions, cities, and so forth) that exist as parts within that whole. The histories produced by all these parts do not, as Sewell feared, move the whole forward. Rather, sometimes changes in parts drive the dynamics of the capitalist world-system, whereas the decline of parts can lead to major crises in the capitalist world-system. What world-systems scholars, including Wallerstein, have sought to show is not a lawlike or nomothetic schema of the capitalist world-system, but rather how the so-called whole and the parts interact, and what kinds of dynamic relationships are created between them. With this perspective in mind, the nineteenth century in China must have been a turning point and a watershed if we look at it through a theoretical lens of incorporation.

There's a pivotal question in examining China's incorporation process theoretically and historically: When did China's incorporation begin and how long did it take to complete? Quite a number of researchers have claimed that a fixed period of China's incorporation process was the key determinant in describing a clear picture of China's integration into the capitalist world-economy: Dilip Basu viewed 1757 as the beginning point of China's incorporation process, while Alvin So preferred the 1830s.[86] In a similar vein, Jang Yong Soo argued that, after the First Opium War, East Asian civilization became a part of the capitalist world-economy.[87] Nevertheless, their arguments have two clear inherent limits. First, although they have presented different time periods for when China's incorporation process began, most of them did not present a date or time period when it ended. I argue that it ended in the 1890s.

Second, there has been a great deal of controversy over exactly when China's incorporation process began; nonetheless, many researchers often omitted the globalized tea trade in connection with China's incorporation process. Tea played an important role in trade with European countries. China was a major tea producer, with tea accounting for nearly 15 percent of its total exports from 1762 to 1785.[88] According to Peter Perdue, from 1786 to 1830, the total amount of tea sold by the East India Company (EIC) doubled, and the total export of northern Fujian tea increased from 48 percent to 73 percent of the crop.[89]

By stressing the role of the international tea trade in explaining the initial stage of China's incorporation process, I assert that China was beginning to integrate into the capitalist world-economy in the mid- and late eighteenth century. Then why was China's tea trade of the 1780s important in explaining the initial stage of China's incorporation process? Before answering this question, why did European countries including Britain strive to build a trade network with China in securing tea? Unlike tea consumption in East Asia, tea drinking in the West only became possible through long-distance overseas trade. While Korean and Japanese tea consumption involved importing seeds and learning cultivation skills from China in order to grow tea locally, European countries imported commodified teas and consumed them without local cultivation. This was in stark contrast to the European countries' import substitution for China's silk and porcelain, which included the use of silk textile machinery in Bologna, the production of French faience during the seventeenth and eighteenth centuries, and Chinese-style porcelain produced by Meissen Porcelain Manufactory of Germany. In the absence of local cultivation, Europe's tea consumption depended entirely on trade with China. In addition, unlike other tea cultivating countries in Asia, until the early nineteenth century China was the only country that could export a significant amount of tea.[90] Before European powers, especially Britain, cultivated tea in places like Assam and Ceylon, they had to rely on tea from China. Furthermore, given that China was not interested in imports from Britain, it can be inferred that Britain was more desperate for tea trade than China. Why then did China cede control of the tea trade to Europeans and become part of the global commercial network in the 1780s?

This question brings a significant world-historical event back into play. Since the first tea arrived in Europe around 1610 on Dutch ships[91] and the Canton system (1758–1842) was established, Qing China took the initiative in trading with Western merchants. They controlled Western countries' tea trade. For example, the Chinese government fixed "the number of the China-bound ships and their crew members, the sorts and amounts of trade goods, and the amounts of funds to be sent from the Dutch Republic on these ships to China each year"[92] when the Vereenigde Oostindische Compagnie (VOC) entered into Canton. Shortly afterward, however, China began to lose control of the tea trade when Britain started exporting Indian opium to China.[93]

Until the late eighteenth century, Britain gained no competitive advantage over rival countries in the tea trade. Rather, the VOC played an important role in redistributing Chinese tea to Europe.[94] The Dutch and the VOC stood almost alone among European states that could afford to continue and stabilize the tea trade. The Dutch and VOC, relatively free from the Seven Years' War, fostered China's tea trade while other European counties did not. Under the Dutch monopoly of the tea trade, Britain and other European countries had to highly depend on the Dutch's redistribution (or reexport) of Chinese tea. By not only distributing Chinese tea into the domestic market but also reexporting them to other European countries, the VOC reaped huge profits, whereas most other European countries had to depend on the smuggling trade to make up for a deficiency in legal tea imports.[95] Nonetheless, the end of the Seven Years' War and the return of peace to Europe drove Britain and other European countries into the tea trade (both legally and illegally).[96]

Competition in the tea trade led Britain to use physical violence to protect its interests. Britain declared war on the Dutch on December 20, 1780, the so-called Fourth Anglo-Dutch War (1780–1784), on the pretext of Dutch support for the American War of Independence (1775–1783). One of Britain's intentions, however, was to achieve dominance over the tea trade[97] and to establish a monopoly of the trade by forcing out Dutch merchants in China;[98] as a result, the dominant position of the Dutch in the tea trade declined. Their defeat in the war seared an unforgettable lesson in the Dutch mind: "trade without war, and war without trade cannot be maintained."[99] On the other hand, Britain's subsequent dominance of the tea trade paved the way for Britain's presence in China after the first two East India Company ships sailed to Dinghai in 1755[100] (see also figure 1.1).

Figure 1.1. Commodities brought from China by the British East India Company. *Source*: Created by the author, based on Tsu-yu Chen 陈慈玉, Jindai zhongguo chaye de fazhan xing shijie shichang 近代中国茶业的发展与世界市场 [The development of the Chinese tea trade in the modern world market]. Studies of Modern Economy Series, No. 6 (Zhongyang yanjiuyuan jingji yanjiu suo, 1982), 9.

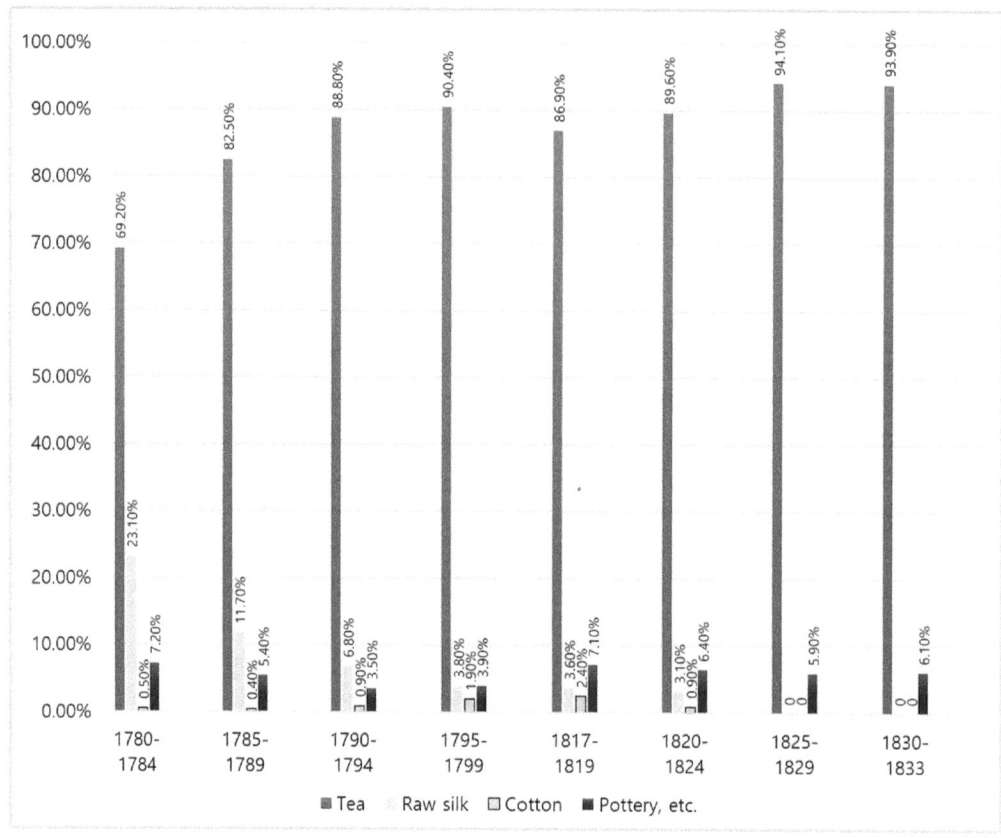

In China the primary purpose of the English East India Company's commercial activities was to secure a sufficient quantity of Chinese tea and to supply Britain, as seen in figure 1.1 and in this report by the House of Commons:

> The main object of the Company's trade with China is the provision of Tea for the consumption of the United Kingdom, under the regulations of the Act of the 24th Geo. 3. C. 38, usually called "The Commutation Act," which require that the Company shall from time to time send orders for the purchase of such quantities of Tea, and provide sufficient ships to import the same, as, being added to the stock in their warehouses and to the quantities ordered and not arrived, shall amount to a sufficient supply for the keeping a stock at least equal to one year's consumption, according to the sales of the last preceding year, always beforehand.[101]

The Chinese tea trade, led by British merchants, continued even after the EIC's commercial monopoly was abolished in 1832. For instance, Jardine Matheson and Company (*yiheyanghang* 怡和洋行) successfully filled the void in the Chinese tea market by developing its own tea brand, employing tea tasters, guaranteeing the excellent quality of the tea, and using high-speed sailing boats. In particular, the high-speed sailing boats owned by the company[102] played an important role in maintaining the British-led tea trade and earning enormous economic profits in that maintenance of tea leaf freshness was at a premium in Britain. Due to the speedy tea transportation in high-speed sailing boats, Jardine Matheson and Company could earn more profit than their competitors.[103]

How, then, were the patterns and organization of tea production in China affected by Britain? Unlike the tea trade with the Dutch, the China's tea trade was conducted to the advantage of Britain since the 1780s,[104] whereas China found it difficult to control the tea trade. This is because, first of all, China did not gain a competitive advantage over Western merchants, in particular British merchants, due mainly to the consecutive bankruptcy of Hong merchants. Under the Canton system, Hong merchants, who were the foreign trade agents of Qing officials, led the way in trading with Western merchants. However, because the Qing's goal in running the Canton system was to enforce compliance rather than expand trade, both Hong merchants and Western merchants were subject to strict discipline, regulation, and the tyranny of Qing officials. Hong merchants had to pay huge amounts of money as tariffs. They were also asked to pay additional taxes, such as a tax for the national defense, a tax for the celebration of the emperor's birthday, and a tax for public works. Worse, they suffered from the extortion of local officials. The tax payments to the government or the money lost through extortion was not invested in trading; as a result, this brought about a liquidity crisis.[105] As the trading of Hong merchants slowed for lack of funds, they had to sign loan agreements with high interest payments to Western lenders. The high interest rates (up to 20 percent per annum)[106] of their foreign creditors pushed Hong merchants into insolvency:[107] "The list of bankrupts included Howqua (Puiqua) in 1789, Eequa in 1790, Shy Kinqua in 1795, Munqua in 1797, Geowqua in 1798, Ponqua and Gnewqua in 1810, and Patqua (Exchin) in 1882; Munqua was so embarrassed that he killed himself."[108] The Qing government did not take Hong merchants' consecutive bankruptcies seriously; it therefore did nothing to resolve the problem. Rather, the Qing government, which considered default on monetary debt to foreigners as an absolute disgrace, pushed Hong merchants to discharge their debts, while turning a blind eye to Western merchants' predatory lending. The regime also made preposterous demands to Hong merchants under the pretext of tax collection. Such unfavorable business conditions and the rapid increase in debt, even though the Hong merchants were outward-looking and enjoyed monopolistic business with Western merchants, drove them to economic insolvency.

Second and more important, Britain gained control over opium production in India and exported a significant amount of opium to China in return for tea imports.

By using legal and illegal (smuggling) routes in the opium trade, Britain overturned trade deficits stemming from the tea trade. In turn, China encountered pressure to respond to Britain's demands by increasing tea production because the economic benefits associated with the tea trade did not compensate for the trade deficits due to opium imports.[109] Conversely, from the British point of view, dominance of the tea trade was epoch-making and became an overriding factor in penetrating China, the biggest market in Asia.

If China's tea trade opened its incorporation process, the First Sino-Japanese War (1894–1895) marked the end of China's incorporation process. The war delivered the demise of the traditional international order (the so-called China-centered world order) in East Asia.[110] It simultaneously represented Japan as one of the non-European powers that had become a great power in Asia and engaged deeply in China's incorporation process. The First Sino-Japanese War was a seminal event in the global history of the late nineteenth century and was inextricably linked with China's incorporation process, yet it remains one of the least-studied areas in incorporation studies. In addition, unlike an erroneous assumption that the First Sino-Japanese War was a mere military competition over regional hegemony, this war led China deeper into the interstate system logic of the modern world-system. Peter Gue Zarrow stresses that the 1890s was a transition period from empire to modern nation; by the 1890s, "Chinese elites were beginning to think about what would come after empire."[111] Put differently, the result of this war was not limited to the decline (and passing) of the Chinese empire or the hegemonic transition from China to Japan in East Asia. In a broader context, it ushered in China's entrance into the West-oriented interstate system.

China had a powerful influence over the East Asian region at least until the outbreak of the First Sino-Japanese War.[112] For instance, the China-Korea Treaty (also described as Chosŏn-Qing Communication and Commerce Rules) that was forged in 1882 epitomized a typical attempt to extend China's politico-economic influence. China's influence was sharply sapped in East Asia due to the defeats of the Opium Wars and aggressive penetration of colonial powers, so the Qing forged the treaty with Korea in order to sustain its political and economic influence; however, China could not sustain the China-Korea Treaty because of its unexpected and ignominious defeat in the First Sino-Japanese War. Not only was China's political influence on Korea doomed to disappear, but Taiwan was also ceded to Japan after the war. Consequently, China was incorporated as a periphery.[113]

This strongly implies that the exploitation and the exercise of political and economic power backed by military force started in earnest beginning with the First Sino-Japanese War. The Treaty of Shimonoseki allowed Japan to establish industrial factories in Qing territory. Prior to this, foreign factories were not allowed in China, and only a small number existed. However, this treaty granted to Japan opened up opportunities for foreign investment in industry and paved the way for economic imperialism. In addition, the Treaty of Shimonoseki included the cession to Japan of rights in the province of the Liaodong Peninsula of southern Manchuria. Because of the cession of the Liaodong Peninsula, geographically located in Manchuria, it signified to the Qing Empire the loss of part of the national home to the colonial powers.

I have briefly shown how China's incorporation process began in the 1780s and ended in the 1890s. Toward the end of the nineteenth century, the capitalist world-economy incorporated China completely; after that, China became a part of the modern world-system. Based on such a newly conceptualized idea, I will examine China's incorporation process in detail in chapter 2.

Chapter 2

China's Incorporation Process

Production, New Classes, and Geography

China as a whole was invaded by a swarm of adventurers from many nations during this period. Smuggling, trading in opium, the coolie traffic, evasion of duties, dealing in arms and other contraband, were engaged in by all sides.

—T. Roger Banister, *A History of the External Trade of China, 1834–81*

Silver, Opium, and Tea

This study of China's incorporation enables us to describe in detail the historical conjuncture between nineteenth-century China and the transnational entity. This chapter presents changes in production, class, and geography that emerged during China's incorporation process.

There is much evidence that China's incorporation process brought about socioeconomic changes in Chinese society, even though every historical evidence of China's incorporation process has a unique history. First, I will discuss the intricate relationships between silver, opium, and tea.

The initial connection between the capitalist world-economy and the Ming was formed by the global circulation of silver. As one of the exogenous forces that led to China's integration into the world-economy, China's silver trade was significant. After the Ming government established a silver standard for tax payments, silver became a necessary currency. Nevertheless, because of the lack of silver deposits in China, the Ming and Qing governments had to import massive amounts of silver through international trade; from 1500 to 1800, China became one of the main end markets for world silver.¹ It may well be that the Chinese government could hardly be free from the vicissitudes of silver's value in international trade.

Because silver was one of the major commodities in the world economic system and that silver was circulated globally, the value of silver could not be controlled by the Chinese government. Spain and Japan actively participated in the international silver trade with China yet they were relatively liberated from the China-led international order. China found it difficult to control the silver trade; on the contrary, the more China needed silver from the outside, the more China was vulnerable to fluctuations in the international value of silver. To obtain silver, China traded porcelain, tea, and raw silk. Later, this relentless silver flow across the globe paved the way for the penetration of the capitalist world-economy because a massive outflow of silver, due to Britain's radical change in traded commodities, triggered the start of China's incorporation process. The initial silver outflow from China was caused by the opium trade with Britain, which grew sharply in the second half of the eighteenth century and peaked in the nineteenth century. The more China depended on the British Empire's opium the more the volume of silver outflow increased in China.

Why did Britain export (Indian) opium to China? Three things can be considered as an answer to this. First, it was the unproductive overproduction of Britain that stood out from the middle of the nineteenth century. Britain used international trade on a global scale to solve its unproductive surplus. J. A. Hobson pointed out that chronic poverty in Britain was caused by the continued production of "unproductive surpluses," and that the way Britain chose to deal with this problem was imperialism.² Based on Hobson's theoretical perspective, we can see how Britain's unproductive surplus led to imperialism and the development of a British-led triangular trade. Britain, colonizing the Indian subcontinent, disrupted the handicraft weaving industry in villages in India. By exporting cheap and machine-made British textiles to India, a large quantity of British textiles flowed into the Indian market, and Indian textiles were quickly replaced by British products. And India somehow had to pay for imported British textiles. How was this possible? To pay for British textiles, India exported tea and jute, but that was not enough. Britain then pushed Indian farmers to grow opium and export it to China.³ In other words, to solve overproduction and surplus in the British textile industry, British capitalists destroyed India's handicraft-based weaving industry, incorporated the Indian market as an exclusive market for British products, and induced India to cultivate opium and export it to China.

Second, the Battle of Plassey (1757), which in turn led to colonization across India, placed a huge financial burden on the British East India Company. Fortunately, the British East India Company was victorious in this battle, but the EIC's debts incurred to fight the Nawab of Bengal and his French allies were growing enormously. One way to solve this financial problem was the triangular trade between India, China, and Britain. The EIC made huge profits by selling Indian opium to China while importing Chinese tea to the British market.⁴

Third, there was a sharp increase in the consumption of Chinese tea in Britain. In England afternoon tea was a pleasant ritual and a midday respite, as evidenced by Henry James's novel *The Portrait of a Lady* (1881). Angela McCarthy and T. M. Devine noted that "according to one estimate, annual per capita consumption of tea in Britain rose more than 300 percent between the 1830s and the 1880s, from 1.48 pounds in 1836 to 5 pounds in 1885."[5] The working class in Britain was no exception: They had enjoyed drinking tea since the eighteenth century.[6]

Driven mainly by Britain's pursuit of the tea trade with China,[7] massive amounts of silver entered China in the eighteenth century. The growth of the tea-silver trade contributed to China's fiscal stability for the first time. European countries (including Britain) found it difficult to import silver from other continents in the nineteenth century because of Mexico's independence from Spanish rule, the economic slowdown of the European world-economy, Britain's silver shortage,[8] and the global decline in the silver supply in the early nineteenth century.[9] Given that "Europe had been buying tea in China since the early eighteenth century but found no acceptable payment other than silver,"[10] the growth of tea consumption in Britain exceeded the silver outflow. The British also tried to sell some luxury items like furs, shark fins and edible bird's nest, pearls, sandalwood, Indian cotton, and Vietnamese sugar in the Chinese market, but they did not have much success, and the shortage of silver pushed the British into a corner over time.

To stop the silver outflow from Britain, the British government needed a major breakthrough and found it in exporting opium to China in return for tea. The British East India Company, for the first time, introduced cotton to replace silver. Cotton exports, however, soon faced a problem because China itself produced cotton. Thus, for China, cotton imports were not attractive. Instead of cotton, Britain began to export opium via India. To offset "Britain's need to pay China for increasing consumption of Chinese tea"[11] the EIC concentrated its energy on producing Indian opium, which was designed for export to China.[12] Figure 2.1 gives a clear picture of which regions of India concentrated on producing opium that was exported to China.

The production of opium from poppies was very complex and required specialized manual labor. Growing poppies requires fertile soil, proper moisture control, frequent fertilization, and a lot of skill and attention to detail. Poppies are a winter crop, so they are planted in the fall after other crops have been harvested. When spring arrives, the flowers bloom, fall off, and go to seed. The seeds are enclosed in a thick husk and are harvested before they are fully mature, when a knife is inserted into the husk surrounding the seeds and lightly squeezed, releasing a white juice that turns into a sticky black mass. The opium is harvested by cutting the seeds in the morning and evening to let the juice flow out and then in the afternoon collecting the black, hardened mass, which is the raw opium. The process of obtaining raw opium requires skill and long hours of labor. The sheath should not be cut too deeply, and each cut should yield less than half a gram. It takes more than twenty careful cuts to get a

Figure 2.1. Shipments of Indian opium to China, 1795–1840. *Source*: Created by the author, based on Tan Chung, *China and The Brave New World: A Study of the Origins of the Opium War (1840–42)* (Carolina Academic Press, 1978), 85.

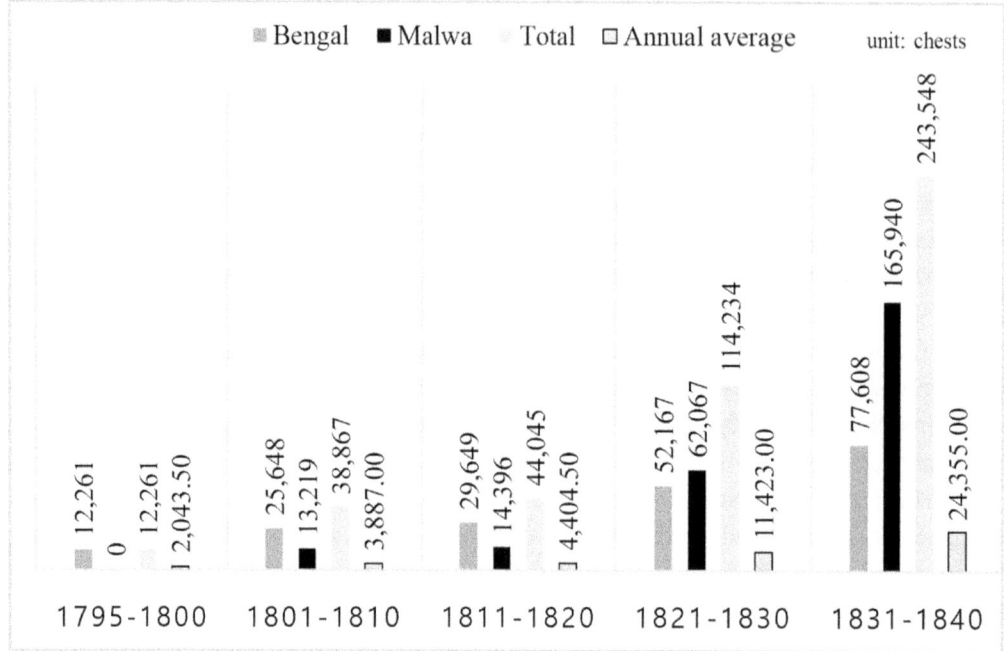

ten-gram chunk. Raw opium is dried several times to form a hard lump of opium. This process also requires a lot of care. Opium cultivators can't just dry them in the sun; instead, they need to turn raw opium over periodically and make sure it doesn't get wet from the rain. Growing poppies to produce opium is so labor-intensive that few farmers cultivated them before the market became large.[13] However, with large quantities of opium being exported to China, opium cultivation and trade became the goose that laid the golden egg.

Britain produced opium in India and exported it to China. In 1729, only 200 chests of opium were exported to China; however, before long, British's opium exports had begun to increase dramatically; they continued to do so until 1838 (4,570 chests in 1800, 23,570 chests in 1832, and 40,000 chests in 1838).[14] For Britain, the exchange of traded commodities was the best choice during the difficult silver shortage. Britain's so-called state merchandizing monopoly[15] made it easier and more effective for the East India Company to facilitate the opium trade. By changing the commodities it traded Britain was able to stop the silver outflow and enjoyed a tremendous trade surplus due to the opium trade, including smuggling.[16]

This does not mean that the British were the only ones exporting opium to China. Merchants from other countries also participated in the Chinese opium trade, and competition among merchants led to unprecedented volumes of opium exports to China. By the end of the eighteenth century, the Chinese opium market was monopolized by the British colonial government in Calcutta, India. The colonial government carefully managed their opium export system to maintain their monopoly, but it could not last long. There are no secrets in the marketplace, and the opium market quickly attracted speculators and competitors. Recognizing the commodity value of opium, traders sought other sources of supply outside of the colonial monopoly in Bengal, for example, Persian (or Parsi) traders sourced opium from Malwa in India,[17] and American traders sourced opium from Smyrna in Turkey, competing with the colonial government in Calcutta. Private merchants secured their interests by challenging the Calcutta colonial government's monopoly on the opium trade. They were not in a position to trade as laxly as the Calcutta colonial government, and they took the initiative to smuggle opium in order to reap more economic benefits. Increased opium smuggling led to collusion between Chinese criminal organizations that moved opium inland from the Chinese coast and Chinese officials who turned a blind eye to the smuggling.[18]

The way brokers operated also played an important role in stimulating the opium trade. Since brokers earned commissions based on the volume of consignments they received, the volume of consignments was more important than the profit on the sale. In practice, the brokers kept a certain amount of commission for each box of opium, even if the selling price of opium fell. Because of this revenue structure, increasing the amount of opium sent to China became a top priority for the brokers. In turn, China's opium market became the center of a transnational commodity network.[19] Caused by increasing quantities of imported opium, the circulation web of imported opium extended not only in littoral zones but also in inland areas.[20] To quote Marx and Engels, the irresistible temptation of opium as a commodity is "the heavy artillery with which it batters down all Chinese walls."[21]

What destructive effects did opium imports have on China? First, opium imports created a lot of socioeconomic problems in Chinese society: "The harmful consequences of the opium consumption swept over the whole Chinese society. The opium consumption brought about thief, make country sick, and pushed people into the depth of misery."[22] "When we think about the opium trades led by the so-called Christian nation, England's opium trades deserved to be harshly criticized. The damage of opium is harmful beyond all description. Anyone living in Chinese society was soon to find out how opium damaged Chinese capacities at an alarming rate."[23] "The harmfulness of opium influenced individuals to begin with, but then started to influence families, and in the end, influenced the country and future generations."[24] In fact, opium smoking expanded to all classes of men, from the Manchu officers and soldiers of the upper class to coolies and peasants of the lower class. Chinese Navy officers even helped to bring opium into Chinese territory.[25]

Second, to meet domestic demand, illegal opium cultivation soared in Chinese territory. Just as the British people became hooked on Chinese tea's astringent taste, often mixed with sugar, more and more Chinese men became addicted to British-Indian opium, leading to the exponential growth of opium imports by China. However, opium imports from outside the country were wholly inadequate to meet the demand, resulting in opium cultivation in China. Opium cultivation in Chinese inland areas steadily increased; according to a report by governmental officials (1831), opium was widely cultivated in Taizhou, Ningbo, Shaoxing, Wenzhou, and Yanzhou of Zhejiang Province.[26] Another governmental report (1838) noted that the opium poppy was cultivated in Guangxi, Guizhou, and Sichuan Province.[27] In the late nineteenth century, for example, poppy cultivation in Sichuan expanded tremendously due to its high price and ease of transportation. In inverse proportion to the expansion of poppy cultivation, paddy and other agricultural land shrank, and the famine that struck eastern Sichuan in 1897 coincided with the shrinkage of arable land, leading to a food crisis.[28] The opium poppy was also widely cultivated in Xinjiang Province.[29]

According to Isabella Bird Bishop, who traveled to Sichuan in the late nineteenth century, opium houses were as common in Sichuan as taverns in the slums of London. And Bishop confessed to having heard rumors of a couple so addicted to opium that they sold all their possessions, even their daughter, because they couldn't control their desire to smoke it.[30] Opium consumption was so deeply embedded in Chinese life that the Chinese themselves used to say, "if you want to take revenge on your enemy, you don't have to beat him or kill him, you just have to seduce him and make him smoke opium."[31] In summary, opium was cultivated in many parts of southwestern China in the early and mid-nineteenth century, which sickened Chinese society.

In response to the increase in opium consumption, cultivation, and trade, Qing bureaucrats proposed exterminatory measures that would eradicate opium-related problems. In July 1813, Qing bureaucrats, including those of the Ministry of Justice (*xingbu*, 刑部), mandated punishments for opium consumers:

> When government officials smoked opium, they had to withdraw from their office. They also received one hundred stroke (*zhang* 杖), beating with a large stick on either the back buttocks or legs and cangue (*jiaxiang* 枷項) for two months. When soldiers and civilians smoked opium, they received one hundred strokes, beating with a large stick on either the back buttocks or legs and cangue for one month. Those who sold opium or opened opium dens would also be punished in accordance with previous regulations.[32]

In 1815, they also discussed ways to prevent foreign opium ships from entering Chinese territory. Jiang Youxian proposed a strong antiforeign opium ship plan—"foreign ships laden with opium would be deported and these ships would never trade commercially with China"—to the Jiaqing Emperor.[33] Other bureaucrats like Li Hong Bin tried to prevent the opium exports of foreign countries through diplomacy: "Given the fact the opium came from the West, we [Chinese government] let each government of Western countries know our strong antiopium policies to stop their opium export."[34] Despite various antiopium measures of Qing bureaucrats, the consumption of opium swept China with unstoppable momentum. As more and more Chinese men were addicted to opium, the opium imports of China had grown exponentially.

Third, and most importantly, continued opium imports aggravated the problems of China's silver-based fiscal system.[35]

The 1811 statement by Su-leng-e (苏楞额, 1742–1827), a Manchurian who served as a senior government official, shows how much China worried about the silver outflow caused mainly by the opium trade: "If they [the foreign merchants] do snatch silver taels and each year ship overseas one million several hundred thousand [taels] . . . then there will be cause for concern for both the state's finances and the people's livelihood."[36] As seen in table 3.1, in 1818 China's silver was the second largest export item in dealing with Britain (for China's bullion shipments to India, 1801–1858, see figure 2.3).

In 1822 the Daoguang Emperor ordered the viceroy of Liangguang (Guangdong and Guangxi) to curb the silver outflow and opium smuggling.[37] Despite this measure China's silver outflow accelerated, while a flourishing illegal opium trade continued in littoral zones. The emperor took stronger "anti opium-silver trade measures" in 1830.

Figure 2.2. Silver holdings by the central government, 1777–1843. *Source*: Created by the author, based on Jin Cao and Dennis O. Flynn, "Global Quantification and Inventory Demand for Silver in China," *Revista de Historia Económica* 38, no. 3 (2020): 9–10.

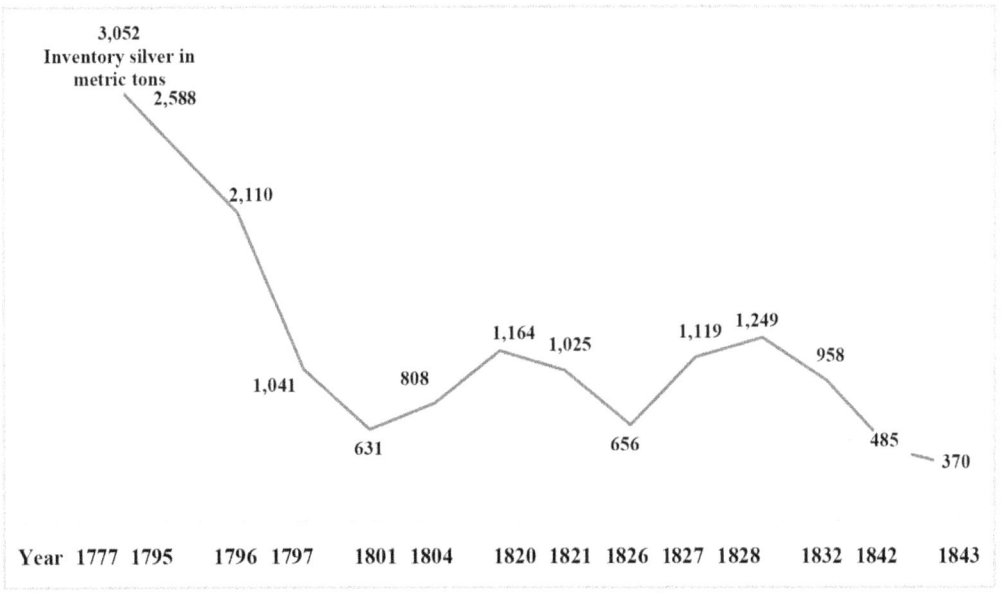

Table 2.1. The Export Trade of Canton, 1818 Season (Values in dollars)*

	Company	British Private	Total	American	Other Flags	Total
Goods						
Ships (number)	16	35	51	44	—	95
Ships (tonnage)	21,500	27,500	49,000	15,410	—	64,410
Exports:						
Tea	5,507,065	436,566	5,943,631	—	—	—
Raw Silk	182,271	632,030	814,301	—	—	—
Silk Piece Goods	—	300,000	300,000	—	—	—
Nankeens**	166,167	550,000	716,167	—	—	—
Tutenague***	—	480,634	480,634	—	—	—
Other Commodities	90,100	1,726,965	1817,065	—	—	—
Silver	400,000	2,688,679	3,088,679	—	3,000,000†	6,088,679

*Hosea Ballou Morse, *The Chronicles of the East India Company Trading to China 1635–1834*, vol. 3 (Harvard University Press, 1926), 345.

**Nankeens is a durable pale yellowish or brownish yellow cotton fabric originally loomed by hand as well as the trousers made from it.

***In Chinese, 白銅 (*baitong*) means nickel-copper-zinc alloy. The Chinese have been producing an alloy of nickel and copper (often combined with zinc), which has the luster and hue of silver. It is much harder than silver and does not fade easily when used. Since the early eighteenth century, it has been widely used as a substitute for real silver to produce various household items such as candlesticks, brush holders, and small desk accessories. In the eighteenth century, it was imported into Europe in small quantities and used by European craftsmen to make household items that imitated silver products.

†Large amounts in bullion from Macao to India.

He banned the use of silver in the international opium trade, mandated monitoring of ships, punishments for bureaucrats who were involved in silver outflow, the monitoring of opium smuggling, and a crackdown on opium dens.[38] Nonetheless, the Qing government could not stop the mounting silver outflow and illegal opium imports;[39] in particular, the galloping increase in silver outflows led to inflation of the value of silver in China. Gideon Nye Jr. (1812–1888), an American diplomat, art collector, writer, and merchant who worked in the East India and China trade, argued that "since opium has spread its baneful poison through China, the quantity of silver exported has been yearly on the increase, till its price has become enhanced, the copper coin

Figure 2.3. China's bullion shipments to India, 1801–1858 (in 000s rupees). *Source*: Created by the author, based on John F. Richards, "The Opium Industry in British India," *Indian Economic and Social History Review* 39, nos. 2–3 (2002): 170–71.

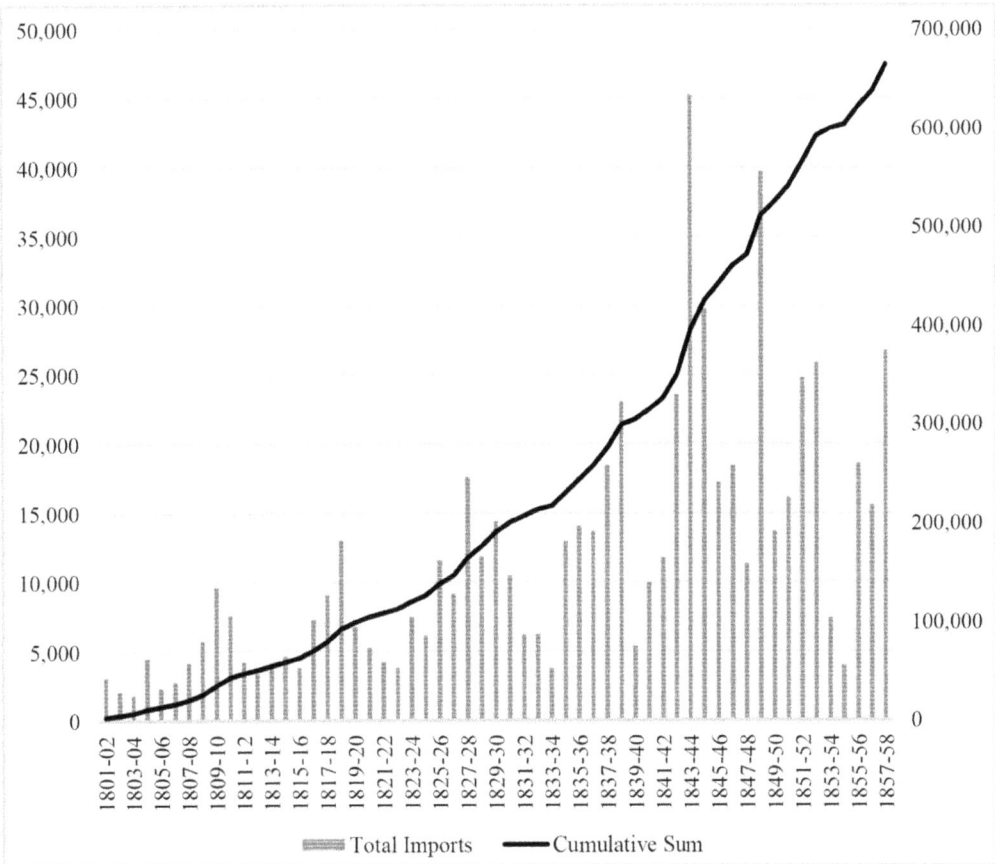

depreciated, and the land and capitation taxes, the transport of grain, and the gabel [import tax], all alike hampered."[40]

By the 1830s the previous balance had been completely reversed.

The Chinese government suffered from inflation in the value of silver,[41] and in response the government imposed a surcharge on taxpayers; in fact, the drain of silver led to an increase in the value of copper in relation to silver. This severely impacted peasants, tradesmen, and small merchants as the taxes were levied in silver but collected in copper. Worse, these taxpayers could not afford to pay the increased taxes after 1800 because they were exploited by state officials through embezzlement and bribes[42] and because of the economic downturn.[43] The taxpayers' accumulated tax delinquency compromised the finances of the Qing Empire.

Table 2.2. Qing Regime's Opium Prohibition, 1729–1836*

Year	Action Taken
1729	The Qing regime criminalized smoking, selling, and operating opium dens.
1780	The Qing regime banned the smoking and sale of opium.
1796	The Qing regime banned the importation of opium (even as a medicine).
1800	The Qing regime banned the importation of opium and the cultivation of opium in inland areas.
1810	The Qing regime banned the smoking of opium and ordered foreign merchants to stop smuggling.
1813	The Qing regime finalized a ban on the sale of opium and penalties for selling opi-um.
1814	The Qing regime ordered the blockade of opium smuggling in Guangdong.
1815	The Qing regime searched foreign ships to stop them from bringing in opium.
1817	The Qing regime made it clear to foreign merchants that they were prohibited from trading in opium.
1821	The Qing regime ordered Hong merchants to closely monitor the importation of opium by foreign merchants.
1822	The Qing regime cracked down on the navy's involvement in opium smuggling.
1823	The Qing regime prohibited aiding and abetting opium smuggling and established penalties.
1829	The Qing regime enacted laws prohibiting the outflow of silver and the smuggling of opium.
1830	The Qing regime banned the retailing of opium and enacted related penalties and banned the cultivation of opium.
1831	The Qing regime established severe penalties for opium smokers.
1832	The Qing regime banned the smuggling of opium by sea.
1834	The Qing regime ordered the water forces in Guangdong to chase away (opium) unloading ships.
1836	The Qing regime orders a thorough investigation into the realities of the opium trade.

*Zhenggu Bao 鮑正鵠, *Yapianzhanzheng* 阿片戰爭 [The Opium War] (Xinzhishicubsanshe, 1954), 50–54.

Combined with the opium trade with Britain, Britain's increasing demand for tea and the aggressive and adventurous British merchants caused China to experience pressures on tea production. Because an increase in export-oriented crops was closely connected with external demand[44] and the development of effective agricultural space in pursuit of large-scale tea production connected Chinese rural areas to Western merchants, the rise of tea cultivation in China can be viewed as an initial moment of the incorporation process. China's abrupt increase in tea cultivation arose from an unavoidable choice to meet the West's demand; as a result, China became the largest exporter of tea in the world. This brought about a radical change in crop cultivation in the central and southeastern regions of China.

Fujian Province became the center of tea cultivation.[45] The Wuyi Mountains (武夷山) in Fujian Province joined the fast-growing area cultivating tea for export. The gazetteer of Fujian (*Fujianxuzhi* 福建續志, 1769) showed how the Wuyi Mountains were turned into a tea-cultivating area in the late eighteenth century: "In the past, the Wuyi Mountains were known as a secluded area where scholars, commoners, and bandits coexisted. It is now called a tea garden or tea village after clearing the land for tea farms. Tea trees covered Wuyi Mountains and tea pickers flocked into the mountains. The number of tea pickers is over ten thousand."[46] As can be seen in the quotation, since the nineteenth century, export-oriented tea cultivation of the Wuyi Mountains became more prominent than the song lyrics of Zhu Xi who boasted about the outstanding scenery of Wuyi Mountains.[47]

Along with these mountains, Mount Niaoshi (*niaoshishan* 鳥石山) and the upper reaches of the Min River (*minjiang* 閩江) in Fujian Province were also transformed into tea-cultivating areas. For instance, the mountain farmers in Minbei area transformed rice cultivation into tea cultivation. As a result, rice paddies on high hills and small-size mountains were uprooted.[48] After the Second Opium War, Western companies opened processing branches in tea-producing areas such as Fuzhou. Not only was Fujian Province transformed into a tea production region, but Anhui Province also began cultivating black tea in response to international demand.[49]

Taiwan was transformed like the Fujian and Anhui areas. When Taiwanese ports were opened by the Peking Treaty (1860), mountain slopes in Taiwan were turned into important tea-cultivating areas. According to the records of the China Imperial Maritime Customs, it was difficult to see tea trees on the mountains fifteen years earlier, but tea trees covered up mountains by the late 1870s.[50] Rice paddies on the Taoyuan Plateau were also converted to tea cultivation areas.[51] Tamsui in Taiwan became an especially important area for the cultivation of tea that was exported to European and American markets, and British merchants especially focused on the tea trade in Taiwan.[52]

As figure 2.4 shows, the tea cultivation of Taiwan increased sharply in response to outside demand. In addition, Fusan Huang, Lin Manhong, and Ueng Jiyin's statistical data show that much of Taiwan's tea was exported to Britain.

In sum, nineteenth-century Fuzhou and Taiwan became centers for commodified tea production, illustrating Benjamin J. Marley's statement that the relationship between "the development of specific commodities" in commodity frontiers and "the expansionary nature of capitalism" generated "place-specific commodity production."[53]

Indeed, as China became a part of the capitalist world-economy, some of its tea cultivators and merchants could not stand apart from the seamless web of the international division of labor. Domestically, to meet a robust growth in demand, mainly from the international market, many tea farms relied upon an organized network of male workers from surrounding villages. As sociopolitical turmoil like the Taiping Rebellion prevented tea farms from hiring tea workers from neighboring towns, many seasonal workers were

Figure 2.4. The export of Taiwanese tea, 1866–1885. *Source*: Created by the author, based on Fusan Huang, Lin Manhong, and Ueng Jiyin, eds., *Maritime Customs Annual Returns and Reports of Taiwan, 1867–1895*, in two vols. (Institute of Taiwan History, Academia Sinica, 1997).

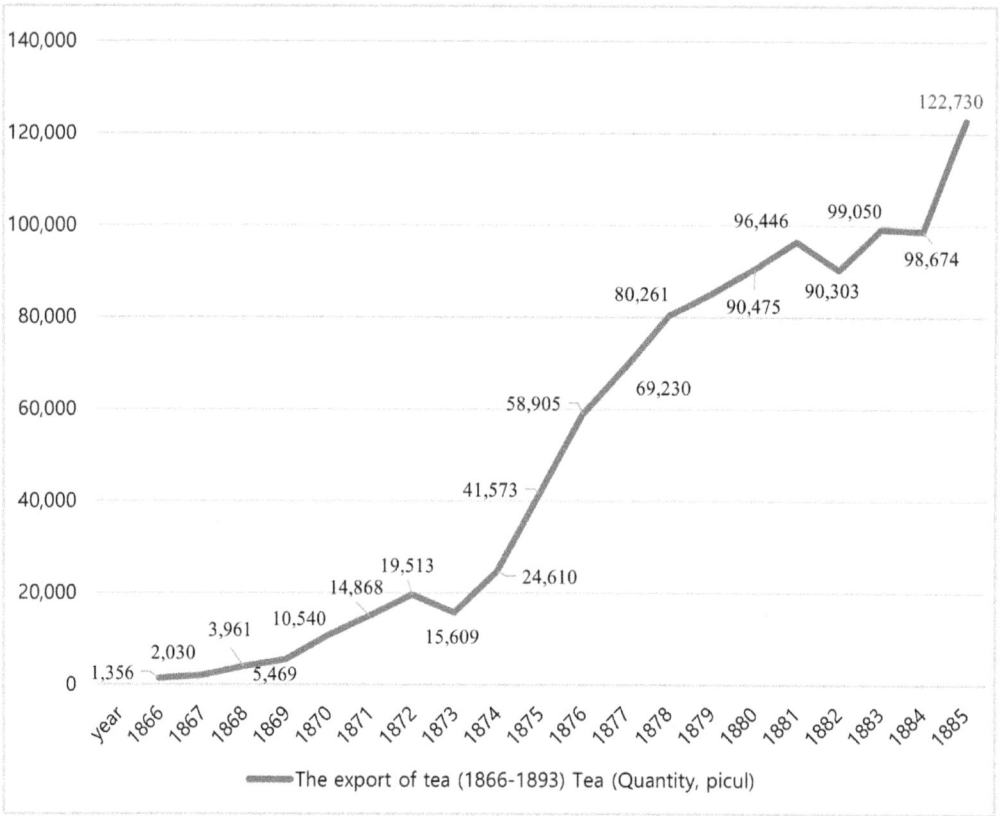

recruited for tea production. Hundreds of seasonal migrant workers who lived in the mountains of the central and southern provinces flocked to Fuzhou for tea cultivation and then returned to their hometowns at the end of the season.[54] The number of these so-called shack people (*pengmin* 棚民) increased due to the enlargement of tea-cultivating areas.[55] As Rev. Justus Doolittle (1824–1880), an American Board missionary to China, noted, "In the suburbs of Fuhchau [Fuzhou], there are many establishments where large numbers of young men, women, and children are industriously employed during the tea season in sifting and sorting the leaves."[56] Additionally, before the invention of tea-roasting machines, the process of roasting tea depended upon human labor. For example, according to Fan He Jun, tea workers in the 1930s were burning eighteen sticks for about twelve hours a day.[57] Given that producing tea was very labor-intensive, it is not surprising that many women were engaged in tea cultivation in southern China.[58] Not only did Chinese women inhabiting these areas work in tea cultivation areas, but many nonnative tea dealers also moved to tea-trading places like Hankou.[59]

In addition, many tea factories (*chachang* 茶厂) were established in the mid-nineteenth century to produce large amounts of tea efficiently:

> In the two *xian* 縣 [Jianyang and Chongyang, in the Quning tea-growing area of Fujian] . . . there are innumerable tea factories (*chachang*). . . . In Quning *xian* alone . . . there are no less than a thousand. The large ones employ over a hundred workers, the small ones several dozen; so in the thousand-odd factories there are ten thousand workers. Several thousand visiting merchants and porters, in an endless stream, block the roads and delay travellers. They also plant tea on low-lying land and pay rent for hill land. . . . Recently these tea plantations have spread far and wide in the four *xiang* 乡; even deep in the Wanshan mountains there are plantations.[60]

According to Andrew Liu, at the end of the nineteenth century, individual tea factories employed from a hundred to a thousand tea workers.[61] When China's tea exports peaked, "a network of coastal warehouse merchants" (tea warehouses) also emerged.[62]

Internationally, Chinese tea workers were moved to Assam, a tea production area in eastern British India. After Robert Bruce first discovered native tea trees in Assam in the 1820s and British explorers pinpointed the location of tea forests in the 1830s,[63] the British regime in India struggled to turn the Assam region into tea plantations. Although ecological conditions were suitable for tea agriculture, plantation managers found it difficult to find laborers. People native to the Assam region lacked tea cultivating skills, and, according to plantation managers' words, were so lazy and indisposed to work that they were not suitable for plantation work.[64] For tea planation managers faced with a labor shortage, Chinese tea workers were the best alternative, as they were seen as industrious and experienced in growing Chinese teas. Lord William Bentinck, a governor general of British India, proposed the recruitment of Chinese tea cultivators living in Penang and Singapore.[65] William Griffith, a naturalist and botanist, also argued that "a sufficient number of first-rate Chinese cultivators and manufacturers, both of black and green teas" should be hired.[66] To meet the demands of Charles Alexander Bruce, Robert Bruce's brother, British deputy G. J. Gordon was even dispatched to China to hire Chinese tea laborers. Chinese tea workers were eagerly welcomed by the tea plantation owners of British India, even though there were some problems in hiring competent Chinese tea growers.[67] Thus, it is not an exaggeration to say that Chinese labor helped to begin the British tea plantations in Assam.[68]

However, China faced an economic disaster after Britain diversified its tea imports. After India successfully began cultivating tea, British merchants reduced their dependency on Chinese tea imports:[69] "The ratio of exportation between Indian and Chinese tea was 1 to 10 in the early 1870s, but the ratio became close to 1 to 1.2 in the late 1880s."[70] As a result, China's share of the global tea supply dropped by 50 percent between 1872 and 1896.[71]

Plus, in the global tea market, tea plantations in the British colonies were able to respond to supply and demand more flexibly than Chinese tea producers. In other words, they could respond to market signals like "expand tea production when demand increases; curtail tea production when demand falls." In contrast with the colonial powers' tea plantations, tea cultivation in China remained small-scale and relatively unresponsive to the fluctuations of the global tea market. Because the tea trade was entirely controlled by Britain, and the Qing government did not protect or support tea-related business, China's tea cultivators—especially small-size tea farming households that depended disproportionately on the Western tea market—suffered from reduced tea exports, as well as tough competition over export markets.[72] As a consequence of the sharp decrease in tea exports, "a valuable trade has dwindled to the most meagre dimensions. Thousands of acres (in China) must have gone out of cultivation."[73]

The decline of tea exports exposed the vulnerability of China's tea cultivators to the vagaries of the international tea market. When tea prices fell, tea-industry workers, like tea pickers and tea sellers, lost their jobs: "After 1881 [seventh year of the Guangxu Emperor], . . . those who opened tea houses had dissipated their fortunes over the years."[74] This was not confined just to tea-related workers; government officials also had difficulty collecting transit dues (*likin* 厘金), or the inland tax on tea: "The decrease last year in the inland duties levied upon tea amounted to 150,000 Haikwan taels, and in that levied upon sundries 50,000 Haikwan taels, making a total falling-off in revenue of 200,000 Haikwan taels."[75] Not only were Chinese merchants unable to profit sufficiently from the tea trade, but other tea-related workers, like the artisans who decorated tea chests and boxes and the boatmen and laborers who loaded tea for export, also lost their jobs.[76]

The decline in Chinese tea cultivation influenced the economic conditions of port cities. In fact, Fuzhou and Xiamen's tea exports dropped off sharply as a result of the

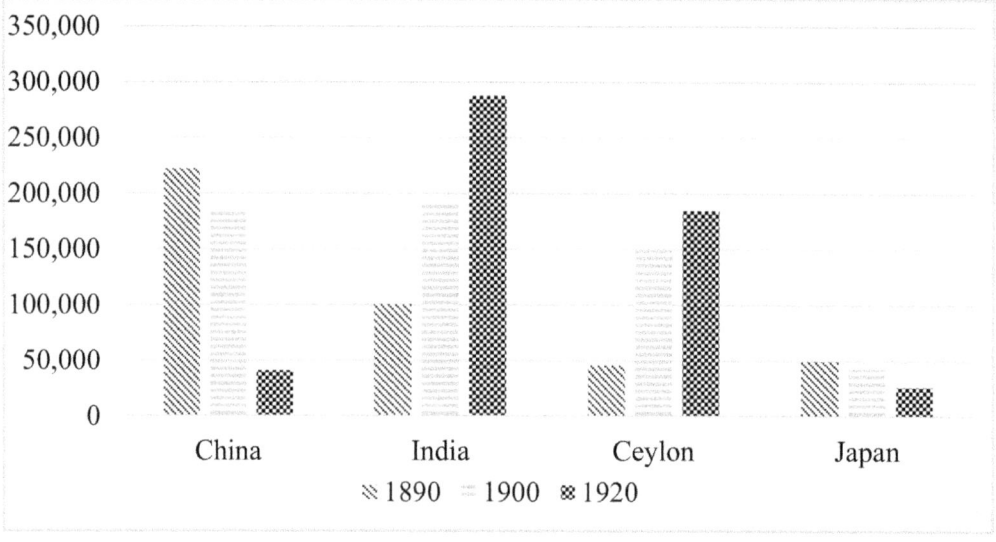

Figure 2.5. Tea exports from China, India, Ceylon, and Japan to the world, 1890–1920. *Source*: Created by the author, based on Ciyu Chen, *Jindai zhongguo chaye de fazhan xing shijie shichang* [The development of the Chinese tea trade in the modern world market] (Zhongyang yanjiuyuan jingji yanjiu suo, 1982), 324–25.

Figure 2.6. Statistics of China's tea-exporting countries, 1862–1920. *Source*: Created by the author, based on Ciyu Chen, *Jindai zhongguo chaye de fazhan xing shijie shichang* [The development of the Chinese tea trade in the modern world market] (Zhongyang yanjiuyuan jingji yanjiu suo, 1982), 306–7.

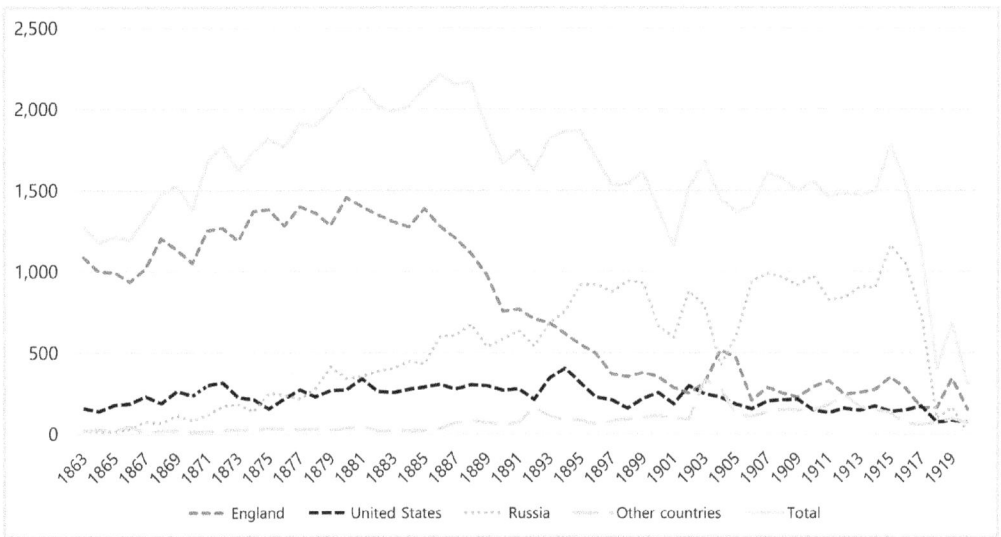

diversification of the tea trade.[77] Both cities suffered irreversible economic damage due to the precipitous decline in tea exports; Fuzhou narrowly escaped the collapse of the tea market by increasing (re-)exports to other Chinese ports, while Xiamen (Amoy) suffered acutely from the decline.[78] China's international tea trade allows us to recognize the rise and decline of port cities because there was a deep relationship between China's tea-producing areas and the port cities, as an important transportation node (see figure 2.7).[79]

Worse, by the second half of the nineteenth century, Western merchants had successfully penetrated major areas of the tea trade in China and become deeply involved in the tea industry. As a consequence, many Chinese tea cultivators were gradually subordinated to Western merchants. Zuo Zongtang 左宗棠 (1812–1885) argued that "Western merchants built many tea storages and dealerships. By using steamships, they also got the [tea-related] news quickly. [As a result of this], while Fujian teas had been heavily dependent on Western merchants, the latter did not need to deeply depend on Fujian teas."[80] In the 1860s, tea accounted for more than 60 percent of the Qing Empire's earnings from foreign exports; however, by the 1930s, under the Republic of China, that number hovered "around five percent."[81] On the other hand, the share of Indian tea in the UK market increased from 2.84 percent to 30.35 percent between 1864 and 1885. Not only that, but the share of Ceylon tea increased from 2 percent to 36 percent between 1885 and the late 1890s.[82]

Figure 2.7. China's major port cities' export volume of tea, 1843–1920. *Source*: Created by the author, based on Ciyu Chen, *Jindai zhongguo chaye de fazhan xing shijie shichang*, [The development of the Chinese tea trade in the modern world market] (Zhongyang yanjiuyuan jingji yanjiu suo, 1982), 228–30.

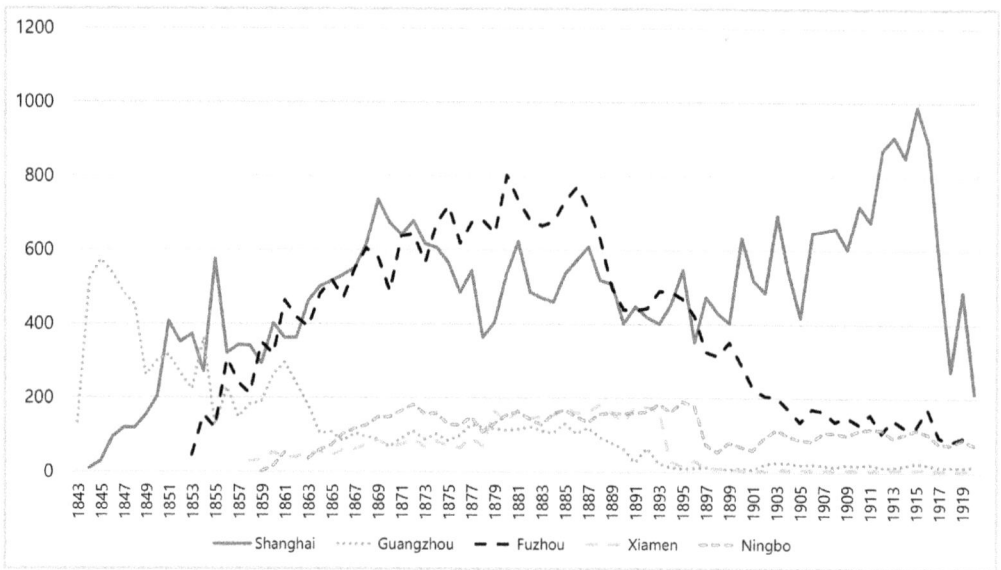

In sum, focusing on the incorporation process allows us to recognize how the ongoing British demand for tea and the exclusive British-China tea trade system generated a tea boom in southeast China until the mid-nineteenth century and a sudden collapse in the late nineteenth century—and, as a consequence, how the transnational commodity network created under the dynamics of the global capitalism influenced China's tea market, tea industry, and port cities.

The overarching influence of China's tea export was not confined to socioeconomic aspects. China's ecological conditions inexorably degraded in the nineteenth century. Anne Osborne insisted that various forms of socioeconomic activities expanded during the eighteenth and nineteenth centuries—for example, the increase in commercial crop cultivation like tobacco, hemp, indigo, and ramie; the demand for firewood; overcutting timber and bamboo; and increasing the number of mines—led to ecological degradation in the lower Yangtze region.[83] In a similar vein, Robert Marks noted that an increase in cash crop cultivation following China's incorporation process into the capitalist world-economy led to serious ecological consequences, along with changes in China's agricultural land use patterns. Chinese tea is no exception.[84] The rise of Chinese tea cultivation, driven by the growth of tea exports, produced several environmental problems. As large swaths of forest were turned into tea-cultivating areas, the rich biodiversity of natural habitats was decreased dramatically, and soil erosion increased as a result of the deforestation and land clearance that was part of transforming areas for tea cultivation.[85] Driven by commercial specialization for tea export, for instance, mountain farmers in the Minbei area transformed areas of rice cultivation into areas of tea cultivation, thereby uprooting rice paddies and forests from high hills and small mountains. This led to landslides that damaged lowland cultivation: "The Jianyangshan of Fujian Province had a lot of valleys that produced a stream of spring water. Recently reclamation for tea cultivation within Jianyangshan caused trouble. . . . When Jianyangshan had heavy rain, sandy soils washed down and the fertile soil of lowlands was turned into gravelly patches. As a result, grains of the lowland could not grow. . . . Fistfights broke out between tea cultivators of mountains and lowland cultivators and it led to a lawsuit."[86] In the 1870s, American missionary Rev. J. E. Walker recorded the ecological problems of tea cultivation areas in Shaowu: "The hills were originally covered with a thick growth of grass, bushes and trees the roots of which retain the rainwater to feed the fountains which irrigate the rice-fields. But from the almost bare ground of the tea-hills the whole rain-fall rushes off in torrents, causing the fields to suffer first by flood and then by drought. Old tea-fields may sometimes be seen with the slides cut deep with ditches worn out by the water and all productive soil washed away."[87] In response to the environmental problems the governor of Anhui and Zhejiang, and central government officials like Lang Baochen and Tao Shilin, pointed out the soil erosion caused by shack people and the locals' reclamations of forest, and asked them to restrict cash crop farming, including tea cultivation. However, this measure was not effective and did not help protect environmental conditions.

Reckless tea cultivation, spurred by external trade, aggravated China's natural disruptions, which indicates that China's ecological disasters can be contextualized within the capitalist universe.[88] In Jason Moore's view, this is because the expansive nature of capitalism created ecological crises in newly incorporated areas.[89] After the local ecosystem became integrated into the capitalist world-economy, the ecological system of China's tea cultivating areas became labor- and capital-intensive, which consequently brought about environmental degradation.[90] Stephen Bunker and Paul Ciccantell have presented persuasive arguments about why newly incorporated areas, resulting from "the systemic expansion of the exploitation of nature via a division of labor on increasingly global scale,"[91] faced ecological difficulties. They argued that industrial countries in the capitalist world-system have continuously drawn external areas into the capitalist system so that they could have cheap and stable access to the crops and raw materials of those newly incorporated areas. Incorporated areas that faced the structural pressure of the international division of labor had to export their crops or raw materials, even though they suffered from increasing production costs, export competition with other underdeveloped countries, and ecological damage.[92]

In the nineteenth-century capitalist world-system, opium, silver, and tea combined in a variety of ways to bring China into the system. It seems pointless to try to determine which of these combinations was the most central. The Indian colonial government, the British East India Company, speculators, opium dealers, Chinese opium brokers and retailers, Chinese opium smokers, the flow of silver into China, the emergence of export-oriented tea cultivation, and the socioeconomic and ecological changes in China associated with tea exports all played their part in China's incorporation into capitalism.

In thinking about China's process of incorporation into the capitalist world-economy, another key issue is the appearance of new social classes mirroring the politico-economic powers of the colonial powers. In the next section, I discuss the appearance of these new social classes during the incorporation process.

A Rise of New Classes in China's Incorporation Process

A deep understanding of a society's class structure during a certain period helps us to interpret the society's socioeconomic conditions (e.g., the mode of production) and its dynamics; a class structure itself gave rise to the class division formed by social relationships of production and class conflicts. Furthermore, it informs approximate structural conditions of class-related phenomenon; for instance, within a peasant-centered society, there is little chance of a social revolution led by an industrial proletariat; however, through the emergence of an industrial proletariat, even if it is small compared to the number of peasants, we can detect a change in society.

For this reason, at a time when a social structure is drastically changing, we find it easy to examine the formation of (new) social classes.[93] Indeed, tracing the new social classes in a given society helps us better understand social transformations.[94] Seen from this angle, I intend to focus on the relationships between the new classes that occurred in China's incorporation process. This perspective contrasts with a common idea of past comparative historical studies that the rigid and rarely changing class structure of the ancien régime led to the decline of late imperial China.[95] I assume that the social origins, membership, characteristics (consciousness, identity, solidarity), and concentration, including the location and developmental paths of the new social classes, had been derailed from the path dependency of the class formation of imperial China. In doing so, I reveal the fact that the rise of new classes correlates with China's incorporation process.

Two Theoretical Premises for New Classes

When a precapitalist society becomes more integrated with global capitalism, new classes, suited for the logic of the capitalist system, were created. I here cover several new classes, first the coolies observed mainly on an international level, and then compradors and capitalists observed mainly on a domestic level. Not surprisingly, the incorporation of a precapitalist society into the capitalist world-economy brought about significant disruption in old political governance and socioeconomic systems, while fostering new classes inextricably linked to foreigners, compradors and coolies, in order to give colonial powers access to markets and produce cheap labor in the incorporated areas. Thus, the new classes created by the penetration of the capitalist world-economy acted as a bridge between colonial powers and the incorporated area's economy or served themselves as a new and cheap labor force within the international division of labor system. China was no exception: China's incorporation process into the capitalist world-economy turned the nineteenth century into an era of unparalleled change and it gave rise to new classes. Then how do we define the new social classes that emerged during China's incorporation process? In answering this question, I proceed from two premises.

First, the social class conception is not invariable. Nor is a new social class formed entirely by internal dynamics. Although many define a social class as an organized group that shares economic interests and socioeconomic status, social scientists and historians have developed various social class conceptions. There are many different theoretical conceptions of social class, and it is inappropriate to lump a variety of (social) class conceptions into one category. I mainly address the new social classes that emerged during China's incorporation process here to simplify the argument and to avoid an absolute methodological internalism in analyzing new classes. To that end, I will distinguish the rise of new classes in nineteenth-century China from the existing social classes of late imperial China and stress that the new classes appear due to the direct or indirect influences of the capitalist world-economy.

Second, social class in any given society is not static but fluid. The class structure could be changed by the gradual or radical changes of economic structure or sociopolitical transformations. Regarding this, Wallerstein's idea enables us to figure out the rise of new classes and their transitional movements during China's incorporation process.

> Social class as a concept was invented within the framework of the capitalist world-economy and it is probably most useful if we use it as historically specific to this kind of world-system. Class-analysis loses its power of explanation whenever it moves towards formal models and away from dialectical dynamics. Thus, we wish to analyze here classes as evolving and changing structures, wearing ever-changing ideological clothing, in order to see to whose advantage it is at specific points of time to define class-memberships in particular conceptual terms. What we shall attempt to show it that alternative perceptions of social reality have very concrete consequences for the ability of contending classes to further their interests.[96]

Wallerstein presents a changeable and evolving class conception in the context of specific moments of time, particular places, and the conditions of development of the capitalist world-economy. Terrence K. Hopkins echoed this point and noted that "the theoretical conditions and processes of 'class-formation' are themselves continually transformed in the course of capitalist development."[97] Hence, "the bourgeoisie is not a static phenomenon"[98] and conceptions of the proletariat cannot be eternal or fixed.[99]

Wallerstein's idea of class was shared by (or partially influenced by) Marx and Marxist historians and was often used to combine historical context with class analysis of the capitalist mode of production.[100] They considered social and economic class as a historical construction and a result of the social-historical process and relationship, in particular because of its flexible capability. Wallerstein also stressed class formation over a long period of time and foregrounded an organization of human relationships that could be changed in the context of historical time and the dynamics of a transnational entity.[101] In Wallerstein's analysis, "a variety of different mechanisms of labor control is possible and used in capitalism, ranging from slavery and indentured servants to free labor,"[102] as long as laborers were formulated and reformulated within the globalized capitalist system.[103] Not only are laborers formed by the dynamics of historical capitalism, but the bourgeoisie also perforce emerged within the logics of the world-economy, according to Wallerstein. It implies that social classes within a society are sometimes structured and restructured by the operating mechanisms of the world-economy. In fact, as China was incorporated into the capitalist world-economy in the nineteenth century, Chinese society experienced massive social structural changes that led to the rise of new social classes. To pinpoint more closely the types of new classes, I will distinguish the rise of Chinese new classes between the international level and the domestic level.

THE RISE OF A NEW CLASS IN ITS INTERNATIONAL ASPECTS

As a new class, coolies were created by the influences of the capitalist world-economy. The cheap labor of a newly incorporated area is essential in expanding the boundary of the capitalist world-economy because it attracts foreign capital. In other words, it is not surprising that the Chinese coolie emerged during China's incorporation process: The continual re-creation of cheap labor stemming from newly incorporated areas plays a key role in replenishing established workers,[104] and it also serves to help weave a seamless web of the international division of labor system[105] or capital accumulation.[106]

The appearance of new and cheap labor was not shaped by the voluntary participation of laborers or the policies of the Chinese government but produced by the logic of the world-economy. In the long run, the capitalist mode of production established a globalized labor market network and brought new laborers into the New World's plantation areas.[107] Especially since the abolition of the slave trade in the nineteenth century and the improvement of commerce and human transportation, the New World's plantations established by the colonial powers sought a substitute for slave labor. In 1842, Lord Elgin addressed the Jamaican parliament, stating that a great experiment (i.e., the abolition of slavery, completed by 1838) had been carried out in the colonies of the West Indies, and he saw great promise in the new wage laborers (i.e., indentured laborers) who would work on the sugar plantations.[108] However, things did not turn out as Lord Elgin had anticipated. After the abolition of slave labor, sugar plantation areas like Jamaica, Trinidad, and British Guiana, where labor was relatively scarce relative to arable land, had difficulty securing labor, and what is worse, freed slaves in the region tended to pursue independent farming rather than working on plantations. As a result, plantation owners no longer had the reliable plantation workers they needed to produce sugar. This, in turn, led to a decline in sugar production, an increase in sugar prices, and dissatisfaction in core countries that consumed sugar. In simple terms, a sufficient number of plantation laborers were needed to produce enough sugar.

Chinese coolies, who were less costly and more industrious than African slaves, fulfilled the requirements.[109] This strongly implies that Chinese coolies can be contextualized in the migration of workers in the nineteenth century, which was mainly controlled by the politico-economic strategies of the colonial powers. In the context of world-systems analysis, I will reexamine the rise of coolie labor in describing China's incorporation process; Chinese coolies were a critical component of each and every phase of the process. How and why coolie labor emerged in China as explicit evidence of China's incorporation process is the crux of the question I must answer. I will examine connections between labor movements and the incorporation process under the conditions of the global expansion of the capitalist world-economy.

Coolie, by its very nature, is a new concept referring to migrant laborers in the nineteenth and early twentieth centuries. As is well-documented, (Chinese) coolies were referred to in Chinese as *kuli* 苦力[110] or piglet (*zhuzai* 猪仔)[111], a vulgar expression of *kuli*. These Chinese words represented hard manual labor. The coolie agreement was called a labor contract (*Gu-gong-he-tong* 雇工合同), according to Evelyn Hu-Dehart.[112] Nonetheless, there is an unfinished controversy over the definition. Hu-Dehart defined Chinese coolies as legal and documented workers; at the same time, however, they represented a third category between free and slave labor. In her account, coolies were described as a distinctive working class that was neither slave nor free. To borrow Giovanni Arrighi's phrasing, the coolie "stands in the grey between coercion and consent."[113] The conceptual vagueness relative to the Chinese coolie is also noted by Walton Look Lai, who argues that "it also raises serious questions (which cannot be discussed here) about whether the Latin American Chinese indentured servants were in practice significantly different from slaves, regardless of what the new (Cuban or Peruvian) deemed them to be."[114] Lai's question did not mean that it necessarily had to be answered. By posing a question, he showed how difficult answering it was.

Although it is difficult for Chinese coolies to be placed in a category between free and slave, those who suffered from low pay, harsh working conditions, and unjust discrimination were scarcely better off than African slaves in practice. The double meaning of "coolie," consequently, complicates our ability to agree on a definition. It is in part attributed to the coercive power of the nineteenth-century international division of labor system because it presents a yawning gap between the conception and reality of the Chinese coolies. Conceptually, it obviously remolded (forced) slave trades to (voluntary) indentured labor, but in reality voluntary indentured labor was another form of the labor exploitation system. For instance, a Chinese man "remains a slave to die there"[115] on the Chincha Islands of Peru. The predatory activities (e.g., kidnapping, fraud, and violence), rather than peaceful and lawful activities, became the guiding light of Chinese coolie recruitment,[116] coolie ships,[117] and coolie labor. Let us now take a closer look at the rise of Chinese coolies caused mainly by the predatory practices of colonial powers.[118]

At the world-historical moment when the capitalist world-economy penetrated China in the nineteenth century, colonial powers, encountering unrelenting pressure to meet Europeans' demand for sugar, actively intervened in raising coolie laborers to secure the labor force: "Labor flows from South China expanded rapidly from 1850 to the 1870s, sending workers to newly emergent cash crop economies around the world. These flows were most strongly determined by outside forces."[119] This strongly indicates that the capitalist world-economy pushed Chinese laborers into the international division of labor after the abolition of the African slave trade; since the Treaty of Ghent (1814), Britain and the United States had agreed to make efforts to end the African slave trade.[120] To be specific, Britain banned British participation in the slave trade in 1807, the US in 1808. Slavery was abolished in British possessions by 1838. While they had yet to effectively ban the international slave trade, they still had to seek a substitute labor force for the mines and factories in Peru and sugar plantations in the West Indies and Cuba.

Sugar plantations were among the critical reasons the global capitalist economy was desperate to find substitute labor. Before the Haitian Revolution (1791–1805), Haiti was a primary location that exported sugar to the world market. Because they were heavily dependent on a workforce of African slaves, however, Haiti's sugar plantations came face-to-face with a production crisis in the aftermath of the Haitian Revolution. Following Haiti's slave revolution, the "European state imposed an embargo on Haitian sugar, driving Haiti out of the sugar market. In 1791, Haiti's sugar production had reached 78,696 tons. After the revolution, sugar production steadily dwindled, down to a half ton in 1835."[121] As Haiti's sugar production decreased, other colonized areas rose rapidly as sugar production areas. Among them was Cuba, which became a center of sugar production. In fact, the number of sugar plantations in Cuba increased sharply after the 1780s: "In 1775, there were 473 sugar plantations on the island; in 1817, there were over 780; and by 1850, the number had exceeded 1,750."[122] Supplying Chinese coolies was a well-timed solution for plantation owners who had a chronic shortage of labor power. Consequently, 125,000 Chinese indentured laborers were sent to Cuba from 1847 to 1874.[123]

What is of special interest here is the fact that the dramatic rise of the Chinese coolies was not spontaneous but artificial. The opening of China's ports in the mid-nineteenth century enabled Western merchants to intervene in Chinese immigration and change its pattern. Lower classes in South China were a prime target for Western merchants.[124] The coolie trade flourished mainly in Fujian and Guangdong Provinces in southern China, because these regions not only have many ports but also have geographical features that allow them to frequently contact Western merchants. Of the Chinese coolies, the Wenzhou, Hokchiu, Hokkien, Teochiu, Cantonese, Henghua/Hokchia, Hakka, and Hailam were overwhelmingly in the majority.[125] Before the 1840s Chinese who emigrated abroad were largely restricted to Southeast Asia and their migration was facilitated by Chinese junks, but after the Opium Wars Western ships began to penetrate into the "the traditional junk monopoly of passenger trade."[126]

After the 1840s, Chinese workers dispersed not only into Southeast Asia but also into the Americas. In the case of the recruitment and transportation of Chinese coolies who moved to Peru or Cuba, outside forces were vital due mainly to a serious labor shortage on the plantations of Cuba, Peru, and Brazil caused by the abolition of the slave system and an increasing number of plantations.[127]

As discussed earlier, the decoupling of a continuous extension of the globalized commodity chain and a reduction in the number of cheap laborers due to the abolition of the slave trade brought about a labor shortage on the large-scale plantations of colonies or peripheral areas. The existing laborers of European colonies or peripheral areas were hardly enough to cover the extended production lines—thus the import of Chinese coolies was an alternative to relieve the manpower shortage. This indicates that the ongoing pressure for more competitive pricing implicitly and explicitly forced merchants and plantation owners to bring Chinese laborers who lived outside the world of the capitalist world-economy into the ambit of the capitalist world-economy.[128]

Since the importation of cheap laborers was the only means of sustaining labor-intensive and export-oriented plantations,[129] colonial powers encouraged plantation owners to recruit indentured laborers. Just as they used cheap African slavery on plantations, they also brought Chinese coolies to their own plantations: "Their fathers [Europeans] destroy Caribs; their sons weep for Caribs and grind up negroes; their grandsons pity negroes, and put Coolies, Chinese, and whatever other unresisting race they can lay hands on into the mills."[130] Thanks in part to their cheap labor, Chinese coolies, "as the pioneers of Chinese coolie-trade,"[131] were already introduced in 1847 into Cuba.

Chinese coolies' movements were not restricted to Cuba or Peru. In contrast with Indian migration, which was confined to the Afro-Asian world or Caribbean islands, coolies were scattered all over the world. There were traces of Chinese coolies even in the Dutch plantation colony of Suriname in South America (see table 2.3).

Table 2.3. Indentured Laborers in Suriname*

Place of Origin	Men	Women	Boys	Girls	Total
West Indies	538	368	128	113	1,147
Holland	73	3	1	1	78
China	444	6	7	7	464
Java	93	—	—		93
Total	1,148	377	136	121	1,782

*Great Britain, House of Commons, "Enclosure in No. 37, Immigration Report for the Year 1875," in *Slave Trade No. 3 (1877), Reports Respecting the Condition of Coolies in Surinam* (1887), 76.

Chinese coolies indeed were exported to the British Caribbean island of Dominica, where they specialized in export-oriented coffee cultivation, and the French island of Guadeloupe, where they specialized in export-oriented sugar cultivation and suffered from intensive exploitation due to labor shortages.[132] They were even introduced to Tahiti and Brazil.

Not only were Chinese coolies moved to European colonies but also to Hawaii. The natural advantages of Hawaii, such as its tropical climate and fertile soil, drove plantation owners to cultivate sugar. Relatedly, as "the native race [of Hawaii] has continued to decline in numbers"[133] and the Reciprocity Treaty in 1876 (which concerned free trade duties between Hawaii and the United States) was enacted, the large-scale sugar plantations of Hawaii needed, and were able, to import foreign laborers. To fill the labor shortages, large numbers of Chinese, Korean, and Japanese laborers were absorbed by the sugar plantations of Hawaii. The Chinese population increased sharply "from 364 to 18,254" between 1852 and 1884.[134] For sugar plantation owners, these Chinese coolies were a suitable solution because it was easier to control Chinese coolies than native Hawaiian workers who often ran away from the plantations.

To secure Chinese coolies as a valuable cheap labor source, Western merchants used every means available, in part by employing Chinese crimps (see figure 2.8 [3A]).[136] Chinese crimps were known for using any means, including kidnapping and fraudulent contracts, to recruit contract workers. The role of Chinese crimps was significant when we are reminded of Arnold Meagher's account that "most foreigners felt that crimps were indispensable."[136] At a time when crimps were dying to get coolies, Cantonese were unsafe to walk the streets even in daylight. This is because, if necessary, they kidnapped Chinese men without any qualms. The historical records of kidnapping in obtaining Chinese coolies are reflected in the following accounts:

> Cha-yin, a Chinese (taken from American ship), states: I am 35 years of age and unmarried; a workman employed on the White Cloud Mountain. About fifteen days ago I was seized by ten Chinese armed with swords and

pikes. I cried out, but no one came to me; it was night. I was dragged away to Tung-poo, near Whampoa. I was taken on board a boat and foreign vessel. I refused and was beaten; taken and tied up with a rope, then beaten with the flat part of a sword. I was taken on board a foreign ship; asked by foreigners if I was willing to emigrate; said no; was again put on board the Chinese boat and beaten afresh, the same as before, and threatened that if I did not consent to emigrate when asked again, I should be killed. I consented under fear. I do not know of any coolies having been killed in that way, but it was said among the coolies that some had been beaten to death. I received one dollar to purchase something to eat; was middling well treated on board the foreign ship; fed twice a day; did not see anyone beaten on board that ship.[137]

I was out of employment when an acquaintance asked me if I would like to go abroad and work for his master at eight dollars a month, pay to commence on my departure in the ship, and an advance of wages given when signing the contract. The offer was too tempting to be rejected without a few inquiries, so I asked him where he wanted me to go; but he could not—or would not—tell me exactly, stating that his master was at Macao collecting his men, and if I wished to go he would send me down to him, when I could make my own arrangements. I accordingly agreed to go, and, with a note from him, he dispatched me in the first junk leaving Canton, giving at the same time some instructions to the master of the junk which I could not hear, any further than that he would introduce me to his master on our arrival, which he did by marching me straightway into a barracoon, where, after a night's lodging, I was informed of my situation (not the eight dollars a month one of course), but a seven years' one at three dollars. I swore a little, you may depend, when I discovered the utter hopelessness of my position—for which I was informed, if I did not mend my manners, they would find means to make me, a fact I did not doubt; therefore, I was not many days in the "man-trap" before I was only too glad to get anywhere out of it. So here I am, like many more unfortunate fools, and all I wish for now is a heavy course upon the hairless head of the villain who brought my transportation.[138]

Ung-cheong-po, a Tartar (taken from an American ship), states: About twelve days ago I was selling herbs in the streets of Canton; it was in the south suburbs. A man (Chinese) came up and asked me to go to Honam, to fetch something to Canton; got into a boat and was taken to Chang-chow. I objected to go to that place, and was struck. I was placed on board a foreign ship, and asked if I would go to a foreign country; I declined. The foreigner said I was to be taken back as I had refused to go. I was again put into the kidnapping boat, and beaten on my back with the flat of a sword;

> I received four blows, and was told I must, when on board the foreign ship, say I was willing to go, or I should be killed. I said I would rather die than go. I was kept below on the foreign ship; my dress was changed, and I was not allowed on deck. There were 189 coolies down in the place; we had plenty of room and plenty to eat; all were unwilling to go, and had been kidnapped. Six days ago I was brought away from the foreign ship.[139]

These gripping narratives of kidnapped people represented well not only the horrors of being kidnapped but how often kidnapping occurred.

Why did Western merchants go so aggressively into such a transportation business? Among their motives for the coolie trade, their profit motivation was the most important: "As time went on and the profits of the coolie-trade grew more and more tempting, piracy and wholesale kidnapping were resorted to for the purpose of filling vessels which otherwise could not be loaded with sufficient rapidity."[140] In 1860, the *New York Times* reported on the profit that could be obtained from the coolie trade: "Thirty dollars a-head or more were being paid last year for coolies delivered on board; arrived at Havana, the 'contracts' could be sold at $400 a-head."[141] This shows that income drove them to become shameless coolie traders.[142]

In conclusion, the central driving force of the nineteenth-century capitalist world-economy drew indentured labor mainly from India and China; this was a new paradigm of labor migration. In particular, the transformation from the slave trade to the indentured labor system, combined with China's incorporation process, pushed Chinese laborers into the international division of labor within the modern world-system. I insist that the increase of Chinese coolies was part of China's incorporation. The reason could be accounted for by Wallerstein's idea of the importance of an external arena's exports in illustrating its incorporation process. A distinctive feature observed in Chinese coolie migration, affiliated with its incorporation process, is its globalizing pattern. Rather than being restricted to European colonies, the migration of Chinese coolies spread all over the world beginning in the nineteenth century. It reminds us to consider the ways in which Chinese coolies' migration emerged as a major source for the labor supply of the entire capitalist world-economy (see figure 2.9 [3B]).

Unlike Chinese coolies who moved to the core states' colonial plantations, most others who entered the United States became mine workers during the Gold Rush, sugar cane workers, or railway workers as a result of the westward expansion, and later as a substitute for the labor of black slaves, in southern areas like Memphis, Tennessee (see figure 2.8. [3C] and figure 2.9 for distribution of the Chinese by state).[143]

Just as Chinese coolies faced severe working conditions on the plantations, Chinese migrants in United States also suffered from institutional and racial discrimination; during the second half of the nineteenth century Chinese men residing in the United States did not have legal protection and were not allowed to become U.S. citizens. The state of California imposed a mining tax and poll tax on Chinese miners. Indeed, as many unskilled and low-paid white laborers moved to California by the 1870s, these white

Figure 2.8. The rise of new economic classes within the logic of the capitalist world-economy. *Source*: Created by the author.

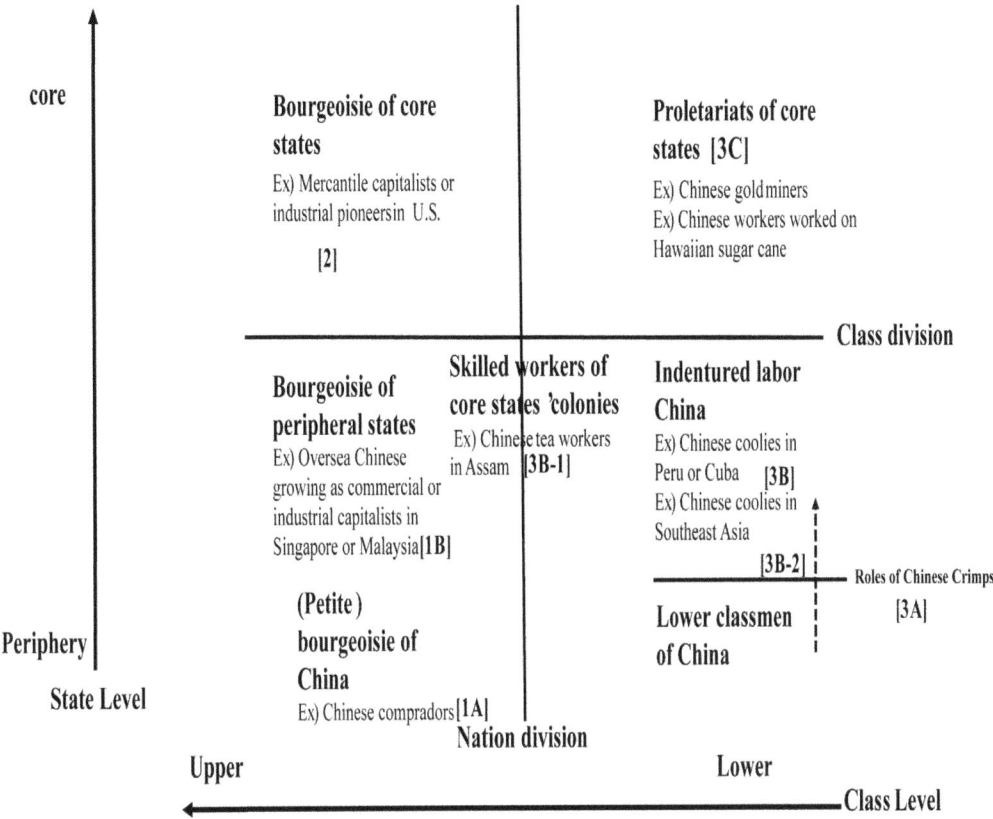

workers agitated for the exclusion of Chinese immigrants. In this sense, it is inappropriate to argue that Chinese coolies in core or semiperipheral countries (e.g., those with better working conditions, higher wages, and some legal protections for white workers or citizens) faced better conditions than migrated workers to peripheral countries during China's incorporation process. Indeed, taking into account the fact that both Peruvians and Chinese coolies in the United States were in difficult working conditions, the state capacities of Peru and the United States did not seem to be directly linked to the political, economic, and social inequality of the Chinese coolies living there. It means that the following claims are not convincing: Chinese coolies in Peru demonstrate the degree to which the less powerful individuals of a hierarchical trans-societal entity accept their political, economic, and social inequality due mainly to weak state power or as compared with coolies in Peru, Chinese workers in the United States demonstrate the degree to which the less cheap and exploitable individuals of a hierarchical interstate system benefit relatively from state power. This, in turn, reveals the fact that applying Arghiri Emmanuel's "concept of unequal exchange" to examine the distinction between Chinese coolies in Peru and Chinese workers in the United States is inappropriate.

Having separated two groups ("coolies" and "workers of core states"), the "migrated but skilled Chinese workers" (e.g., tea cultivators) who received better treatment than coolie laborers began to emerge. In the tea cultivation areas of core states' colonies (e.g., Assam) Chinese tea makers were employed by tea plantation owners. Due mainly to Chinese tea makers' "'jealously guarded' art of processing leaves to produce black and green tea,"[144] they were eagerly welcomed at tea plantations (see figure 2.8. [3B-1]). It indicates that migrated but skilled Chinese workers (e.g., tea makers in Assam) in the capitalist world-economy demonstrate the degree to which the more advantaged individuals of a hierarchical trans-societal entity use their skills to their advantage. Moreover, many Chinese emigrated to Southeast Asia due mainly to labor demands from European powers that colonized Southeast Asian countries. For mass production of commodities (e.g., rice, rubber, tin, palm oil, coconut, tobacco, opium, coffee) in labor-intensive plantations and mines created for export to the global market and regional triangular trade,[145] colonial powers in Southeast Asia attracted large numbers of cheap labor from China and India. In the process of recruiting coolie laborers, European colonial powers also used Chinese brokers close to criminal gangs to secure more labor (see figure 2.8. [3B-2]). Yet not all Chinese who emigrated to Southeast Asia were reduced to the lower classes. Rather, some of the Chinese who moved to Singapore or Malaysia grew into commercial or industrial capitalists in industrial fields such as mining, plantations, rice refining, or the sugar business to the point of dominating the local economy. A small number of Chinese immigrants colluded with colonial administrations and helped European powers' colonial rule to take root in Southeast Asia. In return for close cooperation Chinese received political and economic benefits from the colonial administrations in Southeast Asia (see figure 2.8 [1B]).[146]

In addition, Chinese wealthy merchants, influenced by the impacts of the capitalist world-economy, were also created in core countries. Unlike domestic merchants living on the Chinese mainland, some merchants migrated to core states and became mercantile capitalists there during China's incorporation process (see figure 2.8. [2]). The merchant class represented only a small part of the total Chinese population in the United States, and even among them, most were not those who brought great wealth with them from China, but rather those who had worked long and hard as laborers in the United States and then became businessmen. For example, Lee Chew was born in a farming village of the Guangzhou Prefecture. After arriving in California, Lee Chew worked as a maid in an American family for two years and saved $410. He then opened a laundry in a mining town, and after three years, he increased his capital to $2,500. Finally, he settled in New York City and ran a grocery store.[147] As another example, Chy Lung set up his business in San Francisco's Chinatown.[148] Lue Gim Gong (1859–1925) developed a brighter and sweeter and cold-resistant orange in Florida called the Lue Gim Gong orange; Ah Bing created the Bing cherry while working on a farm in Milwaukee, Oregon. Chien Lung also gained great wealth through successful potato cultivation in San Joaquin County, California. Those Chinese mercantile capitalists or agricultural innovators and pioneers of core countries were distinguished from domestic

figure 2.9. Distribution of the Chinese by US state (1860, 1870, and 1880). *Source*: Created by the author, based on the US Bureau of the Census, *Compendium of the Tenth Census* (Washington, DC: Government Printing Office, 1885), 334.

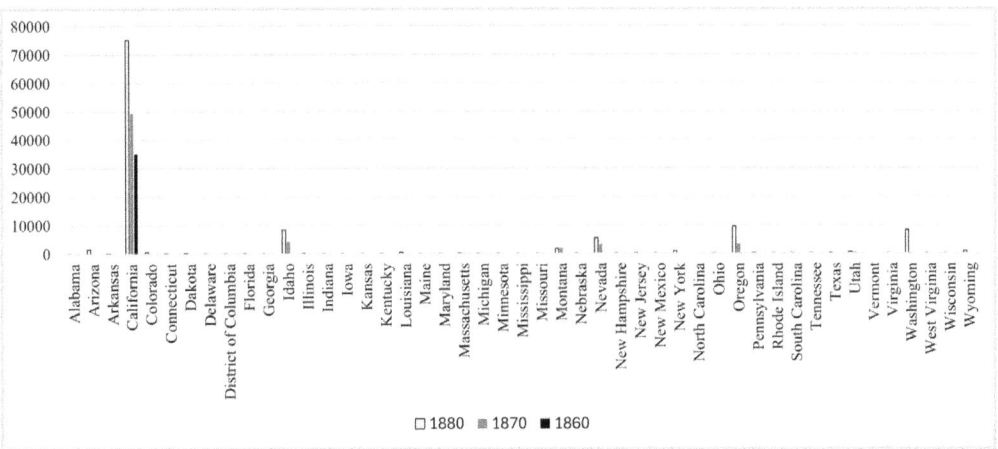

merchants living in China because they were constituted in the context of a differential degree of politico-economic circumstances within the capitalist world-economy. Consequently, the network chain of the capitalist world-economy created a different development path for Chinese merchants.

The Domestic Aspects of the Rise of a New Class

The class system of the Qing changed with the rise of new classes. If the emergence of coolies in globalized sugar plantations, tea makers in core states' colonies, and gold mine workers in United States are considered as the rise of new classes in its international aspect during China's incorporation process, the emergence of compradors can be interpreted as the rise of a new class in its domestic aspect (see figure 2.8. [1A]). Compradors were a group of Chinese who supported foreign traders in China, and they were also involved in the investment, trade, economic, and political exploitation by foreign traders or institutions. As Hao Yen-Ping has noted, the comprador class "was among the first in modern China to stress the importance of commercial and industrial advances as opposed to military development and the Confucian social order."[149] Western companies, especially banking industry and steam navigation companies, were dedicated to finding and hiring Chinese compradors to help link the indigenous trade network and the world-economy.[150] Chinese compradors served to reduce errors in interpretation and translation, notarized important transaction documents, and helped Western merchants to use unfamiliar Chinese currency and to learn Chinese market conditions or China's commerce-related customs that related to their own businesses. The increasing demand for compradors would, in turn, lead to an increase in their numbers by the late nineteenth century.[151] In China "alone there were roughly 700 compradors in 1870, and as many as 20,000 in 1900."[152]

Prior to the 1840s, the roles and authority of compradors were extremely limited. Compradors who spoke foreign languages and learned Western management skills were in charge of connections between Western merchants and Chinese merchants after the Cohong system's establishment in 1760. During the Cohong system period (c. 1760–1839), the government-controlled trading system constrained their authority. As China opened up to foreign trade and began to get incorporated into the world-economy, however, their role grew, and some of them emerged as major international merchants.[153]

Compradors, especially those who signed employment contracts, made an effort to ensure that their foreign employers received maximum returns in all their business dealings. They often did so at the expense of other native-Chinese merchants or Chinese national interests.[154] After the rise of the compradors, Western merchants snugly ensconced themselves in the Chinese market. Nonetheless, characterizing compradors as the nouveau riche is inappropriate. They did not have lifestyles characterized by what Thorstein Veblen called "conspicuous consumption" and did not pursue profligate spending. Their deft command of a foreign language, excellent accounting skills, and assiduousness in their accumulation of wealth could be a stepping-stone for turning themselves into new and independent industrial or bank capitalists. Some compradors accumulated wealth that played an important role in developing Shanghai's banking business from the 1840s to the 1900s.[155] Others, like Xu Run 徐潤 (1838–1911), Tang Jingxing 唐景星 (1832–1892), Zheng Guanying 鄭觀應 (1842–1923), and later Yu Qiaqing 虞洽卿 (1867–1945) gained upper-class status through their own wealth. In significant contrast to members of the imperial family or the gentry class who were directly or indirectly connected to the ruling system of the Qing regime, compradors depended heavily on private, trust-based, and market-oriented relations and valued the right to make themselves independent and self-disciplined capitalists.[156] In addition, new groups such as professional salaried workers and urban proletarians began to emerge in port cities.[157]

This rise in new classes might be dubbed "a rise of new classes generated by China's incorporation process" because it occurred through the dynamics of the capitalist world-economy. Yet it does not imply that the members of the new classes could represent a breakthrough for the old, established class system of the Qing. In fact, their appearance was only half a success due mainly to their lack of class consciousness (i.e., a transition from a "class in itself" to a "class for itself" in Marxist terminology[158]). Although the new class (e.g., the compradors) may have shared a feeling of solidarity, their class identity was too weak to strengthen collective identification and to constitute political organizations. In addition, peasant-centered Chinese society precluded new economic classes from fostering "change agents," which led to class struggles in the socioeconomic aspect. As Sucheta Mazumdar notes, "Peasants emerge not as irrational participants or as helpless victims but as active agents who, in pursuing their material interests, may ally with gentry and landlords."[159] The socioeconomic circumstance of local areas, which induced peasants to share common interests with gentry or landlords, brought about a strong loyalty to the local powers. With a few extreme exceptions stemming from economic ruin or political disorders, small-holding peasant proprietors had no reason to fight against the ancien régime. Furthermore, peasants (and local powers) strongly opposed any kind of socioeconomic change that might end up in depriving them of their rights to the land. This deep socioeconomic trend—"the enserfment of direct producers"[160] and the collusion between peasants and local powers in maintaining agricultural society—led them to oppose socioeconomic changes ushered in by the new economic classes. For these reasons, China's new classes could not organize political or economic organizations and turn themselves into revolutionaries who overthrew the ancien régime or the existing and old class system. Yet we shouldn't underestimate the emergence of these new classes; those who were tied to the logic of the capitalist world-economy brought new blood to the sclerotic Qing class system.

The Geographical Transformation

Perhaps no transformation in China's incorporation process was more variable than that of the port cities in the nineteenth century. The theoretical framework of the incorporation process tries to reveal the distinctive driving force and dynamics of the Europe-oriented world-system on a global scale. For example, Wallerstein addresses what is so special about the modern world-system, how it developed as an independent entity within a long historical context, and how it transformed not only European societies but also non-European societies into a globalized entity. It offers us a historical path for the capitalist world-economy that fundamentally reconstituted China's space dynamics.

In the context of China's incorporation process, in the next section I will investigate how Chinese port cities were transformed. As Fairbank aptly insists, "the new treaty system in China was intended to . . . express the ideals of Britain's worldwide commercial expansion,"[161] and Chinese port cities became the outposts for Western commercial encroachment. Although analyzing the relationship between Chinese port cities and the world-economy is a central aim of this section, I do not intend this as a rigidly doctrinal approach because it cannot provide and cover the whole picture of nineteenth-century China's spatial change. Rather, to track the transformation of a new Chinese geography shaped by its relationship with the outside world and to explore diverse forms of the spatial reconstructions of nineteenth-century China that connected with the effects of the world-economy, I deal with a gradual transition from an economy isolated from global capitalist logics to one connected by the effects of the world-economy. Specifically, I will track (a) the gradual transition from a river network to a coastal network, (b) major port and inland cities' socioeconomic changes, and (c) port city–hinterland relationships. The evidence I will present suggests that China's spatial changes were, in at least one sense, coupled with the dynamics of the world-economy.

The Transition from River Networks to Coastal Networks Under the Influence of the Capitalist World-Economy

The transformation of port cities has broader implications for the gradual transition from river networks to coastal networks. Before discussing it in detail, we may consider urban developmental paths in the late imperial era. Chinese cities underwent a major transformation in the nineteenth century, and before that century, Chinese cities had very different development paths from those in the West.[162]

Suzhou city is a representative example of China's autonomous city formation process in a long historical context, which was different from European cities because the distinction between urban and rural was not clear. As Bozhong Li aptly notes, compared with preindustrial Europe, the continuity between urban and rural was evident in the psychological, social, and material aspects of the Chinese people.[163] Premodern Suzhou and other Chinese cities characteristically contained rural life and agricultural activities within them, while much of the urban economic activity, such as commercial banking and manufacturing, was located or concentrated outside the city walls or in the urban suburbs. "Urban features extended themselves and their impact beyond the city, while rural elements were also welcomed in the city."[164] Thus, urban and rural China were open to each other, and there was no clear pattern of spatial utilization separating urban and rural China. Li's argument promotes awareness of the inappropriateness of European standards when we apply them unconditionally to late imperial Chinese cities. The developmental pattern of late imperial Chinese cities is different enough in many regards that the "urban-rural continuum" may well be neglected by those who are familiar only with the ideal type of Western city formation. Since westernized city formation and developmental patterns do not fit late imperial Chinese cities, it seems absurd to use it as the standard to judge all late imperial Chinese cities.

Since the nineteenth century, however, China's urban development has not been free of Western influence. The patterns of urban development in China that began to emerge as the country was incorporated into the capitalist world-system resembled those in the West, at least outwardly, but also took a different direction of development. The most prominent geomorphological changes were the decline of interdependent river networks and the rise of coastal networks and a transition from river networks to coastal networks.

These transitions built upon relationships between geography, politics, and commercial networks during late imperial times. The commercial developments and population growth in the Yangtze River basin in late imperial China were remarkable. Before China began to incorporate into the capitalist world-economy, China's river networks, which were interlocked with waterways and the Grand Canal, played a decisive role in the development of commerce and inland cities. As influential as the economic and commercial development that centered around the Grand Canal was, its construction and operation was an important act of governance for the Ming and Qing regimes.

During late imperial China, flood control projects were considered an important policy of the government, and the construction, maintenance, and repair of the Grand Canal project linking Beijing and Jiangnan was one of the most important projects that the Ming and Qing regimes were responsible for. Before announcing the move of the capital from Nanjing to Beijing (1421), the Yongle Emperor showed great interest in the work of the Grand Canal connecting Beijing to southern China. The areas of *hetonghe* 會通河 and *qingjiangpu* 清江浦[165] were key to the opening and reopening of the Grand Canal. As maintenance work in these two major zones was successfully completed in 1415 Beijing was turned into a new commercial center and an area that was capable of accelerating commercial transactions and the transport of tribute grain (*caoyun* 漕運) between Beijing and southern China. Accordingly, discussion of reestablishing Beijing as the new imperial capital began to gain strength: "As the waterway is built and (re)established, the amount of the transport tribute grain sharply increased, the number of merchants grew, and commodities were plentiful in Beijing. Many people were pleased with this, so we should not delay making Beijing our new capital."[166]

The maintenance of the Grand Canal was an important national project even in the Qing Empire. For example, one of the main reasons behind Kangxi's first imperial tour of inspection (*xunxing* 巡幸) to Jiangnan in 1684 was to check riparian works. During the Qing regime, flooding of the Yellow River occurred frequently. The Kangxi Emperor understood that constructing and repairing riparian works was not easy and

Figure 2.10. *Qing Yiming Dayunhe Detu* [Map of the Grand Canal from Beijing to the Yangzi River in the late eighteenth or early nineteenth century]. *Source*: Metropolitan Museum of Art, Friends of Asian Art Gifts, 2003. Public domain.

had to be performed whenever necessary. Through documents exchanged with government officials and discussions, he confessed: "I have not seen the construction site of an embankment, which was difficult for me to grasp of how fast and strong the Yellow River is and how firmly the embankment is being repaired."[167]

After that, the Kangxi Emperor visited Suqian 宿遷 in the Jiangnan region for the first time, and expressed his feelings that "the Yellow River has been detrimental to the people for a long time in that the embankment often collapsed and the water overflowed. I am finally able to observe the Yellow River and the construction site of the embankment, which I have only heard of,"[168] and then he began to inspect the embankment site. In addition, Kangxi told a local official that "I always paid attention to the riparian works" and then added that "the operation of the Grand Canal in the Yellow River is an important matter, so I urge you to do everything you can to manage the embankment and dredging so that the Yellow River does not overflow."[169]

The important aim of the Qianlong Emperor's tour of the south, as well as that of the Kangxi Emperor, was to inspect public works and the current state of Jiangnan Province, especially the river control works including "the construction of dams, dikes, seawalls, dredging waterways, [which] required the timely regulation of reservoirs, overflow channels, and drainage canals linking dozens of rivers and lakes."[170] And the target of attention to manage embankments was the Yellow River. Qianlong witnessed a terrible scene caused by flood damage during the Southern Tour of 1756: "One saw the cadaverous and the hungry, their bodies barely covered in thread bare blue tatters, limping, some with no shoes; truly, the effects of the deluge spread all around."[171]

In addition, in the Jiangnan region Hangzhou and Nanking were major trading centers, populated urban areas, and economically well developed because they were interconnected by waterways.[172] Also, due to the development of the canal system, canal cities had already become economically developed centuries earlier.[173] For example, Hangzhou, Suzhou, Wuxi, Huaian, Xuzhou, and Liaocheng were already economic centers in late imperial China.[174] Yangzhou, for example, experienced unprecedented economic development because it sits atop the meeting point for the Yangtze River and the Grand Canal. Consequently, Yangzhou became home to a great many markets, guild halls, accommodations, and entertainment facilities.[175]

Indeed, under the canal system, merchant groups who made better use of the waterways enjoyed commercial advantages.[176] The Huizhou merchants were a characteristic example of a merchant group with such Grand Canal advantages. From the dynasty's inception in 1636, the Huizhou merchants had gained the trust of the Qing government by cooperating with reconstruction efforts (e.g., rebuilding schools and religious facilities, riverbank revetment, and relief work), and by providing the Qing's military forces with financial aid. In return for politico-economic support, the Huizhou merchants were granted a monopoly on the salt trade.[177] In addition, the Huizhou merchants fostered a culture of generosity to ensure a stronger community. To set up public services, they devoted their private fortune to improve the quality of

Figure 2.11. Interconnections among inland cities through waterways. *Source*: Created by the author using a map from Wikimedia Commons, Groverlynn. CC BY-SA 4.0. Public domain.

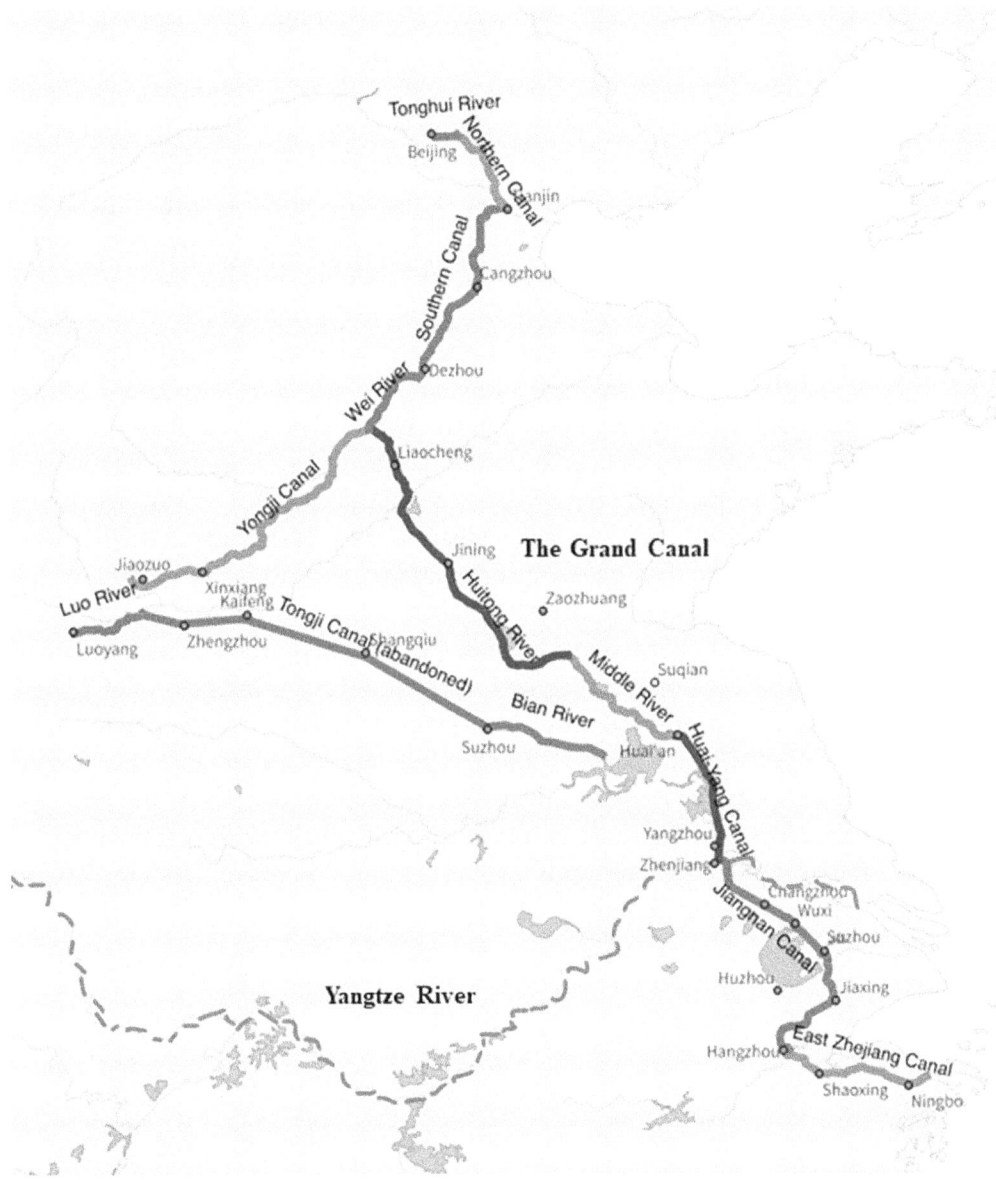

life of local communities. The more their activities played such a vital role the more their influence expanded.[178]

As the capitalist world-economy penetrated China, however, coastal cities like Amoy, Hong Kong, Fuzhou, Shantou, and Shanghai showed marked increases in urban growth. Unlike the urban growth of Grand Canal cities, which depended entirely on domestic trade, urban growth in coastal cities was at the mercy of international trade.

Spaces that have been incorporated into the capitalist system embody geographical extensions of capitalism and play a role in "a forward leap of the forces of production" or "new modalities of production."[179] As Henri Lefebvre argues, the incorporation of China's coastal cities into capitalism created new forms of production relations and the development of productive forces. Conversely, after the First Opium War economic activity in the Grand Canal cities slowed due mainly to the rise in foreign steamships transporting tribute rice.[180] The penetration of these foreign steamships into domestic transportation meant that the transportation businesses of the Grand Canal cities began to lose ground.[181] The presence of British armed forces during the First Opium War indeed accelerated the decline of the canal economy. For instance, when the British blocked the operation of the canal system in 1842, commercial trade and the grain tribute were hit hard.[182] As the Grand Canal and waterways through the Yangtze River became insignificant the economic dominance of Huizhou merchants was on the verge of collapse. However, the decline of the Grand Canal cities does not imply a total cessation of economic activity. To borrow Lefebvre's words again,[183] these cities were incorporated into the multilayered structure of the capitalist world, which was composed of local, regional, national, and global markets. Merchants and cities took on different roles than they had before incorporation.

In contrast to the cities of the Grand Canal the coastal cities came into the spotlight, becoming centers of international trade due to their easy access to sea routes and ocean shipping after China opened its ports to trade. With the integration of China's cities into the capitalist world-economy, port cities were forced to cooperate under the influence of Western merchants. Drawing upon the socioeconomic transformation of the coastal cities for evidence, the following section argues that the capitalist world-economy penetrated the port cities. In effect, China's incorporation into the capitalist world-economy was contingent upon the connection of port cities to Western merchants in the nineteenth century.

TRANSFORMATION OF MAJOR CITIES UNDER PRESSURE FROM THE CAPITALIST WORLD-ECONOMY

Shanghai

Shanghai, a significant port city, became a hub of international trade led by European merchants in the capitalist world-economy. Although it was less developed than other major cities like Hangzhou and Suzhou in the Jiangnan area before the 1840s, it was more commercially advanced than rural towns in the inland areas. However, after the 1840s Shanghai became a British, French, and American international trading concession.[184] The rapid development of Shanghai's infrastructure was a major factor that attracted Westerners to the city, which had gas lighting, a drainage system, the telegraph, daily newspapers in Chinese, rickshaws, electricity, running water, tram lines, and the first

Figure 2.12. *Shanghai xian cheng xiang zu jie quan tu*, 1884 [Complete map of Shanghai County walled city and foreign settlements]. *Source*: Library of Congress, Geography and Map Division.

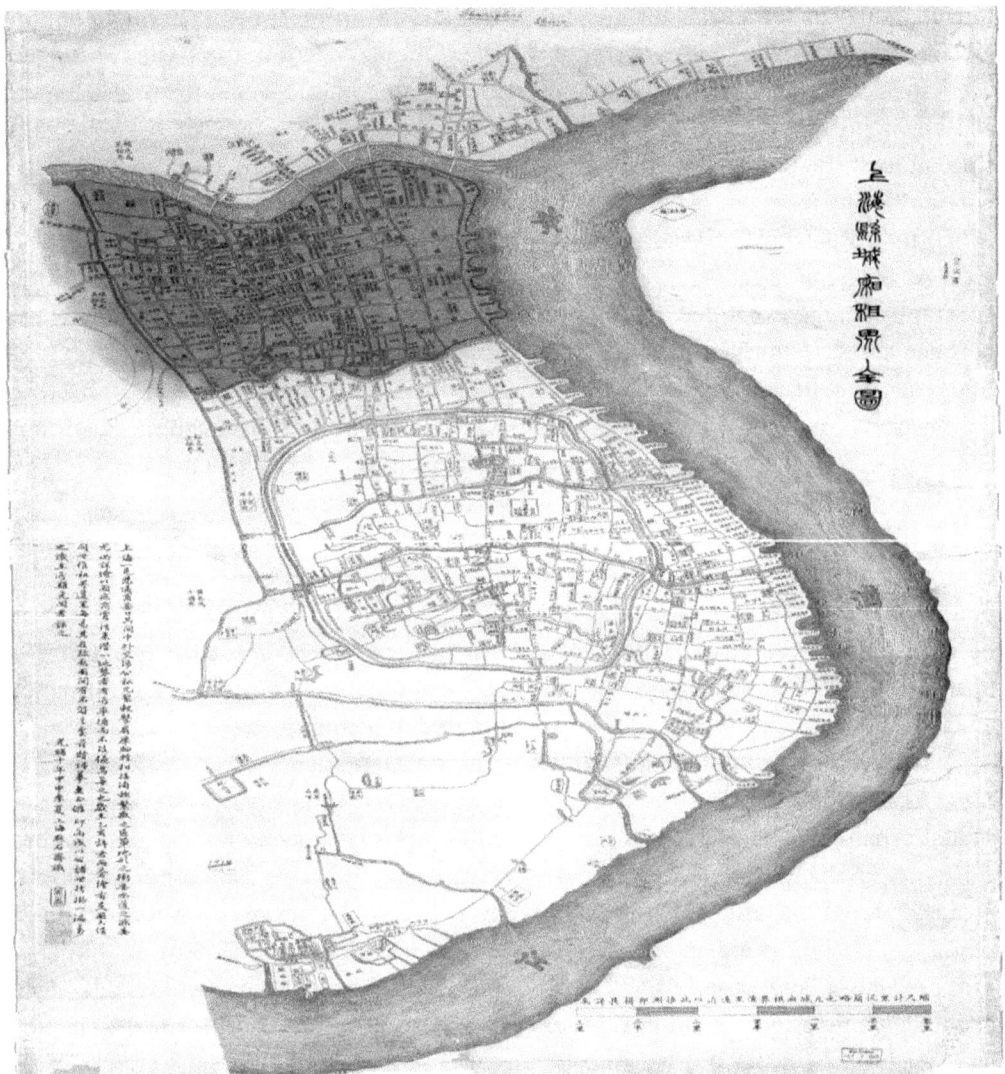

automobiles in the late nineteenth and early twentieth centuries.[185] The Shanghai Bund on the waterfront had a wide, well-paved street that could accommodate multiple carriages, and it also had a modern street with streetlights and Western-style buildings.[186]

The continued growth of Shanghai's international settlement over time indicated the satisfaction of the foreigners who lived in the city with its amenities.[187] Shanghai became a hub for foreign trade, growing along with its Western population.[188] Initially, only a few Western merchants were allowed into Shanghai, but after the Opium Wars many foreign traders came to take advantage of its strategic location along the Yangtze River.[189] According to Robert Fortune, Shanghai was the most important port for foreign trade on the coast of China, and this led to an increase in public attention toward the city.[190] After the abolishment of the Cohong system in the 1840s, Shanghai's economic dominance in international trade was uncontested. Shanghai also served another important role in international trade, functioning as a hub for re-exportation since at least the late nineteenth century: "The trade in re-exports of foreign goods to Foreign Countries is almost entirely centered at Shanghai. The largest market is Japan, which took Re-exports to the value of Hk. [Hong Kong] Tls. [taels] 1,624,335."[191]

As Shanghai established itself as China's most significant trading hub, the city's geographical area expanded, leading to the breakdown of the traditional relationships between cities. Historically, the size of Chinese cities was determined by their political functions, as reflected in the area or length of their walls. Beijing was 6,320 hectares in the late nineteenth century; Nanjing was 4,055 hectares; Hangzhou, Xian, and Chengdu were each about 1,200 hectares; Taiyuan 840 hectares; Wuchang, 635 hectares; Guangzhou, 520 hectares.[192] The size of traditional Chinese cities was structured as a hierarchical formation in accordance with their political importance or functions. In contrast with older, traditional Chinese cities that were at the mercy of patrimonial politics, the geographical expansion of Shanghai, under the influence of the West, was decoupled from the city's traditional pattern of evolution. The urban expansion of Shanghai resulted in the decline of the traditional city while a new spatial formation emerged under the influence of the capitalist world-economy.

The transformation of Shanghai is evident in its landscape, which reflects the city's rapid assimilation of Western culture. As Anthoney D. King notes, the "physical and spatial urban form actually constitute as well as represent much of social and cultural existence."[193] Shanghai's westernized architecture, seen in house decoration, malls, and arcades, played a significant role in stimulating the consumption of Western culture. In the 1880s, in particular, travelers to Shanghai were confronted with an authentic European-style landscape in the Zhang Garden.[194] The new flat and wide roads in the Shanghai Concession were a novelty to the Chinese, who were accustomed to narrow and winding alleys that turned into muddy water when it rained and were now suitable for carriages to run on. Li Wei Qing compared the roads built in the Shanghai concession with the roads in the old town and revealed the reason why the concession was preferred by people: "The roads in the concession run in all directions, whereas the streets in the old town are narrow. The concession is always kept clean, with no dust even when wagons run through, and as a result, its residents have a deep love for their land. There is also a department responsible for cleaning the roads in the old town, but the stench from the canals is overwhelming and the backwaters are lined with ditches and latrines. The old town is so impoverished that it cannot be compared to the concession."[195]

More importantly, Shanghai's embrace of westernized architecture for housing provides evidence of China's acculturation and played a major role in stimulating the consumption of Western culture. The emergence of westernized housing in the transition to capitalism, in fact, led to an increase in demand for energetic and advanced Western images (or messages). To paraphrase Jean Baudrillard, the appearance of westernized housing in Shanghai cannot be defined by its use but rather by what it signifies; and what it signifies was almost entirely determined by Chinese people's longing for Western culture.[196] In this sense, the emergence of Western housing in Shanghai was a fetish of Western modernity to which Chinese people aspired, rendering old, indigenous, and traditional architectures valueless and inferior against Western culture.

In conclusion, the advanced urbanization of Shanghai coincided with the decline of premodern traditional cities, the development of international trade, the consumption of Western culture, and the recompartmentalization of port city residents along class and race lines.

Hong Kong

Hong Kong is another example of a city that underwent a transformation as it became part of the capitalist world-economy.[197] In the early 1800s, Hong Kong was a small island where the locals depended on fishing for their livelihood, even though there was some growth in agriculture during the Mongol era. However, in the latter half of the nineteenth century Hong Kong underwent a significant change when it became a hub for international trade. This transformation led to an increase in Western-style buildings as more foreign settlements were established in the area.[198]

Furthermore, Hong Kong emerged as a prime location for global trade during the mid-nineteenth century due to the increased influx of European manufactured goods.[199] Serving as a Western economic hub, Hong Kong managed over 20 percent of China's total exports and more than a third of its import trade by the 1880s. According to an article in the *Hong Kong Daily Express* on July 20, 1899, the city was praised for its thriving commerce: "Hong Kong being an absolutely free port for the entrance at all foreign goods . . . is the entrepôt for merchandise destined for other ports in the Orient, and well-established steamship lines radiate from this center in every direction." This was not an exaggeration.

Many Western businesses involved in international shipping began to set up commercial operations in Hong Kong once the city became accessible to them. Jardine Matheson and Company emerged as the leader among these Western companies in Hong Kong's international trade. Following Hong Kong's transfer to Britain in 1843, Jardine Matheson and Company established an office in East Point and later relocated its head office from Scotland to Hong Kong.[200] The company was responsible for constructing much of Hong Kong's commercial and trading infrastructure, including

Figure 2.13. Waterfront of the Central District in Hong Kong, 1867. *Source*: University of Hong Kong. Used with permission.

warehouses, docks, and shopping centers. Indeed, it established Hong Kong's first ice plant, cotton textile factory, and sugar mill, as well as the Hong Kong Tramways and public transport system. Numerous other Western corporations, such as maritime insurance companies and shipping businesses, also entered Hong Kong.[201]

What's more, various types of business were introduced to Hong Kong, and one of these was as a place to import opium from outside. Po-keung Hui reports that "by 1880, China imported about 45% of opium from Hong Kong."[202] Hong Kong also functioned as a significant entrepôt for exporting goods such as silk, tea, and porcelain. The emergence of Hong Kong as an international trading hub was mainly due to Western involvement. After the formal acceptance of the Treaty of Nanking in 1843, Britain proclaimed Hong Kong a free port under the protection of British law and removed all trade restrictions. Following the establishment of the Hong Kong free port an active foreign trading community quickly emerged.[203] This strongly suggests that Hong Kong's socioeconomic development was not a spontaneous process but was rather the outcome of British control.[204]

Taking matters one step further, the British colonial government enlarged the geographic size of Hong Kong after it was ceded to Britain. The Convention Between the United Kingdom and China respecting an extension of Hong Kong Territory, signed in Peking on June 9, 1898, enabled this expansion to begin. The British government explicitly stated that "an extension of Hong Kong territory is necessary for the proper defense and protection of the Colony,"[205] making it clear that Hong Kong's territorial expansion was driven solely by Britain's national interests. The first colonial expansion of Britain in the 1840s laid the foundation for and shaped Hong Kong's territorial acquisition, while the second colonial expansion of Britain in the 1890s laid the groundwork for and influenced its territorial extension.

Canton

Canton, a port city of the Qing Empire, was transformed into a base for the capitalist world-economy to penetrate China's southern mainland. Canton was a coastal city in Guangdong Province, and it was the only entry point for Western merchants into China until the Opium Wars. Canton flourished due to its position as one of the largest markets in the Qing dynasty and its exclusive and unique international trading system, the Canton system. There were many Chinese interested in trading with the British in the vicinity of Canton,[206] and Canton, as Henry Ellies, one of the members of the Amherst Embassy (1816–1817) noted, was a place where ships of many nations traded, and was busier than any other city in China.[207] Western traders also considered Canton an ideal location for international trade due to its geographical advantages, such as safe anchorage and proximity to the major trading ports of Southeast Asia and India. The Thirteen Factory system in Canton was a significant trading hub in East Asia where Western and Chinese merchants could conduct business. As a result, foreigners could easily locate Chinese men who spoke Pidgin English and see a variety of foreign flags in Canton.[208]

Canton's reputation for illegal trade was what drew most Western merchants to the city; the coastal areas of Canton, in particular, saw a widespread opium smuggling.[209] Canton's geographic location could account for this as it was the closest Chinese port city to the ports of India. The British East India Company produced most of the opium in Bengal and Malwa, with most of the opium from these centers being exported to China.[210] The sea route between Calcutta in India and Canton in China was the shortest distance between the two countries; thus this route received significant attention from private traders. Many of these private traders were engaged in opium smuggling, which was a business venture that required short transportation distances due to the uncertainty of the trade. Consequently, Canton was an attractive location for reckless British profit-seekers.

Canton, however, went through a significant economic decline after the First Opium War. The number of treaty ports for British trade and residence increased from one to five cities, causing Canton to lose its importance as a trading hub. Just as the "the older center of oceanic trade (of the Indian subcontinent)—Masulipatnam, Surat,

Figure 2.14. The Canton Bund, 1915. Source: Presbyterian Research Centre. Used with permission.

and Hugli—declined in importance, beginning to cede place to new centers linked to European trade, like Calcutta, Bombay, and Madras,"[211] Canton also ebbed in importance as an international trading hub. As Canton's role in foreign trade declined, the city experienced a sudden economic downturn in the 1860s.[212]

To make matters worse, the Second Opium War and the Taiping Rebellion added to Canton's misery as it left the city in ruins, making it difficult for the economy to recover.[213] As a result, many Cantonese migrated to Hong Kong in search of better opportunities and stability from the Taiping threat and the Second Opium War.[214] Unlike Shanghai and Hong Kong, Canton faced an economic downturn, losing its Western merchants in the aftermath of the Second Opium War. To examine the increase in Shanghai's international trade volume and the simultaneous decline in Canton's trade, I compare the customs revenue of Shanghai and Canton from the 1840s to the 1870s (see figure 2.15).

These statistics reflect the woeful economic conditions of Canton after the Second Opium War and help support the notion that Western-led commercial activities damaged Canton's economy. That said, it may be too simplistic to attribute Canton's economic downturn to any single reason. Many factors, such as the fiscal difficulties experienced by local government or the frequency of resistance movements such as the Taiping rebels, might be considered.

Still, the changing structure of commercial activities in Canton, led by Western merchants, was one of the main factors behind Canton's economic downturn, at least to some degree.

Figure 2.15. Customs revenue from 1841 to 1872. *Source*: Created by the author, based on Jerome Ch'en, *State Economic Policies of the Ch'ing Government, 1840–1895* (Garland, 1980), 189.

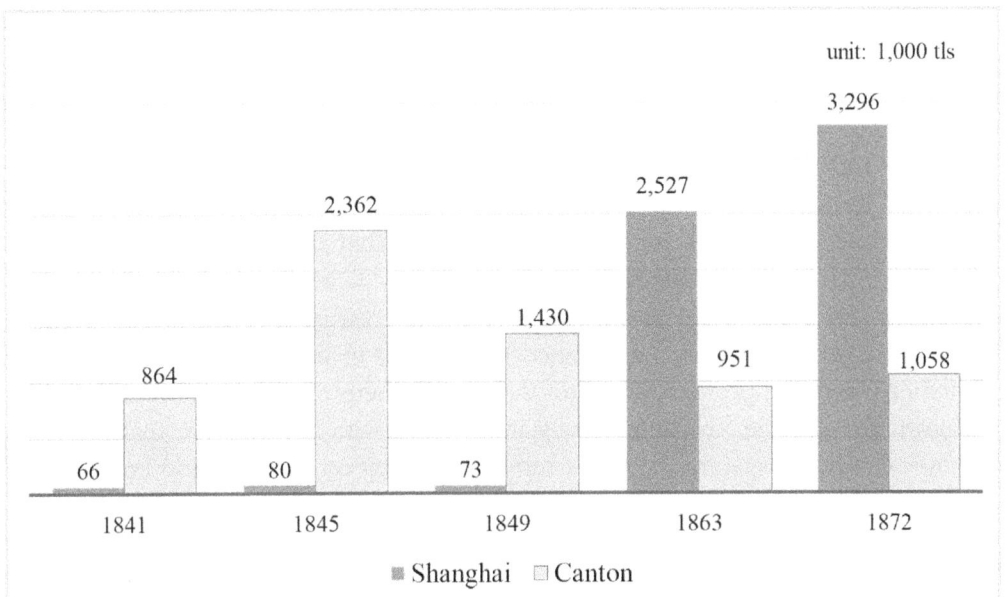

Hankou

China's incorporation into the capitalist world-system transformed port cities such as Hong Kong and Shanghai into international commercial centers. However, not all Chinese port cities moved toward rapid modernization or economic boom, as evidenced by the case of Canton. In addition, some inland Chinese cities went through a different development process as compared to the coastal port cities. Hankou is a prime example. Hankou is a city in Hubei Province, an inland city with well-developed waterways located at the confluence of the Yangtze and Han Rivers (*Han Jiang* 漢江). In geopolitical terms, Hankou was a place where Western influence remained fairly limited, unlike Hong Kong, which was ceded to the British after the First Opium War, or the five ports (Guangzhou, Xiamen, Fuzhou, Ningbo, and Shanghai), which were forcibly opened by the British. Hankou was designated a trading port in 1861, and steamships from many countries came to trade there.[215]

From then on Hankou emerged as a new center for international commerce, and one of the most popular items exported from the city was tea. First, the tea trade flourished in Hankou beginning in the nineteenth century because of Russia's rapidly growing demand for Chinese tea. William Rowe, repeating data from a Soviet scholar, argued that the volume of tea passing through the central market in Kiakhta in Siberia increased by 600 percent between 1802 and 1845.[216] Russia's tea trade continued to flourish even after Hankou was opened as a treaty port; in 1880, for example, about fifteen hundred tons of tea were shipped on the old route to Siberia along the Han River. Russian merchants had been active in the city even before Hankou was turned into a treaty port, and once Westerners were officially allowed to live there by treaty, they came to make up a significant percentage of the foreign community. Russian merchants traded primarily with merchants from Hanyang and Wuchang where they purchased Chinese tea and offered their woolen goods to Chinese merchants. Russian merchants then shipped their tea north through Shanxi transportation brokers with whom they had dealt for generations.[217] Second, from the second half of the nineteenth century, Western merchants also began to show interest in the tea trade in Hankou. After the center of overseas trade shifted to Shanghai in the 1840s the tea-producing plantations of the upper Yangtze regions—located there for the purpose of shipping tea down the Yangtze—became closely intertwined with the Hankou market. From a geo-economic perspective, Hankou served as an important gathering point for tea from the upper and middle Yangtze areas, and many British merchants actively traded there after the opening of Hankou.[218]

Unlike Shanghai and Hong Kong, however, the interior of the city was not dictated by colonial powers but rather maintained and controlled by the city's autonomous economic organizations (e.g., tea guilds) and their independent business practices. For example, Hankou tea merchants organized guilds to negotiate taxes with the government. The tea firms or tea warehouses acted as financial guarantors during the

Figure 2.16. *Coolies Unloading Tea at Hankow, 1900*. Source: Library of Congress, Prints and Photographs Division. Public domain.

tea-trading season, which allowed itinerant merchants to bring tea more easily and quickly from producing areas to Hankou. Plus, when foreign merchants boycotted in protest against the tea prices set by the Hankou tea guild and its bylaws in 1833, guild members who did not succumb to the pressure of foreign merchants took a hardline response like "Chinese tea merchants did not sell teas to foreign merchants."[219] Rowe added that the highly specialized merchant class that existed in Hankou, unlike other Chinese port cities that were characterized as colonial cities or managed under the influence of Western merchants, utilized their own networks and drove the commercial development of Hankou.[220] Amid these macro changes in China's incorporation process into the capitalist world-system Hankou had shown a different development path from other coastal port cities.

Finding the Logic of Incorporation in the Local: City-Hinterland Relationships

Another aspect of China's spatial reorganization during its incorporation process was the relationship between the city and the hinterland, which was influenced by the capitalist world-economy. In the nineteenth century, Chinese port cities, created by the expansion of the modern world-system, compelled their hinterlands to collaborate with global commercial networks. Regarding the hierarchical city-hinterland relationships, Albert Feuerwerker argued: "These thousands of basic markets, of which Skinner estimates there were 63,000 early in the twentieth century, were linked in turn to two higher level markets—intermediate and central—and ultimately to the great trading cities of the coast such as Tianjin, Shanghai, and Canton."[221] To gain a better understanding of this relationship between the port cities and their hinterlands, which were absorbed into the capitalist world-economy's sphere of influence, I investigate them further.

Obviously, the influences of the capitalist world-economy were evident in Chinese port cities, both directly and indirectly, despite the Chinese government's efforts to limit colonial powers' entry since the mid-nineteenth century. In addition, the economically connected hinterlands were also exposed to the logics of the capitalist world-economy. Rhoads Murphey offers a clue as to how large port cities were interdigitated with their hinterlands: "The third level of smaller regional or provincial service centers was represented by places like Changsha, Chungking, Foochow, or Wu-chou, all of them also part of the treaty port hierarchy."[222] The inhabitants of rural areas had few opportunities to meet Western merchants or to trade with them (or Western countries) directly, even though China had already opened its doors to them; nonetheless, the major port cities were directly connected to the inhabitants of the hinterlands. Various goods and coolie workers, both available for export, were produced in the hinterlands of port cities. While these hinterland goods might not have been transferred to the ships of Western merchants directly, they were nonetheless moved through port cities before being loaded aboard Western ships. In this regard, the hinterlands were embedded in the means of production, albeit weakly (see figure 2.17).

To explore the intricate and multidimensional issues related to the city-hinterland relationship, I propose three types of relationships and their complex interactions with the capitalist world-economy. The first type is the city-hinterland relationship through export commodities, exemplified by the connections between Shanghai and its hinterlands. Shanghai was a critical transshipment hub during the Treaty Port Era (1870–1925), with foreign trade at its heart.[223] Due to its proximity to the major silk-producing regions in the lower Yangtze basin and tea cultivation areas in the southern mountains or hills, many Western merchants viewed Shanghai as the primary transshipping point. Therefore, the hinterlands of Shanghai specialized in producing export commodities, while Shanghai focused on transshipping goods to foreign markets.[224] As a transshipment hub, Shanghai played a vital role in exporting Chinese goods to international commercial networks and connecting with its hinterlands under the influence of the capitalist world-economy.

The relationship between Chinese port cities and their hinterlands was strengthened by the export of tea. The more tea cultivation was commercialized, the more the two regions were integrated into the capitalist world-economy. Amoy, as a port city, played a significant role in the reexport of Taiwanese tea, while Taiwan, as a hinterland, cultivated tea. In Canton, the cultivation and export of tea also tied the city to its hinterlands, with two transport routes for black tea to Canton. One was the Town of sing-csun (near the Bohea hills) > Csong-ngan-hien > Ho-keu > Kan- chew-fu > Ky-ngan-fu > She-pa tan > Canton, while the other was Nan-gan-fu > Kau- chew-fu > Nan-hyong-fu > Shau-chew-fu > Canton.[225] The relationship between the hinterlands and port cities in connection with the world market was not limited to the tea trade. Cotton, as an export trade item produced in the northern plains of China, attracted foreign traders, and stimulated the integration of much of northern China into the world market. Through cotton exports, Tianjin, as a re-exporting hub and port city, played a role in connecting the northern plains of China where cotton was produced with the globalized commercial network of the capitalist world-economy.[226]

Figure 2.17. Port city–hinterland relationships during the incorporation process. *Source*: Created by the author.

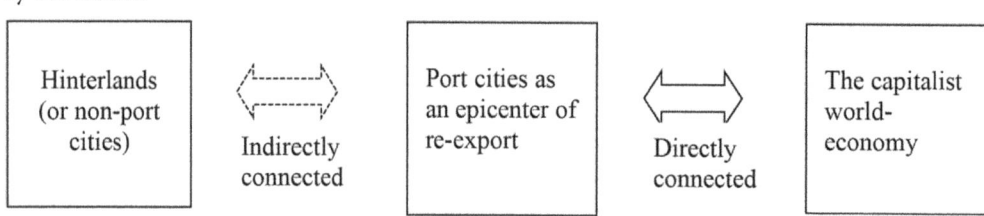

Second, the relationship between port cities and their hinterlands went beyond the export of crops and commodities and included the export of Chinese laborers. Hong Kong and its hinterland areas exemplify this relationship, as Chinese laborers were transported through the port city to work in various countries.[227] Western merchants played a crucial role in maintaining this connection between the hinterlands and Hong Kong. Many peasants from southern China moved to port cities like Hong Kong due to poor economic conditions, political instability, and ethnic conflicts. China's nineteenth-century economic crisis can structurally be attributed to unprecedented population growth. Faced with economic difficulty, many peasants had to leave their homelands and become coolie laborers. Between the late eighteenth century and the mid- to late nineteenth century, the Qing government confronted a series of large and small rebellions. Due to these long-lasting social uprisings the late Qing could not halt the exodus of labor, although it did officially prohibit emigration until at least 1859. This resulted in the movement of Chinese workers throughout all regions of the world, becoming enmeshed with the reorganization of the international division of labor, transforming them into the subordinated laborers of the production network of capitalism. Due to ethnic conflicts between Hakka and Punti in the Hakka–Punti clan wars of the nineteenth century and for political reasons like "the prominent Hakka involvement in the Taiping Rebellion,"[228] Hakka people found it difficult to stay in mainland China; as a result, they emigrated from China and became coolies. They were then transported to work in different countries like Peru and Cuba, or British colonies like Jamaica, Guyana, British Malaya, and Trinidad and Tobago. Hong Kong's reputation as a hub for the coolie trade led to a population increase, with many migrants from the hinterlands seeking employment opportunities[229] or being sold into coolie labor.

The migration of a large number of Foshan inhabitants abroad illustrates the reasons and manner in which they left their homes and became migrant laborers via Hong Kong. Foshan, situated in central Guangdong Province, encountered an unparalleled period of urban expansion from 1730 to 1830 owing to the rapid growth of the iron manufacturing, pottery, and textile industries. Furthermore, Foshan acted as a significant center for the collection and distribution of rice produced in Guangxi and Hunan Provinces, with twenty-three rice mills in Foshan in the early eighteenth century. Given Foshan's status as a hub for industrial activity and distribution during its prime, it is unsurprising that many individuals relocated to the area. However, as of the late nineteenth century, the primary internal and international trade routes shifted to coastal areas, leading to a decline in the inland transportation system and Foshan's prosperity. This resulted in the emigration of a significant number of Foshan's population to Hong Kong to move abroad. Hong Kong was perceived as the point of contact between Foshan and foreign nations by those leaving their hometown.[230]

Not only was Hong Kong connected to the hinterlands, but Swatow (Shantou) and Xiamen were also coupled with the hinterlands under the influence of the capitalist world-economy. Trade agents for coolies would send brokers, including crimps, to Shantou's hinterlands to recruit coolie laborers. If a certain number of coolies were recruited, they would be transported to Shantou and wait until oceangoing ships were ready to depart. According to Chi-cheung Choi, "from 1852 to 1853, more than 3,450 coolies were sent through the coolie business. In 1855, the number increased to 6,300."[231] Xiamen played a significant role in exporting indentured laborers as it served as an exit for overseas Chinese. James Tait, a British merchant, used the Merchant Consulship system to ship Chinese laborers from Xiamen to destinations such as the West Indies, Cuba, Peru, and Australia to solve the labor shortages there. From 1847 to 1853, a total of 8,281 Chinese coolies were shipped overseas from Xiamen, which became a coolie trade center.[232] Likewise, the relentless penetration of Western merchants also drew laborers from the hinterlands into the international division of labor system.

The third point to consider is the relationship between port cities and hinterlands, which evolved over time as the hinterlands played an important role in supplying subsistence to the port cities. As the port cities became international commercial centers, they became increasingly reliant on grain from the countryside. By examining the degree of grain dependence of port cities, we can determine the degree of connectivity between port cities and hinterlands. Although I did not have quantitative data for grain supply in the nineteenth century, Dwight Perkins found that provinces such as Sichuan, Hunan, Hubei, and Jiangxi supplied grain to urban areas, suggesting that a substantial amount of grain from these hinterlands was likely sent to port cities.[233]

To recap, the neglected history of the relationship between port cities and hinterlands sheds new light on China's incorporation process. What was novel was not simply the subordination of the hinterlands to the port cities when China began to be incorporated into the capitalist world-economy, but the evolving pattern of China's incorporation process, which resulted in a distinctive formation of port city–hinterland relationships. This spatial reorganization created a new system of spatial order characterized by accessibility to the globalized commercial network and the international division of labor system.

Concluding Remarks

In *The Modern World-System*, Immanuel Wallerstein broke new ground when he argued that capitalism did not arise separately in different states but arose in northwestern Europe and then went on to serially incorporate other parts of the globe. In tracing this historical narrative Wallerstein assumed that trade between world-systems was a trade in "preciosities" until the process of incorporation. However true this may have been of the Americas, it fails to adequately encapsulate the trade between the emerging capitalist world-economy and late imperial China. For instance, the flow of silver from the Americas, either via Europe or directly through the Manila galleons, was essential for the fiscal system and circulation of money as late imperial China adopted a silver-based currency even though it was chronically deficient in silver supplies. Without inflows from the Americas, it is hard to imagine how the imperial economy could have survived and grown. Indeed, in the case of Europe, especially in England, the consumption of Chinese tea starting in the eighteenth century was not considered to be luxury consumption due mainly to the increased drinking of Chinese tea by the middle and lower classes. The exchange of preciosities between the European world-economy and late imperial China cannot contain the whole picture of trading relationships. Worse, an exclusive emphasis on the luxury trade between the European world-economy and late imperial China cannot explain how the qualitative change of trading relationships affected China, which triggered China's incorporation process (which in turn means that China's commercial network deepened into the capitalist mode of production). Unlike Wallerstein's theoretical assumption, I reformulated China's incorporation process, shedding new light on the changing relationships between late imperial China (as a world empire) and China's incorporation process.

When was China's incorporation process and what did it experience? Since around the 1780s, the power of the world market forced China to enter a triangular production-distribution network comprising silver, opium, and tea. Then, due to surging opium imports, China faced a silver shortage. Worse, the silver shortage compelled China to transform domestic-oriented activities into export-oriented activities. Among these, tea cultivation was central; in effect, China experienced population movement for tea cultivation, geographical reorganization for tea exports (e.g., the rise of the port city as a transshipment place), and environmental change (e.g., frequent landslides due to erosion caused by increased tea cultivation). At a time when Chinese tea was becoming ensconced in the world market, Chinese tea exports sharply declined due to the diversification of tea cultivation areas; not only did India cultivate tea for export, but so did Japan and Sri Lanka. The strategy of Britain—diversification of tea export areas—brought about severe competition in tea supply. The more non-Chinese areas had second-mover advantage from the world tea market, the more Chinese tea faced international competition. Such fierce competition in the world market drove China into a crisis of tea cultivation.

In addition, the rise of new classes played an important role in fostering China's incorporation process. Throughout the nineteenth century, new social classes brought China and the colonial powers together. For instance, compradors connected China with colonial powers within Chinese territory, whereas coolies connected China with colonial powers outside of Chinese territory. Especially when it comes to the rise of Chinese coolies, China was a (cheap) labor producing area that supplied the European colonies' plantations. To sustain and develop commodity production operated by the input of new and cheap laborers, Chinese coolies were essential. Undergirding this Chinese migration pattern was the expansion process of the nineteenth-century capitalist world-system imposed by the stimulus of global production and the more sophisticated international division of labor network.

Another sign of China's incorporation process can be found in its geographical reorganization. Under the influence of the capitalist world-economy, China's river- and Grand Canal–based networks (and inland cities) declined, while port cities grew (although there were exceptions such as Hankou), linked to the expanding capitalist world-economy and centered on the Western-oriented commercial activities. Such commercial activities of the port cities were not limited to their own geographical boundaries; on the contrary, their commercial sphere extended to their hinterlands.

Chapter 3

China's Incorporation Process

The Interstate System

When the Western family of nations reached into the Far Eastern world, it found itself confronting another family of nations under the leadership of China. Clashes arose between these two mutually exclusive systems and in the end the advancing Western one eclipsed the other.

—Immanuel Chung-Yueh Hsü, *China's Entrance into the Family of Nations: The Diplomatic Phase, 1858–1880*

We also began to see the transformation of the Chinese polity from empire to nation, beginning in the latter decades of the nineteenth century.

—Paul A. Cohen, "How Has the Study of China Changed in the Last Sixty Years?"

The decline of the Qing Empire that started in the nineteenth century was exceptional because it did not lead to another similar patrimonial-bureaucratic empire. Throughout China's history, the centralized political organization that sustained the dynasties existed for thousands of years.[1] However, the collapse of the Qing Empire did not repeat previous dynastic transitions where a lesser ruler created a new dynasty. This implies that historical signs of an imperial disintegration and an imperial transition to a modern state caused by outside influences appeared in the nineteenth century; the alternatives were never realized—the Qing Empire itself did not abandon empire status or remain as a rump state like the Southern Song (1127–1279). It also avoids the flat and old-fashioned assumption that the disintegration of the Qing Empire and its transition to a modern state was created due merely to the enfeeblement of the center's authority, the rise of local powers, and the invasion of neighboring countries. China, which stumbled "from one crisis to the next," can be identified as a "metamorphosis" of an ancien régime into a modern state,[2] and no deadly blow was struck at the Qing Empire until the early nineteenth century.

To understand the end of the Qing Empire and its transition toward a modern state, while eschewing the fallibility of the dynastic cycle conception, I use the conception of China's incorporation process. According to Wallerstein, before the nineteenth century the Qing Empire was a world empire and can be defined as a monolithic political organization (or system), which redistributed surplus that originated from many local (or mini) markets in the empire's territory;[3] however, the political system of the Qing Empire had been transformed into a modern state since it was incorporated into the capitalist world-economy. In stressing the political restructuring of incorporated areas, Wallerstein writes that "the incorporation of new zones into the capitalist world-economy involved their political restructuring as well as a series of modern states."[4] As Wallerstein points out, China experienced a decline of the ancien régime and began to accept the logics of the interstate system. It is not different from the fact that China, unlike in the past, had to follow geopolitical logics formed by the capitalist world-economy.

What does it mean that a modern state fits with the logics of the interstate system? Basically, a territorial container and independent political system within the capitalist world-economy is a modern state, historically evolved from northwestern Europe. Unlike a variety of political systems of the premodern era that developed on the outer rim of the capitalist world-economy or from a world empire such as China, all states of the modern world-system were fundamentally formulated by the interstate system.[5] This indicates that the historical origin of capitalism and the mechanism of capital accumulation were not formed within the territory of a nation-state. They were formulated or reformulated by the logics of the world market, operating beyond the boundary of the state.

In framing this conceptualization of the interstate system, I also insist that the emergence and rise of the interstate system went hand in hand with the historical process of capitalist expansion. As Arrighi noted, "The modern system of rule has been closely associated with the development of capitalism as a system of accumulation on a world scale."[6] The interstate system that evolved from the West is the single most important factor in capitalist development and in itself contributes to shoring up the capitalist world-economy.[7] Chase-Dunn also points out the importance of the interstate system in sustaining the world-system network and in developing the capital accumulation process: the "inter-state system itself is the fundamental basis of the competitive commodity economy at the system level. Thus, the interaction of world market and state system is fundamental to an understanding of capitalist development and its potential transformation into a more collective rational system."[8] Based on

Chase-Dunn's arguments, the boundary of the interstate system has been expanded by means of the coercive intervention of strong states and in proportion to capitalist development.

Given the premise that the logic of the transnational system becomes more pervasive as the boundaries of the capitalist world-economy expand, political and institutional change in the incorporated areas can be part of the process of incorporation. And political movements of the newly incorporated areas toward a westernized political system paved the way for capital accumulation.[9] For this, the capitalist world-economy often induced (or forced) incorporated areas to transform their traditional or old political regimes into a modern state during and after their incorporation processes. This political reorganization of the incorporated areas served as the "political underpinning of the mobility of capital" and "the institutional basis for the continuing expansion of capitalist development";[10] consequently, incorporated areas were deeply entrenched in the structural and hierarchical (or core-periphery) political system of the capitalist world-economy. In this chapter I examine how the Opium Wars and the establishment of the Qing's new diplomatic apparatus made room for colonial powers to ensconce themselves in the Chinese market.

To recap, an external arena's acceptance of interstate rules of the capitalist world-economy has the following features. First, incorporated areas experienced political changes as the inevitable result of accepting and adapting Western-oriented politics during and after its incorporation process. Second, an external arena's state-building process was linked with the production and distribution system of global capitalism. Most importantly, the newly created government policies or state apparatus of incorporated areas explicitly or implicitly helped to expand the capitalist mode of production globally. Third, as an external arena is integrated into the interstate system of the capitalist world-economy, most incorporated areas tended to be placed at a relatively disadvantageous position; as a result, most peripheral countries often suffered from unequal treaties with semiperiphery or core countries.[11]

"Under what conditions and by what paths"[12] could we observe the decline of the Qing Empire and its transition to a state coupled with the interstate logics of the capitalist world-economy? In attempting to answer this knotty question I first investigate how European countries developed interstate systems distinguished from the international relationships of late imperial China. This helps us to understand the qualitative differences in both state formation and international relations between European countries and late imperial China and state formation and international relations between late imperial China and incorporating (or incorporated) China. Next, I examine military collisions between Europe and China (including why China was defeated in the Opium War) and the European colonial presence in China during the nineteenth century and how it contributed to the presence of Western merchants in China and China's incorporation process. After that, I will examine how the Qing Empire, after the Opium War, tried to combine interstate logics with domestic logic and establish a new form of political regime in response to the specific expectations or requirements of the capitalist world-economy. Finally, I will elucidate how the Qing Empire adopted various interstate regulations, including the territorial concept of a modern state and international law.

The European and Chinese Dynamics Compared

The interstate relationships of Western Europe, based in the competition among European territorialized states, served as a watershed of the European great divergence.[13] According to this interpretation, a fragmented interstate system led European states to struggle with each other, which consequently triggered the development of war-making capabilities.

Charles Tilly stresses the fact that the emergence of competitive relations with neighboring countries brought about Europe's rise.[14] Just as Weber considered a "monopoly of the legitimate use of physical force within a given territory"[15] as an essential feature of the modern state, Tilly also viewed the monopolization of violence by European monarchs as the start of the modern state. For example, the Tudor monarchs of England launched the demilitarization process of great lords and Louis XIII initiated the disarmament of the great rebel lords while protecting their citizens against external foes.[16] Under such a fundamental rule—people have the right to safety against external attacks as a trade-off for abandoning the means of violence—each European monarch successfully eliminated all rivals in his or her territory and became a holder of military power up through the late eighteenth century. Internally, by monopolizing the means of violence, the governmental apparatus of Western Europe successfully disarmed the lords of their armies. Externally, each European country could build up military strength to check and overcome rival countries or to destroy all challengers under the pretext of protecting its own citizens against outside enemies. Striving for "advantages of power within a secure or expanding territory" paved the way toward the reinforcement of European countries' war-making capability and consequently led them to fall into unprecedented economic and military competition, including wars.[17]

An interstate competition helped not only the military and economic advance of each European state but also the technological progress and the institutional breakthrough of the entire European society. According to Stephan R. Epstein, competition between European states resulted in the development of a culture where elites were eager to recruit skilled craftsmen to create products for them, and it led to experimentation, dissemination, and adaptation of institutions, particularly in war finance.[18]

The competition between nation-states in Western Europe that emerged during their growth was unique and extended beyond Europe's borders. As European countries worked to modernize themselves into states, they also focused on exploring new trade routes. Portugal's success in the spice trade, which resulted in significant economic gains, prompted other European countries to pursue similar opportunities. According to Wallerstein, "No doubt overseas expansion has been traditionally linked with the interests of merchants, who stood to profit by the expanded trade, and with the monarchs who sought to ensure both glory and revenue for the throne."[19] The prosperity of Portugal's long-distance sea trade motivated other European nations to establish "coherent nation-states obtaining politico-commercial advantages" through sea routes.[20] Indeed, there was a geopolitical or geoeconomic reason why northwestern Europe had striven to open new routes: As the Ottoman Empire, with its "conquests of the Black Sea, Red Sea, and much of the Mediterranean," controlled access to the seas since the late fifteenth century,[21] European traders had to find another trading route that was free from the Ottomans' maritime hegemony. Consequently, the Ottoman blockade of the European merchants' international activities, ironically, promoted Europe's discovery of the New World.

These achievements not only marked the beginning of a new era of interstate competition in Europe but also expanded beyond the continent's borders (see figure 3.1).[22]

What is the significance of Europe's expansion resulting from interstate competition, such as the rivalry between the Dutch and the English? I argue that the first interstate competition of Europe, formed by the elimination of internal rivals like the great lords, was nominally oriented toward defense (the protection of people from

Figure 3.1. Diagrammatic representation of an analytical framework of the West's modern state transition. *Source*: Created by the author.

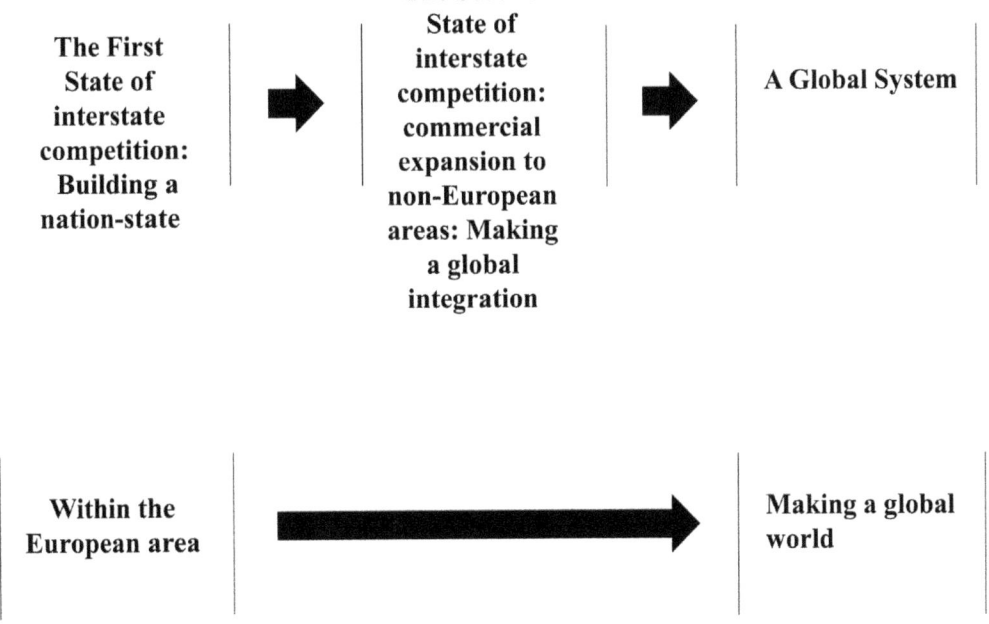

outside enemies) and its interstate competition based on enhancement of national competitiveness was limited to European space. However, the second interstate competition of Europe, formed by the opening of new sea routes, was primarily oriented to expand to the rest of the world. It drove each European state to be aggressive and violent. And its interstate competition went beyond the bounds of European territory.[23]

To get resources beyond Europe, European nation-states needed to work closely with merchants who took the lead in overseas expansion. According to Weber, the partnership between rising states and privileged capitalist powers played a significant role in the creation of modern capitalism, leading to a competitive struggle between large, equally powerful political structures that had a global impact.[24] David Landes explains that European society was shaped by its distinct geography, which separated countries from each other and prevented conquest by a single superpower and oppressive behavior from neighbors or rivals.[25] This fragmentation enabled greater cultural, commercial, and technological development. The competitive and relatively equal relationships among European countries not only drove commercial expansion outside of Europe but also facilitated the development of a dominating and exploitative form of capitalism, allowing European countries to establish global hegemony.

Qing China's development of statehood and international relations seemingly differed from Western Europe's interstate systems characterized by government's monopoly of violence in exchange for people's safety against outside threats, a collaboration between the state and the mercantile-financial elites, and geopolitical expansion to non-European areas.

Yet recent Chinese historians have sought to show that the Qing Empire's expansionist policies were no different from those of Western European countries, and that many Europeans were involved in the production of the Qing Empire's geography and cartography. Influenced partially by the theories of postcolonialist scholars like Louis Hevia or Lydia Liu who have debunked the Eurocentrism embedded in the discourse on modern state formation and colonial expansion,[26] Laura Hostetler and Emma Jinhua Teng regard the wars of conquest in Xinjiang, Tibet, and Burma and the territorial expansion of the seventeenth and eighteenth centuries as equivalent to European colonial expansion.[27] Furthermore, they point to how Jesuit missionaries were involved in the mapping of the Qing Empire in the seventeenth century as historical evidence for a global connection between Qing China and the West. In a similar vein, Peter Perdue argues that the Qing Empire, backed by the Jesuits' outstanding negotiating skills, was able to sign the Treaty of Nerchinsk with Russia in 1689.[28] This allows for the recognition that westernized ideas and scientific skills or techniques were significantly reflected in the maps of the Qing Empire.[29] Hostetler extended this view in striving to find historical clues to Qing China's transition to a modern state, by comparing Qing Empire maps with world maps and identifying the scientific and modern characteristics of Chinese maps.[30] These studies have emphasized China's internal dynamics in the formation of a modern Chinese state. This approach, however, tends to fall into the epistemological quagmire of a China-centered view. For example, Kirk Wayne Larsen interpreted the relationship between Qing China and Chosŏn in the late nineteenth century and early twentieth centuries as an extension strategy of Qing imperialism.[31] In contrast with the predominant conception that considers nineteenth-century China as a victim of Western colonialism, Larsen insisted that the Qing Empire tried to maintain "its large multi-ethnic empire" during the nineteenth century.[32] In addition, Larsen offers a new interpretation of nineteenth-century China's role in the world-economy, writing that "China in particular appears to have been far more significant, even, central, to the functioning of the world economy," and that "China has rejoined the stream of global history as an equal."[33] Larsen's interpretation of Qing China is thought-provoking, but his overstatement regarding late Qing China tends to exclude the Qing government's abjection caused by colonial penetrations in the nineteenth century. Although Hostetler suggests a hybrid approach,[34] she also has a strong tendency to think of eighteenth-century Qing China as the center of the global world. This evidently results in another form of Sinocentrism or "Orientalism in reverse." Reverse Orientalism refers to the opposite of Orientalism, as a distorted narrative created by the East (or West). It often espouses Asian culture, tradition, economy, and politics and, furthermore, portrays Asian civilizations and values as vastly superior to the West, while ignoring the impact of the West or the connected histories of the West and the East.[35] To avoid this "Orientalism in reverse" one should not disregard the influence of the West on East Asian countries, nor conflate the developmental paths of each East Asian country.[36]

In light of this, I here emphasize the different forms of state management and interstate relations between Europe and Qing China. After getting rid of rivals within its territory[37] and forming a governmental apparatus, the first consideration of the ruling regime in Qing China was obtaining legitimate domination, given that the Qing rulers pursued and developed patrimonial governance. During the Qing regime, all government officials had the primary duty of safeguarding the emperor and his relatives, such as Aisin Gioro Hala (the imperial family of the Qing regime),[38] even though the ruling regime didn't have complete control over local elites like the gentry class.[39] Qing China's state-makers derived their power from the hereditary charisma of the emperor's family. Therefore, the ruling regime aimed to grant the emperors and their family absolute power by implementing an efficient internal governance system that prioritized the protection of the royal family. For this reason, the nature of government itself was very private, and the emperor was often perceived as the father figure of all people.[40] Furthermore, the empire was maintained by the act of hereditary rule, so the object of loyalty of officials and gentlemen converged on the emperor and the dynasty.

For the very same reason, when the hereditary charisma of the royal family was not granted by local lords, civil war or rebellions broke out.[41] In fact, antigovernment groups, discontented with Manchu governance, were organized at the beginning of the Qing regime. Though the Qing rose to power in Beijing in 1644, South China was not pacified due mainly to the Revolt of the Three Feudatories from 1673 to 1681.[42]

This alerted the Qing regime to the dangers of localized rebellions even though Qing forces suppressed this revolt.

To forestall such well-armed rebel forces and enhance sociopolitical stability, the Qing regime used both hard-line and conciliatory policies. As a hard-line policy, the early Qing regime strengthened punishments for rebels, outlaws, and Ming loyalists, which was intended to prevent social unrest or uprisings. As a conciliatory policy, the Qing regime accepted and embraced the Ming's institutional and cultural legacy. The judicial and tax policies conducted by Dorgon in the early days of the Qing Empire were piecemeal reforms that were not qualitatively different from those of the Ming dynasty.[43] Qing state-makers were also dedicated to accepting the bureaucratic officialdom of the Ming; they tried to minimize any political disorder caused by the power vacuum.[44] More importantly, Manchus sought to identify themselves as a bastion of China's cultural heritage to inherit the patrimonial governance of their immediate predecessor, which helped strengthen the centralism of the Qing regime.[45] The Qing employed traditional Confucian practices such as "conducting ceremonies, providing pardons, conducting examinations, selecting officials, and issuing decrees in the manner of previous rulers"[46] that were ingrained in the Ming bureaucracy to inspire devotion from state bureaucrats. In doing so, the Qing regime could get steadfast loyalty from state officials.[47] While obtaining state bureaucrats' loyalty in the central government, the Qing regime also indirectly ruled local areas via its support from the local gentry[48] because the Qing's political authorities failed to expand their governance to the point where they could administer state or public affairs at the local levels through their own agents.[49] The Qing regime, in turn, obtained legitimate domination from the central to local and from state bureaucrats to the gentry class while anti-Manchu secret societies (e.g., the Triads, the Society of the Heaven and the Earth) remained relatively covert.[50]

A combination of patrimonial governance, Confucian ideology, and Confucian elites made it possible for Manchu emperors to have the domination continuum—regardless of opposition generated by the establishment of a new empire through Manchu invasions—and the Qing regime consequently monopolized physical force. However, the Qing regime's monopoly on physical force was contrasted with that of Western European countries in that it originally aimed to prevent anti-Qing groups from breaking out in rebellions and to pursue ideological and institutional stabilization. China's economic system, characterized by a labor-intensive agricultural system, well-regulated irrigation, and the growth of trade, did not lead to the predatory and oligopolistic economy that modern European countries pursued. Although China's economic system was not good for the accumulation of capital or the development of labor-saving devices it was skillfully sustained for a long time.[51] In addition, in the process of state formation during the Ming and Qing eras, Confucian ideology and patrimonial governance resulted in extreme reluctance to generate economic inequality between commoners, excepting socioeconomic inequality between ruling elites and commoners. According to Hung, the Confucianist state regarded merchants and other commoners as children who were entitled to equal protection from the state—as if the state were a paternal figure.[52] Safeguarding the poor from the exploitation of profit-seeking merchants was akin to protecting a younger sibling from an older one's bullying. Consequently, despite the emergence of a monetary economy, markets, cities, and merchant guilds during the Qing regime, there was no significant connection between the ruling authorities and the financial or commercial elites, and this, unlike in Western countries, prevented the transformation into a capitalist system.[53]

From an international perspective, in contrast with the situation of the European world that had triggered unprecedented interstate competition through each country's "interdependence of state making and war making" since the 1600s,[54] the China-centered world order did not lead to neighboring countries competing against the Chinese empire.[55] Rather, Qing China used Confucian ideology to establish hierarchical relationships with neighboring countries. That is, Qing China applied China-centered Confucian politics—the whole world revolved around China because China was the center of the world and "halfway between heaven and earth"[56]—onto international relationships. The idea of a so-called centripetal Sinocentric world order was embodied in Qing China's tributary system.[57] Primarily, the Qing regime compelled or induced neighboring nations to join the tributary system led by China to ensure that they received guarantees of peace and trading opportunities.[58] In return for these benefits, all tributaries had to conform to a China-centered world order. Thus, the Qing regime, through the tributary system, sought to establish hierarchical relationships with tributary states,[59] which ultimately resulted in a Sino-centric world order in the Asian region. This hierarchical order with neighboring nations did not foster any motivation for the transformation of its international order or stimulation for expansion into nontributary territories.[60] In simple terms, late imperial China's diplomatic system focused on hierarchized diplomatic relations over culture, politics, and social status rather than economic interests, which, in turn, served to deter military conflict between the Qing and its neighbors.[61]

Synthesis

The competition among European states, which was distinct from the China-centered international order, played a crucial role in the development of European countries' ability to make war. Additionally, this competition led to the expansion of non-European regions. However, the idea that Western Europe's "great divergence" was followed by an escalation of interstate competition offers little explanation for what occurred in non-European areas. For example, although Tilly examined various uses of state-controlled violence such as "war making," "state making," "protection," and "extraction,"[62] he did not apply his insights to the transformation of non-European areas that were affected by the penetration of European powers.[63]

To put it another way, Tilly did not delve deeply into questions such as how and why non-European nations, including Qing China, adopted Europe's interstate system logics, nor did he analyze what occurred within Chinese society during and after the country's acceptance of Europe's interstate rules. Moreover, not only did Tilly overlook these questions, most comparative historical sociologists have not addressed the far-reaching effects of European interstate logics on Qing China, nor have they provided an in-depth analysis of the transformations experienced by Qing China due to its acceptance of Europe's interstate rules.

Rather than focusing solely on identifying similarities or differences between Europe's interstate system and the China-centered international system, my intention is to trace Qing China's adoption of the West's interstate rules and its impact on the Qing regime, including political transformations during and after China's incorporation process. To accomplish this, I will first discuss the Opium Wars and their effect on China, as they played a critical role in transforming imperial China into a modern state within the capitalist world-economy.

Opium Wars: Clashes Between Two Differently Evolved Socio-Military Systems and China's Defeat

Based on the historical fact that China did not take a submissive attitude toward the West prior to the Opium Wars, we can infer that these wars altered China's relationship with the West and weakened the Qing's stability. Indeed, the Opium Wars served as a transformative event that allowed colonial powers to penetrate Chinese territory, and their persistent politico-economic intrusions hastened the decline of the Qing regime. To assess the impact of the Opium Wars, I will begin by examining the military development of the Qing. For the Qing, the Opium Wars were an unexpected disaster, as their military troops proved unable to withstand the assaults by British soldiers who inflicted heavy casualties on the Chinese army. Through a comparison of the military paths of the Qing Empire and the British Empire, I aim to shed light on why the Qing was forced to endure military defeats and what the Opium Wars meant to the Qing.[64]

A Military Legacy of Late Imperial China

As previously mentioned, during the late imperial period China was characterized by a patrimonial-bureaucratic system that focused on maintaining an agricultural empire through irrigated rice cultivation and labor-intensive activities.[65] One of the main military threats to such a large agricultural empire was posed by nomadic incursions. According to Palat, "pastoral nomads" were the biggest problem for China.[66] After the expulsion of the Mongolian tribes during the Ming dynasty, the Ming regime intervened in the Mongols' internal power struggles to prevent them from creating a united nomadic empire that could compete with the Ming. Despite the fact that Dayan Khan

(1464–1517) reunified the Mongols under the name of the "great Yuan dynasty," the Ming regime was successful in containing the growth of Mongol power.[67]

Ming China attempted to develop cavalry in order to effectively defend against nomadic incursions, since the latest firearms were ineffective against the nomadic warriors: "Guns had hardly been fired when the [Manchu] swords had reached the [Ming soldiers'] necks."[68] To obtain horses used by armies, the Ming instituted a "tea-horse market" in present-day Gansu and Qinghai through the government's monopolistic position in the tea market;[69] however, due to insufficient financial resources, the Ming bureaucracy was unable to acquire the number of horses that were required by Ming troops. As a result, the Ming cavalries were incapable of defending border areas against large numbers of the armed cavalry of nomadic tribes, particularly in Manchuria.

In contrast with the Ming's powerless cavalry, Manchu society had relatively developed cavalry regiments that played an important role in leading military victories like the Battle of Sarhu in 1619[70] and the Battle of Ssanglyeong in 1637.[71] Palat concludes that "the speed and maneuverability of light cavalries in much of continental Asia stifled the development of firearms."[72] A key part of late imperial China's military formation, especially the Qing's, goes hand in hand with the development of cavalries. To enable agile military operations and develop striking power that was vastly superior to firearms in battlefields, well-drilled cavalries and large numbers of horses were required; however, during the Opium Wars, Qing armies had to defend and counterattack British armies at sea and on rivers. Given the fact that the Qing's military forces were neither familiar with nor drilled to participate in naval battles, it came as no surprise that the Qing Empire faced disastrous defeats in the Opium Wars.

THE OPIUM WARS AND THEIR IMPACT ON CHINA

Undoubtedly, the Opium Wars of the 1840s played a crucial role in China's integration into the capitalist world-economy. Although there were prior indications of tension between China and Britain (e.g., the *Lady Hughes* incident in 1784 or Admiral Drury's occupation of Macao in 1808), the Opium Wars brought about significant changes in the East Asian region's international situation and unprecedented politico-economic transformations in China.[73] Stephen Platt argues that the Opium Wars had the most significant impact of any major event on China's modern history.[74]

To investigate the Opium Wars' effects on the Qing regime's international relationships and its incorporation process, this study examines the Opium Wars' diplomatic and politico-economic causes. I will establish a historical context for the military confrontation between China and European powers in the nineteenth century. Additionally, I will explain the different politico-economic motives behind the battles of the Opium Wars and the reason for China's defeat. By comparing England's military technologies and weapons with China's, I will expound on why China suffered a military defeat and why Chinese reformers sought to adopt advanced military technologies from the West. Lastly, this study examines how the Opium War hastened China's incorporation process into the capitalist world-system.

Causes of the Opium War

Before addressing questions about the Opium War, such as what occurred during the war, why China was defeated, and how the war contributed to China's incorporation process, I pose the question of how China came to be involved in such a devastating conflict in 1842. The politico-economic aspect—the use of military force for diversification of export markets, Canton's high port tax on British merchants, conflicts between British opium brokers and Chinese officials—was the immediate cause of the Opium War.

Yet what is often missing in assessing the origins of the Opium Wars is the nonpolitical or economic aspects. This leaves us with a problem of explaining how these factors—especially diplomatic relations—contributed to a rush to war in the nineteenth century. We can start with Western perceptions of the Qing government. Before the First Opium War, the closed-door policies (*biguanzishou* 闭关自守) were central to the Qing's foreign policy even though some ports occasionally were opened to the outside. The Qing sustained the closed-door policy because of a fear of Western countries' aggressive trading activities: "It is written in the Chinese books that European are warlike boisterous people, who always seek to invade the eastern countries, where they come to trade."[75] More importantly, Chinese officials believed that an increase in international trade activities might undermine China's socioeconomic stability. Guan Tong's (1780–1831) argument lends support to this idea in that international trade had done more harm than good: "When foreign products entered China, these are for one person, whereas when my wealth and products entered their own countries, these are for three persons. Because of the Western's weird technologies—our wealth flowed out of the country. . . . Given the fact China became poor, I cannot but worry about our security."[76] Guan Tong's view, based on national security, rests on nationalism and, in his view, the uselessness of international trade. China's limited international trade and sea ban policies (*haijinzhengce* 海禁政策),[77] however, roused Western countries' antipathy: Montesquieu said that China was governed by despotic rule. After Britain's proposal aiming to open trade in 1792 was denied by the Chinese government, Robbins Macartney, Britain's first envoy to China, also criticized China: "The Empire of China is an old, crazy, first-rate Man of War, which a fortunate succession of and vigilant officers have contrived to keep afloat for these hundred and fifty years past."[78]

In 1816, Lord William Amherst (1773–1857) left London for China as the second envoy, in charge of a group of ten others, also known as envoys. The envoys traveled by ship to Tientsin and then overland to Beijing, as arranged with the Qing regime. The envoys arrived at the Old Summer Palace (*Yuanmingyuan* 圓明園) in Beijing twenty days after landing, but the emperor abruptly canceled their meeting. The envoys were angry, but they were forced to leave Beijing that day.[79] The envoys' negative impressions of China were reinforced during their four-month return journey from Beijing to Guangzhou. They were able to observe Chinese society in much greater freedom than during the previous Macartney mission. Although the envoys observed different parts of the country over a long period of time, their accounts of their experiences uniformly emphasized China's backwardness.

The strict diplomatic and legal sanctions against Western merchants imposed by the Canton system were also an important factor in the Opium Wars. The Canton system, designed by the Qing government, was not initially focused on expanding trade between China and Western countries, but rather on ensuring that Western merchants complied with strict and complex regulations. As such, Western merchants participating in the Canton system could trade only if they complied with these regulations. Western merchants were prohibited from contacting any other Chinese merchants except Chinese Hong merchants, and the Chinese government uniformly controlled the prices of tea and silk that Europeans wanted to buy. Lower-level Chinese officials demanded bribes to inspect the goods brought in by Western merchants, and Western merchants had to comply to ensure that trade went smoothly. Western merchants were not allowed to stay in the Thirteen Factories for the entire year, so they had to go to Macao at the end of their trading under the Canton system, where they would communicate with Chinese Hong merchants and prepare for the next year's trading. Western merchants were also not allowed to bring women into the Thirteen Factories in Canton because Western women might arouse the curiosity of the Chinese and harm their customs. Furthermore, Western merchants were not permitted to report complaints about their trade directly to the local government. Their complaints had to go through Chinese Hong merchants before being reported to local government officials, which was inconvenient and unreliable. From the Western merchants' perspective, there was no guarantee that their complaints about Chinese Hong merchants would reach government officials because those merchants had to go through the complaints in advance.[80]

For Britain, which proposed free trade and developed an interstate system of international relationships, Macartney's and Amherst's disparaging claims were not entirely groundless. Appalled by China's obstinate closed-door polices, Britain realized that military conflicts might be provoked. Of course, China's closed-door policies cannot be regarded as the sole cause of the Opium Wars, but China can still be seen as a troublesome country from Britain's perspective.

Some Western merchants did not abide by these strict regulations. As American trader William Hunter pointed out, by deliberately ignoring the sanctions imposed on them, Western merchants were able to gain a certain amount of comfort within the Canton system: "Everything worked smoothly and harmoniously by acting in direct opposition to what we were ordered to do. We pursued the evil tenor of our way with supreme indifference, took care of our business, pulled boats, walked, dined well, and so the years rolled by as happily as possible."[81]

While some, like William Hunter, were able to adapt and live within the Canton system with a moderate disregard for the discipline imposed on them, others were deeply dissatisfied with the institutional and legal restrictions imposed by the Chinese government. They could not put up with what they considered to be intolerable restrictions, which was focused by their resentment over the *Lady Hughes* affair (1784).[82] A cannon salute fired by the British East India Company's ship *Lady Hughes*, while moored in Huangpu, killed two neighboring Chinese. The British petitioned to have the killings dismissed as unintentional, but the Chinese government was not willing to be lenient. As China's pressure mounted, one of the men aboard the *Lady Hughes* was extradited by the Chinese government, which eventually hanged him. This was the first time British authorities extradited a British criminal to China for trial.

The *Lady Hughes* affair caused a stir in London when it became publicized. The initial reaction was criticism of the East India Company's incompetence: the company should be held accountable for extraditing an innocent man to lose his life.[83] But it didn't take long for this to escalate into a matter of British pride. The committee of representatives that investigated the *Lady Hughes* affair reported that it was a result of Britain's lack of a trading base that was protected by British law. This was followed by discussions in the British cabinet and parliament about no longer following the Qing Empire's foreign trade rules and calls for intervention in Chinese trade, signaling that the relationship between China and Britain had entered a conflict phase. By the time of the First Opium War relations between Britain and China had been deteriorating for decades.

Obviously, the Opium War was partly caused by the strained relationship between Britain and China, but its fundamental cause is closely tied to economic motives.[84] European nations did not hesitate to employ military force to gain exceptional opportunities in new markets outside of Europe.[85] Just as the stupendous preponderance of Portuguese armed forces served to extend their influence in the Indian Ocean world[86] and East Asian world,[87] the advanced armed forces of Britain helped to penetrate Chinese markets.

Private British merchants, particularly those involved in the lucrative trade between Britain, China, and India (such as the opium trade), were severely constrained by the strict regulations imposed by the Qing government. For these merchants, it was imperative to be free from Qing interference and sanctions. As a result, individuals like James Matheson and William Jardine, who believed in a close connection between their economic interests and national honor, actively lobbied for war and provided the British government with military intelligence on China, including through espionage.[88] Additionally, *the Canton Register*, an English-language newspaper in China that reflected the views of the belligerent private merchants, published articles that were pro-British and market-friendly. These articles emphasized the importance of British national interests in China and urged Britain to initiate a war against China.

It is crucial to recognize the strong link between the gunboat diplomacy advocated by these merchants and the outbreak of the Opium War.[89]

The economic motives behind the Opium War highlight the crucial role played by military means in integrating China into the global economy. By waging the Opium War, Britain was able to remove trade barriers that had been central to China's closed policies. This benefited Britain greatly, as evidenced by the significant increase in China's opium trade deficit (1842–1856) and the accelerated export of China's tea to the British market (1842–1881) following the war.[90] The Opium War in this sense was not simply a major naval battle or a military conflict aimed at imperialistic conquest by Britain; rather, it was an economic-driven military conflict aimed at integrating China into the capitalist world-economy.

REFLECTIONS ON THE WAR SITUATION: HOW DID TENSION BETWEEN BRITAIN AND CHINA REACH A BOILING POINT?

It is clear that Britain used military force to establish superiority over China and to turn trading matters stemming from the stringent trade regulations of the Canton system to its own advantage. In contrast, China had a different idea with the Canton system of trading with European countries: Just as the Qing Empire had a tributary relationship through trade, it considered the opening of the Canton system and Western countries' participation in it as an act of economic benevolence from the Qing Empire. For this reason, the Qing Empire viewed British insistence on "changes in China's diplomatic and commercial practices" as a ludicrous suggestion.[91] Moreover, the Qing regime considered diplomatic relationships with the British Empire and foreign trade with British merchants on the coast as a minor issue before and during the Opium War, believing that local authorities could manage matters related to the British.

During William John Napier's tenure as the chief superintendent of trade at Canton in 1834, he became increasingly aware of the difficulty of convincing China to abandon its China-centric international rules. Moreover, he arrived in China with little familiarity with his assignment and the principles of Sino-British diplomatic relations. For example, he was tasked with cracking down on the smuggling of opium on ships found in Chinese waters, arresting and bringing to trial those involved in the smuggling, but the British cabinet was not informed of this. He was also told by the British cabinet that he was to remain stationed in Guangzhou, abiding by Chinese law, but was unaware of local regulations that required him to leave the city at the end of his trading period. Furthermore, the British order that he create a direct channel of communication with Qing government officials was in fact contrary to Chinese custom, which required that Westerners go through Hong merchants to speak to the Qing government.[92] This situation ultimately led to disagreements and friction between Napier and the Chinese authorities. For instance, despite consistently advocating for westernized diplomatic relationships and expanded trade deals, Napier's requests were repeatedly rejected by Governor-General Lu Kun (1772–1835), who believed that Chinese officials should never correspond with Western barbarians.[93] China's firm rejection of the British government's proposals, including equal diplomatic relationships and expansion of trade and their limitations on British movements and access to Chinese facilities,[94] as well as physical violence against British people,[95] fueled dissatisfaction among the British. Unable to resolve the conflict diplomatically, Napier considered using military force to achieve diplomatic and economic goals. However, a large-scale military conflict did not occur, as Napier unexpectedly retired his British warships to Macao, where he died of a fever in October 1834.

John Frances Davis succeeded Napier as the chief superintendent of trade, but his conciliatory attitude toward China did not gain the support of British merchants in China, which led to his resignation in January 1835. George Robinson was then appointed to the position, but like Davis, he also pursued a cautious approach and maintained a peaceful trade routine.[96] However, this approach did not receive the support of the merchants, and he was eventually replaced by Charles Elliot.

When Elliot assumed the role of chief superintendent of trade in 1836, he understood that demanding the expansion of the opium trade and other market demands was not a graceful approach;[97] nonetheless, he had to protect the interests of British merchants who were heavily involved in the opium trade in China. Unlike his predecessors John Frances Davis and George Robinson, Elliot adopted a more aggressive stance toward China in order to reap the economic benefits of the opium trade and shield British merchants from Chinese authorities' sanctions. As a result, he clashed with Imperial Commissioner Lin Zexu 林則徐 (1785–1850).

As interested as Elliot was in his country's economic gain from the opium trade, the Qing government was equally concerned with the social and economic problems created by the influx of opium (e.g., the silver outflow in return for opium import, financial loss due to silver outflow, and social unrest caused by the increase of opium addicts). To stop the opium trade and prevent British merchants from bringing opium to China, the Qing regime dispatched Lin Zexu. Lin received unconventional and sweeping instructions from the Daoguang Emperor, who ordered him to eliminate the evils associated with opium in Guangdong, including opium brokers and sellers, opium warehouses, opium dens, and other matters related to the drug.[98] This order implied that considerable force could be used if necessary. While Lin believed that the distribution, sale, and consumption of opium should be strictly prohibited, he told the emperor that war with Britain in Chinese coastal areas should be avoided.[99] Lin wanted to stop the spread of opium sales and consumption through decisive, strict, and swift action, but he did not intend to escalate this into war. However, regardless of his true intentions, his bold action to ban the distribution and consumption of opium was seen as a major threat by the British.

Elliot and Lin had their first conflict when Lin seized opium from British merchants by force. Lin had taken a hard stance against the opium trade, which was led by foreign merchants, blaming it for the increase in opium consumption and addiction in China. He warned that any foreign-owned ships carrying opium would not be allowed to enter or trade with China. When Chinese officials found opium on foreign ships, they confiscated the opium and other goods and punished the merchants according to Chinese law.[100] Lin also burned any illegal opium seized from foreign traders. In 1839, after realizing that British merchants exclusively monopolized the opium trade, Lin wrote a letter to Queen Victoria to complain about it[101] in an attempt to discourage the British from producing and exporting opium to China.[102]

Commissioner Lin's strict restrictions and harsh punishments for the British-led opium trade caused fear among British merchants. As a result, Elliot and the merchants moved to Macao, but this did not mean that Elliot abandoned his primary duty of establishing a legal and institutional framework in China that would allow British merchants to conduct opium transactions with Chinese merchants. Despite Lin's stern warnings, Elliot and the pro-free-trade British merchants disregarded them and viewed his opium confiscations as an oppressive abuse of power.

Lin believed that British merchants' opium trade could not be eradicated as long as they remained in Macao and Elliot did not pledge to ban illegal opium transactions. To impose stronger sanctions on the British in Macao, Lin requested that the Portuguese authorities stop providing them with supplies and fuel. He even visited Macao to prohibit opium trade in the area. This led to the first military confrontation between Elliot's warships and Chinese naval vessels on September 4, 1839. Although the British won, Elliot requested more troops to protect the merchants, fulfill his duty of establishing safeguards for their opium trade, and prepare for future battles. In response to Elliott's request, the British government dispatched British troops to China in February 1840 and the British Parliament voted for war in April of the same year.

THE FIRST REASON FOR CHINA'S DEFEAT: POOR COMMUNICATION AND THE INCOMPETENCE OF MILITARY COMMANDERS

The approval of the British Parliament for military action marked the beginning of one of the most unjust wars in global history. Clearly, the British started an unjustifiable war, but the Qing Empire was unable to defeat the British. On the contrary, the Qing Empire was crushingly defeated. The empire's inexperience in waging war was evident in the many battles against the British during the Opium War. An important factor that contributed to the Qing army's one-sided defeat in almost every battle was the incompetence of its leadership and a miscommunication system based on mistrust. After the army led by Lin Zexu was defeated and Dinghai was captured by the British, Emperor Daoguang dismissed Lin and replaced him with Qi Shan 琦善 (1786–1854)

in order to advance the fight and negotiations with the British. In his negotiations with the British, Qi Shan attempted to calm the emperor's anger and to obtain what the emperor considered important goals like the withdrawal of the British fleet and the return of the stolen territory (Zhoushan) from the British, on the one hand, and to offer the British permission to trade in opium in restricted areas on the condition that they accept the emperor's demands, on the other. Although his negotiations were temporarily successful and he obtained the withdrawal of the British fleet and the promise of returning Zhousan, his negotiating methods were improvised rather than based on careful consideration of objective data and information.

Even though the war with Britain was not over, Qishan disbanded the militia organized by Lin Zexu during the negotiation process and made no plans for troop reinforcements. In this situation, the Qing troops were unable to prevent the British from infiltrating the country following the breakdown of negotiations. Worse, when the British took control of Hong Kong, Qishan did not report it to the emperor. Instead, it was Iliyang 怡良 (1791–1867), governor of Guangdong, who reported the British occupation of Hong Kong: "Since Qishan came to Guangzhou, he has never informed me about how he handles things. Suddenly, I heard a rumor that Elliot had hoisted the flag in Hong Kong and proclaimed that all the inhabitants were British subjects. The truth of the rumor cannot be verified, and many people are suspicious. I sent my admirals and generals to ascertain the truth of the rumor. . . . The rumors of the barbarians [British] taking over Hong Kong was true, and I was furious when I heard the news."[103]

Qishan's incompetence and irresponsibility aggravated the situation on the Chinese side, and he was eventually forced to step down by the emperor. Qishan's dismissal left Guangzhou temporarily in a command vacuum, and Chinese troops suffered a series of disastrous defeats. Yang Fang 楊芳 (1770–1846), a Han Chinese general and diplomat, was then assigned to fight the British, but his folkloric beliefs led him to consider British cannons as witchcraft, and he collected chamber pots used by women as a way to weaken British cannons. Yang Fang believed that rafts stacked with chamber pots would emit a negative energy (*yinqi* 陰氣) that would blind the British, which would in turn neutralize their cannons. He then believed that by ramming boats full of phosphorus into British ships, he would be able to sink them. Yang Fang's impractical and superstition-based plan ultimately led to defeat. In reality, whenever the British ships fired their cannons Qing soldiers were busy fleeing, and the rafts stacked with chamber pots simply floated in place.

Despite the loss of the battle due to his flawed strategy, Yang Fang, fearing reprimand and punishment, did not properly communicate the news of the defeat to the emperor. Based on misinformation, the emperor completely misjudged the battle situation, and this poor communication and subsequent misjudgment would continue throughout the war.

The Second and More Important Reason for China's Defeat: An Unbridgeable Gap Between Britain and China in Military Power

During the Opium Wars the Qing's technological and naval capabilities were far inferior to those of the British. This clearly created an insurmountable difference and played a huge role in demoralizing the Qing army. From the very beginning of the Opium War, China, facing the invading British armed forces, was at a disadvantage due to its insufficient military strength, especially in terms of naval forces. The advanced naval power of the British put the Chinese armed forces in a challenging situation they had not experienced before. This nightmare began for China when the British government officially declared war on the Qing Empire. Despite no longer being landlocked after the conquest, the Qing Empire did not focus on increasing its naval power. Instead, it concentrated on developing forces to win land battles, such as improving cavalry regiments. After the Emperor Kangxi put down the Revolt of the Three Feudatories (*sanfanzhiluan* 三藩之亂) (1673–1681) and conquered the whole of China, the Qing began wars of conquest, but most of the areas they conquered were located on the continent. Although the Qing deployed warships to conquer Taiwan and nearby islands in the 1620s, 1660s, and 1680s, the capabilities of their naval power were quite limited,[104] and they had no motivation to improve it as their focus was on land conquests.[105] In addition, the resistance movement of Zheng Jing, the eldest son of and successor to Zheng Chenggong, who took part in the Revolt of the Three Feudatories, led at least partially to the Qing regime's prohibition on ships bearing firearms. Due to strong policies against armed ships, the Qing could not develop sea-based military capabilities.[106] For these reasons, during the Opium Wars China had no navy[107] capable of fighting a British naval vessel like the *Nemesis*, a shallow-draft armored ship, that sailed up Chinese rivers.[108]

The Qing court, which was relatively focused on inland affairs, had limited information about the geography of the world's oceans. The Complete Map of Sea Ports (*Haikou Quantu* 海口全圖), drawn for military purposes in 1800, shows the locations of European countries—Germany (*Huangqi*), Denmark (*Linyin*), Netherlands (*Helan*), France (*Folangxi*), England (*Yingjili*), Portugal (*Putaoya*), Africa, Arabia, India, Russia, Japan, Southeast Asia (Vietnam and Thailand), Australia (*Dashishan*), and the Arctic Ocean. Although the map lists the locations and seaports of many countries, it does not include seaport information, naval power information, or detailed or accurate coastlines for each country.[109] This limited access to information about major overseas seaports and shallow knowledge of the military capabilities of major maritime nations would prove to be a fatal blow to Qing China about forty years later.

To make matters worse, over half of the 242 naval vessels of the Fujian water force (*shuishi* 水師) were being fixed or awaiting repair on the eve of the Opium War so these vessels were out of combat for the duration.[110] At the time when the Qing encountered British armed forces, their inferior quality of cannon and cannon-related military technologies such as "the quality of iron used in the cannon," "casting technology," "the quality of projectiles," "a system for the regular repair and replacement of cannon," "the quality of the powder," and "the quality of cannon manufacture" led Qing soldiers to encounter a woeful situation in battles.[111] Qing cannons could not penetrate the metal-plated hulls of British warships, while the Qing's coastal fortifications and river forts could not withstand fierce bombardment by British warships. The Battle of Humen serves as a clear example of this: even though it was considered the most heavily defended point on the coast,[112] it was unable to withstand the continuous British cannon fire and was ultimately captured by the British army.

Not only were the British armed forces adept at water-based warfare but they were also competent in land-based warfare. For example, at the Battle of Xiamen, Yan Botao (颜伯焘, 1792–1855), the commander in chief, spent six months building an impregnable fortress using granite, which was believed to be the strongest building material in the world.[113] However, the garrison fell to the British army shortly after the outbreak of the battle, despite the fact that the fortress walls withstood the British cannon fire. Yan Botao underestimated the British capacity for land-based warfare, and the British, who had superior firepower, were able to succeed in their landing operation. They landed on the eastern beach of the Xiamen fortress and quickly occupied the entire southern coast with minimal casualties, one of the main reasons for the Qing's defeat in this battle.[114]

The British military had a significant advantage during the Opium Wars due to their mastery of both water-based and land-based warfare, aided by the development of steam-powered ships.[115] The use of steam engines allowed the British navy to navigate the canals and easily reach inland areas of China.[116] Furthermore, the strength of iron ships powered by steam technology far surpassed the outdated Chinese junk ships, leading to quick and easy British victories.[117]

In reality, the Opium Wars were heavily one-sided. While many expected China's military to be a match for the British forces, the British navy was clearly superior. After experiencing repeated losses in large-scale battles, Chinese troops recognized the significant gap in military capabilities between themselves and the British,[118] and it even overwhelmed Chinese commanders with a sense of defeat before battle: "Witnessing the British ships first-hand, Ilibu (伊里布, 1772–1843), a Chinese commander, seems to have realized that it would be impossible to retake Dinghai by force, though he dared not say so explicitly."[119]

In addition, British amphibious warfare, characterized as "a frontal naval attack combined with a land attack to the side and rear,"[120] pushed Qing forces into desperate situations. When the Battle of Zhenjiang—the final battle of the Opium War—culminated in British victory, the Qing government concluded that there was no alternative but to sign a humiliating peace treaty. In the Opium War, Qing forces suffered nearly thirty thousand casualties, most of them in battles. Even more tragically, civilian casualties were also significant. Property damage in the British-occupied cities was also enormous. With regard to the situation that the Qing encountered, Tsiang Tingfu made the following argument: "There is a special relationship between China and the West. Before the Opium War, we were unwilling to treat them as equals; after the Opium War they were unwilling to treat us as equals."[121]

Aftermath of the Opium War: The Political and Institutional Reforms

The Opium War resulted in a significant shift in Chinese society and the East Asian region, as noted by Warren I. Cohen.[122] This marked the beginning of the decline of the ancien régime, which was caused by external pressures rather than the dynastic cycle. This was a revolutionary change for China, leading to its entry into the interstate system of the capitalist world-system. Following the defeat in the Opium War and the politico-economic pressure from the West, China carried out political reforms, namely the Self-Strengthening Movement and the establishment of the Zongliyamen, the prototype Foreign Affairs Office. The Qing government attempted to reform political institutions and revive the ancien régime in response to the politico-economic pressure after the Opium Wars. The Self-Strengthening Movement (c. 1861–1895) was a notable but ultimately unsuccessful attempt at political-institutional reform that primarily focused on adapting advanced Western technology and armaments;[123] although this does not mean the Self-Strengthening Movement focused exclusively on military aspects (see tables 3.1a-b).

The tables presented here indicate the wide-ranging reforms implemented by the Qing government, including economic, educational, and military reforms. One of the key aspects of the Self-Strengthening Movement was the establishment of modernized manufacturing companies, both government-supervised and merchant-managed. The movement emphasized the importance of sending Chinese students to study abroad, which led to notable achievements in fields such as railway construction, as exemplified by Zhan Tianyou 詹天佑 (1861–1919).

In addition, the Qing regime established the *Tongwenguan* 同文館 (School of Combined Learning) in 1862. At the Tongwenguan, students were taught foreign knowledge, modern Western science, and foreign languages. Although the Tongwenguan was modeled after the *Eluosi Wenguan* 俄羅斯文館 (or Russian College) (established in 1708), which was created to prepare for security threats to China's northwestern borders, it was a new institution that had not been previously seen in Chinese history. This was because the Tongwenguan offered a combination of foreign languages and international academic disciplines, which was a novel concept in Chinese education.

The Tongwenguan aimed to train linguists for the purpose of serving diplomatic affairs. At the time, China faced a disadvantage in international negotiations because it lacked proficient linguists who could communicate effectively with foreign diplomats. As a result, China often found itself in unfavorable treaty agreements. The Tongwenguan

Table 3.1a. Projects of the Self-Strengthening Movement, 1860–1870

Military Reforms	Economic Reforms	Educational Reforms	Studying Overseas
	Established government-supervised and merchant-managed companies	Aimed at training translators and military officials and learning knowledge about the West and natural science	
—蘇州洋砲局 (Suzhou Foreign Artillery Bureau, 1863) —江南機器製造總局 (Machine Manufacture of Jiangnan, 1865) —金陵機器製造局 (Nanjing Arsenal, 1865) —福州船政局 (Fuzhou Arsenal, 1867) —天津機器製造局 (Tianjin Arsenal, 1867)		—京師同文館 (Foreign language school at Beijing, 1862) —上海廣方言館 (Foreign Language school at Shanghai, 1863) —廣州同文館 (Foreign Language school at Guangzhou, 1864) —福州船政學堂 (Foochow Shipbuilding Institution, 1866)	— 120 Chinese students were sent to the United States to learn advanced knowledge between 1872 and 1881 (Chinese Educational Mission) — Students of Foochow Shipbuilding Institution were sent to France and Britain in 1875 and 1876 — Seven military officials were sent to Germany in 1876

Table 3.1b. Projects of the Self-Strengthening Movement, 1871–1880

Military Reforms	Economic Reforms	Educational Reform	Studying Overseas
—蘭州機器局 (Lanzhou Arsenal, 1871) —四川機器局 Sichuan Arsenal (1877)	—輪船招商局 (Steamship Navigation Company, 1872) —雲南銅鑛 (Yunnan Copper Mines, 1874) —基隆煤鑛 (Mining in Taiwan, 1875) —湖北廣濟興國煤礦 (Hubei Guangji Xingguo Coal Mine, 1875) —開平鑛務局 (Kaiping Mining Bureau, 1877) —天津電報總局 (Tianjin Telegraph General Administration, 1879)	—天津水師學堂 (Tianjin Navy College, 1880)	

trained linguists who could speak foreign languages fluently and serve as interpreters in diplomatic affairs. By doing so, China aimed to limit the disadvantages of not understanding the language when negotiating treaties and to become more self-reliant in diplomatic matters. This was an effort to level the balance of power and prevent the unfair treaties era from occurring again. According to Pan Lin, the Tongwenguan played a demonstrative role in shifting the paradigm of Chinese humiliation and educational backwardness.[124] The school's focus on linguistics and international relations represented a shift away from traditional Chinese education and signaled a willingness to embrace modernization and internationalization. By training competent linguists, China was able to improve its standing in international negotiations and assert itself as a capable diplomatic player. The Tongwenguan implemented a new curriculum that included subjects such as mathematics, chemistry, geology, mechanics, and international law, which were based on foreign curriculum. The instructors for these courses were foreigners. By studying these fundamental disciplines, students were equipped with the necessary skills to participate more effectively in both domestic and international affairs.[125]

Despite the focus on nonmilitary aspects of modernization, the primary motivation behind the Self-Strengthening Movement was China's military weakness, as evidenced by its outdated weapons and inferior naval forces. As a result, the Qing government sent officials to Western countries to learn advanced technologies and made efforts to modernize munitions factories. Under the motto "use the superior abilities of the barbarians to dominate the barbarians" (*shi yi zhi changji yi zhi yi* 师夷之长技以制夷),[126] the Qing regime attempted to modernize to catch up to the West. This led to the adoption of Western military technology and armaments,[127] as well as the establishment of shipyards and arsenals in key locations such as Nanjing, Shanghai, and Fuzhou.[128]

Yet the Self-Strengthening Movement did not achieve significant results. Despite the production of breech-loading rifles at the Jiangnan Arsenal, the rifles were much more expensive to produce than imported Western rifles and their performance was inferior. Similarly, shipbuilding efforts did not yield cost-effective or technologically competitive vessels. Moreover, the shipyards suffered from a lack of funding, and corruption in the construction contracts made it difficult to produce high-quality weapons and ships. Roy Bin Wong characterizes the outcome as a "poor fit between blueprints for change and current realities," resulting in the failure of China's Self-Strengthening Movement.[129]

More importantly, in analyzing the failure of the Self-Strengthening Movement we may need to think carefully about the following question—Why did the central government not lead this reform effort? Although many central government officials and literati agreed on the importance and necessity of the Self-Strengthening Movement,[130] why were regional viceroys and central administrative officers including Li Hongzhang entrusted with the key reform tasks?[131] This is probably due to opposition to the indiscriminate entry of foreign cultures and technologies; Confucian-oriented and conservative government officials as well as local gentry instead prioritized Confucian doctrines.[132] For instance, Wo Ren 倭仁 (1804–1871), a grand secretary, strongly argued that the pursuit of Western education would lead to the displacement of the Confucian principles that formed the basis of social values and ethics.[133] Since a significant number of conservate elites had hostile feelings toward modernization and westernization,[134] it would have been difficult for the central government to actively implement the Self-Strengthening Movement. Therefore, while sympathizing with the importance and necessity of the reform movement, it was impossible to come up with an active and comprehensive modernization policy at the central government level, and as a result, it remained an unfinished reform project. Li Hongzhang's views also were not much different. Li tended to think that China's political system, traditions, cultures, and customs were superior to those of the West, and that the only thing China could learn from the West was science and technology, such as guns, artillery, ships, and machinery. Liang Qichao 梁啓超 (1873–1929) pointed out that the failure of the Self-Strengthening Movement led by Li Hongzhang was based on false preconceptions about Western societies (i.e., the competitiveness of Western societies did not come from their social and political institutions, culture, and the thinking and behavior of their people, but from their science and technology).[135] This meant that the Self-Strengthening Movement was only half learning about the West.

The failure of the Self-Strengthening Movement may also have resulted from problems with the utilization of human resources within the Qing bureaucracy. Chinese historians like Kwang-Ching Liu note that the numerous diplomatic, defense, and domestic political tasks imposed on Li Hongzhang prevented him from focusing on the Self-Strengthening Movement, and as a result, he found it difficult to properly train the Beiyang Fleet he established in the run-up to the First Sino-Japanese War.[136]

Financial issues also played a role. Li Hongzhang recognized that the Japanese were buying newer and more advanced warships, but he could no longer afford to add to his fleets. One of the most serious problems he was facing was a lack of funds, as the Empress Dowager Cixi had diverted money that should have gone to the navy to build a new summer palace. In addition, the Qing government did not provide enough compensation for individual viceroys' reform projects. All the government could do for them was give them the status of official bureaucrats, which could only be awarded when their projects were successfully completed. Consequently, the viceroys who had a desire for government positions were only interested in becoming bureaucrats, not trying to remain technical experts who improved their professional skills.

Implicit or explicit Western hindrance was another factor that prevented the Qing government from succeeding in its modernization project. One fundamental principle of interstate system logic is that strong states' involvement in incorporated areas aims to dominate these markets in advance and get more material resources from the incorporated areas.[137] The nineteenth-century European powers focused more of their attention on the Chinese market than on any other East Asian country and therefore used their military, political, and economic means to achieve their goals. In the course of China's incorporation process, Western nations intentionally interfered in state affairs to prevent China from transforming politically as an effective modern state. Given that the colonial powers' hidden aim was to dominate China's market, they tried to "reduce the Qing to dependency or peripherality within the world-economy."[138] William Rowe's approach points to the importance of acknowledging outside influences when trying to make sense of the Chinese failure. Stephen Thomas echoed this point, noting that "foreign intervention deprived Ch'ing [Qing] China of much of the sovereignty and resources needed for successful industrialization and indirectly undermined industrialization by accentuating domestic weakness."[139] Based on their analysis, one may well ask how pressure by foreign powers hindered Chinese modernization rather than asserting that the absence of a Chinese self-generative and self-propelling capability for modernization offers a plausible explanation for China's socioeconomic-political decline.

The interference of colonial powers in China's reform efforts had a significant impact on the country's finances. Following a series of unequal treaties in the 1840s, China was compelled to "limit tax rates" and eliminate "arbitrary fees and corruption on imports and exports."[140] Due to the pressure exerted by colonial powers on international trade, as well as being shortchanged in trade deals, the Qing government faced a long-standing trade deficit that eventually led to foreign debts. As a result, Western financial intervention became more invasive, not only limiting China's ability to manage its finances autonomously but also restricting reform efforts. By the end of the nineteenth century, the central government's financial situation had been further worsened by military and indemnity loans.[141]

Finally, the failure of the Self-Strengthening Movement was attributed to the defeat of the Li Hongzhang–led Beiyang Army, which was formerly inherited from the Huai Army, in the Sino-French War[142] and the First Sino-Japanese War. After a series of military defeats the Self-Strengthening projects led by Li Hongzhang and other reform-minded bureaucrats were pushed to a corner due mainly to fiscal difficulties and the strong opposition of conservative officials, and it consequently ended in a failure.

To summarize, the colonial powers aimed to make the self-sufficient Chinese empire a subordinate player in the global hierarchy. The Qing government's unsuccessful reform, influenced by Western intervention and military defeats, marked a turning point in China's incorporation into the world-system. The failure of the Self-Strengthening Movement to preserve the old political regime hastened the Qing Empire's move away from the ancien régime.

The Establishment of the Zongliyamen: A Failed Reform

The capitalist world-economy, which had a significant impact on China following the Opium Wars, had a far-reaching influence that extended beyond military reform. This led to a change in diplomatic relations and the emergence of a new state bureaucracy, with Chinese government officials implementing a series of institutional changes influenced by the interstate system of the world-economy. This deepening involvement in the world-economy resulted in a change in the perception of the colonial powers by the Qing government and the emergence of foreign affairs officers as key players in the Qing government. In 1861, the Chinese government established the Zongliyamen 總理衙門, a proto–foreign office, and appointed foreign affairs officers, including Chinese diplomatic representatives, to oversee Western-related business and important political issues.

Prior to establishing the Zongliyamen, a significant governmental institution responsible for handling foreign relations in the Qing dynasty was the Ministry of Rites (*libu* 禮部) and *lifanyuan* 理藩院. The *libu* was in charge of diplomatic affairs with tributaries such as Korea, Ryukyu, Vietnam, Laos, Thailand, Sulu (in the Philippines), Netherlands, Myanmar, Spain, Italy, Portugal and England,[143] and trading partners (*hushi zhuguo* 互市諸國) such as Japan, Cambodia, Indonesia, Philippines, France, and so on, while *lifanyuan* administered the non-Han settlements of Inner Mongolia, Xinjiang, Qinghai, and Tibet. Due to the absence of formidable competitors or challengers in East Asia until the nineteenth century, the Qing Empire's foreign relations apparatus was primarily focused on the strength of the tribute system.

Another governmental apparatus central to the foreign affairs of Qing regime was *Hui-tong-si-yi-guan* 會同四譯館, which served as the residence for envoys from the Four Tributary States.[144] At the *Hui-tong-si-yi-guan*, a group of Qing government officials was responsible for handling diplomatic business such as receiving and accommodating tribute-bearers, translating and transmitting their memorials to the emperor, overseeing their business dealings with Chinese merchants, and organizing imperial audiences, banquets, and rewards.[145] Even when the Dutch envoys Peter de Goyer and Jacob de Keyzer visited Beijing in 1656 and British envoys Lord Macartney and Amherst came to China in 1793 and 1816, respectively, the *Hui-tong-si-yi-guan* continued to manage diplomatic matters according to the rules of the tributary system.

As Western intervention in China grew, however, the Qing government had to change the list of tributaries and trade partners and felt the need to establish a new governmental agency focused on foreign affairs.[146] First, the Qing regime rewrote the tributary lists. In the unfavorable international situation caused by the modern but unequal treaties with colonial powers,[147] the Qing had to revise the list of tributary countries. In fact, many countries that were considered tributaries about eighty years previously, such as Ryukyu, Thailand, Sulu, the Netherlands, Myanmar, Spain, Italy, Portugal, and England, were excluded from the list. Second, unlike other East Asian countries (e.g., Korea, Vietnam), Japan was not classified as a tributary of China.[148]

It is worth noting that the list of tributaries and trade partners was changed during China's incorporation process, but an equally important change was the establishment of the new diplomatic organization. The creation of this department was prompted by requests from Western officials who often faced challenges delivering important messages to high-ranking officials in China.[149] For instance, in 1804, Lord Castlereagh, a British envoy, was unable to deliver an official letter to the Chinese government, and Lord Palmerston's letter to the grand secretaries in 1840 received no response. During the Opium War, Palmerston's negotiation letter was delivered to the Daoguang Emperor with significant translation errors,[150] exacerbating the communication difficulties between China and the West. Even after the Treaty of Nanking was signed in 1842, these communication issues persisted. In response to requests from colonial powers, the Chinese government established an official institution for foreign affairs to address these challenges.

More importantly, establishing official Chinese diplomacy was crucial for colonial powers to integrate their merchants into Chinese society. Without the involvement of the Chinese government in protecting foreign merchants and enabling free trade, the entry of Western merchants into Chinese markets was often delayed or disrupted.[151] Western merchants sought to minimize their risk in international commercial trades and thus expected Chinese diplomacy to facilitate communication with Western countries, protect their property in China, and ensure free and secure access to the Chinese market. They hoped for a system similar to Edward I of England's Carta Mercatoria, which provided favorable trade conditions for foreign merchants in England.[152]

The colonial powers' requests for a diplomatic presence in China were reflected in the Treaties of Tientsin. As Western diplomats began to reside in Peking according to the treaty, the Qing government realized the necessity of a new state apparatus to handle its foreign affairs,[153] including diplomatic maneuvering and navigating the complex diplomacy of European countries, which local governments had little power to control. Notwithstanding, building such an apparatus within the China-centered diplomatic framework was not easy, as it risked unsettling existing relationships. Despite these concerns, the Qing government established and ran the new foreign agency. This move marked a critical turning point in China's diplomatic relations, as it abandoned its superior stance and accepted the logic of the interstate system. The establishment and strengthening of the Zongliyamen played a pivotal role in this shift.[154]

When the Zongliyamen was first established, it was intended to be temporary, but due to the increasing diplomatic demands of foreign powers, ongoing contacts with Western nations, and the demands of modern diplomacy emerging from reform-minded Qing bureaucrats, it was maintained and operated until 1901. At its inception in 1861, the Zongliyamen was tasked with a wide range of duties including customs, secret documents, and even postal services, without clear guidelines for its operation. However, from 1864 to 1901, the Zongliyamen shifted its focus to foreign affairs, with officials specializing in seven distinct areas: Britain, France, Russia, the United States, coastal defense, diplomatic protocol, and storage of diplomatic documents. These areas were partly reflective of the interests of the colonial powers (see table 3.2).

According to table 3.2, the Zongliyamen had various functions, including safeguarding China from external threats, protecting overseas workers, conducting diplomatic

Table 3.2. Seven Diplomatic Affairs of the Zongliyamen*

Britain	Diplomatic negotiations with Britain and the Austro-Hungarian Empire, custom services of trade ports
France	Diplomatic negotiations with France, the Netherlands, Spain, and Brazil, the protection of missionary work, affairs relating to the recruitment of overseas workers
Russia	Diplomatic negotiations with Russia and Japan, trade routes on land, affairs relating to the border areas
United States	Diplomatic negotiations with the United States, Ger-many, Peru, Italy, Sweden, Norway, Belgium, Den-mark, and Portugal, protection of overseas workers
Coastal defense	Defense of southern and northern coastal areas, Yangtze River navy, protection of coastal areas with artillery batteries, dockyard affairs, purchase and production of steamships, guns and cannons, ammunition, machineries, electric wire, and affairs relating to railways and mining
Diplomatic protocol	Sending and receiving governmental documents
Storage of diplomatic documents	Compilation and proofreading of the governmental documents of *zongligeguoshiwuyamenqingdang* [Qing records in the office for the general manage-ment of affairs concerning the various countries]

*Wen jie Li 李文杰, *Zhongguo jin dai wai jiao guan qun ti de xing cheng (1861–1911)* 中国近代外交官群体的形成 (1861–1911) [The emergence of the modern Chinese diplomats] (Sanlianshudian, 2016), 43–44.

affairs with foreign diplomats, overseeing customs business, and importing technology or military weapons from European countries. These tasks were significantly different from China's international relations during the eighteenth century, which focused on managing and controlling neighboring countries, or those of the Ministers at Five Trading Ports (*wukoutongshangdachen* 五口通商大臣), which led diplomatic affairs between the First and Second Opium Wars.

Due to the critical nature of foreign affairs, Prince Gong and high-ranking officials such as grand councilors initially served as ministers of the Zongliyamen. Li Hongzhang, who had exceptional diplomatic skills, also led the Zongliyamen.[155] In fact, Western government officials expressed satisfaction when Li Hongzhang dealt with Western-related business and foreign affairs. By the end of the nineteenth century, the foreign affairs officials working for the Zongliyamen played a crucial role in mediating between the Qing government and foreign countries. This intervention, whether direct or indirect, took place at different levels, including local areas and state-to-state and ministerial-level activities of the center, allowing the Zongliyamen to function as a multilevel operation of the Qing administration.[156] Consequently, the Zongliyamen became a significant center for foreign affairs and a primary channel for conducting diplomatic activities.

Despite the Zongliyamen's attempt to become a specialized agency for foreign affairs, the influence and functions of the Zongliyamen did not last long, due to its weak influence, frequent replacements of the controlling group (ministers), and high dependency on powerful leaders. Shmuel Noah Eisenstadt observed that power struggles within central governments often involve bureaucratic apparatus vying for control over "some of the main centers of power."[157] In such struggles, smaller and weaker governmental apparatus with less influential leaders often have to follow the decisions of stronger bureaucratic administrative organs. The Zongliyamen, as a newly established, small-sized, and relatively weak political apparatus within the central bureaucracy, was not an exception to this dynamic. Therefore, it was not able to formulate major policies in foreign relations on its own within the central political organs.

Furthermore, the Zongliyamen's chief executives served for less than a decade on average, which hindered the development of their diplomatic skills.[158] The Zongliyamen's reliance on charismatic authority, a traditional type of domination (*Herrschaft*) identified by Max Weber, prevented it from becoming a stable and long-lasting bureaucracy. When the leadership of the Zongliyamen was composed of powerful political elites, such as grand councilors, it had a significant influence in foreign affairs. However, when the leadership consisted of lower-ranking officials, the Zongliyamen's influence was limited. The fluctuation in the *Zongliyamen*'s role and influence, drawing upon the rank of political elites, failed to sustain an independent bureaucratic organization. To replace the Zongliyamen, a Board of Foreign Affairs (*Waiwupu* 外務部) was established as a regular ministry, and it conducted foreign affairs until the fall of the Qing in 1912. However, neither the Zongliyamen nor the *Waiwupu* enjoyed exclusive executive authority over Chinese foreign affairs or "extensive policymaking powers."[159]

A Restructured Demarcation: Making a State Border

The modern nation-state's territorial sovereignty must meet the fundamental requirement of clearly demarcating its territory, and this form of territorial sovereignty is shaped by the global system of nation-states.¹⁶⁰ Border control is a central characteristic of the modern state, and initiating it requires a demarcation project, as controlling borders necessitates setting boundaries.¹⁶¹ At the world-systems level, the process of demarcation was a geographical redrawing of the earth's surface, which restructured the territorial space of incorporated areas according to interstate system logics. The demarcation project of an incorporated area was intentionally designed in response to the pressures of interstate system rules, and not an autonomous, natural, or predetermined history.

If colonial powers' intervention into China's political affairs was escalated by the Opium Wars, the Qing government's response was a demarcation project, a self-directed process of change toward the interstate system.¹⁶² State-making is often called "state formation" in the interstate system logics of the modern world-system. This occurs when the external arena is incorporated into that system. The theoretical perspective underlying this analysis focuses on Qing China's transition to modern statehood, which was initiated by the penetration of interstate system logics. In the context of global geopolitics, there is a power imbalance that pressures states to adhere to state boundaries.¹⁶³ Qing China had to discipline itself by following interstate system rules during its incorporation process.

Based on this perspective, I mean to distinguish the boundaries of the modern state from those of the Chinese empire insofar as the modern state tends to claim a specified locus of sovereignty and self-legitimating boundary lines through negotiations with neighboring countries and the fortification of border defenses, while rejecting overlapping or blurred concepts of the border area that were sustained by the Chinese empire's universal rules or cultural assimilation policies. In this case, the conception of the border of the modern state was clearly distinguished from that of the Qing. Plus, given that the demarcation project played a crucial role in transforming the Qing Empire into a modern state, it is essential to consider the historical account of this project. As it is assumed that the modern world-system's flexibility compelled or coerced incorporated areas to define their territorial boundaries, I will explore how China's territorial boundaries were formed.¹⁶⁴

The Qing Empire did not grasp the significance of territorial boundaries until the onset of incorporation. As noted by Alexander Woodside, the Qing emperors held an unfavorable perception of border areas until the late nineteenth century. For them and their officials, border regions were depicted negatively, often as places of banishment, and thus viewed as spaces that engendered cycles of crisis and disaster.¹⁶⁵

Furthermore, before beginning the process of incorporation, the Qing Empire did not consider it necessary to delineate clear territorial boundary lines. In fact, the Qing regime was apprehensive about the idea of demarcating specific boundaries. When the Kangxi Emperor's territories were mapped by the Jesuits, traditionalists were outraged because it reduced the Middle Kingdom's status to that of its neighbors.¹⁶⁶ Therefore, it is unsurprising that the borders of the Qing Empire as a global entity were disjointed, poorly defined, and lacked clear boundaries. Even during the late seventeenth to mid-eighteenth century, when the Qing Empire expanded its territories, determining the borders was a challenging task. For instance, the Qianlong Emperor (c. 1735–1796) personally went on a foreign expedition and led a successful campaign from 1747 to 1791.[167] Over fifty years, he engaged in "the Zunghar, Ili, and Muslim campaigns (1755–59), two wars to suppress rebellious Jinchuan minorities in [the] Sichuan province (1747–49, 1771–76), wars in Burma (1766–70), Annam (Vietnam, 1788–89), and Taiwan (1787–88), and two wars against the Gurkhas in Nepal (1790–92)"[168] and prevailed in all these wars of conquest over this period.

The Qing Empire's successful conquests and integration of new frontiers led to alterations in China's borders. Consequently, the Qing government took steps to create maps that would identify the expanded territorial boundaries. In 1760, after the Xinjiang region was assimilated into Qing territory, Emperor Qianlong commissioned the *Qianlong nei fu yu tu* 清乾隆內府輿圖. To ensure that the Hami region's detailed topographical features were included in the map, the Qing government sent Western missionaries to survey it (*Qianlong nei fu yu tu* 1966). Additionally, the Kashgar (*Kashigaer* 喀什噶尔), Tashkent (*Tashigan* 塔什干), and Samarkand (*Samaerhan* 撒马尔罕) regions were represented on the *Qing dai yitong ditu* 清代一統地圖, which replaced the *Qianlong nei fu yu tu*. This map even showed the Arctic Ocean (*Beibingyang* 北冰洋) to the north, the Indian Ocean to the south, and the Baltic Sea (*Boluodehai* 波罗的海), the Mediterranean Sea, and the Red Sea to the west.[169]

Even though the Qing Empire had expanded its territories through a series of wars of conquest, the new boundary lines depicted on their maps were imprecise and ambiguous. Rather than providing an accurate demarcation of Qing territory, the maps highlighted the farthest extent of its rule, serving as a tool to display the empire's power and support its empire-building techniques. Additionally, they served the purpose of governing imperial territory. As a result, the Qing Empire was cautious about drawing distinct and clear boundary lines, as their fundamental principle of international relations was the integration of heterogeneity. This approach aimed to establish a universal and united China-centered world by controlling the empire's borders. The Qing Empire's strategy of incorporating political heterogeneity thus explains why the empire's frontier borders were loose and blurry.

Starting in the 1840s, however, the Qing Empire was unable to sustain its policies because it encountered territorial disputes with foreign powers and suffered from the dissolution of its imperial territory.[170] Among Qing China's territorial disputes during its incorporation process were border disputes with Russia that reversed the Treaty of Nerchinsk (1689) and the Treaty of Kyakhta (1727). This resulted in Qing China ceding its own lands. The Qing Empire had vied with Russia for centuries to control border areas such as Turkestan and the Amur River basin, sometimes achieving politico-military dominance over Russia. It encountered heavy pressure from Britain and France from 1858 to 1860, and Russia had the opportunity to transform itself from a rival empire to a colonial power that was able to force the Qing government to accept unequal terms.[171] Under the terms of the Treaty of Aigun (*Aihuntiaoyue* 瑷珲

條約) in 1858 and the Convention of Peking (*Beijingtiaoyue* 北京条约) in 1860, Russia acquired about one million square kilometers of land in the Amur region.

Russia's territorial expansion to the Chinese borderlands had not yet finished. The nineteenth-century northwestern border disputes between the Qing Empire and Russia revolved around Russian frontier expansion and Qing China's responses to it. After the Convention of Peking, Russia proposed a joint expedition to confirm the border with northwestern Qing China. On the surface, Russia's proposal to demarcate boundaries did not seem to reflect a political intention for territorial expansion. However, Russia intended to expand its eastern frontier areas. In response to Russia's proposal, the Qing government appointed Ming Yi 明誼 (1792–1868), the highest military officer in the outer Mongolia region, and Ming Xu 明緒 (?–1866), a minister in the political district of Xinjiang, to a delegation to negotiate with Russia. Departing from previous treaties such as the Treaty of Aigun and the Convention of Peking, the Qing regime considered this border dispute an important matter of national security.[172] For this reason, Prince Gong earnestly asked Ming Yi to prepare for the negotiations, telling him, "[You can't] cause conflict, and you need to deal with [the] border negotiation in a serious and safe manner. To defeat Russia's territorial invasion, you need to watch how the negotiation process for border disputes develops."[173]

The Qing government's original plan for a cautious and unhurried approach to the border disputes, however, was seriously disturbed by Russia's ambition of forceful incorporation policies and by the Muslim revolts that took place between 1862 and 1871. In August 1863, Russian and Chinese delegations met for the demarcation of borders, even as Russian armies were dispatched to Boluo Lake, Jier Kajia, and the bank of the Tuergen River. Furthermore, the Muslim revolts had spread to the entire Xinjiang area, resulting in the Qing Empire losing control of Urumqi. This unexpected disorder in border regions, as well as Russia's armed intervention, pushed China to negotiate border disputes as a matter of urgency.[174] Faced with such threats, the Qing government could not postpone border negotiations with Russia. China and Russia signed the Treaty of Tarbagatai (*Tachengjieyue* 塔城界約 1864), resulting in Russia gaining vast territories, including the eastern region of Lake Balkhash, the Zaysan-nor region, and Lake Issyk-kul. Russia not only expanded its borders in Central Asia but also incorporated Mongolia.

After successfully suppressing the Muslim revolts in 1871, the Qing government attempted to renegotiate its western borders. To recover its lost territories, the Qing regime appointed Chonghou 崇厚 (1826–1893) as a delegate to Russia. Chonghou, however, hastily signed the Treaty of Livadia (1879) without the permission of the Qing government. According to this treaty, the Qing regime had to pay indemnities to Russia. Worse, Qing China also had to cede the vast lands of West Ili and the land along the Tekes River to Russia in exchange for the return of Ili. After the Qing government realized the extent of Chonghou's disastrous border negotiations, it planned to withdraw from the Treaty of Livadia. In January 1880, the Qing emperor sent Russia a message that the Qing government could not ratify the Treaty of Livadia. To renegotiate the borderlines of the Ili area, the Qing government dispatched diplomat Zeng Jize 曾紀澤 (1839–1890) to Russia. He was able to forge a new border agreement, the so-called Treaty of Saint Petersburg, in July 1881. From the Chinese position, this treaty was progress. Qing China regained the eastern part of the Ili basin area, including the Tekes Valley, even though it did not recover its territories entirely. After re-demarcating the borders, the Qing government produced a map with the old and new borders of Ili between Qing China and Russia (*Yili Zhong-Exinjiu jiehe tu* 伊犁中俄新舊界合圖), reflecting the new border established by the Treaty of Saint Petersburg.[175]

The border disputes with Russia did not end. Although China had ceded territory in the Amur region, Russia intended to continue expanding its territory and had conflicts with China in the border regions. Regarding Russia's insatiable territorial expansion, China found it necessary to prepare for border defense not only in Jilin but also in Heilongjiang Province.[176] In order to defend the military front of Manchuria, China even built fortified positions at Khun-ch'un (*Hunchun* 琿春) for the first time, which reflected the Qing's strong will to defend its borders. In short, the demarcation and re-demarcation of the borders between China and Russia, and the Qing government's foreign and military measures taken for border defense, show how the Qing government was dedicated to drawing clear borders where earlier they had been ill-defined, and defending them. Such attention to borders represents a continuous effort to turn the Qing Empire into a modern state that was contextualized within the interstate system.

Russia was not the only encroacher; European countries also watched thirstily for a chance to acquire the borderlands of Yunnan Province, located in southwestern Qing territory. This also caught the attention of the Qing regime. The Qing government did not rule Yunnan's borderlands directly, though these border territories belonged to Qing China. In place of direct rule, the Qing government gave the leaders of indigenous tribes a degree of administrative autonomy (under the *tusi* 土司 system). In this regard, Yunnan's borderlands could be seen as "a dynamic overlapping border that was continuously remolded by a fluid web of power relations at the local level."[177] This governing practice, however, had different characteristics when compared with the logics of the interstate system that emphasized securing a fixed and clear demarcation of the border. European colonial powers were not about to abandon their expansionist policies and their own concept of demarcation. In fact, Britain's colonial expansion reached the Yunnan borderlands at the end of the nineteenth century, representing a critical turning point in Qing China's border control.

Britain's aggressive geographical expansion into the border areas of the Yunnan region led to a border dispute. Since the 1870s, Britain had made inroads into the Yunnan, Tibet, and Xinjiang regions of Qing China's western frontier, keeping the Qing regime on its toes. In 1874, Britain dispatched an expeditionary force to the border areas between Burma and Qing China. This expeditionary force, led by Horace

Browne (1832–1914), numbered around two hundred explorers, including Augustus Raymond Margary (1846–1875); it was dispatched by the British embassy to explore overland trade routes between British India and Qing China. The expeditionary force was stopped by armed local Chinese populations and had to return to Burma. In 1875, on their way to Shanghai from the Burmese city of Bhamo, Margary and his staff were murdered on the orders of local officials. The British government exercised diplomatic pressure on the Qing government under the pretext of arranging adequate compensation for these deaths.

In order to respond to the British government's requests and to identify Britain's unruly activities in the borderlands of the Yunnan region, the Qing government dispatched Xue Fucheng (薛福成, 1838–1894), the Qing government's ambassador to Britain. Xue realized how vulnerable the border areas of the Yunnan region were to geographical penetrations by the British. However, he allowed British officers to enter the Chinese border areas because he dreaded a military confrontation. This idea was at least partially reflected in the negotiation process, which ended with the Chefoo Convention (*Yantaitiaoyue* 煙臺條約, 1876) between Britain and Qing China. Under this agreement, the Qing government had to issue pass cards when British officers asked to investigate trading routes and trading conditions between India and Tibet, and for travel not only from Beijing to India by way of Tibet but also from India or the border areas of Tibet into Tibet.[178]

With this agreement in place, Britain could dispatch surveyors and cartographers to produce maps. The British government's cartographic efforts created tension over the borders between Qing China and Britain's colonies. As a result of Britain's demarcation project, the Qing government had to draw upon westernized geographic concepts in response to border disputes in Tibet in 1890: "Article III: The Government of Great Britain and Ireland and the Government of China engage reciprocally to respect the boundary as defined in Article I and to prevent acts of aggression from their respective sides of the frontier."[179]

Due mainly to the encroachment of foreign powers, China's border areas were turned into contested spaces during the second half of the nineteenth century and the opening years of the twentieth century. Given that supporting Western traders' trespass on border areas of China resulted in their politico-economic advantages,[180] Chinese border areas that were adjacent to colonial powers' territories became a prime target of colonial powers. This led Britain and Russia to keep pressuring China to redraw border lines. As a response to the colonial powers' coercive and forcible requests, China had to carry out demarcation projects continuously. China's ongoing demarcation projects turned China's border areas into contested places, which enabled foreign merchants to invent new trading routes.

For instance, after the Sikkim-Tibet Convention of 1890 and the attached Trade Regulations of 1893, British India successfully invaded Tibet (1903–1904) and ensured a new trade route encompassing Nepal and the western Himalayas.¹⁸¹ Just as Britain got economic profits from the border trade by penetrating Chinese border areas and turning them into contested areas, Russia's territorial expansion to the Chinese border areas also enabled Russian merchants to get economic profits from border trade with China. Until the 1860s, Russian merchants in Kyakhata gained no competitive advantage over Chinese merchants in the tea trade. As a result, they had to depend heavily on the Shanxi traders' redistribution of Chinese tea; however, the treaty of 1862, conferring upon Russian traders the right of tax-free commerce in the border areas of China and other concessions, enabled Russian merchants to stimulate tea trades in Chinese territory. It allowed Russian tea companies such as S. W. Litvinoff & Co, Tokmakoff, Molotkoff, & Co, and Molchanoff, Pechatnoff, & Co to start tea businesses in China. In addition, as they benefited from low taxes and various trade routes (e.g., the land route at Kyakhata and Xinjiang, the sea route connecting Canton and Shanghai to Vladivostok, and the Trans-Siberian Railway), Russian tea merchants gained an advantage in their competition with the Shanxi traders. In particular, the completion of the Trans-Siberian Railway provided Russian tea merchants with both speedy delivery and reduced shipping costs.¹⁸² Consequently, Britain and Russia obtained economic advantages through territorial encroachment and territorial acquisition, whereas Chinese merchants, who suffered from territorial loss and enduring border disputes, could not realize benefits from the border trades.

In summary, the process of border demarcation played a crucial role in China's transition from a world empire to a modern nation-state. Through this process, China was able to reshape its borders from those of a global empire to those of a modern state, which fostered its incorporation process.

Acceptance of International Law (*Wanguogongfa* 萬國公法)

The non-European areas' incorporation of the capitalist world-economy has implicitly or explicitly induced incorporated areas to adopt international orders, resulting in the transformation or destruction of previously established non-European legal and spatial orders. The capitalist world-system is not only a particular way of organizing the international division of labor system and capital; it is also a set of universal and standardized rules about a global community.¹⁸³ Specifically, European international law has been an effective means of redirecting legal norms in incorporated regions, making them uniform and interstate, in accordance with the capitalist world-economy. China, during its incorporation process, also accepted the international law system, resulting in a significant self-directed transformation.¹⁸⁴ American lawyer Henry Wheaton pointed out in 1866 that China's acceptance of international law was "the most remarkable proof of the advance of Western civilization in the east."¹⁸⁵

Background

The traditional view that international law is solely based on European principles has recently been challenged. Instead of attributing the creation of international law solely to Europe, some scholars argue that non-European countries have made significant contributions to the principles of international law. Lauren Benton emphasizes that the involvement of non-European areas and interactions between European powers and non-European countries, rather than European legacies and practices alone, led to the development of the global legal regime.[186] Moreover, the existence of the race-based extraterritorial privileges of European colonial powers in non-European areas was not unique, as Qing China already had such privileges, including economic (e.g., receiving hedges against economic inflation), social (e.g., occupational benefits), and legal privileges (e.g., prohibition on corporal punishments during interrogation) ones for the Eight Banners.[187]

These explanations tend to reject the Eurocentric and linear view of history that sees Europe as the originator of international law, with universal values and norms that all should follow. However, this perspective is not a panacea. This is because it sometimes masks the power dynamics in which European countries exerted their influence on non-European regions. While there is no clear conclusion on the extent of colonial powers' impact on nineteenth-century Chinese society, it is undeniable that Western European countries formed unequal relationships with non-European countries through coercive colonial expansion. These relationships allowed colonial powers to gain a dominant position in the international legal system. Simultaneously, as important as the legal imperium of European powers embedded in the international legal system was, the conventional understanding of international law (that is, the Eurocentric idea of international legal studies) tends to disregard the roles of non-European countries in the globalization process of international law. To track the dynamics of China's acceptance of international law and its role in the global spread of international law, I use the logics of China's incorporation process into the modern world-system as my theoretical framework to analyze the roles that China played in shaping global international law.

After the Opium Wars, the Qing regime's consistent underestimation of the West began to cease because the Qing Empire was encircled by the relentless penetration of colonial powers; the regime could no longer ignore their politico-economic aggression. With growing interconnections with colonial powers, the Qing regime had to learn Western diplomatic norms and rules in order to play a far more active role in sustaining itself. The Qing government's acceptance of the international law system began with the translation of Henry Wheaton's *Elements of International Law* (*Wanguogongfa* 萬國公法) in response to both formal and informal pressure from Western countries. With this translation Western countries expected Chinese officials to learn Western international rules and norms.[188] Regarding this, Prince Gong stated that "examining this book, I found it generally deals with alliances, laws of war, and other things. Particularly it has laws on the outbreak of war and the check and balance between states."[189] Zheng Guanying, who wrote the article "*Lun Gongfa*" 論公法 (On public law), also contended that "it was important for China to understand the similarity and differences between Chinese and international laws in order to conduct international interactions."[190] Reform-minded Chinese intellectuals and bureaucrats, such as Duan Fang 端方(1861–1911), Li Hongzhang, and Zeng Jize, who were at pains to prevent further aggressive penetrations by foreign countries, were also enthusiastic about the idea of the *Wanguogongfa* because they began to acknowledge that ignorance of international law was a disadvantage in the political competition among nation-states.[191]

The introduction, interpretation, and utilization of Wheaton's *Elements of International Law* brought about a significant change in China's understanding of the rules, procedures, and privileges of Western nations, as well as the definition of international law. This book played a pivotal role in shaping the nineteenth-century Qing Empire's perspective on these matters. To gain a deeper understanding of the impact of this book on Chinese society, I will conduct a thorough analysis of its contents and its subsequent influence.

Logics of International Law

Before discussing Wheaton's *Elements of International Law*, it is important to recognize that the popular image of international law, of China's acceptance of international law, has typically favored reciprocal relationships among nations based on unanimous consent, while often disregarding uneven power dynamics among countries within the interconnected capitalist world-economy emphasized thus far. Despite Sir Frederic Bruce's endorsement of Wheaton's *Elements of International Law* as a peaceful way to acknowledge the principles of Western nations,[192] it functioned as another form of interstate system penetration in practice.

Although international law is meant to establish equal treatment of strong and weak states, the reality is quite different. As Richard Horowitz notes, powerful states can break international law with impunity, while weaker states must comply with the coercive diplomacy of stronger states, particularly during times of conflict.[193] Moreover, colonial powers did not seek to establish an equal trading partnership or a comradely relationship with China but rather viewed China as a means of maximizing their own political and economic gains. Thus, the political and economic relationship between the West and China was unilateral and unequal. Due to the strong and persistent pressures exerted by the West, China was forced to be defensive and the Qing eventually accepted Western norms within international relationships.

In the international law system, consent and coercion practices were used to subjugate newly incorporated areas to existing member states and to encourage (and sometimes force) these areas to adopt the logic of the interstate system and embody its values. China's acceptance of Wanguogongfa can thus be seen as acquiescence to the hegemonic world order, as Robert W. Cox and A. Claire Cutler have argued.[194] As a matter of fact, the *Wanguogongfa* that is in line with the westernized interstate system intended to push China to adopt the logic of the interstate system. Wheaton himself came up with an explanation as to why the *Wanguogongfa* was introduced in China: "The same remark may be applied to the recent diplomatic transactions between the Chinese Empire and the Christian nations of Europe and America, in which the former has been compelled to abandon its inveterate anti-commercial and anti-social principles, and to acknowledge the independence and equality of other nations in the mutual intercourse of war and peace."[195] Wheaton clearly showed an unfavorable attitude toward China's isolationist policy or Sino-centric system. He viewed China's old international relations as narrow or exclusive and therefore untenable.

Two Dreams in One Bed (*Tongchuangyimeng* 同床異夢)

To avoid becoming a victim of the colonial powers, China needed to learn the diplomatic style of the West, including both minor and serious diplomatic affairs, as revealed in negotiations between European and non-European countries. By accepting the international law system, China hoped to secure equal status with colonial powers and free itself from military and economic coercion. Wheaton's assertion that "all sovereign states are equal in the eyes of international law, whatever may be their relative power" was particularly appealing to the Qing government, which struggled to fend off the relentless penetrations by colonial powers.[196]

After the Qing government translated and published the *Wanguogongfa*, they used it to handle diplomatic disputes with Prussia. One such instance was the *Dagukouchuanboshijian* 大沽口船舶事件, which occurred in the spring of 1864 when Prussia, allied with Austria, was at war with Denmark.[197] G. von Rehfues, the Prussian ambassador to China, captured three Danish ships near the port of Dagu while he was on a Prussian ship en route to Beijing via Tianjin.[198] His action triggered a diplomatic spat between China and Prussia. The Zongliyamen took charge of resolving this diplomatic conflict and protested Prussia's misuse of power in accordance with the principles of the *Wanguogongfa*.

The Qing government utilized the principles of the *Wanguogongfa* to determine China's territorial waters, and this had a bearing on the outcome of this conflict.

> The term "coasts" includes the natural appendages of the territory which rise out of the water, although these islands are not of sufficient firmness to be inhabited or fortified; but it does not properly comprehend all the shoals which form sunken continuations of the land perpetually covered with water. The rule of law on this subject is *Terra dominium finitur, ubi*

finitur armorum vis; and since the introduction of fire-arms, that distance had usually been recognized to be about three miles from the shore.[199]

Subsequently, the Qing government employed the principles of the *Wanguogongfa* to demonstrate that Prussia had unlawfully captured Danish ships within Chinese territory.

> One of the exceptions to the general rule, laid down by the text-writers, which subjects all the property of the enemy to capture, respects property locally situated within the jurisdiction of a neutral state; but this exemption is referred to the right of the neutral state, not to any privilege which the situation gives to the hostile owner. . . . Not only are all captures made by the belligerent cruisers within the limits of this jurisdiction absolutely illegal and void but captures made by armed vessels stationed in a bay or river, or in the mouth [of] a river, or in the harbor of a neutral state, for the purpose of exercising the rights of war from this station are also invalid.[200]

Based on the norms of the *Wanguogongfa*, the Qing government pushed Prussia into a corner. This was because capturing Danish ships in Chinese waters went against international norms, leaving Prussia at a disadvantage. Prussia, which found it difficult to secure procedural justification for the capture of the Danish ships, backed down from its diplomatic conflict with China. As a consequence, Prussia released all three Danish ships.[201] The resolution of the *Dagukouchuanboshijian* showcased the Qing government's diplomatic skill and helped China understand the significance of international laws. Additionally, it facilitated China's acceptance of international laws.

Nevertheless, the *Wanguogongfa* did not establish equal relations between China and the colonial powers as it could not liberate itself from nineteenth-century international law's Orientalism (a way in which Europe, as a civilized world, should be distinguished from non-European areas as an uncivilized world). Wheaton himself recognized this inequality: "Is there a uniform law of nations? There certainly is not the same one for all the nations and states of the world. The public law, with slight exceptions, has always been, and still is, limited to the civilized and Christian people of Europe or to those of European origin."[202]

Wheaton's principle, which stated that all states are equal, was not actually his true intention, as evidenced by his comments. He did not believe in making all states equal under international law but rather favored European countries heavily in the international law system. The *Wanguogongfa* standard assumed a hierarchy of states, particularly between the "civilized" European world and the "uncivilized" non-European world.[203] The principles of the *Wanguogongfa* that identified a set of European civilizations entitled to access non-European continents were a result of imperial expansion, which was inherent in the forced-consent expansion strategies of colonial powers.[204] The idea of sovereignty, according to Wallerstein, did not imply total autonomy but rather indicated the existence of limits on the legitimacy of interference by one state in the operations of another state.²⁰⁵ The more the Qing government relied on the logic of *Wanguogongfa*, the faster the China-centered international order was undermined, and the deeper China became involved in the logic of the interstate system led by colonial powers.

CONSEQUENCES

Contrary to the desires of the Qing regime, international law functioned as a fundamental principle for the expansion of the international world order led by Western society, and the acceptance of international law represented a de facto recognition that China had become a part of the interstate system. Through the international law system, the interstate system of the capitalist world-economy induced China to become a part by using techniques such as "consent" and "coercion" stemming from the international law system. This system, as a transnationally constituted power, further contributed to justifying politico-economic penetration by foreign powers. For instance, according to the *Wanguogongfa*, "Laws of trade and navigation cannot affect foreigners, beyond the territorial limits of the State, but they are binding upon its citizen, wherever they may be. . . . Commercial treaties, which have the effect of altering the existing laws of trade and navigation of the contracting parties, may require the sanction of the legislative power in each State for their execution."²⁰⁶

These statements imply that Chinese laws governing foreign traders in China could be limited. The intention behind this is that, in some cases, commercial treaties between foreign powers and China could counteract China's legal sanctions. In other words, the international law system, increasingly linked to global orders by the logic of the capitalist world-economy's spread across the planet, prioritized the commercial expansion of colonial powers and undermined the policy space of incorporated areas. This benefited Western merchants in China and colonial powers that entered into commercial agreements with China. Accepting the *Wanguogongfa*, which took the form of a means of capitalist and colonial expansion, was crucial for China's incorporation into the capitalist world-economy.

In addition, to secure and expand their political and economic interests in China, colonial powers disregarded China's territorial sovereignty, which was protected by international law. The presence of colonial powers in China served as a reminder that accepting the rules of international law did not resolve issues stemming from China signing unequal treaties. Despite going against the fundamental principles of international law, which allow individual states to determine their internal or external policies without outside interference, colonial powers exerted more effort to gain politico-economic benefits during the late Qing dynasty and early Republican period. Among the many privileges granted to colonial powers, concessions in China provided a means of increasing their presence in the country.

The practice of granting foreign enclaves in China gained momentum after the First Opium War. During this war, the British, Americans, and French began residing in

Shanghai and demanding residences for foreigners. The Qing regime found it difficult to refuse due to the coercive gunboat diplomacy employed by these countries. As a result, these three countries obtained concessions with extraterritorial rights in Shanghai. Subsequently, other colonial powers also acquired extraterritorial rights. According to Wang Jianlang, these concessions were initially established to provide foreigners with living spaces in China; however, colonial powers gradually gained control over "urban planning, administration, police matters, and judicial discretion" in these concessions while prohibiting Chinese from living there.[207] The practice of foreign concessions in China continued even after the demise of the Qing Empire (see table 3.3).

Table 3.3. Foreign Concessions in China, 1911*

Concession by Area (areas included = Shanghai, Gulangyu, Tianjin, Hankou, Zhenjiang, Xiamen, Guangzhou, Jiujiang, Hangzhou, Suzhou, Chongqing)	Year (from establishment to dissolution)	Area (in *mu** 1 mu = 666 m²)
Shanghai International Settlement (Britain and United States)	1863–1945	33,503
Shanghai French Concession	1849–1943	2,135
Gulangyu International Settlement	1903–1945	2,000
British Concession in Tianjin	1860–1943	6,149
French Concession in Tianjin	1861–1946	2,360
German Concession in Tianjin	1895–1917	4,200
Japanese Concession in Tianjin	1898–1943	2,150
Russian Concession in Tianjin	1900–1920	5,474
Belgian Concession in Tianjin	1902–1931	740.5
Italian Concession in Tianjin	1901–1947	771
Austro-Hungarian Concession in Tianjin	1901–1917	1,030
British Concession in Hankou	1861–1927	795
German Concession in Hankou	1895–1917	630
Russian Concession in Hankou	1897–1923	414
French Concession in Hankou	1896–1946	400
Japanese Concession in Hankou	1898–1943	2,150
British Concession in Zhenjiang	1861–1929	156
British Concession in Xiamen	1852–1930	24.6
British Concession in Guangzhou	1859–1945	264
French Concession in Guangzhou	1859–1945	66
British Concession in Jiujiang	1861–1927	150
Japanese Concession in Hangzhou	1897–1943	900
Japanese Concession in Suzhou	1897–1943	483.9
Japanese Concession in Chongqing	1897–1943	701.3

*Jianlang Wang, *Unequal Treaties and China* (Silkroad Press, 2016), 4–5.

Colonial powers used judicial rights to their own advantage. Their extraterritorial jurisdiction rights—the exercise of judicial authority, encompassing both criminal and civil cases[208] over their own citizens in China and "the application of their own laws to the determination of their personal and property rights"[209]—was a kind of "nonterritorial imperialism"[210] or legal imperialism[211] in that colonial powers expanded their legal authority in China and showed contempt for the Chinese laws imposed on foreigners in China.

An interesting feature of this system was the existence of plural extraterritorial rights, with many colonial powers vying to extend their extraterritoriality in China. This resulted in a legally pluralistic environment, particularly evident in early twentieth-century Shanghai where numerous consular courts coexisted, often competing for jurisdiction and not cooperating with each other.[212] The increasing use of extraterritorial jurisdiction in this context was a visible outcome of China's incorporation process.

In sum, the penetration strategies of the interstate system through international law were effective. The principle of the Chinese government's translation, acceptance, and exploitation of Wheaton's *Wanguogongfa* lies in the fact that all nations are equal before international law; they take no heed, however, of the imperial expansion embedded in the *Wanguogongfa*. This strongly implies that China's international relationships, which were gradually assimilated into the interstate system, were subjected to politico-economic control by imperial rules. Furthermore, colonial powers, which did not give up their interests in China, passed over the principles of the international law while enforcing extraordinary extraterritorial jurisdiction on the Qing and Republican regimes.[213]

Concluding Remarks

This chapter has examined how state formation, international relations, and the military development of Europe and the Qing Empire evolved differently before China's incorporation process. The Qing Empire's state formation was not much different from that of the Ming even though the Qing Empire's governing practices were unique and distinctive. Similar to the Ming, the Qing Empire used and expanded the China-centered tributary system to achieve long-term stability through political hierarchy with neighboring countries. The Qing regime's views about maritime expansion was much more negative than those of the Ming government. This belief became more pronounced after the successful territorial expansion of the late eighteenth century. Also, in contrast to the military path taken by European countries, particularly the British Empire, the Qing Empire's path to military development began on the steppes, which were the original homeland of the Manchu people located in the northeast area of China. As the Manchu people's central stage was located inland, their essential war-fighting style and military organization were developed to suit ground combat. In this sense, the Manchu people were dedicated to producing well-trained cavalrymen who played a critical role on ground battlefields.

The Qing Empire had sunk into a state of complacency with little expansion through naval power. In contrast, interstate competition, enormous resources brought from the New World, and technological innovations turned European countries into fiscal military states (or war-prone states) and led to a quantum leap in naval power. Among European countries, Britain emerged as a leading maritime power in the eighteenth century, and its military expansion, stirred by economic profits, finally reached Chinese territory in the early nineteenth century. Against Britain's free-trade imperialism, which encompassed the use of armed force, the Qing government's stronger measures against the opium trade and against extension of international commerce heightened discontent by Britain, which led it to take military actions. When Chinese armies led by Imperial Commissioner Lin sealed off Macao on August 16, 1839, the Opium War started. However, for China a dark portent appeared in the first battle (the Battle of Chuenpi) of the Opium War. The Qing armies consequently did not stand a chance against the combined might of naval forces and the more advanced weapons of the British and the Opium War ended in the defeat of the Qing Empire.

The ravages of the two Opium Wars marked a watershed in China's political transformation. As an outcome of the Opium Wars, China opened its doors to the colonial powers and its isolationist and China-centered international relations began to wane. If its defeat in the Opium War marked the initial stage of China's decline in international relations, the middle stage began with the failure of the Self-Strengthening Movement. In comparison to other regions that underwent political changes during the incorporation process in the nineteenth and early twentieth centuries.—for example, South Asia underwent political unification of the subcontinent; the Russian Empire experienced little change in its territorial extent; the Ottoman Empire changed from a centralized political regime to fragmentation; South Africa experienced a decline of large-scale chiefdoms—China struggled to restore its centralized authoritarian regime even as it ended in failure. In this sense, the Qing Empire's political change during and after the incorporation process is quietly distinctive from other incorporated areas; notwithstanding, what is explicit is that the inevitable corollary to the Qing regime's failure of restoration did not intend to highlight Qing's abject situation. Rather, it gave greater prominence to a political change in the context of the incorporation process. The key point of the political change after the failure of the Self-Strengthening Movement is the irreversible decline of the ancien régime and the acceptance of interstate system logics. Although there were some last spasms of resistance to the interstate system logic (e.g., the anti-imperialism of the Boxer Rebellion), these could not withstand the tide of incorporation.

In addition, explicit or implicit Western pressure after the Opium Wars caused the Qing government to make a momentous political change and establish the Zongliyamen. Officials in the Zongliyamen, as a new governmental organization, aimed to handle urgent and important foreign affairs. For this, the Zongliyamen officials had to be disciplined, with Western protocols and westernized internal orders. Their efforts partially served China's entrance into the interstate system; nonetheless, it culminated in the collapse of the Zongliyamen due to the underdevelopment of its bureaucratic organization.

I also provide evidence in this chapter to support the argument that China transitioned from being a world empire to becoming a state within the interstate system. This was due to the pressure exerted by colonial powers, which led to the Qing regime renouncing its imperial status and accepting Western standards. The Qing government actively sought to establish clear and non-overlapping borderlines, in contrast to the blurred and overlapping borders of eighteenth-century China. The Qing government's acceptance of international law and its practical application further demonstrated its gradual adoption of westernized codes. The government's translation of *Wanguogongpa* and its use in diplomatic matters such as *Dagukouchuanboshijian* revealed the Qing government's struggle to adapt to the logic of the interstate system.

Chapter 4

Global Geopolitics

The Rise of Pacific Powers and Their Impact on China's Incorporation Process

It is not China that is falling to pieces; it is the powers that are pulling her to pieces!

—Sir Robert Hart, March 12, 1899, quoted in Langxin Xiang,
The Origins of the Boxer War: A Multinational Study

The process of China's incorporation in the nineteenth century, especially after the second half of the century, proceeded more complexly in the midst of this huge transnational power dynamic. Most of all, the geopolitical dynamics of the nineteenth century world-system led to the rise of Pacific powers, which enabled China's incorporation process to enter a new stage.[1]

For researchers of macro or macro-comparative history, the nineteenth century world has been characterized as a century with a unique feature: Europe's influence over the world.[2] They argue that there was no other century in which Europe was at the height of its power, and that the nineteenth century marked the peak of European influence. However, this perspective does not seem to apply to China's incorporation process in the late nineteenth century. While it is true that the changes that originated in Europe in the nineteenth century had an unprecedented impact on the rest of the world, paradoxically, new non-European powers (i.e., Pacific powers) emerged from European influence. These non-European powers tried to secure their interests in China by cooperating and competing with the European powers, which led to China's incorporation process into the capitalist world system.

Based on the definition of the nineteenth-century global world offered by Radhika Desai, newly industrialized countries such as Japan, Russia, the United States, and

Germany identified themselves as formidable contenders for global hegemony rather than being subordinated to an established global order under British hegemony.[3] This contention resulted in competitive imperialism and multipolarity. This is often referred to as the competition between colonial powers over resources and markets in China (or "the scramble for China").[4] However, unlike this view, I divide the colonial powers into European powers and Pacific powers, and here focus on the role of the Pacific powers that appeared at the end of China's incorporation process. Note that most of the emerging powers came mainly from the Pacific region. If nineteenth-century Russia was regarded as a linchpin of Pacific powers, Russia, Japan, and the United States were the key axes of Pacific powers. Table 4.1, table 4.2, and table 4.3 show the Pacific powers' dynamics across time and space.

Table 4.1. Total Population of the European and Pacific Powers, 1890–1938 (millions)*

	1890	1900	1910	1913	1920	1928	1938
European powers	125/42	136/45	149/50	152/51	126/42	142/47	158/53
Pacific powers	219/73	255/85	300/100	324/108	288/96	332/111	391/130

*Paul Kennedy, *The Rise and Fall of the Great Powers: Economic Change and Military Conflict from 1500 to 2000* (Random House, 1987), 199.

**The European powers are Britain, France, and Germany. The Pacific powers are the United States, Russia, and Japan.

***Total/average population of the European and Pacific powers.

Table 4.2. Energy Consumption of the European and Pacific Powers, 1890–1938 (in millions of metric tons and coal equivalent)*

	1890	1900	1910	1913	1920	1930	1938
European powers	252/84	331/110	398/133	445/148	436/145	459/153	508/169
Pacific powers	163/54	283/94	539/180	618/206	742/247	883/294	971/324

*Paul Kennedy, *The Rise and Fall of the Great Powers: Economic Change and Military Conflict from 1500 to 2000* (Random House, 1987), 201.

**The European powers are Britain, France, and Germany. The Pacific powers are the United States, Russia, and Japan.

***Total/average energy consumption of the European and Pacific powers.

Table 4.3. Total Industrial Potential of the European and Pacific Powers in Relative Perspective, 1880–1938 (UK in 1900 = 100)*

	1880	1900	1913	1928	1938
European powers	126/42	208/69	322/107	375/125	469/156
Pacific powers	79/26	188/63	400/133	650/217	768/256

*Paul Kennedy, *The Rise and Fall of the Great Powers: Economic Change and Military Conflict from 1500 to 2000* (Random House, 1987), 201.

**The European powers are Britain, France, and Germany. The Pacific powers are the United States, Russia, and Japan.

***Total/average energy consumption of the European and Pacific powers.

Indeed, these Pacific powers sought and expanded their own politico-economic interests, competing with existing European powers. Britain began to enforce a non-interference policy in the political affairs of East Asian countries in the 1890s because it encountered serious challenges from Germany in Europe, the United States in the North Atlantic region, and Russia in Central Asia, and was not capable of exerting its dominant influence in the East Asian region. In contrast with the stagnation of British power in East Asia, especially China, the influence of Pacific powers over China's affairs continued to expand. This indicated that the rise of Pacific powers opened a new era in China's incorporation process.[5]

As opposed to a conventional analysis that often plays down the impact of the Pacific powers in assessing China's incorporation process, I seek to find the roles of Pacific powers in China's incorporation process. I first examine how each Pacific power emerged and became a new impetus for the capitalist world-system and then discuss how they exerted influence on China's incorporation process. Here, to present a new central axis of the capitalist world-system led by the unprecedented growth of the Pacific powers and to show the impact of Pacific powers on China's incorporation process, I touch upon three major events. The first is the advance of the United States into the Pacific region, which began in the late nineteenth century; the second is the entry of Russia into China, which began in earnest after the nineteenth century; the third is the rise of Japanese power and its imperialist aggression against Korea and China.

The Rise of the United States as a Pacific Power

The remarkable rise of the United States in the international community of the late nineteenth and early twentieth centuries conjures up images signally focused on an inseparable relationship between the US and Europe as a part of Atlantic history. Yet a profound and wider investigation into the origins and development of US hegemony reveals that the position of the United States as a powerhouse in the international community is closely related to its expansion into the Pacific region. Such realities do not mean that economic and political ties between the Atlantic Ocean world and the United States are not significant to the United States attaining global hegemony in the late nineteenth century. I instead suggest that the powerful presence of the US in the Pacific region is as important as the political-economic couplings between the United States and Europe. As described by Patrick O'Brien, "the United States began to project power outwards into its 'home waters' which just happened to be the Atlantic and Pacific oceans" during the closing of the frontier and during the age of imperialism (1870s–1910s).[6] To put my point of view a little more precisely, for late nineteenth-century America the Atlantic Ocean was like a late afternoon sun setting over the horizon, like a past glory, still hot but past its peak, while the Pacific Ocean was like a sun rising over the horizon at dawn, like a future glory—albeit a less hot one—looming over the horizon.

The United States lacked the economic and military capacities to challenge British world hegemony until the early nineteenth century.[7] American political independence from Britain and development of the cotton trade and protectionist policies between 1816 and 1832,[8] however, transformed the United States into a newly emerging independent-industrial state. After the mid-nineteenth century, the agricultural revolution led by the introduction of agricultural machinery like reapers and threshers and the spread of agricultural education and modern scientific farming made it possible to turn the United States into one of the largest agricultural countries in the world.[9] After the Civil War, full-fledged market development in the western United States provided American capitalists with a new space for capital accumulation. In line with the rapid transition to an industrialized and capitalized society, the share of wage workers in the total working population rose to about 40 percent by the 1860s.[10]

Additionally, "protection of domestic industry against competition from core imports"[11] and "the high rate of investment"[12] played a major role in shaping the foundation of American industrial capitalism. The advancement of the railway network, which had been expanded in step with the American frontier, made it possible to closely link East and West.[13] As Fredrick J. Turner pointed out, American westward expansion, the carving out of the West and the subsequent establishment of settlements there, was not a simple replication of the settlement patterns of New England or the mid-Atlantic coastal regions first settled by European immigrants. It was a struggle to break free of the old tradition of Europe, a bloody struggle with Indian tribes and French and Mexican soldiers, and the creation of a new American identity that was distinct from the European identity of settlers: "Thus, the advance of the frontier has meant a steady movement away from the influence of Europe, a steady growth of independence on American lines."[14] In establishing a distinctly American identity in the midst of change through the settlement of the wilderness, the pioneers rejected the traditional authorities, political institutions, and religious values of Europe as well as of the mid-Atlantic region they had left behind. As they pioneered the West, they sought an unconstrained life and created a new type of pioneer democracy based on the land they colonized. Turner noted that as free land disappeared by the end of the nineteenth century in the United States, the American frontier spirit shifted from "the expansion of space" to "the expansion of American capitalist industry." American industrial capitalists, having amassed sufficient wealth, extended their enthusiasm to new industries and saw themselves as pioneers of a new environment:

> At the same time the masters of industry, who control interests which represent billions of dollars, do not admit that they have broken with pioneer ideals. They regard themselves as pioneers under changed conditions, carrying on the old work of developing the natural resources of the nation, compelled by the constructive fever in their veins, even in ill-health and old age and after the accumulation of wealth beyond their power to enjoy, to seek new avenues of action and of power, to chop new clearings, to find new trails, to expand the horizon of the nation's activity, and to extend the scope of their dominion.[15]

The growth of industrial capitalism in the United States was as dynamic as that in Europe, but with distinctive features. Similar to Europe, the United States launched a steady stream of new technology-based products. For example, the goods or industries invented or popularized in the United States in the nineteenth century, such as the "McCormick's reaper, Jackson Roberts' wheat-threshing machine, new cotton looms, the first use of coking coal in blast furnaces to make steel, a highly efficient water turbine, the clipper ship *Sea Witch*, the newest rotating printing cylinder, telegraph, and the Colt 45 revolver," fueled the rapid development of American capitalism.[16]

While industrial capitalism accelerated, it also created a distinctive American capitalist character. In driving the phenomenal development of capitalism in the United States, the radical changes in management methods like the rise of "multi-unit, multi-functional, and multi-industrial enterprise" were equally as important as the increase in capital accumulation rates and the development of infrastructure.[17] American firms exploited policies that favored the long-term stability and growth of the firm over the short-term maximization of profit margins,[18] which led not only to changes in production relations but also to the acquisition of autonomy in corporate management. In response to economies of scale, managerial capitalism emerged in the late nineteenth and early twentieth centuries, with "visible" firms taking the place of "invisible" market principles and assuming the functions of coordinating the flow of production and distribution of goods and allocating funds and labor.[19] In this process, the ownership and management of firms were separated, and a new class of salaried

CEOs (chief executive officers) emerged, forming a new managerial class. Alfred Chandler points out that the "visible hand principles" of bringing managers to the forefront of corporate activity ultimately created a new form of capitalism in the United States.

In contrast with the rapid pace of capitalist growth within US territory, however, its oversea expansion was extremely limited until the first half of the nineteenth century due mainly to internal reasons (e.g., United States' focus on Atlantic trade and territorial expansion in America like the Louisiana Purchase in 1803, the Florida cession in 1819, Texas annexation in 1845, the Mexican-American War from 1846 to 1848). For this reason, it is no wonder that the United States gained no competitive advantage over Britain in the tea trade with China even though Americans were attracted by the delightful flavor and taste of Chinese tea as much as the British were. American companies and merchants got into the Taiwanese tea industry (e.g., tea cultivation in Taiwan and its export to the US) after the first US merchant vessel (the *Empress of China*) arrived in Canton in 1784. Robert Morris (1734–1806), a Philadelphian financier, who led the first oversea investment in China, commented: "I am sending some ships to China in order to encourage others in the adventurous pursuits of commerce."[20] The financial success of the *Empress of China* was an important stepping-stone in subsequent US-China trade. According to Hao Yen-P'ing, the quantity of tea that Canton exported experienced a significant increase over the years, rising from 880,100 pounds in 1784 to 3,093,200 pounds in 1790, and a staggering 5,665,067 pounds in 1800.[21] During the period from 1820 to 1850, the quantity of tea that Americans consumed was between ten million and twenty million pounds, "numbers that impress with their sheer size."[22] The American traders provided Chinese merchants with silver, Appalachian ginseng, sandalwood, furs, and Turkish opium in exchange for Chinese teas. There are also merchants who made their fortunes through trade with China, such as the Forbes family from Boston, who became wealthy through intermediary trade linking the United States, England, India, and China. John Cleve Green returned home in 1839 with millions of dollars from the fortune he made in Guangzhou and invested in railroads, making him very wealthy.[23] With the expectation that China could become a new center for overseas trade, the United States became interested in the balance of power between the colonial powers in China,[24] as can be seen in this 1853 communication from Humphrey Marshall, the first American commissioner to China, to US Secretary of State William L. Marcy:

> I think, then, that almost any sacrifice should be made by the United States to keep Russia from spreading her Pacific boundary, and to avoid her coming directly to an interference in Chinese domestic affairs; for China is like a lamb before the shearers, as easy a conquest as were the provinces of India. Whenever the avarice or the ambition of Russia of Great Britain shall tempt them to make the prizes, the fate of Asia will be sealed, and the future Chinese relations of the United States of America may be considered as

closed for ages, unless now the United States shall foil the untoward result by adopting a sound policy. It is my opinion that the highest interests of the United States are involved in sustaining China—maintaining order here, and gradually engrafting on this worn-out stock the healthy principles which give life and health to government, rather than to see China become the theatre of widespread anarchy, and ultimately the prey of European ambition.[25]

The argument of John Jay in *The Federalist Papers* are also worth listening to, in terms of the need to check the British monopoly on the Chinese market: "In the trade to China and India, we interfere with more than one nation, inasmuch as it enables us to partake in advantages which they had in a manner monopolized, and as we thereby supply ourselves with commodities which we used to purchase from them."[26] In addition, a certain amount of economic desperation also spurred expansion into the Pacific (including China). To address the overcapacity that had become a drag on US economic growth in the 1870s and 1880s, caused by the overbuilding of railroads and an oversupply of silver as mines in the American West were developed, the United States needed to open up new markets in the Pacific.[27] As a consequence, between 1895 and 1905, exports from southern US cotton producers to China more than tripled, reaching nearly $35 million.[28] However, unlike the British traders who benefited from the EIC's well-established tea trade routes or the British government's administrative support, American traders depended almost entirely on their own capacities to make inroads into the Chinese tea market.[29] These opposing approaches were similarly applied to those who entered China. Robert Hart, a British diplomat, was supported by the Maritime Customs Administration, but W. A. P. Martin, an American missionary, expanded his influence in China on his own.[30]

From the late nineteenth century, however, the United States' frenetic pace of economic and military expansion enabled its advance into the Pacific region.[31] Captain A. T. Mahan argued that the United States would need to develop a strong naval force on the Pacific and Atlantic coasts and within three thousand miles of San Francisco so that no nation could threaten it. He also advocated a naval buildup for American expansion.[32] And for those who were called "robber barons"[33] and advocates of American expansionism in the late nineteenth century, the United States' push into China was taken for granted because they believed the prosperity of United States depended on trade in the Pacific. In this sense, it was not a surprise that President McKinley stressed that the annexation of Hawaii created a strategic foothold in an emerging market of the Pacific.[34] US expansion into the Pacific was signaled by the acquisition of such far-flung Pacific territories as Alaska (1867), Hawaii (1898), the Philippines (1898), and penetration into East Asian countries, such as the Perry Expedition to Japan in 1853–1854, the United States expedition to Korea in 1871,[35] and, finally, by the opening of Panama Canal in 1914.[36] And the ultimate destination was China. In fact, US exports to China more than doubled during the last five years of the nineteenth century.[37]

Although exports to China increased, the US ran a trade deficit with China for several decades, from 1865 to 1901.[38] Furthermore, the volume of US-China trade was no greater than the volume of US-Japan trade during the same period.[39] Nevertheless, US expansion into Asia continued, and this expansion signaled the beginning of American hegemony in the late nineteenth century.[40] As Julian Go aptly notes, the "far West" plan of the United States has been an expression of its will to expand its influence not only in California but also in Japan and China.[41] Merchants in New York, Boston, and Philadelphia participated in opium trafficking, tea trading, and the porcelain trade with British merchants. American clipper ships were high-speed sailing ships that promoted international trade with China. The Lowells, Girards, Astors, Lows, Griswolds, and Copes, including Bostonian Russell Sturgis, made their fortunes through trade with China.[42]

US Secretary of State William Seward contended that the United States' entry into Asia would help expand its global influence. The basis of this strong oversea expansion strategy was the dramatic increase of the United States' share of world GDP. During the 1820s, the United States held less than 2 percent of the world's GDP, while Britain had a share of 5 percent. However, by the 1870s, the situation had changed as the United States surpassed Britain in its share of the world's GDP.[43]

Combined with a gradual decline of British hegemony in the late nineteenth century,[44] the remarkable increase in US military capacities contributed to the swift growth of American hegemonic power in the Asia-Pacific region.[45] The Spanish-American War of 1898 became a watershed that enabled the United States to promote its overseas expansion. The strong expansionist sentiment of the United States led to a desire to annex neighboring countries, especially Cuba, that had been under the control of Spain. This in turn led to a war with Spain. Victory in this war gave the US control over Cuba, Puerto Rico, the Philippines, and Guam. This paved the way for the United States to enact aggressive imperialist policies.[46] This was a "turning point in the geopolitical posture of the United States"[47] and opened a path toward "the Greater United States."[48] Captain Arthur MacArthur's argument—"a commanding and progressive nation would only materialize when we secure and maintain the sovereignty of the Pacific"[49]—was never empty words.

The UK's predominant position in the Pacific was the obstacle that the United States had to overcome to become hegemonic in the region. Britain was an opponent the US had to compete with, albeit fearfully.[50] John Quincy Adams argued that the United States had a right to all the shores of the Pacific Ocean, whether Britain liked it or not.[51] For private American merchants who clamored for international trade and free trade and tried to expand their commercial activities to Pacific areas including China, the predominant position of British chartered companies was a major barrier that had to be overcome. US efforts to advance its political-economic interests sometimes brought about acrimonious relations between the US and Britain. Caleb Cushing, an American Democratic politician and diplomat in the 1840s, wrote a letter to President

John Tyler portraying the UK's actions in the Pacific Rim as a politico-economic threat to the US. According to Cushing, British power could be "the immense future peril" not only for United States' territorial possessions but also for all the US's "vast commerce on Pacific."[52]

Amid the growing anti-British sentiment, the aggressive economic penetration of the US into the Pacific region including China created a more equal relationship with British power.[53] For example, in 1882, as the British Empire sent warships to China to benefit their merchants, the United States sent its warships to Shanghai to facilitate cotton merchants' economic activities.[54] Gathering momentum from increasing exports to China, the United States government carried out the Open Door Policy (1899) to get more commercial opportunities and benefits from China.[55] Outwardly, this policy aimed at mediating the competing interests of European and Pacific powers in China; however, for old established European powers in China like Britain, it meant that they surrendered their monopolistic benefits in China. The purpose of the Open Door Policy was to create favorable conditions for relative newcomers like the United States. With the United States' aggressive penetration into China, Britain began to consider the United States as one of its great commercial rivals.

The Entry of Russia into China

In the late nineteenth century the United States of America's rise was at least as exceptional as that of European powers. Of even more concern for Britain, however, was Russia's advance to the west and south in the nineteenth century.[56] Russia, incorporated into the capitalist world-system in the eighteenth century, sought to grow its power alongside the great powers of Europe while at the same time rushing to expand into East Asia, including Siberia.[57] Russia's expansion into East Asia was clearly linked to its expansion into the Pacific. Before discussing this expansion let's look at Russia's industrialization after its incorporation.

Throughout the first half of the nineteenth century the most prominent sector was the cotton textile industry, where capitalist competition was introduced. In St. Petersburg, the first Russian industrial joint-stock companies were established for cotton spinning, the most famous of which was the Russian Cotton Spinning Company, founded in 1835 with a capital of 3.5 million rubles. In the 1840s and 1850s, a number of large mills were established, including Petrovsky, Spasskaya, and others. As a result, between 1842 and 1860 the number of cotton spinning mills in Russia skyrocketed from nineteen to fifty-seven. The mills, some of which were among the largest in the world, employed 41,295 workers. By the early 1860s, the Stieglitz mill on the banks of the Neva River employed 1,300 workers.[58]

By the 1880s, thanks to the Great Reforms under Alexander II and the influx of foreign capital, Russia was entering the mature phase of the Industrial Revolution.

For example, between 1860 and 1895, cast iron production increased 4.5 times, coal mining increased thirty times, and the number of steam engines doubled from 1875 to 1892. In addition, the introduction of steam engines in the oil industry from the 1870s led to an exponential increase in oil production. Changes in the labor market were also prominent. Until the 1860s, workers were serfs or sharecroppers on hereditary or state-owned land, but with the Emancipation reform of 1861, the composition of the labor force began to be dominated by freedmen who moved to the cities. In the second half of the nineteenth century the volume of foreign trade increased rapidly. In 1861, trade totaled 430 million rubles, while by 1900 it had nearly tripled to 1.3 billion rubles.[59] Although railroad construction in Russia did not begin until 1838, and only 1,626 kilometers of railroad had been built by 1860, by 1914 this number had grown to 73,022 kilometers.[60] Moreover, the average annual population growth rate in Russia between 1870 and 1913 was higher than the average annual population growth rate between 1500 and 1820 and that between 1820 and 1870.[61]

But can nineteenth-century Russia be considered one of the Pacific powers? Located between Europe and Asia, Russia had long been a civilization with its own unique development between the two continents. As Alberto Masoero points out, the transcontinental position of the Russian state allowed it to absorb both Eastern and Western cultures at the same time.[62] At different times, Russia has strongly expressed its European features and identity, at other times it has expressed its desire to be distinct from Europe, and it also has shown its ties to Asia and its Asian identity. The period of Russia's strongly European identity was during the reign of Peter the Great in the early eighteenth century. Peter the Great undertook far-reaching reforms of the Russian state and society, which, in a nutshell, were to bring the excellence of European civilization to Russia. For him, Europe in the early eighteenth century stood out as superior to any other region on earth because of its material wealth, excellence in learning and the arts, rational state and social systems, and even the moderation of its climate. He therefore sought to bring this European civilization to Russia and Europeanize Russia.[63]

However, the Europeanization of Russia (or the desire for European civilization) did not last for long. From the turn of the nineteenth century Russians questioned the European identity that Russia had sought, especially the Slavophile intellectuals, who noted the uniqueness of Russian culture and the unique development of Russian history. At the same time, they strongly opposed the idea of European superiority and the Europeanization of Russia. They called for the severing of ties between Russia and Europe, emphasizing the violence, irresponsible egoism, and the individuals and societies that were driven by material interests and desires that European societies had produced.

They also drew attention to how Russia's internal expansion (or colonization) was peaceful (in their view) and developed organically and naturally, contrasting it with European expansion, which was based on violence and brutality. In his book *Russia and Europe*, Nikolay Danilevsky (1822–1885) argued that Russia's eastward expansion was a "predestined space" prepared for Russia's future. He pointed to the uniqueness and distinctiveness of the Slavic peoples identified in the east as the foundation of Russian identity and noted that this space encompassed vast swaths of Russian territory stretching to the Pacific Ocean. Mikhail Petrovich Pogodin (1800–1875), a court historian of the Russian Empire, noted that unlike European societies that grew through the logic of conquest and revolution, the Russian state expanded its territory through voluntary submission.[64] In a similar vein, linguist Vladimir Ivanovich Lamanskiy (1833–1914) argued that Europe was, properly speaking, a peninsula of Asia.[65]

Indeed, from the late nineteenth century, Russia's imperial sphere expanded toward the Asia-Pacific. In the 1860s, the vast Amur and Ussuri River valleys were ceded by the Qing Empire, and in 1871 the Central Asian cities of Samarkand and Tashkent were also occupied by Russian forces. The newly acquired regions of the Russian Empire had an Asian identity, and to elicit voluntary submission from these Asians, some Russian scholars referred to Russians as the descendants of the former Mongol Empire. In this regard, Esper Ukhtomsky (1861–1921) argued that the Russian tsars were descendants of Genghis Khan, not the rulers of Byzantium, and therefore had a cultural affinity with Eastern peoples and peaceful coexistence.[66] Even among Russian bureaucrats, there was a growing sense that the center of gravity of the country was shifting eastward.[67] In sum, similar to the United States, Russia began to see its expansion into Asia as a way of gaining energy and vitality from the new world and began to internalize an Asia-Pacific identity for itself. This can be seen in Russia's movements toward Asia in the nineteenth century.

Boosted by powerful armies and economic industrialization, Russia began to expand its sphere of influence to Afghanistan and central and southern Asia including China. This was partly in line with plans to maintain and develop the tea trade with China. While serving as finance minister, Sergei Witte (1849–1915) advocated for the construction of the Trans-Siberian Railway, citing the need for a smooth tea trade with the Qing Empire. In 1892, Witte argued that tea production in India and Assam was taking a toll on the Qing's international tea trade, which would sooner or later collapse in the face of new and fierce competition. In this situation, Russia's construction of the Trans-Siberian Railway would quickly transport Qing tea to Europe, giving the Qing a new opportunity to export tea while allowing Russia to compete on an equal footing with British cotton, woolen goods, and metal products in the Qing market. The railroad would also significantly increase the mobility of Russia's East Asian fleet, enabling it to operate quickly in the event of political disturbances in Europe or East Asia, and would go a step further to give Russia an advantageous position in trade in the Pacific region.[68]

Russia's interest in the Chinese market and its plans to expand into Central Asia, however, sounded like a disaster for Britain. Britain was fearful of Russia's military inroads into Central Asia because Russia's territorial expansion might reach the borderlands of India. For Britain, the most urgent task was to protect India from Russia's territorial penetration. To forestall Russia's further aggression, Britain fought several wars with Russia, which was called "the Great Game" until 1895. Due to Britain's military restraint on Russia's expansion plan, Russia's territorial expansion toward India was put on hold. The "Great Game" was over when the British and the Russians eventually designated Afghanistan as a neutral buffer zone.

However, this was not the end; the military and political confrontation between Britain and Russia over competition in China became acute. Unlike Britain's penetration into China via ocean routes, approaching the Qing Empire from the south, Russia penetrated China via land routes, approaching the Qing Empire from the north. By using not only gunboat diplomacy but also conciliatory gestures toward the Qing Empire, Russia made efforts to expand its southern territories. Through a series of unequal treaties (the 1858 Treaty of Aigun and the 1860 Convention of Peking) between the Qing Empire and Russia, Russia took over six hundred thousand square kilometers located between the Amur River and the Stanovoy Range and parts of Outer Manchuria. Simultaneously, Russia insinuated herself into the Qing regime's favor by providing China with diplomatic advice and supplies, while condemning British and French armies' brutal depredations during the Second Opium War (e.g., the destruction of the Old Summer Place).

Russia's expansion toward China brought about much anxiety in Britain, which led to conflicts between Russia and Britain over Russia's acquisition of Port Arthur in Manchuria in 1898. Port Arthur was located in between the borderlands of China, Russia, and Korea and this area was considered a strategic place for colonial powers to penetrate Northeast Asia. For this reason, losing Port Arthur was deemed as a serious challenge and encroachment on British interests in China; however, at the time when Russia took Port Arthur, Britain could not take any preventative measures, due mainly to its weak army, with regard to the Russian army's entrance into Port Arthur. Russia's aggressive penetration pushed Britain to change its foreign policy in China; to check Russia's further inroads, the British government allied itself with Japan in the Anglo-Japanese Alliance of 1902.

Britain and Russia clashed sometimes violently over Xinjiang.[69] After the British conquest of Punjab and Kashmir in 1849, British interest in Xinjiang continued to grow as did that of Russia. In fact, "while the British pushed north from Kashmir and the Punjab, Russia expanded southward, effectively annexing Central Asia during the 1860s and 1870s."[70] Between 1870 and 1880, the British sent Indian pilgrims, traders, and expeditions to Xinjiang to look at geopolitical trends related to Russia's expansion into China.[71] Russians countered by advocating their own exploratory missions to seek out advantages against Britain: "Nature has left open for us a broad gate to India. These are the regions the Russian explorers ought to examine and toward which the attention of the Russian Government ought to be directed . . . in view of the immense advantages which we should gain from a discovery of England's most vulnerable point."[72] Some Britons even argued that Britain's entry into Central Asia would have to be extended to the Aral and Caspian Seas, deep inside Russian territory.

On the other hand, Russia was outraged by Britain's aggressive territorial expansion strategies because "Tsarist officials had all along regarded Central Asia as predestined to be Russia's prize."[73] Russian intellectuals and bureaucrats truculently criticized Britain's advance into Central Asia and emphasized that measures should be taken against Britain's aggressive territorial expansion.[74]

Another conflict between Britain and Russia occurred when Russia made inroads in Tibet. After the Qing Empire's conquest of Tibet in the 1720s, Tibet became one of the empire's protectorates; however, as the Qing Empire became decadent in the nineteenth century its influence on Tibet waned. The encroachment of Britain and Russia upon Tibet further debilitated the Qing's authority in Tibet in the late nineteenth century. After the 1870s, Britain de facto had greater political influence than the Qing Empire over Tibet.[75]

With Tibet under nominal Qing Empire suzerainty in the late nineteenth century, Britain tried to expand its politico-economic influence on Tibet to block Russia's territorial expansion. Britain was concerned about a Russian expedition marching into Tibet, given the fact that Russia's penetration into Tibet became a serious threat to the British Raj's border area security. Russian explorer Nicholas Przeworski visited Tibet in 1879–1880, making British concerns real. What is worse, conflicts between Britian and Russia were fueled by the pro-Russian policies of Thubten Gyatso (1876–1933), the thirteenth Dalai Lama, and the spread of rumors alleging secret contacts between Tibet and Russia or that "China had handed over Tibet to Russia."[76]

Against the pressing danger originating from Russia's expedition to Tibet, British troops led by Colonel Francis Younghusband were dispatched to Tibet in 1903 and signed the Treaty of Lhasa with Tibet in the following year.[77] This treaty was a one-sided agreement designed to maximize the politico-economic interests of Britain. First, it allowed Britain to trade in Tibetan areas like Yadong, Gyantse, and Gartok; second, Tibet had to pay an enormous indemnity to Britain; third, Britain could intervene in Tibetan affairs while denying the Qing Empire's suzerainty; and fourth, Britain blocked the political influence of Russia in Tibet.

Russia and the Qing Empire strongly opposed the lopsided and unequal treaty of Lhasa and it led Britain to repudiate the treaty.[78] A new treaty, called the Anglo-Chinese Convention (1906), gave China control of Tibet. "For Russia, the establishment of real Chinese authority in Tibet was a positive development."[79] In return, Russia had to acknowledge the fact that Afghanistan was under the influence of Britain. Russia also had to stop its territorial expansion in Central Asia.

The First Sino-Japanese War and the Rise of Japanese Power

In the preceding section, I delineated the geopolitical history of the United States and Russia, which emerged from the Pacific region in the late nineteenth century. US and

Russian advances into the Pacific region confirmed that East Asia, including China, came under pressure not only from established European powers but also from the rising power of the US. However, the Pacific powers cannot be equated only with the United States and Russia. Another Pacific power, Japan, emerged in the late nineteenth century.

Japan quickly became a semiperipheral country after its opening and incorporation into the capitalist world-system. There are many reasons for Japan's rapid transformation into a semiperipheral country and a colonial power. First, Japan had been in constant contact with foreign powers even before the opening of its ports in 1853. In doing so, the Japanese constantly imported information, learning, and technology, and adopted them where necessary. As a result, the Saga Domain successfully built Japan's first reverberatory iron furnace in 1850, and from 1853 onwards it cast a significant number of iron cannons. The Satsuma Domain, Saga Domain, and Mito Domain built steamships, and just before the Meiji reforms, the Satsuma Domain installed a modern cotton spinning factory. Even the Saga Domain modernized the Takashima coal mine with British technical assistance.[80] Second, although colonial powers continued to put pressure on Japan from the 1840s onward, not only was this external pressure not as great as that exerted on China, but colonial powers themselves were not able to prioritize their relationship with Japan; this created a so-called breathing space for Japan.[81] Although Japan had unequal treaties with the colonial powers, each of these countries could not afford to turn their attention to Japan due to other events that befell them.[82] Moreover, for the colonial powers, trade with Japan was suboptimal. In quantitative terms, it was not as large as trade with China,[83] and investment in Japan by the major colonial powers was negligible.[84] Third, Japan took advantage of this breathing space to rapidly succeed in government-led industrialization. Japan had made a significant economic leap even before the opening of the door. From 1639 to 1868, Japan's population grew, agricultural output increased, new crops were planted, and cities grew larger.[85] The development of a merchant class (e.g., *ton'ya*) to serve the growing Japanese economic system was also prominent, as the commercial activities of the samurai and aristocracy were restricted.[86] Japan's industrialization grew rapidly after the Meiji reforms. By the end of the nineteenth century, Japan's output of goods and services had quadrupled compared to the previous century, and its contribution to total industry grew rapidly. Much of the infrastructure necessary for the development of an industrial economy, such as transportation, communications, ports, and financial institutions, had been built, and the factory goods industry had become a key sector of growth, albeit on a smaller scale.[87] The government played an important role in enabling this rapid industrialization. As Alvin So and Stefan Chiu point out, although Japan was incorporated into the capitalist world-system in the mid-nineteenth century,[88] the Meiji elites at home quickly centralized government, undertook a dynamic economic transformation, claimed protectionism,[89] and engaged in overseas imperialist ventures of their own.[90] In turn, Japan became a new powerhouse in East Asia.[91]

Most of all, the First Sino-Japanese War served to reorganize the world order in East Asia. Before the war broke out in the 1890s, the Qing Empire and Japan concluded the 1871 Sino-Japanese Friendship and Trade Treaty, a treaty of peace and goodwill in which both countries pledged not to "violate opposing country's borders." However, before long the Qing regime came into conflict with Japan over "the tributary state," especially about the status of the Ryukyu Kingdom. The Qing Empire viewed the Ryukyu Kingdom as one of their vassals while Japan did not acknowledge this. This is because Ryukyu had tributary relationships with Japan after the sixteenth century, and furthermore, Japan strove to incorporate the Ryukyu Kingdom into its own territory. The Qing Empire tried to influence the Ryukyu Kingdom; however, due mainly to internal disorders in China (the Dungan Revolt, 1862–1877) and border disputes with Russia over the Ili region, the Qing regime could not pay attention to this conflict. Japan coercively stopped the tributary relationship between the Qing Empire and the Ryukyu Kingdom and incorporated it into Japanese territory in 1879. The Qing Empire did not effectively respond to the new status of the Ryukyu Kingdom; however, the conflict between the Qing Empire and Japan over the status of Qing tributary states did not end.

Conversely, the conflict escalated over Korea. The simplest explanation of the First Sino-Japanese War is that the Qing Empire and Japan fought over influence in Korea.[92] Since Korea lacked any viable means not only to escape the Qing's overwhelming shadow but also to thwart Japan's penetration, Korean territory became a place where Japan could test its strength against the Qing Empire. One critical reason the Qing Empire fought Japan was Japan's political ambition to occupy Korea and invade China thereafter. Such ambition can be confirmed in influential writer Yukichi Fukuzawa's comment that "we shall someday raise the national power of Japan so that not only shall we control the natives of China and India as the English do today."[93] As he hoped, Japan's GNP nearly tripled and the Japanese government increased its military expenditures dramatically between 1885 and 1899; in 1880, Meiji Japan's military spending accounted for 19 percent of all government's spending but exceeded 30 percent by 1890. Intoxicated with national greatness, Japan distinguished itself from other, decaying Asian countries, while catching up to the armed forces of other Western imperialist powers.[94] A strong tendency to compete on par with the advanced colonial powers induced Japan to embrace an imperial spirit, warlike tendencies, and expansionist practices. Consequently, the remarkable economic development and massive increase in military spending in the late nineteenth century turned Japan into an economic-military giant and directed its eyes to East Asia. By seeking to maximize its national interest and join the imperialist club, Japan found Korea an attractive target due in part to geopolitical priorities. Korea's geopolitical location in the East Asian continent was especially fortuitous for Japan to conduct its imperialistic expansion toward China; the northern borders of Korea were an important gateway to the northeastern provinces of China. On this ground, Japan believed that Korea could serve as a bridgehead for its aggressive territorial expansion. Japan, as the first step toward imperialist expansion into Korea, intervened in the tributary relationships between China and Korea. While Japan revealed its ambitions for invasion, the regent Heungseon Daewongun 興宣大院君 (1821–1898), a Korean political leader, had insisted on isolationism since the mid-nineteenth century, except for maintaining the tributary relationship with the Qing Empire. Korea, at that time, had not established diplomatic relations with any other country except Qing China.

In contrast to considerable knowledge of the Western world among Chinese and Japanese in the late 1860s and first half of the 1870s, knowledge of the Western world in Korea was limited to a handful of works written by Chinese in the immediate aftermath of the Opium Wars. Kim Byŏnghak 金炳學 (1821–1879), a leading high-ranking official and brilliant scholar, told King Gojong that the United States was nothing more than a motley band of immigrants when the United States expedition to Korea (or Western Disturbance in the Shinmi Year, 1871) resulted in over two hundred Korean army soldiers being killed by American gunfire.[95] He advised King Gojong that there was no need to be overly afraid of Americans. Many Chosŏn intellectuals and officials, including Kim Byŏnghak, argued that it was important to hold fast to a policy of isolation to preserve their civilization.[96] As a result, Japan as well as Western countries found it difficult to enter or trade with Korea. Despite Korea's policy of isolation, Japan's tenacious efforts (and constant pressure) induced Korea to open its doors, and in 1876 Japan and Korea signed the Kanghwa Treaty, an unequal treaty that forced Korea to allow Japanese and foreign trade. After 1876 the Chinese government (and merchants) in Korea faced severe competition from the Japanese government (and merchants) with respect to the politico-economic interests of Korea.

The Qing regime was wary of the ambitions of colonial powers and Japan to advance into Korea, and it drastically changed its existing Korean policy in the 1870s and 1880s.[97] From the mid-seventeenth century to the end of the nineteenth century, the Qing's policy toward Korea was based on suzerain-vassal relations (*zongfan* 宗藩) or tributary relations; within this, the empire maintained a policy of not interfering in Korea's internal affairs and diplomacy. However, around the 1870s and 1880s, the Qing began to actively intervene in Korea's internal affairs and diplomacy to enhance the Qing's diplomatic status through suzerainty and to maximize China's political and economic interests in Korea. To that end, the Qing government informed the colonial powers of the special relationship between the Qing and Korea while entrusting competent officials with work related to Korea.

The main figures of the Qing regime who led the change in Qing Korean policy were Li Hongzhang and Yuan Shikai. While Li gave instructions on Korean policy outside Korean territory, Yuan, dispatched to Korea, participated in the state affairs of Korea. From Li and Yuan's points of view, the Japanese were the biggest competitive force undermining the traditional Qing-Korea relationship and threatening the politico-economic interests of the Qing in Korea. Accordingly, they kept a wary eye on the expansion of

Japanese power in Korea. For example, regarding the political situation in Korea, Yuan wrote a letter to Li stating that Korean bureaucrats who were fooled by Japanese forces (*fanning* 翻弄) seemed to be in a maze, not realizing their mistakes. The king of Korea also seemed to be deceived by Japan's crafty advice that Korea should try to break the traditional Qing-Korea relationship and seek independence from the Qing. Yuan wrote that "therefore, it is necessary to take measures in advance to prevent Korea's betrayal of the Qing."[98] Upon receiving this letter, Li responded to Yuan that "I was also concerned that Korea's bureaucrats were seduced by the Japanese and betrayed China."[99]

To stay abreast of the competition with Japanese merchants in Korea,[100] Yuan encouraged Chinese merchants to enter Korea and took an active role in protecting China's socioeconomic interests. For instance, to facilitate the convenience of Chinese merchants who planned to enter Korea, Yuan arbitrarily issued dozens of *Hojo* 護照 (passports) in advance from *Tongriamun* 統理衙門 (a proto foreign and trade office of Korea) and then provided them to Qing merchants entering Korea.[101] In addition, Yuan not only ignored Chinese smugglers' entry into Korea, he sometimes promoted their smuggling trade there.[102] As Qing merchants' smuggling became prevalent, the Japanese ambassador in Korea demanded that the Korean government strictly block Qing merchants' smuggling trade and punish smugglers.[103] As a way to compensate for damages caused by the Korean government's insufficient measures against smuggling, Japan demanded the additional opening of ports.[104] This request from Japan, however, was not accepted due to the interference of Yuan;[105] he argued that the opening of Korean ports should only follow consultation with the Qing court.[106] Yuan implicitly sought to block Japan's economic advancement into Korea.

As much as Yuan, Li Hongzhang made diplomatic efforts to carry out China's interests in Korea. In 1881, Li Hongzhang said to the Chinese emperor, "Even if Korea's state affairs are running independently, the Korean kings have been receiving investiture from the Qing regime for a long time. Korea is a vassal of the Qing."[107] In diplomatic communications with Mori Arinori, the Japanese minister in China, Li Hongzhang kept arguing that because Korea was a vassal or tributary of the Qing Empire, Japan's claim that Korea was an independent country was inappropriate. The origin of this dispute stemmed from Mori's claim that "Korea was an independent state, so Japan considered it as an independent sovereign state." The Zongliyamen responded that "Korea was a tributary state of the Qing Empire."[108] "I think that Korea became a tributary state of the Qing was taken for granted not only in China but also in the Western world." Therefore, if Japan invaded Korean territory, it would have violated the Sino-Japanese Friendship and Trade Treaty of 1870.[109] When Li Hongzhang met Mori in China (January 24, 1876), his diplomatic stance on Korea was not unlike that of the Zongliyamen. In rebuttal to Mori's claims that "Korea and India are in Asia, but both are not a tributary state of Qing,"[110] Li asserted that "if Japan invades Korea, the Qing government will not tolerate it"[111] and he added that such Japanese aggression will "break a friendship between China and Japan and result in getting nowhere."[112]

As such, the Qing Empire and Japan were constantly in conflict over their politico-economic interests in Korea, the degree of intervention in Korea's state affairs, and Korea's status in the international community. Indeed, a series of important political events (e.g., the Imo Incident in 1882,[113] the Gapsin Coup in 1884, and Kim Ok-gyun's assassination in Shanghai in 1894[114]) expanded the arenas (economic, political, and military) of Sino-Japanese competition. The trigger point for military collision between China and Japan was the Donghak Peasant Revolution (or movement) of 1894. The Korean government could not subdue it successfully and was forced to ask the Qing for military intervention. Without informing Japan, the Qing sent troops to suppress the revolution. From the perspective of the Japanese government, the Qing's unilateral military intervention seemed like "the fox guarding the chicken coop." Japanese military forces promptly entered Korea on the pretext that the Chinese had not informed Japan in advance: "When about 3,000 Qing troops arrived in Seoul, the Japanese cited the Convention of Tientsin and sent in about 8,000 troops of their own."[115] Soon after, in July 1894, Japanese troops conquered Gyeongbokgung, the main royal palace of Korea. They formed a new pro-Japanese cabinet that abolished all the old treaties with the Qing and drove Chinese military forces out of Korean territory.

Acting as though its military support had been requested by the Korean government,[116] the Japanese army and navy fought with China between 1894 and 1895. Japanese troops won a series of battles, including the Battle of Pungdo in July 1894, the Battle of Seonghwan in July 1894, the Battle of Pyongyang in September 1894, the defeat of the Beiyang fleet in September 1894, the Battle of Yalu River in October 1894, the Battle of Lüshunkou in November 1894, and the Battle of Weihaiwei in 1894–1895. By early 1895 China was incapable of continuing the war. In April 1895, consequently, the Chinese government signed the Treaty of Shimonoseki with Japan at the Qing's request.[117] This treaty guaranteed Korea's independence and liberated it from China's tributary system. In sum, the Qing Empire attempted to use Korea as a fulcrum to revive (or maintain) a Sino-centric world order but failed due to Japan's aggressive expansion into Korea.

The First Sino-Japanese War helped to further integrate China into the interstate system in that China gave up the tributary system. Outwardly, the war and its consequences did not seem to correlate with China's integration into the interstate system of the capitalist world-economy, but, in reality, it catalyzed China's incorporation process in two ways. First, China did not continue its traditional tributary relationships after its defeat in the war. Several decades earlier, before China and Japan were at war, China tried to sustain the China-centered tributary system in East Asia, which inspired reverence and fear among East Asian countries. China's effort to rebuild the old international order, however, was in vain after its abject defeat in the war. Put differently, China never actually abandoned its tributary system; rather, it was the world, and especially Japan, that abandoned China. Japan aimed to invade the Asian continent and ultimately China itself. In this sense, the defeat in the war signified a coup de grace to the declining China-centered international system, and China was consequently forced to accept the interstate system of the capitalist world-economy.

Second, the First Sino-Japanese War brought awareness of China's weakness[118] and enlightened China as to why it had to renounce the tributary system and accept the interstate system. Along with this, Chinese intellectuals began to view Japan's successful incorporation into the capitalist world-system and modernization in a positive light. The most dramatic quantitative manifestation of this is the surge in the number of Chinese students in Japan. In 1896, thirteen Chinese students were the first to study in Japan, and by 1905, the number of Chinese students in Japan was estimated at eight thousand to ten thousand, and up to twenty thousand in 1906.[119]

The result of the First Sino-Japanese War shocked the international community because most Western and Asian countries had, until the mid-nineteenth century, a common belief that no other Asian countries could compete with the Chinese empire's economic and military power. Still, it took less than fifty years for Japan to reverse it. Although Japan's incorporation process began later than that of China, it quickly accepted the logic of the interstate system. In contrast with China, which was not dedicated to the adoption of the Westernized international order, Japan's active and rapid acceptance of the interstate system allowed its successful transformation. After seeing Japan's dedication to insert "itself into the upper level of the international pecking order,"[120] and its victory in the First Sino-Japanese War, both the international community and the Qing government, as well as Chinese intellectuals, had to face reality: the need to accept the interstate system and abandon a China-centered world order.

After the First Sino-Japanese War, British power declined amid the rise of Japanese power in China. European powers, especially Britain, did not foresee that Japan would win the scramble for China. In the wake of the initial success of the opium trade, Britain had believed that the Qing Empire was a magnet for new investment. To establish a more active politico-economic presence in China, Britain went to war against the Qing Empire. As a result, Britain had the predominant influence in China at least until the 1860s, but, after that, Pacific powers gained economic and political advantages from China by competing (and sometimes collaborating) with Britain and other European powers.[121] Through consecutive victories in two wars in 1894–1895 and 1904–1905, Japan's political influence in China, among the Pacific powers, had been strengthened. In contrast, Britain was caught off guard by Japan when it strove to check Russia's territorial expansion in China and Central Asia. Lawrence James concludes that Britain's defeat in competition with Japan and a decline of British hegemony in China was a decisive change: "British political paramountcy in China ended in 1895. The sudden and complete collapse of China in the 1894–95 Sino-Japanese War signaled the country's weakness to the rest of the world."[122]

On the other hand, Japan's economic presence in China had grown significantly since the late nineteenth century and came close to (or surpassed) that of Britain by the early twentieth century as shown in figure 4.1.

Figure 4.1. Comparison of British and Japanese interests in China, 1899–1931. *Source*: Created by the author, based on Peter Duus, "Trade and Investment," in *The Japanese Informal Empire in China, 1895–1937*, ed. Peter Duus, Ramon H. Myers, and Mark R. Peattie (Princeton University Press, 1989), 3.

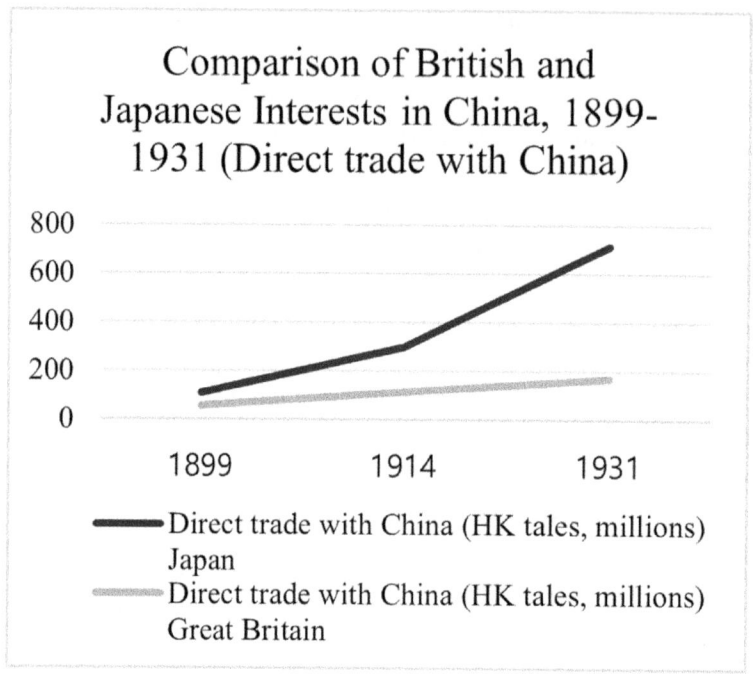

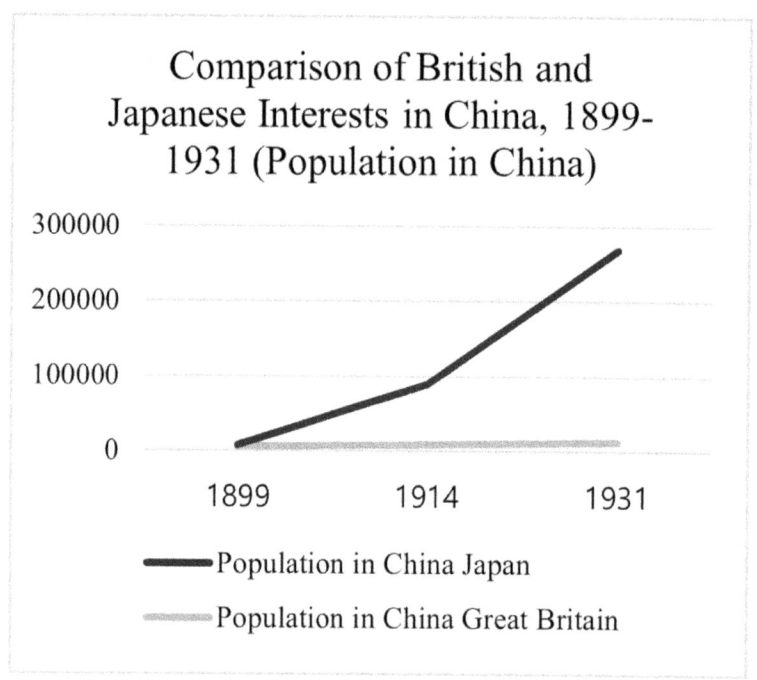

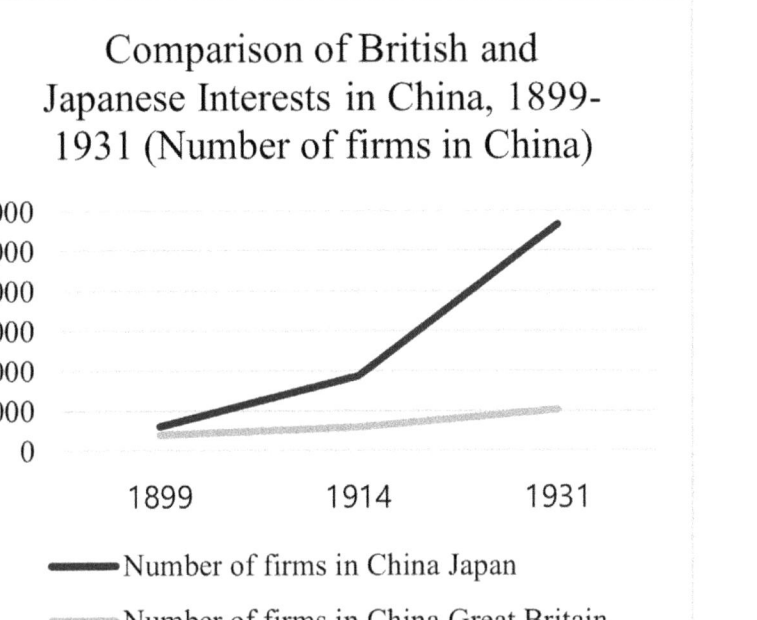

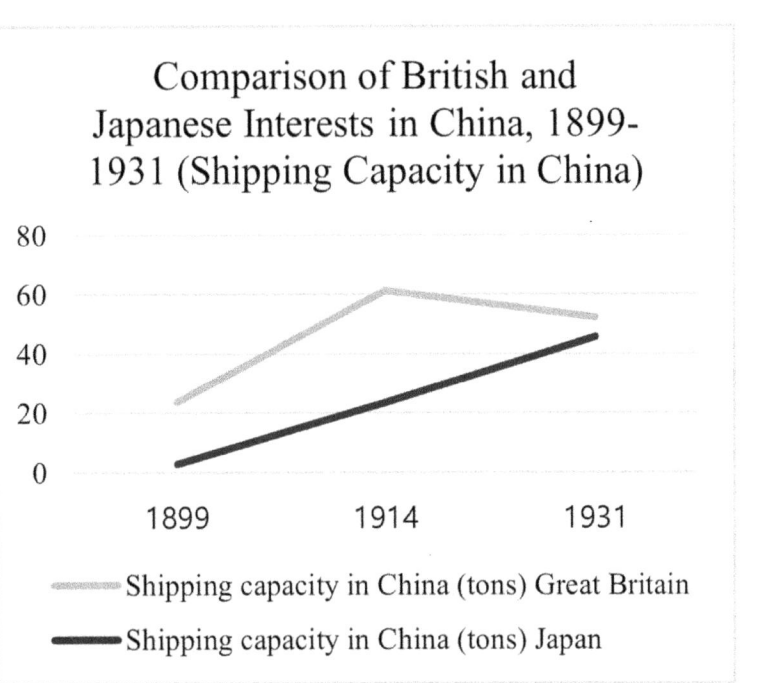

Japan tried to increase its dominant influence not only in Korea but also in China under the pretext of "Asia for the Asians" (or Pan-Asianism).[123] On the other hand, Britain could not help but acknowledge that its influence over China was waning at the outset of the twentieth century.

Examining the presence of Pacific powers—the rise of the United States, Russia, and Japan—as an important factor in the nineteenth-century capitalist world-system helps highlight two important facts. First, the Pacific powers gradually served as the pivot of the Asia-Pacific region. Second, they, and especially Japan, infiltrated China after the second half of the nineteenth century. I will further explicate the historical narratives of Pacific powers within the world-system and their relationships with China.

The Roles of the Pacific Powers in the Incorporation of Manchuria into the Capitalist World-System

Russia and Japan, the two major Pacific powers, expanded into Manchuria in China's northeast to obtain control of the region's rich resources and its geopolitical value; thus, they were central to China's incorporation into the capitalist world-system in the late nineteenth century. This contested space for colonial powers was distinct from the earlier domination of European powers in the incorporation process in southern China.[124] The incorporation of the Manchurian region into the capitalist world-system provides an interesting historical narrative, not only because of the distinctive features identified in its incorporation into the capitalist world-system but also because the presence of Pacific powers can be identified in the incorporation of the Manchurian region.[125]

Soybeans were the first major export crop from Manchuria that integrated the region into the world-economy. Manchurian ports were opened in the late nineteenth century and the ban on soybean exports was lifted in 1863. Expecting to reap many economic benefits from the soybean trade, Britain requested that the Qing regime change its policies, and the Qing government was forced to allow soybeans to be shipped abroad.[126] This led to a large number of domestic and foreign ships entering Manchurian ports every year to acquire soybeans and soybean-related products, which were then exported to Japan, Hong Kong, Southeast Asia, and Europe (see figure 4.2).

As can be seen in figure 4.2., soybean exports from Yingkou grew steadily from 1872 to 1901, and Manchurian exports continued to increase thereafter.[127] The fact that soybeans were the main export-oriented agricultural product of Manchuria confirms that the balance of power in East Asia in the first half of the twentieth century was not in favor of the European powers, but in favor of the Pacific powers. For example, after the Russo-Japanese War, a global shortage of linseed and cottonseed led British traders to utilize Manchurian soybeans as an oilseed, which in turn led to Manchurian soybeans reaching European markets. However, British merchants did not gain long-term control of Manchurian soybean exports. Rather, it was Japanese

Figure 4.2. Soybeans and related products: Export statistics from Yingkou, 1872–1901. *Source*: Created by the author, based on Yang she lian 杨余练 et al., *Qingdai dongbei shi* 清代东北史 [History of northeast China during the Qing dynasty] (Liaoning jiaoyu chubanshe, 1991), 454.

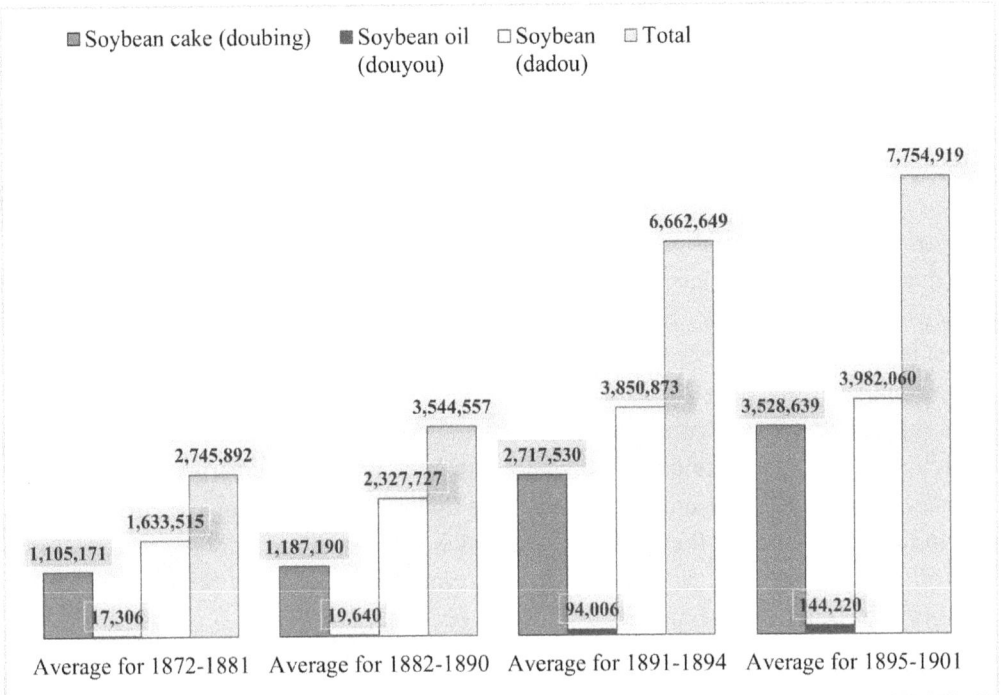

merchants and companies that occupied Manchuria that gained control of Manchurian soybeans.

The second major change is the formation of modern Manchurian cities. The growth of major cities, including port cities, and their transformation into modernized and capitalized spaces can be explained in terms of Manchuria's incorporation into the capitalist world-system. Earlier, I explained how the urban spaces of Shanghai, Hong Kong, and Canton were linked to the incorporation of China. Unlike these cities in the southern part of China, the cities in Manchuria were more under the influence of the Pacific powers, and their transformation into modern and capitalist spaces resulted in unprecedented changes in urban space compared to the pre-nineteenth century. As Ryu Jiwon points out, prior to the eighteenth century, major cities in Manchuria tended to be governed by Qing policies toward the Manchurian region like strengthening protection and control over the region or prioritizing military and defensive functions.[128] However, despite the Qing government's ban on Han Chinese entering Manchuria, natural disasters such as crop failures, droughts, and floods occurred one after another in the eighteenth century, causing the Qing government to have no choice but to send Han Chinese refugees to Manchuria. In addition, in the mid-to-late nineteenth century, when the door was opened by the impact of colonial powers, European and Pacific powers moved into key locations in Manchuria and new cities began to be created.[129] Qu Xiaofan identifies the period after the signing of the 1861 Treaty of Aihun and the Treaty of Tianjin as the time of transition for cities in modern Manchuria and identifies three characteristics of these new urban areas.[130] The first was the emergence of a modern urban mercantile system. This included the influx of foreign goods and the entry of foreign merchants, the development of commodity markets, and the rise of industrial and commercial capitalists including compradors. Second was the transition to a dualistic or pluralistic structure of the urban environment and the emergence of numerous public facilities. The unprecedented modernization of major cities in Manchuria led to the coexistence of traditional agricultural culture and modern commercial culture, and several public facilities were established that transformed Manchurian cities into newly formed commercial and capitalist spaces. The third was the creation of civil society organizations based on commerce. With the emergence of modern industry and commercialization in Manchuria's major cities, those engaged in commerce and industry established their own autonomous and sometimes closed organizational networks to protect their rights, marking the emergence of a new bourgeois network with its own independent and representative civic leaders.[131]

The cities of Yingkou and Dalian in Manchuria were prime examples of commercialized and capitalist spaces. In 1861, at the insistence of the British, Yingkou was opened, and from then on major imperialist powers set up consulates and began their own commercial activities in the city. As Yingkou served as a gateway between Manchuria and the capitalist world-economy, its maritime transportation and commerce developed rapidly, and through Yingkou, Manchuria's in-demand exports, especially soybeans, reached markets throughout China, as well as Japan, Russia, and Europe.

While Yingkou was first opened by Britain, a European power, Dalian's first opening was led by one of the Pacific powers, Russia.[132] As Russia scouted the Pacific coast for acquisition of an ice-free port, it set its sights on Dalian. In 1896, Russia signed the Sino-Russian Secret Treaty with Li Hongzhang, who visited Moscow, and gained agreement from the Chinese government for Russian ships to use Chinese ports in wartime. The following year (1897), when Germany occupied Jiaozhou Bay, Russia sent warships to capture Lüshun and Dalian based on the agreement with Qing China. In 1898, Russia sought to extend its occupation of Lüshun and Dalian by signing the Convention for the Lease of the Liaotung Peninsula with the Qing government, obtaining from Beijing the right to occupy the peninsula for twenty-five years. From then on, Russia began to develop Dalian's port in earnest; with the first phase of construction completed in 1903, Dalian Port was transformed into a place where twenty-five ships of twenty-five hundred tons could berth simultaneously, with a cargo handling capacity of two hundred thousand tons.[133] In addition, Russia connected

Dalian to the continental railway between Europe and Asia, making it a logistics center with the capacity to transport not only by sea but also across the continent. As a result, Dalian's commerce and industry developed rapidly, and by the outbreak of the Russo-Japanese War in 1904, the total population of Dalian had reached about forty thousand.[134] After taking control of Dalian from Russia following the Treaty of Portsmouth (1905) and the end of the Russo-Japanese War, Japan made Dalian the largest trading port in Northeast Asia and a bridgehead to Manchuria. As a result, in the 1920s, Dalian had the second highest foreign trade volume among China's five largest ports (Guangzhou, Shanghai, Hangu, Tianjin, and Dalian).[135]

Throughout the first half of the twentieth century, Japan was the main force behind the transformation of modern Manchurian cities. Especially from the moment they were converted into Japanese colonial cities, Manchurian cities became conduits for the transmission of Japanese institutions, politics, economy, and culture to the colonies. As such, they were spaces where Manchurian urbanites could directly or indirectly experience industrialization and modernization,[136] and this colonial urban development was carried out under Japanese influence, on the one hand, and according to a capitalist world-system logic, on the other. After the establishment of the Japanese puppet state of Manchukuo in 1932, modern Manchuria was physically transformed into a new modern urban and colonial space, and the Manchukuo state advocated "the cooperation and harmony of five ethnic groups (Japanese, Korean, Manchu, Mongolian, and Han Chinese)," the founding sprit of Manchukuo state. In reality, Manchuria was a region where racism and hierarchized ethnic classification were practiced.[137] In fact, after the Mukden incident and the establishment of the Manchukuo state in 1932, Japan induced large-scale migration of Koreans to Manchuria,[138] where many of them lost their original settlements and were forced to become poor laborers in Manchurian cities.[139] In addition, the socioeconomic and occupational status and living space of Japanese and non-Japanese (Chinese and Korean) within Manchurian cities were often formed on the basis of ethnic discrimination. Discrimination in food rationing, with Japanese colored in blue, Koreans in yellow, and others in red, caused the most visceral frustration and anger.[140]

It is important to note that the racial and ethnic discrimination and occupational hierarchies that operated within the Manchurian state were linked to the vertical division of labor in the global economy. The global vertical division of labor within the colonial economy, created as that economy joined the capitalist world-economy, ensured stability and continuity for the colonial economy, and conversely, the colonial economy provided the capitalist world-system with new low-wage workers and resources for capital accumulation. Racism based on a rigid ethnic hierarchy and ethnic discrimination was the magic formula that enabled capital accumulation to be maximized, production costs to be minimized, and social and political disruption costs to be reduced.[141]

In summary, the rise of modern Manchuria was linked to the creation of modern capitalist spaces, and notably, these urban spaces combined with the capital and human and material resources of Pacific powers, resulting in advancements in productivity and the emergence of new forms of capitalist production. Furthermore, the transformation of Manchurian cities into modern and capitalist spaces was linked to the geographical expansion of the capitalist world-system and of capitalist modes of production and networks to places where more capital was formed. Manchuria's connection to the capitalist world-system meant that the region was connected to the international division of labor system (e.g., export-oriented soybean cultivation in Manchuria), the goods produced in the region were synchronized with global commodity networks (e.g., exporting soybeans and receiving imports from abroad in return), and the capitalists and workers of the Manchurian region were inextricably linked to global commodity markets (e.g., the emergence of compradors and workers in foreign stores and factories).[142]

On the other hand, the logic of capitalist modes of accumulation—exploitation, violence, and unequal exchange in capitalized spaces—emerges in incorporated territories. By tracing the development of modern Manchuria, we may see historical evidence of this. For example, when the Qing government granted British merchants' request for soybean trading rights in Manchuria, Chinese merchants who already owned soybean distribution rights in Manchuria had to compete with colonial powers' merchants, and some of them suffered economic losses. In addition, after the Japanese invasion of Manchuria, they forced the new downtown area of Yingkou to be sold at a loss, and worse, starting in the 1910s, the Japanese policy of making Dalian the center of international commerce in Manchuria led to the decline of Yingkou, which had previously established itself as an international import and export port.[143] Furthermore, Japan actively induced Korean migration to the large Manchurian cities, where many Korean migrants had to face ethnic discrimination.[144]

In some cases, the clash between European and Pacific powers changed the direction of the city's development. In the late nineteenth century, Qingdao had to face unprecedented outside influence from Germany. Before the 1890s Germany's interest in overseas expansion and colonization increased, but it did not have the political and economic advantages within China that other colonial powers had. In November 1897, following the murder of a German missionary in Shandong Province, Germany occupied Jiaozhou Bay by force. After that Germany also acquired railroad concessions and mining rights in Shandong.

Under German influence (1897–1914), Qingdao's urban landscape and industrial structure were reorganized, especially the German efforts to build infrastructure such as sea lanes, railroads, and roads. Before German occupation the region's industry was dominated by agriculture and fishing. There were also people engaged in commerce, construction, and home-based handicrafts, but commerce was mainly connected to the coastal cities of Shanghai and Ningbo, and the area was not a center for overseas trade. During the German occupation, however, the area was transformed into a modern and capitalist space as modern infrastructure was built, and trade, small- and medium-sized shipyards, and electric factories began to enter Qingdao. Most of all, it was trade and commerce that breathed new vitality into the Qingdao economy during the German occupation. The construction of Qingdao port and the Qingdao-Jinan Railway connected Qingdao with the rest of Shandong and the world, and as a result, the city's domestic and international trade volume increased dramatically. During this period, the main products exported from Qingdao were straw weaving (*caobian* 草編), peanuts, and peanut oil, while the main products imported were textiles, cotton, and oil. In addition, shipyards, railroad locomotive factories, electric factories, and breweries were built with German capital.

While trade and commerce in Qingdao grew rapidly under German occupation, Qingdao was transformed into a modern industrial city during Japanese occupation (First Japanese Occupation, 1914–1922; Second Japanese Occupation, 1938–1945). Around 1920, Japanese capital entered Qingdao in earnest, and in 1922, there were 116 companies headquartered in the city, 73 companies with branches or offices, and more than 5,000 Japanese self-employed workers in Qingdao.[145] In addition to textiles, many modern manufacturing industries operated in Qingdao, including the chemical, food, machinery, mining, and cement industries. The socioeconomic development of Qingdao under Japanese occupation was different from that under German occupation, which can be attributed to the differences in Japanese and German access to China. While Germany's entry into Qingdao was a limited and indirect mode of domination through a leased territory, Japan's entry into Qingdao was more extensive and direct, and from the 1930s onward, Japanese control of Qingdao was linked to its colonial rule over Manchuria. For this purpose, Japanese capital became more active in Qingdao, and the industrial structure of Qingdao became increasingly dependent on Japanese capital.[146]

The Railway Concession: A Case Study of How the Rise of Pacific Powers and China's Incorporation Process Were Interconnected

Building on the incorporation approach to modern Manchurian dynamics, I argue that Manchurian geoeconomic and geopolitical transformations in the late nineteenth and early twentieth centuries were inextricably linked to the Pacific powers. Furthermore, that Pacific powers were also deeply involved in China's railroad construction, which is one of the key events critical to a comprehensive understanding of China's incorporation into the capitalist world-system.

After the First Sino-Japanese War, colonial powers, hoping to acquire Chinese territory, obtained leased territories from the Qing Empire: in 1898, Jiaozhou Bay and its harbor Qingdao was ceded to Germany, Port Arthur was ceded to Russia, and Weihaiwai and the Kowloon Peninsula were ceded to Britain in the same year.[147] In the following year, Guangzhouwan was ceded to France.[148] In the race for spoils in China, major pillars of foreign imperialism even concluded a bilateral agreement to prevent strife between them.¹⁴⁹ In the Anglo-German Convention of October 1900 (especially Article 3), Britain and Germany agreed to a tacit arrangement in establishing spheres of interest in Chinese territory, while excluding China. It indicated that "colonial powers vacillated between imperialist competition and collaborating in joint actions against the Qing Empire."¹⁵⁰ Yet, a bird's-eye view of how the competition surrounding Chinese railway concessions worked is nowhere better expressed than in conflicts between European and Pacific powers and the rise of Pacific powers in China.

Supported by their respective governments, European powers such as Belgium, Britain, Germany, and France, along with Pacific powers like Russia and the United States, participated in China's railway construction. As a result, by 1911, over 90 percent of China's railways were under the control of colonial powers.¹⁵¹ This created a balance of power and mutual controls in China that ironically prevented any single colonial power from taking over the entire railway system.¹⁵² It provided a new kind of leverage due to the fact that extra-European countries, which are often underrated in China's massive political transformations, played a significant role in complicating China's incorporation process.¹⁵³

In 1876, foreigners and European merchants, such as Jardine and Matheson, constructed the first railway in China, which was unauthorized. It faced opposition from local government officials and the gentry and was eventually abandoned. Subsequent railway construction in China was slow until 1894, when there was a sudden surge in construction between 1895 and 1911, resulting in the completion of 9,253 kilometers of track. European and Pacific powers participated in this railway building to advance their politico-economic interests.¹⁵⁴ These powers wished to use the Chinese railways for secure and cost-effective coal transportation,¹⁵⁵ as well as to gain access to China's interior provinces. The combination of railways and steamships strengthened spatial ties between Western colonial powers and non-Western colonial powers,¹⁵⁶ and so the colonial powers were motivated to develop China's railways.

Despite the oppressive tactics of colonial powers in building China's railways, the Chinese government itself struggled to build railway lines. Wei Yuan 魏源 (1794–1856) mentioned that a train (*huolunche* 火輪車) could accommodate a thousand people and travel about forty-four miles per hour.¹⁵⁷ Xu Jiyu 徐继畬 (1795–1873) asserted that the train could run seventy-three miles a day.¹⁵⁸ In August 1874, the *Wanguogongbao* introduced information about American railroads and noted that hundreds of thousands of people were using them.¹⁵⁹ Especially after the disgraceful defeats of the Sino-Japanese War, reformers and intellectuals like Liu Mingchuan 劉銘傳 (1836–1896), Xue Fucheng, Guo Sungtao 郭嵩燾 (1818–1891), Li Hongzhang, Wang Wenshao, and Zhang Zhidong believed that the establishment of railways was important to accomplish China's economic development and industrialization.¹⁶⁰ To overcome national crises, in July 1895, Emperor Guangxu stressed the need to develop railroads, establish machine factories, mint coins, and develop mines.¹⁶¹

Unfortunately, the Qing government lacked the financial resources to invest in such projects. Moreover, the railway initiatives proposed by the regime failed to garner significant interest from Chinese citizens and domestic capital.[162] Due to the Chinese government's failure to attract domestic investment, the Qing government had to rely on foreign loans to fund their railway construction projects,[163] which resulted in significant problems.

First, the Chinese government had to rely heavily on colonial powers for the necessary funds to construct railways, which suggests that the railway projects were primarily guided by the colonial powers' intentions, despite nominal control by the Qing bureaucracy. As a result, many Chinese railways were built to serve the politico-economic interests of the colonial powers, rather than the Qing government's original goal of modernizing China through railway development. Second, the Chinese government aimed to prevent any one colonial power from dominating railway construction by encouraging competition among them. The Qing regime believed that the longer the competition among the great powers persisted and the longer the planned railway construction period extended, the less likely it was that China's railway construction would be controlled by a superpower.[164] Although this tactic proved partially effective in creating a balance of power among colonial powers, the Qing government did not have the deep pockets to sustain railway construction and a sufficient political and military capacity to defend against penetration by the colonial powers. Contrary to the Qing regime's expectations, the intense competition among European powers for railway concessions allowed Pacific powers such as Russia and Japan to enter the race for concessions, making the situation increasingly difficult to control.

France led the efforts to obtain railway privileges in China.[165] While France appeared to be mainly focused on acquiring territory in or near China, such as Tonkin (1883–1886) or Yunnan Province, commercial and economic interests were more important than territorial expansion. Tonkin is in northern Vietnam, and before the Sino-French War Vietnam was a tributary state of the Qing Empire. Compared to other colonial powers, France did not gain much economic advantage from dealing with China in the late nineteenth century. Therefore, France's railway concession, which was oriented toward commerce, reflected its economic ambitions. When negotiating the Treaty of Tianjin in 1885 with China, French drafts included a clause reserving a thousand kilometers of the future Chinese railway network for construction by French industry.[166] Although Li Hongzhang did not agree to France's proposal, offering instead a vague promise that China would seek France's help when building a railway network, France persistently demanded the railway concession and eventually gained access to the Beijing-Hankou Railway.[167] This railway was constructed between 1897 and 1906 by the Société d'études des chemins de fer en Chine, which was made up of a group of French and Belgian banks and leading construction companies from both countries.[168]

France aimed to accelerate its market entry into China by investing capital in railway construction. However, the French government's investment did not meet its expectations, as French capitalists were not attracted to the government's aggressive plan to enter China. They rejected the government's request for investment by citing the flimsy security for the Chinese railway. The decoupling between the efforts of

French bureaucrats and diplomatic officials such as Jules Ferry, Charles de Freycinet, and Théophile Delcassé, who were committed to participating in Chinese railway construction, and the tepid response of French capitalists who were reluctant to invest in Chinese railways, prevented France from leading the race for Chinese railway concessions. As Comte de Bezaure observed, "China will escape from us like India escaped from us before, only this time not because of the inferiority of our arms or our diplomacy, but because of the invincible inertia of our capitalists."[169] A dearth of venture capitalists was one of the essential reasons why France was one step behind in China's railway competitions.

Beginning in the second half of the nineteenth century, Britain invested significant funds in railway construction abroad. As a result, they led the construction of railways in non-European countries such as Canada, New Zealand, Australia, India, Jamaica, Argentina, Mexico, Guiana, South Africa, Uganda, and Mauritius between the second half of the nineteenth century and the early twentieth century.[170] For example, after intervening in the construction of railroads in Brazil in 1856, British economic control over Brazil was strengthened.[171] In order to fulfill the proactive policies of the British government, British capitalists invested large sums of money into foreign railway construction. In 1914, Britain invested £1.531 million in railway capital around the world, or 41 percent of their total investment overseas that year.[172]

Britain also saw Chinese railway construction as a promising investment opportunity and joined the competition for railway concessions. With a well-established business network in China, the British Empire achieved significant railway concessions. The first modern railway built in China was the Woosung Railway, constructed and operated by Britain. This railway connected a 14.9 km section from the American enclave in the Shanghai International Settlement to Woosung. Construction of the Woosung Railway began in December 1874 and was completed in June 1876.[173]

By 1898, Britain successfully acquired railroad concessions in China, which extended across more than ten provinces in the north China Plain and the lower Yangtze River Delta region, and included the Guangzhou-Kowloon railway line, Tianjin-Pukou railway line (with Germany), and Shanghai-Ningbo railway line.[174] However, social unrest in China, competition from other colonial powers, and strong resistance from locals hindered Britain from gaining the expected political and economic benefits from railway construction. Worse, the collapse of the Qing regime in 1911 was followed by the rise of military factionalism and internal war. For these reasons, many of China's railway loans, which were "mainly secured on current earnings," went into default.[175] Consequently, Britain suffered an enormous loss from the railway loans.

Although not as active and progressive in China's railroad construction as the British, the United States was also interested in Chinese railroad construction. American capital played a significant role in building the Hu-Guang Railroad.[176] US secretary of state Philander C. Knox strongly encouraged US capitalist and government participation in Chinese railroad construction.[177] Although the US wrangled with Chinese authorities about the Hu-Guang railroad, which resulted in excluding a branch line from Ching-men-chour to Hanyang from the original Hu-Guang railroad construction, the US invested in the railroad.

Russia's interest in obtaining railway concessions in China was sparked by the completion of the Trans-Siberian Railway in 1891. The railway was built to address border disputes between Russia and China, promote Russia's steel and cotton exports, and facilitate overland trade between the West and China. However, it wasn't until the First Sino-Japanese War that Russia began actively seeking railway privileges in China. Japan's unexpected victory in the war, and its subsequent acquisition of the Liaotung Peninsula and Port Arthur, posed a threat to Russia. To counter this threat, Russia, along with Germany and France, exerted pressure on the territory that Japan acquired during the war, in what is known as the Tripartite Intervention of 1895. Japan, fearing international isolation, had to withdraw from the Liaotung Peninsula and Port Arthur.

Russia also tried to improve diplomatic relations with China under the pretext of national defense against Japan's encroachment. To that end, Russia stood surety for China's reparations stemming from the First Sino-Japanese War. Russia's conciliatory policy worked so well that China, in response, granted a railway concession, the Chinese Eastern Railway, to Russia in 1896.[178] Russian finance minister Sergei Witte strongly advocated the construction of Russian railroads in Manchuria. Although some foreign officials in the Russian government opposed the construction of the Chinese Eastern Railway, Witte argued that it would facilitate Russia's interests in the competition between the competing imperialist powers for control of Manchuria, that the Chinese Eastern Railway would provide Russia with easy access to China proper, and that it would revitalize Vladivostok, the main Russian port near Manchuria.[179]

Russia didn't stop there. China had agreed to a defense alliance with Russia that was negotiated in secret between Witte and Li Hongzhang; Russia used it as a stepping-stone to expand Russia's control over Manchuria and to promote economic and military penetration into the interior of China. When Germany acquired Kiautschou Bay in 1897, Russia dispatched warships to Port Arthur in the name of protection against Germany's sudden penetration, while coercing the Qing government to grant the concession of the South Manchuria Railway running from Changchun to Dalian. The Qing government, horrified at this unexpected turn of events, was unable to resist Russian pressure and granted a concession for the construction of the railway, which Russia opened in 1901.

However, Russia's forceful and aggressive expansion strategies provoked a backlash from China and from other colonial powers. The Boxer Rebellion (1899–1901) provided momentum for Japan to reenter the competition for China and form a compact with Britain, the Anglo-Japanese Alliance of 1902, to counteract Russia's expansion. As a result of this alliance, Russia's aggressive expansion into China was halted, and Russia was forced to cede the Chinese Eastern Railway and the South Manchuria Railway to Japan after the Russo-Japanese War.[180] Japan's acquisition of the South Manchuria

Railway played a critical role in establishing and expanding Japan's presence in China, as it became crucial to managing the Kwantung territory and safeguarding Japan's special rights and interests in the area.[181]

There is little doubt that the South Manchuria Railway was deeply connected to Japan's expansionist policies and national interest. By controlling the main trunk line in southern Manchuria, Japan hoped to expand its commercial interests, develop the Manchurian economy, and allow Japanese labor and capital to settle in the region, making it an integral part of the motherland's economy. Goto Shinpei, the first president of the South Manchuria Railway, hoped that as many as one million Japanese would move to Manchuria to work in agriculture and mining. Their presence would perpetuate Japanese control over Manchuria, which would become part of the expanded Japanese Empire.[182]

The true winner of the railway concessions was Japan. Japan was a latecomer in the struggle for these concessions, yet it benefited from certain advantages that ironically gave it an edge over other colonial powers. Japan faced fewer potential threats such as resistance from locals or competition from European powers. As a result, Japan's comparative advantage grew and became insurmountable. The strategic value of the railway lines, particularly the South Manchuria Railway, allowed Japan to penetrate the Manchurian economy and establish an economic and military presence in the region.[183]

In sum, the railway concessions obviously show how China's incorporation process in the late nineteenth and early twentieth centuries was turned into a battleground by colonial powers. Pacific powers that emerged in the late nineteenth century competed with each other and European powers for China's resources. In a situation where the influence of European powers in China had declined while those of Pacific powers in China had increased after the nineteenth century, the continued decline of the Qing regime's governing capabilities led to the end of an older era. It was no less than the beginning of a new era.

Concluding Remarks

The conclusion of the First Sino-Japanese War clearly marked the end of China's tributary system, as the country suffered an unexpected and humiliating defeat. This defeat resulted in the disappearance of China's influence on neighboring countries, while Japan emerged as a powerful political and economic force in East Asia. The war's damage forced China to relinquish its status as a world empire, and Japan's subsequent rise significantly impacted China's integration into the capitalist world-economy. As a result of the "slicing of the Chinese melon" by European and Pacific powers, many sectors of the Qing Empire were divided among these powers for economic gain.[184] However, despite this exploitation, China did not become a colony of any Western nation due to the balance of power between European and Pacific powers, as well as the decline of Pax Britannica in the late nineteenth century. Instead, the United States, Russia, and Japan, all relatively free from European control, were the main beneficiaries of China's resources. The slow progress of China's incorporation into the world-economy was due to the struggles between European powers and Pacific powers, resulting in a structural disequilibrium. This can be characterized as China's incorporation process under multicentric powers.[185]

The next chapter focuses on the resistance movements that occurred during China's incorporation process. While the politico-economic penetration by colonial powers had a significant impact on this process, the resistance movements played an equally important role in shaping its dynamics. Through an examination of the different forms of resistance movements in China, I will reconceptualize Chinese historical processes positioned at the apex of China's complex incorporation.

Chapter 5

China's Backlash Against the Penetration of the Capitalist World-Economy

> Divinely aided Boxers, United-in-Righteousness Corps Arose because the Devils Messed up the Empire of yore.
> They proselytize their sect, and believe in only one God,
> The sprits and their own ancestors Are not even given a nod.
> Their men are all immoral; Their women truly vile.
> For the Devils it's mother-son sex That serves as the breeding style.
> . . .
> When at last all the Foreign Devils Are expelled to the very last man, The Great Qing, united, together, Will bring peace to this our land.
>
> —Boxer poem cited in Joseph Esherick, *The Origins of the Boxer Uprising*

During an external arena's incorporation process into the capitalist world-economy, there have been many different types of large or small-scale resistances within the incorporating society. In general, the process of incorporating an external arena into the capitalist world-economy was not a linear progression solely driven by Western intrusion. The resistance movements of the incorporated areas, at various levels of strength, also shape the dynamics of the incorporation process.[1] The world-systemic perspective of Eric Wolf and John R. Hall expressed concern about the conquest of incorporated areas by central states without historical narratives of the responses of the periphery (or "micro-groups").[2] However, contrary to their concerns, several world-systems scholars have paid considerable attention to the responses of incorporated areas to explain the full expansion process of the modern world-system.[3]

For example, chiefdoms in southern Africa established centralized military systems to protect themselves from the world-economy's destructive forces,[4] while Caribbean colonists sometimes resisted British and French colonial trades.[5] Rural revolutions in Mexico were strongest when capitalist agriculture penetrated most deeply,[6] and Bolivian peasants and workers resisted the oppression of economic penetration.[7] Pirates in the Atlantic frontier also participated in resistance movements during their incorporation into the capitalist world-economy.[8]

While various types of resistance have been studied in the context of incorporation, there are some limitations in applying the existing theoretical framework to China. First, the resistance studies in incorporation studies have primarily focused on the physical, military, and economic responses to penetration of outside forces, with less attention paid to the cultural and ideological responses to the penetration of these forces. It is difficult to understand the resistance that emerged in the Chinese incorporation process without considering the importance of culture and ideology in exploring the modes of resistance and the cultural and ideational resources of resistance. This is because the Confucian ideological system created a common belief system that offset the differences between social classes with asymmetrical political, economic, and social resources in late imperial China, and it also brought together various groups within Chinese society under the banner of "anti-Western" to voice their criticism of Western values. In fact, the conservative central bureaucrats, intellectuals, and gentry who valued the Confucian values, lifestyles, and political organizations based on Confucian ideology were the most vocal opponents of China's incorporation process into the capitalist world-system, and they also strongly criticized the colonial powers for their Christian ideology and Western ideas, along with their Eurocentric views. Therefore, if we only consider the material, military, and economic responses of the Chinese people to the incorporation process, we may omit an important part of the resistance movement. Second, many of the existing studies on resistance to the incorporation process show a strong tendency to analyze resistance only within the territory of incorporation. However, if this theoretical framework is applied to China's incorporation, it may render invisible important historical resistance movements that can be identified in China's incorporation process, for example, the resistance movements of coolies who were compelled by external pressure to go abroad.

Hung Ho-Fung, who analyzed Chinese resistance movements during the Qing Dynasty, categorized resistance movements into two main types: "state engaging-based protests"[9] and "state-resisting protests."[10] The former is a movement to request the expansion of the state's role or demand the rights of the people, while the latter is a movement against the state's activities or intervention. The number of "state engaging-based protests" shows a steady increase from 1645 to 1760 and then a sharp decline in the second half of the eighteenth century. On the other hand, the number of "state-resisting protests," which increased sharply in 1645, declined until 1760, and then increased sharply again in the second half of the eighteenth century. This suggests that antistate resistance movements were strong in the early Qing period, resistance movements demanding state participation were stronger in the early and middle years, and antistate resistance movements were strong again in the late eighteenth century.

Hung, in summary, explained the various resistance movements during the Qing dynasty in terms of their relationship with the state. Despite his intriguing and pioneering work, he fails to depict how various resistances have been created in relation to the outside world since the nineteenth century. Given this limitation, I here aim to examine the multiple types of resistance movements created during China's incorporation process.

Following the initial military attacks and the resulting shock to Chinese society, strong resistance movements began to emerge after the First Opium War. These movements can be divided into three categories: (1) resistance by government officials against Western influence, (2) resistance by the gentry class who adhered to Confucian principles, and (3) resistance by Chinese coolies who experienced fraud, suppression, violence, and harsh working conditions. Typically, the resistance movements of conservative Qing officials rejected Western-friendly policies and served to hinder China's westernization either directly or indirectly. The resistance movements of the gentry class were characterized by their adherence to Confucian ideas, anti-Christian sentiment, and opposition to Western privileges in China. Finally, the resistance movements of Chinese coolies who entered the international division of labor system can be observed on coolie ships and plantations.

Conservative Government Officials

The state bureaucrats, who were one of the primary elite groups during the Qing reign, were staunchly in support of the continuation of the ancien régime. When the Manchus ousted the Ming in 1644 and reestablished a centralized bureaucracy, they heavily relied on the bureaucratic officialdom of the Ming due to its several advantages. First, after the Manchus conquered China in the mid-seventeenth century, they had difficulty in governing large areas of the country due to a lack of human resources. Hence, "Manchurians were forced to rely—as any dynasty had to be before them—on the schooled administrators who had managed China since time beyond human memory."[11] By maintaining the previous bureaucratic system, the Qing state-makers minimized any political disorder caused by the power vacuum. Second, the Ming's patrimonialism, which held that all power comes from the emperor's authority, equally helped strengthen the centralism of the Qing regime.

Why did Ming bureaucrats accept the rule of the Manchus, whom they once had regarded as less-civilized tribesmen? To answer this question, it is worth noting the relationship between Confucian governance and state bureaucracy. The Confucian scriptures, state bureaucrats, and the cultural and political governance of premodern

China have a long history of ties. The interpretation of the sacred Confucian texts and the political practice based on this interpretation led state bureaucrats to create and maintain the political doctrine that made imperial autocracy possible. Thus, state bureaucrats who were committed to Confucian doctrine became the guardians of their ruling power, while at the same time they become the proponents of Heaven—the ontological origin of rulers with will and morality in Confucianism, and the ultimate criterion for the morality, legitimacy, and legitimacy of rulers' governance.

During periods of dynastic transition, due to social and political turmoil, the state bureaucracy temporarily lacked precise and consistent standards of loyalty, but once a new regime was established, and the new regime implemented a Confucian-based rule, the state bureaucracy conformed to the system and became a key force in defending and supporting the new rulers.

Apart from the state bureaucracy, of course, the Qing imperial family also intervened heavily in private academia to depoliticize the Chinese literati and make them support the Qing government. Thus, if literati used words that were disrespectful to the Manchu or Mongols, they could be punished, but academic freedom was widely recognized as long as it did not pertain to political affairs.[12] In other words, while the Qing emperor blatantly discouraged intellectuals from political engagement, at the same time, the Manchu regime actively encouraged academic freedom for Chinese scholars. This is evidenced by the Qing patronage of the development of the evidence movement (*kaozheng* 考證) and its extensive imperial publication.[13]

The Qing regime established and maintained its ruling system by adopting the Confucian order and by the unwavering loyalty of the state bureaucracy. The Qing court established new and powerful organizations, such as the Grand Council (*junjichu*), to strengthen royal authority.[14] The court also operated the Eight Banner system to maintain the Qing's distinct ethnic identity.[15] As Mark Elliott explains, the Eight Banners, as a military organization and a socio-military class, played a central role in shaping and sustaining "pax Manjurica."[16]

Nevertheless, Manchu-oriented political institutions were not separable from the Confucian system of governance. Rather, Manchu-oriented political institutions combined with Confucian governance helped secure their pluralistic and multiethnic governance. Compared to the Confucian-based governance of the Ming, the Qing court's Confucian governance system changed only in its attributes, but not in its essence. The system of governance established through Confucian texts provided intellectuals and state officials with reasons for maintaining public order, while also affirming an important reason for the existence of state power. By inheriting Confucian ideology the Qing regime could gain unwavering loyalty from state officials. Indeed, China's imperial examination system (*keju* 科举), used as a recruitment tool for state bureaucrats, played an important role in inspiring the loyalty of bureaucrats with Confucian thinking.[17] As it served to reproduce ideologically homogenous state officials, the imperial examination system itself helped to sustain the existing political order, while producing strong Confucian-oriented government officials who rejected unorthodox ideas or policies that were friendly toward the West.

It was not surprising in this regard that government administrators who adhered to Confucian principles for maintaining social order and loyalty to Qing political authority became an epicenter of political resistance movements. However, it would be wrong to assume that all government officials resisted the West. In reality, from the mid-nineteenth to the early twentieth centuries, government officials had two opposing viewpoints toward the West. After being defeated in the First Opium War, those who were impressed by the advanced military and technology of the West were willing to endorse the idea of adopting Western-oriented approaches to modernize China's outdated military weapons, manufacturing industries, and ineffective bureaucratic system. Such sociopolitical movements spurred political and military reforms. On the other hand, those who strongly advocated for preserving the Confucian-based traditional order tended to view the West's entry as an encroachment of barbarism, leading them to resist accepting Western knowledge and technology. To simplify, in the former case, they tried to compensate for what China lacked, such as outdated technology, military forces, and premodern political systems, while in the latter case, those who disdained Western knowledge and technology relied on the values of China's long-standing civilization.

Many of the vehemently conservative officials were associated with the censorate, the Hanlin Academy, and the Board of Rites. Most of these government agency conservatives had one thing in common—their "intellectual and professional consideration attached closely to Confucian traditionalism"[18] and the traditionalists' strong adherence to Confucianism and traditionalism formed the basis of their antiforeign stance.[19]

This also can be employed to explain the strong sensitivity of the imperial bureaucrats who often resisted the reframing of the Chinese traditional order or long-lasting government organizations. Conservative government officials, following the old order, resorted to the time-honored method of sharply criticizing the establishment of the Zongliyamen and were contemptuous of its official authority as they deemed it to reflect a set of Western-oriented political reforms. Unlike Prince Gong and his supporters, who were dedicated to expanding the authority and roles of the Zongliyamen, conservative officials were unhappy with its functions, especially diplomatic negotiations. They believed that if the Chinese government followed Western instructions through the Zongliyamen, China would be placed in a miserable situation. They argued that the unconditional acceptance of Western requests and the granting of privileges to Westerners would jeopardize Confucian and China-centered traditions.[20] For government officials who upheld traditional values, the Westernization project seemed like an insane idea.[21] Beijing and provincial officials such as Weng Tonghe 翁同龢 (1830–1904), Tu Renshou 屠仁守 (1832–1904), and Wang Wenshao 王文韶 (1832–1908) pointed out that Western-oriented reforms would cause social and political chaos.[22] Regarding the West's disrespect for China, Ma Jianzhong 馬建忠 (1845–1900) claimed that foreign ministers showed disrespect toward the Chinese government and hindered government officials at treaty ports, while foreign merchants, regardless of the size of their countries, illegally occupied Chinese territory.[23]

After adherents of Confucianism, high-ranking officials in the central government, such as Qi Junzao (祁寯藻 1793–1866), Li Tangjie 李棠階 (1798–1865), and Li Hongzao 李鴻藻 (1820–1897), who shared similar views, served as a counterbalance to government officials who were more inclined toward the West. Although they were not formally organized, they supported conservative arguments. Following the Tianjin Massacre of 1870,[24] these conservatives gained more influence in the central government. Prince Chun—a political opponent of Prince Gong—submitted a memorandum urging that "in the future all matters of defense and foreign policy be discussed in court conferences including officials outside the Zongliyamen."[25] In the increasingly unfavorable atmosphere of Western intrusion, his suggestion was accepted.

In addition, conservative officials strongly opposed the reformers' efforts to build railway lines in China, arguing that there were few economic benefits to be gained and that foreign powers would use the construction for their own economic gain. Reformers like Guo Sung Tao 郭嵩燾 (1818–1891) believed that railway construction could help create new jobs and stimulate the economy, particularly in the mining industry.[26] However, opponents believed that it would lead to the displacement of traditional labor-intensive transportation industries and that it would be detrimental to China's traditional values, such as geomancy. They also feared that railways would make it easier for foreign powers to intervene in times of political turmoil.

Anti-Western feelings of the *qingyi* 清議 (or *ch'ing-i*)—low and middle ranking officials—also emerged in the governmental bureaucracy.[27] As a conservative political organization the *qingyi* stalwarts, by using various vehicles (e.g., official memorials, poems, essays, and folk songs), enshrined lofty Confucian values, while condemning anti-Confucian sentiment.[28] The Confucian motivation of the *qingyi* turned into criticisms of foreign-inspired modernization policies after the Tianjin Massacre.[29] One *qingyi* member requested a policy of war against the French military forces after the Tianjin Massacre.[30] Another *qingyi* member, Zhang Zhidong, advocated war with Russia during the border disputes with Russia in the 1870s.[31] Although their radical and impulsive arguments did not last long, and their political opinions were not heavily represented in making governmental policies, the cumulative effect of the *qingyi* was not negligible. In fact, their vitriolic attack on reformers like Guo Songtao, who showed a favorable attitude toward westernization, resulted in his resignation from office.

The unfavorable diplomatic situation and staunch opposition from conservative officials posed significant obstacles for government officers who led political reforms in late Qing China. The situation worsened with the removal in 1860 of Prince Gong, a reform-minded leader, and the rise of the conservative Empress Dowager–led party.[32] Although the young Guangxu was newly crowned emperor, Empress Dowager Cixi ruled the Qing Empire on behalf of the Guangxu Emperor. The Empress Dowager and Yuan Shikai, who had the support of traditional officials, purged intellectuals

China's Backlash Against the Penetration of the Capitalist World-Economy | 199

who advocated reform, including Kang Youwei 康有為 (1858–1927), Liang Qichao 梁啓超 (1873–1929), Tan Sitong 谭嗣同 (1865–1898), Yang Rui 杨锐 (1857–1898), Lin Xu 林旭 (1875–1898), Liu Guangdi 劉光第 (1861–1898), Kang Guangren 康廣仁 (1867–1898), and Yang Shen Xiu 杨深秀 (1849–1898). They also removed the young Guangxu Emperor, who had designed and led a Hundred Days' reform in 1898, aimed at institutional, educational, and political reforms, including transitioning to a constitutional monarchy.³³ And, in the urgency of the situation, with allied forces marching on the palace in 1900, Cixi allegedly ordered the killing of Guangxu's consort, the Pearl Concubine, by throwing her into a well. In Chinese history, a ruthless monarch, like the Yongle Emperor of the Ming, could sometimes be a charismatic figure who expanded the empire's territory and elevated its authority. Cixi's ruthlessness, however, failed to steer the Qing Empire in the right direction. As mentioned in Chapter 3, one of the causes of the failure of the Self-Strengthening Movement, she diverted funds allocated for improving the Qing navy to build a luxurious summer palace in Beijing between 1886 and 1902.

Under such circumstances, new plans for foreign affairs, such as a new lineup for diplomatic negotiations and Western-related policy directions, were canceled or revised by the traditional Six Boards (*liubu*, 六部). The Zongliyamen's efforts to reform foreign affairs were met with opposition from conservative officials, ultimately leading to the failure of the reform movement. This shift toward conservatism resulted in the strengthening of the political power of Empress Dowager Cixi and her conservative allies.³⁴

I contend that the anti-Western sentiments of government bureaucrats were linked to their deep-rooted allegiance to the traditional social order based on Confucian principles. Despite the fact that this order had lost much of its strength as a result of successive military defeats by colonial powers, these bureaucrats felt compelled to maintain it. However, the incongruity between the behavioral patterns of traditional bureaucrats and the logic of the capitalist world-economy ultimately weakened the Qing regime during its integration into the global economy.³⁵

Gentry and Lower-Class People

In the Ming and Qing eras, the gentry class held significant power over many local communities.³⁶ In principle, the gentry class men comprised both government bureaucrats and degree holders like *shengyuan* (生員) or *jiansheng* (監生) who passed the China's imperial examination. However, in reality, most gentry class men were degree holders who passed the first stage exam. When the number of people in the gentry class grew, while the size of the government bureaucracy was limited in Qing times, the gentry class's role increased in managing and controlling local communities. As Fei Hsiao-Tung noted, "The traditional town is the seat of the gentry."³⁷

Their source of power came from their cultural background and education, which was based on Confucianism. In Pierre Bourdieu's theoretical term, the gentry class members were successful in maintaining and passing down their *cultural capital* stemming from Confucian education and practices. The gentry class's exclusive identity had been retained not only by maintaining their Confucian lifestyle but also by inculcating Confucian ideas in younger generations.[38]

Within Confucianism, of course, different subtypes of disciplines emerged at different times. For instance, scholars in the early Qing reign, stimulated by the maladies of *Yangmingism* (陽明學) and the collapse of the Ming regime, emphasized the need for practical learning embodied in the rise of the evidence movement. The evidence movement in the seventeenth and eighteenth centuries emphasized a sociocultural order based on empirical and inductive research methods. In the reality of the decline of the state during and after the nineteenth century, *kaozheng xue* 考證學 (evidential learning)·was no longer recognized as a discipline capable of reforming reality. Wei Yuan 魏源 (1794–1857), for example, pointed out that *kaozheng xue* was mired in literary minutiae: "After the middle of the Qianlong year, intellectuals from all over the country promoted *kaozheng xue*. This movement was especially prevalent in the Jiangnan region. . . . However, it restricted the thinking of the country's intelligent and talented people and led them down a futile path."[39] Fang Dongshu 方東樹 (1772–1851) noted that few of the hundred suggestions put forward by *kaozheng* scholars actually achieved anything.[40] Wei Yuan and Fang Dongshu criticized *kaozheng xue*, and then, about two hundred years later, historian Ray Huang concluded that *kaozheng* scholars lacked a material environment that enabled them to engage in independent contemplation, and as a result, they were unable to break free from the Confucian social values that had taken root under the rule of the literati bureaucracy.[41] In other words, even if they identified themselves as pragmatists, their values were so closely aligned with Confucian values that they were unable to generate any new currents of thought beyond Confucianism.

In the nineteenth century, as the impact of Western forces shook Chinese society and internal social turmoil intensified, *kaozheng* went into decline. As a result of the decline of *kaozheng* scholarship, the academic community in the Jiangnan region declined, and bureaucrats and intellectuals from Hunan and Guangdong Provinces became prominent. These elites revered traditional *Song Xue* 宋學 (Song dynasty academic thought) rather than *kaozheng* and sought to channel their academic interests in *kaozheng* into moral and social reform. For example, in the mid-nineteenth century, the Hunan scholar and bureaucrat Zeng Guofan was a supporter of *Song Xue*.[42] In other words, while it is true that *kaozheng* was interested in astronomy, mathematics, land reclamation, and science and technology, it was ultimately a current within the Confucian framework, not an intellectual and ideological alternative for a volatile Chinese society that was experiencing unprecedented changes brought about by the West. Rather, many gentry class members who did not find social reform alternatives in *kaozheng* were predisposed to put Confucian ethics ahead of everything else. It naturally could be an absolute and sole criterion when the gentry evaluated and judged

Western culture. In their view, Western culture and its civilization were often worthless to Chinese society.[43]

Looking at it this way, the opposition to Western influence from both conservative government officials and the gentry class had the same underlying motivations. Some Confucian radicals even took it a step further, advocating for the complete exclusion of Western knowledge and religious beliefs from Chinese society. In their view, Christian missionaries were the primary targets of criticism since they not only challenged the social and cultural dominance of the gentry class but also opposed Confucian values and practices, such as ancestor worship. Confucian radicals were alarmed by these extreme ideas and practices of the missionaries and actively resisted their presence, as well as Western culture and commerce.

Then, how did the gentry class's value system clash with those of Westerners, particularly Christian missionaries? It is impossible to answer this question without considering the role of Confucianism in the gentry class. I believe that there were religious doctrines of Confucianism that underpinned their strong anti-Western sentiment. Although not all members of the gentry class considered themselves authentic followers of Confucian ethics, the Confucian value system was crucial to their recognition of material and nonmaterial elements of culture.

Max Weber's idea that "religion is one of the antennae of human sensibility"[44] especially fits the gentry class's epistemological structure and the ways in which they made sense of their social world.[45] In comprehending their religious beliefs, attention to the content of Confucian doctrine is significant because it in itself represents a universal and dominant discourse and furthermore endows the gentry with ideological legitimacy. Judged from a Weberian perspective, Confucianism had "world affirmation,"[46] and Confucian believers in the gentry class tried to establish the ideal world of Confucianism under the guidance of gentlemen (*junzi* 君子).[47] As a result, Confucianism was characterized by a "complete absence of expectations in regard to another world and any compensation there"[48] and the "devout remained oriented fully to mundane, terrestrial life."[49] This predisposed Confucian believers to believe that an ideal world was possible through quality education. In Confucian education, the most important practice was to be a Confucian ideal man, having not only "grace and dignity" but also "ceremonial and ritualist propriety."[50] In China, from the earliest times, there were many Confucian schools and academic conventions intended to discipline and promote Confucian rituals and manners (from "the self-discipline for developing *humaneness* (*jen* 仁)," "filial piety," "marital fidelity," and "noble devotion to our country" to "art collection" and "tea ceremony") because these sociocultural rituals provided followers with formalized acts and a deep-seated sentiment for credence.

Considering that gentry class members were the prime movers of the Confucian moral system and its rituals and one of the last bastions as a transmitter of the Confucian way,[51] many of them had been thoroughly indoctrinated into the Confucian mindset. Such a mindset—the Confucian ideal world can be established in the real world—produced a deification of Confucian values, an aura of exclusiveness, and exclusive, dismissive attitudes to non-Confucian ideas,[52] which ended in a feeling of hostility toward Christian principles and an uncompromising stand against Christian missionaries.[53] The gentry's antipathy to foreigners was most marked in anti-Christian sentiment.[54] Yu Yue 俞樾 (1821–1907), a prominent scholar, and Wang Bingxie 王炳燮 (1823–1874), who once worked on Li Hongzhang's staff, asserted that all that China could get from the West was old and obsolete.[55] Furthermore, because some of Christianity's doctrines ideologically influenced the Taiping Heavenly Rebellion, Chen Baochen 陳宝琛 (1848–1935) believed that Christianity would cause many internal rebellions and disorders in China.[56]

In addition, to maintain their privileged status in society, the gentry class refused to embrace Christianity. They saw the missionaries as a threat to their power and influence because they challenged the gentry's leadership and intellectual authority, disrupted China's social structure, endangered Confucianism, and undermined belief in China as the center of the world. Some missionaries' hostile feelings toward Confucianism and the gentry class fueled anti-Christian sentiment in the gentry class. For instance, William Muirhead of the London Missionary Society argued that "until the incubus of Confucianism is removed, we have no hope in reference to China."[57] One Protestant missionary pointed out the stubborn and conservative attitudes of the gentry and said that "there lies almost nothing but cunning, ignorance, rudeness, vulgarity, obscenity, coupled with superstition, vainglory, arrogant assumption and inveterate hatred of everything foreign."[58]

What was worse, Christian missionaries' penetration into the inland areas had reverberations that shocked gentry-led communities. Unlike Matteo Ricci of the late sixteenth century who visited China to convert the upper classes to his religion,[59] the nineteenth-century Christian missionaries who went to China with merchants tried to convert not only upper-class individuals but also the lower stratum of the literati and the lower class. Under the protection of the treaties, Christian missionaries could make deeper inroads into Chinese society. At the end of the nineteenth century, missionaries began not only to take part in government affairs but also to advise local officials and to get involved in their work. For example, during the 1890s, Timothy Richard, a Baptist missionary, established substantial connections with Chinese officials at both the local and central levels, ultimately playing a role in the Hundred Days' reform.[60] Furthermore, missionaries began to exert an influence on Chinese legal proceedings that were formerly reserved exclusively for the gentry. Indeed, missionaries founded institutions such as orphanages, hospitals, and schools, and supplied diverse social services such as famine and flood relief and medical care.[61] As a result of this, by the year 1870, there were close to four hundred thousand Chinese individuals who had converted to Christianity and 250 Western priests and ministers serving in the church. However, in just fifteen years, this number experienced a significant boost to 558,980 Chinese converts, representing a growth of almost 30 percent. Prior to the onset of the First World War, the number of Chinese Christians continued to rise, reaching an estimated total of 1.5 million.[62]

In general, Chinese gentry looked askance at active proselytizing by Christian missionaries because they were highly concerned about Confucian orthodoxy and local stability being undermined. The deeper the Christian missionaries penetrated into the Chinese mainland, the angrier Chinese gentry members became about the aggressive and dramatic evangelism of the missionaries. For example, missionaries' acquisition of landed property was a cause of disputes between the gentry class and missionaries. The gentry class strongly resisted missionaries' land purchases in China[63] because gentry class members often regarded "building a church" as a fiendish enterprise and thus, they believed, it brought disasters or sinister incidents to their own community.[64] The gentry class, inclined to superstitious beliefs, expressed their hostility by making inflammatory anti-Christian pronouncements and issuing and disseminating anti-Christian manifestos.[65]

The gentry's hostility toward Christianity was not solely due to ideological differences with Christianity, despite the doctrines of Western religions causing some tension. The gentry class primarily clashed with Westerners over socioeconomic interests, as the West's economic and religious influence undermined the gentry's socioeconomic foundation. The gentry—as cultural leaders, Confucian advocates, and conflict mediators—had previously enjoyed socioeconomic and political advantages in local communities with little difficulty. For gentry elites, most of all, the stability of rural areas was important for them to enjoy "tax privileges on their landed property." Based on this stability, they "could easily expand their holdings and became the dominant landholders, living on fixed rent collected from tenants."[66] However, the entry of the West in China destabilized local communities due to the movement of peasants from the hinterlands to port cities or overseas, for example, as Chinese coolies. This caused a population decrease and changes in the economic environment in local communities. Furthermore, the massive influx of opium brought into China through foreign trade led to a significant outflow of silver, which caused an increase in the value of silver within China. As a result of this opium trade, southern China experienced a scarcity of silver, which had a detrimental effect on the region's economic stability. The opium trade expanded at an alarming rate, including through illicit smuggling, putting the health of individuals from all levels of society in danger. People from Canton, who had easy access to opium, were vulnerable to addiction. It is reasonable to assume that the health of Cantonese people exposed to opium deteriorated due to the physical harm that opium causes to the addicts' bodies or the way it worsens their mental health.[67]

The Chinese gentry believed that the socioeconomic decline of China was caused by the presence of Westerners in the country. As a response to colonial powers' political and economic interventions, the gentry initiated resistance movements. One notable example is the anti-Western movement led by the gentry in Canton, which was characterized by military conflicts between the British army's regular troops and two distinct types of gentry-led anti-Western movements. The first type was led by intermediary gentry class members such as Yang Yongyan (楊永衍 1818–1903) and Kong Jixun (孔繼勳 1792–1842), who acted as mediators between the local government and gentry militias. They donated funds to the local government, but they also provided the gentry militias with critical military intelligence.[68] The second type was characterized by rural leaders and gentry militias autonomously organizing military groups and participating in local defense missions. Even though their military organizations were not sanctioned by the central government, they played a crucial role in the anti-Western movements by providing insurgents with collective and social ideology and taking part in armed exercises.[69]

The gentry militia's armed conflicts with the West reached a culmination in 1841. The so-called Sanyuanli Incident of 1841 showed how both the gentry militia and local citizens successfully resisted the British army.[70] Thousands of lightly armed gentry militia members and local citizens besieged a British military force, killing four British soldiers. Obviously, this was interpreted as a skirmish from the point of view of the British army, but it was a watershed event in modern China because it ignited the antiforeign movement and provided an all-too-rare moment of success for gentry militia and local citizens' military operations in China.[71] This successful military movement even gained the attention of foreign countries: "At least in the Southern provinces, the mass of people takes an active, nay, a fanatical part in the struggle against the foreigners. They poison the bread of the European community at Hong Kong."[72] Following the Sanyuanli Incident Cantonese people's antiforeignism became widely known, including among Englishmen.

Such gentry-led antiforeign movements spread like wildfire in Canton and Guangdong Provinces. *The Chinese Repository*, an English language journal for Protestant missionaries published in Canton, described Canton's antiforeign movements as follows:

> Early in the evening, the British flag-staff was set on fire, and burning upwards till the whole was on fire; a shout from the mob when it fell told their triumph. Meanwhile the British factor was fired, and the verandah, chapel-belfry and skylight were soon burning furiously.[73]

> *"Shat fan-Kuei, ta fan-Kuei"* (kill the foreign devils, beat the foreign devils), rang and re-echoed through all the streets in the vicinity of the foreign factories. Hundreds of the basest of men were already collected and many hundreds more were hastening to the scene of riot.[74]

> The gentry and elders of San-yuan-li, Nan-ngan, and other villages ninety-two in number, assembled at the Shing-ping shie-hioh, hereby declare the impossibility of living under the same heavens with the English rebels, and swear to destroy them.[75]

The first two news articles reveal that Canton's antiforeign movements were nonanecdotal, and the last news article shows that the gentry had a strong aversion to the entry of the British and took the lead in antiforeign movements.

In addition, the gentry circulated pamphlets that portrayed the missionaries as lacking originality, being malevolent, and immoral. One of the most widely known works denouncing Christianity, *Death Blow to Corrupt Doctrines*, was written by gentry members. In this book, the gentry criticized Christianity for disregarding ancestor worship and imperial authority: "The Christian religion, in not allowing divine honors to the tablets of emperors and ancestors, and forbidding to sacrifice to deceased parents, most certainly seeks to abolish under heaven the relations which men sustain to the emperor and to parents."[76]

If the gentry's anti-Western movements occurred as a response to the cultural-ideological challenges of Western missionaries and the politico-economic penetrations of the colonial powers, the lower class's anti-Western movements occurred due mainly to anti-Christian sentiment. The lower class, which had steadfast traditional values and conservative instincts, tended to have antipathy toward the aggressive and dominant mindset of Christian evangelism, which in China, in the view of lower class, was not unlike imperial expansion.[77] Of course, Chinese attitudes toward Westerners, sometimes combined with superstition, became more hostile toward foreign missionaries. Isabella Bird Bishop, who traveled through Chinese inland areas along the Yangtze River in the late nineteenth century, noted that "slanders against the missionaries were circulated and believed, and the special one that they stole and ate infants, or used their eyes and hearts for medicines, was disagreeably current in Kuan Hsien."[78] Nevertheless, the reason why the lower classes were so exclusionary and aggressive toward missionaries was that they were bound by long-standing traditional customs and the Confucian order.[79] As such, they did not look favorably upon the arrival of foreign missionaries in their communities and feared them.

Furthermore, the overly confident and sometimes arrogant activities and colonial mindset of foreign missionaries caused great resentment among the lower classes. In fact, one aggressive Christian missionary, Sherwood Eddy, who touted the slogan "the Evangelization of the world in this generation," insisted that China was a primary target for missionary work.[80] Furthermore, Christian missionaries advocated for the Opium Wars under the pretext of the spread of Christian virtue.[81] Karl Gützlaff, a Protestant missionary who was allied with the British government, was in charge of interpretation services during the First Opium War and signed the treaty thereafter.[82] Some missionaries even identified themselves as having the mindset of merchants.[83] Charles Denby, an American minister and a defender of commercial expansion, contended that "missionaries are the pioneers of trade and commerce. The missionary, inspired by holy zeal, goes everywhere, and by degrees foreign commerce and trade follow."[84] Lurking beneath the aggressive attitude of Western missionaries to some degree was a desire for Western economic encroachment.[85]

Such hidden motives behind the propagation of Christianity brought on a growing antipathy toward foreign missionaries. Soon after the Treaty of Shimonoseki was signed, anti-Christian sentiment spread in southwest China; a massive anti-Christian riot occurred in Chengdu and violence spread to the west and south of Sichuan Province. In August 1895, the *zhaijiao* 齋教 group started an anti-Christian riot at *Gutian* 古田 in Fujian Province. The so-called Kucheng Massacre caused quite a number of missionary casualties. The *New York Times* reported that "the Rev. Dr. Stewart and his wife and one child were burned to death in their house. The Misses Yellow and Marshall, the two Misses Saunders, the two Misses Gordon, and Miss Newcombe were murdered with spears and swords. Miss Codrington was seriously wounded about the head. This dispatch confirms the report that the Rev. H. S. Phillips and Dr. Gregory of Hartford escaped. Both of them were wounded."[86] The Boxer movement arose from hostility toward Christianity, though it had other causes such as rural poverty and conflicts between landlords and tenants. The Boxer Uprising in the late 1890s was triggered by the Society of the Divine Word's aggressive missionary activities in Shandong Province. The primary targets of the Boxer movement were foreign religions, missionaries, and Chinese converts rather than foreign economic imperialism.[87] Despite repeated riots by the lower class in many rural areas, local government officials were inattentive to the growing violence (e.g., personal injuries and property damage) against missionaries.[88] Goaded by public agitation, some Christian missionaries consequently had to leave the Chinese mainland.

Coolies

The emergence of coolie labor played a significant role in China's incorporation process, which involved socioeconomic changes and the expansion of the international division of labor system. The importance of coolie migration in this process is widely recognized. Nevertheless, within Chinese incorporation studies, coolies' resistance movements have been disregarded or viewed as an incidental event or at best an epiphenomenal indicator of more fundamental resistance movements. The assumption, implicitly or explicitly, behind such reasoning is that coolies' resistance movements occurred outside of China. Unlike this approach, I examine coolies' resistance movements as an important antisystemic movement to capitalist logics.

Resistance Within Chinese Territory

Before I analyze the resistant movements of Chinese coolies, I will briefly explain the poor reputation of Westerners associated with coolie trade increased in nineteenth-century China and how it affected the formation of antipathy toward the oppressive nature of coolie labor and the coolie trade in Chinese society. Since the 1840s, bad rumors about coolies like "the white barbarians of Cuba not only abused the Chinese but ate them as well"[89] or "white people beat Chinese peoples and took them by force" began to circulate. Although the former turned out to be false, the latter—nefarious activities in recruiting Chinese coolies like breaches of contract, an increase in deceptions (including subterfuges), kidnapped victims, and involuntary emigration hiding in the coolie trades—turned out to be true. After that, coolie-related business brought about popular indignation in China. The resistance movements to the coolie trade rose up in cities and their adjoining districts where coolie-trade crimes were prevalent. Hostile feelings toward the coolie trade in Chinese society greatly increased, especially in port cities.

Case 1

Opposition to the coolie trade arose first in Xiamen, the place where the nineteenth-century Chinese coolie trade began. Xiamen had six coolie trading companies (Messrs Tait & Co 德記洋行, Hyde, Hodge & Co 海德洋行, Tait & Co. 德記洋行, Turner & Co 杜勒洋行, Robert & Co. 捷記洋行, and Smeird & Co 沙米爾德洋行), five of which were British-owned companies.[90] Around 1850, coolie recruitment was actively carried out in Xiamen by the coolie trade companies. Coolie labor was unfair and illegal, and hostility toward the coolie trade in the local community increased.

In 1852, after hearing the news that more than eight thousand coolie workers were needed in Cuba, coolie recruiters in China committed numerous illegal acts, including drafting fake contracts, to find new Chinese workers in Xiamen. When this happened, local residents in Xiamen showed strong hostility to the coolie recruitment activities and the coolie trade, and several placards were put up in protest. In November 1852, a coolie recruiter working for Syme, Muir, and Company was arrested by Chinese local authorities on charges of kidnapping while recruiting coolies. Immediately, Syme, Muir, and Company helped the arrested coolie recruiter escape from the local authority's prison.[91] Upon hearing the news, local people in Xiamen were furious and staged a protest. At that time, local residents' demonstrations reached the point of destroying the camp where the coolie workers were temporarily housed. Protesters stormed the camp several times and threw stones at the soldiers defending the camp. During the protest, two British soldiers were attacked, one of whom was seriously injured. When news of the riot became known to British army units, who were anchored nearby, they dispatched marines under the justification of protecting the lives and property of the British. British marines opened fire on the demonstrators, killing eleven or twelve Chinese demonstrators and injuring dozens. The demonstrators disbanded.[92]

Case 2

Opposition to the coolie trade reached a peak in Guangzhou. Even before overcoming the pain of defeat in the First Opium War, the locals of Guangzhou were enraged by the growing number of coolie abductions. Local residents of Guangzhou resorted to collective violence against the kidnappers, those who hired the kidnappers, or those suspected of being kidnappers. "Several known kidnappers were murdered in the streets by the mob of Canton."[93] Furthermore, in April 1859, the Chinese merchant community in Guangzhou made an official request to foreign consuls to urge an end to the coolie kidnapping. In January 1858, foreign allied commanders concerned about the safety of the Guangzhou area issued a decree to stop the kidnapping of coolies; nonetheless, as coolie abductions continued, allied commanders pressed local governments to legalize Chinese emigration. Judging that these commanders were of little help, Bo Gui 柏貴 (1793–1859), governor of the province of Guangdong, declared that if the kidnappers were caught, they would be put to death, and if anyone captured the kidnappers and brought them to the government office, he (or she) would earn a reward of $40.[94]

Case 3

Resistance to the coolie trade spread to Shanghai. The coolie trade was expanded in Shanghai when it was reborn as an international commercial center. Due mainly to the inhumane and illegal acts carried out against coolies, the residents of Shanghai had a great antipathy to the coolie trade. For example, in April 1858 two French ships carrying Chinese coolies, the Admiral Baudin and Indien, left Shanghai and sailed for the French colonies of Martinique and Guadeloupe. And in July of the same year, another French ship, the Gertrude, was moored in the Wusong area of Shanghai to pick up Chinese coolies. However, the Chinese coolies who had previously boarded the vessel attempted to escape. The sailors immediately opened fire on the fleeing coolies, killing and drowning about forty Chinese coolies. When the dead bodies of the coolies floated in the river, the people of the area were horrified and realized that those who had done this were connected to the coolie trade. The residents of Shanghai were furious. About five thousand of them armed with clubs and knives attacked two British sailors, mistaking them for coolie ship sailors, resulting in one British sailor being killed and another seriously injured. Horatio N. Ray, an inspector of China Maritime Customs, and Reverend John Hobson, a missionary, tried to restrain the crowd. However, the excited crowd became angry at the intervention of the inspector and missionary, and even used violence against them. As a result, Horatio N. Ray was stabbed several times and Reverend John Hobson was severely beaten.[95] Hostility toward foreigners grew. According to Shanghai officials, foreigners pretended to treat the Chinese in a friendly and favorable way, but their real purpose was exactly the opposite: they were dedicated to inveigling and entrapping Chinese laborers into the slave market. For example, a government official of Shanghai insisted that one should "let the people of towns and villages with joint effort and united heart set upon and kill every foreigner that is associated with natives professing his doctrine in the teaching of religion, that the kidnapping of men may be put a stop to."[96] It was against this background of a sense of common danger that the coolies' resistance movement was launched, because, for Chinese citizens, the increase in Chinese coolies produced by coercive and violent mechanisms was seen as a new threat to social security.

Yet, resistance activities extended beyond antipathy to the illegal and inhumane coolie trade and coolie recruitment that took place in Chinese territory. This is because Chinese coolies raised their voices themselves and continued to fight against the terrible working conditions as well as the hard and long voyage.

Resistance Outside Chinese Territory

In chapter 2, I argued that the rise of the Chinese coolie is one piece of evidence to confirm China's incorporation process and suggested that their overseas migration and contract labor in migrant areas needs to be understood within the logic of the capitalist world-system. Capitalist production, which entails an endless process of capital accumulation, does not eliminate the effective labor exploitation mechanism, as the axial division of labor involving integrated production processes is necessary to identify a system that is capitalistic in nature.[97] The rise of Chinese coolies during this period, resulting from a significant transition from slavery-based labor to Chinese coolies on global plantations, played a crucial role in extending and developing the global network of labor exploitation. Coolie manpower was geared toward the cultivation of export-oriented crops like sugar.

Although coolie labor appeared to have fewer constraints than slavery due to its fixed-term labor agreement, it was actually a more intricate form of labor exploitation. This was due to several factors. First, the use of coolie labor did not lead to any improvement in working conditions or a reduction in working hours since there were limited labor-saving technologies or machinery available. On the contrary, coolies were subjected to harsh and inhumane working conditions with long hours of grueling labor and poor sanitary conditions. Chinese coolies were required to work either seven or nine hours each day and work for three hundred sixty days a year. Furthermore, if they were unable to work the full number of hours stipulated in their contract, they could be detained at the end of their contract to make up for the shortfall, and even punished physically.[98]

The absence of legal safeguards for most Chinese coolies working on plantations is the second issue. Although the coolie contract regulations were put in place to safeguard the rights of coolie workers, such as the right to work freely, the recognition of personal property, and a system for reporting labor violations, they were hardly ever enforced. These rules, which aimed to secure workers' rights, were essentially useless; historian Evelyn Hu-Dehart refers to them as "a mere piece of paper."[99] Given that there were few protection laws for coolie laborers, labor contracts paradoxically were an effective legal device to bind coolies to the plantations.

The third issue is that Western merchants, along with Chinese crimps, utilized deceitful tactics toward Chinese laborers, making it difficult to detect the exploitation of coolie labor once a contract was established. Western merchants purposely withheld information about the harsh working conditions on the plantations, preventing Chinese laborers from fully comprehending the challenges of coolie labor. By providing incomplete information on coolie labor and working conditions, these merchants shifted all the associated risks of coolie contracts onto the coolies themselves. As a result of facing coercive and cunning labor exploitation tactics, Chinese coolies were left with no choice but to resist.[100]

The resistance movements of Chinese coolies had two key characteristics. First, the geographical scope of these movements extended beyond China's borders, as coolie migration was widespread across the world. Second, the ultimate target of the coolies' resistance movement was the brutal and predatory capitalist mechanism in that the trans-societal world-economy led by colonial powers forced Chinese coolies to comply with the mechanisms of the international division of labor system.

Not only was Chinese society hostile to the coercion embedded in coolie-related business, but Chinese coolies also tenaciously resisted the international coolie trade. The prevalence of their resistance movements was the highest outside China, in that the spatial boundary of the resistance movements was not limited to Chinese territory. It even took place on coolie ships. In spite of the fact that various types of coolie mutiny cannot be generalized as a unified resistance formation, a typical resistance method of the coolies was arson on the voyage.[101] This news article in the *Hong Kong Daily Press* showed that Chinese coolies often set fires on the ship when they resisted:

> Another of those terrible tragedies which are constantly taking place in connection with Macao coolie trade, has to be recorded. It will be recollected that the Chief-Justice recently alluded to the ship *Dolores Ugarte*, which has been taking in a cargo of coolies at Macao. This vessel, it appeared, sailed on the 4th instant with 665 coolies on board, and two days afterwards it was burnt to the water's edge within twelve hours sail of Hong Kong, the current opinion being that the vessel was set on fire by the coolies. The crew and eight coolies escaped to Macao in the boats and fifty other coolies were rescued by a junk and brought on to Hong Kong.[102]

Although not all coolie mutinies were identical, Jiali Peng's comprehensive study identified multiple types of Chinese coolie incidents (see appendix 1). Interestingly, Peng's study found that some mutinies were well organized and prepared. In the case of well-structured coolie incidents, each coolie had systemic and tactical resistance behaviors to increase the associated power of collective behaviors.

Various explanations have been offered for why rebellions occurred on coolie ships: panic among coolies, the anger of coolies at coercive and deceptive contracts, or the deprivation of liberty. However, the main cause of coolie mutinies was the high mortality rate, which was between 25 and 30 percent during the first fifteen years of the coolie trade. Statistical data shows the number of coolies that died on various voyages, such as that of a British ship in 1856 that left Hong Kong with 332 workers, of which 128 died on the way to Cuba, while on another British ship, carrying 298 workers to Peru, 135 Chinese workers died that same year. In 1872, on a Peruvian ship carrying 739 Chinese workers to Peru, 192 coolies died en route[103] (see figure 5.1).

The transport of Chinese coolies to Europe's colonial plantations was ongoing during the nineteenth century, with the global economic system's expansion into China. However, the maritime transport system used was similar to that of slave transport, and some ships used were originally ships that transported enslaved Africans.[104] On the voyage, coolies were treated as de facto slaves and crammed into the coolie ships.[105] Limited space and overcrowding led to the rapid spread of contagious diseases, resulting in high mortality rates. Some coolies, faced with inhumane treatment, even committed suicide. Consequently, there were widespread rumors about the high mortality rate on the ships, and many coolies were deeply fearful before embarking. This fear ultimately led to mutiny. For the coolies, a mutiny was not a fight for labor rights or better living conditions, but rather a desperate struggle for survival.

Figure 5.1. The death rate of coolies on ships at sea, 1847–1873. *Source*: Created by the author, based on Jiali Peng 彭家禮, "Shijiu Shiji Xifang Qinluezhe Dui Zhongguo Lugong Di Lulue" 十九世纪西方侵略者对中国劳工的掳掠 [The seizure of Chinese labor by Western invaders in the nineteenth century]," in *Huagong Chuguo Shi Ziliao Huibian* 華工出國史料匯編 [Collection of historical documents concerning the emigration of Chinese laborers], vol. 4, ed. Chen Hansheng 陈翰笙 (Zhonghua Shuju, 1981), 207.

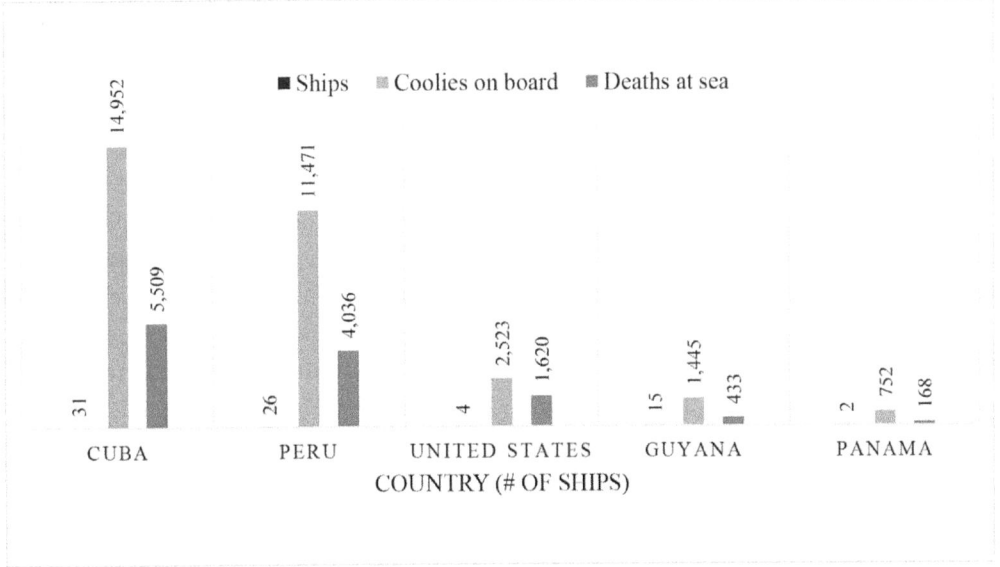

Coolies not only resisted on the coolie ships but also led resistance movements on the plantations. Upon arrival at the plantations, coolies were severely restricted in their movements and the plantation managers used the courts to maintain discipline.[106] The managers used whips to coerce coolies into working harder[107] and to obtain their unquestioning obedience. The primary aim of coolie discipline was to enforce longer working hours. Chinese coolies had a hard time adjusting to the unfamiliar and difficult training they had to undergo before beginning work on the plantations, where they faced much harsher working conditions. An 1876 official report by a Chinese government commission revealed the exploitation of coolies on Cuban plantations:

> The labor, too, on the plantations is shown to be excessively severe, and the food to be insufficient; the hours of labor are too long, and the chastisements by rods, whips, chains, stocks, &c., &c., productive of suffering and injury. During the past years a large number have been killed by blows, have died from the effects of wounds and have hanged themselves, cut their throats, poisoned themselves with opium, and thrown themselves into wells and sugar caldrons. It was also possible to verify by personal inspection wounds inflicted upon others, the fractured and maimed limbs, blindness, the heads full of sores, the teeth struck out, the ears mutilated, and the skin and flesh lacerated, proofs of cruelty to the eyes of all.[108]

To begin with, Chinese coolies resorted to running away from the plantations as a means of resistance. Since they lacked any bargaining power to protect themselves against the inhumane working conditions, escaping from their workplaces became their only option. This resulted in a high number of identified fugitive coolies in late nineteenth-century Cuba. Some of these fugitives even joined antigovernmental organizations and engaged in fighting against the Cuban government. The situation became so severe that in 1870 the Cuban government took action to suppress the growth of the Chinese coolie population in Cuba. One of the measures taken was the immediate deportation of Chinese immigrants who did not possess letters of domicile in Cuba.

Other forms of resistance employed by Chinese coolies were to commit suicide, refuse to work, and sometimes even engage in strikes. As Philip Kuhn points out, some of the unlucky Chinese workers who went to Peru had to collect guano along the coast.[109] This was a dangerous and painful task; many felt they had no choice but to commit suicide. Equally devastating was coolies' opium dependence. Many Chinese coolies who had difficulty in hard labor and homesickness became addicted to opium because it made tolerable the physical pain of hard labor and alleviated emotional distress.[110] The most extreme act of resistance was murder: "A Chinaman in some altercation stabbed the overseer of the estate; the populace seized him likewise and committed him to the flames."[111] Considering that this is a brief report, it is difficult to completely understand the coolie's murder case. Nonetheless, what is clear is that the news—murder by a Chinese coolie—sent shock waves through plantation society.

Despite infrequent murders of overseers most coolies' resistance movements were concentrated on self-defense. Anxious to protect themselves, coolies tried to escape from harsh working conditions and from coolie ships. If they did not succeed, they committed suicide or sometimes murder. Unlike the nineteenth-century Chinese coolies who migrated to Southeast Asia, coolies moved to Cuba and Peru had to pioneer everything from scratch given that there were no existing Chinese networks.[112] This led to a situation in which the first generation of Chinese workers had to endure all the economic, social, cultural, and emotional difficulties and trauma,[113] which sometimes brought about extreme forms of resistance.

Concluding Remarks: Three Different Paths of Resistance

As China became increasingly integrated into the global capitalist system, there was a rise in the number of Chinese coolies, proto-capitalists, proto-proletariats, and state apparatuses that conformed to the evolving world order based on capitalism. However, traditional Chinese society also tried to protect itself from the destructive and coercive forces of the capitalist system. In light of this, I will compare and contrast three different paths of resistance taken by China.

Conservative government officials led a campaign against the West to safeguard the traditional political system. Both high-ranking and low- to middle-ranking officials opposed the westernization promoted by the Zongliyamen. These conservative elites aimed to preserve the China-centered world order and rejected Western-oriented reforms. As they sought to maintain the ancien régime to uphold social stability and Confucian political ethics, reform movements were viewed as akin to invading forces. To protect the Qing Empire's "self-conscious political community,"[114] conservative bureaucrats decried reform-minded Confucian scholars.

The Zongliyamen faced criticism from conservative officials who opposed its promotion of Western-oriented diplomacy and believed it undermined China's traditional political order. These officials sought to weaken the Zongliyamen's influence, viewing it as a betrayal of China's superior position in diplomatic relations. Their resistance movements ultimately led to the decline of the Zongliyamen. Despite causing conflicts and political divisions between reform-minded officials and conservative officials, the conservative officials' resistance movements were successful in achieving their goals.

The gentry class also opposed the infiltration of the capitalist world-economy in political, cultural, and military terms, and they were regarded as another resistance group. As they were staunch defenders of Confucian values and the traditional order, they vigorously expressed anti-Christian sentiments,[115] particularly after the mid-nineteenth century. Thus, it was not unexpected for them to actively participate in resistance movements as they were the guardians of local areas who organized gentry militias. In some cases, they were able to achieve success, such as in the Sanyuanli Incident, by receiving strong support from the local people. Their resistance movements sometimes led to military conflicts with colonial powers, indicating that they, with the support of local citizens, engaged in fierce battles against the colonial powers.[116]

The cultural capital of Confucian ethics was shared by both the governmental bureaucrats and the gentry class, but their relationship became increasingly strained. Interestingly, the gentry class began to distance itself from the Qing bureaucracy after the devastating defeats of the two Opium Wars, despite their long-standing collaboration under the early and mid-Qing regime. Having experienced the Opium Wars, some bureaucrats realized that the empire's technological and military power was inferior to that of the colonial powers. The more they were afraid of the scientific and military superiority of colonial powers, the less they criticized them. Such a fainthearted response alienated many of the anti-Western gentry. Against this backdrop, some of the local gentry took collective actions. They began to criticize central authorities and organize local representative assemblies. However, given that the politicization of the gentry class was not pertinent to the direction of the Qing's political reform, the protection of national interests in response to the predatory penetrations of the West, or the political reform model, but turned into the pursuit of their own privileges,[117] it resulted in deepening divisions and social unrest.

Relationships between the state elites and the gentry class were further strained by racial conflicts between Manchus and Han Chinese.[118] Anti-Western movements were partly influenced by these racial conflicts, which led radical Han Chinese elites to challenge the legitimacy of Qing authorities.

Coolies, unlike state elites and the gentry class, lacked political and social power to resist the penetration of the capitalist world-economy's international division of labor system into China. They were vulnerable as Western merchants recruited or kidnapped them without any protection from the Chinese government. Moreover, their resistance often took place outside Chinese territory, leaving them with no support they could call on. Consequently, their resistance was mainly carried out through individual actions. Coolies' resistance aimed to secure their survival and liberate themselves from labor exploitation, which led to extreme resistance methods. While some of their resistance resulted in success, it often came at the cost of opponents' deaths, while others resulted in coolies' deaths and most ended in failure.

Overall, the resistance movements of the different groups toward colonial powers' penetration took on diverse forms, with varying processes, objectives, and outcomes, depending on the resources available for their resistance and the circumstances they faced.

Table 5.1. Typology of Three Resistance Movements to the Colonial Powers

Source of resistance	Mobilization of resources	Process	Aims	Result
Government officials	Political power	Power struggles in central bureaucracy	Blocking Western-oriented reforms	Success
Gentry class	Cultural capital and hegemonic leadership in local communities	— Development of local-based military forces — Combined with lower class	— Anti–Western civilization — Objection to Western missionaries	Partial success
Coolies	Individualized abilities	Escape, suicide, murder, mutiny	— Survival — Extrication from labor exploitation	Failure including coolies' deaths

Conclusion

The Development and Outcomes of China's Incorporation Process

East-West relations over the past 500 years present two main puzzles. The first concerns the extraordinary geographical expansion of the European system of states. By 1850 or shortly before, that system had come to encompass the entire globe, thereby reducing the China-centered tribute-trade system to a regional subsystem of a now European-centered global economy. What is most puzzling about this tendency—which is what we shall understand by "the rise of the West"—are its modest origins. On the eve of its first major expansion across the Atlantic and around the Cape in the late fifteenth century, the European system of states was a peripheral and chaotic component of a global economy that had long been centered on Asia. In spite of this first expansion, two centuries later no European or American state had managed to create within its domains a national economy that could match the size, complexity and prosperity of the Chinese economy. And yet, within the short span of another century, tiny "Great" Britain was poised to incorporate within its domains the entire Indian subcontinent, and then, in cooperation and competition with other Western powers, to turn China from the center into a peripheral component of the global economy. How can we explain this turnaround?

—Giovanni Arrighi, Po-keung Hui, Ho-fung Hung,
and Mark Selden, "Historical Capitalism, East and West"

Arrighi, Hui, Hung, and Selden pose intriguing questions about why the Qing Empire suddenly went from a path of prosperity to a path of decline during the nineteenth century and how China entered and became a part of the capitalist world-economy. In response to the former question, Fairbank affirmed Liang Qichao's perspective and briefly concluded as follows: "To understand the collapse one must appreciate the earlier success, for it had been so great that China's leaders were unprepared for disaster."[1] Nevertheless, as discussed in the introduction, issues related to the unprecedented and rapid decline of late imperial China remain controversial and have become one of the biggest debates in modern Chinese history; this decline continues to fascinate researchers today. Compared to the first question, however, the second question—How did late imperial China came to be part of the capitalist world-system?—has received much less attention in historical sociology and history. The first and second questions are not disconnected. In order to provide a reasonable and convincing answer to the second question, it must be viewed in conjunction with the first: The sudden decline of China in the nineteenth century and its incorporation into the capitalist world-system are inextricably linked.

In this conclusion, I will revisit the traces of China's incorporation process to reilluminate the significance of a new world-systems method—incorporating dynamics. This methodological approach enables us, first, to provide a new account of the unprecedented historical events of nineteenth-century China. Second, I will discuss the outcomes of China's incorporation process. Finally, I will examine how China's incorporation process is at least partially linked to China's transition to capitalism.

A New Approach to China's Incorporation

My analysis of the China's incorporation process started by discussing the effectiveness of the world-systems approach. In order not to subsume this approach in the welter of historical complexities, while shedding a new light on nineteenth-century China's history, I used world-systems analysis. In chapter 1 I introduced new approaches—incorporating dynamics—to analyze China's multilayered and interwoven processes of change. The use of incorporating dynamics helps to create some reasonably complex incorporation studies. By using incorporating dynamics I analyze some important but unelucidated historical events that occurred during and after the incorporation process. For example, incorporating dynamics enables us to examine city-hinterland relationships that were difficult to confirm or impossible to study with the past world-systems methods of Wallerstein and McMichael; incorporating dynamics is sensitive to the relation between parts within the whole. If we take nineteenth-century China's export-oriented commodity production and the export of these goods as a telltale sign of China's incorporation process into the capitalist world-system, we may focus on the interconnections between cities (part 1) and hinterlands (part 2) that reach beyond the boundary of a single city (or area). Specifically, relationships between Shanghai and its hinterlands show how China's production of export commodities connected port cities and their hinterlands. Shanghai was a perfect place for transshipment. During the Treaty Port Era (1870–1925), "the heart of foreign trade is Shanghai."[2] Given that Shanghai was close to the major silk-producing areas in the lower Yangtze basin and tea cultivation areas in the mountains or hills of southern China, many Western merchants regarded Shanghai as the most important transshipment point. This means that the hinterlands of Shanghai specialized in producing export commodities, whereas Shanghai focused more on transshipments destined for foreign markets. Shanghai, in its capacity as a transshipment hub, played a significant role in exporting Chinese goods to the international commercial network; Shanghai was also connected to its hinterlands under the influence of the capitalist world-economy.

Furthermore, the incorporating dynamics in this book allow us to see how national or regional changes combine within the capitalist world-system. The unprecedented transformation of Chinese society in the nineteenth century was brought about by the penetration of two different kinds of colonial powers. One was the European powers centered on Britain and France (part 1), and the other was the Pacific powers centered on Japan, Russia, and the United States (part 2). While the European powers exerted enormous influence mainly in the first and middle periods of China's incorporation process, the Pacific powers became involved in China's incorporation process since the mid and late periods. I call this the plurality of foreign powers. For instance, the British-led opium trade played a crucial role in opening China's doors and compelled China to grow crops for export, especially tea. On the other hand, the unprecedented transformation of Manchuria shows how Russia and Japan became deeply involved in the incorporation of China. From the mid-nineteenth century Manchuria's primary agricultural product, soybeans, was transformed into an export-oriented crop, and Manchuria's major cities were turned into modernized and capitalist spaces.

I also refer to the competition between European and Pacific powers within China's incorporation process as the competition between European and Pacific powers for China's resources. There were sharp conflicts between these powers over railway concessions. The Qing government had been attempting to construct railways since the late nineteenth century as part of its reform project, but due to financial difficulties it was forced to grant concessions to colonial powers in exchange for foreign loans. European powers, such as France, England, and Germany, as well as Pacific powers, including Russia, Japan, and the United States, were in fierce competition to secure these concessions from the Qing government.

Incorporating dynamics not only identifies how parts are connected in the transnational dynamics of the capitalist world-system but also how the connections and combinations of parts affect the maintenance, change, and development of the capitalist world-system. So how did China's incorporation into the capitalist world-system change the dynamics of the capitalist world-system in the nineteenth century? First, China's incorporation into the capitalist world-system changed international relations between China and its neighbors. The tributary system that had been centered on China until the nineteenth century collapsed, and China's influence over its neighboring tributaries declined. The collapse of the tributary system due to China's incorporation into the capitalist world-system left areas that were once tributaries of China vulnerable to invasion by colonial powers. As a result, the Ryukyu Kingdom became a part of Japan, and Korea experienced Japanese colonization and was incorporated into the capitalist world-system.[3]

Second, China's incorporation into the capitalist world-system allows us to see the emergence of the Pacific powers (United States, Japan, and Russia), which was a foreshadowing of the long-term rise of the Asia-Pacific world. Since its incorporation into the capitalist world-system in the eighteenth century, Russia steadily increased its influence in the Asia-Pacific region. While Russia maintained equal relations with Western Europe, it also exerted considerable influence over its neighbors, consolidating its geopolitical dominance. The Crimean War (1853–1856), albeit unsuccessfully, provides an indication of the extent of Nicholas I (1796–1855)'s expansionism at the time and the extent to which Russia was recognized as a military power in Europe.[4] As Wallerstein notes, in fact, Russia was intent on consolidating its control and influence over southeastern Europe, the Black Sea, and the Caucasus region.[5] Moreover, in the nineteenth century, Russia was eager to expand into Asia and it engaged in the Great Game with Britain over control of Central and South Asia. The Trans-Siberian Railway was a major national project that marked Russia's expansion into the Asia-Pacific region in the nineteenth century. From the first meeting of the Russian Railroad Committee on December 10, 1892, plans for the Trans-Siberian Railway were drawn up, and the construction of the railway was carried out simultaneously in different regions. After the completion of the Trans-Siberian Railway, industrial development occurred along the railroad in the eastern Siberian region, and the dramatic increase in rail transportation capacity facilitated Russian foreign trade. The construction of the railroad led to the parallel development of industries related to the railroad (e.g., metallurgy, the iron and steel industry, and the machinery industry) and extensive migration to eastern Siberia. In other words, the Trans-Siberian Railway not only strengthened the economic, cultural, and social connections between the east and west of Russia; it also enhanced Russia's capital accumulation. Furthermore, in the late nineteenth century, Russia's push into the frontier regions of the Qing Empire resulted in significant territorial gains for Russia at the expense of the Qing. Russian expansion toward China was later than the major European powers, including Britain. Yet Nikolai Muraviev (1850–1908), governor general of the Russian Far East in the late nineteenth century, carried out a bold and aggressive expansionist policy that resulted in the acquisition of huge territories from the Qing Empire. Russia's expansion into the Amur and Ussuri regions was primarily motivated by the need to gain access to the Pacific Ocean. The Amur and Ussuri regions were the gateway to the Pacific Ocean for Russia, which had lost the Crimean War. To accomplish this, the Russian government built a large Russian settlement along the Ussuri River and promoted Vladivostok as an important strategic hub. As a result, Russia emerged as a state with a stronger state capacity than other regions incorporated during the same period (e.g., West Africa, the Ottoman Empire, the Indian subcontinent) and as a geopolitical power in the Asia-Pacific region.

In the late nineteenth century the rise of another important Pacific power, Japan, was an important counterweight to European power in the Asia-Pacific region. Even before the Meiji Restoration in the mid-nineteenth century, Japan's Tokugawa shogunate had been keenly observing the imperialist aggression of major colonial powers. The frequent presence of Russians on Sakhalin and Hokkaido Islands, the borderlands between Russia and Japan in the late eighteenth century, and the Opium War in China in 1840 led Japanese intellectuals to warn of a crisis facing Japan. A young intellectual named Fujita Yukoku (1774–1826), writing to the daimyo, said: "In the north, there is a cunning country called Russia, which aims to usurp Japan and is always planning to go south."[6] With regard to world affairs, Aizawa Yasushi (1782–1863) pointed out that the world was no different from the Warring States period that China had experienced in the past.[7] Although there was a heightened sense of crisis, there were various options promoted within Japan (such as a closed-door policy, the expulsion of the foreigners, and an open-door policy) regarding the outlook of the world situation and the response to foreign intrusion. Soon after, however, with the outbreak of the Opium War in China (1840–1842) and the arrival of Admiral Perry's Black Ships (1853) off Edo Bay in Japan, Japan's closed-door policies were greatly curtailed, and the open-door policy gradually became the dominant view. Accordingly, from the late 1850s onward, nation building through trade became the basic line of the Tokugawa shogunate.[8] Nevertheless, the shogunate's political system was unable to cope with these massive sociopolitical changes. Although a series of reforms (the Ansei Treaties, 1858; Bunkyū Reforms, 1861–1864; Keiō Reforms, 1864–1867) were carried out to introduce Western institutions at the end of the shogunate, the lack of political leadership and weak political unity within the shogunate were insufficient to embrace all the new social changes. Japan could not handle the sudden and unexpected external shocks through changes from below. All that remained was reform from above, which brought about an unprecedented political revolution. The Meiji Restoration, the centralized reforms led by the Japanese samurai class, transformed Japan's old system into a westernized one, not dissimilar to the political and economic logic of the modern world-system.[9] The Meiji Restoration in Japan was quite successful, and, for Japan, the outcome of the First Sino-Japanese War heralded the emergence of a new Pacific power in East Asia. In the mid-to-late nineteenth century, even if the global economy was no longer a solar system revolving around its sole star, Britain,[10] British hegemony still exerted enormous influence around the world. But even Britain could not have foreseen the emergence of Japan as a major power in the Asia-Pacific region. When the First Sino-Japanese War broke out, Britain thought that China would not be defeated by Japan, but contrary to expectations, Japan defeated China easily. Japan even won the Russo-Japanese War. Afterward, Japan rushed to gain control of Korea and hastened its expansion into China. While Japan wielded great influence in the region, Britain stepped back from East Asia. After the Russo-Japanese War Japan's penetration into China began in earnest. As a result, Japan surpassed the British in scale of direct trade with China, the number of British residents in China, and the number of companies that had a significant influence on China before the war.[11]

While the rise of Japan and Russia in the Asia-Pacific world should be noted, the United States was even more important. The United States began emerging as a Pacific power in the mid-to-late nineteenth century. The United States emerged on the world stage during this period and became a global hegemon in the first half of the twentieth century through the two world wars. The rise of the United States, especially in the Pacific region, was the decisive moment when the Pacific power pushed the Atlantic power out of the center of the capitalist world-system. As Norman Davies has argued, the American variant of Western civilization after World War Two was no longer a European replica, but a new one, and the US no longer had to rely on Europe to run the global political and economic system. The new hegemony of the United States, albeit slowly, shifted the center of gravity of the capitalist world-system away from the mid-Atlantic and toward the Pacific Rim.[12]

In summary, the Pacific powers, as observed in China's incorporation process, had grown to challenge the European powers. Furthermore, the geographical and geopolitical rise of the Asia-Pacific region, shaped by the integration of East Asia into the capitalist world-system in the long nineteenth century, gradually shifted the center of the capitalist world-system from the Atlantic to the Pacific. Consequently, incorporating dynamics help us to trace the dynamics of the parts created by the connections, combinations, and competitions of the parts, which can reveal regional dynamics and even geopolitical changes in the capitalist world-system.

Consequences of Chinese Incorporation

The Qing Empire had a well-established imperial bureaucracy and experienced commercial prosperity and geographical expansion before it became part of the capitalist world-economy. While the Manchus who governed the empire tried to maintain their own ethnic identity and culture, they sometimes adopted political and social institutions from the preceding Ming dynasty. Although there were several moments of internal crisis, the Qing regime had sufficient politico-military capabilities to suppress rebellions and repel external threats due to its successful empire-building projects. However, when the capitalist world-economy encroached on China starting in the late eighteenth century, the Qing regime experienced extensive revolts, social and economic losses, and environmental degradation caused by export-oriented crop cultivation. Fiscal difficulties caused by opium imports and silver outflows and an increase in opium addicts exacerbated the situation. The decline of the central governance system also contributed to these problems. The Qing regime attempted political reforms several times to address these difficulties, including a series of military and political reforms under the leadership of Prince Gong, Zeng Guofan, and Li Hongzhang, but they failed due to the strong opposition of conservative bureaucrats who wanted to preserve the autocratic monarchy of the Qing Empire. The only partial success of reform-minded bureaucrats' political reforms was not remarkable considering the old regime's fundamental goal was to maintain the existing order of society without radical sociopolitical changes that would threaten the patrimonial bureaucracy or Confucian ideology.[13]

Nor did the conservatives help revitalize Qing society. The strong influence of the conservatives within the Qing government was short-lived in the late nineteenth century. The conservative Qing regime was toppled by the disastrous Boxer Rebellion (1899–1901). The Boxer Rebellion was an antiforeign movement that combined the power of conservative Qing bureaucrats, the gentry class, and an ignorant and superstitious populace. Over one hundred thousand people were killed in the rebellion. Because the movement was thoroughly crushed by the colonial powers, the Qing regime and its conservative bureaucrats had to bear the brunt of the responsibility for the movement's destructive behavior. Immanuel Hsü's study summarizes the disastrous consequences of the movement.[14] First, the allied occupation of Beijing, followed by Russia's entry into Manchuria, accelerated the division of China among the colonial powers. While the failure of the Boxer Rebellion did not lead to the immediate collapse of the Qing Empire, it did significantly diminish the Qing's international standing. Second, the Boxer Protocol, forced on China after the rebellion failed, severely infringed on Chinese sovereignty. From the ban on arms imports, to the presence of foreign troops in diplomatic zones, to the right to deploy foreign troops from Beijing to the coast, the Qing's sovereignty was severely damaged. Third, over nine hundred million taels in reparations, including interest, had to be paid in foreign currency, which multiplied the Qing's financial difficulties. Fourth, after the Boxer Protocol, Beijing's foreign ministers formed a powerful diplomatic corps, whose power sometimes exceeded that of the Qing court. Fifth, the destructive and impulsive behavior of the Boxers led the international community to perceive the Qing Empire as a barbaric state. Sixth, many Chinese believed that the Qing court's ability to lead had all but collapsed, and they were no longer bent on reviving it, but rather on establishing a new government through revolution.

In the midst of the threat of Qing court collapse, Empress Dowager Cixi and the conservative bureaucrats acknowledged the need to renew state institutions and modernize the country and considered partially allowing the upper classes to participate in policymaking. Dowager Cixi's promise in 1906 to begin preparatory work for a constitutional convention, and the Qing emperor's announcement in late 1908 of his plans to enact a constitution within nine years, signaled a thorough break with tradition. In 1909, the popularly elected provincial councils (*ziyiju* 諮議局), composed of elite male representatives from each provincial unit, were established. As a political body modeled after European precedents, it was unprecedented in premodern Chinese history. In the first decade of the twentieth century, the Qing government also established specialized government departments, banned opium cultivation, expanded railroad construction, established universities and other new educational institutions, and abolished the civil service examination system.

Although the political and institutional reforms undertaken by the Qing government after 1901 appeared remarkable and radical on the surface, in reality the regime was still conservative and more concerned with protecting its own interests. For example, despite the establishment of the popularly elected provincial councils, the Qing government strictly controlled the expression of ideas. Those who were involved in the reforms cared more about personal gain than the prospects of the Qing. The Manchu government was concerned with protecting itself from attacks by Han Chinese and foreigners. The local gentry initially opposed the Qing government's reforms but changed their attitudes when they saw them as beneficial to their interests. Consequently, political reforms were not enough to revive a vast empire that was already in decline.

Worse, the Qing Empire suffered a series of military defeats and large-scale social revolts such as the Taiping Rebellion[15] and the Boxer Rebellion that caused its old military system to almost break down. The Opium Wars, the Sino-French War, and the First Sino-Japanese War were some of the significant military defeats that contributed to this deterioration. The disintegration of, and conflict within, the ruling elites, including conservative bureaucrats vs. reform-minded government officials and intellectuals, Manchu elites vs. Han Chinese elites, and the rise of local-based militia generals who were free from the central government's influence,[16] combined with the decline of the Confucian state system, brought about the Qing Empire's demise. These changes in political ideology and social division accelerated the Revolution of 1911. However, the revolution did not result in the emergence of a more centralized and bureaucratic political regime. On the contrary, the early Republican government fostered political and class conflicts, and the state-building efforts during this period were plagued by political turmoil that was no better than that at the end of the Qing regime.[17] Combined with political chaos, "the expansion of the capitalist world-system did not improve human welfare" in late nineteenth and early twentieth-century China.[18]

Economically, after China became part of the capitalist world-economy, it did not experience a significant increase in export volume. In fact, in 1890, Chinese exports accounted for less than 1 percent of the country's gross domestic product, and from 1913 to 1990, Chinese exports did not exceed 3 percent of GDP.[19] According to Shannon R. Brown, the economic impact of colonial powers on the Chinese economy in the nineteenth century was limited and insignificant.[20] This was due to the increase in industries substituting for imports, such as opium production in China, the "inapplicability of much Western technology in China," and geographical constraints. Even with the growth of domestic industry, the Chinese economy did not show sustained growth. Modern industry still barely exceeded 10 percent of the nation's net domestic product in 1911, coupled with a lack of institutional arrangements to sustain capitalist industrialization.[21] Furthermore, although a new class of capitalists had emerged in Chinese society starting in the nineteenth century, they lacked class consciousness to call themselves a capitalist class, and individual capitalists remained stuck in a traditional and premodern mindset.²² Albert Feuerwerker also concludes that until the early twentieth century, commercial farming based on capitalist principles was rare in China.²³

These studies suggest that late nineteenth- or early twentieth-century China did not have an export-oriented economic structure or socioeconomic modernization and experienced relatively limited Western impacts. Nonetheless, these studies do not undermine my argument that China was incorporated into the capitalist world-system in the nineteenth century. This is because, as Wang Xi briskly put it, from 1840 on, "internal and external causes often intermingle and interact, and it is often difficult to disentangle the various threads."²⁴ We may distinguish two types of situations created by the combination of internal and external factors: the first is where the internal economic structure is changed by external influences. The rapid increase in international opium trade from the late eighteenth century led to a sharp increase in opium consumption among Chinese people, which in turn led to the growth of opium-growing areas in China. The second is the weakening of internal premodern or feudal systems, which expose them to external influences. For example, the deterioration of land ownership relations in rural areas—the "intensified exploitation of tenants, loss of authority of landowners, spread of decadence and poverty"²⁵—and bloody civil wars, such as the Taiping Rebellion, forced many poor peasants to migrate abroad, where Chinese coolies were exposed to the influence of the capitalist world-system without any protection.

More importantly, emphasizing Western impacts is not intended to squeeze all kinds of historical evidence of China's economic changes into the mold of the connected histories between colonial powers and China. Rather, I try to pinpoint the nineteenth century as the starting point of changes in China's economic structure, not as a portrait of a completely transformed Chinese economy or a full-blown stage of China's capitalist transition.

If we cut a cross-section of China's economic system as it changed during and after the nineteenth century, we may observe a picture of the coexistence of a unique Chinese market economy and the logics of the capitalist world-system. For example, in China's major coastal areas, such as Shanghai and Hong Kong, and in regions with strong foreign influence, such as Manchuria, the logics of the capitalist world-system prevailed, while we would find that most inland areas still maintained a traditional economic system based on smallholder farming. In other words, to a certain extent, Shanghai, Hong Kong, and Manchuria had experienced capitalist industrialization under Western influence since the mid-to-late nineteenth century, while many inland areas remained in the traditional Chinese market economy. However, this approach makes it difficult to track the evolution of the Chinese economy over the long term. I thus argue that we need to track change over long periods of time in the modern Chinese economy. At the beginning of the changes in China's economic structure, China was exposed to coercive penetration by colonial powers and influenced by a weak force of the capitalist mode of production. Put differently, in the nineteenth century, China's precapitalist agrarian society began to dissolve and was partially turned into a modernized, industrialized, and capitalized society by the encroachment of colonial powers, though its process was slow, and its effect was limited. Nevertheless, there are two main reasons for claiming that this period is the point at which change begins. First, after the nineteenth century, China could not return to the precapitalist economic system. The second is that China did not opt out of the network of the capitalist world-economy after its incorporation process. Given that the Chinese economy has functioned as a part of global capitalism since the nineteenth century,[26] it is plausible to argue that nineteenth-century China was slowly beginning to change, as distinguished from pre–nineteenth-century China's noncapitalist economy.[27]

In terms of the spatial dynamics, treaty ports had been further developed after completing China's incorporation process. For example, we can compare the total of five port cities in the early nineteenth century (after the First Opium War) with the number of forty-eight port cities that opened to foreign powers in the early twentieth century. The geographical location of port cities extended from central and South China seaports to North China seaports (e.g., Tianjin, Yantai), Yangtze River ports (e.g., Hankow, Nanking), southwestern China inland ports (e.g., Nanning, Simao), and Manchurian ports (e.g., Dalian, Harbin). These Chinese port cities had opened their doors to colonial powers, allowing foreigners from a wide range of core economic countries to undertake capitalist experiments. Chinese treaty ports were reconstructed to facilitate capitalist modes of production and became an epicenter of new social movements like women's liberation, manifested in anti-foot-binding efforts and an increase in female education. However, the development of treaty ports (or port cities) cannot be lumped into the same category because the developmental pattern of port cities, combined with the influence of colonial powers, was distinctive. For instance, Hong Kong was turned into a Western city under British rule, whereas the port cities of Manchuria (e.g., Yingkou and Dalian) had been developed by forming indispensable connections with economic penetration by Russia and Japan. Hinterlands also experienced economic changes, such as the establishment of modern Chinese enterprises (e.g., the Dasheng cotton mill in northern Jiangsu Province[28]), even though "hinterland areas increasingly fell behind the coastal areas in real incomes and social welfare."[29]

In terms of a geopolitical perspective, nineteenth-century China's unprecedented transformations, caused by European and Pacific powers, ended by shaping an incorporation conjuncture. What were the results of the penetration of these two imperial groups? Obviously, China did not become a colony of a dominant colonial power due to the checks and balances of multiple foreign powers. This can be regarded as one of the idiosyncratic characteristics of China's incorporation process. It was lucky that China avoided becoming a colony; the Qing government's decline left Chinese territory wide open to penetration by colonial powers, and European powers and Pacific powers competed—and occasionally cooperated—to exploit China.[30] China did not experience the full colonial authority of a dominant colonial power, and thus nationalists and reformists like Sun Yat-sen successfully led Chinese people to overthrow an autocratic old regime, to arouse national consciousness, and to introduce "new culture" and "new thought" like social Darwinism and Marxism.[31] In port cities like Shanghai and Hong Kong, modernized Chinese capitalists began to appear and compete with Western merchants.

This, however, may not have redounded to China's advantage. Pressured by the competition of foreign powers, China experienced severe economic crises and social dislocation throughout its incorporation process. Unlike colonies that eventually regained sociopolitical stability through the centralized management of an absolute colonial power or colonial government (albeit at the cost of exploitative relationships), conservative Qing government officials, reformists, and foreign powers vied for opposed politico-economic interests. This sparked political and social turmoil in Chinese society. Worse, after the collapse of the old regime, the rise of warlords increased sociopolitical conflict without a successful effort to revitalize the Chinese economy.[32] To jostle for extending territory, all warlords were dedicated to extorting money from peasants; furthermore, their "military requisitions drove many peasants from their lands."[33] In retrospect, China's long-term internal disorder, which had been started by peasant-based rebellions in the late eighteenth century, through the penetrations of the colonial powers (including several wars of aggression) over the whole of the nineteenth century, lasted to the rise of warlords in the early twentieth century. This social disruption drove Chinese society into a prolonged economic depression and fragmented social and political relations. The social turbulence caused by the rise of warlords in turn merely created a new disorder for the beleaguered Chinese society.

In addition, after the 1890s, China's position in the capitalist world-system and the direction of its development were largely determined by the Pacific powers rather than by the European powers. Although European influence remained strong in some parts of China, such as Hong Kong, the overall political and economic situation of China was shaped by its geopolitical and geoeconomic relations with the Pacific powers. Above all, Japan's presence in China stood out. Japan created Manchukuo (a puppet state) in Manchuria and made a serious push into mainland China.[34]

Starting from the 1890s, discontent toward colonial powers increased due to the seizure of Chinese territories, discrimination between Western and Chinese people in concessions, internal divisions among colonial powers and military factions, and more aggressive economic and ideological influences. In addition, China's awakening (between 1919 and 1949) brought about a broader set of revolts: "Some were specific expressions of protest against the core-periphery relationship, manifest in anticolonial demonstrations. Other revolts went beyond the specifically colonial relationship to challenge the capitalist world-economy itself."[35]

China's resistance movements against the colonial powers became more widespread and frequent, leading to the emergence of political parties and large-scale mobilization. Anti-imperialist sentiment was often combined with Chinese nationalism, which inspired educated individuals and businessmen to call for Chinese national autonomy. The evolutionary worldview of Yan Fu 嚴復 (1854–1921), which emphasized the "survival of the fittest," made it clear to Chinese society how precarious their political situation was and how international relationships were often based on unequal power dynamics. This worldview had a significant influence on Chinese intellectuals, who began to advocate for Chinese nationalism as a means of promoting cultural and national identity and resisting imperialism.

Conservative intellectuals were also supportive of anti-imperialist sentiments. For instance, Gu Hongming 辜鴻銘 (1827–1928), a strong proponent of traditional and Confucian principles, criticized the predatory aggression of European civilization, which he likened to a "Trojan horse" that would destroy Chinese civilization from within.[36] Additionally, pro-Western intellectuals who had led political reforms during the late Qing Empire became targets of criticism following its downfall, as their reform projects lacked an anti-imperialist perspective. This sociopolitical climate created a strong combination of anti-imperialist and nationalistic sentiments, with Chinese intellectuals emphasizing national integrity and instilling patriotism in the people's minds while also inspiring anti-imperialist sentiment. These intellectual movements contributed to popular mobilization and the development of a contentious collective identity. The emphasis on patriotism also led to the rapid spread of Chinese nationalism after the 1890s, serving as a defense against the aggressive and violent encroachments of colonial powers.

For example, the primary target of Chinese nationalism in the late nineteenth and early twentieth centuries was the United States. The Chinese Exclusion Act, passed by Congress in 1882 and signed by President Chester A. Arthur, is a testament to the prevalence of racist "yellow peril" ideas in American society at the time. It was an ethnic discrimination policy aimed at controlling the Chinese population in the United States while regulating the legal immigration of Chinese nationals. To protest the discriminatory treatment of the Chinese and the excessive enforcement of the Chinese Exclusion Act, many Chinese merchants, intellectuals, and students in China and Southeast Asia organized anti-American boycotts in 1904–1905, which naturally led to the rise of Chinese nationalism.[37]

Another noteworthy resistance movement that combined nationalism and anti-imperialism was the railroad reclamation movement to reclaim financial and construction interests in railroads from foreign companies. While modern industry was encouraged and practiced for the sake of the nation's wealth, as advocated by major nineteenth-century reformers, the Qing government's financial shortfalls forced it to borrow from foreign banks to build its railroads. The Qing government's financial problems eventually forced it to hand over the right to build railroads to foreign companies. Some local gentlemen, merchants, and bureaucrats realized this and argued that the right to build and manage railroads was linked to national interests and sovereignty and should be reclaimed by China. The Guangzhou-Hankou Railroad was the first response to these claims. In 1904, "merchant leaders of the Seventy-Two Guilds and the Nine Charitable Halls in Canton organized several well-attended meetings asking for the return to Chinese hands of the construction and financing rights for this railway,"[38] and demanded this from the China Development Company, a British company. In late 1907, representatives of gentlemen and merchants in Zhejiang Province reclaimed the right to lay the railroad line from a British company and raised capital by issuing $5 shares payable in five-year installments.[39] These movements to reclaim Chinese railroad building interests manifested themselves in ways that combined—sometimes violently—antiforeign nationalism with Chinese economic nationalism.

The combination of nationalist and anti-imperialist movements reached a peak in 1919, during the May Fourth Movement. This movement was led by college students in Beijing, who were mobilized to resist Japan's expansionist policies. During the First World War, Japan and Yuan Shikai, the emperor of China, made a secret agreement known as the Twenty-One Demands in 1915. This agreement included provisions for Japan's seizure of German ports and operations in Shandong Province, extending Japan's leasehold in the South Manchuria Railway zone, and extending Japan's sphere of influence in eastern Inner Mongolia and southern Manchuria. The Chinese people were outraged by the Twenty-One Demands, as it provided fodder for another invasion of Chinese territory without any benefits to China. However, China had to wait until the end of the First World War to attempt to nullify the Twenty-One Demands. In 1919, a Chinese delegation participated in the Paris Peace Conference to regain territories in Shandong Province from Japan and annul the Twenty-One Demands. Unfortunately, Britain, France, and Italy sided with Japan and agreed that Japan would retain the territorial entitlements formerly held by Germany in Shandong Province.

During the Paris Peace Conference China's requests were rejected, and the disappointing news was delivered to China. Subsequently, three thousand students marched to the Gate of Heavenly Peace, and not only students but also intellectuals like Chen Duxiu 陳獨秀 (1879–1942), Li Dazhao 李大釗 (1889–1927), and Lu Xun 魯迅 (1881–1936) and the public harshly criticized the two-faced attitudes of colonial powers, especially Japan, and the government's inability to respond to the encroachments of these powers. Despite the Beijing government's arrest of over thirty students who participated in the demonstration, the anti-imperialist movement did not stop. On the contrary, it spread to other major cities such as Tianjin, Shanghai, Nanjing, and Wuhan. The May Fourth Movement, which involved a wide variety of Chinese people, became a turning point in the development of the systematization, popularization, and politicization of the anti-imperialist movement. From that point on, both the Kuomintang (KMT) and the Communist Party of China (CPC) began using the anti-imperialist movement as an important tool in mobilizing mass support,[40] and this tradition, rooted in the anti-imperialist movement, has continued ever since.[41]

In addition to antiforeign and nationalist movements, there were also movements organized by industrial workers. Although the unskilled nature, high turnover, lack of class consciousness, and regional and occupational divisions of Chinese industrial workers in the early twentieth century limited their ability to develop as an independent social group, they did lead the kind of underclass collective action that can be seen within early Chinese industrialized societies. For example, between 1900 and 1910 forty-six factories in Shanghai, each with more than five hundred workers, employed a total of seventy-six thousand workers, and thirty-six labor strikes occurred during this period. The strikes were motivated by strong feelings of dissatisfaction with poor working conditions and low wages and were sometimes very violent, including the destruction of machinery.[42]

In conclusion, at the time when China's incorporation process was completed Chinese society was in a state of disorder. Both the Qing regime and the early Republican government could not afford to bring about sociopolitical stability. The local warlords who jostled for territory tried to sustain their politico-military powers while milking the peasants in their own base areas.[43] Colonial powers did not abandon their political interests in Chinese territory despite the collapse of the old regime. As distinctive aspects of China's social atmosphere and a reaction of the encroachments of colonial powers, socialist movements, nationalist movements, anti-imperialist movements, and collective action by workers grew stronger in Chinese society. Finally, even though foreign merchants were nibbling away at China's economic base, their business expansion in China was still limited. China's export-oriented economic activities were also a small part of China's GDP. However, this does not imply that China was liberated from the influence of the capitalist world-economy. China, as a part of that global economy, rather began to take, albeit slowly, a new way: not a reversion to a traditional economy but the development of a capitalist society.[44]

China's Capitalist Transition

A thought-provoking finding of this book on China's incorporation is the nature and history of China's capitalist transition. This urges us to more closely analyze the nature of China's historical capitalism. There is no doubt that China has undergone momentous changes since China's incorporation process was completed. The politico-economic changes during the last one hundred years (1890s–1990s) turned China into one of the fastest-growing capitalist states in the world-economy even though China underwent terrifying ordeals during the Great Chinese Famine of 1959–1961 and the Cultural Revolution, 1966–1976. Together, these events resulted in the deaths of tens of millions of Chinese from famine and political violence and radically disrupted Chinese society.

To link China's incorporation with its capitalist transition, I argue that Chinese society's capitalist transition was mainly initiated by the penetration of the capitalist world-economy. This perspective contrasts with a theory of the "germination of capitalism (or sprouts of capitalism)" (*zibenzhuyimengyalun* 資本主義盟芽論) in China.

This theory is based on the premise that China developed a market economy because of its own dynamics. Mao Zedong initiated the emphasis on the domestic aspects for understanding China's economic development (or the rise of capitalism). He argued as follows: "As China's feudal society had developed a commodity economy, and so carried within itself the seeds of capitalism, China would of herself have developed slowly into a capitalist society even without the impact of foreign capitalism."[45] Since Mao's assertions, the germination of capitalism theory has been spotlighted by Chinese researchers. If studies about the "germination of capitalism" are arranged chronologically, Kong Jingwei first asserted that the germination of capitalism appeared in the Tang and Song dynasties (618–1279) fostering a merchandization of agricultural products, labor employment, and the handicraft industries;[46] Qian Hong argued that the laboring class and the separation of the proprietary and laboring classes appeared in the late Yuan and early Ming era;[47] lastly, Shang Yue insisted that it was not until the late Ming and mid Qing that advances in the textile industry in Suzhou and Hangzhou appeared.[48] Deng Tuo, in a similar vein, noted that commodity production and labor employment developed between the late Ming and early and mid-Qing eras.[49] Although I acknowledge the importance of internal forces within China, I believe that China's transition to capitalism was triggered by external influences.

In a similar vein, I don't believe that studies of the European capitalist transition can be directly applied to China. Since the 1970s, the concept of a "pre-capitalist society's transition to capitalist society" in England has been spotlighted in historical sociology. This theory focuses on the increase in productivity created by technological innovations and the increasing division of labor, and the appearance of proletariats as a diverse group of dispossessed workers,[50] a transition from a self-sustaining economy to a money economy fueled by commercial revolution,[51] structural changes of class relations in promoting a quantum leap of agricultural productivity,[52] and urban growth.[53] These England-centered capitalist transition theories gave subsequent researchers considerable room to examine a fruitful question: Why did only modern Europe historically have a successful capitalist transition while late imperial China did not? These studies seem plausible, but a couple of vexing questions arise: Compared with eighteenth-century England, did non-European areas' capitalist transition go through similar steps? As non-European areas proceeded with capitalist transitions, were they left alone to run their own socioeconomic and political changes and to experience economic prosperity, technological innovations, and urban growth without any intervention from foreign powers? Conversely, did they not have any developmental delay or underdevelopment imposed on them by colonial powers? Previous studies have been criticized due to the overgeneralization of England's (or Europe's) case while ignoring the distinctive underdevelopment of capitalism in non-European areas.[54] And more importantly, the insufficient attention to interconnections between the West and non-West has often led to omitting the roles of the West in formulating non-European areas' capitalist transitions.[55] In fact, a far too limited understanding of Western impacts on China's capitalist transformation has often produced a hereditary bias of Europe-centered ideas. By reiterating the idea of "the transition to capitalism" as tied to notions of modern Europe and using Europe's capitalist transition as a frame of reference, they have tried to find negative signs in late imperial China, as a case of a failed transition to capitalism, while sidelining relationships between the West and non-West or the influences of European capitalism in explaining China's capitalist transition.

Theoretically, I don't believe that China has followed the ways Western societies have implemented capitalism. Such a typology encompasses steps like this: a series of (1) socioeconomic conditions such as the emergence of private ownership of the means of production and wage labor, technological development,[56] and urban expansion, (2) political conditions such as the passage of the Poor Law, the Statute of Artificers, and the Act of Settlement in England,[57] (3) religious ethics or ideological devices such as the emergence of the Puritan work ethic[58] or the rise of liberal doctrines,[59] and (4) expropriation of the labor of racialized subjects within the periphery.[60]

For those reasons, I presuppose that China's capitalist transition did not seem to conform to the normative typology of Britain's or Europe's transitions. Within the literature of world-systems research, an external arena's incorporation process highlights an expansion of the European-led capitalist mode of production constituting a set of ongoing connections between core and periphery states. This theoretical framework attempts to apprehend non-European areas' capitalist transition not as a clone of European states but as a result of the global expansion of the capitalist system and the various relationships between non-European areas (almost all of them peripheries) and colonial powers (almost all of them core countries) within the long-lasting web of a trans-societal entity.

In this book, I postulated that China's incorporation process marked a turning point of capitalist transition. Identifying China's incorporation process with capitalist transition is not a completely arbitrary decision because both the incorporation process of China and China's capitalist transition represent a situation in which late imperial China's unprecedented socioeconomic changes, caused by Western impacts, were derailed from the path dependence of the internal dynamics. Although comparative historical studies have discussed the fact that imperial China or late imperial China seems to have undergone commercial development, the precapitalist Chinese economy did not continuously "flow back into ever-expanding markets and increasing production."[61] As Jack Goldstone notes, there were merely "periodic efflorescences."[62] In turn, the golden age of late imperial China enabled it to undergo commercial development, urban growth, and a population increase; nonetheless, late imperial China did not enter a new phase in a capitalist transition.

Given that (a) Europe's, in particular England's, capitalist transition took a different path from non-European areas' capitalist transition, and (b) the commercial advance, market development, and economic affluence of late imperial China were so discontinuous that its ephemeral glory never reached the level of the capitalist transition, I argue that the Western impacts are the most important factor to consider in analyzing nineteenth-century China's capitalist transition. This theoretical framework consequently is based on two assumptions: that late imperial China never experienced structural socioeconomic changes for the transition to capitalism, and that its transition processes were never present without the penetration of the colonial powers. It highlights the fact that precapitalist China was turned into a capitalist economy due mainly to the Western impacts. What China's capitalist transition calls attention to is that the history of China's capitalist transition needs to be regarded as a part of the long-term global dynamics of capitalism. In this regard, I capture China's incorporation process and its capitalist transition within a single category.

Drawing on two theoretical assumptions, in this book I laid out the reorganization of the production process as shaped by the relationships between the capitalist world-economy and China. Considering that it would seem logical to encompass both the encroachment of colonial powers and China's response in exploring the occurrence of a transition, I suggest a couple of historical examples. The first is the rise of the tea industry.

During the nineteenth century and into the early twentieth century, export-oriented tea cultivation accounted for a fairly small proportion of the overall agricultural structure.[63] Moreover, by the end of the nineteenth century, the volume of Chinese tea exports had declined sharply due to tea plantations in colonial Assam and Ceylon and Japanese tea exports. In addition, compared to the tea plantations owned by the colonial powers in the nineteenth century, the size of Chinese tea farms was relatively small. Nevertheless, the nineteenth-century Chinese tea industry created a transnational network of production and distribution that China had never experienced before. Most of all, the tea industry played a role in boosting the nineteenth-century Chinese economy. In the 1860s and 1870s, tea accounted for 40 percent of all Chinese exports. Before China's opium imports rose, foreign silver, obtained from the tea exports, alleviated the economic downturn in the country.[64] Indeed, until the 1890s, participants in the Fujian tea industry made enormous profits from tea exports. As a more provocative perspective on the rise of Chinese capitalism, Andrew Liu argues that the activities of early modern tea merchants in China and their labor-intensive accumulation, focusing on labor efficiency and rationalization of management, led to the country's early modernization.[65] In fact, the Chinese tea industry made important economic changes in the nineteenth century. Tea merchants became more involved in tea production, which meant that their role in the industry expanded. Furthermore, beginning in the nineteenth century, some had begun to own and operate their own tea factories. Increasing attention to tea merchants in the nineteenth century enables us to recognize how China's private merchants were gradually turned into capitalists.

Second is the rise of the new class of compradors. Since the nineteenth century, compradors had played a significant role in connecting Western merchants to the Chinese market. For instance, in 1868, Tong King-Sing 唐景星 (1832–1892), Jardine Matheson's comprador, wrote a letter in which he discussed how he did his work:

> I have been always aiming at something which I can feel proud to offer to your firm, but have not yet succeeded and I have every hope that something will soon be under my command. You may rest sure that so long as I have the honor to be in your service I will do my best in looking after the interest of your house and I can say that ever since I entered the service, I might have a little error in my judgment, but I never have robbed or squeezed you in the slightest degree as most of Chinese servants do. Having received a thorough Anglo-Chinese education I consider squeezing the Employer is a sinful & mean act.[66]

As Tong King-Sing's letter confirms, the compradors made significant efforts to serve the interests of the Western companies that employed them. As a result, Western merchants penetrated the Chinese market without difficulty. And, by cooperating with Western merchants, compradors could accumulate economic wealth. Later, some compradors even successfully turned themselves into industrialists or bankers in the late nineteenth or early twentieth centuries. Tong King-Sing was one of the earliest modern entrepreneurs, both in that he was involved in the early years of modern Chinese industries like "steamship, steam-driven mining equipment, and railway," and in that "he succeeded in organizing commercial capital into joint-stock companies that issued shares to the public."[67] He also had the ability to combine the resources of Chinese merchants and the Qing government with the technical know-how of Europeans and Americans. His entrepreneurial achievements did not result in the sustained success of his business, nor did his and others' achievements lead to a systemic transformation of the Chinese economic structure. Yet his business acumen and his entrepreneurial behavior can be considered as an example of the changes in Chinese society during and after China's incorporation process.

Not only did compradors with an entrepreneurial mindset rise in Chinese society, but Chinese proletarians began to emerge during nineteenth-century China's capitalist transition. Industrial workers first appeared in Guangdong and Zhejiang Provinces, where they worked in foreign-owned shipyards or ship repair factories, and in Hong Kong after the Opium War. This first generation of industrial workers, composed mainly of professional craftsmen from the cities, was also responsible for the technical training of most of the workers needed in the state-owned and foreign enterprises that developed after 1860. The increase in the number of industrial proletarians, from about 100,000 in 1890 to 661,000 in 1912, reflected the influx of large numbers of unskilled laborers into the cities. Most of these workers, including many women and child laborers, came from rural backgrounds and became part of the urban poor.[68]

When looking at Shanghai in the late nineteenth or early twentieth centuries, we can find urban poor who filled Shanghai's slums and became unskilled or semiskilled urban workers such as rickshaw pullers, wheelbarrow and handcart operators, and dockworkers.[69] A large portion of the urban poor in Shanghai were peasants or the demimonde of the southern areas who had moved to Shanghai to avoid cataclysmic communal and political chaos like the Taiping Rebellion and to find jobs. In addition, as the textile industries developed, about four thousand laborers worked for the Shanghai Cotton Cloth Mill (*Shanghai jiqi zhibu ju* 上海機器織布局) beginning in 1889. By 1911, "the silk-reeling industry in Shanghai had expanded to such an extent that there were 49 factories, 13,738 boilers, 40,000 to 50,000 women workers, and an annual production of 20,000 piculs."[70] In the textile factories, the majority of downtrodden laborers were women or children. The proportion of female and child laborers at forty-three textile workforces was 58.8 percent and 20.5 percent, respectively. Nonetheless, the monthly wages of the typical female worker (between $4.50 and $6) and child workers ($3) were much lower than those of male workers ($15–$20).[71] They worked twelve hours a day on average in factories, except in the case of textile factories, where fourteen hours a day was typical. Foreign-owned factories closed on Sunday, while many Chinese-owned factories closed only once or twice a month. The workers broke for lunch for a mere fifteen minutes and were monitored and regulated when they went to the restroom. Child laborers in textile factories had to pull cocoons out of boiling water and were subject to thrashing by supervisors.[72]

In conclusion, the emergence of new classes that were separate from their social origins, membership, characteristics such as consciousness and identity, and concentration, including the location of the old classes, was a new socioeconomic phenomenon. Although the members of the new classes did not confront the old classes and thus could not represent a breakthrough for the old and established class system of the Qing dynasty, they at least partially served to foster a new socioeconomic environment.

The third element of the transition was the emergence of capitalist space. Nineteenth-century China's unprecedented geographical changes led to the decline of river-based commercial networks, the rise of coastal cities, and the development of new city-hinterland relationships. Given that Chinese spatial dynamics were forced to connect with the logics of the globalized capitalist world-system, this could be interpreted as an essential part of China's incorporation process. Such changes in the physical fabric of Chinese cities resulting from China's incorporation process gave rise to conflicting results. First, the internal dynamics of China's spatial transformation were predisposed to suppressing the emergence of a capitalist–industrial economy. Unlike Britain's eighteenth-century transition to capitalism, which stemmed from the Industrial Revolution, the early stage of China's capitalist mode of production involved a transplanted form of capitalism that emerged following China's penetration by colonial powers. This contrasting tendency was largely a product of capitalism itself. Following the emergence of the capitalist world-system in Europe, it quickly came to operate on the basis of unequal or forced exchanges between core countries in Europe and peripheries in non-European areas. Given that the continuous growth of politico-economic power for the core at the expense of the periphery's disproportionately small share of wealth was central to the development of the capitalist world-system,[73] nineteenth-century

China's geographical changes were initiated not for creating indigenous industrial capitalism but as a place for exploitation of the capitalist space economy. Viewed in this light, China's geographical transformation seems largely unrelated to China's economic advance. Rather, it seems that China's geographical transformation was about promoting uneven geographical development between core countries and China, with Chinese port cities assuming their subordinate place in the capitalist world-system.

However, the exclusive emphasis on the unequal relationship between penetrating European powers (especially Britain) and China's geographical changes often overlooks the benefits that China received from this arrangement. Taking a long-term perspective, both China's geographical transformation and incorporation helped to accelerate its transition to capitalism. As Richard Walker notes, "Capital invariably creates for itself in its process of geographic generalization a 'reserve' of places, in a fashion analogous to the creation of an industrial reserve army of workers."[74] Chinese port cities were not only a place of exploitation but a potential zone that can be considered a fully developed capitalist space. The more Chinese port cities contributed to accelerating the circulation of capital accumulation the faster these port cities drew attention from Western merchants. The influx of Western merchants and their capital investment turned Chinese port cities into a place for capitalist development, and they consequently served rising new Chinese merchant groups. In fact, the new merchant groups (e.g., compradors, traders, bankers, and speculators), ironically, began to emerge in the port cities where the unevenness between colonial powers and China was concentrated. In addition, China's incorporation process into the capitalist world-system paved the way for the expansion of Chinese trading networks and businesses overseas, many of which were centered on the coastal-border cities (coastal cities with the characteristics of a border city) where Chinese had migrated in large numbers. Because of the Opium Wars and large-scale uprisings in the nineteenth century, the Qing government's control over the international movement of commodities and people loosened, thus opening the door to new opportunities for overseas Chinese businesses. The trade in opium and coolies provided overseas Chinese businesses with the capital to expand, eventually leading to a rise in the number of Chinese-owned businesses abroad. Moreover, these Chinese businesses played an important role in the development of many coastal-border cities and led in no small way to contemporary China's economic development.[75]

The fourth important factor was the role of the Chinese government. Becoming a part of the interstate system consequently brought about the reconstitution of certain components of China's political system and its political changes, which served to connect China to the capitalist world-economy; the Qing Empire's Western-oriented political and institutional changes directly or indirectly spurred China to turn from a precapitalist society into a capitalist society.

In contrast with the point of view of the theory of underdevelopment that imperial powers brought about major constraints on Chinese industrialization because of unequal exchanges between these powers and China, the intervention from imperial powers—though it may be understood as an unintended result—played a pivotal role in late nineteenth-century Qing China's industrialization, in particular between 1870 and 1897,[76] and an equally important role in early twentieth-century China's capitalist transition. Deng Kent, in this regard, insisted that "the NTR [Nanking Treaty Reform[77]] represented the first step a long line of reforms in post-Opium War history."[78] Inspired by labor-saving modern industries of the West, the Chinese government began to launch state-led industrialization policies. Under a pragmatic economic policy like "government-supervision and merchant-operation" (*Kuan tu shang pan* 官督商瓣), the Qing government provided many new industries with financial and institutional aid. For example, the China Merchants' Steam Navigation Company (1872), the Kaiping Coal Mines (1877), Imperial Telegraph Administration (1881), Hanyang Ironworks (1890), and Shanghai Cotton Cloth Mill (1889) benefited from government loans.

The establishment and operation of the China Steamship Company, for instance, was the first example of Qing scholarly bureaucrats taking action to compete with Western companies entering China. The Qing government needed a reliable means of transporting tribute rice, which was regularly shipped from the Yangtze River provinces to Beijing. However, the Qing government was dissatisfied that since the mid-nineteenth century many Chinese merchants had been transporting their goods on Western steamships within China's waterways. In response, the Qing government spearheaded the creation of the China Merchants' Steam Navigation Company. This company was the first transportation company to use modern technology, with 80 percent of its startup capital provided by the Chinese people. With government support, the company was given an exclusive contract to transport tribute grain from the Yangtze River to Beijing, and the monopoly prevented the establishment of other competing Chinese steamship companies.

In addition, when the Kaiping Coal Mines first started its business, the Qing government gave it positive aid to prevent imperial powers from obtaining mining concessions. The Qing government also conferred on the Imperial Telegraph Administration "a monopoly over introduction of telegraphy in China."[79] The Shanghai Cotton Cloth Mill enjoyed patent rights and avoided foreign competition in China at least until 1895 thanks in part to the Qing government's institutional support. The government's strong support helped to create momentum to move forward in a capitalist transition.[80]

The government-supervision and merchant-operation business was a state-driven business model rather than a market-driven model. Rather than a Western-style business model of holding shareholder meetings to elect a board of directors and all officers, it was a uniquely Chinese business model of hiring one or a few government-connected managers and giving him (or them) near-absolute control of the business. This had a number of effects. Most of all, by delegating absolute power to managers, the role of a watchdog to oversee a company's accounting and books became notoriously weak. As a result, managers often used the company's public funds for their own personal purposes, and there were unfair hiring processes, such as hiring relatives of managers to fill positions. In addition, the company's operations were often determined by government intervention and policies rather than market principles, which made it difficult for the company to make profits.

At the Kaiping Coal Mines (1877), under Tong King-Sing, a chief manager, and his merchants' associates, the company made a profit. And Tong was recognized as a conscientious and capable manager. However, after Tong's death in 1892, the new general manager, Chang Yen-mao 張燕謀 (1846–1913), did not run the company as efficiently as Tong, nor was he able to attract investment from merchants. As a result, the Kaiping Coal Mines was forced to rely on foreign loans and be controlled by foreigners.[81]

However, the negative consequences of the government-supervision and merchant-operation businesses were an inevitable outgrowth of China's capitalist transition. The individuals and groups who founded the enterprises could not have transformed Chinese society on their own, nor could they have survived in the jungle-like ecosystem of the capitalist world-system. Furthermore, under the conditions of colonial powers' relentless invasion and the impossibility of an autonomous capitalist transition, the Qing court sought to embrace modern market principles in a way that would be less disruptive to the existing socioeconomic system. Accordingly, it paid more attention to businesses that could be controlled by the government and spurred the development of government-led businesses through gradual reforms. It operated through a combination of traditional and modern business practices rather than the expanded reproduction of capital based on the cold market principle noted by Karl Marx.

It was a compromise between newness and tradition, and here we observe how capitalist enterprises and entrepreneurs with Chinese characteristics survive. Some entrepreneurial officials led the success of several enterprises—for example, the Hua-hsin Mill (established 1916), the Lanchou Official Mining Company (1908), the Chee Hsin Cement Company (1889), and the Dah Sun Mill (1895)—but they were not capitalist entrepreneurs from a modern perspective. They sometimes diverted public funds for personal use, made more profits through cronyism than through rational management, and used all sorts of tricks to get more subsidies from the government. They used informal connections with the government to run their businesses, and they were inextricably linked to politically influential people who could protect them.[82] In doing so, they introduced a unique type of business to the Chinese market, one that was certainly new and unheard of in premodern China.[83]

China's nineteenth-century gestures to open up its society to capitalism were also evidenced by new market-oriented administrative and legal regulations (although these attempts were rendered obsolete by the collapse of the Qing court). On January 21, 1904, the Qing government first promulgated the "General Rules for Merchants" and the "Company Law." These were followed by "laws on company registration" (1906), "bankruptcy" (1906), and "patent rights" (1906). These institutional and legal instruments had some success: by 1908, the number of officially registered companies had reached 272, and they represented virtually all of China's modernized enterprises.[84] The new administrative codes and laws were driven by the idea that privately run companies could contribute to the country's industrial development, which in turn manifested itself in the Qing government's protection of private enterprise.

In addition, the municipal council, as a governmental apparatus that was a replacement for local government, played an important role in building business infrastructure like port facilities, public roads, and transportation, which helped to transform Chinese port cities into capitalist space. As Marie-Claire Bergère apply notes, after the Qing's governmental authority collapsed in 1911, the municipal council proved "itself capable of organizing the representative associations and of setting up the procedures of deliberation and cooperation, and the institutions of self-government."[85] Especially during the early twentieth century, the Shanghai City Council improved public facilities, developed its own merchant militia, and standardized tax collection.[86] even though the concessions made during late Qing China and under the Republic of China—establishing institutional approval for colonial powers to govern and occupy a port city (or parts thereof)—forcibly connected Chinese port cities to global capitalism.

In sum, if we accept the idea of a capitalist transition in China in the nineteenth century as an initial stage of China's capitalist transition, we may trace a long-term developmental path of Chinese capitalism. Of course, studies on these theoretical assumptions should be investigated thoroughly. Nevertheless, if I were to summarize China's incorporation process into the capitalist world-system and its transition to capitalism in the nineteenth century in one word, it would be *commencement*.[87] It was both a graduation from the old era and a new beginning. During the long nineteenth century, numerous transitional and sometimes disconnected events occurred. This book is an attempt to understand it as a continuous process. In this respect, I believe the theorical idea of the long-term developmental path of Chinese capitalism will present a new way forward for the study of Chinese capitalism.[88]

Appendix

Chinese Coolies' Incident Records on the Coolie Ships, 1850–1872

	Sailing date	Name of the ship	Ship's flag	Captain	Export port	Destination	Number of coolies	Contents
1	1850.2.14	Lady Montague	England	Smith	Hong Kong	Callao, Peru	450	Many coolies got sick, three hundred coolies died. When the ship arrived in Peru, a riot broke out.
2	1850.9.7	Albert	France	Pain	Hong Kong	Peru		When the ship returned to Hong Kong (October 2), the captain, manager, and some crew members were killed by coolies. As the ship arrived in Hong Kong some coolies escaped, while others were arrested by Hong Kong policemen.
3	1851.12.6	Victory	England	Mullen	Amoy	Peru	355	January 26, 1852, when the ship arrived in Singapore, the captain, employees, crew members including cooks were killed by coolies. The ship was anchored off two small islands in the Gulf of Siam.
4	1852.1.20	Beatrice	England	Edwards	Hong Kong	Peru	300	As the ship sprang a leak, the ship entered Singapore. At that time, coolies started riots.

	Sailing date	Name of the ship	Ship's flag	Captain	Export port	Destination	Number of coolies	Contents
5	1852.1.24	Spartan	England	Marshal	Amoy	Sydney	254	In the middle of sailing, coolies started riots. The captain and a lot of crew members were seriously injured and many coolies also died. The ship entered Singapore.
6	1852.3.20	Robert Bowne	U.S.A.	Bryson	Amoy	San Francisco	410	Coolies excited riots. A small number of crew members were killed.
7	1852.8.23	Lord Elgin	England	MacLellan	Amoy	Guyana	110	A high death rate of coolies due to edema. More than forty-five coolies died.
8	1852.9.25	Panama	England	Fisher	Amoy	Cuba		Coolies excited riots. The ship entered Singapore.
9	1852.9.24	Columbus	England	Holton	Amoy	Cuba	266	Many coolies died.
10	1852.10.13	Gertrude	England	Campbell	Amoy	Cuba	350	Coolies attempted to riot. October, 28, 1852, the ship entered Singapore. Some employees were injured.
11	1853.3.8	Rosa Elias	Peru	Barclay	Hong Kong	Peru	200	Coolies excited riots. The captain, crew members, employees were killed.
12	1853.8.18	British Sovereign	England	Harris	Amoy	Cuba		Coolies excited riots. A high death rate of coolies on the ship. The captain, the chief mate, and crew members died.

continued on next page

Chinese Coolies' Incident Records on the Coolie Ships, 1850–1872 (Continued)

	Sailing date	Name of the ship	Ship's flag	Captain	Export port	Destination	Number of coolies	Contents
13	1854	Samlock	England		Hong Kong	Australia		The ship, which went ashore on a rock, sprang a leak. When the ship entered Singapore, coolies scattered and escaped.
14	1854	三桅船	England		Hong Kong	Australia		The ship, which went ashore on a rock, was lost near the Sulu Sea.
15	1855.10	Waverly	U.S.A.	Wellman	Amoy	Cuba	442	A high death rate: As soon as the captain began to sail, he died. More than a hundred coolies died and forty-five coolies were missing.
16	1856.3.13	John Calvin	England	Thornhill	Hong Kong	Cuba	298	A hundred and ten coolies died.
17	1856.3.26	Sea Witch	U.S.A.		Amoy	Cuba	600	The coolie ship was sunk off the Cuban coast. Two hundred fifty coolies were rescued whereas 150 died.
18	1856.4.2.	Duke of Portland	England	Seymour	Hong Kong	Cuba	332	One hundred thirty-two coolies died on the voyage.
19	1857.1.29	Anais	France	Carignac	Shantou	Cuba		When the ship began to sail, coolies excited riots. The captain, manager, and some of the crew members were killed by coolies. After that, coolies took over the ship.

	Sailing date	Name of the ship	Ship's flag	Captain	Export port	Destination	Number of coolies	Contents
20	1857.2.9	Henrietta Maria	Holland	Bakker	Macao	Cuba	350	About two hundred coolies were missing. The captain suffered external injuries. It seemed that there were riots on the ship.
21	1857.4.1	Gertrude	England	Wardrop	Hong Kong	Cuba		Coolies excited riots and about 33–40 crew members were killed.
22	1857.3.17	Gertrude	England		Shantou	Cuba	428	Coolies assembled a crowd to excite riots. The captain and crewmembers counterattacked against the coolies. As a result, about thirty coolies were injured while 209 coolies committed suicide by jumping into the sea. Some of the coolies carried out an arson attack on the ship. The fire was extinguished and the ship returned to Hong Kong.
23	1857.10.14	Kate Cooper	U.S.A.		Macao	Cuba	650	As the ship entered an Indonesian port, the coolies broke out in a riot but it was quickly suppressed.

continued on next page

Chinese Coolies' Incident Records on the Coolie Ships, 1850–1872 (Continued)

	Sailing date	Name of the ship	Ship's flag	Captain	Export port	Destination	Number of coolies	Contents
24	1859.9	Mastiff	U.S.A.					The ship was on fire while sailing. One hundred seventy-four coolies were picked up by a passing English ship.
25	1859.10.8	Flora Temple	England	Johnson	Macao	Cuba	850	On October 14, after the storm . . . the ship struck a rock. The captain and crew members got into a boat and they reached a port area of India . . . and were rescued. However, the ship sank and 850 coolies were missing.
26	1859.11.26	Norway	U.S.A.		Macao	Cuba	1,038	Five days after the voyage began, the coolies excited a riot. They carried out an arson attack, but the fire was extinguished. One hundred and fifty who took the lead in the riot were sacrificed.
27	1861	Leonidas	England	Wood				Before sailing, a riot occurred near the Amoy fortress.
28	1861.5.3	Ville d'Agen	France	Fourson	Macao	Pondicherry		Coolies excited a riot and a shipwrecked ship returned to Hong Kong.
29	1865.9	Deardel Mare	Italy	Glacamo	Macao	Peru	550	When the ship arrived in Haiti, only 162 coolies survived.

	Sailing date	Name of the ship	Ship's flag	Captain	Export port	Destination	Number of coolies	Contents
30	1865.12.3		England		Huangpu	Guyana	400	On December 11, at 4:30 p.m., the coolies broke out in a riot. The captain was thrown into the sea. Coolies ordered the chief mate to return the ship to Hainan Island off China.
31	1866.2.3	Therese	Italy	Boloro	Macao	Peru	296	Sixty-three days after a voyage, . . . coolies excited a riot. They killed twelve employees and crew members and the ship returned to Macao.
32	1866.3.8	Jeddo	England	West	Amoy	Guyana	480	When the ship passed an Indonesian port, the ship was on fire. Due to the fire, about two hundred coolies died.
33	1866.3.17	Napolean Canavaro	Italy	Denmore	Macao	Peru		Coolies set a ship on fire.
34	1866.7.28	Providenza	Italy	Videnwayige	Macao	Peru	380	When the ship was discovered at the Hakodate coast of Japan, only forty-two coolies survived but there was no European among the survivors.

continued on next page

Chinese Coolies' Incident Records on the Coolie Ships, 1850–1872 (Continued)

	Sailing date	Name of the ship	Ship's flag	Captain	Export port	Destination	Number of coolies	Contents
35	1866.10.10	Eugene Adile	France	Frudden	Macao	Peru		Coolies excited a riot. The captain was killed and a lot of crew members and employees were injured. Five coolies who took the lead in the riot were sacrificed while thirty coolies escaped to the sea.
36	1869.1.19	Frederic	Philippines	Nicaise	Hong Kong	Peru	379	On February 5—the day after the ship's arrival in Batavia—the ship was on fire. Captain, crew members, and 366 coolies were rescued.
37	1869.4.24	Tamask	France	Roune	Macao	Cuba	235	When the ship arrived at Sunda Strait, coolies excited a riot. The captain was killed and the ship was returned to Batavia. The new captain was appointed and the ship kept sailing.
38	1869.12	Uncowak	Italy	Rosciano	Macao	Peru	548	Coolies excited a riot and also carried out an arson attack.
39	1870.5.4	Doroles Ugarte	El Salvador	Caray	Macao	Peru	650	Two days after a voyage, coolies set a ship on fire. Six hundred coolies were burned to death. Captain, crew members, and employees escaped by a small boat.

	Sailing date	Name of the ship	Ship's flag	Captain	Export port	Destination	Number of coolies	Contents
40	1870.5.28.	Maria Luz	Peru	Herreira	Macao	Peru		When the ship passed the sea of Japan (East Sea), coolies excited a riot. The Japanese government released the coolies and let them return to China.
41	1870.10.4	Nouvelle Penelope	France		Macao	Peru	300	Coolies excited a riot. The captain and many crew members and employees were killed. About thirty-five coolies who took a boat escaped. The ship returned to Macao.
42	1871.5.4.	Don Juan	Peru		Macao	Peru	650	Two days after a voyage, the ship was on fire. The captain, crew members, and employees took to a boat and escaped from the ship. On the contrary, a few coolies escaped from the ship while others who were imprisoned from the ship were burned to death or were suffocated to death. Also many coolies were trampled to death due to the collision. Finally only fifty coolies were rescued.

continued on next page

Chinese Coolies' Incident Records on the Coolie Ships, 1850–1872 (Continued)

	Sailing date	Name of the ship	Ship's flag	Captain	Export port	Destination	Number of coolies	Contents
43	1872.8.26	Fachoy	Spain		Macao	Cuba	1,005	Four days after the voyage, coolies excited a riot three times in succession and carried out an arson attack on the ship. Crew members and employees fired a gun at the coolies. Three coolies were killed and about ten or fifteen coolies were tied by using their pigtails. And then, they took off coolies' clothes and lashed coolies with a whip. Blood of coolies streamed down the deck.... And then coolies who excited a riot were imprisoned under the law.
44		Louisa	France					Coolies excited a riot and they requested to sail back to China.
45		Carolin	France					Coolies excited a riot. Crew members fired a gun at the coolies. Four coolies were killed and the rest of the coolies were imprisoned under the law.

	Sailing date	Name of the ship	Ship's flag	Captain	Export port	Destination	Number of coolies	Contents
46		Ville de Sanro	France					Coolies excited a riot. Crew members fired a gun at the coolies. Twelve coolies were killed and the rest of the coolies were imprisoned under the law. The sailors drove the ship to the Sai Kung.
47		Winged Racer	U.S.A.	Coran	Shantou	Havana	700	Before sailing, the captain lashed sixty coolies with a whip. For this reason, a riot broke out.
48		Challenger	U.S.A.	Kearny	Shantou	Havana	900	After sailing, . . . the first riot broke out. When the ship arrived at Havana, the captain, seven crew members, and about 150 coolies died.

Source: Jiali Peng, "Shijiu Shiji Xifang Qinluezhe Dui Zhongguo Lugong Di Lulue," 210–19.

Notes

Introduction

1. Andrew B. Liu, *Tea War: A History of Capitalism in China and India* (Yale University Press, 2020).

2. Gregory Clark, *A Farewell to Alms: A Brief Economic History of the World* (Princeton University Press, 2008).

3. Jürgen Osterhammel, *The Transformation of the World: A Global History of the Nineteenth Century*, trans. Patrick Camiller (Princeton University Press, 2014).

4. Kenneth Pomeranz, *The Great Divergence: China, Europe, and the Making of the Modern World-Economy in the Asian Age* (University of California Press, 2000); Jack A. Goldstone, *Why Europe? The Rise of the West in World History 1500–1850* (McGraw-Hill, 2009).

5. Some China researchers may not agree with this claim. See Daniel McMahon, *Rethinking the Decline of China's Qing Dynasty: Imperial Activism and Borderland Management at the Turn of the Nineteenth Century* (Routledge, 2015); William T. Rowe, *Speaking of Profit: Bao Shichen and Reform in Nineteenth-Century China* (Harvard University Press, 2018); Wensheng Wang, *White Lotus Rebels and South China Pirates* (Harvard University Press, 2014). However, the nineteenth-century decline of China that I am arguing here has two different meanings. One is the fall of the ancien régime. The other is China's transition from the ancien régime to a modern and capitalist society. In other words, the decline of the Qing Empire in the nineteenth century that I am claiming here implies an epoch of great transformation.

6. The long walls of the Bogue forts,

> So strong, so thick;
> The great general's confident air,
> So full of pride.
> But the black barbarians came from afar,
> Invaded this land of peace,
> Nightly belched their cannon-fire
> Before our towered gates.
> Admiral Kuan falls and dies in bitter battle,

> Sitting, looking, none to save,
> Who can pity him?
> The women of Guangdong weep to the gods above.
> White bones lie across fields,
> Flocks of sheep asleep.

Sun I-yen, quoted in Fredric Wakeman Jr., *Strangers at the Gate: Social Disorder in South China, 1839–1861* (University of California Press, 1966), 11.

    7. Max Weber, *From Max Weber*, ed. H. H. Gerth and C. W. Mills (Oxford University Press, 1958), 20.

    8. Robert Frost, "The Road Not Taken," in *Mountain Interval* (Henry Holt and Company, [1916] 1931), 9.

    9. A distinct trend in recent early modern Chinese studies is to consider the period from 1600 to the 1800s as a renaissance period for China. See Angus Maddison, *Chinese Economic Performance in the Long Run*, 2nd ed. (OECD, [1998] 2007); Jack A Goldstone, *Revolution and Rebellion in the Early Modern World* (University of California Press, 1991); Roy Bin Wong, *China Transformed* (Cornell University Press, 1997); Shaohua Zhan, *The Land Question in China: Agrarian Capitalism, Industrious Revolution, and East Asian Development* (Routledge, 2019). During the early and middle years of the Qing Empire, China maintained and developed an empire comparable to that of European countries of the same period, driven by market expansion and state centralization. See Robert M. Marsh, "Weber's Misunderstanding of Traditional Chinese Law," *American Journal of Sociology* 106, no. 2 (2000): 281–302; Evelyn S. Rawski, "The Qing Formation and the Early-Modern Period," in *The Qing Formation in World-Historical Time*, ed. Lynn A. Struve (Harvard University Press, 2004), 207–41. Explosive population growth, a constant influx of silver, and a unified domestic market led to the rise of a new merchant class and the development of cities (especially in the Jiangnan region). See Ho-Fung Hung, *Protest with Chinese Characteristics: Demonstrations, Riots, and Petitions in the Mid-Qing Dynasty* (Columbia University Press, 2011), 24; Bozhong Li 李伯重, "Zhongguo chuanguo shichang de xingcheng, 1500–1840" (中国全国市场的形成 1500–1840), *Qinghua daxue xuebao* 清华大学学报 4 (1999): 48–54. In the mid-eighteenth century, the Qing Empire operated a rational fiscal system, resulting in a high degree of fiscal solvency (see Goldstone, *Revolution and Rebellion*, 204). In addition, new institutions (e.g., the Grand Council, *junjichu* 軍機處) and techniques of centralized rule (e.g., the secret place memorial system or memorial to the throne, *zouzhe* 奏摺) were introduced. See Beatrice S. Barlett, *Monarchs and Ministers: The Grand Council in Mid-Ch'ing China, 1723–1820* (University of California Press, 1991). As Hung noted, the Grand Council allowed the emperor and his closest advisors to deal effectively and clandestinely with pressing matters of the empire, even though its original aim was to wage wars against the Zunghar (Hung, *Protest with Chinese Characteristics*, 29). In practice, the Yongzheng Emperor was able to exercise strong and active imperial power through the Grand Council. The secret place memorial system helped the emperor to secure a secret channel of communication between himself and local bureaucrats. By using the secret place memorial system, the emperor was able to quickly and secretly gain access to information about events in the provinces and expand his influence over these bureaucrats.

10. Barry Buzan and George Lawson, *The Global Transformation* (Cambridge University Press, 2015); Barrington Moore Jr., *Social Origins of Dictatorship and Democracy: Lord and Peasant in the Making of the Modern World* (Beacon Press, 1966).

11. Nan Bingwen, 南炳文, "Mingqingshiqi gudai zhongguoshehuide zhongjieliqi jiaoxun" 明清时期古代中国社会的终结及其教训 [Lessons from the end of ancient Chinese society in the Ming and Qing], Henan Shifandaxue xuebao 河南师范大学学报 32, no. 6 (2005): 1–3; Xianqing Zhang, 张显清, "Wanming shehuibianqian yu zhongguo zaoqi jindaihua" 晚明社会变迁与中国早期近代化 [Social changes in the late Ming dynasty and China's early modernization], *Hebei xuekan* 河北学刊 28, no. 1 (2008): 63–67.

12. Andrew Gordon, *A Modern History of Japan: From Tokugawa Times to the Present* (Oxford University Press, 2003), xi.

13. Émile Durkheim, *The Rules of Sociological Method* (University of Chicago Press, [1895] 1938), 139.

14. Charles Tilly, *Big Structures, Large Processes, Huge Comparisons* (Russell Sage, 1984), 82.

15. Sung He Ru, "The Critical Appraisal of Existing Comparison Methods: Bringing the Connected Histories into Chinese Stagnation Studies," *Journal of Asian Sociology* 48, no. 2 (2019): 241.

16. Max Weber argued that Europe had turned into a "disenchanting world" since the advent of modern society, but that non-European regions, including China, were still strongly influenced by tradition and magic, and thus referred to them as "magic gardens."

17. Max Weber, *Methodology of Social Sciences*, ed. Edward A. Shils and Henry A. Finch (Free Press, 1949), 92.

18. For instance, Marx insisted that the traditional Chinese economy experienced a substantial change caused by unprecedented imports of foreign manufacture. According to him, China's cotton spinners had difficulty competing with British cotton manufacturers because imported machine-spun yarn was cheaper than domestic manufactured goods. Dona Torr, *Marx on China 1853–1860: Articles from the New York Daily Tribune* (Lawrence and Wishart, 1968), 3.

19. Karl Marx, "On Imperialism in India," in *The Marx-Engels Reader*, ed. Robert C Tucker (W. W. Norton, 1978), 658.

20. Marx, "On Imperialism in India," 658. Based on the theory of linear development, which takes the development path of Western Europe as the only absolute standard, Marx argued that Asian societies, unlike Western Europe, not only lacked the concept of private land ownership but also did not have the feudal production system (which was based on the class relationship between peasants and lords) that emerged in medieval Europe. In other words, Marx argued that Asia did not have a capitalist production system because it lacked the feudal lords that existed in precapitalist European societies, which made the capitalist production system possible, and because it also lacked private land ownership.

21. Alexander Anievas and Kerem Nişancioğlu, *How the West Came to Rule: The Geopolitical Origins of Capitalism* (Pluto, 2015), 4.

22. By comparing Western society with China, they have revealed a wide range of causes for Chinese stagnation. Examples are China's less-developed military force: Linda Weiss and John M. Hobson, *States and Economic Development: A Comparative Historical Analysis* (Polity, 1995)—in particular, relatively weak naval forces: Pamela Kyle Crossley, *Orphan Warriors:*

Three Manchu Generations and the End of the Qing World (Princeton University Press, 1990); the lack of formal rationality: Sybille Van Dear Sprenkel, "Urban Social Control," in *The City in Late Imperial China*, ed. William G. Skinner (Stanford University Press, 1977), 609–32; the "lack of free market and institutionalized property rights" and the deprivation of "economic potential of its scientific expertise" under totalitarian rule: David S. Landes, "Why Europe and the West? Why Not China," *Journal of Economic Perspectives* 20, no. 2 (2006): 6–7; the shortage of livestock capital: see Eric L. Johns, *The European Miracle: Environments, Economies, and Geopolitics in the History of Europe and Asia* (Cambridge University Press, [1981] 2003); the lack of scientific culture: see Margaret Jacob, *The Cultural Meaning of the Scientific Revolution* (Alfred A. Knopf, 1988); Benjamin Nelson, *On the Roads to Modernity: Conscience, Science, and Civilizations, Selected Writings by Benjamin Nelson* (Rowman and Littlefield, 1981); less-developed agricultural technologies: see Lynn White Jr., "What Accelerated Technological Progress in the Western Middle Ages?," in *Scientific Change*, ed. A. C. Crombie (Basic Books, 1963), 272–91; the absence of radical and innovative social change—such as constraints facing working women in late imperial China: Jack A. Goldstone, "Gender, Work, and Culture: Why the Industrial Revolution Came Early to England but Late to China," *Sociological Perspective* 39 (1996): 1–21; antagonism between state and civil society or the market economy: John A. Hall, *Powers and Liberties: The Causes and Consequences of the Rise of the West* (Blackwell, 1985); the scarcity of institutional mechanisms to support technological progress: Joel Mokyr, *The Lever of Riches: Technological Creativity and Economic Progress* (Oxford University Press, 1990); Joel Mokyr, "Why Was the Industrial Revolution a European Phenomenon?," *Supreme Court Economic Review* 10 (2003): 27–63; the underdevelopment of public goods and formal-legal institutions: see Carol H. Shiue and Wolfgang Keller, "Markets in China and Europe on the Eve of the Industrial Revolution," *American Economic Review* 97 (2007): 1189–1216; the Malthusian trap of late imperial China: see Susan Naquin and Evelyn S. Rawski, *Chinese Society in the Eighteenth Century* (Yale University Press, 1987); Kang Chao, *Man and Land in Chinese History: An Economic Analysis* (Stanford University Press, 1986); high quantitative growth but decrease in per-capita productivity: Mark Elvin, *The Pattern of the Chinese Past: A Social and Economic Interpretation* (Stanford University Press, 1970); and growth without development: see Philip C. C. Huang, *The Peasant Family and Rural Development in the Yangzi Delta, 1350–1988* (Stanford University Press, 1990).

23. Robert Brenner and Christopher Isett, "England's Divergence from China's Yangzi Delta: Property Relations, Microeconomics, and Patterns of Development," *Journal of Asian Studies* 61 (2002): 609–62.

24. Weber examined how only westernized cities supported the development of capitalism. To distinguish between Western and non-Western cities (including in China), Weber suggested an ideal type of Western city: it contains "a court of its own and at least partially autonomous law," "a related form of association," and "partial autonomy": Max Weber, *The City*, ed. Don Martindale and Gertrud Neuwirth (Free Press, 1958), 81. He concluded that Chinese cities had no urban community, separation from kinship relations, citizenship, or the political and military autonomy of a city. In sum, China did not have Western-type cities.

25. Peter Saunders, *Social Theory and the Urban Question*, 2nd ed. (Hutchinson, 1986); Brian Elliott and David McCrone, *The City: Patterns of Domination and Conflict* (Macmillan, 1982).

26. Pomeranz, *Great Divergence*, 31.

27. Pomeranz, *Great Divergence*, 332.

28. Ho-Fung Hung, "Agricultural Revolution and Elite Reproduction in Qing China: The Transition to Capitalism Debate Revisited," *American Sociological Review* 73 (2008): 569–88.

29. Ho-Fung Hung, *The China Boom: Why China Will Not Rule the World* (Columbia University Press, 2016), chap. 2.

30. On the contrary, generations of scholars who have attempted to trace capitalist development in Europe have proposed necessary material conditions such as "property rights including free labor, markets, and the concentration of industrial and mercantile wealth" and ideal conditions such as culture or religious ethics that facilitate the development of capitalism: Mark Cohen, "Historical Sociology's Puzzle of the Missing Transitions: A Case Study of Early Modern Japan," *American Sociological Review* 80, no. 3 (2015): 605. Douglass C. North and Robert Paul Thomas considered the existence of private property rights as a watershed in the capitalist transition of Europe; see Douglass C. North and Robert Paul Thomas, *The Rise of the Western World* (Cambridge University Press, 1973). Fernand Braudel asserted that major Western cities, standing at the forefront of capitalist expansion, had grown by imitating each other: Fernand Braudel, *Afterthoughts on Material Civilization and Capitalism* (Johns Hopkins University Press, 1977). Randall Collins views the existence of a formal-rational law system as an essential part of capitalist development in that the calculable law enables the entrepreneurial organization of capital and fosters a prosperous economic system. Randall Collins, *Weberian Sociological Theory* (Cambridge University Press, 1986). The ideal approach is another keyword to understand capitalist transition in Europe. Max Weber was interested in the value orientations of (world) religions and argued that Protestant religious ethics have an affinity with the development of modern capitalism. Dominant religious doctrines produce not only different lifestyles in each society but also different ideas of the development path: Max Weber, *The Religion of China: Confucianism and Taoism*, ed. Hans H. Gerth (Free Press, [1915] 1951. Shmuel Noah Eisenstadt insists that cultural, social, and political pluralism and competition for revolutionary change led to the capitalist transition of the West: Shmuel Noah Eisenstadt, *European Civilization in Comparative Perspective* (Norwegian University Press, 1987). Jack A. Goldstone stresses a fusion of material and ideal aspects ("broad civic participation, protection of individual rights, and capitalist economic organization") and ideal aspects ("personal freedom based on toleration" and an "engineering culture") in explaining the development of Western capitalism: Goldstone, *Revolution and Rebellion*, 485; Jack A. Goldstone, "The Rise of the West—or Not? A Revision to Socio-Economic History," *Sociological Theory* 18, no. 2 (2000): 175–94.

31. Chun Lin, "Marxism and the Politics of Positioning China in World History," *Inter-Asia Cultural Studies* 13, no. 3 (2012): 450. Here, methodological internalism means a separation of causal factors from external or interpenetrating influences.

32. Theda Skocpol, *States and Social Revolutions: A Comparative Analysis of France, Russia, and China* (Cambridge University Press, 1979).

33. Charles Tilly, "War Making and State Making as Organized Crime," in *Bringing the State Back In*, ed. Peter Evans, Dietrich Rueschemeyer, and Theda Skocpol (Cambridge University Press, 1985), 169–87.

34. Charles Tilly, *Coercion, Capital, and European States, AD 990–1990* (Basil Blackwell, 1990), 190–91.

35. Eric R. Wolf explained how the dynamics of the global market led to the decline of premodern rural societies in China (e.g., an increasing gap between traditional political control and agricultural activities, market fluctuations caused by Western impacts). See Eric R. Wolf, *Peasant Wars of the Twentieth Century* (University of Oklahoma Press, 1969). Jeffrey M. Paige examined the various forms of rural class conflict or social movements under global capitalism and, albeit indirectly, provided important theoretical clues as to why China's rural social movements have taken place with the support of socialist parties. See Jeffery M. Paige, *Agrarian Revolution: Social Movements and Export Agriculture in the Underdeveloped World* (Free Press, 1975). Notwithstanding their invaluable theoretical ideas or historical evidence, Wolf and Paige both argued that the radical changes in rural China occurred in the early or mid-twentieth century, not in the nineteenth century.

36. Gurminder K. Bhambra, "Comparative Historical Sociology and the State: Problems of Method," *Cultural Sociology* 10, no. 3 (2016): 335–51.

37. Stephen Platt, *Imperial Twilight: The Opium War and the End of China's Last Golden Age* (Knopf Doubleday, 2018).

38. Carl A. Trocki, 1999. *Opium, Empire and the Global Political Economy: A Study of the Asian Opium trade 1750–1950* (Routledge, 1999), 88.

39. Tansen Sen, *India, China, and the World: A Connected History* (Rowman and Littlefield, 2017).

40. Ssu-yü Teng and John K. Fairbank, *China's Response to the West: A Documentary Survey, 1839–1923* (Harvard University Press, [1954] 1979), 1. The Chinese empire's abrupt decline caused by the West's unexpected penetration reminds us of a C. P. Fitzgerald's metaphor: "to the amazement of all, within and without, the great structure . . . suddenly collapsed, leaving the surprised Europeans still holding the door handle"; Bruce Cumings, "The World Shakes China," *The National Interest* 43 (1996): 29.

41. John K. Fairbank, *Trade and Diplomacy on the China Coast: The Opening of the Treaty Ports 1842–1854*, vol. 1 (Stanford University Press, [1953] 1969), 6.

42. *Gojongsilrok* 高宗實錄 19 (October 17, 1882).

43. Kirk Wyne Larsen, "From Suzerainty to Commerce: Sino-Korean Economic and Business Relations During the Open Port Period (1876–1910)," PhD diss., Harvard University, 2000.

44. Jin-A Kang, *Tongsunt'aeho: Tongashia Hwagyo Chabon'gwa Kŭndaejosŏn* [Tongshunti-Chinese merchant network in East Asia and modern Korea] (Kyŏngbuk National University Press, 2011).

45. Sech'angyanghaeng 世昌洋行 is a trading company established in 1884 as the Jemulpo branch of the German firm Meyer & Co.

46. *Ch'ongnigyosŏpt'ongsangsamuamun* (總理交涉通商事務衙門) (同順泰號借款合同, [Loan Contracts of Tongshuntai], 1892.

47. Tongsunt'ae had a close relationship with the Chosŏn government. The intimacy between the two can be confirmed in several cases. In December 1893, Anhakchu 安學柱, a government official, visited Tongsunt'ae and offered to sell 5,000 *kŭn* 斤 of ginseng that the Chosŏn government owned; *Tongsunt'aewangbongmunsŏ* 同順泰往復文書 12 (December 10, 1893). Tongsunt'ae helped the resident officers of the Qing and Chosŏn governments in ordering ships to Japan; *Tongsunt'aewangbongmunsŏ* 同順泰往復文書 1 (January 28, 1894).

48. The major Chinese lottery tickets circulated in Korea were *Kangnamch'aep'yo* 江南彩票, *Kyojuch'aep'yo* 膠洲彩票, and *Hobukch'aep'yo* 湖北彩票.

49. Tongsunt'ae obtained the Han River navigation rights and set up its own steamboat company with steamboats running between between Inch'ŏn, Map'o, and Yongsan. At the same time, Tongsunt'ae also started transportation services linking the Yongsan wharf and Seoul. At the end of the 1920s, Tongsunt'ae even owned 70 percent of the taxis in Seoul (Kang, *Tongsunt'aeho*, 97).

50. There is an example of a cooperative environment between the Qing and Chosŏn governments regarding the isolation policy. In June 1832 the British merchant ship *Lord Amherst* appeared on the coast of Chungcheng Province to negotiate trade with Korea. Upon request, the Chosŏn government immediately sent a diplomatic document, which contained the following content that "although Chosŏn territory was one of the Chinese empire's tributaries, the Chosŏn government, in keeping with the Chinese empire's will, blocked entry of the British merchant ship"; *Sunjosilrok* 純祖實錄 32 (July 21, 1832). In response to this, the Daoguang Emperor delivered silk to praise the loyalty of Chosŏn; *Qingshigao* 清史稿 vol. 526 (1977): 14593.

51. Zhongyang yanjiuyuan jindaishi yanjiusuobian 中央研究院近代史研究所編, *Qingjizhongrihanguanxishiliao* 清季中日韓關係史料 [Historical materials on China-Japan-Korea relations in the Qing period], vol. 2 (Zhongyang yanjiuyuan jindaishi yanjiusuo, 1972), 25–26.

52. Zhongyang yanjiuyuan jindaishi yanjiusuobian, *Qingjizhongrihanguanxishiliao*, 27.

53. Byŏksu Kwŏn, *Kŭndae hanjunggwan'gyesaŭi chaejomyŏng* [A reexamination of the modern history of Korea-China relations] (Hyeyan, 2007), 22–23.

54. Mary C. Wright, "The Adaptability of Ch'ing Diplomacy: The Case of Korea," *Journal of Asian Studies* 17, no. 3 (1958): 363–81.

55. For an argument that the Qing Empire did not want Chosŏn to move away from its tribute system, see Key-hiuk Kim, *The Last Phase of the East Asian World Order: Korea, Japan, the Chinese Empire 1860–1882* (University of California Press, 1980), chap. 2.

56. The "impact-response" approach to China's encounter with the West has also been challenged by others, such as Paul A. Cohen who foregrounded indigenous factors in China's historical path: Paul A. Cohen, *Discovering History in China: American Historical Writing on the Recent Chinese Past* (Columbia University Press, ([1984] 2010). Yet Cohen's approach, focusing on the indigenous factors in Chinese history, can also be criticized because it fails to break with "the China-West binary that has animated much of the discussion of Western imperialism in China" and put nineteenth-century China into a global context: Louis J. Hevia, *English Lessons: The Pedagogy of Imperialism in Nineteenth-Century China* (Duke University Press, 2003), 11.

57. Joseph W. Esherick, "Harvard on China: The Apologetics of Imperialism," *Bulletin of Concerned Asian Scholars* 4, no 4 (1972): 9–16.

58. Mao Tse-tung (Zedong), "The Chinese Revolution and the Chinese Communist Party," in *Selected Works of Mao Tse-Tung*, vol. 2 (Pergamon, 1965), 310.

59. Harold R. Isaacs, *The Tragedy of the Chinese Revolution*, 2nd rev. ed. (Stanford: Stanford University Press, [1938] 1961).

60. Albert Feuerwerker even argues that there is little historical basis for the claim that foreign capitalism destroyed (or exploited) China's handicraft industry, or that the entry of colonial powers into China kept Chinese industry underdeveloped. See Albert Feuerwerker,

"Economic Trends in the Late Ch'ing Empire, 1870–1911," in *The Cambridge History of China. Late Ch'ing 1800–1911*, vol. 2, pt. 2, ed. John K. Fairbank and Kwang-Ching Liu (Cambridge University Press, 1980, 15).

61. While the impact-response approach emphasizes the two-sided aspects of Western aggressive penetration and China's response to it, the colonial approach tends to focus more on the unilateral aspect of Western ruthlessness and unprecedented penetration into China. Nevertheless, the two theoretical approaches have common aspects in that social and economic instability increased in late-Qing China along with Western development, and traditional ideologies and the old regime's political system fell into decline. Although the late Qing period embraced westernized ideas and institutions and carried out reforms, it did not prevent the decline of the Qing Empire. Furthermore, both of these approaches basically assume that the Ming and Qing dynasties were part of the same long-standing Chinese empire. However, the new Qing history, which questions the fundamental notion that the Ming and Qing are part of the single and continuous long-standing Chinese empire, emphasizes that the Qing empire should be qualitatively distinguished from the Ming.

62. Evelyn S. Rawski, "The Non-Han Peoples in Chinese History," *East Asian Library Journal* 10, no. 1 (2001): 197–222; Evelyn S. Rawski, "The Qing Empire During the Qianlong Reign," in *New Qing Imperial History: The Making of Inner Asian Empire at Qing Chengde*, ed. James A. Millward, Ruth W. Dunnell, Mark C. Elliott, and Philippe Forêt (Routledge, 2004), 15–21; Joanna Waley-Cohen, "The New Qing History," *Radical History Review* 88 (2004): 193–206.

63. William T. Rowe, *China's Last Empire: The Great Qing* (Harvard University Press, 2009).

64. Sun Lin, "Writing an Empire: An Analysis of the Manchu Origin Myth and the Dynamics of Manchu Identity," *Journal of Chinese History* 1 (2017): 93–109.

65. Mark C. Elliott, *The Manchu Way: The Eight Banners and Ethnic Identity in Later Imperial China* (Stanford University Press, 2001), 98.

66. Patricia Berger, *Empire of Emptiness: Buddhist Art and Political Authority in Qing China* (University of Hawai'i Press, 2003).

67. Evelyn S. Rawski, "Presidential Address: Reenvisioning the Qing: The Significance of the Qing Period in Chinese History," *Journal of Asian Studies* 55, no. 4 (1996): 834.

68. Kwangmin Kim, *Borderland Capitalism: Turkestan Produce, Qing Silver, and the Birth of an Eastern Market* (Stanford University Press, 2016).

69. Charles Maier, "Consigning the Twentieth Century to History: Alternative Narratives for the Modern Era," *American Historical Review* 105 (2000): 807–31.

70. Peter C. Perdue, *China Marches West: The Qing Conquest of Central Eurasia* (Harvard University Press, 2005), 409. In a similar vein, Joanna W. Cohen and Nicola Di Cosmo argue that the Qing Empire's rule over inner Asian areas like Tibet was a process of colonization: Joanna W. Cohen, "Religion, War, and Empire in Eighteenth-Century China," *International History Review* 20, no. 3 (1998): 336–52; Nicola Di Cosmo, "Qing Colonial Administration in the Inner Asian Dependencies," *International History Review* 20, no. 2 (1998): 287–309. Wu Li-Wei refutes Di Cosmo and Cohen's claim, saying that there was no such westernized concept of colonialism or colonization in premodern China. Furthermore, he pointed out that even if the term *colonization* is applied to the period of expansion of the Qing Empire, it is difficult to use it uniformly because the historical conditions of the northwest, northeast, and southwest regions of the Qing Empire were different. See Li-Wei Wu 吴莉苇, "18 shijiou renyan

lide qingchao guojia xingzhi–cong <zhonghuadiguoquanzhi> dui xinan shaoshu minzhu de miaoshu tanqi" 18 世纪欧人眼里的清朝国家性质—从《中华帝国全志 》对西南少数民族的描述谈起 [European views of the nature of the Qing government in the eighteenth century: Some notes on Du Halde's description of non-Han groups in southwest China], *Qingshiyanjiu* 清史研究, no. 2 (2007): 28–38.

71. Perdue, *China Marches West*, 527.
72. Perdue, *China Marches West*, 549.
73. Perdue, *China Marches West*, 564.
74. Perdue, *China Marches West*, 552.
75. The Torghuts are one of the Mongolian clans. The Torghuts, who migrated to the Volga River region of Russia in the 1630s, maintained cooperative relations with Russia. However, due to excessive interference and religious conversion demands made by Peter the Great and Catherine II to the Torghuts in Russia, they left Russia in 1771 and became subordinate to the Qing Empire. Qianlong Emperor welcomed their submission and completed the conquest of Eurasia.
76. Perdue, *China Marches West*, 552.
77. William Atwell, "Notes on Silver, Foreign Trade, and the Late Ming Economy," *Ching-shih went'I* 3, no. 8 (1977), 5. Also see, George Bryan Souza, "Convergence Before Divergence: Global Maritime Economic History and Material Culture," *International Journal of Maritime History* 17, no. 1 (2005): 17–28; see also Om Prakash, "The Portuguese and the Dutch in Asian Maritime Trade: A Comparative Analysis," in *Merchants, Companies, and Trade: Europe and Asia in the Early Modern Era*, ed. S. Chaudhury and M. Morineau (Cambridge University Press, 1999), 175–88.
78. Niels Steensgaard, "The Dutch East India Company as an Institutional Innovation," in *Dutch Capitalism and World Capitalism*, ed. Aymard Maurice (Cambridge University Press, 1982), 235–257.
79. William G. Skinner, "Regional Urbanization in Nineteenth-Century China," in *The City in Late Imperial China*, ed. William G. Skinner (Stanford University Press, 1977), 211–49.
80. Osterhammel, *Transformation of the World*, 260–61.
81. Wellington K. K. Chan, "Government, Merchants, and Industry to 1911," in *The Cambridge History of China*, vol. 11, pt. 2, *Late Ch'ing 1800–1911*, ed. John K. Fairbank and Kwang-Ching Liu (Cambridge University Press, 1980), 418; Philip Kuhn, *Rebellion and Its Enemies in Late Imperial China: Militarization and Social Structure, 1796–1864* (Harvard University Press, 1970); Philip C. C. Huang, *The Peasant Economy and Social Change in North China* (Stanford University Press, 1985).
82. Elizabeth J. Perry, *Rebels and Revolutionaries in North China, 1845–1945* (Stanford University Press, 1980), 33–38.
83. Rhoads Murphey, *The Treaty Ports and China's Modernization: What Went Wrong?* Papers in Chinese Studies 7 (University of Michigan, 1970), 57.
84. Lin Man-houng, "China's 'Dual Economy' in International Trade Relations, 1842–1949," in *Japan, China, and the Growth of the Asian International Economy, 1850–1949*, ed. Kaoru Sugihara (Oxford University Press, 2005), 179.
85. Even Chinese historians such as Robert Gardella and Richard Von Glahn who accepted Western effects on China faltered in their quest for China's incorporation process. See Robert

Gardella, *Harvesting Mountains: Fujian and the China Tea Trade, 1757–1937* (University of California Press, 1994); Robert Gardella, "Tea Processing in China, Circa 1885," *Business History Review* 75, no 4 (2001): 807–12; Richard Von Glahn, *The Economic History of China: From Antiquity to the Nineteenth Century* (Cambridge University Press, 2016). They have tended to find a middle (but ambiguous) ground between China's rapid and enormous transformations led by the outside effects of the global capitalist economy and an unchanging Chinese economy deeply rooted by indigenous and long-standing market institutions. According to Gardella and Von Glahn, to a certain degree the global capitalist economy influenced the Chinese market; nonetheless, China was not subsumed by the global capitalist economy.

86. In this sense, the challenge of recent Chinese historians, such as William Rowe, Perdue, and Roy Bin Wong, to small-scale analysis is worth listening to, whether dominant Chinese historians who are habituated to use small-size units in Chinese historical research accept their emphasis on international or world historical context or not; William T. Rowe, "Introduction: City and Region in the Lower Yangzi," in *Cities of Jiangnan in Late Imperial China*, ed. L. C. Johnson (State University of New York Press, 1993), 1; Perdue, *China Marches West*, 6; Roy Bin Wong, "China and World History," *Late Imperial China* 6, no. 2 (1985): 1–11.

87. Frederick W. Mote, "A Millennium of Chinese Urban History: Form, Time, and Space Concepts in Soochow," *Rice University Studies* 59, no. 4 (1973): 44.

88. Donna Brunero, *Britain's Imperial Cornerstone in China: The Chinese Maritime Customs Service, 1854–1949* (Routledge, 2006).

89. Philip Kuhn, *Origins of the Modern Chinese State* (Stanford University Press, 2002).

90. Kuhn, *Origins of the Modern Chinese State*, 21.

91. Kuhn, *Origins of the Modern Chinese State*, 21.

92. Kuhn, *Origins of the Modern Chinese State*, 22.

93. Kuhn, *Origins of the Modern Chinese State*, 90.

94. Kuhn, *Origins of the Modern Chinese State*, 90.

95. Kuhn, *Origins of the Modern Chinese State*, 96.

96. Stephen Kalberg, *Max Weber's Comparative Historical Sociology* (Polity, 1994), 5.

97. Emily Honig, *Creating Chinese Ethnicity: Subei People in Shanghai, 1850–1980* (Yale University Press, 1992), 14–15.

98. Immanuel Wallerstein, *The Modern World-System III* (Academic Press, 1989).

99. Terrence K. Hopkins and Immanuel Wallerstein. "Capitalism and the Incorporation of New Zones into the World-Economy," *Review* (Fernand Braudel Center) 10, no 5 (1987): 763–79.

100. Dipesh Chakrabarty, *Provincializing Europe: Postcolonial Thought and Historical Difference* (Princeton University Press, 2000), 6.

101. Giovanni Arrighi and Beverly J. Silver, introduction to *Chaos and Governance in the Modern World System*, ed. Giovanni Arrighi and Beverly J. Silver (University of Minnesota Press, 1999), 22.

102. The creation and prosperity of capitalism is related to the (modern) state's capacities; see Masser Tiago Appel, "Why Was There No Capitalism in Early Modern China," *Brazilian Journal of Political Economy* 37, no. 1 (2017): 167–88; Ho-Fung Hung, "The Global, the Historical, and the Social in the Making of Capitalism," in *Global Historical Sociology*, ed. Julian Go and George Lawson (Cambridge University Press, 2017), 163–81. Such a perspective rejects state-centrism. It also rejects instrumental Marxism, which stresses Marx's idea that the modern state is nothing more than a committee to manage the collective affairs of the entire

bourgeoisie: Karl Marx and Friedrich Engels, *The Communist Manifesto* (Yale University Press, ([1848] 2012). As Joseph Schumpeter puts it, we should not accept the idea that "the world was resolved to play the capitalist game": Joseph Schumpeter, *Business Cycles: A Theoretical, Historical, and Statistical Analysis of the Capitalist Process*, vol. 2 (McGraw-Hill, 1939), 671. This view emphasizes an interrelationship between capitalists (or a capitalist system) and the state rather than a judgment as to whether capitalists (or the state) can trump the state (or capitalists). In this sense, Fernand Braudel's statement is worth considering: "Capitalism only triumphs when it becomes identified with the state, when it is the state." At least when it comes to the definition and characteristics of capitalism, Braudel's and Marx's ideas appear to be in agreement (Braudel, *Afterthoughts on Material Civilization and Capitalism*, 64).

103. Adam Smith, *An Inquiry into the Nature and Causes of the Wealth of Nations* (Clarendon, 1976), 26–27.

104. Giovanni Arrighi, "China's Market Economy in the Long Run," in *China and the Transformation of Global Capitalism*, ed. Ho-Fung Hung (Johns Hopkins University Press, 2009), 22–49; Eric H. Mielants, *The Origins of Capitalism and the Rise of the West* (Temple University Press, 2007); Immanuel Wallerstein, *European Universalism: The Rhetoric of Power* (New Press, 2006).

105. Fernand Braudel, *Civilization and Capitalism, 15th-Eighteenth Century: The Wheels of Commerce*, vol. 2 (Harper and Row, 1982), 588–89.

106. Henri Lefebvre, *The Production of Space*, trans. Donald Nicholson-Smith (Blackwell, 1991), 276.

107. Regarding Europeans' monopolistic practices in the maritime trades, see Walter Rodney, *How Europe Underdeveloped Africa* (Howard University Press, 1974), 75–76. Immanuel Wallerstein, in a similar vein, stressed monopolization in capitalism: "Capitalism is being defined as the zone of concentration, the zone of a relatively high degree of monopolization"; see Immanuel Wallerstein, "Braudel on Capitalism, or Everything Upside Down," *Journal of Modern History* 63, no. 2 (1991): 356. Emily Erikson demonstrates that one of the monopolizing practices used by the English East India Company to accumulate economic benefits was "controlling market opportunities and restricting competition": Emily Erikson, *Between Monopoly and Free Trade: The English East India Company, 1600–1757* (Princeton University Press, 2014), 3. Li Bozhong pointed out that the driving force of historical development during the early period of economic globalization was based on greed and plunder; Li Bozhong 李伯重, *Huo qiang yu zhang bu: zao qi jing ji quan qiu hua shi dai de Zhongguo yu Dong Ya shi jie* 火枪与账簿: 早期经济全球化时代的中国与东亚世界 [Guns and ledgers: China and the East Asian world in the early era of economic globalization] (Sheng huo, du shu, xin zhi san lian shu dia, 2017).

108. Anievas and Nişancioğlu, *How the West Came to Rule*, 67; see also Janet L. Abu-Lughod, *Before European Hegemony: The World System, A.D. 1250–1350* (Oxford University Press, 1989).

109. Prasannan Parthasarathi, *Why Europe Grew Rich and Asia Did Not* (Cambridge University Press, 2011), 10.

110. Karl Marx, *Capital Volume One* (Vintage, 1977), 915.

111. Leon Trotsky, *The History of the Russian Revolution* (Pluto, [1933] 1977), 27.

112. Thomas D. Hall, "Incorporation into and Merger of World-Systems," in *Routledge Handbook of World-Systems Analysis*, edited by Salvatore J. Babones and Christopher Chase-Dunn, 37–55 (New York: Routledge, 2012).

113. Immanuel Wallerstein, *The Modern World-System III* (Academic Press, 1989), 129–30.

114. Immanuel Wallerstein, "Incorporation of Indian Subcontinent into Capitalist World-Economy," *Economic and Political Weekly* 21, no. 4 (1986): 28–39. Unlike Wallerstein's perspective, recent studies of incorporation are concerned not only with political and economic changes in the incorporated areas but also with processes of cultural assimilation. Caleb Bush (2005), for example, using the example of the Diné (Navajo) who became more assimilated into middle-class American culture, argued that an incorporation process is never-ending. Even if the economic part of the incorporated area is completed (i.e., the dependent peripheralization of the incorporated area identified in economic terms), Bush argued, it does not end there but leads to cultural assimilation: Caleb M. Bush, "Reconsidering Incorporation: Uneven Histories of Capitalist Expansion and Encroachment, Native America," *Studies in Political Economy* 76 (2005): 83–109.

115. In contrast to Wallerstein's perspective (the automatic integration of the external arena with the expansion of the capitalist world-system), Thomas Hall adds the concept of a frontier between the external arena and the incorporation process. According to Hall, the areas where external arenas come into contact with the capitalist world-system are often called frontiers, and by examining the emergence, transformation, and elimination of frontiers, researchers are able to trace the historical trajectory of the incorporation process. Thomas D. Hall, "Incorporation into and Merger of World-Systems," in *Routledge Handbook of World-Systems Analysis*, ed. Salvatore J. Babones and Christopher Chase-Dunn (Routledge, 2012), 47. In a similar vein, Nick Kardulias points out that cultural change (of incorporated areas) occurs at a high pace in contact zones. He emphasizes the importance of studying places of contact to uncover the nuances of cultural contact and interaction processes: Nick Kardulias, "Negotiation and Incorporation on the Margins of World-Systems: Examples from Cyprus and North America," *Journal of World-Systems Research* 13, no. 1 (2007): 55–82. Contrary to Wallerstein's idea that incorporation was a uniform process that depended on the balance of class forces, levels of technology, and structures of power between the capitalist world-economy and the areas being incorporated, Christopher Chase-Dunn and Donald Hall argue that there were two distinct processes involved: "effective or real incorporation" and "nominal or formal incorporation": Christopher Chase-Dunn and Donald Hall, *Rise and Demise: Comparing World-Systems* (Routledge, 1997), 63. In the former, an external arena's intrinsic and long-standing production and reproduction systems dissolve and are subsumed into the globalized economic system during its incorporation into the capitalist world-economy, while in the latter, despite incorporation, dominant production and reproduction systems of incorporated areas do not collapse or disintegrate. Moreover, in contrast with Wallerstein's idea about the incorporation process, which omitted the various forms of transformation that occur during the external arena's incorporation process, Chase-Dunn and Hall conceptualized "incorporation as a continuum that ranges from weak to strong" (Chase-Dunn and Hall, *Rise and Demise*, 61). In doing so, they intended to offer specific and multilateral pictures of the process of change in the incorporated regions.

116. Immanuel Wallerstein, "The Rise and Future Demise of the World Capitalist System: Concepts for Comparative Analysis," *Comparative Studies in Society and History* 16, no. 4 (1974): 388; see also Immanuel Wallerstein, "The Present State of the Debate on World Inequality," in *The Capitalist World-Economy: Essays by Immanuel Wallerstein* (Cambridge University Press,

1979), 58; Immanuel Wallerstein, *World-Systems Analysis: An Introduction* (Duke University Press, 2004).

117. Philip McMichael, "Incorporating Comparison Within a World Historical Perspective: An Alternative Comparative Method," *American Sociological Review* 55, no. 3 (1990): 385–86.

118. Wallerstein, "Rise and Future Demise," 390.

119. McMichael, "Incorporating Comparison," 386.

120. Terrence K. Hopkins and Immanuel Wallerstein, "Structural Transformations of the World-Economy," in *Dynamics of World Development*, ed. Richard Rubinson (Sage, 1981), 233–62.

121. Mary Backus Rankin, "Social and Political Change in Nineteenth-Century China," in *Historical Perspective on Contemporary East Asia*, ed. Merle Goldman and Andrew Gordon (Harvard University Press, 2000), 42–84; Samee Ullah Kahn Lashari, "From the Periphery to the Semi-Core: A World-System Analysis of the Fall and Rise of China and the Indian Subcontinent (1757–2014)," PhD diss., Northern Arizona University, 2017.

122. Immanuel Wallerstein, "Incorporation of Indian Subcontinent," 34.

123. Immanuel Wallerstein, "Dependence in an Interdependent World: The Limited Possibilities of Transformation within the Capitalist World-Economy," in *The Capitalist World-Economy: Essays by Immanuel Wallerstein* (Cambridge University Press, 1979), 75; see also Kwangkuan Lee, " 'Getting Prices Right Again?' An Actor-Oriented World-Systems Approach to the Transformation of the South Korean Labor Regime, 1987–2010," PhD diss., State University of New York at Binghamton, 2012, 15.

124. Immanuel Wallerstein, "Dependence in an Interdependent World," 76.

125. Giovanni Arrighi, *Adam Smith in Beijing: Lineages of the Twenty-First Century* (Verso, 2007), 337–38. On of the economic contributions of Chinese sojourners or overseas Chinese (*huaquio* 华侨) to China, see Sucheng Chan, *This Bittersweet Soil: The Chinese in California Agriculture, 1860–1911* (University of California Press, 1986); Michael Godley, *The Mandarin-Capitalists from Nanyang: Overseas Chinese Enterprise in the Modernization of China, 1839–1911* (Cambridge University Press, 1982); Gary G. Hamilton, "Overseas Chinese Capitalism," in *Confucian Traditions in East Asian Modernity*, ed. Tu Wei-ming (Harvard University Press, 1996), 328–42; Gary G. Hamilton, "Hong Kong and the Rise of Capitalism in Asia," in *Cosmopolitan Capitalists: Hong Kong and the Chinese Diaspora at the End of the 20th Century*, ed. Gary G. Hamilton (University of Washington Press, 1999), 14–34; Jessieca Leo, *Global Hakka: Hakka Identity in the Remaking* (Brill, 2015); Lynn Pan, *Sons of the Yellow Emperor: A History of the Chinese Diaspora* (Kodansha International, 1994), chap. 11.

126. Dwight Perkins, "China's Prereform Economy in World Perspective," in *China's Rise in Historical Perspective*, ed. Brantly Womack (Rowman and Littlefield, 2010), 118. With regard to the role of foreign capital in China's economic modernization between the mid-nineteenth and early twentieth centuries, see Chi-ming Hou, *Foreign Investment and Economic Development in China, 1840–1937* (Harvard University Press, 1965).

127. In contrast with the absolutizing subjugation of colonies stemming from a theory of imperialism, Wallerstein asserted that incorporated areas can be divided into three categories ("territorial units," "sometimes sovereign," and "sometimes colonized"); see Immanuel Wallerstein, "From Feudalism to Capitalism: Transition or Transitions," in *The Capitalist World-Economy: Essays by Immanuel Wallerstein* (Cambridge University Press, 1979), 145.

128. Here, only European countries are civilized countries, and Asian and other non-European countries are semicivilized or barbarian nations; see Lydia H. Liu, "Kŭlloböl hisŭťori yŏn'guŭi saeroun pangbŏp" [A new way to study global history], in *Segyejilsŏwa munmyŏngdŭnggŭp* [The global order and the standard of civilization], translated by Ch'a T'aekŭn (Gyoyudang Press, 2022), 11–30.

129. Mary Louise Pratt, "Arts of the Contact Zone," *Profession* (1991): 33–40.

130. Geoculture refers to a set of ideas, values, and norms that were widely accepted throughout the world-system and subsequently imposed restrictions on social behavior, city, region, and nation-state.

131. Lydia H. Liu, *The Clash of Empires: The Invention of China in Modern World Making* (Harvard University Press, 2006).

132. Stanley Aronowitz, "A Metatheoretical Critique of Immanuel Wallerstein's 'The Modern World System,'" *Theory and Society* 10, no. 4 (1981): 503–20; David Washbrook, "South Asia, the World System and World Capitalism," in *South Asia and World Capitalism*, ed. Sugata Bose (Oxford University Press, 1990), 40–84.

133. Marshall Sahlins, "Cosmologies of Capitalism: The Trans-Pacific Sector of 'the World-System,'" *Proceedings of the British Academy* 74 (1988): 1–51; Thomas D. Hall, "Incorporation into and Merger of World-Systems," in *Routledge Handbook of World-Systems Analysis*, ed. Salvatore J. Babones and Christopher Chase-Dunn (Routledge, 2012), 37–55.

134. Regarding Wallerstein's explanations on China's incorporation process, see Immanuel Wallerstein, *The Modern World-System III* (Academic Press, 1989), p. 168.

135. Immanuel Wallerstein, *The Modern World-System I* (Academic Press, 1974), 347.

136. Philip McMichael, "World-Systems Analysis, Globalization, and Incorporating Comparison," *Journal of World-Systems Research* 6, no. 3 (2000): 68–99. According to world-systems analysis, the whole refers to the logics of the capitalist world-economy like an international division of labor system, the hierarchical relationships of the interstate system (e.g., unilateral transfers of labor and capital between core and periphery), and the transnational commodity and capital network. However, unlike Wallerstein's idea of the whole, McMichael argued that the whole refers to "a conceptual procedure, rather than an empirical or conceptual premise" (McMichael, "Incorporating Comparison," 391) and thus "the whole emerges through the action of its parts" (McMichael, "Incorporating Comparison," 394). On the contrary, there are different levels and forms of parts that are the constituent elements of the whole. For instance, there are relatively large parts like (modern) states, and relatively small parts like cities or regions.

137. Karel Kosik, *Dialectics of the Concrete: A Study on Problems of Man and World* (D. Reidel, 1976), 22.

138. As such, it posed no methodological idea for the multiple forms of interpart relationships, which is evidenced in how it follows a prominent world-systems researcher's choice of research design. Influenced by Antonio Gramsci's idea of hegemony at the national level, Marx's idea of capital accumulation, and Philip McMichael's idea of incorporating comparison, Giovanni Arrighi presented an inseparable relation between the territorial logic of power and the capitalist within the capitalist world-economy. See Giovanni Arrighi, *The Long Twentieth Century: Money, Power, and the Origins of Our Times* (Verso, [1994] 2010). This resulted in emphasizing the expansion of territorial-based capitalism and hegemonic transition that were

played out in the capital accumulation process (C-M: material accumulation, M-C: financial accumulation) and political capacities (e.g., leadership and governance) (Arrighi and Silver, introduction to *Chaos and Governance*, 22). However, Arrighi's research ended up in methodological territorialism, which insisted on a single unit of analysis of the state (including the city-state). If I may borrow the rhetoric of physics, Arrighi reduced the state to an atomic unit that could no longer be divided. Unlike Arrighi's methodological territorialism, José Itzigsohn pointed out that the dynamics of units that are physically smaller than the state, such as a region or a local place, can also be related to the logics of the capitalist world-system: "Global processes are mediated by institutional structures at the local level"; José Itzigsohn, "World-Systems and Institutional Analysis—Tensions and Complementarities: The Cases of Costa Rica and the Dominican Republic," *Review* (Fernand Braudel Center) 24, no. 3 (2001): 439–68. The part in a part-whole relationship is not a single fixed unit (i.e., the state) but rather consists of multiple forms.

139. Giovanni Arrighi, Takeshi Hamashita, and Mark Selden, "The Rise of East Asia in Regional and World Historical Perspective," in *The Resurgence of East Asia: 500, 150 and 50 Year Perspective*, ed. Giovanni Arrighi, Takeshi Hamashita, and Mark Selden (Routledge, 2003), 4.

140. Arrighi, Hamashita, and Selden, "Rise of East Asia," 13.

141. Takeshi Hamashita, "Tribute and Treaties: Maritime Asia and Treaty Port Networks in the Era of Negotiation, 1800–1900," in *The Resurgence of East Asia*, ed. Giovanni Arrighi, Takeshi Hamashita, and Mark Selden (Routledge, 2003), 23.

142. Device Bilotti, *The Rise of East Asia: Rethinking Theories of Economic Development* (IPRASTAH, 1997), 118–19.

143. According to Charles Tilly, Wallerstein's world-systems analysis used both "individualizing" and "encompassing" comparisons (Tilly, *Big Structures, Large Processes, Huge Comparisons*, 83–84); however, to show more detailed and specific encompassing comparisons of Wallerstein's world-systems analysis, an idea of the interpart relationships is essential. As Tilly rightly pointed out, Wallerstein's "encompassing" comparison tended to focus merely on the single function or role of core, semiperiphery, and peripheral parts that were operated through the relationships with the whole. However, the various relationships between parts cannot be explained only by the unified criteria of core, semiperipheral, and peripheral conditions. As will be discussed later, interpart relations are sometimes organically connected, or conversely have disconnected from each other. Indeed, parts coexist in the same time-space without any connection.

144. *Yizhangxianzhi* 宜章縣志 [Local Gazetteer of Yizhangxian] vol. 10 (1941), 122.

145. Hyŏngkwŏn Chŏn, *Chungguk Kŭnhyŏndae Sangin'gwa Mulgabyŏn-dong: Honam Chiyŏksahoe Yŏn-gu* [Chinese modern and contemporary merchants and price fluctuations–a study of the Honam community] (Hyeyan, 2021), 43–44.

146. Smith, *Wealth of Nations*, 220.

147. Stanley J. Stein and Barbara H. Stein, *Silver, Trade, and War: Spain and America in the Making of Early Modern Europe* (Johns Hopkins University Press, 2000).

148. Many existing sociological studies that mainly focused on the changes in Chinese society in the nineteenth century and the relationship between China and the global world tended to be used in secondary literature. In contrast, this study uses various types of archival data.

Chapter 1

1. One is Immanuel Wallerstein's approach; the other is Philip McMichael's approach (i.e., incorporating comparison).

2. Peter D. Phillips, "Incorporation of the Caribbean 1650–1700," *Review* 10, no. 5 (1987): 781–804; Reşat Kasaba, "Incorporation of the Ottoman Empire," *Review* 10, no. 5 (1987): 805–47; William G. Martin, "Incorporation of Southern Africa, 1870–1920," *Review* 10 no. 5 (1987): 849–902.

3. Frances V. Moulder, *Japan, China, and the Modern World-Economy* (Cambridge University Press, 1977); Dilip Basu, "The Peripheralization of China: Notes on the Opium Connection," in *The World System of Capitalism: Past and Present*, ed. Walter L. Goldfrank (Sage, 1979), 171–87.

4. Alvin Y. So, "The Process of Incorporation into the Capitalist World-System: The Case of China in the Nineteenth Century," *Review* 8, no. 1 (1984): 91–116.

5. The Sanyuanli Incident was a military collision between the British army and an irregular force composed of gentry members and Guangzhou citizens. It occurred on May 29, 1841. This was the first Chinese people's spontaneous mass struggle against foreign invasion, and it led to a victory by the Chinese forces. With regard to the military combat deployments of the Sanyuanli Incident, see So, "Process of Incorporation," 98–99.

6. So, "Process of Incorporation," 112.

7. Alvin Y. So, *The South China Silk District: Local Historical Transformation and World-System Theory* (State University of New York Press, 1986), 54.

8. So, *South China Silk District*, 66.

9. So, *South China Silk District*, 69.

10. So, *South China Silk District*, 70. In addition, according to So, northern and central China had favorable responses to the entrance of Westerners and their capital investments, while southern China opposed them fiercely (So, "Process of Incorporation," 111). He insisted that China's political incorporation process was decoupled from economic incorporation, depending on separation between central and southern China's political authority.

11. Alvin Y. So and Stephen Chiu, *East Asia and World-Economy* (Sage, 1995).

12. The dynastic cycle indicates that all Chinese dynasties in the premodern era followed a repetitive and identical pattern of power characterized by peace and prosperity in the upswing when a new line of emperors was established. During this period, the population increased, and the economy developed. Later, civil war, misery, and population decline occurred during the downswing when the dynasty became old and feeble. An important aspect is that a motive for change in the dynastic cycle was not external pressure but internal pressure, like revolts. See Skocpol, *States and Social Revolutions*, 75.

13. So and Chiu, *East Asia and World-Economy*, 45–49.

14. Victor Nee and James Peck, "Introduction: Why Uninterrupted Revolution?," in *China's Uninterrupted Revolution: From 1840 to the Present*, ed. Victor Lee and James Peck (Pantheon, 1975), 6.

15. James Peck, "Revolution Versus Modernization and Revisionism: A Two-Front Struggle," in *China's Uninterrupted Revolution: From 1840 to the Present*, ed. Victor Nee and James Peck (Pantheon, 1975), 90.

16. Yen-P'ing Hao, *The Commercial Revolution in Nineteenth-Century China: The Rise of Sino-Western Mercantile Capitalism* (University of California Press, 1986); Hanchao Lu, *Beyond the Neon Lights: Everyday Shanghai in the Early Twentieth Century* (University of California Press, 1999).

17. Hao, *Commercial Revolution in Nineteenth-Century China*, 354–55.

18. Alvin Y. So, *Social Change and Development: Modernization, Dependency, and World-System Theory* (Sage, 1990), 259.

19. Giovanni Arrighi and Jessica Drangel, "The Stratification of the World-Economy: An Exploration of the Semiperipheral Zone," *Review* 10, no. 1 (1986): 9–74.

20. With regard to the qualitative features of dependency theory, see Theotonio Dos Santos, "The Structure of Dependence," *American Economic Review* 60, no. 2 (1970): 231–36; So, *Social Change and Development*, part 2, chapter 5. Regarding qualitative

differences between dependency theory and world-systems analysis, see Stephen K. Sanderson, *Social Transformations: A General Theory of Historical Development* (Rowman and Littlefield, 1999), 209–10.

21. During the late imperial eras, many merchants based in the coastal regions of southern China traveled to the Indian and Pacific Oceans, especially in Southeast Asia, on junks (ships) to exchange material goods with various cultures. China's junk trade played a key role in China's expansion of its maritime influence across Asia and beyond. A typical example of China's junk trade was the "Pacific and Southeast Asian trade" between the 1750s and 1830s: Sucheta Mazumdar, *Sugar and Society in China: Peasants, Technology, and the World Market* (Harvard University Press, 1998), 111. Though no reliable quantitative data of the volume of export within the Pacific and Indian Oceans is available, "Tian Rugang, extrapolating from the tonnage of shipping, has estimated that Chinese shipping in the Pacific and Indian Ocean was around 85,000 tons annually at this time. The total tonnage of the British East India Company, at Canton, on the other hand, never exceeded 30,000 tons annually" (Mazumdar, *Sugar and Society in China*, 112–13).

22. Hao, *Commercial Revolution in Nineteenth-Century China*, 6, 8.

23. Rebecca Jean Emigh, "The Power of Negative Thinking: The Use of Negative Case Methodology in the Development of Sociological Theory," *Theory and Society* 26, no. 5 (1997): 666.

24. Ravi R. Palat, *The Making of an Indian Ocean World-Economy, 1250–1650: Princes, Paddy Fields, and Bazaars* (Palgrave Macmillan, 2015).

25. For a detailed discussion of unequal exchange, see Christopher Chase-Dunn and Richard Rubinson, "Toward a Structural Perspective on the World-System," *Politics and Society* 7, no. 4 (1977): 453–76; Immanuel Wallerstein, "World-Systems Analysis: Theoretical and Interpretative Issues," in *World Systems Analysis: Theory and Methodology*, ed. Terence K. Hopkins and Immanuel Wallerstein (Sage, 1982), 91–103.

26. Stephen C. Thomas, *Foreign Investment and China's Industrial Development, 1870–1911* (Westview, 1984), 35.

27. Lu, *Beyond the Neon Lights*, 52.

28. Arrighi and Drangel, "Stratification of the World-Economy," 56.

29. Giovanni Arrighi, "The Development Illusion: A Reconceptualization of the Semiperiphery," in *Semiperipheral States in the World-Economy*, ed. W. G. Martin (Greenwood, 1990), 11–42.

30. Wallerstein, *Modern World-System III*, 138–39.

31. Buzan and Lawson, *Global Transformation*, 30.

32. See Pomeranz, *Great Divergence*, chap. 6.

33. Wallerstein, *Modern World-System I*, 41.

34. Terence K. Hopkins and Immanuel Wallerstein, "Commodity Chains in the World-Economy Prior to 1800," *Review* 10, no. 1 (1986): 157–70; David Northrup, *Indentured Labor in the Age of Imperialism, 1834–1922* (Cambridge University Press, 1995).

35. Wallerstein, *Modern World-System III*, 129.

36. Dennis O. Flynn, *World Silver and Monetary History in the 16th and 17th Centuries* (Variorum, 1996); Dennis O. Flynn and Arturo Giraldez, "Cycles of Silver: Global Economic Unity Through the Mid-Eighteenth Century," *Journal of World History* 13, no. 2 (2002): 391–427; Richard Von Glahn, "Money-Use in China and Changing Patterns of Global Trade in Monetary Metals, 1500–1800," in *Monetary History in Global Perspective, 1500–1808: B6 Proceedings, Twelfth International Economic History Congress*, ed. Clara Eugenia Nuñez (Universidad de Sevilla, 1998), 51–59.

37. Since the sixteenth century, Chinese silk had been exported to Europe, a trade initially monopolized by Spanish merchants. They paid silver in exchange for Chinese silk; however, starting in the late sixteenth century, the Spanish monopoly declined due mainly to intense competition from the British East India Company. In Europe, Chinese silk was regarded as a precious item and it also was used in "luxurious bed hangings, blankets and dresses" until China was incorporated into the capitalist world-economy in the nineteenth century; Hanna Hodacs, *Silk and Tea in the North: Scandinavian Trade and the Market for Asian Goods in Eighteenth-Century Europe* (Palgrave Macmillan, 2016), 92. Since the eighteenth century, China's raw silk was more popular than finished silk products due mainly to the "maturing of Britain's silk-weaving industry" (Ronald C. Po, "Tea, Porcelain, and Silk: Chinese Exports to the West in the Early Modern Period," *Oxford Research Encyclopedia of Asian History*, April 26, 2018, 15; https://doi.org/10.1093/acrefore/9780190277727.013.156). From 1887 until the fall of the Qing Empire, China's raw silk became China's single most important export, surpassing tea (Feuerwerker, "Economic Trends in the Late Ch'ing Empire," 26; So, *South China Silk District*, 69–71).

38. Although when it entered the European market remains debatable, Chinese porcelain, in particular Jingdezhen blue and white porcelain, enthralled the European upper classes with its elegance, delicate decoration, and durability during the Ming dynasty. Import of Chinese porcelain began in earnest when Portuguese merchants arrived in China in the early sixteenth century. When the VOC replaced the Portuguese in most of the porcelain trade in the seventeenth century, it imported close to "43 million pieces of porcelain from China." Other European countries including Britain, France, Sweden, and Denmark also imported Chinese porcelain from the early seventeenth to the late nineteenth centuries (Po, "Tea, Porcelain, and Silk," 9).

39. Peter Gordon and Juan José Morales, *The Silver Way: China, Spanish America and the Birth of Globalization, 1565–1815* (Penguin, 2017), 27.

40. William Lytle Schurz, *The Manila Galleon* (E. P. Dutton, 1939), 15.

41. Between the seventeenth and early nineteenth centuries, large quantities of American silver, which was considered "contraband silver," had entered China through land and sea routes: Jin Cao and Dennis O. Flynn, "Global Quantification and Inventory Demand for Silver in China," *Revista de Historia Económica* 38, no. 3 (2020): 421–47.

42. Schurz, *Manila Galleon*, 63–64.

43. China also exported sugar through European international commerce in the early seventeenth century. China exported sugar to the Dutch when "events in distant Brazil reduced [sugar] supplies to the Amsterdam refineries" (Mazumdar, *Sugar and Society in China*, 3). As the demand for Chinese sugar increased in the global market, in particular the European market, China even developed labor-saving technology in the sugar-manufacturing industry.

44. Francesca Bray, *The Rice Economy: Technology and Development in Asian Society* (Basil Blackwell, 1986); Dennis O. Flynn, "Big History, Geological Accumulations, Physical Economics, and Wealth," *Asian Review of World History* 7 (2019): 80–106; Sucheta Mazumdar, "The Impact of New World Food Crops on the Diet and Economy of China and India, 1600–1900," in *Food in Global History*, ed. Raymond Grew (Westview, 1999), 58–78; Ming Wan, "The Monetarization of Silver in China: Ming China and Its Global interactions," in *China's Development from a Global Perspective*, ed. M. D. Elizalde and J. Wang (Cambridge Scholars, 2017), 274–96.

45. Before 1750, there was no rapid population increase; on the contrary, the Chinese population declined in the mid-seventeenth century due to wars, banditry, and epidemics. For example, "for Guangdong province, the population fell from 9 million to 7 million; Guangxi's population declined from 3.4 million to 2.8 million between 1640 and 1661." Ramon H. Myers and Wang Yeh-Chien, "Economic Development, 1644–1800," in *The Cambridge History of China*, vol. 9, pt. 1, *The Ch'ing Empire to 1800*, ed. Willard J. Peterson (Cambridge University Press, 2002), 565. But the Chinese population soon increased because, first, the Manchu government carried out large-scale population movements from overpopulated areas to underpopulated areas that had an abundance of cultivable land. Among underpopulated areas "Szechwan [Sichuan] area was the largest recipient of immigrants from 1650 to 1850"; Ping-ti Ho, *Studies on the Population of China, 1368–1953* (Harvard University Press, 1974), 141. The government provided new immigrants not only with draft animals and seeds but also with tax exemptions. As a result, agricultural productivity increased, and the quality of life also improved. It brought about the rise of the birth rate in China. Second, the Kangxi Emperor's tax remission policies eased the tax burden on the Chinese population; in "1701, more than 90,000,000 taels of taxes had been remitted and by 1711 the total amount of taxes remitted had exceeded 100,000,000 taels" (Ho, *Studies on the Population of China, 1368–1953*, 210). Tax exemption benefits brought increases in the real income of taxpayers, improving their economic condition. Third, improvements in economic conditions prevented Chinese people from practicing infanticide. According to William T. Rowe, infanticide was "a routine practice of family planning" due to lack of food and rising living costs: "Social Stability and Social Change," in *The Cambridge History of China*, vol. 9, pt. 1, *The Ch'ing Empire to 1800*, ed. Willard J. Peterson (Cambridge University Press, 2002), 477. However, economic affluence after 1680 *controlled* mortality such as infanticide. As a result, the growth of the Chinese population continued. Fourth, the Kangxi Emperor established pediatric clinics to inoculate infants in 1687. As a result of this, for example, "over one-half the registered population of Beijing was regularly inoculated through state clinics": James Lee and Wang Feng, *One Quarter of Humanity: Malthusian Mythology and Chinese Reality* (Harvard University Press, 1999), 46). The extension of inoculation to infants reduced infant mortality.

46. Ho, *Studies on the Population of China*, 281–82. As a method for measuring the population, the Qing regime used household registrations called as the *baojia* 保甲 system. (Of course, it was used not only for controlling the movement and activities of people but also

for surveillance.) Generally, a *jia* (甲) was composed of 100 households and a *bao* (保) was composed of 10 *jia*, all of which were supervised by an elected head. The head of each unit was responsible for maintaining public order and maintaining records of the local population census. According to the *baojia* 保甲 system record, between 1750 and 1850, that is, over about 100 years, the population of China increased by more than 250 million.

47. Naquin and Rawski, *Chinese Society in the Eighteenth Century*, 25.

48. Jonathan Schlesinger, *A World Trimmed with Fur: Wild Things, Pristine Places, and the Natural Fringes of Qing Rule* (Stanford University Press, 2017), 131–32.

49. Leonard Blussé, *Strange Company: Chinese Settlers, Mestizo Women and the Dutch in VOC Batavia* (Foris Publications, 1986).

50. Jennifer Wayne Cushman, *Fields from the Sea: Chinese Junk Trade with Siam During the Late Eighteenth and Early Nineteenth Centuries* (Cornell University Press, 1993), frontispiece.

51. Edgar Wickberg, "Organization of Overseas Migration," in *Cosmopolitan Capitalists: Hong Kong and the Chinese Diaspora at the End of the 20th Century*, ed. Gary G. Hamilton (University of Washington Press, 1999), 35–55.

52. Wallerstein, *Modern World-System I*, 41.

53. Many Mexicans, also, had begun to treat cotton, which was imported from China, as a necessity, since many consumed Chinese imports (Gordon and Morales, *Silver Way*, 34).

54. Alexander Anievas and Kerem Nişancioğlu, "Why Europe? Anti-Eurocentric Theory, History and the Rise of Capitalism," *Spectrum Journal of Global Studies* 8, no. 1 (2017): 84; Andre Gunder Frank, *ReOrient: Global Economy in the Asian Age* (University of California Press, 1998); Andre Gunder Frank and Barry K. Gills, "The 5,000 Year World System: An Interdisciplinary Introduction," in *The World System: Five Hundred Years or Five Thousand?*, ed. Barry K. Gills and Andre Gunder Frank (Routledge, 1993), 3–58.

55. Wallerstein, in fact, noted that "the transition from feudalism to capitalism involved first of all the creation of a world-economy. That is to say, a social division of labor was brought into being through the transformation of long-distance trade from a trade in 'luxuries' to a trade in 'essentials' or 'bulk goods,' which tied together processes that were widely dispersed into long commodity chains": Immanuel Wallerstein, *Unthinking Social Science: The Limits of Nineteenth-Century Paradigms* (Temple University Press, 2001, 73). He believed that Western Europe (or the European world-economy) achieved its capitalist transition due mainly to a successful massive transformation from luxury trade to essentials or bulk goods trade. His statement provides us with a glimpse of one side of his Eurocentric idea.

56. Gang Deng, "The Foreign Staple Trade of China in the Pre-Modern Era," *International History Review* 9, no. 2 (1997): 283.

57. In a critical tone, Mazumdar pointed out that Wallerstein's theoretical approach to China's incorporation did not capture China's socioeconomic changes well (Mazumdar, *Sugar and Society in China*, 114–15).

58. Wallerstein, *Modern World-System III*, 167.

59. For instance, contrary to Wallerstein's view, which paid little heed to the importance of China's international trade, Dennis Flynn argued that worldwide trade connections in the sixteenth century were initiated and evolved not only by European powers but also by Asian powers' participation (e.g., China and Japan) (Flynn, "Big History, Geological Accumulations," 100).

60. Immanuel Wallerstein, "The West, Capitalism, and the Modern World-System," in *China and Historical Capitalism*, ed. Timothy Brook and Gregory Blue (Cambridge University Press, 1999), 15.

61. Gordon and Morales, *Silver Way*, 83.

62. Prior to China's incorporation, the Chinese trade network paid little attention to the expansion of its trade boundary as an effective means of profit-seeking activities. Economic advantages, unlike for European countries, were not a big consideration for sustaining China-centered tributary relationships. Chinese trade networks were used to maximize political deals. The Chinese empire, to that end, often gave gifts of higher value than what was received as tribute. Given that the economic costs of China's tributary system were subordinated to political stability between China and its tributary states, the Ming and Qing regimes did not have any strong motives to foster risk-taking merchants who sought economic profits from international trade. Of course, some Chinese merchants made enormous economic profits through international trade; however, in contrast with the quantum leap in international trade of Europe that enabled it to develop risky ventures between the state and the mercantile-financial elites, the late imperial Chinese regime did not go hand in hand with mercantile elites for advanced international trade.

63. Lincoln Paine, *The Sea and Civilization: A Maritime History of the World* (Knopf, 2013), 448.

64. Philip Kuhn, *Chinese Among Others: Emigration in Modern Times* (Rowman and Littlefield, 2008).

65. For instance, the Vereenigde Oostindische Compagnie (VOC) expanded its trading monopoly by flexibly accepting the rituals and customs required by local powers in Japan and Java: Leonard Blussé, *Visible Cities: Canton, Nagasaki, and Batavia and the Coming of the Americans* (Harvard University Press, 2008), 34–37.

66. Holden Furber, "Asia and the West as Partners Before 'Empire' and After," *Journal of Asian Studies* 28, no. 4 (1969): 711–21.

67. Two or three decades before China was incorporated into the capitalist world-system, China began to feel a great sense of crisis from Western ships that regularly appeared on its shores. For example, in April 1755, a memo to the emperor from Admiral Wu Jinshseng of Zhejiang Province concerning a *hongmaoren* 紅貓人 (red-haired people) ship that appeared in Ningbo of Zhejiang Province shows this well: *Qinggaozongshilu* 清高宗实录 489 (May 1755). *Hongmaoren* usually referred to a Dutch person, but it had gradually been extended to a general term for Westerners. Wu Jinshseng, who lacked knowledge of European nationalities, called the Western ship that entered the Ningbo a "Hongmaoren's ship." However, it was a ship of the British East India Company. In the following year (June 15, 1756), another Hongmaoren's ship docked again at Ningbo to try to trade with China. When Wu Jinshseng's memo reached Emperor Qianlong, the emperor realized that their repeated visits to China were due mainly to a desire to trade with China. Emperor Qianlong believed there must be Chinese traders or brokers (*yahang* 牙行) seeking economic interests who were involved in the frequent visits of Westerners so he ordered government bureaucrats to conduct a thorough investigation. Then, on November 10, 1757, an order was issued to prevent repeated visits of Westerners. The order blocked Western ships in all ports except Guangzhou; *Qinggaozongshilu* 清高宗实录 550 (November 1757).

68. *Gongzhongdang Yongzhengchao zouzhe* 宮中檔雍正朝奏摺 8 (National Palace Museum [Taipei], 1977), 836–38.

69. W. A. P. Martin, *A Cycle of Cathay or China, South and North with Personal Reminiscences* (Fleming H. Revell, 1900), 160.

70. Ching-huang Yen (Yan Qinghuang), *Coolies and Mandarins: China's Protection of Overseas Chinese During the Late Ch'ing Period (1815–1911)* (Singapore University Press, 1985), 154–68.

71. Li Hongzhang 李鴻章, *Lihongzhang quanji* 李鴻章全集 [The complete works of Li Hongzhang], vol. 6 (Anhuijiaoyu chubanse, 2008), 342–43.

72. Philip Kuhn, *Chinese Among Others: Emigration in Modern Times* (Rowman and Littlefield, 2008), 141–42.

73. The Ming and Qing did not consistently prohibit maritime trade. For example, in 1684, the Kangxi Emperor ordered the establishment of customs in four coastal areas (Shanghai, Ningbo, Xiamen, and Guangzhou).

74. Yü Ying-shih even points out that capitalism did not arise in China first because of China's totalitarian politics and the resulting setbacks in maritime expansion: Yü Ying-shih, *The Religious Ethic and Mercantile Spirit in Early Modern China* (Columbia University Press, 2021).

75. Gungwu Wang, "Merchants Without Empire: The Hokkien Sojourning Communities," in *The Rise of Merchant Empires: Long-Distance Trade in the Early Modern World, 1350–1750*, ed. James D. Tracy (Cambridge University Press, 1990), 400–421.

76. Unlike past Chinese maps drawn with China as the center, what is unique about this map, estimated to have been created around 1608, is that the center of the map is the South China Sea. While inland China was treated as insignificant on the map, the maritime routes in the South China Sea in the seventeenth century were marked in great detail. As can be easily guessed from the fact that the center of the map is the South China Sea, the main users of this map were Chinese maritime merchants traveling in and out of the South China Sea.

77. An English lawyer named John Selden donated this map to Oxford University in 1654. It is an important old map in terms of showing the overseas expansion of the Chinese during the Ming. This map contained the world that the Chinese at the time knew, "from the Indian Ocean in the west to the Spice Islands in the east, Java in the south, Japan in the north": Timothy Brook, *Mr. Selden's Map of China: The Spice Trade, a Lost Chart and the South China Sea* (Profile Books, 2013), xx. The Selden Map of China can be found at https://seldenmap.bodleian.ox.ac.uk/.

78. Kuhn, *Chinese Among Others*, 21.

79. William H. Sewell Jr., "The Temporalities of Capitalism," *Socio-Economic Review* 6, no. 3 (2008): 518.

80. William H. Sewell Jr., "Three Temporalities: Toward an Eventful Sociology," in *The Historic Turn in the Human Sciences*, ed. Terence McDonald (University of Michigan Press, 1996), 248.

81. D. W. Tomich, *Slavery in the Circuit of Sugar: Martinique and the World-Economy, 1830–1848*, 2nd ed. (State University of New York Press, 2016), 16.

82. Immanuel Wallerstein, "Reflections on an Intellectual Adventure in Special Symposium on the Modern World-System, Vol, I–IV," *Contemporary Sociology* 41, no. 1 (2012): 9.

83. Immanuel Wallerstein, "World System Versus World-Systems: A Critique," *Critique of Anthropology* 11, no. 2 (1991): 191.

84. Sung Hee Ru, "A Comparison of Weber's and Wallerstein's Historical Methods," *Journal of Asian Sociology* 52, no. 1 (2023): 39.

85. Arrighi and Silver, "Introduction," 1–36; Richard E. Lee and Dale Tomich, "Method and Practice in World-Systems Analysis: An Introduction to the Collection," *Review* 39, no. 1 (2016): 1–12; McMichael, "Incorporating Comparison," 385–97; Ru, "Comparison of Weber's and Wallerstein's Historical Methods," 33–64.

86. Basu, "Peripheralization of China," 171–87; So, "Process of Incorporation," 91–116; So, *South China Silk District*, 55.

87. Yong Soo Jang, "A World-Systems Perspective on the Sociocultural History of East Asia: The Cases of China, Japan, and Korea," PhD diss., State University of New York at Albany, 2004.

88. De-Chen Tao 陶德臣, "Lun qing dai cha ye mao yi de she hui ying xian" 论清代茶叶贸易的社会影响 [The social influence of the tea trade in the Qing dynasty], *Shixuiyuekan* 史学月刊 5 (2002): 90.

89. Peter C. Perdue, "Is Pu-er in Zomia? Tea Cultivation and the State in China," Agrarian Studies Colloquium, October 24, 2008, https://agrarianstudies.macmillan.yale.edu/sites/default/files/files/colloqpapers/07perdue.pdf, 12. At the same time, "Minbei exports to Russia grew to up to 7.6 million pounds per year, or 76% of total exports to Russia in 1850. The remote highlands had established remarkably long connections with the global markets of Eurasia" (Perdue, "Is Pu-er in Zomia?," 12).

90. Chris Nierstrasz, *Rivalry for Trade in Tea and Textiles: The English and Dutch East India Companies (1700–1800)* (Palgrave Macmillan, 2015), 7.

91. Kit Chow and Ione Kramer, *All the Tea in China* (China Books and Periodicals, 1990), 14.

92. Yong Liu, *The Dutch East India Company's Tea Trade with China, 1757–1781* (Brill, 2007), 14.

93. Of course, not all the EIC's attempts to expand its commercial network to China ended in success. For instance, in the late eighteenth century, the EIC tried to penetrate the Chinese market by using overland routes (Bengal-Tibet-China); however, the Qing's presence in Tibet prevented "trading activities through overland routes between Bengal and Tibet" (Sen, *India, China, and the World*, 252).

94. Unlike the Estado da India's international trades, which inhibited the development of maritime trades in the long run, the Dutch companies, especially the Vereenigde Oostindische Compagnie, actively participated in local trade. The VOC, for instance, earned money by selling goods purchased in one region of Asia to other regions of Asia. The massive profits, which came from "a permanent circulating capital" in Asia, at least partially helped the VOC to take the initiative in the international tea trade with China: Niels Steensgaard, *The Asian Trade Revolution of the Seventeenth Century: The East India Companies and the Decline of the Caravan Trade* (University of Chicago Press, 1974), 140. As another very salient point, the VOC enjoyed a monopoly on the tea trade in the European market by dominating the junk trade in advance.

95. Cheung Hoh and Lorna H. Mui, "Smuggling and the British Tea Trade Before 1784," *American Historical Review* 74, no. 1 (1968): 48. In the case of Britain, associated with an increase of tea-smuggling activities, high taxation on tea was another problem. Regarding this, Adam Smith argued that "the high duties which have been imposed upon the importation of many different sorts of foreign goods, in order to discourage their consumption in Great Britain,

have in many cases served only to encourage smuggling" (Smith, *Wealth of Nations*, 881–82). To eradicate tea smuggling and lower taxation on tea, Britain enacted the Commutation Act of 1784, and, as a result, the tax on tea dropped 119 percent to 12.5 percent: Denys Forrest, *Tea for the British: The Social and Economic History of a Famous Trade* (Chatto and Windus, 1973), 73. On the contrary, Hoh and Mui insist that the illegal tea trade, at least before the 1780s, contributed to promoting the international and domestic trade of Britain and helped to grow the British economy (Hoh and Mui, "Smuggling and the British Tea Trade," 73).

96. Since European powers realized that international trade with China was lucrative, Britain, France, the Netherlands, Denmark, and Sweden hoped to tap into the Chinese market after the seventeenth century. The VOC and the EIC were vying for a tea monopoly, and the EIC won this competition due mainly to the administrative support of the British government and Britain's massive advantages from its victory in the Seven Years' War. The EIC and Britain consequently pulled ahead of European competitors in China.

97. Liu, *Dutch East India Company's Tea Trade*, 152.

98. Femme Gaastra, "War, Competition and Collaboration: Relations Between the English and Dutch East Indian Companies in the Seventeenth and Eighteenth Centuries," in *The Worlds of the East India Company*, ed. H. V. Bowen, Margarette Lincoln, and Nigel Rigby (Boydell Press, 2002), 49–68.

99. Robert Parthesius, *Dutch Ships in Tropical Waters: The Development of the Dutch East India Company (VOC) Shipping Network in Asia, 1595–1660* (Amsterdam University Press, 2010), 38.

100. Boris P. Torgasheff, *China as a Tea Producer* (Commercial Press, 1926); Robert B. Marks, *Tigers, Rice, Silk, and Silt: Environment and Economy in Late Imperial South China* (Cambridge University Press, 1998).

101. Great Britain, House of Commons, *First Report from the Select Committee on the Affairs of the East India Company* (China Trade), 1830, viii.

102. For instance, the *Sylph*—one of Jardine Matheson and Company's high-speed sailing ships—completed the long distance from Calcutta to Macao in the record time of seventeen days and seventeen hours.

103. Jin-A Kang, "Yanghaeng: Tongashiaŭi kugyo sangin" [Western companies: Western merchants in East Asia], in *Segyeŭi taesangindŭl* [The great merchants in history] (National Research Council for Economics, Humanities, and Social Sciences, 2016), 143–87.

104. Peer Vries points out the importance of the 1780s as the starting point of the tea-opium trade between China and Britain; Peer Vries, *State, Economy and the Great Divergence: Great Britain and China, 1680s–1850s* (Bloomsbury, 2015). The dropping of import duties on tea through the Commutation Act of 1784 resulted in a decrease in foreign tea-smuggling, on the one hand, and reduced dependency on tea imports coming from the VOC, on the other hand; John K. Fairbank and Merle Goldman, *China: A New History*, 2nd ed. (Harvard University Press, 2006), 196.

105. Song-Chuan Chen, *Merchants of War and Peace: British Knowledge of China in the Making of the Opium War* (Hong Kong University Press, 2017), 44.

106. Around the same time (circa 1780–1840), the interest rates in Britain were between 4 percent and 5 percent.

107. Ernest John Eitel, *Europe in China: The History of Hong Kong from the Beginning to the Year 1882* (Kelly & Walsh, 1895), 67–68; Michael Greenberg, *British Trade and the Opening*

of China, 1800–1842 (Cambridge University Press, 1951), 64–65.

108. James R. Gibson, *Otter Skins, Boston Ships, and China Goods: The Maritime Fur Trade of the Northwest Coast, 1785–1841* (University of Washington Press, 1992), 194.

109. Bang Yue, "Ch'amuyŏki chŏngnarae mich'in younghyang" [The tea trade's impacts on the Qing Empire], master's thesis, Pusan University, 2013.

110. S. C. M. Paine, *The Sino-Japanese War of 1894–1895* (Cambridge University Press, 2003).

111. Peter Gue Zarrow, *After Empire: The Conceptual Transformation of the Chinese State, 1885–1924* (Stanford University Press, 2012), 4.

112. Marquis Tseng [Zeng Jize], "China: The Sleep and the Awakening," *Chinese Recorder* 18 (1887), 152.

113. As a unequal relationship, peripheral countries provide labor and materials to core and semiperipheral countries and are also in a situation where they do not occupy a relative political-geopolitical advantage in their relations with neighboring countries. After incorporation, China was forced to sign unequal treaties with several imperialist powers (core countries like Britain). At the same time, it had to endure political, economic, and geopolitical losses in its relations with semiperipheral countries (e.g., Japan and Russia). As a result, it also gave up the China-centered tributary relationship with its neighbors (e.g., Korea, Vietnam) and experienced territorial losses like Taiwan and Hong Kong. And a significant number of Chinese laborers had to move to overseas plantation farms and send materials such as Chinese tea or raw silk to core and semiperipheral countries.

Chapter 2

1. China had silver mines, but the central government strictly enforced a ban on private businesses running silver mining due to the increase of socioeconomic instability if private companies monopolized or oligopolized silver mines. Timothy Brook, *Vermeer's Hat: The Seventeenth Century and the Dawn of the Global World* (Bloomsbury Press, 2008), 160, 172. Worse, by the late Qing period the few silver mines were depleted. Relatedly, the story of *Guangxinfuzhi* in Jiangxi Province illustrates how minerals including silver in the area were depleted in late Qing period: "It is said that there used to be many minerals in Guangxinfu, but now there is none. The Book of *Shangraoxianzhi* records that gold, silver, and iron came out of Guangxinfu, the Book of *Yanshanxianzhi* records that copper and zinc came out of Guangxinfu, and the Book of *Yiyangxianzhi* records that copper and iron came out of Guangxin, but all of them were mined during the Ming Dynasty, and now there is no ore." *Guangxinfuzhi* 廣信府志 [Local Gazetteer of Guangxin] (1872), 145.

2. J. A. Hobson. "Free Trade and Foreign Policy," *Contemporary Review* 74 (1898), 178.

3. David Harvey. *The Anti-Capitalist Chronicles* (Pluto, 2020), chap. 12.

4. Fredric Wakeman Jr., *The Fall of Imperial China* (Free Press, 1975), 123–25; threefold expansion of the opium trade, 126.

5. Angela McCarthy and T. M. Devine, *Tea and Empire: James Taylor in Victorian Ceylon* (Manchester University Press, 2017), 61.

6. Gregory Clark Michael Huberman and Peter H. Lindert, "A British Food Puzzle, 1770–1850," *Economic History Review* 48, no. 2 (1995): 215–37; C. H. Denyer, "The Consumption

of Tea and Other Staple Drinks," *Economic Journal* 3, no. 9 (1893): 33–51; J. R. Ward, "The Industrial Revolution and British Imperialism, 1750-1850," *Economic History Review* 47, no. 1 (1994): 44–65. In fact, tea with sugar, as a substitute for rum and gin, was often consumed by workingmen, which led English workers to help develop self-disciplined drinking and eating habits under the capitalist mode of production: Sidney W. Mintz, "Food and Concepts of Power," in *Food and Agrarian Orders in the World-Economy*, ed. Philip McMichael (Praeger, 1995), 3–13. Mintz, in another study, insisted that the British working class's new practices, drinking tea and sugar, contributed to solving the problem of working-class alcoholism, which fostered the successful industrialization of Britain: Sidney W. Mintz, "Food, Culture, and Energy," in *Food and Globalization: Consumption, Markets and Politics in the Modern World* (Berg, 2008), 21–35.

7. In the period between 1660 and 1760, the British East India Company's tea imports from China accounted for 71 percent of Chinese imports to Britain: Kirti N. Chaudhuri, *The Trading World of Asia and the English East India Company, 1660–1760* (Cambridge University Press, 2006), 507–48. According to Ralph Davis, who analyzed the customs records of Britain between 1834 and 1836, the British East India Company's tea imports from China accounted for 80 percent of Chinese imports; see Ralph Davis, *The Industrial Revolution and British Overseas Trade* (Leicester University Press, 1979).

8. Ho-Fung Hung, "Imperial China and Capitalist Europe in the Eighteenth-Century Global Economy," *Review* 24, no. 4 (2001): 473–513.

9. Man-houng Lin, *China Upside Down: Currency, Society, and Ideologies, 1808–1856* (Harvard University Press, 2006).

10. Wallerstein, *Modern World-System III*, 167.

11. John F. Richards, "The Opium Industry in British India," *Indian Economic and Social History Review* 39, nos. 2–3 (2002): 163.

12. Paul Wilson Howard, "Opium Suppression in Qing China: Responses to a Social Problem, 1729–1906," PhD diss., University of Pennsylvania, 1998.

13. Kyung-Ho Suh. *Ap'yŏnjŏnjaeng* [The Opium War] (Ilchokak, 2020), 67.

14. Jonathan D. Spence, *The Search for Modern China* (Norton, 1990), 129, 149.

15. The state merchandizing monopoly bears the stamp of British mercantilism. In effect, British "commercial organizations acted as its political arm abroad": Jane T. Merritt, *The Trouble with Tea: The Politics of Consumption in the Eighteenth-Century Global Economy* (Johns Hopkins University Press, 2017), 14. For example, the British government empowered the EIC to use political and military means when EIC merchants invested in maritime adventures or traded with foreign countries.

16. Of course, before the nineteenth century, opium was used and distributed in Chinese society. At that time, however, opium was often used as medicine and was sometimes consumed by upper class men like the literati and government officials (for relieving stress) or wealthy merchants (for facilitating business deals). Also, Portuguese merchants participated in the trade in opium, which had been exported to China since the early sixteenth century; "the amount of opium exported to China remained relatively small . . . until the middle of the following century when Britain extended its control over the country" (Howard, "Opium Suppression in Qing China," 40). Meanwhile, after the late eighteenth century opium imports by Chinese society increased sharply once Britain took the competitive edge away from Portugal in opium

exports. Afterward, lower-class Chinese were vulnerable to the use of opium; Qichen Huang 黃啓臣 and Zheng Weiming 鄭煒明, *Aomen jingjisi bainian* 澳門經濟 四百年 (Macau economy, four hundred years) (Aomen jijinhui, 1994), chap. 8.

17. Indian merchants were often overlooked by important participants in the opium trade. Under the rule of the British Empire, Indian merchants, especially Parsis, a minority Indian religious group, strove to take advantage of the opium trade beginning in the eighteenth century. The Parsis did not monopolize the opium market of India, but their deep involvement in the opium trade made a significant contribution to the development of Indian and imperial economies; Jesse S. Palsetia. *Jamsetjee Jejeebhoy of Bombay: Partnership and Public Culture in Empire* (Oxford University Press, 2015), 35. While acting as mediators between the British merchants and China during the early nineteenth century, eleven Parsi companies operated in Canton, which outnumbered the nine American firms (Palsetia, *Jamsetjee Jejeebhoy of Bombay*, 26). Jamsetjee Jejeebhoy, inter alia, played an important role in accelerating the opium trade between British India and China by creating strong ties with Hong merchants in China. His close connection with Hong merchants prevented Chinese merchants from developing a negative impression of Jejeebhoy, which led to the success of his trading enterprise.

18. Suh, *Ap'yŏnjŏnjaeng*, 176–77.
19. Suh, *Ap'yŏnjŏnjaeng*, 153–55.
20. Lin, *China Upside Down*, 90.
21. Marx and Engels, *Communist Manifesto*, 77.
22. *Wanguogongbao* 萬國公報 452 (1877), 3985.
23. *Wanguogongbao* 萬國公報 454 (1877), 4038.
24. *Wanguogongbao* 萬國公報 459 (1877), 4177.
25. *Yapianzhanzhengdanganshiliao* 鸦片战争档案史料 [Archival historical materials on the Opium War], vol. 1 (Shanghairenminchubanshe, 1987), 771.
26. *Yapianzhanzhengdanganshiliao*, 1:90.
27. *Yapianzhanzhengdanganshiliao*, 1:446.
28. Isabella Bird Bishop. *The Yangtze Valley and Beyond*, vol. 2 (G. P. Putnam's Sons and John Murray, 1900), 281.
29. *Yapianzhanzhengdanganshiliao*, 1:675–77.
30. Bishop, *Yangtze Valley and Beyond*, 283.
31. Bishop, *Yangtze Valley and Beyond*, 507.
32. *Yapianzhanzhengdanganshiliao*, 1:6.
33. *Yapianzhanzhengdanganshiliao*, 1:18.
34. *Yapianzhanzhengdanganshiliao*, 1:64.
35. Lin, "China's 'Dual Economy,'" 179–97. For quantitative data on the outflow of silver from Guangzhou between 1827 and 1834, see Zhongping Yan et al. 嚴中平 等著, *Zhongguo jindai jingjishi tongji zhliao xuanji* 中國近代經濟史統計資料選輯 [Selected statistics of modern Chinese economic history] (Kexuechubanshe, 1955), 33.
36. Willard J. Peterson. "Early Nineteenth-Century Monetary Ideas on the Cash-Silver Exchange Ratio," in *Papers on China*, vol. 20 (Harvard University Press, 1966), 40.
37. *Yapianzhanzhengdanganshiliao*, 1:45.
38. *Yapianzhanzhengdanganshiliao*, 1:68–70.
39. Greenberg, *British Trade*, 142.

40. Gideon Nye, *The Morning of My Life in China: Comprising an Outline of the History of Foreign Intercourse from the Last Year of the Regime of Honorable East India Company, 1833, to the Imprisonment of the Foreign Community in 1839* (Canton, 1873), 56.

41. The Qing government failed to modify or develop alternatives to the silver-based tax system that might have enhanced the power of the central government. The result was a long period of weakening of the Chinese fiscal system covering most of nineteenth century. In a silver inflation crisis, Wang Liu 王鎏 (1786–1834) put forth a monetary proposal, *Qianbi chuyan* 鈔幣芻言 (Preliminary remarks on copper coins), to allow paper currency, as a standard for tax payments, to be introduced to substitute for silver. However, his proposal was not accepted due to a strong backlash from intellectuals and government officials who expressed concern about a strong possibility that this would open the way to counterfeit currency. In addition, the opponents of Wang Liu's proposal did not want to repeat the mistakes of the past; previous Chinese dynasties had repeated failures whenever they issued paper currency due mainly to the low levels of trust of paper currency (Lin, *China Upside Down*, chap. 4).

42. Nancy E. Park, "Corruption in Eighteenth Century China," *Journal of Asian Studies* 56, no. 4 (1997): 967–1005.

43. Frank, *ReOrient*, 273–74.

44. Feng Xu 徐峰, "Shangye yu jindaizhongguo chengshihuade qidong, 1840–1895 商业与近代中国城市化的启动, 1840–1895) [Trade and the start of urbanization in modern China, 1840–1895], *Beifangluncong* 北方论丛 2 (2008): 78–82.

45. Rev. Justus Doolittle. *Social Life of the Chinese*, vol. 1 (Sampson Low Son & Marston, 1866); Y. M. Yeung and David K. Y. Chu, *Fujian: A Coastal Province in Transition and Transformation* (Chinese University Press, 2000).

46. Juenong Wu 吴觉农, *Zhongguo difangzhi chaye lishi ziliao xuanji* 中国地方志茶叶历史资料选辑 [Selection of historical materials on tea from Chinese local gazetteers) (Nongye chubanshe, 1990), 301.

47. Zhu Xi (1130–1200), who had a profound effect on the development of Neo-Confucianism, composed lyrics praising Wuyi Mountain for its outstanding natural environment: "There are agathodaimon spirit (*xianling* 仙靈) on Wuyi Mountain and the cold current at the foot of the mountain is clear. If you want to know some outstanding places, listen to the song two or three times" (in the middle of *Jiuqu zhao ge* 九曲棹歌).

48. Yifeng Dai 戴一峰, "Zai lun jin dai minjiang shang yu shanqu de shangpin shengchan" 再论近代闽江上游山区的商品生产 [More research on commodity production in the mountain area of the upper Min River in modern times], *Zhongguo shehui jingjishi yanjiu* 中国社会经济史研究 4 (1989): 61.

49. Fang Xing, "The Role of Embryonic Capitalism in China," in *Chinese Capitalism, 1522–1840*, ed. Xu Dixin and Wu Chengming (Macmillan, 2000), 402–29.

50. Imperial Maritime Customs, 1, *Statistical Series. Nr. 4, Reports on Trade at the Treaty Ports*, 1878 (1879), 211.

51. Robert Gardella. "Reform and the Tea Industry and Trade in Late Ch'ing China: The Fukien Case," in *Reform in Nineteenth-Century China*, ed. P. A. Cohen and J. E. Schrecker (Harvard University Press, 1976), 71–79.

52. Man-houng Lin. 林滿紅, *Cha tang zhangnao ye yu Taiwan zhi sheshui jingji bianqian 1860–1895* 茶、糖、樟腦業與台灣之社會經濟變遷 *(1860–1895)* [The tea, sugar, and camphor industries and socioeconomic change of Taiwan, 1860–1895) (Lien-ching publishing, 1997).

53 Benjamin J. Marley, "The Coal Crisis in Appalachia: Agrarian Transformation, Commodity Frontiers, and the Geographies of Capital," *Journal of Agrarian Change* 16, no. 2 (2016): 227.

54. Gardella, *Harvesting Mountains*, 43–44.

55. Liu Min and Liu Xiusheng explained where the shack people were and how they survived during the Ming and Qing periods: see Liu Min 刘敏, "Lunqingdaipengmindehujiwenti" 论清代棚民的户籍问题 [On the problem of the household registration of shack people in the Qing period], *Zhongguo shehui jingjishi yanjiu* 中国社会经济史研究 1 (1983): 17–26; Liu Xiusheng 刘秀生, "Qingdaiminzheganwandepengminjingji" 清代闽浙赣皖的棚民经济 [The economy of shack people in the Fujian-Zhejiang-Jiangxi-Anhui area in the Qing period], *Zhongguo shehui jingjishi yanjiu* 中国社会经济史研究 1 (1988): 53–60. Anne Osborne explained how shack people mobilized for tea cultivation: Anne Osborne, "The Local Politics of Land Reclamation in the Lower Yangzi Highlands," *Late Imperial China* 15, no. 1 (1994): 10.

56. Doolittle, *Social Life of the Chinese*, 1:49.

57. He Jun Fan 范和钧, "Tunxi chaye diaocha" 屯溪茶业调查 [Survey on the Tunxi tea industry], *Guoji Maoyi Daobao* 国际贸易导报 9, no. 4 (1937): 113–35. The twenty-hour days of hard work roasting tea took a heavy toll on the laborers' bodies. Some suffered from body aches or exhaustion. Others were struck down by sunstroke (Fan, "Tunxi Chaye diaocha," 120–22).

58. James W. Davidson, *The Island of Formosa, Past and Present* (Kelly and Walsh, 1903); Delia Davin, "Women in the Countryside of China," in *Women in Chinese Society*, ed. Margery Wolf and Roxane Witke (Stanford University Press, 1975), 243–73; Weijing Lu, "Beyond the Paradigm: Tea-Picking Women in Imperial China," *Journal of Women's History* 15, no. 4 (2004): 19–46.

59. William T. Rowe. *Hankow: Commerce and Society in a Chinese City, 1776–1889* (Stanford University Press, 1984).

60. Qi Shi and Fang Zhuofen, "Embryonic Capitalism in Agriculture," in *Chinese Capitalism, 1522–1840*, ed. Xu Dixin and Wu Chengming (Macmillan, 2000), 155.

61. Liu, *Tea War*, 57.

62. Liu, *Tea War*, 57.

63. Jayeeta Sharma, " 'Lazy' Natives, Coolie Labour, and the Assam Tea Industry," *Modern Asian Studies* 43, no. 6 (2009): 1287–1324.

64. H. A. Antrobus, *A History of the Assam Company, 1839–1953* (Private printing by T. and A. Constable, 1957).

65. *Assam: Sketch of Its History, Soil, and Production, with the Discovery of the Tea-Plant, and of the Countries Adjoining Assam* (Smith Elder and Co, 1839), 23.

66. William Griffith, "Report on the Tea Plant of Upper Assam," in *Transactions of the Agricultural and Horticultural Society of India, Volume 5* (Agricultural & Horticultural Society of India, Calcutt, 1838), 175.

67. This was mainly due to the high wages requested by Chinese laborers, their difficulty in adapting to the new climate, and the employment of unskilled Chinese workers.

68. Nitin Varma, *Producing Tea Coolies? Work, Life, and Protest in the Colonial Tea Plantations of Assam, 1830s–1920s* (Humboldt-Universität, 2011).

69. Relatedly, but unsurprisingly, the tea plantations that the British established in India, Sri Lanka, and elsewhere were large-scale enterprises, even though the production process of tea is labor-intensive. The tea-collecting trip of Robert Fortune (1813–1880) is an interesting example of how tea could be cultivated outside of China. In order to transplant tea cultivation

to the Indian colony of Assam in 1848 the British East India Company collected teas from China. In fact, the EIC asked Fortune to collect the finest teas produced in China. He often disguised himself as a Chinese merchant since his activities were forbidden to foreigners. Fortune collected both samples of fine teas and seedlings of the tea plants that could be planted in India. Fortune embarked on a tea-collecting trip to China to collect green teas from Zhejiang and Anhui Provinces. Leaving Shanghai, he traveled through Hangzhou in Zhejiang Province and came to a green tea factory on the Yangtze River. He then traveled to Songluoshan 松蘿山 in Anhui Province to collect tea before returning to Shanghai. The purpose of his second trip was to collect black tea from the Wuyi Mountains in Fujian Province. From Ningbo he traveled through Zhejiang and Jiangxi Provinces to reach the Wuyi Mountains, where he could collect a famous tea, *daponggpao* 大红袍. He then travelled to Pucheng in Fujian Province before returning to Shanghai. Through his secret and illegal tea-collecting trips many Chinese teas were transported to the Assam region of India, where they were transformed into Assam tea.

70. Chen, *Jindai zhongguo chaye de fazhan*, 342.

71. Lin, *Cha tang zhangnao*, 19. For statistical data on the decline in tea export volume in the late nineteenth and early twentieth centuries, see Yan et al., *Zhongguo jindai jingjishi tongji zhliao xuanji*, 74.

72. Christopher Thomas Gardner, "Amoy Emigration to the Straits," *China Review* 22, no. 4 (1897): 621–26. See also figure 3.5 and figure 3.6.

73. The Statistical Department of the Inspectorate General of Customs, "Foochow Trade Report," in *Returns of Trade and Trade Reports*, vol. 4—*Southern Coast Ports* (Statistical Department of the Inspectorate General of Customs, 1905), 356.

74. China, *Imperial Maritime Customs*, Tea, 1888. 2-Special Series no. 11 (1889), 106.

75. Foreign Office, Great Britain, "George Phillips to John Walsham, Foochow, April 3, 1890," in *Diplomatic and Consular Reports, Annual Series*, no. 726 (Great Britain, Foreign Office), 9.

76. Foreign Office, Great Britain, "George Phillips to John Walsham, Foochow, April 3, 1890," 9.

77. Thomas P. Lyons, *China Maritime Customs and China's Trade Statistics, 1859–1948* (Willow Creek Press, 2003).

78. Arnold Wright, *Twentieth Century Impressions of Hongkong, Shanghai, and Other Treaty Ports* (Lloyd, 1908).

79. The principal cause of declining overseas demand may be attributed to domestic factors. It is an undeniable fact that the increased cost of tea production, heavy taxation on the tea industry, and the deteriorating quality of Chinese tea and the creation of fake tea (e.g., mixing tea and iron crumbs) meant Chinese tea was left behind in the international competition of the second half of the nineteenth century: Ciyu Chen 陈慈玉, Jindai Zhongguo chaye zhi fazhan 近代中国茶业之发展 [The development of the modern Chinese tea industry] (Beijing, Zhongguo renmin da xue chu ban she, 2013), 259–74. This explanation is limited in important respects by its primary concern with the decline of the Chinese tea industry. This view, focusing on internal causes, tends to ignore external conditions in furthering the collapse of the Chinese tea industry.

80. Zontang Zuo 左宗棠, Zuo Wenxiang gong quan ji 左文襄公全集 [The collected works of Zuo Zongdang], ed. Yang shulin 楊書霖, vol. 2, bk. 19 (Wenhaichubanshi, 1979), 759.

81. Liu, *Tea War*, 232.

82. Erika Rappaport, *A Thirst for Empire: How Tea Shaped the Modern World* (Princeton University Press, 2017).

83. Anne Osborne, "Highlands and Lowlands: Economic and Ecological Interactions in the Lower Yangzi Region Under the Qing," in *Sediments of Time: Environment and Society in Chinese History*, ed. Mark Elvin and Liu Ts'ui-jung (Cambridge University Press, 1998), 203–24.

84. Marks, *Tigers, Rice, Silk, and Silt*, 180–81.

85. Tea requires a deep soil layer, humus-rich soil, and a moist but well-drained location (Anne Osborne, "Barren Mountains, Raging Rivers: The Ecological and Social Effects of Changing Land Use on the Lower Yangzi Periphery in Late Imperial China," PhD diss., Columbia University, 1989, 75). In addition, the spacing between the tea plants must be kept constant. If it rains heavily in this situation, it can create serious soil runoff and landslides.

86. Shengshao Chen, 陈盛韶, "Wensulu" 問俗錄 [An investigation of customs records], in *Sikuweishoushujikan* 四库未收书辑刊 [Collection of books not included in Siku], vol. 6 (Beijing chubanshe, [1826] 2000), 230.

87. Rev. J. E. Walker. "Shao-Wu in Fuh-Kien: A Country Station," *Chinese Recorder and Missionary Journal* 9, no. 5 (1878), 348.

88. Nancy Fraser argues that countries at the center of the capitalist world-system often caused the socio-ecological destruction of peripheral regions through trade relations. "From the silver mines of Potosi to the slave plantations of Saint-Domingue" (Fraser, *Cannibal Capitalism* [Verso, 2022], 95), the capitalist core exploited the land and labor of the periphery until it was exhausted, leaving a trail of environmental and social damage in its wake. Fraser notes that capitalism has "a cannibalistic and extractive relationship" with nature to the lands and peoples that it exploits (Fraser, *Cannibal Capitalism*, 83).

89. Jason W. Moore, "Amsterdam Is Standing on Norway Part II: The Global North Atlantic in the Ecological Revolution of the Long Seventeenth Century," *Journal of Agrarian Change* 10, no. 2 (2010): 188–227.

90. Jason W. Moore, "Sugar and the Expansion of the Early Modern World-Economy: Commodity Frontiers, Ecological Transformation, and Industrialization," *Review* 23, no. 3 (2000): 409–33.

91. Stephen G. Bunker and Paul S. Ciccantell, "Economic Ascent and the Global Environment: World-Systems Theory and the New Historical Materialism," in *Economy and the World-System*, ed. Walter L. Goldfrank, David Goodman, and Andrew Szasz (Greenwood, 1999), 107.

92. See Stephen G. Bunker and Paul S. Ciccantell, *Globalization and the Race for Resources* (Johns Hopkins University Press, 2005), 90.

93. On the long-standing elites, especially the gentry class, in late imperial China, see Chang-li Chang, *The Chinese Gentry: Studies on Their Role in Nineteenth-Century Chinese Society* (University of Washington Press, 1955); Ping-ti Ho, *The Ladder of Success in Imperial China: Aspects of Social Mobility, 1368–1911* (Columbia University Press, 1962); Kung-chuan Hsiao, *Rural China: Imperial Control in the Nineteenth Century* (University of Washington Press, 1960).

94. Because the rise of new social class means a deviation from the (previous or existing) class structure, it can spark a society's unprecedented transformations. And in an extreme case, the new social class has the potential for sociopolitical violence or for social revolution (Skocpol, *States and Social Revolutions*, 4–5).

95. For example, Barrington Moore Jr. insisted that the gentry class, a dominant class in late imperial China, made considerable efforts to sustain not only economic wealth but also high status (Moore, *Social Origins of Dictatorship and Democracy*, 165). This fossilized the gentry-centered class system and gave other classes few opportunities for transforming society. As a result, late imperial Chinese society did not create profit-seeking and adventurous entrepreneurs, and thus it did not escape from the static and unchanged gentry-class system and eventually faced stagnation. In a similar vein, Theda Skocpol insisted that it was impossible for a new class to overturn the gentry-class-centered society because the gentry class had close links with central and local government officials (Skocpol, *States and Social Revolutions*, 71–72). The powerful gentry class's influence that was formed by collaboration with bureaucrats restricted the growth of a new class. As a result, the engine of socioeconomic changes in late imperial China was lost and Chinese society remained in stagnation.

96. Immanuel Wallerstein, "Class-Formation in the Capitalist World-Economy," *Politics and Society* 5, no. 3 (1975): 367.

97. Terence K. Hopkins. "Notes on Class Analysis and the World-System," *Review* 1, no. 1 (1977): 68.

98. Immanuel Wallerstein, "Class Conflict in the Capitalist World-Economy," in *The Capitalist World-Economy: Essays by Immanuel Wallerstein* (Cambridge University Press, 1979), 286.

99. Giovanni Arrighi, Terrence K. Hopkins, and Immanuel Wallerstein, "Rethinking the Concepts of Class and Status-Group in a World-System Perspective," *Review* 6, no. 3 (1983): 302.

100. For instance, see Karl Marx, *Wage-Labour and Capital & Value, Price and Profit* (International Publishers, [1933] 1990); E. P. Thompson, *The Making of the English Working Class* (Victor Gollancz, [1963] 1980).

101. Immanuel Wallerstein, "Class and Class Conflict in Africa," *Monthly Review* 26, no. 9 (1975): 37.

102. Victor D. Lippit, *Capitalism* (Routledge, 2005), 115.

103. For the wide range of modes of labor elaborated by Immanuel Wallerstein, see Chamsy El-Ojeili, "Reflections on Wallerstein: The Modern World-System, Four Decades On," *Critical Sociology* 41, nos. 4–5 (2014): 1–22.

104. Ravi R. Palat, "Curries, Chopsticks, and Kiwis: Asian Migration to Aotearoa/New Zealand," in *Nga Patai: Racism and Ethnic Relations in Aotearoa*, ed. Paul Spoonley, David G. Pearson, and Cluny MacPherson (Dunmore Press, 1996), 38.

105. Chase-Dunn and Rubinson, "Toward a Structural Perspective," 456–57.

106. Philip McMichael, "Pastoralism and Capitalist Development in Nineteenth-Century Australia: A Study of Settler Capital Accumulation," PhD diss., State University of New York at Binghamton, 1979.

107. Tomich, *Slavery in the Circuit of Sugar*, 68–69.

108. Kenneth Pomeranz and Steven Topik, *The World That Trade Created: Society, Culture, and the World Economy, 1400 to the Present* (Routledge, 2013), 180–82.

109. Chinese coolies were particularly suitable for plantation work due to their industriousness and patience in the workplace. See Matthew Pratt Guterl, "After Slavery: Asian Labor, the American South, and the Age of Emancipation," *Journal of World History* 14, no. 2 (2003): 209–41; Leonard Wray, *The Practical Sugar Planter: A Complete Account of the Cultivation and Manufacture of the Sugar Cane According to the Latest and Most Improved Processes* (Smith,

Elder and Company, 1848), 83; Lisa Yun and Ricardo Rene Laremont, "Chinese Coolies and African Slaves in Cuba, 1847–74," *Journal of Asian American Studies* 4, no. 2 (2001): 109. Chinese coolies who migrated from the sugar-producing areas of Fukien Province also had advanced skills in sugar cultivation. This consequently helped boost the efficiency of their work. For these reasons, Chinese workers were pampered by sugar plantation owners.

110. Originally the word *coolie* was used by the Portuguese to describe Indian laborers in the sixteenth century. However, this term was mistakenly connected to the Chinese word *kuli*, "meaning that bitterly hard use of strength": Mae Ngai, "Chinese Gold Miners and the 'Coolie Question' in Nineteenth-Century California and Victoria," *Journal of American History* 101, no. 4 (2015): 1084. At a time when Chinese laborers were being contracted out to the plantations of colonial powers, *kuli* or coolie was used to identify Chinese indentured laborers.

111. Western merchants often called coolies "piglets," indicating the horrible situation of these exploited laborers. They were treated like animals such as pigs, and they were locked up in barracks that were similar to piglet pens until they were shipped overseas; Liping Wong Yip, *From Wah Lee to Chew Keen: The Story of a Pioneer Chinese Family in North Cariboo* (Friesen Press, 2017).

112. Evelyn Hu-Dehart, "Coolies, Shopkeepers, Pioneers: The Chinese of Mexico and Peru," *AMERASI* 15, no. 2 (1989): 106.

113. Arrighi, *Long Twentieth Century*, 28.

114. Walton Look Lai, *Indentured Labor, Caribbean Sugar: Chinese and Indian Migrants to the British West Indies, 1838–1918* (Johns Hopkins University Press, 1993), 266–67.

115. "Peruvian Guano, An Account of the Guano Trade at the Chincha Islands on the Coast of Peru," in *Transaction of the American Institute of the City of New York* (1856), 225.

116. According to the testimonies of Chinese coolies, many of whom were kidnapped and then "forcibly carried on the coolie ships or enticed by the Chinese Coolie brokers on various pretexts to see the vessel" ("Piracy and Murder—the Coolie Trade," *New York Times*, July 21, 1853, https://www.nytimes.com/1853/07/21/archives/piracy-and-murderthe-coolie-trade.html).

117. Regarding the description of coolie ships' remarkable similarities to the miserable conditions of slave ships, see Don Aldus, *Coolie Traffic and Kidnapping* (McCorquodale & Co, 1876), 31. In reference to the wretched conditions on coolie ships, Mo Shixiang also described them as a floating hell (*fudongdiyu* 浮动地狱). See Mo Shixiang 莫世祥, "Gangao kuli maoyiyu yingpu lunzheng" 港澳苦力贸易与英葡论争 [Hong Kong and Macao's coolie trades and the dispute between Britain and Portugal], *Guangzhou shehuikexue* 广东社会科学 2 (2016): 80–89.

118. Domestic factors were the principal cause of increasing numbers of Chinese coolies Unexpected political turmoil, governmental negligence, a Hakka diaspora, and massive population growth pushed members of low-income families to become coolie laborers. Yet this is limited in important respects by its primary concern with China's poor economic conditions, unstable society, and weakening political authority. In fact, these views focusing on internal causes tend to ignore colonial powers' roles in furthering the coolie trade.

119. Adam McKeown, *Chinese Migrant Networks and Cultural Change: Peru, Chicago, Hawaii, 1900–1936* (University of Chicago Press, 2001), 61; June Mei, "Socioeconomic Origins of Emigration: Guangdong to California, 1850 to 1882," in *Labor Immigration Under Capitalism: Asian Workers in the United States Before World War II*, ed. Lucie Cheng and Edna Bonacich (University of California Press, 1984), 220.

120. Foster M. Farley, "The Chinese Coolie Trade, 1845–1875," *Journal of Asian and African Studies* 3 (1967): 257–70.

121. Lisa Yun, *The Coolie Speaks: Chinese Indentured Laborers and African Slaves of Cuba* (Temple University Press, 2008), 12.

122. Arnold J. Meagher, *The Coolie Trade: The Traffic in Chinese Laborers to Latin America, 1847–1874* (Xlibris, 2008), 40.

123. Evelyn Hu-Dehart, "Chinese Coolie Labor in Cuba in the Nineteenth Century: Free Labor of Neoslavery," *Contributions in Black Studies* 12 (1994): 38.

124. "The lowest class of Chinamen were collected under every variety of pretext, there being no Government superintendence or protection, and shipped to Peru and the adjacent Chincha Islands, or to Cuba" ("A Chatter on the Coolie Trade," in *Harper's New Monthly Magazine*, vol. 14, June 1864, 2).

125. Kuhn, *Chinese Among Others*, 31. Of course, Chinese immigration was not limited to southern China. Chinese from Shandong and Hubei migrated to Siberia and South Africa in the early twentieth century or to France during World War I (Meagher, *Coolie Trade*, 66).

126. Meagher, *Coolie Trade*, 133.

127. Brett Clark and John Bellamy Foster, "Ecological Imperialism and the Global Metabolic Rift: Unequal Exchange and the Guano/Nitrates Trade," *International Journal of Comparative Sociology* 50, nos. 3–4 (2009): 311–34. Indeed, *The Report on the Census of Cuba* (1900), officially published by the US government, showed how many coolies were moved to Cuba in the late nineteenth century: "Between 1853 and 1873, there were shipped from China to Cuba 132,435 Chinese." War Department, Director, Census of Cuba, *Report on the Census of Cuba* (U.S. Government Printing Office, 1900), 71.

128. Marquis Tseng [Zeng Jize], "China: The Sleep and the Awakening," *Chinese Recorder* 18 (1887), 149; Walton Look Lai, "Asian Contact and Free Migration to the Americas," in *Coerced and Free Migration: Global Perspectives*, ed. David Eltis (Stanford University Press, 2002), 229–58.

129. Regarding the necessity of cheap labor in sugar or tobacco plantations, see Eric Williams, *Capitalism and Slavery* (University of North Carolina Press, [1944] 1994), 23.

130. "The Coolie Trade," *Debow's Review* 27 (New Orleans, 1859), 299. This quote was apparently a comment on slave owners in Cuba, pretending to criticize them, but in reality agreeing that slave owners should exploit whoever they needed for profit. The history of exploited labor in the U.S. was no different. Caribs were the indigenous people of Cuba.

131. "Emigration and the Coolie Trade in China," *Westminster Review* 100 (July 1873), 80.

132. George Goudie Chisholm, *The Two Hemispheres: A Popular Account* (W. O. Blackie and Co, Printers, 1882), 802–3.

133. Katharine Coman, "The History of Contract Labor in the Hawaiian Islands," *Publications of the American Economic Association* 4, no. 3 (1903), 7.

134. Eleanor C. Nordyke and Richard K. C. Lee, "Chinese in Hawaii: A Historical and Demographic Perspective," *Hawaiian Journal of History* 23 (1989): 201.

135. "The Coolie and Slave Trade: Horrors of the Coolie-Trade a Legalized System of Free Chinese Emigration Important Dispatch from Lord John Russell," *New York Times*, August 16, 1860. https://www.nytimes.com/1860/08/16/archives/city-and-county-affairs-west-washington-market-the-case-not-decided.html; Persia Crawford Campbell, *Chinese Coolie Emigration to Countries Within the British Empire* (P. S. King & Westminster, 1923), xii. Violence and crime

can be easily found in coolie recruitments. With regard to this, see Great Britain, Parliament, House of Commons, *Parliamentary Papers, Correspondence Respecting Emigration from Canton*, Vol. 69, Inclosure 1 in No. 1. Consul Alcock to Sir J. Bowring, Canton, April 12, 1859.

136. Meagher, *Coolie Trade*, 81. Chinese crimps' roles were also significant in luring Chinese people craftily, including underhanded methods like drugs or gambling and abduction: "Emigration and the Coolie Trade in China," *Westminster Review*, vol. 100 (July 1873), 81.

137. Great Britain, Parliament, House of Commons, "Inclosure 26 in No. 13: Deposition of Kidnapped Coolie Brought from Whampoa," *Accounts and Papers*, Thirty-Five Volumes, China; Japan; Syria (24 January–28 August 1860), 99.

138. Aldus, *Coolie Traffic and Kidnapping*, 169–70.

139. George Battye Fisher, *Personal Narrative of Three Years' Service in China* (Richard Bentley, 1863), 304.

140. "Emigration and the Coolie Trade in China," 81.

141. "The Coolie and Slave Trade: Horrors of the Coolie-Trade a Legalized System of Free Chinese Emigration Important Dispatch from Lord John Russell," *New York Times*, August 16, 1860. https://www.nytimes.com/1860/08/16/archives/city-and-county-affairs-west-washington-market-the-case-not-decided.html.

142. In addressing the economic reason for the coolie trade, Meagher's argument is also worth heeding: "The freight of tea from China to the Americas in the early 1850s averaged $19 per ton, or $9,500 for a cargo of five hundred tons. Hence, a ship trading in Chinese emigrants to Cuba or Peru netted a profit of from five to ten times that of a ship trading in tea. These enormous profits attracted ships of all size and types carrying the flags of nineteen nations. Initially, British, French, and Peruvian flags predominated. British bottoms carried the bulk of the emigrants from 1852 to 1854 after United States clippers invaded the China tea trade in 1851 and sent British shipping scrambling for employment" (Meagher, *Coolie Trade*, 144). Meagher's arguments can be viewed as broadly indicating the scale of coolie trade revenue across the Western merchants.

143. Peter Kwong, *Forbidden Workers: Illegal Chinese Immigrants and American Labor* (New Press, 1997).

144. Nitin Varma, *Coolies of Capitalism: Assam Tea and the Making of Coolie Labour* (De Gruyter Oldenbourg, 2017), 18. The tea-making process goes through several phases even after the harvest of tea: "1) withering, 2) fixing leaves, 3) agitating leaves, 4) stir frying, 5) rolling, 6) fermenting, 7) drying" (Lyons, *China Maritime Customs and China's Trade Statistics, 1859–1948*, 64). In addition, the sequence of these processing operations can vary widely depending on the type of tea (green, oolong, or black).

145. JongHo Kim, "Namjungguk'ae hwain net'ŭwŏk'ŭ song saram, chabon, mulcha, kŭrigo munhwaŭi idong: Kŭndae Hwagyo Songgŭm Net'ŭwŏk'ŭŭi Hyŏngsŏnggwa Idongŭi Kujo" [Movement of Chinese people, capital, goods, and culture in the South China Sea: Formation and movement of the modern Chinese remittance network], in *Haeyanggwa megaashia* [The ocean and mega-Asia], ed. Jou KyungChul and Ru Sung Hee (Zininzin, 2023), 186–87.

146. Kuhn, *Chinese Among Others*, 63–65.

147. Shih-shan Henry Tsai, *China and the Overseas Chinese in the United States, 1868–1911* (University of Arkansas Press, 1983), 17.

148. Yong Chen, "The Internal Origins of Chinese Emigration to California Reconsidered," *Western Historical Quarterly* 28, no. 4 (1997): 520; Mei, "Socioeconomic Origins of Emigration,"

232–33; Mae Ngai, *The Chinese Question: The Gold Rushes, Chinese Migration, and Global Politics* (Norton, 2021), 49.

149. Yen-P'ing Hao, "A New Class in China's Treaty Ports: The Rise of the Comprador-Merchants," *Business History Review* 44, no. 4 (1970): 456.

150. Sherman Cochran, *Western, Japanese, and Chinese Corporations in China, 1880–1937* (University of California Press, 2000); Robert F. Dernberger, "The Role of the Foreigner in China's Economic Development, 1840–1949," in *China's Modern Economy in Historical Perspective* (Stanford University Press, 1975), 19–47.

151. Po-keung Hui, "Overseas Chinese Business Networks: East Asian Economic Development in Historical Perspective," PhD diss., State University of New York at Binghamton, 1995.

152. Osterhammel, *Transformation of the World*, 769.

153. Of course, Chinese compradors even worked in noneconomic fields. Between the 1840s and the 1860s, government compradors in Hong Kong worked as official or unofficial staff members of administrative and military apparatuses like the police station (e.g., Mok Shing), post office (e.g., Chun Mau Yung), colonial treasury (e.g., Chow Aaon), and for British troops (e.g., Bu Dingbang, Ahow, and Ayung); however, unlike compradors in the economic field, the colonial government of Hong Kong gradually reduced these government compradors throughout the nineteenth century (Kaori Abe, *Chinese Middlemen in Hong Kong's Colonial Economy, 1830–1890* (Routledge, 2017).

154. Immanuel Chung-Yueh Hsü, *Rise of Modern China* (Oxford University Press, 2000), 429. In terms of compradors' voluntary cooperation with Western merchants ensconcing them in the Chinese market, compradors may be viewed as traitors to the nation or "economic collaborators": Ronald Robinson, "Non-European Foundations of European Imperialism: Sketch for a Theory of Collaboration," in *Studies in the Theory of Imperialism*, ed. Roger Owen and Bob Sutcliffe (Longman, 1972), 120. Nonetheless, they cannot be entirely decried as collaborating elites of the Western merchants because some of them had nationalist sentiments and served to develop the incipient capitalist mode of production in China.

155. Zhaojin Ji, *History of Modern Shanghai Banking: The Rise and Decline of China's Finance Capitalism* (M. E. Sharpe, 2003).

156. Compradors played an important role in making profits for foreign capitalists even after the 1890s. Chinese compradors were hired not only for crossing unfamiliar thresholds (e.g., customs, language) of the Chinese market but also for establishing commercial networks formed by the ties of kinship or regionality. To secure and extend the Chinese market, Western companies like the Standard Oil Company or the British-American Tobacco Company gave compradors or Chinese commission agents a great deal of discretion in planning and developing marketing strategies. For example, Ye Chengzhong, a comprador for Standard Oil, exploited his market network to help Standard Oil achieve incredible growth in its exports in China. Zheng Bozhao (鄭伯昭, 1863–1951), as a comprador of the British-America Tobacco Company, also used "a preexisting social network of experienced tobacco merchants who were bound together by native-place times" (Cochran, *Western, Japanese, and Chinese Corporations*, 50) to expand the company's supply chain. Unlike compradors who collaborated with Western merchants, entrepreneurial bureaucrats—for example, Sheng xuanhuai 盛宣懷 (1844–1916) and Zhou Xuexi 周学熙 (1866–1947)—emerged (Chan, "Government, Merchants, and Industry to

1911," 454–59); they built and ran enterprises while using and depending on governmental support and political protection.

157. Hao Chang, "Intellectual Change and the Reform Movement, 1890–98," in *The Cambridge History of China*, vol. 11, pt. 2, *Late Ch'ing, 1800–1911*, ed. Dennis Twitchett and John K. Fairbank, 274–338 (Cambridge University Press, 1980).

158. See Edward Andrew, "Class in Itself and Class Against Capital: Karl Marx and His Classifiers," *Canadian Journal of Political Science* 16, no. 3 (1983): 577–84; G. A. Cohen, *Karl Marx's Theory of History: A Defense* (Princeton University Press, [1978] 2000); Theotonio Dos Santos. "The Concept of Social Classes," *Science & Society* 34, no. 2 (1970): 166–93; Adam Przeworski, "Proletariat into a Class: The Process of Class Formation from Karl Kautsky's *The Class Struggle* to Recent Controversies," *Politics and Society* 7, no. 4 (1977): 343–401.

159. Mazumdar, *Sugar and Society in China*, 7.

160. Mazumdar, *Sugar and Society in China*, 405–6.

161. John K. Fairbank, "The Creation of the Treaty System," in *Cambridge History of China*, vol. 10, pt. 1, *Later Ch'ing, 1800–1911*, ed. Denis Twitchett and John K. Fairbank (Cambridge University Press, 1978), 216.

162. However, I do not intend to take the Eurocentric path of urban development as a universal standard and apply it to the study of nineteenth-century Chinese cities. Recent comparative historical researchers have launched a strong attack on past researchers' Eurocentric and dichotomous approaches; for example, see Jack Goody, *The East in the West* (New York: Cambridge University Press, 1996), 229; Engin F. Isin, "Historical Sociology of the City," in *Handbook of Historical Sociology*, ed. Gerard Delanty and Engin F. Isin (Sage, 2003), 312–25. Chinese history scholars also criticize classical comparative historical sociologists' amateur knowledge, especially Max Weber's idea of Chinese city history, harshly. William T Rowe, as a prime example, suggested how late imperial Chinese cities like Hankou had westernized characteristics like a remarkable commercial metropolis, discrete political systems, and urban autonomy (Rowe, *Hankow*, 339).

163. Bozhong Li, *Agricultural Development in Jiangnan, 1620–1850* (Macmillan, 1998), 173.

164. Li, *Agricultural Development in Jiangnan*, 173.

165. Young-hun Cho, *Taeunhashidae, 1415–1784* [The age of the Grand Canal, 1415–1784] (Minumsa, 2021), 61.

166. *Ming Taizongshilu* 明太宗實錄, vol. 182 (November 1416).

167. *Qing Shengzushilu* 清聖祖實錄, vol. 117 (October 1684).

168. *Qing Shengzushilu* 清聖祖實錄, vol. 119 (October 1684).

169. *Qing Shengzushilu* 清聖祖實錄, vol. 119 (October 1684).

170. Mark C. Elliott, *Emperor Qinglong: Son of Heaven, Man of the World* (Longman, 2009), 151.

171. Elliott, *Emperor Qinglong*, 150.

172. Thomas A. Metzger, "The Organizational Capabilities of the Ch'ing State in the Field of Commerce: The Liang-huai Salt Monopoly, 1740–1840," in *Economic Organization in Chinese Society*, ed. W. E. Willmott (Stanford University Press, 1972), 9–45.

173. Regarding the economic prosperity of the Jiangnan region, Elliott argued as follows: "In Qianlong's day, Jiangnan accounted for 16 percent of the total agricultural land in the empire

but provided 29 percent of the government's land tax revenue in cash (paid in silver) and 38 percent of its revenue in kind (paid in grain), as well as 64 percent of the tribute grain sent to feed the capital" (Elliott, *Emperor Qinglong*, 78–79).

174. A painting of a thriving Suzhou in the eighteenth century, *Gusu fanhua tu* 姑苏繁华图, hints at how commercially developed the canal cities were at the time: Yanghui Xu 徐扬绘 and Yang Dongsheng 杨东胜, *Gusu fanhua tu* 姑苏繁华图 [Picture of the flourishing Suzhou city in the eighteenth century] (Tianjin Renmin meishu chubanshe, [1753] 2009).

175. Tobie Meyer-Fong, *Building Culture in Early Qing Yangzhou* (Stanford University Press, 2003).

176. Yongtao Du, *The Orders of Places: Translocal Practices of the Huizhou Merchants in Late Imperial China* (Brill, 2015).

177. Ping-Ti Ho, "The Salt Merchants of Yang-Chou: A Study of Commercial Capitalism in Eighteenth-Century China," *Harvard Journal of Asiatic Studies* 17, nos. 1–2 (1954): 130–68.

178. Young-hun Cho, *Daeunhawa chungguksangin: Hoe-yang jiyŏkhuijusangin sŏngchangsa, 1415–1784* [The Grand Canal and Chinese merchants] (Minumsa, 2011). However, the economic activities of these large-scale merchant groups were hardly out of bureaucratic control. The collusion between officials and merchants allowed a small group of merchants to monopolize enormous wealth, which Wakeman called bureaucratic capitalism, adding that corruption frequently occurred under this system (Wakeman, *Fall of Imperial China*, 50).

179. Lefebvre, *Production of Space*, 325–26.

180. Stephen R. Halsey, *Quest for Power: European Imperialism and the Making of Chinese Statecraft* (Harvard University Press, 2015).

181. The decline of the Grand Canal system was also due to a crisis in the grain transport system that operated through the canal. Not only did the bureaucrats exercise massive amounts of corruption through the grain transport system, but the constant accumulation of silt in the canals from floods caused periodic flooding, making it difficult to transport grain tribute and continue commerce through the canals. Susan Mann Johns and Philip A. Kuhn, "Dynastic Decline and the Roots of Rebellion," in *The Cambridge History of China*, vol. 10, pt. 1, *Late Ch'ing, 1800–1911*, ed. Denis Twitchett and John K. Fairbank (Cambridge University Press, 1978), 127.

182. In fact, Morrison, who was well aware of the political affairs in the country, advised the British armies: "[Here is a way] you can threaten Beijing [the Qing government]: Nanjing is a gate way of (the Yangtze River and the Grand Canal). Thus, if you occupied it, and then cut off waterways which connected the North, you can get what you want": *Yifenwenji* 夷氛闻记 [The records of barbarians' rise], vol. 4 (Zhonghuashuju, 1959), 54).

183. Lefebvre, *Production of Space*, 86.

184. Catherine Vance Yeh, "Representing the City: Shanghai and Its Maps," in *Town and Country in China: Identity and Perception*, ed. David Faure and Tao Tao Liu (Palgrave, 2002), 166–202. When it comes to Shanghai's geographical advantage for international trade, see Charles Gutzlaff, *Journal of Three Voyages along the Coast of China in 1831, 1832, and 1833 with Notices of Siam, Corea, and the Loo-Choo Islands* (London: Frederick Westley and A. H. Davis, 1834), 303–304.

185. Michael Marmé, "From Suzhou to Shanghai: A Tale of Two Systems," *Journal of Chinese History* 2, no. 1 (2018): 101.

186. Published in 1876, Ge Yuan xu (葛元煦)'s book *Huyou zaji* 滬游雜記 [Miscellaneous notes on visiting Shanghai] includes an appendix with the addresses of various shops and businesses in Shanghai, major foreign trading companies and halls, and lodgings for travelers. It also lists the piers, routes, and the prices of Shanghai's passenger ships.

187. Wright, *Twentieth Century Impressions*, 62.

188. Wolfgang Keller, Ben Li, and Carol H. Shiue, "Shanghai's Trade, China's Growth: Continuity, Recovery, and Change Since the Opium War," *IMF Economic Review* 61, no. 2 (2013): 336–78.

189. Frederic Wakeman Jr. and Wen-hsin Yeh, introduction to *Shanghai Sojourners*, ed. Frederic Wakeman Jr. and Wen-hsin Yeh (University of California Press, 1992), 1–14.

190. Robert Fortune, *Three Years' Wanderings in the Northern Provinces of China*, 2nd ed. (John Murray, 1847), 110.

191. China, *Imperial Maritime Customs*: Reports on Trade at the Treaty Ports in China (1875), 20.

192. Shiba Yoshinobu. *Chunggukdosisa* [History of Chinese cities], trans. Im dahŭi and Sin t'aekap (Sŏkyŏngmunhwasa, 2008), 79.

193. Anthony D. King, *Global Cities: Post-Imperialism and the Internationalization of London* (Routledge, 1990), 1.

194. Meng Yue. "Re-envisioning the Great Interior: Gardens and the Upper Class Between the Imperial and the 'Modern,'" *Modern Chinese Literature and Culture* 14, no. 1 (2002): 20–21.

195. Wei qing Li 李维清 1993, "Shanghai xiang tu zhi" 上海乡土志 [Chronicles of Shanghai], in *Shanghai fengsu guji kao* 上海风俗古迹考 [A study of Shanghai customs and historic sites], ed. Go bing quan 顾炳权 (Huadongshi fandaxue chubanshe, 1993), 282.

196. Jean Baudrillard, *The Consumer Society: Myths and Structures* (Sage, [1970] 1998), 26,

197. This study does not aim to list the characteristics of the colonized city of Hong Kong, but to show how Hong Kong, one of China's port cities, underwent socioeconomic changes under the pressure of the capitalist world-system. In particular, since the study is limited to the nineteenth century, it does not include the changes in post-nineteenth-century Hong Kong. Unlike the incorporation study, a description of the socioeconomic or cultural situation of Hong Kong after the nineteenth century may be approached from the perspective of a colonial city.

198. John Warner, *Fragrant Harbor: Early Photographs of Hong Kong*, 3rd ed. (John Warner Publications, 1979).

199. Huei-Ying Kuo, "Agency amid Incorporation: Chinese Business Networks in Hong Kong and Singapore and the Colonial Origins of the Resurgence of East Asia, 1800–1940," *Review* 32, no. 3 (2009): 215–21.

200. Carol Matheson Connell, "Jardine Matheson & Company: The Role of External Organization in a Nineteenth-Century Trading Firm," *Enterprise & Society* 4, no. 1 (2003): 113.

201. See, for example, advertisements of the Marine Insurance Company and shipping businesses in *The Daily Advertiser and Shipping Gazette*, January 3 and 10, 1872.

202. Hui, "Overseas Chinese Business Networks," 133.

203. Yin-Ping Ho, *Trade, Industrial Restructuring, and Development in Hong Kong* (University of Hawaii Press, 1992).

204. Nonetheless, viewing Hong Kong's massive transformation under British colonial rule as a role model of capitalist development and praising Hong Kong's contribution to mainland

China's capitalist transition unintentionally seems to point to the benignity and benefits of British colonialism, while disregarding "Chinese–European collaboration" or the roles of Hong Kong settlers in fostering Hong Kong's capitalist transition and development: Law Wing Sang, *Collaborative Colonial Power: The Making of the Hong Kong Chinese* (Hong Kong University Press, 2009), 12–13. To avoid the single-track development of Western intrusion and identify collaboration between Europeans and Chinese in Hong Kong, I support recent researchers' common ground, which focuses on the roles of Chinese collaborators: see John M. Carroll, *Edges of Empire* (Harvard University Press, 2005); Stephanie Po Yin Chung, *Chinese Business Groups in Hong Kong and Political Change in South China, 1900-25* (Macmillan, 1998); Po-keung Hui, "Comprador Politics and Middleman Capitalism," in *Hong Kong's History: State and Society Under Colonial Rule*, ed. Tak-Wing Ngo (Routledge, 1999): 30–45.

205. British Parliamentary Papers, *China 26: Correspondence, Annual Reports, Conventions, and Other Papers Relating to the Affairs of Hong Kong 1882–99* (Irish University Press, 1972), 629.

206. Gao Hao, "The Amherst Embassy and British Discoveries in China," *History* 99 (2014): 585.

207. Henry Ellis, *Journal of the Proceedings of the Late Embassy to China* (Printed for John Murray, Albemarle-Street, 1817), 408.

208. Tan Chung, *China and the Brave New World: A Study of the Origins of the Opium War (1840–42)* (Carolina Academic Press, 1978), 67. Regarding the increase in Canton's international trade volume from 1831 to 1837, see Hosea Ballou Morse, *The International Relations of the Chinese Empire*, vol. 1 (Paragon Book Gallery, 1900), 168.

209. Chung, *China and the Brave New World*, 70.

210. Platt, *Imperial Twilight*, 195.

211. Wallerstein. *Modern World-System III*, 138.

212. Indeed, as unemployment rose in Canton, so did urban crime. Wakeman, *Fall of Imperial China*, 141.

213. Alfred Schinz, *Cities in China* (Gebrüder Bortraeger, 1989).

214. Carl T. Smith, "The Emergence of a Chinese Elite in Hong Kong," *Journal of the Hong Kong Branch of the Royal Asiatic Society* 11 (1971): 74–115.

215. Osterhammel, *Transformation of the World*, 287–88.

216. Rowe, *Hankow*, 124.

217. Rowe, *Hankow*, 124.

218. Rowe, *Hankow*, 125.

219. Joseph Fewsmith, "From Guild to Interest Group: The Transformation of Public and Private in Late Qing China," *Comparative Studies in Society and History* 25, no. 4 (1983): 621.

220. Rowe, *Hankow*, 252–88.

221. Feuerwerker, "Economic Trends in the Late Ch'ing Empire," 40.

222. Rhoads Murphey, "The Treaty Ports and China's Modernization," in *The Chinese City Between Two Worlds*, ed. Mark Elvin and G. William Skinner (Stanford University Press, 1974), 52.

223. Keller, Li, and Shiue, "Shanghai's Trade, China's Growth," 341.

224. Hosea Ballou Morse, *The Trade and Administration of China* (Russell & Russell, [1908] 1920), 263–70.

225. Samuel Ball, "Observations on the Expediency of Opening a New Port in China" (1817), in *Nineteenth-Century China: Five Imperialist Perspectives*, ed. Rhoads Murphey (University of Michigan Press, 1972), 19.

226. Kwan Man Bun, "Mapping the Hinterland: Treaty Ports and Regional Analysis in Modern China," in *Remapping China: Fissures in Historical Terrain*, ed. Gail Hershatter, Emily Honig, Jonathan N. Lipman, and Randall Stross (Stanford University Press, 1996), 181–93. Also, a significant amount of hand-woven cloth produced in Jiangnan Province was exported to Britain and the United States via Canton (Feuerwerker, "Economic Trends in the Late Ch'ing Empire," 18).

227. William G. Skinner, "Chinese Cities: The Difference a Century Makes," in *Cosmopolitan Capitalists: Hong Kong and the Chinese Diaspora at the End of the 20th Century*, ed. Gary G. Hamilton (University of Washington Press, 1999), 56–79.

228. Nicole Constable, "Introduction: What Does It Mean to Be Hakka?," in *Guest People: Hakka Identity in China and Abroad*, ed. Nicole Constable (University of Washington Press, 1996), 13.

229. E. V. Roberts, Ngai-long Sum, and Peter Bradshaw, *Historical Dictionary of Hong Kong and Macau* (Scarecrow Press, 1992); Meliza Ng and Jade Lai King Wong, "Migration in Hong Kong: A Look into the Past at the Exhibition of the Chinese Overseas Collection at the Chinese University of Hong Kong," in *Chinese Overseas: Migration, Research, and Documentation*, ed. Tan Chee-Beng, Colin Storey, and Julia Zimmerman (Chinese University Press, 2007), 359–85.

230. Yoshinobu, *Chunggukdosisa*, 284, 290. This distinct spatial characteristic of Hong Kong—as a Chinese coolie stopover—caused it to develop into an informal hub for the sharing of coolie labor-related information. The Tung Wah Hospital was at the center of this coolie communications network. Established in 1869, the Tung Wah Hospital offered Chinese not only medical care but also served as a meeting place for coolies. Regarding this, see Sang, *Collaborative Colonial Power*, 22–25; Elizabeth Sinn, *Power and Charity: The Early History of the Tung Hua Hospital, Hong Kong* (Hong Kong University Press, 1989); Wickberg, "Organization of Overseas Migration," 38–39.

231. Chi-cheung Choi, "Rice, Treaty Ports and the Chaozhou Chinese Lianhao Associate Companies: Construction of a South China–Hong Kong–Southeast Asia Commodity Network, 1850s–1930s," in *Merchant Communities in Asia, 1600–1980*, ed. Lin Yu-ju and Madeleine Zelin (Pickering and Chatto, 2015), 62.

232. Yeung and Chu, *Fujian*, 33.

233. Dwight Perkins, *Agricultural Development in China, 1368–1968* (Aldine, 1969), 159.

Chapter 3

1. Charles Tilly, *Roads from Past to Future* (Rowman and Littlefield, 1997), 137.

2. Odd Arne Westad, *Restless Empire: China and the World Since 1750* (Basic Books, 2012), 19.

3. Wallerstein, "Rise and Future Demise," 390–91.

4. Immanual Wallerstein, "Antisystemic Movements: History and Dilemmas," in *Transforming the Revolution: Social Movements and the World-System*, ed. Samir Amin, Giovanni Arrighi, Andre Gunder Frank, and Immanuel Wallerstein (Monthly Review, 1990), 15.

5. Immanuel Wallerstein, *The Politics of the World-Economy: The States, the Movements and the Civilizations* (Cambridge University Press, 1984), 33.

6. Arrighi, *Long Twentieth Century*, 32.

7. For a discussion of the interdependence of nations as "the political units of the world-system," see Chase-Dunn and Rubinson, "Toward a Structural Perspective," 455. Samee Ullah Khan Lashari echoed this point and noted that "the state is the frontline agent of the capitalist system" (Lashari, "From the Periphery to the Semi-Core," 26).

8. Christopher Chase-Dunn, "Inter-state System and Capitalist World-Economy: One Logic or Two," in *The Theoretical Evolution of International Political Economy*, ed. George T. Crane and Abla Amawi (Oxford University Press, 1997), 146.

9. To put it another way, the more the boundary of the capitalist world-economy is enlarged, the more the logics of the interstate system become widespread. This consequently affected the incorporating area's political and institutional changes as the capitalist world-economy penetrated into the external arena.

10. Chase-Dunn, "Inter-state System," 151.

11. Unquestionably, unequal treaties were a key means to incorporate China as a subordinate country in the world-system. However, China's case does not provide a one-size-fits-all, universal, and uniform standard for understanding the incorporation of all countries, and therefore cannot be applied to other countries in the same way. For instance, the unequal treaties experienced during China's incorporation were qualitatively different from those experienced by other countries like Korea, the Philippines, Afghanistan, Ireland, Cuba, and Peru that suffered from colonization of their entire territory.

12. Chase-Dunn, "Inter-state System," 6.

13. Giovanni Arrighi, "Reading Hobbes in Beijing: Great Power Politics and the Challenges of the Peaceful Ascent," in *Routledge Handbook of International Political Economy*, ed. M. Blyth (Routledge, 2009), 163–79; Anthony Giddens, *The Nation-State and Violence: A Contemporary Critique of Historical Materialism, Volume II* (University of California Press, 1985); Michael Mann, *The Autonomous Power of the State: Its Origins, Mechanisms and Results* (Basil Blackwell, 1986); William H. McNeill, *The Pursuit of Power* (Basil Blackwell, 1982); A. R. Zolberg, "Origins of the Modern World System: A Missing Link," *World Politics* 33, no. 2 (1981): 253–81.

14. Tilly, *Coercion, Capital, and European States*, 71; Charles Tilly, *Roads from Past to Future* (Rowman and Littlefield, 1997), 137. For a discussion of the competition between the four global powers (Portugal, the Netherlands, Britain, and the United States) over global hegemony since the 1500s, see George Modelski, "The Long Cycle of Global Politics and the Nation-State," *Comparative Studies in Society and History* 20, no. 2 (1978): 214–35; for a discussion of European powers' competition to achieve an Industrial Revolution, see Graeme Donald Snooks, "New Perspectives on the Industrial Revolution," in *Was the Industrial Revolution Necessary?*, ed. Graeme Donald Snooks (Routledge, 1994), 1–26.

15. Max Weber, *Economy and Society. Volume 3*, trans. Guenther Roth and Claus Wittich (Bedminster Press, 1968), 78.

16. Tilly, "War Making and State Making," 174.
17. Tilly, "War Making and State Making," 172.
18. Stephan R. Epstein, "The Rise of the West," in *An Anatomy of Power: The Social Theory of Michael Mann*, ed. John A. Hall and Ralph Schroeder (Cambridge University Press, 2006), 258–59.
19. Wallerstein, *Modern World-System I*, 47.
20. Wallerstein, *Modern World-System I*, 265.
21. Anievas and Nişancioğlu, *How the West Came to Rule*, 115.
22. In this context Palat insisted that "evolving patterns of war- and state-making and associated expansions of circuits of exchange implies that rulers could not afford to be introverted" (Palat, *Making of an Indian Ocean World-Economy*, 74).
23. Tilly, *Coercion, Capital, and European States*, 4.
24. Max Weber, *Economy and Society*, trans. Guenther Roth and Claus Wittich (University of California Press, [1922] 1978), 353–54.
25. David S. Landes, *Wealth and Poverty of Nations* (Little, Brown, 1998).
26. Louis J. Hevia, *Cherishing Men from Afar: Qing Guest Ritual and the Macartney Embassy of 1793* (Duke University Press, 1995); Louis J. Hevia, "Postpolemical Historiography: A Response to Joseph W. Esherick," *Modern China* 24, no. 3 (1998): 319–27; Lydia H. Liu, *The Clash of Empires: The Invention of China in Modern World Making* (Harvard University Press, 2006).
27. Laura Hostetler, *Qing Colonial Enterprise: Ethnography and Cartography in Early Modern China* (University of Chicago Press, 2001); Emma Jinhua Teng, *Taiwan's Imagined Geography: Chinese Colonial Travel Writing and Pictures, 1683–1895* (Harvard University Press, 2004).
28. Peter C. Perdue, "Boundaries and Trade in the Early Modern World: Negotiations at Nerchinsk and Beijing," *Eighteenth-Century Studies* 43, no. 3 (2010): 341–56.
29. See Mario Cams, *Companions in Geography: East-West Collaboration in the Mapping of Qing China (c. 1685–1735)* (Brill, 2017).
30. Laura Hostetler, "Contending Cartographic Claims?," in *The Imperial Map: Cartography and the Mastery of Empire*, ed. James R. Akerman (University of Chicago Press, 2009), 93–132; Laura Hostetler, "Early Modern Mapping at the Qing Court: Survey Maps from the Kangxi, Yongzheng, and Qianlong Reign Periods," in *Chinese History in Geographical Perspective*, ed. Yongtao Du and Jeff Kyong-McClain (Lexington Books, 2013), 7–32.
31. Kirk Wayne Larsen, *Tradition, Treaties, and Trade: Qing Imperialism and Chosŏn Korea, 1850–1910* (Harvard University Press, 2008).
32. Larsen, *Tradition, Treaties, and Trade*, 7.
33. Larsen, *Tradition, Treaties, and Trade*, 8.
34. Hostetler, "Contending Cartographic Claims," 123.
35. Sang'u Yun, "Beijing kŏnsensŏsŭ pip'an: Ramo wa Aligi ŭi nonŭi rŭl chungsim ŭro" [A critical review of the "Beijing Consensus": Focusing on Ramo's and Arrighi's arguments], *Yurasia yŏn'gu* 11, no. 4 (2014): 177.
36. Sung Hee Ru, "Sorry, but G. Arrighi Is Not Almighty: Why Did He Fail to Explain China's Process of Incorporation into the Capitalist World-Economy?," *Journal of Asian Sociology* 49, no. 2 (2020): 268.
37. For example, a considerable number of gentry loyalists were eliminated by the Qing force and some surviving gentry loyalists had to live an eremitical life; Frederic Wakeman Jr.,

The Great Enterprise: The Manchu Reconstruction of Imperial Order in Seventeenth-Century China, Volume 1 (University of California Press, 1985), 674–89.

38. *Hala* means a clan-based community.

39. This does not mean that the whole gentry class was liberated from the influence of patrimonial rules; rather, most of the gentry class supported the existing ruling system while enjoying their class privileges.

40. John K. Fairbank, "Introduction: The Old Order," in *Cambridge History of China*, vol. 10, pt. 1, *Later Ch'ing, 1800–1911*, ed. Denis Twitchett and John K Fairbank (Cambridge University Press, 1978), 21.

41. A hereditary charisma is a variant of charismatic authority. According to Weber, charismatic authority, which is characterized as the extraordinary abilities of individuals, was an important mass mobilization strategy of outstanding leaders. In contrast with "a unique gift of grace charisma" (Weber, *Economy and Society*, 1135) as a typical case of charismatic authority, hereditary charisma did not guarantee followers of the (political) subjugation due to the lack of justified and legitimized authority, which may lead to the revolt of local powers.

42. Mazumdar, *Sugar and Society in China*, 6.

43. Nonetheless, to compensate for the fatal weakness in the Ming fiscal record stemming from incorrect tax registers, Dorgon ordered the first empire-wide cadastral survey (Wakeman, *Great Enterprise*, 464).

44. For example, after the conquest of Beijing Dorgon promised their old salaries to government officials who served in the late Ming regime (Wakeman, *Great Enterprise*, 416) and asked scholarly elites to accept government posts. Many of them accepted Dorgon's request. Song Quan, who was an official at the end of the Ming regime, gave a moral jurisdiction for collaboration with the Qing regime: "I am a minister of the Ming, but the Ming has perished, and there is nothing to belong to. Whoever has the ability to take revenge upon the enemies of the Ming, those murdering bandits, is thereupon my ruler" (Wakeman, *Great Enterprise*, 419).

45. Richard J. Smith, *The Qing Dynasty and Traditional Chinese Culture* (Rowman and Littlefield, 2015), 62.

46. John K. Fairbank, *The United States and China*, 4th ed. (Harvard University Press, 1983), 98–99.

47. As a result of this, "in the later imperial period, subordinate officials were indoctrinated with the ideal of unswerving loyalty to the throne, which led many of them to commit suicide rather than serve a usurper" (Wakeman, *Fall of Imperial China*, 57).

48. Wakeman summarized the roles of local gentry in five ways: (a) "the mediation of legal disputes between peasants," (b) "the supervision of local schools and academies," (c) "the supervision of irrigation works," (d) "the recruiting and training of local militia," and (e) "the proxy remittance of peasants' taxes to the yamen clerks" (Wakeman, *Fall of Imperial China*, 31).

49. Local gentry enjoyed their own sociopolitical benefits in their communities in return for cooperation with the Qing's local and central bureaucracy, which resulted in "patron-client ties."

50. With regard to these secret societies' anti-Qing movements, see Jean Chesneaux, "Secret Societies in China's Historical Evolution," in *Popular Movements and Secret Societies in China, 1840–1950*, ed. Jean Chesneaux (Stanford University Press, 1972), 1–21; Frederic Wakeman Jr., "The Secret Societies of Kwangtung, 1800–1856," in *Popular Movements and Secret Societies in China, 1840–1950*, ed. Jean Chesneaux (Stanford University Press, 1972), 29–47.

51. Arrighi, *Adam Smith in Beijing*, 33; Mark Selden, "East Asia in World History, 1750–21st Century," in *The Cambridge World History*, vol. 7, pt. 1, ed. J. R. McNeill and Kenneth Pomeranz (Cambridge University Press, 2015), 493–525; Kaoru Sugihara, "The East Asian Path of Economic Development: A Long-Term Perspective," in *The Resurgence of East Asia: 500, 150 and 50 Year Perspective*, ed. Giovanni Arrighi, Takeshi Hamashita, and Mark Selden (Routledge), 82–84.

52. Hung, "Agricultural Revolution and Elite Reproduction," 580.

53. Moreover, since the late nineteenth century, the central government's finances had been in a precarious situation due mainly to the cost of suppressing internal rebellions, military expenditures, war reparations, and repayment of foreign loans. In contrast, major Western governments devoted significant resources to education, general administration, and judicial services, which in turn created a climate conducive to the development of private sector commerce and industry (Feuerwerker, "Economic Trends in the Late Ch'ing Empire," 64–65).

54. Tilly, "War Making and State Making," 170.

55. Of course, there was a Hong Taiji (Abahai, 1593–1643) who conducted a war of conquest; he invaded the Chosŏn dynasty twice (1627 and 1636) because of Chosŏn's refusal of tributary relationships. Nonetheless, these are difficult to categorize as "inter-state competitions among countries" because, unlike Western Europe's interstate competition governed by "the collective interests, ambitions, and emotions of these national communities" bearing on the equal relationship and competitive positions between independent states, the Chinese pirates and Chosŏn did not intend to pursue the same status as the Qing Empire (Arrighi, *Long Twentieth Century*, 53).

56. Palat, *Making of an Indian Ocean World-Economy*, 109.

57. Ravi R. Palat, "Spatial Imaginaries of Capitalism: Dynamics of the Northeast Asian Regional Order," *Asian Perspective* 23, no. 2 (1999): 13.

58. From the tributary's perspective, the China-centered tributary system allowed tributary states to establish and sustain independent regimes without China's intervention in their domestic policies. In addition, tributary states often received cultural and economic benefits through the tributary trades with China, which was economically disadvantageous to the Chinese empire.

59. J. K. Fairbank and S. Y. Teng. "On the Ch'ing Tributary System," *Harvard Journal of Asiatic Studies* 6, no. 2 (1941): 135–246. Kim characterized the East Asian international order led by China as a hierarchical relationship based on Confucian philosophy (Kim, *Last Phase of the East Asian World Order*, chap. 1).

60. For a thousand years, the Chinese empire had secured the ideological and political legitimacy of the China-centered world order with Confucian ideology, which basically assumed that China was the center of the world due to the mandate of heaven. Confucian ideology played an important role in spreading and establishing a China-centered world order; Earl H. Pritchard, *The Crucial Years of Early Anglo-Chinese Relations, 1750–1800* (Octagon Books, [1936] 1970). In principle, Confucian ethics were often used to distinguish Chinese (civilized) from non-Chinese (barbarian). Confucian ethics argued that, considering that the emperor of China was a son of heaven (*tianzi*, 天子), all things in the world should be organized and controlled by the will of the Chinese emperor. A classic poem (*shijing*, 詩經), an important Confucian text, noted the sphere of influence of the Chinese emperor: "under the wide heaven, all is the king's land; within the sea-boundaries of the land, all are king's servants." Kung-chuan

Hsiao, *A History of Chinese Political Thought: From the Beginning to the Sixth Century A.D.*, vol. 1, trans. F. W. Mote (Princeton University Press, 1979), 23. In this sense, the rise of a country that challenged or betrayed the orders of the Chinese empire caused disharmony and destruction in the universe composed of an "orderly status-continuum": Mark Mancall, *China at the Center: 300 Years of Foreign Policy* (Free Press, 1984), 21. Preoccupied with Confucian ideology, the China-centered worldview provided all East Asian people with an ideological dichotomy between Chinese and non-Chinese; H. H. Lindsay, *Report of Proceedings on a Voyage to the Northern Ports of China, in the Ship Lord Amherst* (London: B. Fellows, 1833), 68–69. In addition, ordered guidance and learning, based on a China-centered ideology and institutional apparatus (e.g., *koutou* 叩头), were imposed on East Asian civilization; thereby, all East Asian countries had to revolve around China.

61. Tilly, *Coercion, Capital, and European States*, 72.

62. Tilly, "War Making and State Making," 170, 172.

63. Tilly insisted that "states form systems to the extent that they interact, and to the degree that their interaction significantly affects each party's fate. Since states always grow out of competition for control of territory and population, they invariably appear in clusters and usually form systems. The system of states that now prevails almost everywhere on earth took shape in Europe after AD 990, then began extending its control far outside the continent five centuries later. It eventually absorbed, eclipsed, or extinguished all its rivals, including the systems of states that then centered on China, India, Persia, and Turkey" (Tilly, *Coercion, Capital, and European States*, 4).

64. The First Opium War was fought between China and the Britain from 1839 to 1842. The war was triggered by the British-led opium trade and the Qing's campaign to ban it. The Second Opium War took place between China and the Anglo-French coalition from 1856 to 1860. After the First Opium War, when as much trade and openness as the British hoped for was not achieved, the British attacked China in alliance with France, using the Arrow incident (in 1856, Qing officials boarded the ship *Arrow*, a British-registered cargo ship, and forced the British flag to be lowered) as a pretext.

65. Timothy Brook, *The Troubled Empire: China in the Yuan and Ming Dynasties* (Harvard University Press, 2010), 107.

66. Palat, *Making of an Indian Ocean World-Economy*, 69.

67. In fact, in response to Dayan Khan's military threats, the Ming cut their existing political and economic ties with the Mongols and prepared to defend itself against their attacks. Given that the Mongols' economy was overwhelmingly dependent on the Ming trade, the rupture between the Mongols and the Ming led to a decline of the Mongol economic system. The death of Dayan Khan accelerated the dissolution of the tribal union's political and economic system, which ended in the breakup of the union.

68. Nicola Di Cosmo, "Did Guns Matter? Firearms and the Qing Experience," in *The Qing Formation in World Historical Time*, ed. L. A. Struve (Harvard University Press, 2004), 135. Of course, apart from the effective use of firearms, firearms technology advanced in the late Ming dynasty.

69. Palat, *Making of an Indian Ocean World-Economy*, 77. Also see Herrlee Glessna Creel, "The Role of the Horse in Chinese History," *American Historical Review* 70, no. 3 (1965): 668; Pita Kelekna, *The Horse in Human History* (Cambridge University Press, 2009), 149; Gertaude

Roth Li, "State Building Before 1644," in *The Cambridge History of China*, vol. 9, pt. 1, *The Ch'ing Empire to 1800*, ed. Willard J Peterson (Cambridge University Press, 2002), 22.

70. Chongnian Yan 阎崇年, *Nuerhachizhuan* 努尔哈赤传 [A bibliography of Nurhachi] (Beijing Chubanshe, 1983).

71. The Battle of Ssanglyeong in 1637 shows how a shrewd tactical maneuver of the Qing's armed cavalries led to a military success. At this battle the cavalries of the Qing worked in perfect unison under the command of the military leaders. The Battle of Ssanglyeong was one of the major battles between the Qing and Chosŏn during the Manchu War of 1636. Two Chosŏn commanders, Hhu-wan and Min-Young, and soldiers from the province of Gyeongsang marched to Namhansanseong fortress to save King In-jo, who was trapped by a Qing army. It is hard to give an exact number of Chosŏn troops, but thousands of soldiers were mobilized to participate in the battle (*Injosilrok* 仁祖實錄, vol. 33 [December 30, 1636]). The two commanders led their soldiers to Ssanglyeong hill on January 2, 1637, and split the forces side by side to encamp and prepare for the attack. However, the Qing army learned of the opponent's plans and about thirty cavalrymen carried out a surprise attack. Taken by surprise, the Chosŏn soldiers became confused and could not counterattack because they lacked discipline and were mainly gun shooters who needed protection during reloading. The Chosŏn soldiers could not continue shooting after the first volley while being exposed to their enemies. The Chosŏn camp was plunged into confusion, which allowed the Qing troops to carry out an easy attack. Consequently, almost all the Chosŏn soldiers died in the battle. In summary, the Chosŏn troops were routed by the agile movements of a small number of cavalrymen; therefore, they had no time to regroup. As the Chosŏn soldiers rushed around the battlefield in total confusion, Qing troops, waiting in the wings, attacked the Chosŏn camps one by one. The Qing's victory could be attributed to the combat units' shrewd and well-organized military operations.

72. Palat, *Making of an Indian Ocean World-Economy*, 88.

73. John K. Fairbank, *The Great Chinese Revolution: 1800–1985* (New York: Harper Perennial, 1987); Dwight H. Perkins, *East Asian Development: Foundation and Strategies* (Harvard University Press, 2013).

74. Platt, *Imperial Twilight*, xxiii.

75. *Canton Register*, March 10, 1835.

76. Wu Baosan 巫寶三, Feng Ze 馮澤, and Wu Chaolin 吳朝林, *Zhongguo jin dai jing ji si xiang yu jing ji zheng ce zi liao xuan ji, 1840–1864* 中国近代經濟思想与經濟政策資料选辑, 1840–1864 [Selected writings on China's modern economic thought and economic policies] (Ke xue chu ban she, 1959), 238–39.

77. The Qing regime had a sea ban policy to prevent Chinese people from participating in international trade. According to the Laws and Precedents of the Great Qing (*Daqinglüli* 大清律例), leaving Chinese territory and sailing the ocean were prohibited. In 1647, the Shunzhi Emperor, who received a report that there were private ships drifting offshore near Guangdong, stoutly asserted that "it is strictly prohibited": *Qingshizushilu* 清世祖实录, vol. 33 (July 1647). Such a rigid sea ban policy was eased after the Kangxi Emperor's successful suppression of the Revolts of the Three Feudatories. In 1684, China opened the seas for international trade; *Qingshengzushilu* 清圣祖实录, vol. 226 (September 1684). After the Kangxi Emperor declared foreign trade open, many ports, such as Canton in Guangdong Province, Fuzhou and Amoy in Fujian Province, Ningbo in Zhejiang Province, and Shanghai in Jiangsu Province, were

authorized for international trade. The Qing's open-door policies, however, did not last. The Qianlong Emperor, fearing threats from abroad and learning of corruption in Canton, suddenly announced in 1757 that international trade would be allowed only at Canton: (*Qinggaozongshilu* 清高宗实录, vol. 550 (December 1757). The retrenchment to a restricted international trade policy dissatisfied Western merchants.

78. Robbins Macartney, *Our First Ambassador to China* (John Murray Macpherson, 1908), 386.

79. Hao, "Amherst Embassy and British Discoveries," 571.

80. Suh, *Ap'yŏnjŏnjaeng*, 86, 89, 97–98.

81. John M. Carroll, "The Canton System: Conflict and Accommodation in the Contact Zone," *Journal of the Royal Asiatic Society, Hong Kong Branch* 50 (2010): 56.

82. Regarding the importance of the *Lady Hughes* case as the starting point of the Opium War, see Chen Li, "Law, Empire, and Historiography of Modern Sino-Western Relations: A Case Study of the *Lady Hughes* Controversy in 1784," *Law and History Review* 27, no. 1 (2009): 1–53.

83. Suh, *Ap'yŏnjŏnjaeng*, 122.

84. Regardless of whether some British people supported a war with China or not, almost all believed that trade with China was important. For example, even though Richard Cobden fiercely opposed the Anglo-Chinese wars, he welcomed the consequences of the wars—"the opening of China to world trade": D. C. M. Platt, *Finance, Trade, and Politics: British Foreign Policy, 1815–1914* (Clarendon, 1968), 85.

85. The progress of the inseparable relation between commercial benefits and the development of military forces in Western Europe paved the way for making and expanding the European world-economy. Under the European world-economy, European countries did not need to draw on "direct appropriation of the small agricultural surplus produced within a manorial economy by a small class of nobility" (Wallerstein, *Modern World-System I*, 36) because they began to make profits from oversea expansion; since then armaments manufacture has become one of the profitable industries of northwestern Europe. In developing overseas trade, the development of military forces, in particular naval forces, and military technologies was vital to penetrate non-European societies as well as to compete with rivals. As Jeffrey Kentor put it, "Economic and coercive power were the two basic dimensions across which the modern inter-state system evolved": *Capital and Coercion: The Economic and Military Processes That Have Shaped the World-Economy, 1800–1900* (Garland, 2000), 10. The quantum leap of armed force marked the beginning of a new era of the global commercial-military system. The more the commercial-military system has been developed, the more sophisticated and deadly military weapons have been invented in the capitalist world-economy. See Carlo M. Cipolla, *Guns and Sails in the Early Phase of European Expansion, 1400–1700* (Collins, 1965), 137; Paul A. Baran and Paul M. Sweezy, *Monopoly Capital: An Essay on the American Economic and Social Order* (Monthly Review, 1966), 3. Fred M. Gottheil echoed this point and noted that "military production to them is a matter of considerable importance in explaining capitalism's stubborn staying-power": Fred M. Gottheil, "Marx Versus Marxists on the Role of Military Production in Capitalist Economies," *Journal of Post Keynesian Economics* 8, no. 4 (1986): 563.

86. Cipolla, *Guns and Sails*, 137.

87. The *cartaz* system of Portugal—a naval trade license issued by the Portuguese government—was not new. It was established to pursue a trade monopoly in the Indian Ocean

(Palat, *Making of an Indian Ocean World-Economy*, 176) and the Estado de India's control over the Indian Ocean trade was not cost-effective as time went on; see Kirti N. Chaudhuri, *Trade and Civilisation in the Indian Ocean: An Economic History from the Rise of Islam to 1750* (Cambridge University Press, 1985), 65. Rather, Portugal's seaborne trade could reap big profits from engaging transit trades between China and Japan. Under the circumstance that the Ming prohibited direct trade with Japan, Portugal played an important role in connecting the two countries' international trade, which compensated Portugal for the large loss in the Indian Ocean.

88. Frederic Wakeman Jr., "The Canton Trade and the Opium War," in *The Cambridge History of China. Late Ch'ing, 1800–1911*, vol. 10, pt. 1, ed. Denis Twitchett and John K. Fairbank (Cambridge University Press, 1978), 194.

89. The economic benefits that were always preeminent to British government officials became a priority. Charles Elliot (a plenipotentiary of Great Britain) even asked the Qing government to resume trade in Guangzhou though the Opium War was not yet over: Haijian Mao, *The Qing Empire and the Opium War: The Collapse of the Heavenly Dynasty* (Cambridge University Press, 2016), 226–27. International trade had been resumed after making a ceasefire agreement on March 20, 1841, albeit only temporarily; however, Elliot's request for resuming international trade during the Opium War reflected the importance of trade profits and also strongly suggested that the use of Britain's armed forces was related to the trade benefits from China.

90. Lin, *China Upside Down*, 76–78, 96–97.

91. Jane Kate Leonard, *Wei Yuan and China's Rediscovery of the Maritime World* (Harvard University Press, 1984), 76.

92. Suh, *Ap'yŏnjŏnjaeng*, 199–200.

93. Priscilla Napier noted that "imperial officials never argued or pleaded with the barbarians, they just pronounced": Priscilla Napier, *Barbarian Eye: Lord Napier in China, 1834: The Prelude to Hong Kong* (Brassey's, 1995), 226.

94. For instance, a British father and daughter were given a severe reprimand because they rode in a sedan chair of Hong merchants. British merchants' wives were also not allowed to enter the British factories of Canton due to the imperial decree that "it is right to issue strict orders to the chief foreign merchants of every nation, disallowing their bringing foreign women to Canton to reside": Asiatic Intelligence, *The Asiatic Journal and Monthly Register for British and Foreign India, China and Australasia. Volume 7* (Parbury, Allen, and Co, 1832), 28.

95. "For Europeans to wander there was suicidal. Even walkers on the wall of the city [Canton] would sometimes have stones and brickbats hurled at them" (Napier, *Barbarian Eye*, 121).

96. *The Spectator: A Weekly Journal of News, Politics, Literature, and Science, Volume 13* (1840), 274.

97. "If my private feelings were of the least consequence upon questions of a public and important nature, assuredly I might justly say that no man entertains a deeper detestation of the disgrace and sin of this forced traffic on the coast of China than the humble individuals who signs this dispatch." Great Britain, House of Parliament. *Additional Papers Relating to China. No. IV* (1840), 5.

98. *Chou ban yi wu shi mo* 籌辦夷務始末 [The complete account of the management of barbarian affairs], *Tongzhi chao* 同治朝 [The Tongzhi era], vol. 5, 1980, 17.

99. Wakeman, "Canton Trade and the Opium War," 185.

100. Arthur Waley, *The Opium War Through Chinese Eyes* (Stanford University Press, 1958), 34.

101. William Thedore de Bary, Wing-tsit Chan, and Burton Watson, *Sources of Chinese Traditions, Volume 2* (Columbia University Press, 1960), 669–71.

102. To make matters worse, the Wei-hsi murder case (July 7, 1839) escalated tensions between Commissioner Lin and Elliot: Lin Wei-hsi was critically injured and died the following day after being attacked by drunken English and American seamen in the small village of Chien-sha-tsai (Wakeman, "Canton Trade and the Opium War," 189). To indict the murderers of Lin Wei-hsi, Commissioner Lin demanded that Elliott turn over the British culprits to Chinese authorities, but Elliott did not accept Lin's request: J. W. Wong, *Anglo-Chinese Relations 1839–1860: A Calendar of Chinese Documents in the British Foreign Office Records* (Oxford University Press, 1983), 45. Instead of handing the British culprit(s) over to the Chinese government, they were accused, tried, and sent to British prisons according to British laws. This angered Chinese authorities and Chinese people.

103. Suh, *Ap'yŏnjŏnjaeng*, 351–52.

104. Jeremy Black, *Beyond the Military Revolution: War in the Seventeenth-Century World* (Palgrave Macmillan, 2011), 152.

105. The Ming dynasty also lacked apparent motives for developing overseas expeditions. Of course, in 1405, "Cheng Ho [Zheng He 鄭和 1371–1433], as a eunuch admiral, left with a fleet of 63 ocean-going junks who visited many parts of the South Seas. During the next 30 years seven such expeditions set forth, returning each time with abundant information concerning geography and sea routes as well as large quantities of the produce of the isles and India"; Joseph Needham, *Science and Civilization in China I* (Cambridge University Press, 1954), 143. See also Kenneth Chase, *Firearms: A Global History to 1700* (Cambridge University Press, 2003), 50; Sen, *India, China, and the World*, 201–22. Liang Qichao was proud that Zheng He's achievement was the result of an expedition that the West could not match at the time and added that the size and number of ships used in Zheng He's overseas expeditions in the fifteenth century were truly remarkable: Sally K. Church, "The Colossal Ships of Zheng He: Image or Reality?," in *Zheng He: Images and Perceptions*, ed. Roderich Ptak and Claudine Salmon (Otto Harrassowitz, 2005, 155–58. These overseas expeditions, however, suddenly stopped and never happened again until the demise of the Ming. As Wallerstein notes, "the causes of their cession" are unclear (Wallerstein, *Modern World-System I*, 55). If the overseas expeditions were successful, why did the Ming government not continue them? It may have had something to do with the "drain on Treasury funds occasioned by the fitting-out of overseas missions": William Willetts, "The Maritime Adventures of the Great Eunuch Ho," in *Papers on Early South-East Asian History*, ed. Colin Jack-Hinton (Journal of Southeast Asian History, 1964), 38. Young-hun Cho argues that the Ming government was opposed to dispatching more maritime expeditions, which required enormous financial resources and manpower that instead were needed for flood-control work: Young-hun Cho, *Taeunhashidae, 1415–1784* [The age of the Grand Canal, 1415–1784] (Minumsa, 2021), 78–79. The continuous threat from Mongol tribes may be another reason the Ming stopped its overseas expeditions suddenly. There were few chances to develop naval forces once the Ming paid more attention to its northern frontier: Gunageu Wan, " 'Public' and 'Private' Overseas Trade in Chinese History," in *Sociétés et compagnies de commerce en orient at*

dans l'Océan Indien, ed. M. Mollat [S.E.V.P.E.N, 1970], 215–25. Whatever the real reason, it is certain that the Ming stopped overseas expeditions and "the upshot was that the commerce of the Indian Ocean was left to the Arabs and the Portuguese" (Needham, *Science and Civilization in China I*, 144). The main aim of Zheng He's overseas expedition, expansion of maritime tribute at a diplomatic level, was thus qualitatively distinguished from that of Columbus, who sought the expansion of global trade at an economic level.

106. Instead of developing naval power, the Qing government adopted a new strategy called "maintaining sea defense without sea battle" (*Youhaifangerwuhaizhan* 有海防而無海戰). By "sea-defense," it meant coastal defense: "The strategy was: (1) maintaining a strong land force to guard coastal areas, (2) fortification of coastal exits, (3) not building a strong naval fleet, but maintaining a small, compact task force on sea mainly to check piracy and smuggling" (Chung, *China and the Brave New World*, 39).

107. Of course, the Qing Empire had littoral boats; however, these were not equal to the British naval forces. For instance, "the united squadrons of the celestial empire [Qing Empire] are not able to drive away a single merchant ship, manned with a few Europeans" (*Chinese Repository*, vol. 4 [1836], 444).

108. Crossley, *Orphan Warriors*, 117. With regard to advanced British steam power, see Jack A. Goldstone, "The Problem of the 'Early Modern' World," *Journal of Economic and Social History of the Orient* 41 (1998): 249–84; Jack A. Goldstone, "Neither Late Imperial nor Early Modern: Efflorescences and the Qing Formation in World History," in *The Qing Formation in World-Historical Time*, ed. Lynn A. Struve (Harvard University Press, 2004), 242–302; E. A. Wrigley, *Continuity, Chance, and Change: The Character of the Industrial Revolution in England* (Cambridge University Press, 1988). With regard to the advanced iron ship technology of Britain, see Roger Burlingame, "Locomotives, Railways, and Steamships," in *Technology in Western Civilization*, vol. 1, *The Emergence of Modern Industrial Society, Earliest Times to 1900*, ed. Melvin Kranzberg and Carroll W. Pursell (Oxford University Press, 1967), 432; Thomas A. Palmer, "Military Technology," in *Technology in Western Civilization. Volume 1*, ed. Melvin Kranzberg and Carroll W. Pursell Jr. (Oxford University Press, 1967), 500.

109. See the David Rumsey Map Collection (Stanford University) for the image of Haikou Quantu 海口全圖 [Complete Map of Sea Ports], 1800.

110. Mao, *Qing Empire and the Opium War*, 35.

111. Mao, *Qing Empire and the Opium War*, 30–32.

112. Mao, *Qing Empire and the Opium War*, 200.

113. Mao, *Qing Empire and the Opium War*, 280.

114. In fact, only one British soldier was killed and sixteen were wounded at the Battle of Xiamen (Mao, *Qing Empire and the Opium War*, 288).

115. Gerald S. Graham, *The China Station: War and Diplomacy, 1830–1860* (Oxford University Press, 1978), 18–19; Daniel R. Headrick, *The Tools of Empire: Technology and European Imperialism in the Nineteenth Century* (Oxford University Press, 1981), 19.

116. The steamship engine, as a smaller and more powerful machine, allowed smaller boats to travel to the inland areas of China.

117. Arrighi, "China's Market Economy," 30.

118. Chinese warships enveloped in flames demonstrated the asymmetric military capabilities between the West and China during the unexpected and miserable defeat at the Second

Battle of Chuenpi (*chuanbizhizhan* 穿鼻之戰). W. D. Bernard and W. H. Hall described the power of the British navy at this battle in the Pearl River Delta on January 7, 1841:

"The very first rocket fired from the Nemesis was seen to enter the large junk against which it was directed, near that of the admiral, and almost the instant afterwards it blew up with a terrific explosion, launching into eternity every soul on board, and pouring forth its blaze like the mighty rush of fire from a volcano. The instantaneous destruction of the huge body seemed appalling to both sides engaged. The smoke, and flame, and thunder of the explosion, with the broken fragments falling round, and even portions of dissevered bodies scattering as they fell, were enough to strike with awe, if not with fear, the stoutest heart that looked upon it." W. D. Bernard and W. H. Hall, *Narratives of the Voyages and Services of the Nemesis, from 1840 to 1843* (Henry Colburn Publisher, 1844), 271.

Interestingly, the rocket launched from the *Nemesis* was the Congreve rocket that was originally invented by the Indian kingdom of Mysore. In other words, British colonial power sometimes used nonendogenous sources of armaments in the battles of the Opium War. See Luke Cooper, "Asian Sources of British Colonial Power: The Role of the Mysorean Rocket in the Opium War," in *Historical Sociology and World History*, ed. Alexander Anievas and Kamran Matin (Rowman and Littlefield, 2016), 111–26.

119. Mao, *Qing Empire and the Opium War*, 167.
120. Mao, *Qing Empire and the Opium War*, 242.
121. Mao, *Qing Empire and the Opium War*, 416.
122. Warren I. Coburn Cohen, *East Asia at the Center: Four Thousand Years of Engagement with the World* (Columbia University Press, 2000).
123. Charles Desnoyers, "Toward 'One Enlightened and Progressive Civilization': Discourses of Expansion and Nineteenth-Century Chinese Missions Abroad," *Journal of World History* 8, no. 1(1997): 135–56.
124. Pan Lin, *English as a Global Language in China: Deconstructing the Ideological Discourses of English in Language Education*, vol. 2 (Norton, 2014), 63.
125. Bob Adamson, *China's English: A History of English in Chinese Education* (Hong Kong University Press, 2004), 26.
126. Aiguo Lu, *China and the Global Economy Since 1840* (Macmillan, 1999), 19.
127. Prior to the initiation of the Self-Strengthening Movement, a few Hong merchants in Canton dedicated themselves to accepting and utilizing the superior military technologies of the colonial powers. For example, Pan Shichung 潘仕成 (1804–1873), before and after the Opium Wars, invested a large sum of money in manufacturing warships for the Qing forces. He also invited American specialists to show him how to make naval mines. Based on what he learned from the American experts he drew blueprints (e.g., *Gongchuanshuileitushuo* 攻船水雷圖說) of naval mines.
128. Benjamin Elman explains that the Jiangnan Arsenal adapted its machinery to manufacture advanced foreign guns and small arms for military purposes. The arsenal produced a variety of guns modeled after products from the Armstrong factory in Britain and manufactured a total of 110 cannons: Benjamin A. Elman, *On Their Own Terms: Science in China 1550–1900* (Harvard University Press, 2005), 371. The Shanghai Arsenal, established in 1865, was revolutionary in its manufacturing processes and linked Western engineering subjects and texts to practical applications of science. The modern navy yard in the southern city of Fuzhou

focused more closely on naval operations. Under the guidance of Zuo Zongtang the Fuzhou Navy Yard School was opened in 1866 to help build Western-style warships: Anthony C. Sturniolo, "Influences of Western Philosophy and Educational Thought in China and Their Effects on the New Culture Movement," master's thesis, State University of New York at Buffalo, 2016, 17. The school became a central gathering point for foreign employees and encouraged students to study abroad to broaden their knowledge of military science and technology. According to Elman, advanced students went to France to study fortifications, defenses, and gunpowder explosives; two students went to England to study navigation and naval command, while one went to Germany for training in naval mines and torpedoes (Elman, *On Their Own Terms*, 375).

129. Wong, *China Transformed*, 153. In addition, the modernized companies, inspired by the Self-Strengthening Movement, had difficulty in maintaining their business due to a bottleneck in management and the lack of capital: John K. Fairbank, *China: A New History* (Harvard University Press, 1992), 219.

130. Several Chinese elite figures—for example, Huang En-tong 黃恩彤 (1801–1883), Li Shuchang 黎庶昌 (1837–1897), Wang Tao 王韜 (1828–1897), and Ding Richang 丁日昌, 1823–1882)—began to recognize that China faced a changed situation, one the country had not experienced in thousands of years. Some scholar-bureaucrats like Feng Guifen 馮桂芬 (1809–1874) also felt keenly that China had to accept the advanced technologies of the West to overcome these difficulties. See Immanuel Chung-Yueh Hsü, "Late Ch'ing Foreign Relations, 1866–1905," in *The Cambridge History of China*, vol. 11, pt. 2, *Late Ch'ing 1800–1911*, ed. John K. Fairbank and Kwang-Ching Liu (Cambridge University Press, 1980), 156.

131. A number of Self-Strengthening Movement projects had been placed in the hands of individual viceroys. Li Hongzhang was in two positions at the same time; he was a regional viceroy and a central administrative officer.

132. Wakeman, *Fall of Imperial China*, 186.

133. Sturniolo, "Influences of Western Philosophy," 13.

134. Hsü, "Late Ch'ing Foreign Relations," 173.

135. Qichao Liang 梁启超, "Li Hongzhang," in *Yin bingshi heji* 饮冰室合集 [Collected works of Yin Bing Shi], vol. 3 (Zhonghuashuju, 1994), 39.

136. Kwang-Ching Liu, *China's Early Modernization and Reform Movement: Studies in Late Nineteenth-Century China and American-Chinese Relations*, vol. 1, ed. Yung-Fa Chen and Kuang-che Pan (Institute of Modern History, Academia Sinica, 2009), 177.

137. Chase-Dunn and Rubinson, "Toward a Structural Perspective," 470.

138. William T. Rowe, *China's Last Empire: The Great Qing* (Harvard University Press, 2009), 218.

139. Thomas, *Foreign Investment and China's Industrial Development*, 15.

140. Richard S. Horowitz, "International Law and State Transformation in China, Siam, and the Ottoman Empire During the Nineteenth Century," *Journal of World History* 15, no. 4 (2004): 469.

141. Feuerwerker, "Economic Trends in the Late Ch'ing Empire," 66–68.

142. Not long after the end of the Second Opium War, China became embroiled in another war, the Sino-French War (1884–1885). The war cost the Qing a great deal of money and saw the destruction of the Fujian Fleet and the Foochow Arsenal. It confirmed that the Qing's Self-Strengthening Movement was on the wrong track. This was a foreshadowing of

another war, the First Sino-Japanese War, and its serious consequences. See Hsü, "Late Ch'ing Foreign Relations," 99–101.

143. This claim was written from the perspective of late imperial China (Ming and Qing) before its incorporation into the capitalist world-system. From China's perspective, the European countries that sought to establish relations with Ming and Qing were considered tributaries. Of course, China's tributary relations with European countries functioned very differently from those between China and its neighboring countries. In other words, Portugal, the Netherlands, and England were not tributary states to imperial China in the traditional sense that characterized the relationships with countries like Korea or Vietnam. However, during certain periods, these European powers engaged in tributary-like relations or established trade agreements that can be viewed through a similar lens.

For example, the Portuguese engaged in tributary diplomacy by sending tribute missions and gifts to the Chinese emperor, which helped legitimize their trading activities. The first official visit by Portugal was by a delegation (1517–1518) sent to Guangzhou during the Ming Dynasty (1368–1644) by Fernão Pires de Andrade, and the visit was quite successful. The Dutch sought trade with China in the seventeenth century. Initially, they attempted to establish direct trade relations without recognizing the tributary system. However, after conflicts with the Spanish and Portuguese, the Dutch eventually sent tribute missions to China to secure trade rights, particularly during the Qing dynasty. Isaac Titsingh, representing the interests of the Dutch and the Dutch East India Company, visited Beijing for the sixtieth anniversary of the enthronement of the Qianlong Emperor in 1794–96. The British East India Company began trading with China in the late seventeenth century. Initially, they did not engage in tributary relations. In 1793, Lord Macartney led a mission to China to establish trade relations, presenting gifts to the Qianlong Emperor. However, this mission was met with resistance, as the Chinese viewed British trade requests as improper.

144. Although they were called the four tribute states, there were more than four in that Burma, Annam, Japan, Korea, Ryukyu, Sulu (in the southern Philippines), and Laos were included; Sandra L. Bunn-Livingstone, *Juricultural Pluralism Vis-à-Vis Treaty Law* (Martinus Nijhoff, 2002), 4. Before 1748, Hui-tong guan and si-yi-guan were separated from each other. The former was operated under the control of the Hanlin Academy and the latter was operated under the Board of Ceremonies. In 1748, Emperor Qianlong combined "these two kuan (guan) into a single organization known as Hui-t'ung ssu-I kuan (*Hui-tong-si-yi-guan*)": Immanuel Chung-Yueh Hsü, *China's Entrance into the Family of Nations: The Diplomatic Phase, 1858–1880* (Harvard University Press, 1960), 13.

145. S. M. Meng, *The Tsungli Yamen: Its Organization and Functions* (Harvard University Press, 1962), 5.

146. Together with the appearance of diplomatic representatives, officials emerged who were responsible for Western matters including translation work. For instance, Ma Jianzhong 馬建忠 (1845–1900), who studied at a French Catholic school in Shanghai and at the Ecole Libre des Sciences Politiques in Paris, gained expertise in international law and foreign affairs. Later, he became Li Hongzhang's secretary and helped to conduct Qing policy in Korea (1880–1882). Gu Hongming 辜鴻銘 (1857–1928), who studied literature at the University of Edinburgh in Scotland and law in Paris, returned to Penang in China in 1880. Later, he became a secretary to Zhang Zhidong 張之洞 (1837–1909) and served as a director of the Huangpu River Authority

in Shanghai; Marianne Bastid-Bruguiere, "Currents of Social Change," in *The Cambridge History of China*, vol. 11, pt. 2, *Late Ch'ing, 1800–1911*, ed. Denis Twitchett and John K. Fairbank (Cambridge University Press, 1980), 548–49.

147. The following quotation written in the *Qingshigao* in the early twentieth century gives an idea of how afraid China was of the unprecedented penetrations of colonial powers: "The vastness of the Qing Empire's territory far exceeds that of previous dynasties. . . . However, we failed to properly manage and govern the territory that Emperor Kangxi and Qianglong acquired, and consequently allowed outside forces to invade. To the west, we lost Kogand and several territories of badakeshan to Russia; to the south, we lost Vietnam and Myanmar to Britain and France; and to the east we lost Ryukyu and Korea to Japan. . . . What does it mean to protect a country and its borders?" *Qingshigao* 清史稿, vol. 153 (1977), 4482. The *Qinshigao* was compiled at the Qing History Museum 清史館, which was established in 1914 by the Beiyang Government in the early years of the Republic of China, and was finished, albeit not completely, in 1927 after 14 years of compilation.

148. *Qingshigao* 清史稿, vol. 526 (1977): 14575–730. It is interesting to note that Japan is the only East Asian country that is not recorded as a vassal of China; this suggests that China's perception of its neighbors was based on the international situation at the time.

149. Ti Qiang Chen 陳體強, *Zhongguowaijiaoxingzheng* 中國外交行政 [China's diplomatic administration] (Shangwuyinshuguan, [1945] 1983), 11. Disconnections between the Qing emperor and British officials were at least partially attributed to the way Qing bureaucrats communicated with the emperor. Qing officials showed a total disregard for foreign officials' letters, glossed over the fact that they had communicated with foreign officers, or blocked forwarding foreign officers' messages to the emperor because they did not want to take the risk of violating strict lèse majesté laws that prohibited Qing officials from submitting "foreign communications to the emperor that contained language deemed to be rebellious or perverse" (Mao, *Qing Empire and the Opium War*, 136).

150. Mao, *Qing Empire and the Opium War*, 149.

151. With regard to the role of consuls in expanding nineteenth-century capitalism, see Ferry De Goey, *Consuls and the Institutions of Global Capitalism, 1783–1914* (Routledge, 2016). In a similar vein, Colin Flint and Zhang Xiaotong present the term "economic diplomacy," which means the use of diplomatic means in pursuing economic power. See Colin Flint and Zhang Xiaotong, "Historical-Geopolitical Contexts and the Transformation of Chinese Foreign Policy," *Chinese Journal of International Politics* 12, no. 3 (2019): 298.

152. The plan to preserve the interests of Chinese overseas merchants through diplomacy is also evident in English merchants' opposition to the Alcock Convention. When a Chinese delegation traveled to London in 1868, they were welcomed by Queen Victoria and told by the foreign secretary, Lord Clarendon, that Britain would extend to China the same courtesies offered other nations if the Qing Empire made good on the agreements it had concluded with Britain; Clarendon added that he had no intention of exerting any unfriendly and coercive pressure on the Qing government. Clarendon's comments were relayed to Sir Rutherford Alcock, who was instructed to approach treaty revision negotiations with the Qing. The Alcock Convention, signed on October 23, 1869, was the first time since the Opium War that negotiations were conducted on an equal footing and without military threats, and resulted in (a) Britain allowing the Qing to establish a consulate in Hong Kong, (b) raising the duty on opium imports

to 2.5 percent of the price, (c) raising export duties on cotton yarn by at least 1 percent, and guaranteeing most-favored-nation treatment with the understanding that when certain benefits were granted to other foreign powers, they would either obtain British consent or receive the same benefits in return, (d) opening Wenzhou and Wuhu, (e) closing the port of Qiongzhou on Hainan Island, (f) imposing a 2.5 percent additional transportation tax on British cotton yarn imports at ports of entry, (g) granting inland waterway passage for Qing trading vessels leased to foreigners, (h) steamboat passage on Poyang Lake, (i) temporary residency for foreigners in the interior, and (j) Qing consent to the full text of the Commercial Code. Alcock at least regraded the Alcock Convention as negotiated for mutual benefit on an equal footing. However, it was heavily criticized by British merchants because of Alcock's insistence that the Qing be treated the same as Western nations, when in their eyes the Qing were not entitled to the same rights and privileges as Western nations. A larger reason was the terms of the agreement. For example, British merchants believed that the presence of a Chinese consul in Hong Kong would not only allow the Chinese consul to spy for the Qing government, but that their economic activities in Hong Kong would be hindered by the consul's surveillance. As a result, numerous petitions from British merchants opposing ratification of the convention were sent to the British Parliament, and on July 25, 1870, ratification of the Alcock Convention was rejected (Hsü, "Late Ch'ing Foreign Relations," 75–76).

153. Aside from Western pressure, the Qing government, for its part, also needed a professional foreign affairs department because high government officials, in particular the grand councilors who took charge of foreign affairs, had a tough time addressing the large volume of foreign-related work. Not only did the grand councilors wish to build a new governmental apparatus to deal with diplomatic matters, but the provincial authorities, using every trick in the book to avoid the requests of foreign representatives, also wanted to establish a foreign affairs department.

154. See Richard S. Horowitz, "Central Power and State Making: The Zongli Yamen and Self-Strengthening in China 1860–1880," PhD diss., Harvard University, 1998.

155. He was appointed as a minister of the Zongliyamen on October 24, 1896.

156. Jennifer Marie Rudolph, "Negotiating Power and Navigating Change in the Qing: The Zongli Yamen, 1861–1901," PhD diss., University of Washington, 1999, 211.

157. Shmuel Noah Eisenstadt, "Political Struggle in Bureaucratic Societies," *World Politics* 9, no. 1 (1956: 22.

158. Meng, *Tsungli Yamen*, 85–106.

159. Tsai, *China and the Overseas Chinese*, 4.

160. Prasenjit Duara, *Rescuing History from the Nation: Questioning Narratives of Modern China* (University of Chicago Press, 1995), 81.

161. Peter Sahlins, *Boundaries: The Making of France and Spain in the Pyrenees* (University of California Press, 1989). Indeed, making a nation's boundaries is a social, cultural, and political process: Anssi Paasi, "Generations and the 'Development' of Border Studies," *Geopolitics* 10 (2005): 668. It can be recontextualized by external forces (see Sami Moisio and Anssi Paasi, "Beyond State-Centricity: Geopolitics of Changing State Spaces," *Geopolitics* 18 [2013]: 255–66) because "the standardization of space that accompanied European settlement" created a new political geography of the areas affected (John A. Agnew, *Hegemony: The New Shape of*

Global Power [Temple University Press, 2005], 4). By the same token, the drawing of the new boundaries in Qing China, which was shaped by the rules of the European colonial powers, can be understood within the transnational context.

162. Nonetheless, given that China's transition to modern statehood was not a clone of the European model but a result of global geopolitical dynamics, the state formation of Qing China followed a different historical path than that of Western Europe. Here, I make it a proviso that, when colonial powers invaded China and imposed modern state logics in the nineteenth century, China, as an empire, gradually declined while taking the initial steps toward modern statehood.

163. Agnew, *Hegemony*; John A. Agnew, *Globalization and Sovereignty* (Rowman and Littlefield, 2009), 25.

164. When the Qing Empire signed the Treaty of Nerchinsk with Russia in 1689, the Qing already used a Western-style conception of the border: Laura Hostetler, "Imperial Competition in Eurasia: Russia and China," in *The Cambridge World History*, ed. Jerry H. Bentley, Sanjay Subrahmanyam, and Merry E. Wiesner-Hanks (Cambridge University Press, 2015), 303. In addition, after the Treaty of Neschinsk, the Kangxi Emperor thought that the West should recognize a more accurate knowledge of Qing territory and consequently produced the Kangxi Atlas (*Huangyu quanlan tu* 皇輿全覽圖, 1718). Jesuit missionaries employed by the Qing regime applied westernized cartographic techniques to create the Kangxi Atlas (Hostetler, "Early Modern Mapping at the Qing Court," 18). The idea that the Treaty of Nerchinsk and the Kangxi Atlas as geopolitical practices were embedded in the logics of the modern state, however, arouses a certain skepticism. Since the Kangxi Atlas was created and subsequently kept in the office of the palace treasurer, the cartographic practices of Chinese mapmakers followed Chinese methods rather than the modern Western method: D. Cordell Yee, "Traditional Chinese Cartography and the Myth of Westernization," in *Cartography in Traditional East and Southeast Asian Societies*, ed. John B. Harley and David Woodward (University of Chicago Press, 1994), 187. The Qing regime was not greatly influenced by Western cartographic practices in the production of maps, pursuing instead Chinese and traditional mapping practices. In fact, it was not until the end of the nineteenth century that the Sino-Russian border gained significant geopolitical attention (mainly due to railroad projects) and both China and Russia began to realize the importance of a "division of bordered lands in the modern sense": Sören Urbansky, *Beyond the Steppe Frontier: A History of the Sino-Russian Border* (Princeton University Press, 2020), 2.

165. Alexander Woodside, "The Centre and the Borderlands in Chinese Political Theory," in *The Chinese State at the Borders*, ed. Diana Lary (University of British Columbia Press, 2007), 21.

166. Palat, "Spatial Imaginaries of Capitalism," 6–7.

167. Elliott, *Emperor Qinglong*, chap. 6.

168. Joanna Waley-Cohen, "Commemorating War in Eighteenth-Century China," *Modern Asian Studies* 30, no. 4 (1996): 869–70.

169. Hua gang wenhua shuju zong jingxiao 華岡文化書局總經銷, *Qing dai yitong ditu* 清代一統 地圖 [China's national atlas of the Qing dynasty], 中華大典編印會合作 [Compiling and Printing Association in China], 1966.

170. Matthew W. Mosca, *From Frontier Policy to Foreign Policy: The Question of India and the Transformation of Geopolitics in Qing China* (Stanford University Press, 2013).

171. Pamela Kyle Crossley, *The Wobbling Pivot, China Since 1800* (Blackwell, 2010).

172. "[The] Temurtu-nor and Zaysan-nor [regions] are both located in Qing's kalun (guard post). If Russia incorporates both Temurtu-nor and Zaysan-nor . . . it not only takes large territories of Qing but also has [the] kalun of [the] Qing armies. It consequently makes it difficult to thwart invasions from Russia. And those who live in the Temurtu-nor and Zaysan-nor [regions] face a serious foreign intrusion." *Chou ban yi wu shi mo*, Tongzhi chao (同治朝) [The Tongzhi era], vol. 4, 1980, 17–19).

173. *Chou ban yi wu shi mo*, Tongzhi chao (同治朝) [The Tongzhi era], vol. 4, 1980, 20.

174. *Chou ban yi wu shi mo*, Tongzhi chao (同治朝) [The Tongzhi era], vol. 19, 1980, 16–17.

175. Weixin Chen 陳維新, Tong-guangnian jian zongeyili bianjie jiaoshe tantao-yi zhonge dingdingzhi tiaoyue ji jietu weili 同、光年間中俄伊犁邊界交涉探討-以中俄訂定之條約及界圖為例 [Treaty of Saint Petersburg of 1881: A case study of treaties and border maps in the National Palace Museum] (*Kongjianxinsiwei-lishiyutuxuequojixueshuyantaohui*, 2008), 289.

176. James W. Morley, *Sino-Japanese Relations 1862–1927: A Checklist of the Chinese Foreign Ministry Archives* (East Asian Institute, Columbia University, 1965), 12.

177. Eric Vanden Bussche, "Contested Realms: Colonial Rivalry, Border Demarcation, and State-Building in Southwest China, 1885–1960," PhD diss., Stanford University, 2014, 9.

178. Sheng Hu 胡绳, *Cong apianzhanzheng dao wusiyundong* 从鸦片战争到五四运动 [From the Opium War to the May Fourth Movement] (Renmin chubanshe, 1981).

179. Great Britain, The Houses of Parliament. Treaty Series, no. 11, "Convention Between Great Britain and China Relating to Sikkim and Tibet," *Parliamentary Paper C. 6208, 1890*, 1894.

180. Alastair Lamb, *British India and Tibet, 1766–1910* (Routledge and Kegan Paul, [1960] 1986).

181. Alex McKay, "Nineteenth-Century British Expansion on the Indo-Tibetan Frontier: A Forward Perspective," *Tibet Journal* 28, no. 4 (2003): 61–76; Alex McKay, "The British Invasion of Tibet, 1903–04," *Inner Asia* 14, no. 1 (2012): 5–25.

182. Chinyun Lee, "From Kiachta to Vladivostok: Russian Merchants and Tea Trade," *Region* 3, no. 2 (2014): 210. In addition, China's ceding of a border area (Vladivostok) to Russia helped Russian merchants to enjoy economic benefits. Vladivostok, as a northeastern border region between China and Russia and the final destination of the Trans-Siberian Railway, was under the Qing Empire's administration before the Treaty of Aigun in 1858 and the Convention of Peking in 1860. However, thanks in part to the successful Russian territorial expansion to the Chinese borderlands in the late nineteenth century, Russia acquired Vladivostok. Since then, Vladivostok has grown into the biggest commercial and traffic hub in eastern Russia. Vladivostok made a new route possible, connecting China and Russia, which led to the flourishing of Russia's tea trade (Lee, "From Kiachta to Vladivostok," 211). In contrast, since the late nineteenth century Shansi merchants suffered from tax-related disadvantages such as transit dues (*likin*) and high shipping costs and fell behind in the tea competition with Russian merchants.

183. Anthony D. King, *Urbanism, Colonialism, and the World-Economy: Cultural and Spatial Foundations of the World Urban System* (Routledge, 1990), 79.

184. Qinhua He, "The First Integrated Practice of Legal Translation in Modern China: A Study of the Chinese Translation of Elements of International Law, 1864," *Semiotica* 216 (2017): 151–68; Arnulf Becker Lorca, "Universal International Law: Nineteenth-Century Histories

of Imposition and Appropriation," *Harvard International Law Journal* 51, no. 2 (2010): 475–552.

185. Henry Wheaton, *Elements of International Law*, 8th ed., ed. Richard Henry Dana Jr. (Little, Brown, 1866), 22.

186. Lauren Benton, *A Search for Sovereignty: Law and Geography in European Empires, 1400–1900* (Cambridge University Press, 2010).

187. Par Kristoffer Cassel, *Grounds of Judgment: Extraterritoriality and Colonial Power in Nineteenth-Century China and Japan* (Oxford University Press, 2012), 21; Elliott, *Manchu Way*, 197–202. Influenced by the organization of the Jurchen Society's hunting, *mukun*-based blood ties, and its militarily functioning, tribe-centered social-economic community, Nurhaci developed the Eight Banner system. Most of all, the origin of the Eight Banner system stemmed from the *niru*, which was considered a basic hunting unit. The Eight Banners (八旗) were a key component of the Manchu military and social structure. After establishing the Qing, they enjoyed a high social status. Although the main ethnic group of the Eight Banners system was the Manchu, there were also Han military forces, Mongolians, and a small number of Koreans. They were composed of (1) Bordered Yellow Banner (鑲黃旗), (2) Plain Yellow Banner (正黃旗), (3) Plain White Banner (正白旗), (4) Plain Red Banner (正紅旗), (5) Bordered White Banner (鑲白旗), (6) Bordered Red Banner (鑲紅旗), (7) Plain Blue Banner (正藍旗), and (8) Bordered Blue Banner (鑲藍旗).

188. For instance, it was not until the *Wanguogongfa* was published in China that the concept of "rights" (*quanli*) stemming from the Western legal system was officially accepted in China. See Zhuo Yang 楊焯, "Cong「yousi」dao「shuren」: "Right" zai <wanguogongfa>zhong-defanyi" 從「有司」到「庶人」: "right" 在《萬國公法》中的翻譯 [From the right of "the superior" to the right of the "general public": The translation of "right" in the Wanguogongfa], *Bianyi Luncong* 編譯論叢 7, no. 1 (2014): 213–34.

189. Hsü, *China's Entrance into the Family of Nations*, 128.

190. Zhiguang Yin, "Heavenly Principles? The Translation of International Law in Nineteenth-Century China and the Constitution of Universality," *European Journal of International Law* 27, no. 4 (2016): 1018.

191. Zewei Yang, "Western International Law and China's Confucianism in the Nineteenth Century: Collision and Integration," *Journal of the History of International Law* 13 (2011): 285–306.

192. Martin, *Cycle of Cathay*, 234.

193. Horowitz, "International Law and State Transformation," 449.

194. Robert W. Cox, "Gramsci, Hegemony and International Relations: An Essay in Method," *Journal of international Studies* 12, no. 2 (1983): 162–75; A. Claire Cutler, "Gramsci, Law, and the Culture of Global Capitalism," *Critical Review of International Social and Political Philosophy* 8, no. 4 (2005): 527–42.

195. Wheaton, *Elements of International Law*, 22.

196. Wheaton, *Elements of International Law*, 52.

197. Weijian Wang 王维俭, "Pudandagu kou chuan bo shi jian yu xi fang guo ji fa chuan ru zhongguo," 普丹大沽口船舶事件和西方国际法传入中国 [Daguou's ship incident between Prussia-Denmark and China's acceptance of West's international laws], *Xueshuyanjiu* 学术研究 5 (1985): 84–90.

198. *Chou ban yi wu shi mo*, Tongzhi chao (同治朝) [The Tongzhi era], vol. 26, 1980, 29.

199. Wheaton, *Elements of International Law*, 256. Italics in original.

200. Wheaton, *Elements of International Law*, 378, 520–21.

201. *Chou ban yi wu shi mo*, Tongzhi chao (同治朝) [The Tongzhi era], vol. 26, 1980, 30. With satisfactory resolution of the diplomatic conflict, the Zongliyamen, on August 30, 1864, reported the emperor's effective use of the *Wanguogongfa* as follows: "After looking into the principles of the *Wanguogongfa*, we realized that every clause in the *Wanguogongfa* does not fit with the Chinese law system, nonetheless, some clauses of the *Wanguogongfa* would be worth accepting. When Prussia captured Danish ships this year, we (officials of the Zongliyamen) protested the misuse of Prussian power by using clauses of the *Wanguogongfa*. The ambassador of the Prussia admitted its mistakes (and there was no refutation). This is evidence why we consider the *Wanguogongfa*" (*Chou ban yi wu shi mo*, Tongzhi chao (同治朝) [The Tongzhi era], vol. 26, 1980, 32).

202. Wheaton, *Elements of International Law*, 17–18.

203. Horowitz, "International Law and State Transformation," 453.

204. Antony Anghie, *Imperialism, Sovereignty and the Making of International Law* (Cambridge University Press, 2005).

205. Wallerstein, *Historical Capitalism with Capitalist Civilization*, 57.

206. Wheaton, *Elements of International Law*, 151–52, 283.

207. Jianlang Wang, *Unequal Treaties and China* (Silkroad Press, 2016), 4.

208. For instance, a "citizen of the United States who committed a crime in China was triable only by the Consul, or other public functionary of the United States, thereto authorized according to the laws of the United States." This principle applied equally to the civil suits: "a Chinese plaintiff could sue an American citizen only in an American court": Teemu Ruskola, "Colonialism Without Colonies: On the Extraterritorial Jurisprudence of the U.S. Court for China," *Law and Contemporary Problems* 71 (2008): 220.

209. Crawford Bishop, "American Extraterritorial Jurisdiction in China," *American Journal of International Law* 20, no. 2 (1926): 281–99.

210. Ruskola, "Colonialism Without Colonies," 236.

211. Turan Kayaoğlu, *Legal Imperialism: Sovereignty and Extraterritoriality in Japan, the Ottoman Empire, and China* (Cambridge University Press, 2010).

212. Cassel, *Grounds of Judgment*, 7.

213. Indeed, China's embrace of *Wanguogongfa* facilitated the globalization of international law. Translated from the Qing Empire, *Wanguogongfa* was disseminated to Japan and especially to Chosŏn, where it allowed them to learn about the meaning and system of international law and the operation of the Western international order. In August 1882, Gojong, the king of Chosŏn, argued that treaties with foreign countries should be based on the *Wanguogongfa*:

"In recent times, the prevailing conditions of the global world have become quite different from those of the past. The major countries of Europe and America, namely England, France, the United States, and Russia, are devoting themselves to making precise machinery and enriching their countries. They are building ships to travel around the world, and they are making treaties with many countries around the world. The way they are confronting each other with the *Wanguogongfa* is reminiscent of the Spring and Autumn Period. . . . It is based on *Wanguogongfa* that countries make treaties and conduct trade" (*Gojongsilrok* 高宗實錄, vol. 19, August 5, 1882).

Chapter 4

1. Geoffrey Barraclough, *An Introduction to Contemporary History* (Penguin, 1967).

2. Osterhammel, *Transformation of the World*, xx.

3. Radhika Desai, *Geopolitical Economy: After US Hegemony, Globalization and Empire* (Pluto Press, 2013).

4. Wakeman, *Fall of Imperial China*, 199, 206.

5. Feuerwerker, in this sense, argued that Japanese trade experienced significant growth in the 1890s, driven by the provisions of the Shimonoseki Treaty and Japan's involvement in Manchuria afterward (Feuerwerker, "Economic Trends," 50). Concurrently, both the American and Russian portions of China's trade were also on the rise.

6. Patrick O'Brien, "The Pax Britannica and American Hegemony," in *Two Hegemonies: Britain 1846–1914 and the United States 1941–2001*, ed. Patrick Karl O'Brien and Armand Clesse (Ashgate, 2002), 33.

7. Thomas Piketty, *Capital in the Twenty-First Century* (Harvard University Press, 2014), 152.

8. John A. Agnew, *The United States in the World-System: A Regional Geography* (Cambridge University Press, 1987); Dall W. Forsythe, *Taxation and Political Change in the Young Nation, 1781–1833* (Columbia University Press, 1977); Robert B. Zevin, "The Growth of Cotton Textile Production after 1815," in *The Reinterpretation of American Economic History*, ed. Robert W. Fogel and Stanley L. Engerman (Harper and Row, 1971), 122–47.

9. George W. Hoffman, "Nineteenth Century Roots of American World Power Relations: A Study in Historical Political Geography," *Political Geography Quarterly* 1, no. 3 (1982): 285.

10. James Parisot, "The Two Hundred and Fifty Year Transition: How the American Empire Became Capitalist," *Journal of Historical Sociology* 30, no. 3 (2017): 605.

11. Christopher Chase-Dunn, "The Development of Core Capitalism in the Antebellum United States: Tariff Politics and Class Struggles in an Upwardly Mobile Semiperiphery," in *Studies of the Modern World-System*, ed. Albert Bergesen (Academic Press, 1980), 201.

12. Lance E. Davis and Robert E. Gallman. "Capital Formation in the United States During the Nineteenth Century," in *The Cambridge Economic History of Europe*, vol. 6, pt. 2, ed. Peter Mathias and M. M. Postan (Cambridge University Press, 1978), 66.

13. Some American merchants who traded with China hoped that US railroad construction would help them trade with China across the Pacific. For instance, Asa Whitney, a China trader, lobbied for the construction of an east-west railroad in the 1840s because it would not only cross the American continent but would also greatly benefit trade between the United States and China; Margaret L. Brown, "Asa Whitney and His Pacific Railroad Publicity Campaign," *Mississippi Valley Historical Review* 20, no. 2 (1933): 213–14.

14. Frederic Jackson Turner, *The Frontier in American History* (Holt, Rinehart and Winston, 1962), 4.

15. Turner, *Frontier in American History*, 319.

16. Bruce Cumings, *Dominion From Sea to Sea: Pacific Ascendancy and American Power* (Yale University Press, 2009), 76.

17. Alfred D. Chandler, "The United States: Evolution of Enterprise," in *The Cambridge Economic History of Europe*, vol. 6, pt. 2, ed. Peter Mathias and M. M. Postan (Cambridge University Press, 1978), 115.

18. Alfred D. Chandler, *The Visible Hand: The Managerial Revolution in American Business* (Harvard University Press, 1977), 10.

19. Alfred D. Chandler, "The Emergence of Managerial Capitalism," *Business History Review* 58, no. 4 (1984): 473–503.

20. John Jay, *The Correspondence and Public Papers of John Jay, Vol. 3 (1782–1793)* (G. P. Putnam's Sons, 1891), 97.

21. Yen-P'ing Hao, "Chinese Teas to America—a Synopsis," in *America's China Trade in Historical Perspective*, ed. Ernest R. May and John K. Fairbank (Harvard University Press, 1986), 13.

22. John R. Haddad, *America's First Adventure in China: Trade, Treaties, Opium, and Salvation* (Temple University Press, 2013), 58.

23. Suh, *Ap'yŏnjŏnjaeng*, 184.

24. Michael J. Green, *By More Than Providence: Grand Strategy and American Power in the Asia Pacific Since 1783* (Columbia University Press, 2017), 40.

25. "Letter from Humphrey Marshall to Secretary Marcy, July 26, 1853, 33rd Congress, 1st Session," *House Executive Document 123* (1853), 204.

26. Alexander Hamilton, John Jay, and James Madison, *The Federalist and Other Constitutional Papers, Vol. 1* (Albert, Scott & Company, 1894), 24.

27. Kevin Narizny, *The Political Economy of Grand Strategy* (Cornell University Press, 2007), 42.

28. Cumings, *Dominion from Sea to Sea*, 149.

29. Jonathan Goldstein, *Philadelphia and the China Trade 1682–1846: Commercial, Cultural, and Attitudinal Effect* (Pennsylvania State University Press, 1978).

30. Akira Iriye, *Pacific Estrangement: Japanese and American Expansion 1897–1911* (Imprint, 1994), 12.

31. Arang Ha, "Free Labor, Free Trade, Free Immigration: The Vision of the Pacific Community After the Civil War," PhD diss. Rice University, 2021; Minyong Lee, "Circuits of Empire: The California Gold Rush and the Making of America's Pacific," PhD diss., University of Chicago, 2018. While it is debatable what single event triggered the beginning of America's geopolitical and geoeconomic expansion, it is clear that the Gold Rush paved the way for the United States' expansion into the Pacific. As Kenneth Pomeranz and Steven Topik point out, the Gold Rush signaled the United States' new international status, and the westward expansion led the United States to take a keen interest in creating the Panama Canal, which runs through Central America (Pomeranz and Topik, *The World That Trade Created*, 114).

32. Captain A. T. Mahan, "The United States Looking Outward," *The Atlantic* (1890), https://www.theatlantic.com/magazine/archive/1890/12/the-united-states-looking-outward/306348/.

33. Matthew Josephson, *The Robber Barons: The Great American Capitalists, 1861–1901* (Harcourt, Brace, 1934).

34. Brooks Adams, *America's Economic Supremacy* (New York: Macmillan, 1900), 221; Richard H. Immerman, *Empire for Liberty: A History of American Imperialism from Benjamin Franklin to Paul Wolfowitz* (Princeton University Press, 2010), 141.

35. The United States asserted that it may use force in its advance into Japan and Korea.

36. Of course, a direct route between the West Coast and East Asia did not open up until the mid-nineteenth century, when California was admitted as a US state.

37. Walter LaFeber, *The American Age: United States Foreign Policy at Home and Abroad Since 1750* (Norton, 1989), 173.

38. *Statistical Abstract of the United States*, ed. Department of Commerce and Labor (Washington, DC, 1905), 216.

39. *Statistical Abstract of the United States*, 221.

40. Turner had this to say about it: "Having colonized the Far West, having mastered its internal resources, the nation turned at the conclusion of the nineteenth and the beginning of the twentieth century to deal with the Far East, to engage in the world-politics of the Pacific Ocean. Having continued its historic expansion into the lands of the old Spanish empire by the successful outcome of the recent war, the United States became the mistress of the Philippines at the same time that it came into possession of the Hawaiian Islands, and the controlling influence in the Gulf of Mexico. It provided early in the present decade for connecting its Atlantic and Pacific coasts by the Isthmian Canal and became an imperial republic with dependencies and protectorates—admittedly a new world-power, with a potential voice in the problems of Europe, Asia, and Africa" (Turner, *Frontier in American History*, 315).

41. Julian Go, "Waves of Empire: US Hegemony and Imperialistic Activity from the Shores of Tripoli to Iraq, 1787–2013," *International Sociology* 22, no. 1 (2007): 23. Paul Reinsch also noted that Asia was a treasure trove of future human and material resources; see Paul S. Reinsch, *World Politics: At the End of the Nineteenth Century* (Macmillan, 1900), 66.

42. Cumings, *Dominion from Sea to Sea*, 8.

43. Christopher Chase-Dunn, Andrew K. Jorgenson, Thomas E. Reifer, and Shoon Lio, "The Trajectory of the United States in the World-System: A Quantitative Reflection," *Sociological Perspectives* 48, no. 2 (2005): 241–42.

44. Arthur W. Lewis, *Growth and Fluctuations, 1870–1913* (George Allen and Unwin, 1978), chap. 5.

45. Andrew Gamble, "Hegemony and Decline: Britain and the United States," in *Two Hegemonies: Britain 1846–1914 and the United States 1941–2001*, ed. Patrick Karl O'Brien and Armand Clesse (Ashgate, 2002), 132–33.

46. US overseas expansion was partly related to westward or Pacific settlement policy of expansionists like James K. Polk, Franklin Pierce, and James Buchanan in the mid-nineteenth century. See James K. Polk, "James K. Polk's Special Message," February 10, 1847, https://www.presidency.ucsb.edu/documents/special-message-3254. For the expansion policy of Pierce and Buchanan, see Iriye, *Pacific Estrangement*, 7.

47. Hoffman, "Nineteenth Century Roots," 289.

48. Daniel Immerwahr, "The Great United States: Territory and Empire in U.S. History," *Diplomatic History* 40, no. 3 (2016): 377.

49. Bruce Cumings. "Dominion from Sea to Sea: America's Pacific Ascendancy," *Asia-Pacific Journal* 10, no. 7 (2012): 7.

50. Green, *By More Than Providence*, 54.

51. Cumings, *Dominion from Sea to Sea*, 60.

52. Macabe Keliher, "Anglo-American Rivalry and the Origins of U.S. China Policy," *Diplomatic History* 31, no. 2 (2007): 248–49.

53. Tamar Rachel Van, "Cents and Sensibilities: Fairness and Free Trade in the Early 19th Century," *Diplomatic History* 42, no. 1 (2018): 72–89.

54. Sven Beckert, *The Empire of Cotton* (Vintage, 2014).

55. Bruce Cumings, "Archaeology, Descent, Emergence: Japan in British/American Hegemony, 1900–1950," in *Japan in the World*, ed. Masao Miyoshi and H. D. Harootunian (Duke University Press, 1993), 79–111; Department of State, *Papers Relating to the Foreign Relations of the United States with the Annual Message of the President*, transmitted to Congress (1899), 129. For research showing that the Open Door Policy was based on economic objectives, see Iriye, *Pacific Estrangement*, 66.

56. David P. Calleo, *Beyond American Hegemony: The Future of the Western Alliance* (Basic Books, 1987).

57. Regarding Russia's incorporation process into the capitalist world-system, see Wallerstein, *Modern World-System III*, 137.

58. William L. Blackwell, *The Beginnings of Russian Industrialization, 1800–1860* (Princeton University Press, 1968), 46–47.

59. Jun Kee Baek, "Rŏshiaŭi tongashiajŏngch'aekkwa manjumunje" [Russian policy in East Asia and the Manchurian question], in *Ashiaŭi Palk'an, Manjuwa Seo-gu Yŏlgangŭi Chegukchuŭi Chŏngch'aek* [Imperialist policies of Western powers in Manchuria, called the Balkans in Asia] (Tongbugayŏksajaedan, 2007), 38–40.

60. Herbert J. Ellison, "Economic Modernization in Imperial Russia: Purposes and Achievements," *Journal of Economic History* 25, no. 4 (1965): 524. With regard to the economic growth of Tsarist Russia, see Raymond E. Goldsmith, "The Economic Growth of Tsarist Russia 1860–1913," *Economic Development and Cultural Change* 9, no. 3 (1961): 441–75.

61. Maddison, *Chinese Economic Performance*, 377.

62. Alberto Masoero, "Russia Between Europe and Asia," in *The Boundaries of Europe: From the Fall of the Ancient World to the Age of Decolonisation*, ed. Pietro Rossi (De Gruyter, 2015), 192.

63. Mark Bassin, "Russia Between Europe and Asia: The Ideological Construction of Geographical Space," *Slavic Review* 50, no. 1 (1991), 5.

64. Masoero, "Russia Between Europe and Asia," 199.

65. Bassin, "Russia Between Europe and Asia," 9. However, Ramansky was also contemptuous of Asian cultures and civilizations. He treated Asian civilizations as decadent, and he saw Asia as a region with no hope of creating an independent future. Accordingly, Ramansky predicted that in the distant future the entire Asian continent would fall within the sphere of European or Russian conquest and domination (Bassin, "Russia Between Europe and Asia," 13).

66. Masoero, "Russia Between Europe and Asia," 203.

67. Masoero, "Russia Between Europe and Asia," 202.

68. Andrew Malozemoff, *Russian Far Eastern Policy 1881–1904—with Special Emphasis on the Causes of the Russo-Japanese War* (University of California Press, 1958).

69. Demetrius Charles Boulger, *England and Russia in Central Asia* (W. H. Allen & Co., 1879).

70. Michael B. Share, "The Great Game Revisited: Three Empires Collide in Chinese Turkestan (Xinjiang)," *Europe-Asia Studies* 67, no. 7 (2015): 1106.

71. Owen Lattimore, *Pivot of Asia: Sinkiang and the Inner Asian Frontier of China and Russia* (Little, Brown, 1950), 24–44.

72. M. A. Terent'yev, *Russia and England in Central Asia. Volume 2* (London: Routledge, 1876), 114.

73. Lattimore, *Pivot of Asia*, 27.

74. Share, "Great Game Revisited," 1107.

75. Xiuyu Wang analyzed the "local" dimension of the geopolitical changes regarding Tibet. He transcended (a) "a nationalist perspective" that the Tibet region is a part of the centralized Qing regime and that Tibet and the Qing regime united to fight against the colonial powers when they invaded Tibet in the nineteenth century, and (b) "the impact-response approach" that focused on the passive and lethargic response of Tibet to the colonial powers as they penetrated into Tibet. Wang explained how the major local powers emerged in Tibet related to the Qing government on the one hand and the colonial powers on the other. Xiuyu Wang, *China's Last Imperial Frontier: Late Qing Expansion in Sichuan's Tibetan Borderlands* (Lexington Books, 2011). Of the new explanations, Wang's detailed analysis of regional dynamics is insightful; however, he did not sufficiently analyze the multiple types of colonial powers that influenced China in the nineteenth century. As Wang himself admitted, from the mid-nineteenth century the political, economic, and social situation of Tibet was not determined solely by the Qing and its neighbors. Tibet, including eastern Tibet, was gradually influenced by the colonial powers, notably Britain and Russia. The problem is that in the case of colonial powers, unlike Wang's assumption, they are not a unified form. I divide the colonial powers into European powers and Pacific powers and how there were two different types of colonial powers that influenced China's incorporation process. To be specific, I am more interested in how the two different external powers (European and Pacific powers), which were confirmed through the perspective of "the incorporation process of nineteenth-century China," influenced Tibet.

76. Kees Van Dijk, *Pacific Strife: The Great Powers and Their Political and Economic Rivalries in Asia and the Western Pacific 1870–1914* (Amsterdam University Press, 2015), 350.

77. Younghusband's troops attacked the Tibetan army with machine guns, killing two thousand to three thousand Tibetans armed with old-fashioned flintlock rifles. This was the background to Tibet's signing of the treaty.

78. Of course, British incursion in Tibet brought about the Qing government's backlash and counterattack; however, the main target of the Qing was not British-Indian forces but local powers in eastern Tibet (Kham) (Wang, *China's Last Imperial Frontier*, 9).

79. Van Dijk, *Pacific Strife*, 357.

80. E. Sydney Crawcour, "Economic Change in the Nineteenth Century," in *The Cambridge History of Japan*, vol. 5, *The Nineteenth Century*, ed. John W. Hall, Marious B. Jansen, Madoka Kanai, and Denis Twitchett (Cambridge University Press, 1989), 610–11.

81. E. H. Norman, *Origins of the Modern Japanese State* (Pantheon, 1975).

82. Keiji Yamaguchi, *Ilbon'gŭnseŭi Swaegukkwa Kaeguk* [Closed-door policies and the opening of Japan in modern times], trans. Kimhyŏnyŏng (Hyean, 2001), 330. Although external pressure was inflicted on Japan after the 1840s, Japan was still able to adapt. Before Japan's incorporation, it faced constant demands from colonial powers to open its ports, but it did not become a primary target because the colonial powers were preoccupied with various circumstances. For example, the Anglo-Japanese Friendship Treaty (1854) required Japan to open Nagasaki and Hakodate and supply fresh water and provisions to Britain. However,

Britain was dealing with the Crimean War (1854–1856) and could not afford to pay attention to Japan. When the Arrow Incident (1856) occurred in China, Britain declared war on China in collusion with France (Second Opium War). In 1857–1859, Indian mercenaries hired by the British East India Company rebelled against the British (see L. S. Stavrianos, *Global Rift: The Third World Comes to Age* [William Morrow and Company, 1981], 351). France also signed a treaty with Japan, the Treaty of Amity and Commerce (1858), which was also unequal from the Japanese perspective. Japan was required to open Edo, Kobe, Nagasaki, Niigata, and Yokohama as foreign ports of trade, and foreign citizens were granted the freedom to live and trade there. Foreign residents were also granted extraterritorial legal rights. The resulting fixed low import tariffs and the loss of Japanese government control over foreign trade heavily burdened Japan. However, France's subsequent war and colonial occupation of Vietnam and its war with Mexico deprioritized its penetration into Japan. Thus, while Japan agreed to unequal treaties with the colonial powers, Japan was of limited focus. Moreover, trade with Japan was suboptimal for the colonial powers, involving less quantity than trade with China and negligible investment (Moulder, *Japan, China, and the Modern World-Economy*, 97). Because many colonial powers were more interested in China than in Japan (see G. Daniels, "The British Role in the Meiji Restoration: A Re-Interpretive Note," *Modern Asian Studies* 2, no, 4 [1968], 292), and because Japan signed a trade agreement with the US, Japan—unlike China—was not subject to external pressure from multiple colonial powers. Japan had breathing room (Moulder, *Japan, China, and the Modern World-Economy*, 150).

83. W. G. Beasley, "The Foreign Threat and the Opening of the Ports," in *The Cambridge History of Japan*, vol. 5, *The Nineteenth Century*, ed. John W. Hall, Marious B. Jansen, Madoka Kanai, and Denis Twitchett (Cambridge University Press, 1989), 261.

84. Moulder, *Japan, China*, 97.

85. Edwin O. Reischauer and Albert M. Craig, *Japan: Tradition and Transformation* (Houghton Mifflin, 1978), 94–98.

86. Edwin O. Reischauer, *Japan Past and Present*, 3rd ed. (Gerald Duckworth, [1946] 1964), 97.

87. Crawcour, "Economic Change in the Nineteenth Century," 569.

88. So and Chiu, *East Asia and World-Economy*, 57.

89. High-ranking Japanese officials such as Ito Hirobumi argued that Japan should emulate American protectionism and pursue the same policy. See Akira Iriye, "Japan's Drive to Great-Power Status," in *The Cambridge History of Japan*, vol. 5, *The Nineteenth Century*, ed. Marius Jansen (Cambridge University Press, 1989), 738.

90. Iriye, *Pacific Estrangement*, 25.

91. Marie Conte-Helm, *Japan and the North East of England: From 1862 to the Present Day* (Athlone Press, 1989); Kozo Yamamura, "Success Ill-Gotten? The Role of Meiji Militarism in Japan's Technological Progress," *Journal of Economic History* 37, no. 1 (1977): 113–35.

92. Sheila Miyoshi Jager notes that Korea played an important role in the establishment of a new regional order in East Asia at the end of the nineteenth century. See Sheila Miyoshi Jager, *The Other Great Game: The Opening of Korea and the Birth of Modern East Asia* (Harvard University Press, 2023).

93. William R. Nester, *Power Across the Pacific: A Diplomatic History of American Relations with Japan* (New York University Press, 1996), 63.

94. Sandra Wilson, "The Discourse of National Greatness in Japan, 1890–1919," *Japanese Studies* 25, no. 1 (2005): 35–51.

95. In 1866, in order to build a new trade relationship with South Korea, the American armed merchant ship The General Sherman visited South Korea. The General Sherman contacted the Korean officials and demanded trade, but its request was rejected on the grounds that trade with the West was prohibited by Korean law. When the General Sherman's request for trade was rejected, the ship detained a Korean military officer and landed on the island to commit acts of looting. Then, the Koreans were outraged by the atrocities of this ship and set it on fire. This incident was called The General Sherman incident in Korea. As the General Sherman's ship sank off the coast of Korea, the United States asked the Korean government to investigate the incident jointly with Korea. Another reason the United States wanted to jointly investigate the General Sherman incident was to open the port of Korea. The United States had already used gunboat diplomacy to force Japan to open its ports, so it expected that Korea would be able to open its ports easily. At the time, the Korean court was skeptical of this joint investigation by the United States and had no intention of opening Korea. The United States then launched a reconnaissance expedition to Korea in 1867 and 1868. Then, in 1869, Secretary of State Hamilton Fish planned an expedition to Korea when the Ulyssess S. Grant administration was launched. President Grant officially announced the execution of the expedition to Korea in 1870. The United States entrusted Frederick Low, the US Ambassador to China, with full authority and ordered John Rodgers, the commander of the naval fleet of the expedition to Korea, to lead the expedition to Korea. In 1871, the US fleet led by John Rodgers arrived at Kanghwado in Korea via Japan. However, the Korean court at the time had very limited information about the United States. In fact, Kim Byung-Hak, the highest official position in Uijeongbu, referred to the United States as a country made up of small villages, and told King Gojong that it was no different from pirates who valued trade with the United Kingdom and had a habit of looting when they sailed the seas. As information about the United States was very limited, the Korean court had little idea of the U.S. naval power and their national strength. The Joseon court had little information about the United States, so it maintained a tough stance even after exchanging letters with the U.S. fleet led by John Rodgers. As a result, a battle broke out between the two countries, in which the US Navy attacked the Korean army, killing more than 200 Koreans. The Koreans call this incident the Western Disturbance in the Shinmi Year, 1871.

96. Key-hiuk Kim, *Last Phase*, chap. 2.

97. Wang Mingxing and Song Huijuan see the 1870s as the turning point in the Qing Empire's Korean policy. See Wang Mingxing 王明星, Hanguo jindai waijiao yu zhongguo 1861–1910 韩国近代外交与中国, 1861–1910 [Modern Korean diplomacy and China, 1861–1910 (Beijing: Zhongguo shehui kexue chubanshe, 1998); Song Huijuan 宋慧娟, Qing dai Zhong Chao zongfan guanxi shanbian yanjiu 清代中朝宗藩關係嬗變研究 [Transformation of Sino-Korean tributary relations during the Qing dynasty] (Jilin daxue chubanshe, 2007); on the other hands, Zhang Liheng argued the starting point for the Qing Empire's policy change toward Korea occurred during the 1880s: see Zhang Liheng 张礼恒, "Ping jiawu zhan zheng qian qing zheng fu de dui chao zhengce" 评甲午战争前清政府的对朝政策 [The Qing's policy on Korea before the First Sino-Japanese War], Anhui shixue 安徽史学 [Anhui Historiography] 2 (1993): 51–54.

98. Hongzhang Li 李鴻章, *Li Wenxhong gong quan ji* 李文忠公全集 [Complete works of Li Hongzhang], vol. 16, ed. Wu Rulun (Wenhai chubanshe, 1962), September 25, 1884.

99. Li, *Li Wenxhong gong quan ji*, vol. 16, September 25, 1884. Yuan was deeply involved in Korea's diplomacy. For example, in June 1887, the Korean court appointed Pakchŏngyang as the head of the Korean mission in the United States and Shim Sanghak as the head of the Korean mission in England, Germany, Russia, Belgium, and France, and then tried to send them to the United States and the five other countries, respectively (*Gojongsilrok* 高宗實錄 vol. 28, June 29, 1887). Having heard this, Yuan reported the news of diplomatic affairs in Korea to Li Hongzhang and then strongly demanded that the Korean government stop sending missions to Western countries, saying it had not consulted with the Qing court in advance: *Qing Guang xu chaozhongri jiaoshe shijiao* 清光緒朝中日交涉史料 [Historical materials on Sino-Japanese negotiations during the Guang-xi period], vol. 1 (Wenhai chubanshe, 1970), 558. In addition, Yuan threatened to wage war with Korea if the Korean king sent a mission to United States; see Horace Newton Allen, *Aellŏnŭi ilgi* [Horace Newton Allen's diary], trans. Kim Won-Mo (Dankook University Press, 1991), 132.

100. The *Deokheungho* incident in Busan is a representative case of commercial competition between China and Japan; see *Kukan'gugoegyomunsŏ* 舊韓國外交文書 [Old Korean diplomatic documents], vol. 8, *Chŏngan* (清案) 1 (Korea University Press, 1970): 9–10. This incident was a clash between a Chinese merchant and a Japanese merchant at the Japanese residence in Busan in November 1883. Huang Yaodong, who was running a trading store (*Gongxinghao* 公興號) in Kobe, Japan, was trying to open his new store in the Japanese residence in Busan, but a conflict broke out with local Japanese merchants. The Japanese consul attempted to expel Huang Yaodong's employees by force, but he objected to Japan's decision and asked Chen Shu-Tang, the general commissioner of trade, to settle this case. This eventually escalated into a diplomatic issue between China and Japan, leading to the construction of a Qing concession in Korea. The Qing regime provided political assistance to Chinese merchants in securing and expanding their commercial sphere in Korea like the construction of Qing concessions in major port cities in Korea.

101. *Kukan'gugoegyomunsŏ* 舊韓國外交文書 [Old Korean diplomatic documents], vol. 4, *T'ongsŏilgi* 統署日記 2 (Korea University Press, 1974), 450; *Kukan'gugoegyomunsŏ* 舊韓國外交文書 [Old Korean diplomatic documents), vol. 5, *T'ongsŏilgi* 統署日記 2 (Korea University Press, 1974), 213. Obviously, Yuan's behavior disregarded the Korean government's diplomatic principle that all foreigners must obtain a *Hojo* from *Tongriamun* when they entered Korean territory. His arbitrary action made it difficult for the Koran government to manage and control the entry of Chinese merchants.

102. Yang Ja Lee, *Chosŏnesŏŭi wŏnsegae* [Yuan Shikai in Chosŏn] (Shinjisŏwŏn, 2002), 105.

103. *Kukan'gugoegyomunsŏ* 舊韓國外交文書 [Old Korean diplomatic documents], vol. 4, 114–15.

104. *Kukan'gugoegyomunsŏ* 舊韓國外交文書 [Old Korean diplomatic documents], vol. 4, 198–99, 410–11.

105. Of course, the modern East Asian order that China pursued was partially different from that put forward by the colonial powers. In 1886, Li Hongzhang pointed out to the king of Korea the difference between Western and Chinese policies: "Unlike Western rule, which subjugates everything from administrative and financial to military; Qing's governance is dif-

ferent in that it minimizes tributaries' interference in internal affairs": Quan Hexiu 权赫秀, *Jindai Zhonghanguanxi shiliao xuanbian* 近代中韩关系史料选编 [Selected historical materials on Sino-Korean relations in modern times] (Beijing: Shujie zhishi chubanshe, 2008), 296. However, this claim was very different from the actions of Yuan Shikai in Korea.

106. Lee, *Chosŏnesŏŭi wŏnsegae*, 106.

107. *Qingshigao* 清史稿, vol. 526 (1977): 14597–99.

108. Dabohashi Giyoshi, *Gŭndaeilsŏnkwan'gyeŭiyŏn'gu* 近代日鮮關係の研究 [Modern Japanese-Korean relations], trans. Kim Jonghak (Ilchokak, [1940] 2013), 503.

109. Giyoshi, *Gŭndaeilsŏnkwan'gyeŭiyŏn'gu*, 504.

110. Giyoshi, *Gŭndaeilsŏnkwan'gyeŭiyŏn'gu*, 508.

111. Giyoshi, *Gŭndaeilsŏnkwan'gyeŭiyŏn'gu*, 512.

112. Giyoshi, *Gŭndaeilsŏnkwan'gyeŭiyŏn'gu*, 512.

113. The Imo Incident was an uprising in 1882 led by Korean soldiers armed with outdated weapons who were dissatisfied with the treatment they received from the government. The causes of the rebellion were (1) opposition to King Gojong's reform and modernization policies, including the hiring of Japanese military advisors, and (2) frustration over the inadequate food rations for soldiers (rice was used as currency at the time, so soldiers were paid in rice). The Qing army intervened to quell the rebellion.

114. The Gapsin Coup in 1884 was a coup led by reformers including Kim Ok-gyun, Park Yeong-hyo, Philip Jaisohn, and Hong Yeong-sik, who were members of the Enlightenment Party. This was supported directly or indirectly by Japan. After the Imo Incident, Heungseon Daewongun was placed under house arrest by Qing China, and Queen Min came to power. However, the Min clan's regime was able to regain power with the help of the Qing Empire, making it very reliant on the Qing dynasty. Enlightenment Party members, dissatisfied with the situation, launched a coup and killed key figures in the Min clan's regime, and received approval from King Gojong to set up a new government. However, three days later, the coup was crushed by an attack by Chinese troops requested by Queen Min. When the Qing army intervened and the coup failed, the Japanese army, which was supporting the coup, also sent troops in opposition to the Qing army's intervention, and a military clash between the two sides broke out. Kim Ok-gyun, one of the key figures who led the coup, defected to Japan and then went to China to plan a new scheme, but he was assassinated in Shanghai.

115. Crossley, *Wobbling Pivot*, 95.

116. Outwardly, the Japanese government showed no political intentions of imperialist expansion, while continuing to insist that the sole purpose of its political intervention was to help liberate the Korean nation from China: "First, my government [Japanese government] had no desire other than to see Korea's independence and peace established": Munemitsu Mutsu, *Kenkenroku: A Diplomatic Record of the Sino-Japanese War, 1894–95*, trans. Gordon Mark Berger (Princeton University Press, 1982), 41. Before long, however, Japan's ambitions of imperial conquest were exposed under the pretext of the protection of its allies: "The Korean government simply did not know how to comport itself during times of war or peace as an independent state among the nations of the world . . . so [we] keep the Koreans firmly under our control" (Munemitsu, *Kenkenroku*, 93).

117. The Treaty of Shimonoseki provided for "(1) recognition of Korean independence and termination of tribute to China; (2) an indemnity of 200 million taels; (3) cession of

Taiwan, the Pescadores, and the Liaotung Peninsula; (4) the opening of Chungking, Soochow, Hangchow, and Shansi to trade; and (5) the right of Japanese nationals to open factories and engage in industries and manufacturing in China" (Hsü, *Rise of Modern China*, 342).

118. Alexis Krausse, *China in Decay: The Story of a Disappearing Empire*, 3rd ed. (Chapman & Hill, 1900), 383–84.

119. Marius Jansen, "Japan and the Chinese Revolution of 1911," in *The Cambridge History of China*, vol. 11, pt. 2, *Late Ch'ing, 1800–1911*, ed. John K. Fairbank and Kwang-Ching Liu (Cambridge University Press, 1980), 348, 350.

120. Paine, *Sino-Japanese War of 1894–1895*, 111.

121. Fang Zhong Wang 王方中, *Zhong guo jin dai jing ji shi gao (1840 nian–1927 nian)* 中國近代經濟史稿 *(1840 年 –1927 年)* [The economic history of modern China] (Beijing chubanshe, 1982).

122. Lawrence James, *The Rise and Fall of the British Empire* (St. Martin's, 1994), 241.

123. Van Dijk, *Pacific Strife*, 190.

124. Nakami Dasao, "Yŏksa sogŭi manjusang" [Images of Manchuria in history], in *Manjuran muŏshiŏnnŭn'ga* [What was Manchuria], ed. Nakami Dasao (Somyŏngch'ulp'an, 2013), 29. In addition, Japan established a puppet state, the Manchukuo state, where it used Manchuria as a laboratory for creating Japanese-style modernity (Prasenjit Duara, *Sovereignty and Authenticity: Manchukuo and the East Asian Modern* [Rowman and Littlefield, 2003], 250), a place to realize the Japanese "kingly way" (Prasenjit Duara, "Transnationalism and the Predicament of Sovereignty: China, 1900–1945," *American Historical Review* 102, no. 4 [1997], 1036) and Pan-Asianism (Shin'ichi Yamamuro, *Manchuria Under Japanese Dominion*, trans. Joshua A. Fogel [University of Pennsylvania Press, 2006]).

125. Bruce Cumings used a world-systems perspective to analyze the Japan-Korea-Manchuria connections that formed after the Japanese Empire's expansion into Manchuria as the center, semiperiphery, and periphery, respectively. Bruce Cumings, *The Origins of the Korean War: Liberation and the Emergence of Separate Regimes, 1945–1947* (Princeton University Press, 1981), 13–15; Bruce Cumings, "The Origins and Development of the Northeast Asian Political Economy: Industrial Sectors, Product Cycles, and Political Consequences," *International Organization* 38, no. 1 (1984): 1. Carter J. Eckert points out that the Koch'ang Kims, a Korean capitalist family, entered the Manchurian market with Japanese support, using Japanese technology and cheap Korean labor: Carter J. Eckert, *Offspring of Empire: The Koch'ang Kims and the Colonial Origins of Korean Capitalism, 1876–1945* (University of Washington Press, 1991), 177. Daqing Yang further notes that Japan, Korea, and Manchuria were interconnected within Japan's imperial telecommunications network: Daqing Yang, "Colonial Korea in Japan's Imperial Telecommunication Network," in *Colonial Modernity in Korea*, ed. Gi-Wook Shin and Michael Robinson (Harvard University Press, 2000), 173–78. These pioneering studies confirm the connectivity of the East Asian regional system centered on Japan in the first half of the twentieth century, although it is questionable whether this connectivity was hierarchically structured because none of them analyzed the Manchurian region as an independent research topic and its integration into the capitalist world-system. See Suk-Jung Han, "Taedongagongyŏnggwŏn'gwa segyech'ejeronŭi chŏkyonge taehan shiron" [A critique of world-system analysis of the so-called Greater East Asian Co-Prosperity Sphere], *Han'guksahoehak* [Korean Journal of Sociology] 33 (1999): 917–36.

126. Kim Youngsin, "Kaehang, choch'awa kŭndae manjur shinhŭngdoshiŭi hŭnggi" [Open port, lend lease, and the development of the modern city in the Manchuria], in *Kŭndae manju toshi yŏksajiri yŏn'gu* [Historical geographic study of the modernization process in Manchuria] (Tongbugayŏksajaedan, 2007), 78.

127. For instance, "Manchuria's exports of soybeans, soy oil, and bean cake" rose from about 160,000 tons in 1907 to 930,000 tons in 1909, and to 2.72 million tons in 1929 (Richard Evan Wells, "The Manchurian Bean: How the Soybean Shaped the Modern History of China's Northeast, 1862–1945," PhD diss., University of Wisconsin–Madison, 2018), 70–71. Indeed, the increased trade in Manchurian soybeans became an important factor in the migration of many Chinese to Manchuria: Thomas R. Gottschang and Diana Lary, *Swallows and Settlers: The Great Migration from North China to Manchuria* (University of Michigan Press, 2000), 49–50.

128. Jiwon Ryu, "Chŏngdae tongbukchŏngch'aegŭi pyŏnhwae ttarŭn manju toshi sŏnggyŏgŭi pyŏnhwa" [Changes in the character of Manchurian cities in response to changes in the Qing's Northeast policy], in *Kŭndae manju toshi yŏksajiri yŏn'gu* [Historical geographic study of the modernization process in Manchuria] (Tongbugayŏksajaedan, 2007), 18–63. Because Manchuria symbolized the origins of the Qing court and was a cultural space for Manchu identification, the Qing dynasty was careful to keep Manchuria separate from China proper by prohibiting Han Chinese from settling in Manchuria. See Mark C. Elliott, "The Limits of Tartary: Manchuria in Imperial and National Geographies," *Journal of Asian Studies* 59, no. 3 (2000): 603–46.

129. Kim Youngsin, "Kaehang, choch'awa kŭndae manjur," 67.

130. Qu Xiaofan, 曲曉范, *Chunggung tongbung chiyŏng toshisa yŏn'gu* [A study on the history of cities in northeast China), trans. Piao you (Zininzin, 2016).

131. Qu, *Chunggung tongbung chiyŏng*, 28–37.

132. Of course, in both Yingkou and Dalian, the changes in urban structure and appearance, as well as the paths of industrial and urban development, were largely dictated by Japan from the early twentieth century. Furthermore, in the 1910s Japan intentionally constrained Port Yingkou to propel Dalian Port as a new transportation hub (Kim, "Kaehang, choch'awa kŭndae manjur shinhŭngdoshiŭi hŭnggi," 79).

133. Key-hiuk Kim, "Kaehang, choch'awa kŭndae manjur," 88.

134. Key-hiuk Kim, "Kaehang, choch'awa kŭndae manjur," 90.

135. Jingyu Wang 汪敬虞, *Zhungguo Jindai Jingjishi 1895–1927* 中国近代经济史, 1895–1927 [Modern Chinese economic history, 1895–1927] (Renminchubanshe, 1998), 69.

136. Anthony D. King, *Colonial Urban Development: Culture, Social Powers and Environment* (Routledge and Kegan Paul, 1976), chap. 2.

137. Hwytak Yoon, *Manjuguk: Shingminjijŏng sangsangi ingt'aehan pok'amminjokkukka* [Manchukuo: The sun of a new nation] (Hyean, 2013), chap. 8.

138. Suk-Jung Han, *Manjugung kŏn'gugŭi chaehaesŏk: Koeroegugŭi kukkahyogwa, 1932–1936* [Reinterpreting the founding of Manchukuo: State effectiveness in a puppet state, 1932–1936] (Tongadaehakkyo ch'ulp'anbu, 1999), 165. The Mukden Incident refers to the Japanese army's capture of the Manchurian city of Mukden (now Shenyang, located in the Liaoning Province of China) in September 1931. After that, the Japanese army invaded the entirety of Manchuria and established the Japanese-controlled Manchukuo in the region.

139. Keongil Kim et al. *Tongashiaŭi minjogisan'gwa toshi: 20segi chŏnban manjuŭi chosŏnin* [Korean diaspora in Manchurian cities in the early twentieth century] (Yŏksabip'yŏngsa, 2004);

Kim Joo Yong, "Ilchegangjŏmgi haninŭi manju ijuwa toshijiyŏgŭi kujobyŏnhwa" [Korean migration to Manchuria and the changing structure of urban areas during the Japanese occupation), in *Kŭndae manju toshi yŏksajiri yŏn'gu* (Historical geographic study of the modernization process in Manchuria) (Tongbugayŏksajaedan, 2007), 142.

140. Jaeeun Kim, *Contested Embrace: Transborder Membership Politics in Twentieth-Century Korea* (Stanford University Press, 2016), 66.

141. Etienne Balibar and Immanuel Wallerstein, *Race, Nation, and Class: Ambiguous Identities* (Verso, 1991), 33.

142. Manchuria's colonial legacy continued after the fall of the Qing regime. According to Hirata Koji, industrial infrastructure created in Manchuria during the Manchukuo period (e.g., the Showa Steel Works in Anshan city) was converted into state-owned enterprises by the Chinese Communist Party (Hirata, Koji "Steel Metropolis: Industrial Manchuria and the Making of Chinese Socialism, 1916–1964," PhD diss., Stanford University, 2018).

143. Key-hiuk Kim, "Kaehang, choch'awa kŭndae manjur," 79.

144. Kim Joo Yong, "Ilchegangjŏmgi haninŭi manju ijuwa," 142.

145. Kyung-Seon Kwon, "Togil, ilbon chŏmnyŏnggi ch'ingdaoŭi sanŏpkujowa toshinodongja" [Industrial structure and urban workers in Qingdao during the German and Japanese occupations], in *Ch'ingdao: Shingmindoshiesŏ Ch'ogukchŏktoshi-ro* (Qingdao: From colonial city to transnational city), ed. Koo Jiyoung, Kwon Kyung-Seon, and Choi Nack-Min (Sŏnin, 2014), 132.

146. Having been incorporated into the capitalist world-system, Qingdao also experienced the same capitalist logic as Yingkou and Dalian. For example, during the German occupation, European and Chinese settlements in Qingdao were separated, and courts, police stations, train stations, hospitals, and schools were concentrated in European settlements. Kyung-Seon Kwon, "Togil, Ilbon Chŏmnyŏnggi Ch'ingdaoŭi Toshigŏnsŏlgwa Saenghwalgonggan" [Urbanism and living space in Qingdao during the German and Japanese occupations], in *Ch'ingdao: Shingmindoshiesŏ Ch'ogukchŏktoshi-ro* [Qingdao: From colonial city to transnational city], ed. Koo Jiyoung, Kwon Kyung-Seon, and Choi Nack-Min (Sŏnin, 2014), 82. The Chinese, who made up the majority of the urban poor, were living in slums. Although the German colonial government issued a new urban plan in the 1910s that removed the boundaries between European and Chinese neighborhoods, the gap between the two was already irreversible. In addition, Germany seized the mineral resources of Shandong during the occupation. Under Japanese influence, the Japanese government built protection policies and amenities for the Japanese who moved to Qingdao (Japanese residential areas, Japanese schools, and Japanese shrines), which ultimately resulted in the acceptance of discriminatory policies between Japanese and non-Japanese. In addition, Qingdao was to serve as an important forward base for Japan's invasion of China. See Laiqing Yang and Baofeng Sun, "20segi ch'o ch'ingdao ilbonin sahoeŭi hyŏngsŏnggwa pyŏnch'ŏn" [The formation and transformation of Japanese society in Qingdao in the early twentieth century], in *Ch'ingdao: Shingmindoshiesŏ Ch'ogukchŏktoshi-ro* [Qingdao: From colonial city to transnational city], ed. Koo Jiyoung, Kwon Kyung-Seon, and Choi Nack-Min (Sŏnin, 2014), 157–77.

147. British Parliamentary Papers, *China 26: Correspondence, Annual Reports, Conventions, and Other Papers Relating to the Affairs of Hong Kong 1882–99*, 628.

148. Kim, Ki-jung. "Segyech'ejeŭi kuchopyŏntongkwa 19sekihupankiŭi tongyangoekyosa" [The structural changes of the world-system and diplomatic history of the nineteenth-century Orient], *Hangukkwa kukjechŏngch'I* 7, no. 1 (1991): 161–93.

149. Paul Hibbert Clyde, *International Rivalries in Manchuria, 1689–1922* (Ohio State University Press, 1926), 66.

150. Catherine Ladds, "China and Treaty-Port Imperialism," in *The Encyclopedia of Empire*, ed. N. Dalziel and J. M. Mackenzie, August 24, 2015, 3, https://onlinelibrary.wiley.com/doi/epdf/10.1002/9781118455074.wbeoe079.

151. Clarence B. Davis, "Railway Imperialism in China, 1895–1939," in *Railway Imperialism*, ed. Clarence B. Davis and Kenneth E. Wilburn Jr. (Greenwood, 1991), 155–73.

152. Flint and Zhang, "Historical-Geopolitical Contexts," 312.

153. Warren L. Cohen, "The Foreign Impact on East Asia," in *Historical Perspective on Contemporary East Asia*, ed. Merle Goldman and Andrew Gordon (Harvard University Press, 2000), 1–41.

154. Feuerwerker, "Economic Trends," 94.

155. Jürgen Osterhammel, "British Business in China, 1860s–1950s," in *British Business in Asia Since 1860*, ed. R. P. T. Davenport-Hinves and Geoffrey Jones (Cambridge University Press, 1989), 189–216.

156. Buzan and Lawson, *Global Transformation*, 73–74.

157. Yuan Wei 魏源, *Haiguo Tuzhi* 海國圖志 [Illustrated treatise on the maritime kingdoms], vol. 2, ed. Chen Hua 陈华 et al. (Yuelu shushe chubanshe, 1998).

158. Xu Jiyu 徐继畲, *Yinghuan zhilue* 瀛環志略 [A short account of the maritime circuit], vol. 9, 1848.

159. *Wanguogongbao* 萬國公報, vol. 1 ([1876] 1968): 185–88.

160. Arthur Lewis Rosenbaum, "Chinese Railway Policy and the Response to Imperialism: The Peking-Mukden Railway, 1895–1911," *Ch'ing-shih wen-ti'* 2, no. 1 (1969): 38–70. Reformers believed that building railroad lines enriched and stabilized Chinese society. After the Taiping Rebellion, reformers began to think that the peasant class's high unemployment and impoverishment was the main cause of the rebellion. To improve social stability and increase the overall size of the economy, Guo Sungtao advocated government-led railway construction because railroads could in fact create new jobs and help boost the economy. Reformers also expected that railroad building would develop China's mining industry, and it consequently helped to provide the raw materials "for arsenals" and fossil fuel "for warships." Ralph William Huenemann, *The Dragon and the Iron Horse: The Economics of Railroads in China, 1876–1937* (Harvard University Press, 1984), 43.

161. Ji-hwan Kim, *Chŏlloŭi tŭngjanggwa chŏngjo ponggŏnch'ejeŭi punggoe* [The rise of the railway and the collapse of feudalism in the Qing dynasty] (Tongashia, 2019), 29.

162. Huenemann, *Dragon and the Iron Horse*, 40. Opponents believed that there were few economic advantages to railway construction because of foreign powers' intervention for economic gain, the low profitability of railroads, and the increase of unemployed workers in the traditional and labor-intensive transportation industry caused by a heavy dependence on rail transport. They also put forth noneconomic reasons why railway building projects drove China toward destruction. First, they believed railroads would make foreign intrusions easier during periods of political turmoil in China. Not only that, but many Chinese who suffered from "village poverty, rising unemployment and general hardship in popular livelihood" attributed economic difficulties to foreign influence and economic penetration including foreign railways (Hsü, "Late Ch'ing Foreign Relations," 117). Second, given the fact that railway construction

would "level graves, raze cottages, trample fields, and dam streams and rivers up" (Huenemann, *Dragon and the Iron Horse*, 40), it was likely to violate and undermine China's traditional geocultural values like geomancy (*fengshui* 風水).

163. Feuerwerker, "Economic Trends," 65.

164. Lukáš Novotný, "Great Britain, Germany, and the Selected Railway Problems in China, 1907–1908," *Prague Papers on the History of International Relations* 2 (2014): 97.

165. En-Han Lee, *China's Quest for Railway Autonomy 1904–1911* (Singapore University Press, 1977).

166. Robert Lee, *France and the Exploitation of China: A Study in Economic Imperialism* (Oxford University Press, 1989), 30.

167. When it comes to the Beijing-Hankou Railway, it was true that a Belgian company won a concession, but the fact that France provided financial support to the Belgian company should not be overlooked.

168. Bulletin of the American Geographical Society, "The Peking-Hankow Railway," *Bulletin of the American Geographical Society* 38, no. 9 (1906): 555.

169. Lee, *France and the Exploitation of China*, 109.

170. Diane K. Drummond, "Sustained British Investment in Overseas Railways, 1830–1914," in *Across the Borders: Financing the World's Railways in the Nineteenth and Twentieth Centuries*, ed. Ralf Roth and Günter Dinhobl (Ashgate, 2008), 207–23.

171. John Gallagher and Ronald Robinson, "The Imperialism of Free Trade," *Economic History Review* 6, no. 1 (1953): 10.

172. D. K. Fieldhouse, *Economics and Empire, 1830–1914* (Macmillan, 1984), 56.

173. *Wanguogongbao* 萬國公報, vol. 5 ([1876] 1968), 2794. This railroad was in operation from 1876 to 1877 and was abandoned due to local opposition.

174. Lee, *China's Quest for Railway Autonomy*, 16.

175. Osterhammel, "British Business in China," 200.

176. Ja Ia Chong, *External Intervention and the Politics of State Formation: China, Indonesia, and Thailand, 1853–1952* (Cambridge University Press, 2012), 87.

177. Robert E. Hannigan, *The New World Power: American Foreign Policy, 1898–1917* (Philadelphia: University of Pennsylvania Press, 2002), 117–18.

178. Jin Siwon, "Tongpukasia chŏl-to kŏnsŏlkwa chiyŏkkukkakwankyeŭi pyŏnhwa: 19seki hupankwa 20seki ch'opan chekukchuŭi sikilŭl chungsimŭlo" [Railway construction and the change of interstate imperialistic relations in Northeast Asia: From the late nineteenth century to the early twentieth century], *P'yŏnghwayŏnku* 12, no. 2 (2004): 68.

179. Deok kyoo Choi, "Rŏshiaŭi taemanjujŏngch'aekkwa tongch'ŏngch'ŏlto" [Russia's Manchurian policy and the Chinese Eastern Railway], *Manjuyŏn'gu* [Journal of Manchurian Studies] 6 (2004): 5–25.

180. At that time, even if Russia gave up its interests in Korea, it could not abandon its interests in Manchuria, which led to military clashes between Russia and Japan, and Russia did not achieve satisfactory results in the Russo-Japanese War.

181. Masayoshi Noguchi and Trevor Boyns, "The South Manchuria Railway Company: An Accounting and Financial History, 1907–1943," March 15, 2013, 3, https://www.rieb.kobe-u.ac.jp/academic/ra/dp/English/DP2013-08.pdf.

182. Iriye, *Pacific Estrangement*, 174.

183. Yoshihisa Tak Matsusaka, *The Making of Japanese Manchuria, 1904–1932* (Harvard University Asia Center, 2001); Peter Duus, "Japan's Informal Empire in China, 1895–1937," in *The Japanese Informal Empire in China, 1895–1937*, ed. Peter Duus, Ramon H. Myers, and Mark R. Peattie (Princeton University Press, 1989), xxvii.

184. Rowe, *China's Last Empire*, 236.

185. For a discussion of the strong powers' race for resources of weak or peripheral countries, see Christoper Chase-Dunn, "Core-Periphery Relations: The Effect of Core Competition," in *Social Change in the Capitalist World-Economy*, ed. B. Kaplan (Sage, 1978), 159–76; Albert Bergesen, "1914 Again? Another Cycle of Inter-State Competition and War," in *Foreign Policy and the Modern World System*, ed. P. McGowan and C. W. Kegley Jr. (Sage, 1983), 255–73.

Chapter 5

1. Hall, "Incorporation into and Merger of World-Systems," 37–55.

2. Eric R. Wolf, *Europe and the People Without History* (University of California Press, 1982); John R. Hall, "World-System Holism and Colonial Brazilian Agriculture: A Critical Case Analysis," *Latin American Research Review* 19, no. 2 (1984): 43–69.

3. Terry Boswell, "World Revolutions and Revolutions in the World-System," in *Revolution in the World-System*, ed. Terry Boswell (Greenwood, 1989), 1–16.

4. Martin, "Incorporation of Southern Africa, 1870–1920," 865; J. D. Omer-Cooper, *The Zulu Aftermath: A Nineteenth-Century Revolution in Bantu Africa* (Northwestern University Press, 1966).

5. Phillips, "Incorporation of the Caribbean," 781–804.

6. Walter L. Goldfrank, "Theories of Revolution and Revolution Without Theory," *Theory and Society* 7, nos. 1–2 (1979): 154.

7. Brent Z. Kaup, "In Spaces of Marginalization: Dispossession, Incorporation, and Resistance in Bolivia," *Journal of World-Systems Research* 19, no. 1 (2013): 108–29.

8. Nick P. Kardulias and Emily Butcher, "Piracy in a Contested Periphery: Incorporation and the Emergence of the Modern World-System in the Colonial Atlantic Frontier," *Journal of World-Systems Research* 22, no. 2 (2016): 542–64. In world-systems analysis, the resistance movements identified in these studies are also linked to antisystemic movements, which means that the causes, development, and outcomes of resistance are not understood as nationally bound phenomena, but are implicitly or explicitly linked to global forces and Western aggression; Robert MacPherson, "Antisystemic Movement Analysis," *Social Problems* 65 (2018): 492. For further details, see Giovanni Arrighi, Terence K. Hopkins, and Immanuel Wallerstein, *Anti-Systemic Movements* (Verso, 1989); William G. Martin, *Making Waves: Worldwide Social Movements, 1750–2005* (Paradigm, 2008); Jackie Smith and Dawn Wiest, *Social Movements in the World-System: The Politics of Crisis and Transformation* (Russell Sage, 2012).

9. Hung, *Protest with Chinese Characteristics*, 97.

10. Hung, *Protest with Chinese Characteristics*, 58–59.

11. Wolf, *Peasant Wars of the Twentieth Century*, 103.

12. Benjamin A. Elman, *From Philosophy to Philology: Intellectual and Social Aspects of Changes in Late Imperial China* (Harvard University Press, 1984), 15.

13. Elman, *From Philosophy to Philology*, 16. The evidence movement refers to a branch of Confucianism that developed between the late Ming and early Qing periods, focusing on philology and linguistics, and pursuing an objective and empirical attitude.

14. Alfred Kuo-Liang Ho, "The Grand Council in the Ch'ing Dynasty," *Far Eastern Quarterly* 11, no. 2 (1952): 167–82.

15. The rise of the Eight Banner noble families (*baqiguizushijia* 八旗貴族世家) showed how bannermen maintained their lineage and Manchu military tradition in early Qing times. Regarding this, see Bing Yan Lei, 雷炳炎, *Qingdaishehuibaqiguizushijiashiliyanjiu* 清代社会八旗貴族世家勢力研究 [A study on the social power of the Eight Banners aristocratic families in the Qing regime] (Zhongguo Shehui kexue chubanshe, 2016).

16. Elliott, *Manchu Way*, 5.

17. Benjamin A. Elman, *A Cultural History of Civil Examinations in Late Imperial China* (University of California Press, 2000); Joseph R. Levenson, *Confucian China and Its Modern Fate* (University of California Press, 1968).

18. Philip Y. S. Leung, "The Tragic Passage to a New World: The Changing Views and Attitudes of Chinese Intellectuals Toward the West in the Nineteenth Century," in *Modern China in Transition*, ed. Philip Yuen-sang Leung and Edwin Pak-wah Leung (Regina Books, 1995), 26.

19. Regarding the backgrounds of conservative scholar-officials from 1861 to 1884, see Leung, "Tragic Passage," 26–27.

20. Wright, "Adaptability of Ch'ing Diplomacy," 363–81.

21. John K. Fairbank, Edwin O. Reischauer, and Albert M. Craig, *East Asia: Tradition and Transformation* (Houghton Mifflin Company, 1978), 563.

22. Yen-P'ing Hao and Erh-min Wang, "Changing Chinese Views of Western Relations, 1840–95," in *The Cambridge History of China*, vol. 11, pt. 2, *Late Ch'ing 1800–1911*, ed. John K. Fairbank and Kwang-Ching Liu (Cambridge University Press, 1980), 175–76.

23. Jian Zhong Ma 馬建忠, *Shikezhaijiyan* 适可斋记言 [Correspondence and memoranda from prudence room] (Zhonghuashuju, [1894] 1960).

24. The Tianjin Massacre of 1870 refers to an anti-Christian riot that took place in Tianjin. In 1869, the Notre Dame des Victoires orphanage run by the Roman Catholic Church took in orphans from the streets. The problem arose with the way the orphans were taken in: Chinese people were unwilling to send them to orphanages set up by foreigners, so nuns paid the people who brought them in a gratuity for each one. This led to the kidnapping of children by thugs known as orphan brokers. When many of the orphans died in the orphanages, the public became suspicious of the church-run orphanages. Rumors spread that foreigners were performing magic on the children, mutilating their bodies, and taking out their hearts and eyes to make medicines. Henri Fontanier, a French consul, visited the orphanage to investigate, but a large crowd had already gathered around the orphanage. Feeling threatened by the crowd, Fontanier started firing at them; in retaliation, the crowd killed the French consul and his staff, set fire to churches and orphanages, and burned British and American churches and consulates, killing dozens of foreigners and nuns. Strong protests from foreign consuls demanding reparations for the riots and punishment for the rioters were sent to Beijing, and the Chinese government sent a delegation to investigate the incident. The commission led by Zeng Guofan (曾國藩, 1811–1872) recommended the dismissal of the Tianjin prefect and the district magistrate, the

death penalty for fifteen of the rioters, and the banishment of twenty-one others involved in the riot (Hsü, "Late Ch'ing Foreign Relations, 1866–1905," 78–80).

25. Horowitz, "Central Power and State Making," 111.

26. Huenemann, *Dragon and the Iron Horse*, 43.

27. Influenced partially by Taoist principles, *qingyi* originally emphasized naturalness and tried to liberate themselves from political interests, including power relations created in the political arena. *Qingyi* also stressed politics for the public interest, but this was only part of their concerns. When the West penetrated China, *qingyi* became actively involved in secular politics, leading to fundamentalist Confucianism in Qing China.

28. Benjamin Schwartz, *In Search of Wealth and Power: Yen Fu and the West* (Harvard University Press, 1964); Cohen, *Discovering History in China*, 40.

29. Lloyd E. Eastman, "Ch'ing-i and Chinese Policy Formation During the Nineteenth Century," *Journal of Asian Studies* 24, no. 4 (1965): 599.

30. With regard to the militant conservative approach of *qingyi*, see John Schrecker, "The Reform Movement, Nationalism, and China's Foreign Policy," *Journal of Asian Studies* 29, no. 1 (1969): 43–53. Although *qingyi* members upheld traditional values and institutions, they did not do much to help rebuild the ancien régime (Kuhn, *Origins of the Modern Chinese State*, 121–22).

31. Hao and Wang, "Changing Chinese Views of Western Relations," 180.

32. Of course, until the Xinyou Coup (辛酉政變 (1860), Prince Gong and Empress Dowager Cixi were on the same side. Prince Gong joined forces with the Empress Dowager Cixi and Empress Xiaozhenxian to take power from the Sushun-led eight regents—Sushun 肅順 (1816–1861), Duanhua 端華 (1807–1861), Zaiyuan 載垣 (1816–1861), Jingshou 景壽 (1829–1889), Muyin 穆蔭 (?–1864), Kuangyuan 匡源 (1815–1881), Duhan 杜翰 (1806–1866), and Jiaoyouying 焦祐瀛 (1814–1887)—in the Qing bureaucracy, after the death of the Xianfeng Emperor. Their palace coup, called the Xinyou Coup, was successful; however, not much later, a power struggle between them occurred. The Empress Dowager Cixi dismissed Prince Gong on the pretense of his unproductive negotiations with France during the Sino-French War.

33. The Empress Dowager, who was enraged by the Guangxu Emperor's support for the Hundred Days' reform in 1898, even rushed into his bedroom in the middle of the night and took the emperor's authority from him. After the failure of the Hundred Days' reform, Kang You Wei and Liang Qichao, who escaped from the terrible purge of the Empress Dowager, fled to Japan.

34. Were the Empress Dowager Cixi and conservative officials totally apathetic about world affairs and inattentive to the penetration of colonial powers? It is hardly probable they would have paid little attention to a turbulent world situation and its effects on China, which was at an unprecedented juncture with the encroachment of European and Pacific powers. Then how should we interpret such resistance movements to the West? Faced with the West's politico-economic and military penetration and the impending doom of the ancien régime, the Qing government strove to achieve the success of the Self-Strengthening Movement. Reform-minded Confucian scholars in particular grappled with how to deal with Western societies to China's advantage. After the Sino-French War (1884–1885), mainstream Confucian scholars even shifted from resistance to support for the West (Leung, "Tragic Passage to a New World," 34); nonetheless, why did not conservative government officials abandon the revival of the ancien

régime? The answer is probably the absence of alternatives: Those who had long adhered to the patrimonial system were unable to handle the destructive force of the West that accompanied capitalist logic, and therefore reverted to the old, familiar system. Put differently, the colonial powers' penetration brought about resistance movements from conservative officials; still, they had no alternatives but to depend on a regime that was a fulcrum of political interests.

35. According to Arrighi, Hopkins, and Wallerstein, the ancien régime of the incorporated area could have maintained a centralized and strengthening political regime or, on the contrary, could have been transformed into a weak and declining political regime, depending on how each incorporated area responded to the network of the interstate system. In the case of Qing's political regime, it had been jeopardized—albeit slowly—due to the severe decoupling between the conservative-led political regime and the logic of the global capitalist economy (Arrighi, Hopkins, and Wallerstein, *Anti-Systemic Movements*, 22–23).

36. See also Paul K. Chao, *Chinese Culture and Christianity* (University Press of America, 2006), 35.

37. Hsiao-Tung Fei, "Peasantry and Gentry: An Interpretation of Chinese Social Structures and Its Changes," *American Journal of Sociology* 52, no. 1 (1946): 7.

38. Pierre Bourdieu, "The Forms of Capital," in *Handbook of Theory and Research for the Sociology of Education*, ed. John G. Richardson (Greenwood, 1986), 241–58. The gentry class spread Confucian thought widely by establishing schools throughout China, passing on Confucian virtues and values to the next generations: Paul A. Cohen, *China and Christianity: The Missionary Movement and the Growth of Chinese Antiforeignism, 1860–1870* (Harvard University Press, 1963), 83.

39. Yuan Wei 魏源, "Guweitang Waiji" 古微堂外集, in *Weiyuan quanji* 魏源全集 [Complete works of Wei Yuan], vol. 12 (Yuelu shushe, 2004), 283.

40. Dongshu Fang 方東樹, *Han xue shang dui* 漢學商兌 [An assessment of Han learning] (Taiwan shangwu yinshuguan, 1968), 120.

41. Ray Huang, *China: A Macro History* (M. E. Sharpe, 1997), 225.

42. Elman, *From Philosophy to Philology*, chap. 7.

43. Paul A. Cohen, "The Anti-Christian Tradition in China," *Journal of Asian Studies* 20, no. 2 (1961): 169–80.

44. Young Jin Yang, "Durkheim and Weber: Two Approaches to the Study of Religion and Society," PhD diss., University of Chicago, 1986, 76–77.

45. In a similar vein, Talcott Parsons insisted that values in a social system are self-commitments to a role, to a direction of behavior, to a particular type of behavior, and to a set of endorsements: Talcott Parsons, *Structure and Process in Modern Societies* (Free Press, 1960), 172.

46. World-affirmation religions consider this world more valuable than the afterlife, so followers of such religions try to build their own ideal world in this one. By contrast, world-rejection religions (e.g., Buddhism and Protestantism) consider the afterlife more valuable than this world, so followers of world rejection try to gain immortal life in the afterlife. Jürgen Habermas, *The Theory of Communicative Action: Reason and The Rationalization of Society*, vol. 1, trans. Thomas McCarthy (Beacon Press, 1981), 204.

47. On this ground, Confucianism stressed "learning for oneself." Peter K. Bol, "Why Do Intellectuals Matter to Chinese Politics?," in *The China Questions: Critical Insights into a Rising Power*, ed. Jennifer Rudolph and Michael Szonyi (Harvard University Press, 2018), 250.

48. Weber, *Economy and Society*, 527.

49. Stephen Kalberg, *Max Weber's Comparative-Historical Sociology Today: Major Themes, Mode of Causal Analysis, and Applications* (Ashgate, 2012), 147.

50. Weber, *Religion of China*, 227–28.

51. Chang, *Chinese Gentry*, 422.

52. D. E. Mungello, *The Great Encounter of China and the West, 1500–1800* (Rowman and Littlefield, 2005).

53. Jacques Gernet, *China and the Christian Impact* (Cambridge University Press, [1982] 1987), 640.

54. Hsü, "Late Ch'ing Foreign Relations," 116. New members of the gentry who served as military officers in the Hunan army also had a deep antipathy to the missionaries because they thought spreading the gospel could undercut the gentry's moral authority. In addition, the Gelaohui 哥老會 (Elders Brothers Society) was one of the secret societies that fostered anti-Western sentiment in the Hunan area. Because anti-Western sentiments were running high there, it became a center of the anti-Western movement in an area that had once produced the empire's pro-Western officials. See Stephen Platt, *Provincial Patriots: The Hunanese and Modern China* (Harvard University Press, 2007).

55. Hao and Wang, "Changing Chinese Views," 174.

56. Hao and Wang, "Changing Chinese Views," 177.

57. Cohen, *China and Christianity*, 80.

58. John Chalmers, "The Missionary Question," *Chinese Recorder and Missionary Journal* 4, no. 6 (1871), 155.

59. John K. Fairbank, "Introduction: The Place of Protestant Writings in China's Cultural History," in *Christianity in China: Early Protestant Missionary Writings*, ed. Suzanne Wilson Barnett and John Kong Fairbank (Harvard University Press, 1985), 6.

60. Jerome Ch'en, *China and the West: Society and Culture, 1815–1937* (Indiana University Press, 1979), 108.

61. Cohen, *China and Christianity*, 84–85.

62. Ch'en, *China and the West*, 92.

63. Alexander Michie, *The Englishman in China During the Victorian Era, Volume II* (William Blackwood and Sons, 1900), 253.

64. Charles A. Litzinger, "Patterns of Missionary Cases Following the Tientsin Massacre, 1870–1875," *Papers on China* 23 (1970): 87–108.

65. Fairbank, *China*, 223; Cohen, "Anti-Christian Tradition in China," 169.

66. Hung, "Agricultural Revolution and Elite Reproduction," 576.

67. R. M. Martin, *China, Political, Commercial, and Social: In an Official Report to Her Majesty's Government. Volume 2* (J. Madden, 1847), 177. Due to this devastating impact of opium, Canton was a center of resistance to Western influence. Fairbank insisted that Canton was "the capital of two provinces and residence of many officials and great families, a symbol of government prestige as well as local patriotism, far more resistant [to Western intrusion] and defensible than Shanghai" (Fairbank, "Creation of the Treaty System," 227).

68. Wakeman, *Strangers at the Gate*, 37.

69. Wakeman, *Strangers at the Gate*, 38.

70. Although some members of the Society of Heaven and Earth (*Tiandihui* 天地會), one of the secret societies, joined the Sanyuanli Incident, others cooperated with England. For

this reason, I do not put members of the Society of Heaven and Earth into the category of anti-Western groups.

71. For British casualties in the fighting at Sanyuanli, see Mao, *Qing Empire and the Opium War*, 257.

72. Frederick Engels. "Persia and China," in *On Colonialism*, ed. Karl Marx and Frederick Engels (International Publishers, 1972), 123.

73. *The Chinese Repository*, vol. 11 (Canton: Printed For The Proprietors, 1842), 687.

74. *The Chinese Repository*, vol. 15 (Canton: Printed For The Proprietors, 1846), 365.

75. *The Chinese Repository*, vol. 18 (Canton: Printed For The Proprietors, 1849), 217.

76. The Gentry and People, *Death Blow to Corrupt Doctrines: A Plain Statement of Facts* (Shanghai, 1870), 39. During the 1860s, there was a close association between anti-Christian literature spread by the gentry and acts of anti-Christian violence in fourteen out of the eighteen provinces in China (Cohen, *China and Christianity*, 86).

77. Nonetheless, the lower classes, in particular peasants, who lacked "local collective institutions and autonomy" (Theda Skocpol, "Social Revolution in France, Russia, and China: A Comparative-Historical and Structural Analysis," PhD diss., Harvard University, 1975, 240) and strong ties as a social class, often depended on the gentry when they campaigned in anti-imperialist movements.

78. Bishop, *Yangtze Valley and Beyond*, 82.

79. For lower classes in local communities, the possibilities of choice were often influenced by the institutional environment (i.e., political governance based on Confucian thinking) and sociocultural dominant discourses (i.e., Confucian doctrines and beliefs), as well as the ideological preferences like the cultural and semiotic factors of the upper groups (e.g., gentry class or state bureaucrats) with which the lower classes were more closely intertwined. In this sense, it comes as no surprise that the lower classes had a critical attitude toward foreign missionaries.

80. Paul A. Varg, *Missionaries, Chinese, and Diplomats: The American Protestant Missionary Movement in China, 1890–1952* (Princeton University Press, 1958), 3.

81. Chen, *Merchants of War and Peace*, 76; Paul W. Harris, "Cultural Imperialism and American Protestant Missionaries: Collaboration and Dependency in Mid-Nineteenth-Century China," *Pacific Historical Review* 60, no. 3 (1991): 309–38.

82. Jessie G. Lutz, *Opening China: Karl F. A. Gützlaff and Sino-Western Relations, 1827–1852* (William B. Eerdmans, 2008), 91.

83. Of course, not all missionaries agreed with Western merchants' unfair trade practices. Some missionaries believed that the coercive and unequal trades, especially the opium trade between the West and China, had badly affected missionary work in Chinese society; *Wanguogongbao* 萬國公報, vol. 461 (1877), 4232.

84. Joseph W. Esherick, *Origins of the Boxer Uprising* (University of California Press, 1988), 75–76. On cooperation between Western merchants and missionaries to break down the cultural barriers of China, see Fred W. Drake, "E. C. Bridgman's Portrayal of the West," in *Christianity in China: Early Protestant Missionary Writings*, ed. Suzanne Wilson Barnett and John King Fairbank (Harvard University Press, 1985), 89–106; Michael C. Lazich, "Diffusion of Useful Knowledge in China: The Canton Era Information Strategy," in *Mapping Meanings: The Field of New Learning in Late Qing China*, ed. Michael Lackner and Natascha Vittinghoff (Brill, 2004), 305–27; *The Chinese Repository*, vol. 3 (Canton: Printed for the Proprietors, 1834), 382.

85. With regard to the interconnections between the economic globalization of Europe and Christian theologians, see Sang, *Collaborative Colonial Power*, 33; Ivan Strenski, "The Religion in Globalization," *Journal of the American Academy of Religion* 72, no. 3 (2004): 631–52.

86. "Victims Were Tortured; Gross Cruelties Inflicted on the Kucheng Missonaries," *New York Times*, August 5, 1895, https://www.nytimes.com/1895/08/05/archives/victims-were-tortured-gross-cruelties-inflicted-on-the-kucheng-miss.html.

87. Esherick, *Origins of the Boxer Uprising*, 68.

88. As the Boxer movement was extended to Beijing in 1900, eight colonial powers (Britain, Germany, Japan, Russia, France, the United States, Italy, and Austria) dispatched their own armies to China in the name of protecting their people. Empress Dowager Cixi and government officials who opposed the invasion of foreign troops supported the Boxers and fought against the foreign powers (Fairbank, *China*, 230–31). Despite the expectations of Cixi and government officials, the Qing's armed forces and the Boxers were caught off guard by the allied foreign forces. As a result, the Qing regime had to sign another unequal treaty (the Boxer Protocol, 1901). The Boxer Protocol was "a disaster not only for the Qing Empire but for its various twentieth-century successor regimes" (Rowe, *China's Last Empire*, 245) due mainly to the huge reparations forced on China amounting to 450 million silver taels.

89. Yun, *Coolie Speaks*, 21.

90. Yung Gu Jung, "19segi chungban chunggugŭi k'ullimuyŏk" [Chinese coolie trade in the latter half of the nineteenth century], *Tongyangsahakyŏn'gu* [Journal of Asian Historical Studies] 142 (2018): 180.

91. Kuhn, *Chinese Among Others*, 100.

92. Meagher, *Coolie Trade*, 96–97.

93. "American Ships and the Coolie Trade," *New York Times*, August 4, 1860, https://www.nytimes.com/1860/08/04/archives/american-ships-and-the-coolie-trade.html.

94. Meagher, *Coolie Trade*, 109–10.

95. Meagher, *Coolie Trade*, 113–15.

96. Ralph Wardlaw Thompson, *Griffith John: The Story of Fifty Years in China* (Religious Tract Society, 1906), 106–7.

97. Mielants, *Origins of Capitalism*, 24.

98. Great Britain, Parliament, House of Commons, "Report on the Labour Question in the Crown Colonies," in *Reports from Commissioners, Inspectors, and Others*, vol. 18 (1892), 98.

99. Hu-Dehart, "Chinese Coolie Labor in Cuba," 44.

100. The *New York Times* pointed out that it was time for civilized governments to expose the horrific reality of the coolie trade ("Chinese Coolie Mutinies," *New York Times*, October 10, 1870, https://www.nytimes.com/1870/10/10/archives/chinese-coolie-mutinies.html).

101. "A Chatter on the Coolie Trade," 6.

102. "The Daily Press," *Hong Kong Daily Press*, May 9, 1871.

103. Shui Le 乐水, "Xianggang Ceng Shi fanyun qiyue huagong de zhuyao gangkou" 香港曾是贩运契约华工的主要港口 [Hong Kong used to be a major port for the trafficking of indentured Chinese laborers], *Bagui qiaoshi* 八桂侨刊 2 (1997): 11–12.

104. Yun and Laremont, "Chinese Coolies and African Slaves," 111–12.

105. Don Aldus's realistic description of coolie ships gives us a sense of the terrible circumstances: "The bunks for the emigrants consist of two rows of shelves running the whole

length of the ship both sides, as well as down the center. These shelves are six feet wide with an eight-inch footboard secured to the outside to prevent them slipping off. After the shelves and footboards are completed the next operation is to measure and number each bed space, allowing to each man a breadth—out of the length—of from twenty to twenty-four inches, the latter being the legal allowance, but it would appear they are not over particular in this matter, as they seldom exceed twenty-one inches. There is no kind of division between the sleepers—in short, each shelf simply represented one hundred and fifty in a bed" (Aldus, *Coolie Traffic and Kidnapping*, 31).

106. Meagher, *Coolie Trade*, 253.

107. Joseph Beaumont, *The New Slavery—An Account of the Indian and Chinese Immigrants in British Guiana* (Caribbean Press, [1871] 2011), 20.

108. *Chinese Emigration. The Cuba Commission. Report of the Commission Sent by China to Ascertain the Condition of Chinese Coolies in Cuba* (Imperial Maritime Customs Press, 1876), 3.

109. Kuhn, *Chinese Among Others*, 105.

110. Lai, *Indentured Labor, Caribbean Sugar*, 100; Joyce A. Madancy, *The Troublesome Legacy of Commissioner Lin: The Opium Trade and Opium Suppression in Fujian Province, 1820s to 1920s* (Harvard University Press, 2003), 30.

111. Great Britain, Houses of Parliament, "Mr. Jerningham to the Earl of Clarendon, March 9, 1869 (received April 13)," *Respecting the Emigration of Chinese Coolies from Macao* (Harrison and Sons, 1871), 2.

112. Kuhn, *Chinese Among Others*, 104.

113. Kuhn, *Chinese Among Others*, 141.

114. Prasenjit Duara, "De-Constructing the Chinese Nation," *Australian Journal of Chinese Affairs* 30 (1993): 8.

115. Tsou Mingteh, "Christian Missionary as Confucian Intellectual: Gilbert Reid (1857–1917) and the Reform Movement in the Late Qing," in *Christianity in China: From the Eighteenth Century to the Present*, ed. Daniel H. Bays (Stanford University Press, 1996), 73–90.

116. Nonetheless, under the circumstance that the "Chinese gentry had a preponderant organizational position within local communities" (Skocpol, *States and Social Revolutions*, 148) and vertical relationships between the gentry class and local peasants were more prevalent than horizontal relationships among local peasants in local areas (Fei, "Peasantry and Gentry," 8–10), it was difficult to organize peasant-centered anti-Western movements, ruling out the intervention of the gentry class, in Chinese society.

117. Due to the local gentry's politicization pursuing their own economic interests, they often were called "local bullies and evil gentry" (*t'u-hao lieh-shen* 土豪劣紳) (Wakeman, *Fall of Imperial China*, 23). After the politicization of the gentry class, all they did was usurp district magistracies and the "control of local taxing and policing functions to tighten their hold over the exploitation of the peasantry" (Skocpol, *States and Social Revolutions*, 240).

118. After the defeat in the Opium Wars, Chinese bureaucrats and intellectuals who were trained in Confucian ethics and indulged in Sino-centric ideas embraced antiforeignism (Elliott, *Manchu Way*, 23). As a reaction to China's wounded pride and high esteem, hostility to foreign ministers or consuls' haughty attitudes, and an antipathy to aggressive, greedy, and opportunistic Western merchants, antiforeign movements had extended to the sociopolitical sphere. What led to problematic conflict was that Han Chinese political elites and intellectuals began to attribute

this incapacity to the Manchu-centered governmental system; Chün-Tu Hsüeh and Geraldine R. Schiff, "The Life and Writings of Tsou Jung," in *Revolutionary Leaders of Modern China*, ed. Chün-Tu Hsüeh (Oxford University Press, 1971), 197. Han Chinese elites believed that China's impoverishment had become the cause of West's politico-economic intrusions and the Qing government's unjustified governance; see Kauko Laitinen, *Chinese Nationalism in the Late Qing Dynasty: Zhang Binglin as an Anti-Manchu Propagandist* (Curzon, 1990). Such anti-Manchuism was developed by Sun Yat-Sen. Since Sun Yat-Sen considered Han Chinese as the cornerstone of the new nation-state, Han Chinese became an ideological core of the new nation, whereas Manchus were denigrated as a national enemy. He also argued that the Manchus invaded a holy Chinese territory and broke the noble and peaceful spirit of the Han Chinese; Lyon Sherman, *Sun Yat-Sen: His Life and Its Meaning* (Stanford University Press, 1968). Put differently, one of the important tasks was to build a Han Chinese-centered state, while cleaning up the vestiges of the Qing regime. His focus on anti-Manchuism gave partial validity to his revolutionary ideas. Regarding the correlations between anti-Manchuism and the justification of the Chinese revolution, see Edward J. Rhoads, *Manchus and Han: Ethnic Relations and Political Power in Late Qing and Early Republican China, 1861-1928* (University of Washington Press, 2000).

Conclusion

1. Fairbank, "Introduction: The Old Order," 6.
2. Keller, Li, and Shiue, "Shanghai's Trade, China's Growth," 341.
3. Sung Hee Ru, "Historical Geographies of Korea's Incorporation: The Rise of Underdeveloped and Modernized Colonial Port Cities," *Journal of Historical Geography* 76 (2022): 42–55.
4. Boris Kagarlitsky, *Empire of the Periphery: Russia and the World System*, trans. Renfrey Clarke (Pluto, 2008), 192.
5. Wallerstein, *Modern World-System III*, 187.
6. Park Hun, *Meijiyushinŭn ŏttŏk'e kanŭnghaennŭn'ga* [How the Meiji Restoration Came about] (Minŭmsa, 2014), 55.
7. Park, *Meijiyushinŭn ŏttŏk'e kanŭnghaennŭn'ga*, 57.
8. Park, *Meijiyushinŭn ŏttŏk'e kanŭnghaennŭn'ga*, 92.
9. E. D. Westney, *Imitation and Innovation: The Transfer of Western Organizational Patterns to Meiji Japan* (Harvard University Press, 1987); Hamilton, "Hong Kong and the Rise of Capitalism," 14–34.
10. E. J. Hobsbawm, *The Age of Empire 1875–1914* (Vintage, 1989), 317.
11. See Peter Duus, "Japan's Informal Empire in China, 1895–1937: An Overview," in *The Japanese Informal Empire in China, 1895–1937*, edited by Peter Duus, Ramon H. Myers, and Mark R. Peattie, xi–xxix (Princeton University Press, 1989), 3.
12. Norman Davies, *Europe: A History* (Pimlico, 1997), 23.
13. With the dogged firmness of a resolute purpose, the Qing bureaucracy believed that the reform project had to be a part of reestablishing (or rebuilding) the Qing regime and not result in the demise of the emperor (or a decline of the emperor's authority). See Ichiko Chuzo, "Political and Institutional Reform, 1901–11," in *The Cambridge History of China*, vol. 11, pt.

2, *Late Ch'ing 1800–1911*, ed. John K. Fairbank and Kwang-Ching Liu (Cambridge University Press, 1980), 375–415.

14. Hsü, "Late Ch'ing Foreign Relations," 129–30.

15. By interpreting this historical event of the Taiping rebellion, exclusive emphasis on the relationships between the Taiping rebel forces and Qing government may result in inattention to the influences of Western powers. Just as the Netherlands Revolt in the late sixteenth century was influenced and furthered by the interests between European countries (i.e., France, England, and Spain) (Wallerstein, *The Modern World-system I*, 210), the Taiping rebellion broke out under the interactions between internal dynamics and outside influences. In fact, economically, the rise in unemployment in Guangdong and Guangxi Province, after the increase of silver outflow in return for opium import, had an influence on the inception of the Taiping Rebellion and increased the size of the Taiping rebel forces in a short time. In this sense, in 1853 Marx contended that the Taiping Rebellion could be understood as "a sign of China's integration into the global economy": Stephen Platt, *Autumn in the Heavenly Kingdom: China, The West, and the Epic Story of the Taiping Civil War* (Alfred A. Knopf, 2012), 10. Politically, the diplomatic and military intervention of foreign countries made the Taiping Rebellion more complicated and violent. Furthermore, ideologically, a large part of Hong Xiuquan's message of salvation originated from Christian gospel elements like "Fatherhood of God, the life of Jesus, the Trinity, the Eucharist, the parables, and the supreme virtue of love": Yu-wen Jen, *The Taiping Revolutionary Movement* (Yale University Press, 1973), 21. The idea had also taken hold, pushed by Hong Xiuquan, that there was a right to end socioeconomic inequalities, and this view originated from Confucian ideology. Given the fact that the Taiping Rebellion was intertwined with Western powers economically, politically, and ideologically, ignorance of Western powers' intervention is inappropriate. In sum, situating correlations between the Taiping Rebellion and influences of Western powers on the supranational context suggests that the dynamics of the Taiping Rebellion were at least partially determined by larger system-wide processes.

16. Obviously, the Qing regime attempted to place these local elites under state control; however, the Qing's efforts "resulted not so much in enhancing central control over local elites" (Skocpol, *Social Revolution*, 360) when local elites formalized their powers.

17. The political disorder can be in part attributed to the rise of local warlords. During the beginning of China's early Republican era, the factional dissension between warlords prevented the unification of the country. In addition, Chinese warlords helped colonial powers to obtain politico-economic benefits in China in exchange for the purchase of military weapons from Western countries; Jerome Ch'en, *The Military-Gentry Coalition: China Under the Warlords* (University of Toronto–York University, Joint Centre on Modern East Asia, 1979). One must be cautious in arguing deep connections between warlords and colonial powers due mainly to the absence of firm evidence; nonetheless, it is reasonable to say that, explicitly or implicitly, there was at least a political connection between them.

18. Dylan Sullivan and Jason Hickel, "Capitalism and Extreme Poverty: A Global Analysis of Real Wages, Human Height, and Mortality Since the Long 16th Century," *World Development* 161 (2023): 14. https://doi.org/10.1016/j.worlddev.2022.106026.

19. Maddison, *Chinese Economic Performance*, 48, 88.

20. Shannon R. Brown, "The Partially Opened Door: Limitations on Economic Change in China in the 1860s," *Modern Asian Studies* 12, no. 2 (1978): 185.

21. Chan, "Government, Merchants, and Industry," 416.

22. Bastid-Bruguiere, "Currents of Social Change," 558.

23. Feuerwerker, "Economic Trends," 12.

24. Wang Xi, "Approaches to the Study of Modern Chinese History: External Versus Internal Causations," in *China's Quest for Modernization: A Historical Perspective*, ed. Frederic Wakeman Jr. and Wang Xi (University of California Press, 1997), 20.

25. Bastid-Bruguiere, "Currents of Social Change," 591.

26. This includes the Maoist period. According to the world-systems perspective, the economic system of the Maoist period of China is also a part of the capitalist world-system.

27. As another result of China's incorporation, the old labor-intensive guilds like the Chinese handicraftsmen guilds had declined due mainly to the encroachment of Western capitalism: Akira Nagano, *Development of Capitalism in China* (Japan Council of the Institute of Pacific Relations Tokyo, 1931), 18. After labor-saving machines like spinning mills and the factory system were introduced by Western capitalists, the labor of handicraftsmen, the operating spinning wheels and water flour mills, and the handicraft guilds were rendered useless and ineffective, which led to the decline of the old labor-intensive guilds in Chinese society.

28. On the rise of the Dasheng cotton Mill, see Elisabeth Köll, *From Cotton Mill to Business Empire: The Emergence of Regional Enterprises in Modern China* (Harvard University Press, 2003).

29. Von Glahn, *Economic History of China*, 398. In addition, the rural population moved to urban areas or went abroad due to the poverty of rural areas. With regard to the urban-rural gap between 1901 and 1911, see Fairbank, *China*, 235.

30. Cohen, *Discovering History in China*, 144.

31. Timothy Brook, "Capitalism and the Writing of Modern History in China," in *China and Historical Capitalism: Genealogies of Sinological Knowledge*, ed. Timothy Brook and Gregory Blue (Cambridge University Press, 1999), 110–57.

32. Due to the parochialism of warlords, Zhang Peilun was easily defeated by the French navy in the Battle of Fuzhou (1884). At the time, despite Zhang's request for more warships, Li Hongzhang and Zhang Zhidong did not dispatch their warships to Fuzhou (Wakeman, *Fall of Imperial China*, 190).

33. Skocpol, *States and Social Revolutions*, 238.

34. This is partly linked to the US policy toward Japan. In the early twentieth century, the United States was favorable to Japanese expansion in Northeast Asia, as evidenced by the Taft-Katsura Agreement (1905) and the Root-Takahira Agreement (1908), both signed under President Theodore Roosevelt, which recognized Japanese control of Korea and Japan's status in Manchuria. For Roosevelt, the stability of the Pacific world under close cooperation with Japan was more important than American interests in China. See Charles E. Neu, "Theodore Roosevelt and American Involvement in the Far East, 1901–1909," *Pacific Historical Review* 35, no. 4 (1966): 433–49.

35. Flint and Zhang, "Historical-Geopolitical Contexts," 313.

36. Werner Meissner, "China's Search for Cultural and National Identity from the Nineteenth Century to the Present," *China Perspective* 68 (November–December 2006): 45.

37. Akira Iriye, *Across the Pacific: An Inner History of American–East Asian Relations* (Harcourt, Brace, 1967), 94–95.

38. Chan, "Government, Merchants, and Industry," 439.

39. Chan, "Government, Merchants, and Industry," 441.

40. By strongly advocating anti-imperialism, the GMT and CPC had a solid foothold in China. However, unlike the CPC's class-based political struggles, the radical GMT leaders did not agree with the CPC's promotion of class conflict and their class revolution even though both pursued reunification of China and anti-imperialism. This stark difference led to a break with the CPC, and they began to struggle with each other for power and influence in China. The GMT, which had military superiority over the CPC, drove the CPC and the Red Army to the brink of total defeat in the early 1930s. In fact, during the Long March (1934–1935), the CPC and the Red Army were on the verge of annihilation. The CPC was fortunate to survive due mainly to Japan's full-fledged invasion of China in 1937. It led to an alliance between the GMT and CPC to fight the Japanese. While fighting against Japan, the CPC succeeded in eliciting mass mobilization in rural areas through "tax or rent reduction, seizure and redistribution of gentry property, provision of local social services, and protection against marauding armies" (Skocpol, *States and Social Revolutions*, 254). The CPC was not strong enough to compete with the GMT's military forces; however, Japan's full-fledged invasion of China provided the CPC with an opportunity to gain a strong foothold.

41. William A. Callahan, "History, Identity, and Security: Producing and Consuming Nationalism in China," *Critical Asian Studies* 38, no. 2 (2006): 179–208.

42. Bastid-Bruguiere, "Currents of Social Change," 574.

43. Skocpol, "Social Revolution," 373.

44. This informs us that China had a capitalist transition that starkly contrasts with those of European countries, which glamorized internal dynamics as structural conditions thought to be manifest signs of the new stage of capitalist development.

45. Mao, "Chinese Revolution," 309. See also Jie Wu 吳傑, *Zhongguo jin dai guo min jing ji shi* 中国近代国民經济史, [The national economy of modern China] (Renminchubanshe, 1958), 2.

46. Jingwei Kong, 孔经纬, "Zhongguo fengjianshehuizhong zibenzhuyi mengya wenti zhi yanjiu" 中国封建社会中资本主义萌芽问题之研究 [The study of the germination of capitalism in the feudal society of China], *Shixue yuekan* 史学月刊 2 (1955): 3–7; Jingwei Kong, 孔经纬, "Quanyu tangsong shiqi yi you zibenzhuyi mengya de lishishishi" 关于唐宋时期已有资本主义萌芽的历史事实 [Historical facts about the germination of capitalism in the Tang and Song dynasties], *Shixue yuekan* 史学月刊 3 (1956): 13–14.

47. Qian Hong 钱宏, *Yapianzhanzheng Yiqian zhongguo ruogan shougongye bumen Zhong de zibenzhuyi mengya* 鸦片战争以前中国若干手工业部门中的资本主义萌芽 [The handicraft industries of Chinese capitalism's germination prior to the Opium War] (Shanghairenminchubanshe, 1956).

48. Shang Yue 尚钺, "Zhongguo zibenzhuyi shengchanyaosu de mengya jiqi zengzhang" 中国资本主义生产因素的萌芽及其增长 [The germination of China's capitalist production factors and its growth], *Lishiyanjiu* 历史研究 [Historical Research] 3 (1955): 85–133.

49. Deng Tuo, 邓拓, "Congwan li dao qianlong—guanyu zhongguo zibenzhuyi mengyashiqi de yigelunzheng" 从萬曆到乾隆—关于中国资本主义萌芽时期的一个論证 [From Wanli to the Qianlong regime—an argument on the germination period of Chinese capitalism], *lishiyanjiu* 历史研究 [Historical Research] 10 (1956): 1–31.

50. Maurice Dobb, *Studies in the Development of Capitalism* (New York: International Publishers, [1947] 1963).

51. Paul Sweezy, "A Critique," in *The Transition from Feudalism to Capitalism*, ed. R. H. Hilton (Verso, [1976] 1992), 33–67.

52. Robert Brenner, "Agrarian Class Structure and Economic Development in Pre-industrial Europe," in *The Brenner Debate: Agrarian Class Structure and Economic Development in Pre-industrial Europe*, ed. T. H. Aston and C. H. E. Philpin (Cambridge University Press, 1985), 10–63.

53. E. A. Wrigley, "Urban Growth and Agricultural Change: England and the Continent in the Early Modern Period," *Journal of Interdisciplinary History* 15, no. 4 (1985): 683–728.

54. Rebecca Jean Emigh, "Economic Interests and Sectoral Relations: The Undevelopment of Capitalism in Fifteenth-Century Tuscany," *American Journal of Sociology* 108, no. 5 (2003): 1075–1113.

55. Joseph M. Bryant, "The West and the Rest Revisited: Debating Capitalist Origins, European Colonialism, and the Advent of Modernity," *Canadian Journal of Sociology* 31, no. 4 (2006): 403–44; Immanuel Wallerstein, "The Present State of the Debate on World Inequality," in *The Capitalist World-Economy: Essays by Immanuel Wallerstein* (Cambridge University Press, 1979), 49–65.

56. "The handmill gives you society with the feudal lord; the steam-mill, society with the industrial capitalists": Karl Marx, *The Poverty of Philosophy* (Foreign Languages Publishing House, 1954), 109.

57. Karl Polanyi, *The Great Transformation* (Beacon Press, 1964), 86.

58. Max Weber, *The Protestant Ethic and the Spirit of Capitalism* (Routledge, 2001).

59. Polanyi, *Great Transformation*, chap. 13; Immanuel Wallerstein, *The Modern World-System IV: Centrist Liberalism Triumphant, 1789–1914* (University of California Press, 2011). Even within Europe, a single and unified approach to the transition to capitalism has recently been challenged; see Henry Bernstein, "Agrarian Classes in Capitalist Development," in *Capitalism and Development*, ed. Leslie Sklair (Routledge, 1994), 40–71; Robert S. Duplessis, *Transition to Capitalism in Early Modern Europe* (Cambridge University Press, 1997). And it has been suggested that not only socioeconomic factors like class relations but also political and cultural factors are important in the transition to capitalism. For the political factors in the transition to capitalism, see Richard Lachmann, *Capitalists in Spite of Themselves: Elite Conflict and Economic Transitions in Early Modern Europe* (Oxford University Press, 2000). For the cultural factors (e.g., consumerism) in the transition to capitalism, see Sidney W. Mintz, *Sweetness and Power: The Place of Sugar in Modern History* (Penguin, 1985); Werner Sombart, *Luxury and Capitalism*, trans. W. R. Dittmar (University of Michigan Press, 1967). Jack A. Goldstone and Kenneth Pomeranz even emphasized the contingent event or nature of the transition to capitalism in Europe; see Jack A. Goldstone, "Efflorescences and Economic Growth in World History: Rethinking the 'Rise of the West' and the Industrial Revolution," *Journal of World History* 13, no. 2 (2002): 377; Pomeranz, *Great Divergence*, 66.

60. Fraser, *Cannibal Capitalism*, chap. 2.

61. Cohen, "Historical Sociology's Puzzle," 606.

62. Goldstone, "Efflorescences and Economic Growth," 342.

63. Feuerwerker, "Economic Trends," 2.

64. Gardella, "Reform and the Tea Industry," 71–79.

65. Liu, *Tea War*, 45–80.

66. Kwang-Ching Liu, *China's Early Modernization and Reform Movement: Studies in Late Nineteenth-Century China and American-Chinese Relations*, vol. 2, ed. Yung-Fa Chen and Kuang-che Pan (Institute of Modern History, Academia Sinica, 2009), 475–76.

67. Liu, *China's Early Modernization and Reform Movement*, 476–77.

68. Bastid-Bruguiere, "Currents of Social Change," 571–72.

69. Lu, *Beyond the Neon Lights*, 66.

70. Tomoo Suzuki, "Shanghai Silk-Reeling Industry During the Period of the 1911 Revolution," in *The 1911 Revolution in China: Interpretive Essays*, ed. Eto Shinkichi and Harold Z. Schiffrin (University of Tokyo Press, 1984), 49.

71. Gyesun Lim, *Chŏngsa-manjujoki t'ongch'ihan chungkuk* [Qing history: China under rule of the Manchu] (Sinsŏwŏn, 2000), 650.

72. Betty Peh-t'I Wei, *Shanghai: Crucible of Modern China* (Oxford University Press, 1987), 129–30. Regarding the poor working condition of Chinese laborers in Shanghai, see Robert Y. Eng, *Economic Imperialism in China: Silk Production and Exports, 1861–1932* (Institute of East Asian Studies, University of California, 1986).

73. Wallerstein, *Historical Capitalism with Capitalist Civilization*, 30–32.

74. Richard A. Walker, "Two Sources of Uneven Development Under Advanced Capitalism: Spatial Differentiation and Capital Mobility," *Review of Radical Political Economics* 10, no. 3 (1978): 32.

75. Arrighi, *Adam Smith in Beijing*, 333.

76. Thomas, *Foreign Investment and China's Industrial Development*, chap. 5.

77. This refers to reforms by the Qing that followed the Treaty of Nanking.

78. Kent Deng, "State Transformation, Reforms and Economic Performance in China, 1840–1910" (LSE Research Online, 2003), https://eprints.lse.ac.uk/640/1/CUP-final.pdf, 19.

79. Thomas, *Foreign Investment and China's Industrial Development*, 92.

80. In contrast, Wakeman argued that the policy of "government-supervision and merchant-operation" regressed rather than advanced private capitalism in China (Wakeman, *Fall of Imperial China*, 194). He added that it operated as a mechanism for those who had political influence to squeeze merchants' money or to exhaust their capacity, which in turn failed to convert to a merchant-led capitalist economic system. Wakeman's conclusion may help answer the question of why late imperial China did not have a capitalist transition; nonetheless, a government-led or government-involved market economy was qualitatively different from China's previous politico-economic system. First, when faced with the danger of undermining the ancien régime in the nineteenth century, Qing bureaucrats realized that China's relatively unfavorable position within the capitalist world-system was as great a concern as the fears of instability of the socioeconomic system. As a result, they struggled to accept the principles of the capitalist world-system and strived for a capitalist transition although it was debatable whether the appropriate means for such a transition were used. Second, unlike before, Qing bureaucrats tried to protect and maximize the interests of Chinese merchants and workers who emigrated abroad (e.g., Chinese merchants who entered Korea or Chinese coolies who were shipped to Cuba or Peru) as much as the inland merchants and workers.

81. Chan, "Government, Merchants, and Industry," 426.

82. Chan, "Government, Merchants, and Industry," 454–59.

83. A ministry of commerce—a new government department proposed by Sheng Xuanhuai to manage the government's major industrial and commercial schemes—also fell short of expectations (Chan, "Government, Merchants, and Industry," 448–51). Friction with existing departments, financial problems, and corruption prevented it from achieving the expected results. However, these trials and tribulations can be viewed in another light: they were part

of the ongoing process of moving Chinese society away from its traditional roots, and they were the "predestined disruptions" of capitalist modernization transplanted from the outside. Successes and failures in terms of outcomes cannot explain long-term nineteenth-century Chinese social, economic, and institutional change. If success and failure were the only criteria, most of the reform movements that emerged from the nineteenth century would be devalued because they failed in the end.

84. Chan, "Government, Merchants, and Industry," 446–47.

85. Marie-Claire Bergère, *The Golden Age of the Chinese Bourgeoisie, 1911–1937*, trans. Janet Lloyd (Cambridge University Press, 1986), 7.

86. Elvin, *Pattern of the Chinese Past*, 176–96; Debin Ma, "Shanghai-Based Industrialization in the Early 20th Century: A Quantitative and Institutional Analysis," Working Papers of the Global Economic History Network (18/06) (Department of Economic History, London School of Economics and Political Science, 2006), http://eprints.lse.ac.uk/22473/, 19.

87. In a recent study paying attention to this period (1830s–1940s), Peter Thilly pointed to the role of the opium business in developing narco-capitalism: Peter Thilly, *The Opium Business: A History of Crime and Capitalism in Maritime China* (Stanford University Press, 2022). Jonathan Kaufman recounted the story of two Jewish families, the Sassoon and Kadoorie families, who contributed to advancing capitalist space in Shanghai and Hong Kong: Jonathan Kaufman, *The Last Kings of Shanghai: The Rival Jewish Dynasties That Helped Create Modern China* (Penguin Random House, 2020).

88. Of course, one can debate over how China after the 1890s is defined in a world-systems context, because, in this research I mainly examined China's politico-economic changes from precapitalist society to capitalist society during the nineteenth century, excluding the long-term and ongoing capitalist transition between late Qing China and the Republic of China (1912–1949) and the beginning stage of Chinese Communist Party rule (1949–1978). For these reasons, these tentative conclusions await further refinement and correction in the light of further research.

Bibliography

American Archives

Bureau of the Census. *Compendium of The Tenth Census*. US Government Printing Office, 1885.
Department of State. *Papers Relating to the Foreign Relations of the United States with the Annual Message of the President*. Transmitted to Congress, 1899.
"Letter from Humphrey Marshall to Secretary Marcy, July 26, 1853, 33rd Congress, 1st Session." *House Executive Document* 123 (1853): 203–5.
Statistical Abstract of the United States. Department of Commerce and Labor, 1905.
Transaction of the American Institute of the City of New York. 1856.
War Department, Census of Cuba. *The Report on the Census of Cuba*. Government Printing Office, 1900.

Chinese Archives

Chinese Emigration. The Cuba Commission. Report of the Commission Sent by China to Ascertain the Condition of Chinese Coolies in Cuba. Imperial Maritime Customs Press, 1876.
Chou ban yi wu shi mo 籌辦夷務始末 [The complete account of the management of barbarian affairs]. Tongzhi chao 同治朝 [The Tongzhi era]. Vol. 4, 1980.
Chou ban yi wu shi mo 籌辦夷務始末 [The complete account of the management of barbarian affairs]. Tongzhi chao 同治朝 [The Tongzhi era]. Vol. 5, 1980.
Chou ban yi wu shi mo 籌辦夷務始末 [The complete account of the management of barbarian affairs]. Tongzhi chao 同治朝 [The Tongzhi era]. Vol. 19, 1980.
Chou ban yi wu shi mo 籌辦夷務始末 [The complete account of the management of barbarian affairs]. Tongzhi chao 同治朝 [The Tongzhi era]. Vol. 26, 1980.
First Historical Archives of China (中国第一历史档案馆编). *Yapianzhanzheng danganshiliao* 鸦片战争档案史料. Vol. 1. Shanghairenminchubanshe, 1987.
Gongzhongdang Yongzhengchao zouzhe 宮中檔雍正朝奏摺. Vol. 8. National Palace Museum, 1977.
Guangxinfuzhi 廣信府志 [Local Gazetteer of Guangxin]. Vol. 2. 1872. '地理'(物産).

Huang, Fusan, Lin Manhong, and Ueng Jiyin, eds. *Maritime Customs: Annual Returns and Reports of Taiwan, 1867–1895*. Vol. 1, 2. Institute of Taiwan History, Academia Sinica, 1997.
Imperial Maritime Customs. "Reports on Trade at the Treaty Ports in China, 1875."
Imperial Maritime Customs. "Tea, 1888." 2-Special Series no. 11 (Shanghai, 1889).
Imperial Maritime Customs. 1, Statistical series no. 4. "Reports on Trade at the Treaty Ports, 1878." (1879).
Ming Taizongshilu (明 太宗實錄). Vol. 182. November 1416 (永樂 14年 11月), 壬寅條.
Qianlong nei fu yu tu (清乾隆內府輿圖). Guofangyanjiuyuan (國防研究院), Minguo 53. 1964.
Qing dai yitong ditu (清代一統地圖). Huagangwenhuashujuzongjingxiao (華岡文化書局總經銷), 1966.
Qinggaozongshilu 清高宗实录. Vol. 489. May 1755.
Qinggaozongshilu 清高宗实录. Vol. 550. November and December 1757.
Qing Guang xu chaozhongri jiaoshe shijiao (清光緒朝中日交涉史料). 上冊. Wenhai Chubanshe, 1970.
Qing Shengzushilu 清 聖祖實錄. Vol. 117. October 1684.
Qing Shengzushilu 清 聖祖實錄. Vol. 119. October 1684.
Qingshengzushilu 清圣祖实录. Vol. 226. September 1684.
Qingshigao (清史稿). Vol. 153. Zhonghuashuju, 1977.
Qingshigao (清史稿). Vol. 526. Zhonghuashuju, 1977.
Qingshizushilu 清世祖实录. Vol. 33. July 1647.
The Chinese Repository. Vol. III. December. Canton: Printed For The Proprietors, 1834.
The Chinese Repository, Vol. IV. Canton: Printed For The Proprietors, 1836.
The Chinese Repository, Vol. XI, From January to December. Canton: Printed For The Proprietors, 1842.
The Chinese Repository, Vol. XV, From January to December. Canton: Printed For The Proprietors, 1846.
The Chinese Repository, Vol. XVIII, From January to December. Canton: Printed For The Proprietors, 1849.
The Chinese Repository. Vol. 3. Huawenshujufaxing. (1875) 1968.
The Chinese Repository. Vol. 5. Huawenshujufaxing. (1876) 1968.
The Chinese Repository. Vol. 452. August 1877.
The Chinese Repository. Vol. 454. September 1877.
The Chinese Repository. Vol. 459. October 1877.
The Chinese Repository. Vol. 461. October 1877.
Wanguogongbao (萬國公報). Vol. 1. Huawenshujufaxing, (1876) 1968.
Yizhangxianzhi 宜章縣志 [Local Gazetteer of Yizhangxian]. Vol. 10, 1941.
Zhongyang yanjiuyuan jindaishi yanjiusuobian 中央研究院近代史研究所編. *Qingjizhongrihanguanxishiliao* 清季中日韓關係史料. Vol. 2. Zhongyang yanjiuyuan jindaishi yanjiusuo, 1972.

British Archives

British Parliamentary Papers. *China 26: Correspondence, Annual Reports, Conventions, and Other Papers Relating to the Affairs of Hong Kong 1882–99*. Irish University Press, 1972.
Canton Register. March 10, 1835.

Daily Advertiser and Shipping Gazette. January 3 and 10, 1872.

George Jamieson. *Report on the Revenue and Expenditure of the Chinese Empire*. Foreign Office, Miscellaneous Series, No. 415. H. M. Stationery Office, 1897.

Great Britain, Foreign Office. "George Phillips to John Walsham, Foochow, April 3, 1890." In *Diplomatic and Consular Reports, Annual Series*, No. 726. Great Britain, Foreign Office, 1890.

Great Britain, Foreign Office. *Slave Trade, No. 3 (1877). Reports Respecting the Condition of Coolies in Surinam*. Printed by Harrison and Sons, 1877.

Great Britain, House of Commons. *First Report from the Select Committee on the Affairs of the East India Company* (China Trade). 1830.

Great Britain, House of Commons. "Inclosure 26 in No. 13: Deposition of Kidnapped Coolie Brought from Whampoa," *Accounts and Papers*, 35 vols., China; Japan; Syria, January 24–August 28, 1860.

Great Britain, House of Commons. *Parliamentary Papers, Correspondence Respecting Emigration from Canton, Vol. 69, Inclosure 1 in No. 1. Consul Alcock to Sir J. Bowring*. Canton, April 12, 1859.

Great Britain, House of Commons. *Reports from Commissioners, Inspectors, and Others*. Vol. 18, 1892.

Great Britain, The House of Parliament. *Additional Papers Relating to China*. No. IV, 1840.

Great Britain, The House of Parliament. "Mr. Jerningham to the Earl of Clarendon, March 9, 1869 (Received April 13)." *Respecting the Emigration of Chinese Coolies from Macao*. London: Harrison and Sons, 1871.

Great Britain, The House of Parliament. Treaty Series, no. 11. "Convention Between Great Britain and China Relating to Sikkim and Tibet." *Parliamentary Paper C. 6208, 1890*, 1894.

Korean Archives

Ch'ongnigyosŏpt'ongsangsamuamun (總理交涉通商事務衙門), 同順泰號借款合同, 1892.
Gojongsilrok 高宗實錄. Vol. 19, 1882.
Gojongsilrok 高宗實錄.Vol. 28, 1887.
Injosilrok 仁祖實錄. Vol. 33, 1636.
Kuhan'gugoegyogwan'gyebusongmunsŏ (舊韓國外交關係附屬文書). Vol. 4. *T'ongsŏilgi* (統署日記) 2. 高麗大學校出版部, 1974.
Kuhan'gugoegyogwan'gyebusongmunsŏ (舊韓國外交關係附屬文書). Vol. 5. *T'ongsŏilgi* (統署日記) 3. 高麗大學校出版部, 1974.
Kuk'an'gugoegyomunsŏ (舊韓國外交文書). Vol. 8. *Chŏngan* (清案) 1. 高麗大學校出版部, 1970.
Sunjosilrok 純祖實錄. Vol. 32, 1832.
Tongsunt'aewangbongmunsŏ (同順泰往復文書). Vol. 1. January 28, 1894.
Tongsunt'aewangbongmunsŏ (同順泰往復文書). Vol. 12. December 10, 1893.

Secondary Sources

Abe, Kaori. *Chinese Middlemen in Hong Kong's Colonial Economy, 1830–1890*. Routledge, 2017.

Abu-Lughod, Janet L. *Before European Hegemony: The World System, A.D. 1250–1350*. Oxford University Press, 1989.

Adams, Brooks. *America's Economic Supremacy*. Macmillan, 1900.
Adamson, Bob. *China's English: A History of English in Chinese Education*. Hong Kong University Press, 2004.
Agnew, John A. *Globalization and Sovereignty*. Rowman and Littlefield, 2009.
Agnew, John A. *Hegemony: The New Shape of Global Power*. Temple University Press, 2005.
Agnew, John A. *The United States in the World-System: A Regional Geography*. Cambridge University Press, 1987.
Aldus, Don. *Coolie Traffic and Kidnapping*. McCorquodale & Co., 1876.
Allen, Horace Newton. *Aellŏnŭi ilgi* [Horace Newton Allen's Diary]. Translated by Kim Won-Mo. Dankook University Press, 1991.
Andrew, Edward. "Class in Itself and Class Against Capital: Karl Marx and His Classifiers." *Canadian Journal of Political Science* 16, no. 3 (1983): 577–84.
Anghie, Antony. *Imperialism, Sovereignty and the Making of International Law*. Cambridge University Press, 2005.
Anievas, Alexander, and Kerem Nişancioğlu. *How the West Came to Rule: The Geopolitical Origins of Capitalism*. Pluto, 2015.
Anievas, Alexander, and Kerem Nişancioğlu. "Why Europe? Anti-Eurocentric Theory, History, and the Rise of Capitalism." *Spectrum Journal of Global Studies* 8, no. 1 (2017): 70–98.
Antrobus, H. A. *A History of the Assam Company, 1839–1953*. Private printing by T. and A. Constable, 1957.
Appel, Tiago Masser. "Why Was There No Capitalism in Early Modern China." *Brazilian Journal of Political Economy* 37, no. 1 (2017): 167–88.
Aronowitz, Stanley. "A Metatheoretical Critique of Immanuel Wallerstein's 'The Modern World System.'" *Theory and Society* 10, no. 4 (1981): 503–20.
Arrighi, Giovanni. *Adam Smith in Beijing: Lineages of the Twenty-First Century*. Verso, 2007.
Arrighi, Giovanni. "China's Market Economy in the Long Run." In *China and the Transformation of Global Capitalism*, edited by Ho-fung Hong, 22–49. Johns Hopkins University Press, 2009.
Arrighi, Giovanni. "The Development Illusion: A Reconceptualization of the Semiperiphery." In *Semiperipheral States in the World-Economy*, edited by W. G. Martin, 11–42. Greenwood, 1990.
Arrighi, Giovanni. *The Long Twentieth Century: Money, Power, and the Origins of Our Times*. Verso, (1994) 2010.
Arrighi, Giovanni. "Reading Hobbes in Beijing: Great Power Politics and the Challenges of the Peaceful Ascent." In *Routledge Handbook of International Political Economy*, edited by M. Blyth, 163–79. Routledge, 2009.
Arrighi, Giovanni, and Jessica Drangel. "The Stratification of the World-Economy: An Exploration of the Semiperipheral Zone." *Review* (Fernand Braudel Center) 10, no. 1 (1986): 9–74.
Arrighi, Giovanni, Takeshi Hamashita, and Mark Selden. "The Rise of East Asia in Regional and World Historical Perspective." In *The Resurgence of East Asia: 500, 150 and 50 Year Perspective*, edited by Giovanni Arrighi, Takeshi Hamashita, and Mark Selden, 1–16. Routledge, 2003.
Arrighi, Giovanni, Terence K. Hopkins, and Immanuel Wallerstein. *Anti-Systemic Movements*. Verso, 1989.

Arrighi, Giovanni, Terrence K. Hopkins, and Immanuel Wallerstein. "Rethinking the Concepts of Class and Status-Group in a World-System Perspective." *Review* (Fernand Braudel Center) 6, no. 3 (1983): 283–304.

Arrighi, Giovanni, Po-keung Hui, Ho-fung Hung, and Mark Selden. "Historical Capitalism, East and West." In *The Resurgence of East Asia: 500, 150 and 50 Year Perspective*, edited by Giovanni Arrighi, Takeshi Hamashita, and Mark Selden, 259–333. Routledge, 2003.

Arrighi, Giovanni, and Beverly J. Silver. Introduction to *Chaos and Governance in the Modern World System*, edited by Giovanni Arrighi and Beverly J. Silver, 1–36. University of Minnesota Press, 1999.

Asiatic Intelligence. *The Asiatic Journal and Monthly Register for British and Foreign India, China and Australasia*. Volume 7. Parbury, Allen, and Co., 1832.

Assam: Sketch of Its History, Soil, and Production, with the Discovery of the Tea-Plant, and of the Countries Adjoining Assam. Smith Elder and Co., 1839.

Atwell, William. "Notes on Silver, Foreign Trade, and the Late Ming Economy." *Ching-shih went'I* 3, no. 8 (1977): 1–33.

Baek, Jun Kee. "Rŏshiaŭi tongashiajŏngch'aekkwa manjumunje" [Russian policy in East Asia and the Manchurian question]. In *Ashiaŭi Palk'an, Manjuwa Seo-gu Yŏlgangŭi Chegukchuŭi Chŏngch'aek* [Imperialist policies of Western powers in Manchuria, called the Balkans of Asia], 22–69. Tongbugayŏksajaedan, 2007.

Balibar, Etienne, and Immanuel Wallerstein. *Race, Nation, and Class: Ambiguous Identities*. Verso, 1991.

Ball, Samuel. "Observations on the Expediency of Opening a New Port in China." 1817. In *Nineteenth-Century China: Five Imperialist Perspectives*, edited by Rhoads Murphey, 1–23. University of Michigan Press, 1972.

Banister, T. Roger. *A History of the External Trade of China, 1834–81*. Inspector General of Chinese Customs, 1931.

Bao, Zhenggu 鮑正鵠. Yapianzhanzheng 阿片戰爭 [The Opium War]. Xinzhishicubsanshe, 1954.

Baran, Paul A., and Paul M. Sweezy. *Monopoly Capital: An Essay on the American Economic and Social Order*. Monthly Review, 1966.

Barlett, Beatrice S. *Monarchs and Ministers: The Grand Council in Mid-Ch'ing China, 1723–1820*. University of California Press, 1991.

Barraclough, Geoffrey. *An Introduction to Contemporary History*. Penguin, 1967.

Bassin, Mark. 1991. "Russia Between Europe and Asia: The Ideological Construction of Geographical Space." *Slavic Review* 50, no. 1 (1991): 1–17.

Bastid-Bruguiere, Marianne. "Currents of Social Change." In *The Cambridge History of China*, vol. 11, pt. 2, *Late Ch'ing, 1800–1911*, edited by Denis Twitchett and John K. Fairbank, 535–602. Cambridge University Press, 1980.

Basu, Dilip. 1979. "The Peripheralization of China: Notes on the Opium Connection." In *The World System of Capitalism: Past and Present*, edited by Walter L. Goldfrank, 171–89. Sage, 1979.

Baudrillard, Jean. *The Consumer Society: Myths and Structures*. Sage, (1970) 1998.

Beasley, W. G. "The Foreign Threat and the Opening of the Ports." In *The Cambridge History of Japan*, vol. 5, *The Nineteenth Century*, edited by John W. Hall, Marious B. Jansen, Madoka Kanai, and Denis Twitchett, 259–307. Cambridge University Press, 1989.

Beaumont, Joseph. *The New Slavery—An Account of the Indian and Chinese Immigrants in British Guiana*. 1871. Caribbean Press, 2011.

Beckert, Sven. *The Empire of Cotton*. Vintage, 2014.

Benton, Lauren. *A Search for Sovereignty: Law and Geography in European Empires, 1400–1900*. Cambridge University Press, 2010.

Berger, Patricia. *Empire of Emptiness: Buddhist Art and Political Authority in Qing China*. University of Hawaii Press, 2003.

Bergère, Marie-Claire. *The Golden Age of the Chinese Bourgeoisie 1911–1937*. Translated by Janet Lloyd. Cambridge University Press, 1986.

Bergesen, Albert. "1914 Again? Another Cycle of Inter-state Competition and War." In *Foreign Policy and the Modern World System*, edited by P. Mcgowan and C. W. Kegley Jr., 255–73. Sage, 1983.

Bernard, W. D., and W. H. Hall. *Narratives of the Voyages and Services of the Nemesis, from 1840 to 1843*. Henry Colburn Publisher, 1844.

Bernstein, Henry. "Agrarian Classes in Capitalist Development." In *Capitalism and Development*, edited by Leslie Sklair, 40–71. Routledge, 1994.

Bhambra, G. K. "Comparative Historical Sociology and the State: Problems of Method." *Cultural Sociology* 10, no. 3 (2016): 335–51.

Bilotti, Edvige. *The Rise of East Asia: Rethinking Theories of Economic Development*. IPRASTAH, 1997.

Bishop, Crawford. "American Extraterritorial Jurisdiction in China." *American Journal of International Law* 20, no. 2 (1926): 281–99.

Bishop, Isabella Bird. *The Yangtze Valley and Beyond*. Vol. 2. G. P. Putnam's Sons; John Murray, 1900.

Black, Jeremy. *Beyond the Military Revolution: War in the Seventeenth-Century World*. Palgrave Macmillan, 2011.

Blackwell, William L. *The Beginnings of Russian Industrialization, 1800–1860*. Princeton University Press, 1968.

Blussé, Leonard. *Strange Company: Chinese Settlers, Mestizo Women and the Dutch in VOC Batavia*. Foris Publications, 1986.

Blussé, Leonard. *Visible Cities: Canton, Nagasaki, and Batavia, and the Coming of the Americans*. Harvard University Press, 2008.

Bol, Peter K. "Why Do Intellectuals Matter to Chinese Politics?" In *The China Questions: Critical Insights into a Rising Power*, edited by Jennifer Rudolph and Michael Szonyi, 244–51. Harvard University Press, 2018.

Boswell, Terry. "World Revolutions and Revolutions in the World-System." In *Revolution in the World-System*, edited by Terry Boswell, 1–16. Greenwood, 1989.

Boulding, Kenneth E., and Alan H. Gleason. "War as Investment: The Strange Case of Japan." In *Economic Imperialism: A Book of Readings*, edited by Kenneth E. Boulding and Tapan Mukerjee, 240–61. University of Michigan Press, 1972.

Boulger, Demetrius Charles. *England and Russia in Central Asia*. London: W. H. Allen & Co, 1879.

Bourdieu, Pierre. "The Forms of Capital." In *Handbook of Theory and Research for the Sociology of Education*, edited by John G. Richardson, 241–58. Greenwood, 1986.
Braudel, Fernand. *Afterthoughts on Material Civilization and Capitalism*. Johns Hopkins University Press, 1977.
Braudel, Fernand. *Civilization and Capitalism, 15th-Eighteenth Century*, vol. 2, *The Wheels of Commerce*. Harper & Row, 1982.
Bray, Francesca. *The Rice Economy: Technology and Development in Asian Society*. Basil Blackwell, 1986.
Brenner, Robert. "Agrarian Class Structure and Economic Development in Pre-industrial Europe." In *The Brenner Debate: Agrarian Class Structure and Economic Development in Pre-industrial Europe*, edited by T. H. Aston and C. H. E. Philpin, 10–63. Cambridge University Press, 1985.
Brenner, Robert, and Christopher Isett. "England's Divergence from China's Yangzi Delta: Property Relations, Microeconomics, and Patterns of Development." *Journal of Asian Studies* 61, no. 2 (2002): 609–62.
Brook, Timothy. "Capitalism and the Writing of Modern History in China." In *China and Historical Capitalism: Genealogies of Sinological Knowledge*, edited by Timothy Brook and Gregory Blue, 110–57. Cambridge University Press, 1999.
Brook, Timothy. *Mr Seldeon's Map of China: The Spice Trade, a Lost Chart and the South China Sea*. Profile Books, 2013.
Brook, Timothy. *The Troubled Empire: China in the Yuan and Ming Dynasties*. Harvard University Press, 2010.
Brook, Timothy. *Vermeer's Hat: The Seventeenth Century and the Dawn of the Global World*. Bloomsbury, 2008.
Brown, Margaret L. "Asa Whitney and His Pacific Railroad Publicity Campaign." *Mississippi Valley Historical Review* 20, no. 2 (1933): 209–24.
Brown, Shannon R. "The Partially Opened Door: Limitations on Economic Change in China in the 1860s." *Modern Asian Studies* 12, no. 2 (1978): 177–92.
Brunero, Donna. *Britain's Imperial Cornerstone in China: The Chinese Maritime Customs Service, 1854–1949*. Routledge, 2006.
Bryant, Joseph M. "The West and the Rest Revisited: Debating Capitalist Origins, European Colonialism, and the Advent of Modernity." *Canadian Journal of Sociology* 31, no. 4 (2006): 403–44.
Bulletin of the American Geographical Society. "The Peking-Hankow Railway." *Bulletin of the American Geographical Society* 38, no. 9 (1906): 554–56.
Bun, Kwan Man. "Mapping the Hinterland: Treaty Ports and Regional Analysis in Modern China." In *Remapping China: Fissures in Historical Terrain*, edited by Gail Hershatter, Emily Honig, Jonathan N. Lipman, and Randall Stross, 181–93. Stanford University Press, 1996.
Bunker, Stephen G., and Paul S. Ciccantell. "Economic Ascent and the Global Environment: World-Systems Theory and the New Historical Materialism." In *Ecology and the World-System*, edited by W. L. Goldfrank, D. Goodman, and A. Szasz, 107–22. Greenwood, 1999.
Bunker, Stephen G., and Paul S. Ciccantell. *Globalization and the Race for Resources*. Johns Hopkins University Press, 2005.
Bunn-Livingstone, Sandra L. *Juricultural Pluralism vis-à-vis Treaty Law*. Martinus Nijhoff, 2002.

Burlingame, Roger. "Locomotives, Railways, and Steamships." In *Technology in Western Civilization*, vol. 1: *The Emergence of Modern Industrial Society, Earliest Times to 1900*, edited by Melvin Kranzberg and Carroll W. Pursell. Oxford University Press, 1967.

Bush, Caleb M. "Reconsidering Incorporation: Uneven Histories of Capitalist Expansion and Encroachment, Native America." *Studies in Political Economy* 76 (2005): 83–109.

Bussche, Eric Vanden. "Contested Realms: Colonial Rivalry, Border Demarcation, and State-Building in Southwest China, 1885–1960." PhD diss., Stanford University, 2014.

Buzan, Barry, and George Lawson. *The Global Transformation*. Cambridge University Press, 2015.

Callahan, William A. "History, Identity, and Security: Producing and Consuming Nationalism in China." *Critical Asian Studies* 38, no. 2 (2006): 179–208.

Calleo, David P. *Beyond American Hegemony: The Future of the Western Alliance*. Basic Books, 1987.

Campbell, Persia Crawford. *Chinese Coolie Emigration to Countries Within the British Empire*. P. S. King & Westminster, 1923.

Cams, Mario. *Companions in Geography: East-West Collaboration in the Mapping of Qing China (c. 1685–1735)*. Brill, 2017.

Cao, Jin, and Dennis O. Flynn. "Global Quantification and Inventory Demand for Silver in China." *Revista de Historia Económica* 38, no. 3 (2020): 421–47.

Carroll, John M. "The Canton System: Conflict and Accommodation in the Contact Zone." *Journal of the Royal Asiatic Society, Hong Kong Branch* 50 (2010): 51–66.

Carroll, John M. *Edges of Empire*. Harvard University Press, 2005.

Cassel, Par Kristoffer. *Grounds of Judgment: Extraterritoriality and Colonial Power in Nineteenth-Century China and Japan*. Oxford University Press, 2012.

Chakrabarty, Dipesh. *Provincializing Europe: Postcolonial Thought and Historical Difference*. Princeton University Press, 2000.

Chalmers, John. "The Missionary Question." *Chinese Recorder and Missionary Journal* 4, no. 6 (1871): 141–72.

Chan, Sucheng. *This Bittersweet Soil: The Chinese in California Agriculture, 1860–1911*. University of California Press, 1986.

Chan, Wellington K. K. "Government, Merchants, and Industry to 1911." In *The Cambridge History of China*, vol. 11, pt. 2, *Late Ch'ing, 1800–1911*, edited by John K. Fairbank and Kwang-Ching Liu, 416–62. Cambridge University Press, 1980.

Chandler, Alfred D. "The Emergence of Managerial Capitalism." *Business History Review* 58, no. 4 (1984): 473–503.

Chandler, Alfred D. "The United States: Evolution of Enterprise." In *The Cambridge Economic History of Europe*, vol. 6, pt. 2, edited by Peter Mathias and M. M. Postan, 70–133. Cambridge University Press, 1978.

Chandler, Alfred D. *The Visible Hand: The Managerial Revolution in American Business*. Harvard University Press, 1977.

Chang, Chung-li. *The Chinese Gentry: Studies on Their Role in Nineteenth-Century Chinese Society*. University of Washington Press, 1955.

Chang, Hao. "Intellectual Change and the Reform Movement, 1890–98." In *The Cambridge History of China*, vol. 11, pt. 2, *Late Ch'ing, 1800–1911*, edited by Denis Twitchett and John K. Fairbank, 274–338. Cambridge University Press, 1980.

Chao, Kang. *Man and Land in Chinese History: An Economic Analysis.* Stanford University Press, 1986.
Chao, Paul K. *Chinese Culture and Christianity.* University Press of America, 2006.
Chase, Kenneth. *Firearms: A Global History to 1700.* Cambridge University Press, 2003.
Chase-Dunn, Christopher. "Core-Periphery Relations: The Effect of Core Competition." In *Social Change in the Capitalist World-Economy*, edited by B. Kaplan, 159–76. Sage, 1978.
Chase-Dunn, Christopher. "The Development of Core Capitalism in the Antebellum United States: Tariff Politics and Class Struggles in an Upwardly Mobile Semiperiphery." In *Studies of the Modern World-System*, edited by Albert Bergesen, 189–230. Academic Press, 1980.
Chase-Dunn, Christopher. "Inter-state System and Capitalist World-Economy: One Logic or Two." In *The Theoretical Evolution of International Political Economy*, edited by George T. Crane and Abla Amawi, 144–57. Oxford University Press, 1997.
Chase-Dunn, Christopher, and Thomas T. Hall. *Rise and Demise: Comparing World Systems.* Routledge, 1997.
Chase-Dunn, Christopher, Andrew K. Jorgenson, Thomas E. Reifer, and Shoon Lio. "The Trajectory of the United States in the World-System: A Quantitative Reflection." *Sociological Perspectives* 48, no. 2 (2005): 233–54.
Chase-Dunn, Christopher, and Richard Rubinson. "Toward a Structural Perspective on the World-System." *Politics and Society* 7, no. 4 (1977): 453–76.
Chaudhuri, Kirti N. *Trade and Civilisation in the Indian Ocean: An Economic History from the Rise of Islam to 1750.* Cambridge University Press, 1985.
Chaudhuri, Kirti N. *The Trading World of Asia and the English East India Company, 1660–1760.* Cambridge University Press, 2006.
Chen, Ciyu 陈慈玉. *Jindai zhongguo chaye de fazhan xing shijie shichang* 近代中国茶业的发展与世界市场 [The development of the Chinese tea trade in the modern world market]. Studies of Modern Economy Series, no. 6. Zhongyang yanjiuyuan jingji yanjiu suo, 1982.
Chen, Ciyu 陈慈玉. *Jindai Zhongguo chaye zhi fazhan* 近代中国茶业之发展 [The development of the modern Chinese tea industry]. Zhongguo renmin da xue chu ban she, 2013.
Ch'en, Jerome. *China and the West: Society and Culture, 1815–1937.* Indiana University Press, 1979.
Ch'en, Jerome. *The Military-Gentry Coalition: China Under the Warlords.* University of Toronto–York University, Joint Centre on Modern East Asia, 1979.
Ch'en, Jerome. *State Economic Policies of the Ch'ing Government 1840–1895.* Garland, 1980.
Chen, Shengshao 陈盛韶. "Wensulu" 問俗錄 [An investigation of customs records]. In *Siku-weishoushujikan* 四庫未收书辑刊 [Collection of books not included in Siku]. Vol. 6, 227–84. Beijing chubanshe, (1826) 2000.
Chen, Song-Chuan. *Merchants of War and Peace: British Knowledge of China in the Making of the Opium War.* Hong Kong University Press, 2017.
Chen, Ti Qiang 陳體強. *Zhongguowaijiaoxingzheng* 中國外交行政 [China's diplomatic administration]. Shangwuyinshuguan, (1945) 1983.
Chen, Weixin 陳維新. *Tong-guangnian jian zongeyili bianjie jiaoshe tantao-yi zhonge ding-dingzhi tiaoyue ji jietu weili* 同、光年間中俄伊犁邊界交涉探討-以中俄訂定之條約及界圖為例 [Treaty of Saint Petersburg of 1881: A case study of treaties and border maps in the National Palace Museum]. Kongjianxinsiwei-lishiyutuxuequojixueshuyantaohui, 2008.

Chen, Yong. "The Internal Origins of Chinese Emigration to California Reconsidered." *Western Historical Quarterly* 28, no. 4 (1997): 520–46.

Chesneaux, Jean. "Secret Societies in China's Historical Evolution." In *Popular Movements and Secret Societies in China, 1840–1950*, edited by Jean Chesneaux, 1–21. Stanford University Press, 1972.

Chisholm, George Goudie. *The Two Hemispheres: A Popular Account*. W. O. Blackie and Co, Printers, 1882.

Cho, Young-hun. *Daeunhawa chungguksangin: Hoe-yang jiyŏkhuijusangin sŏngchangsa, 1415–1784* [The grand canal and Chinese merchants]. Minumsa, 2011.

Cho, Young-hun. *Taeunhashidae, 1415–1784* [The age of the Grand Canal, 1415–1784]. Minumsa, 2021.

Choi, Chi-cheung. 2015. "Rice, Treaty Ports and the Chaozhou Chinese Lianhao Associate Companies: Construction of a South China–Hong Kong–Southeast Asia Commodity Network, 1850s–1930s." In *Merchant Communities in Asia, 1600–1980*, edited by Lin Yu-ju and Madeleine Zelin, 53–77. Pickering and Chatto, 2015.

Choi, Deok kyoo. "Rŏshiaŭi taemanjujŏngch'aekkwa tongch'ŏngch'ŏlto" [Russia's Manchurian policy and the Chinese Eastern Railway]. *Manjuyŏn'gu* [Journal of Manchurian Studies] 6 (2004): 5–25.

Chŏn, Hyŏngkwŏn. *Chungguk Kŭnhyŏndae Sangin'gwa Mulgabyŏn-dong: Honam Chiyŏksahoe Yŏngu* [Chinese modern and contemporary merchants and price fluctuations—a study on the Honam community]. Hyeyan, 2021.

Chong, Ja Ia. *External Intervention and the Politics of State Formation: China, Indonesia, and Thailand, 1853–1952*. Cambridge University Press, 2012.

Chow, Kit, and Ione Kramer. *All the Tea in China*. China Books and Periodicals, 1990.

Chung, Stephanie Po Yin. *Chinese Business Groups in Hong Kong and Political Change in South China, 1900–25*. Macmillan, 1998.

Chung, Tan. *China and the Brave New World: A Study of the Origins of the Opium War (1840–42)*. Carolina Academic Press, 1978.

Church, Sally K. "The Colossal Ships of Zheng He: Image or Reality?" In *Zheng He: Images and Perceptions*, edited by Roderich Ptak and Claudine Salmon, 155–58. Otto Harrassowitz, 2005.

Chuzo, Ichiko. "Political and Institutional Reform, 1901–11." In *The Cambridge History of China*, vol. 11, pt. 2, *Late Ch'ing, 1800–1911*, edited by John K. Fairbank and Kwang-Ching Liu, 375–415. Cambridge University Press, 1980.

Cipolla, Carlo M. *Guns and Sails in the Early Phase of European Expansion, 1400–1700*. Collins, 1965.

Clark, Brett, and John Bellamy Foster. "Ecological Imperialism and the Global Metabolic Rift: Unequal Exchange and the Guano/Nitrates Trade." *International Journal of Comparative Sociology* 50, nos. 3–4 (2009): 311–34.

Clark, Gregory. *A Farewell to Alms: A Brief Economic History of the World*. Princeton University Press, 2008.

Clark, Gregory, Michael Huberman, and Peter H. Lindert. "A British Food Puzzle, 1770–1850." *Economic History Review* 48, no. 2 (1995): 215–37.

Clyde, Paul Hibbert. *International Rivalries in Manchuria, 1689–1922*. Ohio State University Press, 1926.

Cochran, Sherman. *Encountering Chinese Networks: Western, Japanese, and Chinese Corporations in Chin, 1880–1937*. University of California Press, 2000.

Cohen, G. A. *Karl Marx's Theory of History: A Defense*. Princeton University Press, (1978) 2000.

Cohen, Joanna W. "Religion, War, and Empire in Eighteenth-Century China." *International History Review* 20, no. 3 (1998): 336–52.

Cohen, Mark. "Historical Sociology's Puzzle of the Missing Transitions: A Case Study of Early Modern Japan." *American Sociological Review* 80, no. 3 (2015): 603–25.

Cohen, Paul A. "The Anti-Christian Tradition in China." *Journal of Asian Studies* 20, no. 2 (1961): 169–80.

Cohen, Paul A. *China and Christianity: The Missionary Movement and the Growth of Chinese Antiforeignism, 1860–1870*. Harvard University Press, 1963.

Cohen, Paul A. *Discovering History in China: American Historical Writing on the Recent Chinese Past*. Columbia University Press, (1984) 2010.

Cohen, Paul A. "How Has the Study of China Changed in the Last Sixty Years?" In *The China Questions: Critical Insights into a Rising Power*, edited by Jennifer Rudolph and Michael Szonyi, 288–94. Harvard University Press, 2018.

Cohen, Warren I. *East Asia at the Center: Four Thousand Years of Engagement with the World*. Columbia University Press, 2000.

Cohen, Warren I. "The Foreign Impact on East Asia." In *Historical Perspective on Contemporary East Asia*, edited by Merle Goldman and Andrew Gordon, 1–41. Harvard University Press, 2000.

Collins, Randall. *Weberian Sociological Theory*. Cambridge University Press, 1986.

Coman, Katharine. "The History of Contract Labor in the Hawaiian Islands." *Publications of the American Economic Association* 4, no. 3 (1903): 1–61.

Connell, Carol Matheson. "Jardine Matheson & Company: The Role of External Organization in a Nineteenth-Century Trading Firm." *Enterprise & Society* 4, no. 1 (2003): 99–138.

Constable, Nicole. "Introduction: What Does It Mean to Be Hakka?" In *Guest People: Hakka Identity in China and Abroad*, edited by Nicole Constable, 3–35. University of Washington Press, 1996.

Conte-Helm, Marie. *Japan and the North East of England: From 1862 to the Present Day*. Athlone Press, 1989.

Cooper, Luke. "Asian Sources of British Colonial Power: The Role of the Mysorean Rocket in the Opium War." In *Historical Sociology and World History*, edited by Alexander Anievas and Kamran Matin, 111–26. Rowman and Littlefield, 2016.

Cox, Robert W. "Gramsci, Hegemony and International Relations: An Essay in Method." *Journal of International Studies* 12, no. 2 (1983): 162–75.

Crawcour, E. Sydney. "Economic Change in the Nineteenth Century." In *The Cambridge History of Japan*, vol. 5, *The Nineteenth Century*, edited by John W. Hall, Marious B. Jansen, Madoka Kanai, and Denis Twitchett, 569–617. Cambridge University Press, 1989.

Creel, Herrlee Glessna. "The Role of the Horse in Chinese History." *American Historical Review* 70, no. 3 (1965): 647–72.

Crossley, Pamela Kyle. *Orphan Warriors: Three Manchu Generations and the End of the Qing World*. Princeton University Press, 1990.

Crossley, Pamela Kyle. *The Wobbling Pivot, China Since 1800*. Blackwell, 2010.

Cumings, Bruce. "Archaeology, Descent, Emergence: Japan in British/American Hegemony, 1900–1950." In *Japan in the World*, edited by Masao Miyoshi and H. D. Harootunian, 79–111. Duke University Press, 1993.

Cumings, Bruce. "Dominion from Sea to Sea: America's Pacific Ascendancy." *Asia-Pacific Journal* 10, no. 7 (2012): 1–11.

Cumings, Bruce. *Dominion from Sea to Sea: Pacific Ascendancy and American Power.* Yale University Press, 2009.

Cumings, Bruce. "The Origins and Development of the Northeast Asian Political Economy: Industrial Sectors, Product Cycles, and Political Consequences." *International Organization* 38, no. 1 (1984): 1–40.

Cumings, Bruce. *The Origins of the Korean War: Liberation and the Emergence of Separate Regimes, 1945–1947.* Princeton University Press, 1981.

Cumings, Bruce. "The World Shakes China." *National Interest* 43 (1996): 28–41.

Cushman, Jennifer Wayne. *Fields from the Sea: Chinese Junk Trade with Siam During the Late Eighteenth and Early Nineteenth Centuries.* Cornell University Press, 1993.

Cutler, A. Claire. "Gramsci, Law, and the Culture of Global Capitalism." *Critical Review of International Social and Political Philosophy* 8, no. 4 (2005): 527–42.

Dabohashi Giyoshi. *Gŭndaeilsŏnkwan'gyeŭiyŏn'gu* 近代日鮮關係の研究 [Modern Japanese-Korean relations]. Translated by Kim Jonghak. Ilchokak, (1940) 2013.

Dai, Yifeng 戴一峰. 1989. "Zai lun jin dai minjiang shang yu shanqu de shangpin shengchan." 再论近代闽江上游山区的商品生产 [More research on commodity production in the mountain area of the upper Min River in modern times]. *Zhongguo shehui jingjishi yanjiu* 中国社会经济史研究 4 (1989): 57–64.

Dasao, Nakami. "Yŏksa sogŭi manjusang" [mages of Manchuria in history]. In *Manjuran muŏshiŏnnŭn'ga* [What was Manchuria], edited by Nakami Dasao, 17–32. Somyŏngch'ulp'an, 2013.

Davidson, James W. *The Island of Formosa, Past and Present.* Kelly and Walsh, 1903.

Davies, Norman. *Europe: A History.* Pimlico, 1997.

Davin, Delia. "Women in the Countryside of China." In *Women in Chinese Society*, edited by Margery Wolf and Roxane Witke, 243–73. Stanford University Press, 1975.

Davis, Clarence B. "Railway Imperialism in China, 1895–1939." In *Railway Imperialism*, edited by Clarence B. Davis and Kenneth E. Wilburn, 155–73. Greenwood, 1991.

Davis, Lance E., and Robert E. Gallman. "Capital Formation in the United States During the Nineteenth Century." In *The Cambridge Economic History of Europe*, vol. 6, pt. 2, edited by Peter Mathias and M. M. Postan, 1–69. Cambridge University Press, 1978.

Davis, Ralph. *The Industrial Revolution and British Overseas Trade.* Leicester University Press, 1979.

De Bary, William Thedore, Wing-tsit Chan, and Burton Watson. *Sources of Chinese Traditions*, vol. 2: *From 1600 Through the Twentieth Century.* Columbia University Press, 1960.

Debow's Review. Vol. 27. New Orleans and Washington City, 1859.

Deng, Gang. "The Foreign Staple Trade of China in the Pre-Modern Era." *International History Review* 19, no. 2 (1997): 253–85.

Deng, Kent. "State Transformation, Reforms and Economic Performance in China, 1840–1910." LSE Research Online, 2003. https://eprints.lse.ac.uk/640/1/CUP-final.pdf.

Deng, Tuo 邓拓 1956. "Congwan li dao qianlong—guanyu zhongguo zibenzhuyi mengyashiqi de yigelunzheng" 从萬曆到乾隆—关于中国资本主义萌芽时期的一个論証 [From Wanli to Qianlong regime—an argument on the formative period of Chinese capitalism]. *Lishiyanjiu* 历史研究 [Historical Research] 10 (1956): 1–31.
Denyer, C. H. "The Consumption of Tea and Other Staple Drinks." *Economic Journal* 3, no. 9 (1893): 33–51.
Dernberger, Robert F. "The Role of the Foreigner in China's Economic Development, 1840–1949." In *China's Modern Economy in Historical Perspective*, edited by Dwight H. Perkins, 19–47. Stanford University Press, 1975.
Desai, Radhika. *Geopolitical Economy: After US Hegemony, Globalization and Empire*. Pluto, 2013.
Desnoyers, Charles. "Toward 'One Enlightened and Progressive Civilization': Discourses of Expansion and Nineteenth-Century Chinese Missions Abroad." *Journal of World History* 8, no. 1 (1997): 135–56.
Di Cosmo, Nicola. "Did Guns Matter? Firearms and the Qing Experience." In *The Qing Formation in World Historical Time*, edited by L. A. Struve, 121–66. Harvard University Press, 2004.
Di Cosmo, Nicola. "Qing Colonial Administration in the Inner Asian Dependencies." *International History Review* 20, no. 2 (1998): 287–309.
Dobb, Maurice. *Studies in the Development of Capitalism*. International Publishers, (1947) 1963.
Doolittle, Rev. Justus. *Social Life of the Chinese*. Vol. 1. Sampson Low Son & Marston, 1866.
Dos Santos, Theotonio. "The Concept of Social Classes." *Science & Society* 34, no. 2 (1970): 166–93.
Dos Santos, Theotonio. "The Structure of Dependence." *American Economic Review* 60, no. 2 (1970): 231–36.
Drake, Fred W. "E. C. Bridgman's Portrayal of the West." In *Christianity in China: Early Protestant Missionary Writings*, edited by Suzanne Wilson Barnett and John King Fairbank, 89–106. Harvard University Press, 1985.
Drummond, Diane K. "Sustained British Investment in Overseas Railways, 1830–1914." In *Across the Borders: Financing the World's Railways in the Nineteenth and Twentieth Centuries*, edited by Ralf Roth and Günter Dinhobl, 207–23. Ashgate, 2008.
Du, Yongtao. *The Orders of Places: Translocal Practices of the Huizhou Merchants in Late Imperial China*. Brill, 2015.
Duara, Prasenjit. "De-Constructing the Chinese Nation." *Australian Journal of Chinese Affairs* 30 (1993): 1–26.
Duara, Prasenjit. *Rescuing History from the Nation: Questioning Narratives of Modern China*. University of Chicago Press, 1995.
Duara, Prasenjit. *Sovereignty and Authenticity: Manchukuo and the East Asian Modern*. Rowman and Littlefield, 2003.
Duara, Prasenjit. "Transnationalism and the Predicament of Sovereignty: China, 1900–1945." *American Historical Review* 102, no. 4 (1997): 1030–51.
Duplessis, Robert S. *Transition to Capitalism in Early Modern Europe*. Cambridge University Press, 1997.
Durkheim, Émile. *The Rules of Sociological Method*. University of Chicago Press, (1895) 1938.
Duus, Peter. "Japan's Informal Empire in China, 1895–1937." In *The Japanese Informal Empire in China, 1895–1937*, edited by Peter Duus, Ramon H. Myers, and Mark R. Peattie, xi–xxix. Princeton University Press, 1989.

Duus, Peter. "Trade and Investment." In *The Japanese Informal Empire in China, 1895–1937*, edited by Peter Duus, Ramon H. Myers, and Mark R. Peattie, 3–9. Princeton University Press, 1989.

Eastman, Lloyd E. "Ch'ing-i and Chinese Policy Formation During the Nineteenth Century." *Journal of Asian Studies* 24, no. 4 (1965): 595–611.

Eckert, Carter J. *Offspring of Empire: The Koch'ang Kims and the Colonial Origins of Korean Capitalism, 1876–1945*. University of Washington Press, 1991.

Eisenstadt, Shmuel Noah. *European Civilization in Comparative Perspective*. Norwegian University Press, 1987.

Eisenstadt, Shmuel Noah. "Political Struggle in Bureaucratic Societies." *World Politics* 9, no. 1 (1956): 15–36.

Eitel, Ernest John. *Europe in China: The History of Hong Kong from the Beginning to the Year 1882*. Kelly & Walsh, 1895.

Elliot, Brian, and David McCrone. *The City: Patterns of Domination and Conflict*. Macmillan, 1982.

Elliott, Mark C. *Emperor Qinglong: Son of Heaven, Man of the World*. Longman, 2009.

Elliott, Mark C. "The Limits of Tartary: Manchuria in Imperial and National Geographies." *Journal of Asian Studies* 59, no. 3 (2000): 603–46.

Elliott, Mark C. *The Manchu Way: The Eight Banners and Ethnic Identity in Later Imperial China*. Stanford University Press, 2001.

Ellis, Henry. *Journal of the Proceedings of the Late Embassy to China*. Printed for John Murray, Albemarle-Street, 1817.

Ellison, Herbert J. "Economic Modernization in Imperial Russia: Purposes and Achievements." *Journal of Economic History* 25, no. 4 (1965): 523–40.

Elman, Benjamin A. *A Cultural History of Civil Examinations in Late Imperial China*. University of California Press, 2000.

Elman, Benjamin A. *From Philosophy to Philology: Intellectual and Social Aspects of Changes in Late Imperial China*. Harvard University Press, 1984.

Elman, Benjamin A. *On Their Own Terms: Science in China, 1550–1900*. Harvard University Press, 2005.

El-Ojeili, Chamsy. "Reflections on Wallerstein: The Modern World-System, Four Decades On." *Critical Sociology* 41, nos. 4–5 (2014): 1–22.

Elvin, Mark. *The Pattern of the Chinese Past: A Social and Economic Interpretation*. Stanford University Press, 1970.

Emigh, Rebecca Jean. "Economic Interests and Sectoral Relations: The Undevelopment of Capitalism in Fifteenth-Century Tuscany." *American Journal of Sociology* 108, no. 5 (2003): 1075–1113.

Emigh, Rebecca Jean. "The Power of Negative Thinking: The Use of Negative Case Methodology in the Development of Sociological Theory." *Theory and Society* 26, no. 5 (1997): 649–84.

Emmanuel, Arghiri. *Unequal Exchange: A Study of the Imperialism of Trade*. Monthly Review, 1972.

Eng, Robert Y. *Economic Imperialism in China: Silk Production and Exports, 1861–1932*. Institute of East Asian Studies, University of California, 1986.

Engels, Frederick. "Persia and China." In *On Colonialism*, edited by Karl Marx and Frederick Engels, 120–26. International Publishers, 1972.

Epstein, Stephan R. "The Rise of the West." In *An Anatomy of Power: The Social Theory of Michael Mann*, edited by John A. Hall and Ralph Schroeder, 233-62. Cambridge University Press, 2006.

Erikson, Emily. *Between Monopoly and Free Trade: The English East India Company, 1600–1757*. Princeton University Press, 2014.

Esherick, Joseph W. "Harvard on China: The Apologetics of Imperialism." *Bulletin of Concerned Asian Scholars* 4, no. 4 (1972): 9-16.

Esherick, Joseph W. *The Origins of the Boxer Uprising*. University of California Press, 1988.

Fairbank, John K. *China: A New History*. Harvard University Press, 1992.

Fairbank, John K. "The Creation of the Treaty System." In *Cambridge History of China*, vol. 10, pt. 1, *Late Ch'ing, 1800–1911*, edited by John K. Fairbank, 213-63. Cambridge University Press, 1978.

Fairbank, John K. *The Great Chinese Revolution: 1800–1985*. Harper Perennial, 1987.

Fairbank, John K. "Introduction: The Old Order." In *Cambridge History of China*, vol. 10, pt. 1, *Late Ch'ing, 1800–1911*, edited by John K. Fairbank, 1-34, Cambridge University Press, 197a.

Fairbank, John K. "Introduction: The Place of Protestant Writings in China's Cultural History." In *Christianity in China: Early Protestant Missionary Writings*, edited by Suzanne Wilson Barnett and John King Fairbank, 1-18. Harvard University Press, 1985.

Fairbank, John K. *Trade and Diplomacy on the China Coast*, vol. 1, *The Opening of the Treaty Ports, 1842–1854*. Stanford University Press, (1953) 1969.

Fairbank, John K. *The United States and China*. 4th ed. Harvard University Press, 1983.

Fairbank, John K. and Merle Goldman. *China: A New History*. 2nd ed. Harvard University Press, 2006.

Fairbank, John K., Edwin O. Reischauer, and Albert M. Craig. *East Asia: Traditional and Transformation*. Houghton Mifflin, 1978.

Fairbank J. K., and S. Y. Teng. "On the Ch'ing Tributary System." *Harvard Journal of Asiatic Studies* 6, no. 2 (1941): 135-246.

Fan, He Jun 范和钧. 1937. "Tunxi chaye diaocha." 屯溪茶业调查 [Survey on the Tunxi tea industry] *Guoji Maoyi Daobao* 国际贸易导报 9, no. 4 (1937): 113-35.

Fang, Dongshu 方東樹. *Han xue shang dui* 漢學商兑 [An assessment of Han learning]. Taiwan shangwu yinshuguan, 1968.

Farley, Foster M. "The Chinese Coolie Trade, 1845–1875." *Journal of Asian and African Studies* 3 (1967): 257-70.

Fei, Haiao-Tung. "Peasantry and Gentry: An Interpretation of Chinese Social Structure and Its Changes." *American Journal of Sociology* 52, no. 1 (1946): 1-17.

Feuerwerker, Albert. "Economic Trends in the Late Ch'ing Empire, 1870–1911." In *The Cambridge History of China*, vol. 11, pt. 2, *Late Ch'ing, 1800–1911*, edited by John K. Fairbank and Kwang-Ching Liu, 1-69. Cambridge University Press, 1980.

Fewsmith, Joseph. "From Guild to Interest Group: The Transformation of Public and Private in Late Qing China." *Comparative Studies in Society and History* 25, no. 4 (1983): 617-40.

Fieldhouse, D. K. *Economics and Empire, 1830–1914*. Macmillan, 1984.

Fisher, George Battye. *Personal Narrative of Three Years' Service in China*. Richard Bentley, 1863.

Flint, Colin, and Zhang Xiaotong. "Historical-Geopolitical Contexts and the Transformation of Chinese Foreign Policy." *Chinese Journal of International Politics* 12, no. 3 (2019): 295-331.

Flynn, Dennis O. "Big History, Geological Accumulations, Physical Economics, and Wealth." *Asian Review of World History* 7 (2019): 80–106.

Flynn, Dennis O. *World Silver and Monetary History in the 16th and 17th Centuries.* Variorum, 1996.

Flynn, Dennis O., and Arturo Giraldez. "Cycles of Silver: Global Economic Unity Through the Mid-Eighteenth Century." *Journal of World History* 13, no. 2 (2002): 391–427.

Forrest, Denys. *Tea for the British: The Social and Economic History of a Famous Trade.* Chatto & Windus, 1973.

Forsythe, Dall W. *Taxation and Political Change in the Young Nation. 1781–1833.* Columbia University Press, 1977.

Fortune, Robert. *A Journey to the Tea-Countries of China, Including Sung-Lo and the Bohea Hills.* John Murray, 1852.

Fortune, Robert. *Three Years' Wanderings in the Northern Provinces of China.* 2nd ed. John Murray, 1847.

Frank, Andre Gunder. *ReOrient: Global Economy in the Asian Age.* University of California Press, 1998.

Frank, Andre Gunder, and Barry K. Gills. "The 5,000 Year World System: An Interdisciplinary Introduction." In *The World System: Five Hundred Years or Five Thousand?*, edited by Barry K. Gills and Andre Gunder Frank, 3–58. Routledge, 1993.

Fraser, Nancy. *Cannibal Capitalism.* Verso, 2022.

Frost, Robert. "The Road Not Taken." In *Mountain Interval.* Henry Holt and Company, (1916) 1931.

Furber, Holden. "Asia and the West as Partners Before 'Empire' and After." *Journal of Asian Studies* 28, no. 4 (1969): 711–21.

Gaastra, Femme. "War, Competition and Collaboration: Relations Between the English and Dutch East Indian Companies in the Seventeenth and Eighteenth Centuries." In *The Worlds of the East India Company*, edited by H. V. Bowen, Margarette Lincoln, and Nigel Rigby, 49–68. Boydell Press, 2002.

Gallagher, John, and Ronald Robinson. "The Imperialism of Free Trade." *Economic History Review* 6, no. 1 (1953): 1–15.

Gamble, Andrew. "Hegemony and Decline: Britain and the United States." In *Two Hegemonies: Britain 1846–1914 and the United States 1941–2001*, edited by Patrick Karl O'Brien and Armand Clesse, 127–40. Ashgate, 2002.

Gardella, Robert. *Harvesting Mountains: Fujian and the China Tea Trade, 1757–1937.* University of California Press, 1994.

Gardella, Robert. "Reform and the Tea Industry and Trade in Late Ch'ing China: The Fukien Case." In *Reform in Nineteenth-Century China*, edited by P. A. Cohen and J. E. Schrecker, 71–79. Harvard University Press, 1976.

Gardella, Robert. "Tea Processing in China, Circa 1885." *Business History Review* 75, no. 4 (2001): 807–12.

Gardner, Christopher Thomas. "Amoy Emigration to the Straits." *China Review* 22, no. 4 (1897): 621–26.

Ge, Yuan xu 葛元煦. *Huyou zaji shangjuan* 滬游雜記 [Miscellaneous notes on visiting Shanghai]. Vol. 1, 1876.

Gernet, Jacques. *China and the Christian Impact*. Cambridge: Cambridge University Press, (1982) 1987.
Gibson, James R. *Otter Skins, Boston Ships, and China Goods: The Maritime Fur Trade of the Northwest Coast, 1785–1841*. University of Washington Press, 1992.
Giddens, Anthony. *The Nation-State and Violence*, vol. 2, *A Contemporary Critique of Historical Materialism*. University of California Press, 1985.
Go, Julian. "Waves of Empire: US Hegemony and Imperialistic Activity from the Shores of Tripoli to Iraq, 1787–2013." *International Sociology* 22, no. 1 (2007): 5–40.
Godley, Michael. *The Mandarin-Capitalists from Nanyang: Overseas Chinese Enterprise in the Modernization of China, 1839–1911*. Cambridge University Press, 1982.
Goey, Ferry De. *Consuls and the Institutions of Global Capitalism, 1783–1914*. Routledge, 2016.
Goldfrank, Walter L. "Theories of Revolution and Revolution Without Theory." *Theory and Society* 7, nos. 1–2 (1979): 135–65.
Goldsmith, Raymond E. "The Economic Growth of Tsarist Russia 1860–1913." *Economic Development and Cultural Change* 9, no. 3 (1961): 441–75.
Goldstein, Jonathan. *Philadelphia and the China Trade, 1682–1846: Commercial, Cultural, and Attitudinal Effect*. Pennsylvania State University Press, 1978.
Goldstone, Jack A. "Efflorescences and Economic Growth in World History: Rethinking the 'Rise of the West' and the Industrial Revolution." *Journal of World History* 13, no. 2 (2002): 323–89.
Goldstone, Jack A. "Gender, Work, and Culture: Why the Industrial Revolution Came Early to England but Late to China." *Sociological Perspective* 39, no. 1 (1996): 1–21.
Goldstone, Jack A. "Neither Late Imperial nor Early Modern: Efflorescences and the Qing Formation in World History." In *The Qing Formation in World-Historical Time*, edited by Lynn A. Struve, 242–302. Harvard University Press, 2004.
Goldstone, Jack A. "The Problem of the 'Early Modern' World." *Journal of Economic and Social History of the Orient* 41 (1998): 249–84.
Goldstone, Jack A. *Revolution and Rebellion in the Early Modern World*. University of California Press, 1991.
Goldstone, Jack A. "The Rise of the West—Or Not? A Revision to Socio-Economic History." *Sociological Theory* 18, no. 2 (2000): 175–94.
Goldstone, Jack A. *Why Europe? The Rise of the West in World History, 1500–1850*. McGraw-Hill Education, 2009.
Goody, Jack. *The East in the West*. Cambridge University Press, 1996.
Gordon, Andrew. *A Modern History of Japan: From Tokugawa Times to the Present*. Oxford University Press, 2003.
Gordon, Peter, and Juan José Morales. *The Silver Way: China, Spanish America and the Birth of Globalization, 1565–1815*. Penguin, 2017.
Gottheil, Fred M. "Marx Versus Marxists on the Role of Military Production in Capitalist Economies." *Journal of Post Keynesian Economics* 8, no. 4 (1986): 563–73.
Gottschang, Thomas R., and Diana Lary. *Swallows and Settlers: The Great Migration from North China to Manchuria*. University of Michigan Press, 2000.
Graham, Gerald S. *The China Station: War and Diplomacy, 1830–1860*. Oxford University Press, 1978.

Green, Michael J. *By More Than Providence: Grand Strategy and American Power in the Asia Pacific Since 1783*. Columbia University Press, 2017.

Greenberg, Michael. *British Trade and the Opening of China 1800–1842*. Cambridge University Press, 1951.

Griffith, William. "Report on the Tea Plant of Upper Assam." In *Transactions of the Agricultural and Horticultural Society of India*, vol. 5, edited by Agricultural & Horticultural Society of India, 94–180. 1838.

Griffiths, Percival. *The History of the Indian Tea Industry*. Weidenfeld and Nicolson, 1967.

Guterl, Matthew Pratt. "After Slavery: Asian Labor, the American South, and the Age of Emancipation." *Journal of World History* 14, no. 2 (2003): 209–41.

Gutzlaff, Charles. *Journal of Three Voyages Along the Coast of China in 1831, 1832, and 1833 with Notices of Siam, Corea, and the Loo-Choo Islands*. Frederick Westley and A. H. Davis, 1834.

Ha, Arang. "Free Labor, Free Trade, Free Immigration: The Vision of the Pacific Community after the Civil War." PhD diss., Rice University, 2021.

Habermas, Jürgen. *The Theory of Communicative Action*, vol. 1, *Reason and the Rationalization of Society*. Translated by Thomas McCarthy. Beacon Press, 1981.

Haddad, John R. *America's First Adventure in China: Trade, Treaties, Opium, and Salvation*. Temple University Press, 2013.

Hall, John A. *Powers and Liberties: The Causes and Consequences of the Rise of the West*. Blackwell, 1985.

Hall, John R. "World-System Holism and Colonial Brazilian Agriculture: A Critical Case Analysis." *Latin American Research Review* 19, no. 2 (1984): 43–69.

Hall, Thomas D. "Incorporation into and Merger of World-Systems." In *Routledge Handbook of World-Systems Analysis*, edited by Salvatore J. Babones and Christopher Chase-Dunn, 37–55. Routledge, 2012.

Halsey, Stephen R. *Quest for Power: European Imperialism and the Making of Chinese Statecraft*. Harvard University Press, 2015.

Hamashita, Takeshi. "Tribute and Treaties: Maritime Asia and Treaty Port Networks in the Era of Negotiation, 1800–1900." In *The Resurgence of East Asia*, edited by Giovanni Arrighi, Takeshi Hamashita, and Mark Selden, 17–50. Routledge, 2003.

Hamilton, Alexander, John Jay, and James Madison. *The Federalist and Other Constitutional Papers*. Vol. 1. Albert, Scott & Company, 1894.

Hamilton, Gary G. "Hong Kong and the Rise of Capitalism in Asia." In *Cosmopolitan Capitalists: Hong Kong and the Chinese Diaspora at the End of the 20th Century*, edited by Gary G. Hamilton, 14–34. University of Washington Press, 1999.

Hamilton, Gary G. "Overseas Chinese Capitalism." In *Confucian Traditions in East Asian Modernity*, edited by Tu Wei-ming, 328–42. Harvard University Press, 1996.

Han, Suk-Jung. *Manjugung kŏn'gugŭi chaehaesŏk: Koeroegugŭi kukkahyogwa, 1932–1936* [Reinterpreting the founding of Manchukuo: State effectiveness in a puppet state, 1932–1936]. Pusan: Tongadaehakkyo ch'ulp'anbu, 1999.

Han, Suk-Jung. "Taedongagongyŏnggwŏn'gwa segyech'ejeronŭi chŏkyonge taehan shiron" [A critique of the world-system analysis of the so-called Greater East Asian Co-Prosperity Sphere]. *Han'guksahoehak* [Korean Journal of Sociology] 33 (1999): 917–36.

Hannigan, Robert E. *The New World Power: American Foreign Policy, 1898–1917*. University of Pennsylvania Press, 2002.
Hao, Gao. "The Amherst Embassy and British Discoveries in China." *History* 99 (2014): 568–87.
Hao, Yen-P'ing. "Chinese Teas to America—a Synopsis." In *America's China Trade in Historical Perspective*, edited by Ernest R. May and John K. Fairbank, 11–31. Harvard University Press, 1986.
Hao, Yen-P'ing. *The Commercial Revolution in Nineteenth-Century China: The Rise of Sino-Western Mercantile Capitalism*. University of California Press, 1986.
Hao, Yen-P'ing. "A New Class in China's Treaty Ports: The Rise of the Comprador-Merchants." *Business History Review* 44, no. 4 (1970): 446–59.
Hao, Yen-P'ing, and Erh-min Wang. "Changing Chinese Views of Western Relations, 1840–95." In *The Cambridge History of China*, vol. 11, pt. 2, *Late Ch'ing, 1800–1911*, edited by John K. Fairbank and Kwang-Ching Liu, 142–201. Cambridge University Press, 1980.
Harper's New Monthly Magazine. Vol. 29, June 1864.
Harris, Paul W. "Cultural Imperialism and American Protestant Missionaries: Collaboration and Dependency in Mid-Nineteenth-Century China." *Pacific Historical Review* 60, no. 3 (1991): 309–38.
Harvey, David. *The Anti-Capitalist Chronicles*. Pluto, 2020.
He, Qinhua. "The First Integrated Practice of Legal Translation in Modern China: A Study of the Chinese Translation of Elements of International Law, 1864." *Semiotica* 216 (2017): 151–68.
Headrick, Daniel R. *The Tools of Empire: Technology and European Imperialism in the Nineteenth Century*. Oxford University Press, 1981.
Hevia, Louis J. *Cherishing Men from Afar: Qing Guest Ritual and the Macartney Embassy of 1793*. Duke University Press, 1995.
Hevia, Louis J. *English Lessons: The Pedagogy of Imperialism in Nineteenth-Century China*. Duke University Press, 2003.
Hevia, Louis J. "Postpolemical Historiography: A Response to Joseph W. Esherick." *Modern China* 24, no. 3 (1998): 319–27.
Ho, Ping-Ti. *The Ladder of Success in Imperial China: Aspects of Social Mobility, 1368–1911*. Columbia University Press, 1962.
Ho, Ping-Ti. "The Salt Merchants of Yang-Chou: A Study of Commercial Capitalism in Eighteenth-Century China." *Harvard Journal of Asiatic Studies* 17, nos. 1–2 (1954): 130–68.
Ho, Ping-Ti. *Studies on the Population of China, 1368–1953*. Harvard University Press, 1974.
Ho, Yin-Ping. *Trade, Industrial Restructuring, and Development in Hong Kong*. University of Hawaii Press, 1992.
Hobsbawm, E. J. *The Age of Empire 1875–1914*. Vintage, 1989.
Hobson, J. A. "Free Trade and Foreign Policy." *Contemporary Review* 74 (1898): 167–80.
Hodacs, Hanna. *Silk and Tea in the North: Scandinavian Trade and the Market for Asian Goods in Eighteenth-Century Europe*. Palgrave Macmillan, 2016.
Hoffman, George W. "Nineteenth-Century Roots of American World Power Relations: A Study in Historical Political Geography." *Political Geography Quarterly* 1, no. 3 (1982): 279–92.
Hoh, Cheung, and Lorna H. Mui. "Smuggling and the British Tea Trade Before 1784." *American Historical Review* 74, no. 1 (1968): 44–73.

Hong Kong Daily Express. May 9, 1871.
Hong Kong Daily Express. July 20, 1899.
Honig, Emily. *Creating Chinese Ethnicity: Subei People in Shanghai, 1850–1980.* Yale University Press, 1992.
Hopkins, Terrence K. "Notes on Class Analysis and the World-System." *Review* (Fernand Braudel Center) 1, no. 1 (1977): 67–72.
Hopkins, Terence K., and Immanuel Wallerstein. "Capitalism and the Incorporation of New Zones into the World-Economy." *Review* (Fernand Braudel Center) 10, no. 5 (1987): 763–79.
Hopkins, Terence K., and Immanuel Wallerstein. "Commodity Chains in the World-Economy Prior to 1800." *Review* (Fernand Braudel Center) 10, no. 1 (1986): 157–70.
Hopkins, Terence K., and Immanuel Wallerstein. "Structural Transformations of the World-Economy." In *Dynamics of World Development*, edited by Richard Rubinson, 233–62. Sage, 1981.
Horowitz, Richard S. "Central Power and State Making: The Zongli Yamen and Self-Strengthening in China, 1860–1880." PhD diss., Harvard University, 1998.
Horowitz, Richard S. "International Law and State Transformation in China, Siam, and the Ottoman Empire During the Nineteenth Century." *Journal of World History* 15, no. 4 (2004): 445–86.
Hostetler, Laura. "Contending Cartographic Claims?" In *The Imperial Map: Cartography and the Mastery of Empire*, edited by James R. Akerman, 93–132. University of Chicago Press, 2009.
Hostetler, Laura. "Early Modern Mapping at the Qing Court: Survey Maps from the Kangxi, Yongzheng, and Qianlong Reign Periods." In *Chinese History in Geographical Perspective*, edited by Yongtao Du and Jeff Kyong-McClain, 7–32. Lexington Books, 2013.
Hostetler, Laura. "Imperial Competition in Eurasia: Russia and China." In *The Cambridge World History*, edited by Jerry H. Bentley, Sanjay Subrahmanyam, and Merry E. Wiesner-Hanks, 297–322. Cambridge University Press, 2015.
Hostetler, Laura. *Qing Colonial Enterprise: Ethnography and Cartography in Early Modern China.* University of Chicago Press, 2001.
Hou, Chi-ming. *Foreign Investment and Economic Development in China, 1840–1937.* Harvard University Press, 1965.
Howard, Paul Wilson. "Opium Suppression in Qing China: Responses to a Social Problem, 1729–1906." PhD diss., University of Pennsylvania, 1998.
Hsiao, Kung-chuan. *A History of Chinese Political Thought*, vol. 1, *From the Beginning to the Sixth Century A.D.* Translated by F. W. Mote. Princeton University Press, 1979.
Hsiao, Kung-chuan. *Rural China: Imperial Control in the Nineteenth Century.* University of Washington Press, 1960.
Hsü, Immanuel Chung-Yueh. *China's Entrance into the Family of Nations: The Diplomatic Phase, 1858–1880.* Harvard University Press, 1960.
Hsü, Immanuel Chung-Yueh. "Late Ch'ing Foreign Relations, 1866–1905." In *The Cambridge History of China*, vol. 11, pt. 2, *Late Ch'ing, 1800–1911*, edited by John K. Fairbank and Kwang-Ching Liu, 70–141. Cambridge University Press, 1980.
Hsü, Immanuel Chung-Yueh. *The Rise of Modern China.* Oxford University Press, 2000.
Hsüeh, Chün-Tu, and Geraldine R. Schiff. "The Life and Writings of Tsou Jung." In *Revolutionary Leaders of Modern China*, edited by Chün-Tu Hsüeh, 153–209. Oxford University Press, 1971.

Hu, Sheng 胡绳. *Cong apianzhanzheng dao wusiyundong* 从鸦片战争到五四运动 [From the Opium War to the May Fourth Movement]. Renmin chubanshe, 1981.
Huang, Philip C. C. *The Peasant Economy and Social Change in North China*. Stanford University Press, 1985.
Huang, Philip C. C. *The Peasant Family and Rural Development in the Yangzi Delta, 1350–1988*. Stanford University Press, 1990.
Huang, Qichen 黃啓臣 and Zheng Weiming 鄭煒明. *Aomen jingjisi bainian* 澳門經濟 四百年 [Economic history of Macau]. Aomen jijinhui, 1994.
Huang, Ray. *China: A Macro History*. M. E. Sharpe, 1997.
Hu-Dehart, Evelyn. "Chinese Coolie Labor in Cuba in the Nineteenth Century: Free Labor of Neoslavery." *Contributions in Black Studies* 12 (1994): 38–54.
Hu-Dehart, Evelyn. 1989. "Coolies, Shopkeepers, Pioneers: The Chinese of Mexico and Peru." *AMERASI* 15, no. 2 (1989): 91–116.
Huenemann, Ralph William. *The Dragon and the Iron Horse: The Economics of Railroads in China, 1876–1937*. Harvard University Press, 1984.
Hui, Po-keung. "Comprador Politics and Middleman Capitalism." In *Hong Kong's History: State and Society Under Colonial Rule*, edited by Tak-Wing Ngo, 30–45. Routledge, 1999.
Hui, Po-keung. "Overseas Chinese Business Networks: East Asian Economic Development in Historical Perspective." PhD diss., State University of New York at Binghamton, 1995.
Hung, Ho-Fung. "Agricultural Revolution and Elite Reproduction in Qing China: The Transition to Capitalism Debate Revisited." *American Sociological Review* 73 (2008): 569–88.
Hung, Ho-Fung. *The China Boom: Why China Will Not Rule the World*. Columbia University Press, 2016.
Hung, Ho-Fung. "The Global, the Historical, and the Social in the Making of Capitalism." In *Global Historical Sociology*, edited by J. Go and G. Lawson, 163–81. Cambridge University Press, 2017.
Hung, Ho-Fung. "Imperial China and Capitalist Europe in the Eighteenth-Century Global Economy." *Review* 24, no. 4 (2001): 473–513.
Hung, Ho-Fung. *Protest with Chinese Characteristics: Demonstrations, Riots, and Petitions in the Mid-Qing Dynasty*. Columbia University Press, 2011.
Immerman, Richard H. *Empire for Liberty: A History of American Imperialism from Benjamin Franklin to Paul Wolfowitz*. Princeton University Press, 2010.
Immerwahr, Daniel. "The Great United States: Territory and Empire in U.S. History." *Diplomatic History* 40, no. 3 (2016): 373–91.
Iriye, Akira. *Across the Pacific: An Inner History of American-East Asian Relations*. Harcourt, Brace, 1967.
Iriye, Akira. "Japan's Drive to Great-Power Status." In *The Cambridge History of Japan*, vol. 5, *The Nineteenth Century*, edited by Marius Jansen, 721–82. Cambridge University Press, 1989.
Iriye, Akira. *Pacific Estrangement: Japanese and American Expansion, 1897–1911*. Imprint Publications, 1994.
Isaacs, Harold R. *The Tragedy of the Chinese Revolution*. 2nd rev. ed. Stanford University Press, (1938) 1961.
Isin, Engin F. "Historical Sociology of the City." In *Handbook of Historical Sociology*, edited by Gerard Delanty and Engin F. Isin, 312–25. Sage, 2003.

Itzigsohn, José. "World-Systems and Institutional Analysis—Tensions and Complementarities: The Cases of Costa Rica and the Dominican Republic." *Review* (Fernand Braudel Center) 24, no. 3 (2001): 439–68.

Jacob, Margaret. *The Cultural Meaning of the Scientific Revolution.* Alfred A. Knopf, 1988.

Jager, Sheila Miyoshi. *The Other Great Game: The Opening of Korea and the Birth of Modern East Asia.* Harvard University Press, 2023.

James, Lawrence. *The Rise and Fall of the British Empire.* St. Martin's, 1994.

Jang, Yong Soo. "A World-Systems Perspective on the Sociocultural History of East Asia: The Cases of China, Japan, and Korea." PhD diss., State University of New York at Albany, 2004.

Jansen, Marius. "Japan and the Chinese Revolution of 1911." In *The Cambridge History of China*, vol. 11, pt. 2, *Late Ch'ing, 1800–1911*, edited by John K. Fairbank and Kwang-Ching Liu, 339–74. Cambridge University Press, 1980.

Jay, John. *The Correspondence and Public Papers of John Jay, Vol. 3 (1782–1793).* G. P. Putnam's Sons, 1891.

Ji, Zhaojin. *A History of Modern Shanghai Banking: The Rise and Decline of China's Finance Capitalism.* M. E. Sharpe, 2003.

Jin Siwon. "Tongpukasia chŏl-to kŏnsŏlkwa chiyŏkkukkakwankyeŭi pyŏnhwa: 19seki hupankwa 20seki ch'opan chekukchuŭi sikilŭl chungsimŭlo" [Railway construction and the change of interstate imperialistic relations in Northeast Asia: From the late nineteenth century to the early twentieth century]. *P'yŏnghwayŏnku* 12, no. 2 (2004): 57–85.

Johns, Eric L. *The European Miracle: Environments, Economies, and Geopolitics in the History of Europe and Asia.* Cambridge University Press, (1981) 2003.

Johns, Susan Mann, and Philip A. Kuhn. "Dynastic Decline and the Roots of Rebellion." In *The Cambridge History of China*, vol. 10, pt. 1, *Late Ch'ing, 1800–1911*, edited by Denis Twitchett and John K. Fairbank, 107–62. Cambridge University Press, 1978.

Josephson, Matthew. *The Robber Barons: The Great American Capitalists, 1861–1901.* Harcourt, Brace, 1934.

Jung, Yung Gu. "19segi chungban chunggugŭi k'ullimuyŏk [Chinese coolie trade in the latter half of the nineteenth century]. *Tongyangsahakyŏn'gu* (Journal of Asian Historical Studies) 142 (2018): 171–204.

Kagarlitsky, Boris. *Empire of the Periphery: Russia and the World System.* Translated by Renfrey Clarke. Pluto, 2008.

Kalberg, Stephen. *Max Weber's Comparative Historical Sociology.* Polity, 1994.

Kalberg, Stephen. *Max Weber's Comparative-Historical Sociology Today: Major Themes, Mode of Causal Analysis, and Applications.* Ashgate, 2012.

Kang, Jin-A. *Tongsunt'aeho: Tongashia Hwagyo Chabon'gwa Kŭndaejosŏn* [Tongshunti: Chinese merchant network in East Asia and modern Korea]. Kyŏngbuk National University Press, 2011.

Kang, Jin-A. "Western Companies: Western Merchants in East Asia." In *The Great Merchants in History*, 143–87. National Research Council for Economics, Humanities, and Social Sciences, 2016.

Kardulias, Nick P. "Negotiation and Incorporation on the Margins of World-Systems: Examples from Cyprus and North America," *Journal of World-Systems Research*, 13, no. 1 (2007): 55–82.

Kardulias, Nick P., and Emily Butcher. "Piracy in a Contested Periphery: Incorporation and the Emergence of the Modern World-System in the Colonial Atlantic Frontier." *Journal of World-Systems Research* 22, no. 2 (2016): 542–64.

Kasaba, Reşat. "Incorporation of the Ottoman Empire." *Review* (Fernand Braudel Center) 10, no. 5 (1987): 805–47.

Kaufman, Jonathan. *The Last Kings of Shanghai: The Rival Jewish Dynasties That Helped Create Modern China*. Penguin, 2020.

Kaup, Brent Z. "In Spaces of Marginalization: Dispossession, Incorporation, and Resistance in Bolivia." *Journal of World-Systems Research* 19, no. 1 (2013): 108–29.

Kayaoğlu, Turan. *Legal Imperialism: Sovereignty and Extraterritoriality in Japan, the Ottoman Empire, and China*. Cambridge University Press, 2010.

Keiji, Yamaguchi. *Ilbon'gŭnseŭi Swaegukkwa Kaeguk* [Closed-door policies and the opening of Japan in modern times]. Translated by Kimhyŏnyŏng. Hyean, 2001.

Kelekna, Pita. *The Horse in Human History*. Cambridge University Press, 2009.

Keliher, Macabe. "Anglo-American Rivalry and the Origins of U.S. China Policy." *Diplomatic History* 31, no. 2 (2007): 227–57.

Keller, Wolfgang, Ben Li, and Carol H. Shiue. "Shanghai's Trade, China's Growth: Continuity, Recovery, and Change Since the Opium War." *IMF Economic Review* 61, no. 2 (2013): 336–78.

Kennedy, Paul. *The Rise and Fall of the Great Powers: Economic Change and Military Conflict from 1500 to 2000*. Random House, 1987.

Kentor, Jeffrey. *Capital and Coercion: The Economic and Military Processes That Have Shaped the World-Economy, 1800–1900*. Garland, 2000.

Kim, Jaeeun. *Contested Embrace: Transborder Membership Politics in Twentieth-Century Korea*. Stanford University Press, 2016.

Kim, Ji-hwan. *Chŏlloŭi tŭngjanggwa chŏngjo ponggŏnch'ejeŭi punggoe* [The rise of the railway and the collapse of feudalism in the Qing dynasty]. Tongashia, 2019.

Kim, Jong Ho. "Namjungguk'ae hwain net'ŭwŏk'ŭ song saram, chabon, mulcha, kŭrigo munhwaŭi idong: Kŭndae Hwagyo Songgŭm Net'ŭwŏk'ŭŭi Hyŏngsŏnggwa Idongŭi Kujo" [The movement of Chinese people, capital, goods, and culture in the South China Sea: Formation and movement of the modern Chinese remittance network]. In *Haeyanggwa megaashia* [The ocean and mega-Asia], edited by Jou KyungChul and Ru Sung Hee, 177–213. Zininzin, 2023.

Kim Joo Yong. "Ilchegangjŏmgi haninŭi manju ijuwa toshijiyŏgŭi kujobyŏnhwa" [Korean migration to Manchuria and the changing structure of urban areas during the Japanese occupation]. In *Kŭndae manju toshi yŏksajiri yŏn'gu* [Historical geographic study of the modernization process in Manchuria], 108–56. Tongbugayŏksajaedan, 2007.

Kim, Keongil, et al. *Tongashiaŭi minjogisan'gwa toshi: 20segi chŏnban manjuŭi chosŏnin* [Korean diaspora in Manchurian cities in the early twentieth century]. Yŏksabip'yŏngsa, 2004.

Kim, Key-hiuk. *The Last Phase of the East Asian World Order: Korea, Japan, the Chinese Empire, 1860–1882*. University of California Press, 1980.

Kim, Kwang min. *Borderland Capitalism: Turkestan Produce, Qing Silver, and the Birth of an Eastern Market*. Stanford University Press, 2016.

Kim Youngsin. "Kaehang, choch'awa kŭndae manjur shinhŭngdoshiŭi hŭnggi" [Open ports, lend lease, and the development of the modern city in Manchuria]. Iin *Kŭndae manju toshi yŏksajiri yŏn'gu* [Historical geographic study of the modernization process in Manchuria], 64–106. Tongbugayŏksajaedan, 2007.

King, Anthony D. *Colonial Urban Development: Culture, Social Powers and Environment*. Routledge & Kegan Paul, 1976.

King, Anthony D. *Global Cities: Post-Imperialism and the Internationalization of London*. Routledge, 1990.

King, Anthony D. *Urbanism, Colonialism, and the World-Economy: Cultural and Spatial Foundations of the World Urban System*. Routledge, 1990.

Koji, Hirata. "Steel Metropolis: Industrial Manchuria and the Making of Chinese Socialism, 1916–1964." PhD diss., Stanford University, 2018.

Köll, Elisabeth. *From Cotton Mill to Business Empire: The Emergence of Regional Enterprises in Modern China*. Harvard University Press, 2003.

Kong, Jingwei 孔经纬. "Quanyu tangsong shiqi yi you zibenzhuyi mengya de lishishishi" 关于唐宋时期已有资本主义萌芽的历史事实 [Historical facts about the germination of capitalism in the Tang and Song dynasties]. *Shixue yuekan* 史学月刊 3 (1956): 13–14.

Kong, Jingwei 孔经纬. "Zhongguo fengjianshehuizhong zibenzhuyi mengya wenti zhi yanjiu" 中国封建社会中资本主义萌芽问题之研究 [The study of the germination of capitalism in the feudal society of China]. *Shixue yuekan* 史学月刊 2 (1955): 3–7.

Kosik, Karel. *Dialectics of the Concrete: A Study on Problems of Man and World*. D. Reidel, 1976.

Krausse, Alexis. *China in Decay: The Story of a Disappearing Empire*. 3rd ed. Chapman & Hill, 1900.

Kuhn, Philip. *Chinese Among Others: Emigration in Modern Times*. Rowan and Littlefield, 2008.

Kuhn, Philip. *Origins of the Modern Chinese State*. Stanford University Press, 2002.

Kuhn, Philip. *Rebellion and Its Enemies in Late Imperial China: Militarization and Social Structure, 1796–1864*. Harvard University Press, 1970.

Kuo, Huei-Ying. "Agency amid Incorporation: Chinese Business Networks in Hong Kong and Singapore and the Colonial Origins of the Resurgence of East Asia, 1800–1940." *Review* (Fernand Braudel Center) 32, no. 3 (2009): 211–37.

Kwŏn, Byŏksu. *Kŭndae hanjunggwan'gyesaŭi chaejomyŏng* [A reexamination of the modern history of Korea-China relations]. Hyeyan, 2007.

Kwon, Kyung-Seon. "Togil, ilbon chŏmnyŏnggi ch'ingdaoŭi sanŏpkujowa toshinodongja," [Industrial structure and urban workers in Qingdao During the German and Japanese occupations). In *Ch'ingdao: Shingmindoshiesŏ Ch'ogukchŏktoshi-ro* [Qingdao: From colonial city to transnational city], edited by Koo Jiyoung, Kwon Kyung-Seon, and Choi Nack-Min, 127–56. Sŏnin, 2014.

Kwon, Kyung-Seon. "Togil, ilbon chŏmnyŏnggi ch'ingdaoŭi toshigŏnsŏlgwa saenghwalgonggan" [Urbanism and living space in Qingdao during the German and Japanese occupations]. In *Ch'ingdao: Shingmindoshiesŏ Ch'ogukchŏktoshi-ro* [Qingdao: From colonial city to transnational city], edited by Koo Jiyoung, Kwon Kyung-Seon, and Choi Nack-Min, 75–107. Sŏnin, 2014.

Kwong, Peter. *Forbidden Workers: Illegal Chinese Immigrants and American Labor*. New Press, 1997.

Lachmann, Richard. *Capitalists in Spite of Themselves: Elite Conflict and Economic Transitions in Early Modern Europe*. Oxford University Press, 2000.

Ladds, Catherine. "China and Treaty-Port Imperialism." In *The Encyclopedia of Empire*, edited by N. Dalziel and J. M. Mackenzie, August 24, 2015. https://onlinelibrary.wiley.com/doi/epdf/10.1002/9781118455074.wbeoe079.

LaFeber, Walter. *The American Age: United States Foreign Policy at Home and Abroad Since 1750*. Norton, 1989.

Lai, Walton Look. "Asian Contact and Free Migration to the Americas." In *Coerced and Free Migration: Global Perspectives*, edited by David Eltis, 229–58. Stanford University Press, 2002.

Lai, Walton Look. *Indentured Labor, Caribbean Sugar: Chinese and Indian Migrants to the British West Indies, 1838–1918*. Johns Hopkins University Press, 1993.

Laitinen, Kauko. *Chinese Nationalism in the Late Qing Dynasty: Zhang Binglin as an Anti-Manchu Propagandist*. Curzon Press, 1990.

Lamb, Alastair. *British India and Tibet, 1766–1910*. Routledge & Kegan Paul, (1960) 1986.

Landes, Davis S. *Wealth and Poverty of Nations*. Little, Brown, 1998.

Landes, Davis S. "Why Europe and the West? Why Not China?" *Journal of Economic Perspectives* 20 (2006): 3–22.

Larsen, Kirk Wayne. "From Suzerainty to Commerce: Sino-Korean Economic and Business Relations During the Open Port Period (1876–1910)." PhD diss., Harvard University, 2000.

Larsen, Kirk Wayne. *Tradition, Treaties, and Trade: Qing Imperialism and Chosŏn Korea, 1850–1910*. Harvard University Press, 2008.

Lashari, Samee Ullah Khan. "From the Periphery to the Semi-Core: A World-System Analysis of the Fall and Rise of China and the Indian Sub-continent (1757–2014)." PhD diss., Northern Arizona University, 2017.

Lattimore, Owen. *Pivot of Asia: Sinkiang and the Inner Asian Frontier of China and Russia*. Little, Brown, 1950.

Lazich, Michael C. "Diffusion of Useful Knowledge in China: The Canton Era Information Strategy." In *Mapping Meanings: The Field of New Learning in Late Qing China*, edited by Michael Lackner and Natascha Vittinghoff, 305–27. Brill, 2004.

Le, Shui 乐水. "Xianggang Ceng Shi fanyun qiyue huagong de zhuyao gangkou" 香港曾是贩运契约华工的主要港口 [Hong Kong used to be a major port for the trafficking of indentured Chinese laborers]. *Bagui qiaoshi* 八桂侨刊 2 (1997): 11–12.

Lee, Chinyun. "From Kiachta to Vladivostok: Russian Merchants and Tea Trade." *Region* 3, no. 2 (2014): 195–218.

Lee, En-Han. *China's Quest for Railway Autonomy, 1904–1911*. Singapore University Press, 1977.

Lee, James, and Wang Feng. *One Quarter of Humanity: Malthusian Mythology and Chinese Reality*. Harvard University Press, 1999.

Lee, Kwangkuan. "'Getting Prices Right Again?' An Actor-Oriented World-Systems Approach to the Transformation of the South Korean Labor Regime, 1987–2010." PhD diss., State University of New York at Binghamton, 2012.

Lee, Minyong. "Circuits of Empire: The California Gold Rush and the Making of America's Pacific." PhD diss., University of Chicago, 2018.

Lee, Richard E., and Dale Tomich. "Method and Practice in World-Systems Analysis: An Introduction to the Collection." *Review* (Fernand Braudel Center) 39, no. 1 (2016): 1–12.

Lee, Robert. *France and the Exploitation of China: A Study in Economic Imperialism*. Oxford University Press, 1989.

Lee, Yang Ja. *Chosŏnesŏŭi wŏnsegae* [Yuan Shikai in Chosŏn]. Shinjisŏwŏn, 2002.

Lefebvre, Henri. *The Production of Space*. Translated by Donald Nicholson-Smith. Blackwell, 1991.

Lei, Bing Yan 雷炳炎. *Qingdai shehui baqi guizu shijia shili yanjiu* 清代社会八旗貴族世家勢力研究 [A study on the social power of the Eight Banners aristocratic families in the Qing regime]. Zhongguo Shehui kexue chubanshe, 2016.

Leo, Jessieca. *Global Hakka: Hakka Identity in the Remaking*. Brill, 2015.

Leonard, Jane Kate. *Wei Yuan and China's Rediscovery of the Maritime World*. Harvard University Press, 1984.

Leung, Philip Y. S. "The Tragic Passage to a New World: The Changing Views and Attitudes of Chinese Intellectuals toward the West in the Nineteenth Century." In *Modern China in Transition*, edited by Philip Yuen-sang Leung and Edwin Pak-wah Leung, 7–45. Regina Books, 1995.

Levenson, Joseph R. *Confucian China and Its Modern Fate*. University of California Press, 1968.

Lewis, Arthur W. *Growth and Fluctuations, 1870–1913*. George Allen & Unwin, 1978.

Li, Bozhong 李伯重. *Agricultural Development in Jiangnan, 1620–1850*. Macmillan, 1998.

Li, Bozhong 李伯重. Huo qiang yu zhang bu: Zao qi jing ji quan qiu hua shi dai de Zhongguo yu Dong Ya shi jie 火枪与 账簿: 早期经济全球化时代的中国与东亚世界 [Guns and ledgers: China and the East Asian world in the early era of economic globalization]. Sheng huo, du shu, xin zhi san lian shu dia, 2017.

Li, Bozhong 李伯重. "Zhongguo chuanguo shichang de xingcheng, 1500–1840" 中国全国市场的形成 1500–1840 [Formation of the national market in China, 1500–1840]. *Qinghua daxue xuebao* 清华大学学报 4 (1999): 48–54.

Li, Chen. "Law, Empire, and Historiography of Modern Sino-Western Relations: A Case Study of the *Lady Hughes* Controversy in 1784." *Law and History Review* 27, no. 1 (2009): 1–53.

Li, Hongzhang 李鸿章. *Lihongzhang quanji* 李鸿章全集 [The complete works of Li Hongzhang]. Vol. 6. Anhuijiaoyu chubanse, 2008.

Li, Hongzhang 李鸿章. *Li Wenxhong gong quan ji* 李文忠公全集 [The complete works of Li Hongzhang]. Vol. 16, edited by Wu Rulun. Wenhai chubanshe, 1962.

Li, Wei Qing 李维清. 1993. "Shanghai xiang tu zhi" 上海乡土志 [Chronicles of Shanghai]. In *Shanghai fengsu guji kao* 上海风俗古迹考 [A study of Shanghai customs and historic sites], edited by Go bing quan 顾炳权. Huadongshi fandaxue chubanshe, 1993.

Li, Wen Jie 李文杰. *Zhongguo jin dai wai jiao guan qun ti de xing cheng (1861–1911)*, 中国近代外交官群体的形成 (1861–1911) [The emergence of the modern Chinese diplomats]. Sanlianshudian, 2016.

Liang, Qichao 梁啓超. "Li Hong Zhang 李鴻章." In *Yin bingshi heji* 饮冰室合集 [Collected works of Yin Bing Shi]. Vol. 3. Zhonghuashuju, 1994.

Lim, Gyesun. *Chŏngsa-manjujoki t'ongch'ihan chungkuk* [Qing history: China under the rule of the Manchus]. Sinsŏwŏn, 2000.

Lin, Chun. "Marxism and the Politics of Positioning China in World History." *Inter-Asia Cultural Studies* 13, no. 3 (2012): 438–66.

Lin, Man-houng 林滿紅. *Cha tang zhangnao ye yu Taiwan zhi sheshui jingji bianqian 1860–1895* 茶、糖、樟腦業與台灣之社會經濟變遷 *(860–1895)* (The industries of tea, sugar, and camphor and socioeconomic change of Taiwan, 1860–1895]. Lien-ching Publishing, 1997.

Lin, Man-houng 林滿紅. "China's 'Dual Economy' in International Trade Relations, 1842–1949." In *Japan, China, and the Growth of the Asian International Economy, 1850–1949*, edited by in Kaoru Sugihara, 179–97. Oxford University Press, 2005.

Lin, Man-houng 林滿紅. *China Upside Down: Currency, Society, and Ideologies, 1808–1856*. Harvard University Press, 2006.

Lin, Pan. *English as a Global Language in China: Deconstructing the Ideological Discourses of English in Language Education*. W. W. Norton, 2014.

Lin, Sun. "Writing an Empire: An Analysis of the Manchu Origin Myth and the Dynamics of Manchu Identity." *Journal of Chinese History* 1 (2017): 93–109.

Lindsay, H. H. *Report of Proceedings on a Voyage to the Northern Ports of China, in the Ship Lord Amherst*. B. Fellows, 1833.

Lippit, Victor D. *Capitalism*. Routledge, 2005.

Litzinger, Charles A. "Patterns of Missionary Cases Following the Tientsin Massacre, 1870–1875." *Papers on China* (East Asian Research Center, Harvard University) 23 (1970): 87–108.

Liu, Andrew B. *Tea War: A History of Capitalism in China and India*. Yale University Press, 2020.

Liu, Kwang-Ching. *China's Early Modernization and Reform Movement*, vol. 1, *Studies in Late Nineteenth-Century China and American-Chinese Relations*. Edited by Yung-Fa Chen and Kuang-che Pan. Institute of Modern History, Academia Sinica, 2009.

Liu, Kwang-Ching. *China's Early Modernization and Reform Movement*, vol. 2, *Studies in Late Nineteenth-Century China and American-Chinese Relations*. Edited by Yung-Fa Chen and Kuang-che Pan. Institute of Modern History, Academia Sinica, 2009.

Liu, Lydia H. *The Clash of Empires: The Invention of China in Modern World Making*. Harvard University Press, 2006.

Liu, Lydia H. "Kŭlloböl hisŭt'ori yŏn'guŭi saeroun pangböp" [A new way to study global history]. In *Segyejilsŏwa munmyŏngdŭnggŭp* [The global order and the standard of civilization]. Translated by Ch'a T'aekŭn, 11–30. Gyoyudang Press, 2022.

Liu Min 刘敏. "Lunqingdaipengmindehujiwenti" 论清代棚民的户籍问题 [On the problem of the household registration of shack people in the Qing period]. *Zhongguo shehui jingjishi yanjiu* 中国社会经济史研究 1 (1983): 17–26.

Liu, Xiusheng 刘秀生. 1988. "Qingdaiminzheganwandepengminjingji" 清代闽浙赣皖的棚民经济 [The economy of shack people in the Fujian-Zhejiang-Jiangxi-Anhui Area in the Qing period]. *Zhongguo shehui jingjishi yanjiu* 中国社会经济史研究 1 (1988): 53–60.

Liu, Yong. *The Dutch East India Company's Tea Trade with China 1757–1781*. Brill, 2007.

Lorca, Arnulf Becker. "Universal International Law: Nineteenth-Century Histories of Imposition and Appropriation." *Harvard International Law Journal* 51, no. 2 (2010): 475–552.

Lu, Aiguo. *China and the Global Economy Since 1840*. Macmillan, 1999.

Lu, Hanchao. *Beyond the Neon Lights: Everyday Shanghai in the Early Twentieth Century*. University of California Press, 1999.

Lu, Weijing. "Beyond the Paradigm: Tea-Picking Women in Imperial China." *Journal of Women's History* 15, no. 4 (2004): 19–46.

Lutz, Jessie G. *Opening China: Karl F. A. Gützlaff and Sino-Western Relations, 1827–1852*. William B. Eerdmans, 2008.

Lyons, Thomas P. *China Maritime Customs and China's Trade Statistics, 1859–1948*. Willow Creek Press, 2003.

Ma, Debin. "Shanghai-Based Industrialization in the Early 20th Century: A Quantitative and Institutional Analysis." Working Papers of the Global Economic History Network (18/06), Department of Economic History, London School of Economics and Political Science, 2006. http://eprints.lse.ac.uk/22473/.

Ma, Jian Zhong 馬建忠. *Shikezhaijiyan* 适可斋记言 [Correspondence and memoranda from Prudence Room]. Zhonghuashuju, (1894) 1960.

Macartney, Robbins. *Our First Ambassador to China.* John Murray Macpherson, 1908.

MacPherson, Robert. "Antisystemic Movement Analysis." *Social Problems* 65 (2018): 491–515.

Madancy, Joyce A. *The Troublesome Legacy of Commissioner Lin: The Opium Trade and Opium Suppression in Fujian Province, 1820s to 1920s.* Harvard University Press, 2003.

Maddison, Angus. *Chinese Economic Performance in the Long Run.* 2nd ed. Paris: OECD, (1998) 2007.

Mahan, Captain A. T. "The United States Looking Outward." *The Atlantic*, 1890, https://www.theatlantic.com/magazine/archive/1890/12/the-united-states-looking-outward/306348/.

Maier, Charles. "Consigning the Twentieth Century to History: Alternative Narratives for the Modern Era." *American Historical Review* 105 (2000): 807–31.

Malozemoff, Andrew. *Russian Far Eastern Policy, 1881–1904—with Special Emphasis on the Causes of the Russo-Japanese War.* University of California Press, 1958.

Mancall, Mark. *China at the Center: 300 Years of Foreign Policy.* Free Press, 1984.

Mann, Michael. *The Autonomous Power of the State: Its Origins, Mechanisms and Results.* Basil Blackwell, 1986.

Mao, Haijian. *The Qing Empire and the Opium War: The Collapse of the Heavenly Dynasty.* Cambridge University Press, 2016.

Mao Tse-tung. "The Chinese Revolution and the Chinese Communist Party." In *Selected Works of Mao Tse-Tung, Volume II*, 305–34. Pergamon, 1965.

Marks, Robert B. *Tigers, Rice, Silk, and Silt: Environment and Economy in Late Imperial South China.* Cambridge University Press, 1998.

Marley, Benjamin J. "The Coal Crisis in Appalachia: Agrarian Transformation, Commodity Frontiers, and the Geographies of Capital." *Journal of Agrarian Change* 16, no. 2 (2016): 225–54.

Marmé, Michael. "From Suzhou to Shanghai: A Tale of Two Systems." *Journal of Chinese History* 2 (2018): 79–107.

Marsh, Robert M. "Weber's Misunderstanding of Traditional Chinese Law." *American Journal of Sociology* 106, no. 2 (2000): 281–302.

Martin, R. M. *China, Political, Commercial, and Social: In an Official Report to Her Majesty's Government, Volume 2.* J. Madden, 1847.

Martin, W. A. P. *A Cycle of Cathay.* 3rd ed. Fleming H. Revell, 1900.

Martin, William G. "Incorporation of Southern Africa, 1870–1920." *Review* (Fernand Bradel Center) 10, no. 5 (1987): 849–902.

Martin, William G. *Making Waves: Worldwide Social Movements, 1750–2005.* Paradigm, 2008.

Marx, Karl. *Capital Volume One.* Introduced by Ernest Mandel and translated by Ben Fowkes. Vintage, 1977.

Marx, Karl. "On Imperialism in India." In *The Marx-Engels Reader*, edited by Robert C Tucker, 653–64. W. W. Norton, 1978.

Marx, Karl. *The Poverty of Philosophy*. Foreign Languages Publishing House, 1954.
Marx, Karl. *Wage-Labour and Capital & Value, Price and Profit*. International Publishers, (1933) 1990.
Marx, Karl, and Friedrich Engels. *The Communist Manifesto*. Yale University Press, (1848) 2012.
Masoero, Alberto. "Russia Between Europe and Asia." In *The Boundaries of Europe: From the Fall of the Ancient World to the Age of Decolonisation*, edited by Pietro Rossi, 192–208. De Gruyter, 2015.
Matsusaka, Yoshihisa Tak. *The Making of Japanese Manchuria, 1904–1932*. Harvard University, Asia Center, 2001.
Mazumdar, Sucheta. "The Impact of New World Food Crops on the Diet and Economy of China and India, 1600–1900." In *Food in Global History*, edited by Raymond Grew, 58–78. Westview, 1999.
Mazumdar, Sucheta. *Sugar and Society in China: Peasants, Technology, and the World Market*. Harvard University Press, 1998.
McCarthy, Angela, and T. M. Devine. *Tea and Empire: James Taylor in Victorian Ceylon*. Manchester University Press, 2017.
McKay, Alex. "The British Invasion of Tibet, 1903–04." *Inner Asia* 14, no. 1 (2012): 5–25.
McKay, Alex. "Nineteenth-Century British Expansion on the Indo-Tibetan Frontier: A Forward Perspective." *Tibet Journal* 28, no. 4 (2003): 61–76.
McKeown, Adam. *Chinese Migrant Networks and Cultural Change: Peru, Chicago, Hawaii, 1900–1936*. University of Chicago, 2001.
McMahon, Daniel. *Rethinking the Decline of China's Qing Dynasty: Imperial Activism and Borderland Management at the Turn of the Nineteenth Century*. Routledge, 2015.
McMichael, Philip. "Incorporating Comparison within a World-Historical Perspective: An Alternative Comparative Method." *American Sociological Review* 55, no. 3 (1990): 385–97.
McMichael, Philip. "Pastoralism and Capitalist Development in Nineteenth-Century Australia: A Study of Settler Capital Accumulation." PhD diss., State University of New York at Binghamton, 1979.
McMichael, Philip. "World-Systems Analysis, Globalization, and Incorporating Comparison." *Journal of World-Systems Research* 6, no. 3 (2000): 68–99.
McNeill, William H. *The Pursuit of Power*. Basil Blackwell, 1982.
Meagher, Arnold J. *The Coolie Trade: The Traffic in Chinese Laborers to Latin America 1847–1874*. Xlibris, 2008.
Mei, June. "Socioeconomic Origins of Emigration: Guangdong to California, 1850 to 1882." In *Labor Immigration Under Capitalism: Asian Workers in the United States Before World War II*, edited by Lucie Cheng and Edna Bonacich, 219–45. University of California Press, 1984.
Meissner, Werner. "China's Search for Cultural and National Identity from the Nineteenth Century to the Present." *China Perspective* 68 (2006): 41–54.
Meng, S. M. *The Tsungli Yamen: Its Organization and Functions*. Harvard University Press, 1962.
Merritt, Jane T. *The Trouble with Tea: The Politics of Consumption in the Eighteenth-Century Global Economy*. Johns Hopkins University, 2017.
Metzger, Thomas A. "The Organizational Capabilities of the Ch'ing State in the Field of Commerce: The Liang-huai Salt Monopoly, 1740–1840." In *Economic Organization in Chinese Society*, edited by W. E. Willmott. Stanford University Press, 1972.

Meyer-Fong, Tobie. *Building Culture in Early Qing Yangzhou.* Stanford University Press, 2003.

Michie, Alexander. *The Englishman in China During the Victorian Era, Volume II.* William Blackwood and Sons, 1900.

Mielants, Eric H. *The Origins of Capitalism and the Rise of the West.* Temple University Press, 2007.

Mingteh, Tsou. "Christian Missionary as Confucian Intellectual: Gilbert Reid (1857–1917) and the Reform Movement in the Late Qing." In *Christianity in China: From the Eighteenth Century to the Present,* edited by Daniel H. Bays, 73–90. Stanford University Press, 1996.

Mintz, Sidney W. "Food and Concepts of Power." In *Food and Agrarian Orders in the World-Economy,* edited by Philip McMichael, 3–13. Praeger, 1995.

Mintz, Sidney W. "Food, Culture, and Energy." In *Food and Globalization: Consumption, Markets and Politics in the Modern World,* edited by Alexander Nützenadel and Frank Trentmann, 21–35. Berg, 2008.

Mintz, Sidney W. *Sweetness and Power: The Place of Sugar in Modern History.* Penguin, 1985.

Mo, Shixiang 莫世祥. "Gangao kuli maoyiyu yingpu lunzheng," 港澳苦力贸易与英葡论争 [Hong Kong and Macao's coolie trades and the dispute between Britain and Portugal]. *Guangzhou shehuikexue* 广东社会科学 2 (2016): 80–89.

Modelski, George. "The Long Cycle of Global Politics and the Nation-State." *Comparative Studies in Society and History* 20, no. 2 (1978): 214–35.

Moisio, Sami, and Anssi Paasi. "Beyond State-Centricity: Geopolitics of Changing State Spaces." *Geopolitics* 18 (2013): 255–66.

Mokyr, Joel. *The Lever of Riches: Technological Creativity and Economic Progress.* Oxford University Press, 1990.

Mokyr, Joel. "Why Was the Industrial Revolution a European Phenomenon?" *Supreme Court Economic Review* 10 (2003): 27–63.

Moore, Barrington, Jr. *Social Origins of Dictatorship and Democracy: Lord and Peasant in the Making of the Modern World.* Beacon Press, 1966.

Moore, Jason W. "Amsterdam Is Standing on Norway Part II: The Global North Atlantic in the Ecological Revolution of the Long Seventeenth Century." *Journal of Agrarian Change* 10, no. 2 (2010): 188–227.

Moore, Jason W. "Sugar and the Expansion of the Early Modern World-Economy: Commodity Frontiers, Ecological Transformation, and Industrialization." *Review* (Fernand Bradel Center) 23, no. 3 (2000): 409–33.

Morley, James W. *Sino-Japanese Relations 1862–1927: A Checklist of the Chinese Foreign Ministry Archives.* East Asian Institute, Columbia University, 1965.

Morse, Hosea Ballou. *The Chronicles of the East India Company Trading to China 1635–1834 Volume III.* Harvard University Press, 1926.

Morse, Hosea Ballou. *The International Relations of the Chinese Empire, Volume 1.* Paragon Book Gallery, 1900.

Morse, Hosea Ballou. *The Trade and Administration of China.* Longmans, Greens, (1908) 1920.

Mosca, Matthew W. *From Frontier Policy to Foreign Policy: The Question of India and the Transformation of Geopolitics in Qing China.* Stanford University Press, 2013.

Mote, Frederick W. "A Millennium of Chinese Urban History: Form, Time, and Space Concepts in Soochow." In "Four Views of China," edited by Robert A. Kapp. *Rice University Studies* 59, no. 4 (1973): 35–65.

Moulder, Frances V. *Japan, China, and the Modern World-Economy*. Cambridge University Press, 1977.
Munemitsu Mutsu. *Kenkenroku: A Diplomatic Record of the Sino-Japanese War, 1894–95*. Translated by Gordon Mark Berger. Princeton University Press, 1982.
Mungello, D. E. *The Great Encounter of China and the West, 1500–1800*. Rowman and Littlefield, 2005.
Murphey, Rhoads. "The Treaty Ports and China's Modernization." In *The Chinese City Between Two Worlds*, edited by Mark Elvin and G. William Skinner, 17–71. Stanford University Press, 1974.
Murphey, Rhoads. *The Treaty Ports and China's Modernization: What Went Wrong?* University of Michigan Papers in Chinese Studies 7, 1970.
Myers, Ramon H., and Wang Yeh-Chien. "Economic Development, 1644–1800." In *The Cambridge History of China*, vol. 9, pt. 1, *The Ch'ing Empire to 1800*, edited by Willard J Peterson, 563–646. Cambridge University Press, 2002.
Nagano, Akira. *Development of Capitalism in China*. Japan Council of the Institute of Pacific Relations. Tokyo, 1931.
Nan, Bingwen 南炳文. "Mingqingshiqi gudai zhongguoshehuide zhongjieliqi jiaoxun" 明清时期古代中国社会的终结及其教训 [Lessons from the end of ancient Chinese society in the Ming and Qing]. Henan Shifandaxue xuebao 河南师范大学学报 32, no. 6 (2005): 1–3.
Napier, Priscilla. *Barbarian Eye: Lord Napier in China, 1834: The Prelude to Hong Kong*. Brassey's, 1995.
Naquin Suan and Evelyn S. Rawski. *Chinese Society in the Eighteenth Century*. Yale University Press, 1987.
Narizny, Kevin. *The Political Economy of Grand Strategy*. Cornell University Press, 2007.
Nee, Victor, and James Peck. "Introduction: Why Uninterrupted Revolution?" In *China's Uninterrupted Revolution: From 1840 to the Present*, edited by Victor Nee and James Peck, 3–56. Pantheon, 1975.
Needham, Joseph. *Science and Civilization in China I*. Cambridge University Press, 1954.
Nelson, Benjamin. *On the Roads to Modernity: Conscience, Science, and Civilizations, Selected Writings by Benjamin Nelson*. Rowman and Littlefield, 1981.
Nester, William R. *Power Across the Pacific: A Diplomatic History of American Relations with Japan*. New York University Press, 1996.
Neu, Charels E. "Theodore Roosevelt and American Involvement in the Far East, 1901–1909." *Pacific Historical Review* 35, no. 4 (1966): 433–49.
New York Times. "American Ships and the Coolie Trade." *New York Times*, August 4, 1860. https://www.nytimes.com/1860/08/04/archives/american-ships-and-the-coolie-trade.html.
New York Times. "Chinese Coolie Mutinies." *New York Times*, October 10, 1870. https://www.nytimes.com/1870/10/10/archives/chinese-coolie-mutinies.html.
New York Times. "The Coolie and Slave Trade: Horrors of the Coolie-Trade a Legalized System of Free Chinese Emigration Important Dispatch from Lord John Russell." *New York Times*, August 16, 1860. https://www.nytimes.com/1860/08/16/archives/city-and-county-affairs-west-washington-market-the-case-not-decided.html.
New York Times. "Piracy and Murder—the Coolie Trade." *New York Times*, July 21, 1853. https://www.nytimes.com/1853/07/21/archives/piracy-and-murderthe-coolie-trade.html.

New York Times. "Victims Were Tortured; Gross Cruelties Inflicted on the Kucheng Missionaries." *New York Times*, August 5, 1895. https://www.nytimes.com/1895/08/05/archives/victims-were-tortured-gross-cruelties-inflicted-on-the-kucheng-miss.html.

Ng, Meliza, and Jade Lai King Wong. "Migration in Hong Kong: A Look into the Past at the Exhibition of the Chinese Overseas Collection at the Chinese University of Hong Kong." In *Chinese Overseas: Migration, Research, and Documentation*, edited by Tan Chee-Beng, Colin Storey, and Julia Zimmerman, 359–85. Chinese University Press, 2007.

Ngai, Mae. "Chinese Gold Miners and the 'Coolie Question' in Nineteenth-Century California and Victoria." *Journal of American History* 101, no. 4 (2015): 1082–1105.

Ngai, Mae. *The Chinese Question: The Gold Rushes, Chinese Migration, and Global Politics*. W. W. Norton, 2021.

Nierstrasz, Chris. *Rivalry for Trade in Tea and Textiles: The English and Dutch East India Companies (1700–1800)*. Palgrave Macmillan, 2015.

Noguchi, Masayoshi, and Trevor Boyns. "The South Manchuria Railway Company: An Accounting and Financial History, 1907–1943." March 15, 2013. https://www.rieb.kobe-u.ac.jp/academic/ra/dp/English/DP2013-08.pdf.

Nordyke, Eleanor C., and Richard K. C. Lee. "Chinese in Hawaii: A Historical and Demographic Perspective." *Hawaiian Journal of History* 23 (1989): 196–216.

Norman, E. H. *Origins of the Modern Japanese State*. Pantheon, 1975.

North, Douglass C., and Robert Paul Thomas. *The Rise of the Western World*. Cambridge University Press, 1973.

Northrup, David. *Indentured Labor in the Age of Imperialism, 1834–1922*. Cambridge University Press, 1995.

Novotný, Lukáš. "Great Britain, Germany, and the Selected Railway Problems in China, 1907–1908." *Prague Papers on the History of International Relations* 2 (2014): 85–111.

Nye, Gideon. *The Morning of My Life in China: Comprising an Outline of the History of Foreign Intercourse from the Last Year of the Regime of Honorable East India Company, 1833, to the Imprisonment of the Foreign Community in 1839*. Canton, 1873.

O'Brien, Patrick K. "The Pax Britannica and American Hegemony." In *Two Hegemonies: Britain 1846-1914 and the United States 1941-2001*, edited by Patrick Karl O'Brien and Armand Clesse, 3–64. Ashgate, 2002.

Omer-Cooper, J. D. *The Zulu Aftermath: A Nineteenth-Century Revolution in Bantu Africa*. Northwestern University Press, 1966.

Osborne, Anne. "Barren Mountains, Raging Rivers: The Ecological and Social Effects of Changing Land Use on the Lower Yangzi Periphery in Late Imperial China." PhD diss., Columbia University, 1989.

Osborne, Anne. "Highlands and Lowlands: Economic and Ecological Interactions in the Lower Yangzi Region under the Qing." In *Sediments of Time: Environment and Society in Chinese History*, edited by M. Elvin and L. Ts'ui-jung, 203–24. Cambridge University Press, 1998.

Osborne, Anne. "The Local Politics of Land Reclamation in the Lower Yangzi Highlands." *Late Imperial China* 15, no. 1 (1994): 1–46.

Osterhammel, Jürgen. "British Business in China, 1860s–1950s." In *British Business in Asia Since 1860*, edited by R. P. T. Davenport-Hinves and Geoffrey Jones, 189–216. Cambridge University Press, 1989.

Osterhammel, Jürgen. *The Transformation of the World: A Global History of the Nineteenth Century*. Translated by Patrick Camiller. Princeton University Press, 2014.

Paasi, Anssi. "Generations and the 'Development' of Border Studies." *Geopolitics* 10 (2005): 633–71.

Paige, Jeffery M. *Agrarian Revolution: Social Movements and Export Agriculture in the Underdeveloped World*. Free Press, 1975.

Paine, Lincoln. *The Sea and Civilization: A Maritime History of the World*. Knopf, 2013.

Paine, S. C. M. *The Sino-Japanese War of 1894–1895*. Cambridge University Press, 2003.

Palat, Ravi R. "Curries, Chopsticks, and Kiwis: Asian Migration to Aotearoa/New Zealand." In *Nga Patai: Racism and Ethnic Relations in Aotearoa*, edited by Paul Spoonley, David G. Pearson, and Cluny MacPherson, 35–54. Dunmore Press, 1996.

Palat, Ravi R. *The Making of an Indian Ocean World-Economy, 1250–1650: Princes, Paddy Fields, and Bazaars*. Palgrave Macmillan, 2015.

Palat, Ravi R. "Spatial Imaginaries of Capitalism: Dynamics of the Northeast Asian Regional Order." *Asian Perspective* 23, no. 2 (1999): 5–34.

Palmer, Thomas A. "Military Technology." In *Technology in Western Civilization*, vol. 1, *The Emergence of Modern Industrial Society, Earliest Times to 1900*, edited by Melvin Kranzberg and Carroll W. Pursell Jr., 489–502. Oxford University Press, 1967.

Palsetia, Jesse S. *Jamsetjee Jejeebhoy of Bombay: Partnership and Public Culture in Empire*. Oxford University Press, 2015.

Pan, Lynn. *Sons of the Yellow Emperor: A History of the Chinese Diaspora*. Kodansha International, 1994.

Parisot, James. 2017. "The Two Hundred and Fifty Year Transition: How the American Empire Became Capitalist." *Journal of Historical Sociology* 30, no. 3 (2017): 587–618.

Park Hun. *Meijiyushinŭn ŏttŏk'e kanŭnghaennŭn'ga* [How the Meiji Restoration came about]. Minŭmsa, 2014.

Park, Nancy E. "Corruption in Eighteenth-Century China." *Journal of Asian Studies* 56, no. 4 (1997): 967–1005.

Parsons, Talcott. *Structure and Process in Modern Societies*. Free Press, 1960.

Parthasarathi, Prasannan. *Why Europe Grew Rich and Asia Did Not*. Cambridge University Press, 2011.

Parthesius, Robert. *Dutch Ships in Tropical Waters: The Development of the Dutch East India Company (VOC) Shipping Network in Asia 1595–1660*. Amsterdam University Press, 2010.

Peck, James. "Revolution Versus Modernization and Revisionism: A Two-Front Struggle." In *China's Uninterrupted Revolution from 1840 to the Present*, edited by Victor Nee and James Peck, 57–217. Pantheon Books, 1975.

Peng, Jiali 彭家禮. "Shijiu shiji xifang qinluezhe dui zhongguo lugong di lulue" 十九世纪西方侵略者对中国劳工的掳掠 [The seizure of Chinese labor by Western invaders in the nineteenth century]. In *Huagong Chuguo Shi Ziliao Huibian* 華工出國史料匯編 [Collection of historical documents concerning the emigration of Chinese laborers]. Vol. 4, edited by Chen Hansheng 陈翰笙, 174–251. Zhonghua Shuju, 1981.

Perdue, Peter C. "Boundaries and Trade in the Early Modern World: Negotiations at Nerchinsk and Beijing." *Eighteenth-Century Studies* 43, no. 3 (2010): 341–56.

Perdue, Peter C. *China Marches West: The Qing Conquest of Central Eurasia*. Harvard University Press, 2005.

Perdue, Peter C. "Is Pu-er in Zomia? Tea Cultivation and the State in China." Agrarian Studies Colloquium, October 24, 2008. https://agrarianstudies.macmillan.yale.edu/sites/default/files/files/colloqpapers/07perdue.pdf.

Perkins, Dwight H. *Agricultural Development in China, 1368–1968*. Aldine, 1969.

Perkins, Dwight H. "China's Prereform Economy in World Perspective." In *China's Rise in Historical Perspective*, edited by Brantly Womack, 109–27. Rowman and Littlefield, 2010.

Perkins, Dwight H. *East Asian Development: Foundation and Strategies*. Harvard University Press, 2013.

Perry, Elizabeth J. *Rebels and Revolutionaries in North China, 1845–1945*. Stanford University Press, 1980.

Peterson, Willard J. "Early Nineteenth-Century Monetary Ideas on the Cash-Silver Exchange Ratio." In *Papers on China*, vol. 20, 23–48. East Asian Research Center, Harvard University, 1966.

Phillips, Peter D. "Incorporation of the Caribbean 1650–1700." *Review* (Fernand Braudel Center) 10, no. 5 (1987): 781–804.

Piketty, Thomas. *Capital in the Twenty-First Century*. Harvard University Press, 2014.

Platt, D. C. M. *Finance, Trade, and Politics: British Foreign Policy, 1815–1914*. Clarendon Press, 1968.

Platt, Stephen. *Imperial Twilight: The Opium War and the End of China's Last Golden Age*. Knopf, 2018.

Platt, Stephen. *Provincial Patriots: The Hunanese and Modern China*. Harvard University Press, 2007.

Po, Ronald C. "Tea, Porcelain, and Silk: Chinese Exports to the West in the Early Modern Period." *Oxford Research Encyclopedia of Asian History*, April 26, 2018. https://oxfordre.com/asianhistory/view/10.1093/acrefore/9780190277727.001.0001/acrefore-9780190277727-e-156.

Polanyi, Karl. *The Great Transformation*. Beacon, 1964.

Polk, James K. "James K. Pork's Special Message." February 10, 1847. https://www.presidency.ucsb.edu/documents/special-message-3254.

Pomeranz, Kenneth. *The Great Divergence: China, Europe, and the Making of the Modern World-Economy in the Asian Age*. University of California Press, 2000.

Pomeranz, Kenneth, and Steven Topik. *The World That Trade Created: Society, Culture, and the World Economy, 1400 to the Present*. Routledge, 2013.

Prakash, Om. "The Portuguese and the Dutch in Asian Maritime Trade: A Comparative Analysis." In *Merchants, Companies, and Trade: Europe and Asia in the Early Modern Era*, edited by S. Chaudhury and M. Morineau, 175–88. Cambridge University Press, 1999.

Pratt, Mary Louise. "Arts of the Contact Zone." *Profession* (1991): 33–40.

Pritchard, Earl H. *The Crucial Years of Early Anglo-Chinese Relations, 1750–1800*. Octagon Books, (1936) 1970.

Przeworski, Adam. "Proletariat into a Class: The Process of Class Formation from Karl Kautsky's *The Class Struggle* to Recent Controversies." *Politics and Society* 7, no. 4 (1977): 343–401.

Qian, Hong 钱宏. *Yapianzhanzheng Yiqian zhongguo ruogan shougongye bumen Zhong de zibenzhuyi mengya* 鸦片战争以前中国若干手工业部门中的资本主义萌芽 [The handicraft industries of Chinese capitalism's germination prior to the Opium War]. Shanghairenminchubanshe, 1956.

Qu, Xiaofan 曲曉范. *Chunggung tongbung chiyŏng toshisa yŏn'gu* [A study on the history of cities in Northeast China]. Translated by Piao you. Zininzin, 2016.

Quan Hexiu 权赫秀. *Jindai Zhonghanguanxi shiliao xuanbian* 近代中韩关系史料选编 [Selected historical materials on Sino-Korean relations in modern times]. Shujie zhishi chubanshe, 2008.

Rankin, Mary Backus. "Social and Political Change in Nineteenth-Century China." In *Historical Perspective on Contemporary East Asia*, edited by Merle Goldman and Andrew Gordon, 42–84. Harvard University Press, 2000.

Rappaport, Erika. *A Thirst for Empire: How Tea Shaped the Modern World*. Princeton University Press, 2017.

Rawski, Evelyn S. "The Non-Han Peoples in Chinese History." *East Asian Library Journal* 10, no. 1 (2001): 197–222.

Rawski, Evelyn S. "Presidential Address: Reenvisioning the Qing: The Significance of the Qing Period in Chinese History." *Journal of Asian Studies* 55, no. 4 (1996): 829–50.

Rawski, Evelyn S. "The Qing Empire During the Qianlong Reign." In *New Qing Imperial History: The Making of Inner Asian Empire at Qing Chengde*, edited by James A. Millward, Ruth W. Dunnell, Mark C. Elliott, and Philippe Forêt, 15–21. Routledge, 2004.

Rawski, Evelyn S. "The Qing Formation and the Early-Modern Period." In *The Qing Formation in World-Historical Time*, edited by Lynn A. Struve, 207–41. Harvard University Press, 2004.

Reinsch, Paul S. *World Politics: At the End of the Nineteenth Century*. Macmillan, 1900.

Reischauer, Edwin O. *Japan Past and Present*. 3rd ed., rev. Gerald Duckworth, (1946) 1964.

Reischauer, Edwin O., and Albert M. Craig. *Japan: Tradition and Transformation*. Houghton Mifflin, 1978.

Rhoads, Edward J. *Manchus and Han: Ethnic Relations and Political Power in Late Qing and Early Republican China, 1861–1928*. University of Washington Press, 2000.

Richards, John F. "The Opium Industry in British India." *Indian Economic and Social History Review* 39, nos. 2–3 (2002): 149–80.

Roberts, E. V., Ngai-long Sum, and Peter Bradshaw. *Historical Dictionary of Hong Kong and Macau*. Scarecrow Press, 1992.

Robinson, Ronald. "Non-European Foundations of European Imperialism: Sketch for a Theory of Collaboration." In *Studies in the Theory of Imperialism*, edited by Roger Owen and Bob Sutcliffe, 117–42. Longman, 1972.

Rodney, Walter. *How Europe Underdeveloped Africa*. Howard University Press, 1974.

Rosenbaum, Arthur Lewis. "Chinese Railway Policy and the Response to Imperialism: The Peking-Mukden Railway, 1895–1911." *Ch'ing-shih wen-t'i* 2, no. 1 (1969): 38–70.

Roth Li, Gertraude. "State Building Before 1644." In *The Cambridge History of China*, vol. 9, pt. 1, *The Ch'ing Empire to 1800*, edited by Willard J. Peterson, 9–72. Cambridge University Press, 2002.

Rowe, William T. *China's Last Empire: The Great Qing*. Harvard University Press, 2009.

Rowe, William T. *Hankow: Commerce and Society in a Chinese City, 1776–1889*. Stanford University Press, 1984.

Rowe, William T. "Introduction: City and Region in the Lower Yangzi." In *Cities of Jiangnan in Late Imperial China*, edited by L. C. Johnson, 1–16. State University of New York Press, 1993.

Rowe, William T. "Social Stability and Social Change." In *The Cambridge History of China*, vol. 9, pt. 1, *The Ch'ing Empire to 1800*, edited by Willard J Peterson, 473–562. Cambridge University Press, 2002.

Rowe, William T. *Speaking of Profit: Bao Shichen and Reform in Nineteenth-Century China*. Harvard University Press, 2018.

Ru, Sung Hee. "A Comparison of Weber's and Wallerstein's Historical Methods." *Journal of Asian Sociology* 52, no. 1 (2023): 33–64.

Ru, Sung Hee. "The Critical Appraisal of Existing Comparison Methods: Bringing the Connected Histories into Chinese Stagnation Studies." *Journal of Asian Sociology* 48, no. 2 (2019): 231–61.

Ru, Sung Hee. "Historical Geographies of Korea's Incorporation: The Rise of Underdeveloped and Modernized Colonial Port Cities." *Journal of Historical Geography* 76 (2022): 42–55.

Ru, Sung Hee. "Sorry, but G. Arrighi Is Not Almighty: Why Did He Fail to Explain China's Process of Incorporation into the Capitalist World-Economy?" *Journal of Asian Sociology* 49, no. 2 (2020): 253–80.

Rudolph, Jennifer Marie. "Negotiating Power and Navigating Change in the Qing: The Zongli Yamen, 1861–1901." PhD diss., University of Washington, 1999.

Ruskola, Teemu. "Colonialism Without Colonies: On the Extraterritorial Jurisprudence of the U.S. Court for China." *Law and Contemporary Problems* 71 (2008): 217–42.

Ryu, Jiwon. "Chŏngdae tongbukchŏngch'aegŭi pyŏnhwae ttarŭn manju toshi sŏnggyŏgŭi pyŏnhwa" [Historical geographic study of the modernization process in Manchuria]. In *Kŭndae manju toshi yŏksajiri yŏn'gu* [Historical geographic study of the modernization process in Manchuria], 18–63. Tongbugayŏksajaedan, 2007.

Sahlins, Marshall. "Cosmologies of Capitalism: The Trans-Pacific Sector of 'the World System.'" *Proceedings of the British Academy* 74 (1988): 1–51.

Sahlins, Peter. *Boundaries: The Making of France and Spain in the Pyrenees*. University of California Press, 1989.

Sanderson, Stephen K. *Social Transformations: A General Theory of Historical Development*. Rowman and Littlefield, 1999.

Sang, Law Wing. *Collaborative Colonial Power: The Making of the Hong Kong Chinese*. Hong Kong University Press, 2009.

Saunders, Peter. *Social Theory and the Urban Question*. 2nd ed. Hutchinson, 1986.

Schinz, Alfred. *Cities in China*. Gebrüder Bortraeger, 1989.

Schlesinger, Jonathan. *A World Trimmed with Fur: Wild Things, Pristine Places, and the Natural Fringes of Qing Rule*. Stanford University Press, 2017.

Schrecker, John. "The Reform Movement, Nationalism, and China's Foreign Policy." *Journal of Asian Studies* 29, no. 1 (1969): 43–53.

Schumpeter, Joseph. *Business Cycles*. Vol. 2. McGraw-Hill, 1939.

Schurz, William Lytle. *The Manila Galleon*. E. P. Dutton, 1939.

Schwartz, Benjamin. *In Search of Wealth and Power: Yen Fu and the West*. Harvard University Press, 1964.

Selden, Mark. "East Asia in World History, 1750–21st Century." In *The Cambridge World History*, vol. 7, *Production, Destruction, and Connection, 1750–Present*, edited by J. R. McNeill and Kenneth Pomeranz, 493–525. Cambridge University Press, 2015.
Sen, Tansen. *India, China, and the World: A Connected History*. Rowman and Littlefield, 2017.
Sewell, William H., Jr. "The Temporalities of Capitalism." *Socio-Economic Review* 6 (2008): 517–37.
Sewell, William H., Jr. "Three Temporalities: Toward an Eventful Sociology." In *The Historic Turn in the Human Sciences*, edited by T. J. McDonald, 245–80. University of Michigan Press, 1996.
Shang, Yue 尚钺. "Zhongguo zibenzhuyi shengchanyaosu de mengya jiqi zengzhang," 中国资本主义生 产因素的萌芽及其增长 [The germination of China's capitalist production factors and its growth]. *Lishiyanjiu* 历史研究 [Historical Research] 3 (1955): 85–133.
Share, Michael B. 2015. "The Great Game Revisited: Three Empires Collide in Chinese Turkestan (Xinjiang)." *Europe-Asia Studies* 67, no. 7 (2015): 1102–29.
Sharma, Jayeeta. 2009. "'Lazy' Natives, Coolie Labour, and the Assam Tea Industry." *Modern Asian Studies* 43, no. 6 (2009): 1287–1324.
Sherman, Lyon. *Sun Yat-Sen: His Life and Its Meaning*. Repr. 1938 ed. Stanford University Press, 1968.
Shi, Qi, and Zhuofen Fang. "Embryonic Capitalism in Agriculture." In *Chinese Capitalism, 1522–1840*, edited by X. Dixin and W. Chengming, 147–62. Macmillan, 2000.
Shiue, Carol H., and Wolfgang Keller. "Markets in China and Europe on the Eve of the Industrial Revolution." *American Economic Review* 97, no. 4 (2007): 1189–1216.
Sinn, Elizabeth. *Power and Charity: The Early History of the Tung Hua Hospital, Hong Kong*. Hong Kong University Press, 1989.
Skinner, G. William. "Chinese Cities: The Difference a Century Makes." In *Cosmopolitan Capitalists: Hong Kong and the Chinese Diaspora at the End of the 20th Century*, edited by Gary G. Hamilton, 56–79. University of Washington Press, 1999.
Skinner, G. William. "Regional Urbanization in Nineteenth-Century China." In *The City in Late Imperial China*, edited by William G. Skinner, 211–49. Stanford University Press, 1977.
Skocpol, Theda. "Social Revolution in France, Russia, and China: A Comparative-Historical and Structural Analysis." PhD diss., Harvard University, 1975.
Skocpol, Theda. *States and Social Revolutions: A Comparative Analysis of France, Russia, and China*. Cambridge University Press, 1979.
Smith, Adam. *An Inquiry into the Nature and Causes of the Wealth of Nations*. Clarendon, 1976.
Smith, Carl T. "The Emergence of a Chinese Elite in Hong Kong." *Journal of the Hong Kong Branch of the Royal Asiatic Society* 11 (1971): 74–115.
Smith, Jackie, and Dawn Wiest. *Social Movements in the World-System: The Politics of Crisis and Transformation*. Russell Sage, 2012.
Smith, Richard J. *The Qing Dynasty and Traditional Chinese Culture*. Rowman and Littlefield, 2015.
Snooks, Graeme Donald. "New Perspectives on the Industrial Revolution." In *Was the Industrial Revolution Necessary?*, edited by Graeme Donald Snooks, 1–26. Routledge, 1994.
So, Alvin Y. "The Process of Incorporation into the Capitalist World-System: The Case of China in the Nineteenth Century." *Review* (Fernand Braudel Center) 8, no. 1 (1984): 91–116.
So, Alvin Y. *Social Change and Development: Modernization, Dependency, and World-System Theory*. Sage, 1990.

So, Alvin Y. *The South China Silk District: Local Historical Transformation and World-System Theory*. State University of New York Press, 1986.
So, Alvin Y., and Stephen Chiu. *East Asia and World-Economy*. Sage, 1995.
Sombart, Werner. *Luxury and Capitalism*. Translated by W. R. Dittmar. University of Michigan Press, 1967.
Song Huijuan 宋慧娟. *Qing dai Zhong Chao zongfan guanxi shanbian yanjiu* 清代中朝宗藩關係嬗變研究 [Transformation of Sino-Korean tributary relations in the Qing dynasty]. Jilin daxue chubanshe, 2007.
Souza, G. B. "Convergence Before Divergence: Global Maritime Economic History and Material Culture." *International Journal of Maritime History* 17, no. 1 (2005): 17–28.
Spence, Jonathan D. *The Search for Modern China*. W. W. Norton, 1990.
Sprenkel, Sybille Van Dear. "Urban Social Control." In *The City in Late Imperial China*, edited by William G. Skinner, 609–32. Stanford University Press, 1977.
Statistical Department of the Inspectorate General of Customs. "Foochow Trade Report." In *Returns of Trade and Trade Reports*, vol. 4, *Southern Coast Ports*. Shanghai: Statistical Department of the Inspectorate General of Customs, 1905.
Steensgaard, Niels. *The Asian Trade Revolution of the Seventeenth Century: The East India Companies and the Decline of the Caravan Trade*. University of Chicago Press, 1974.
Steensgaard, Niels. "The Dutch East India Company as an Institutional Innovation." In *Dutch Capitalism and World Capitalism*, edited by Aymard Maurice, 235–57. Cambridge University Press, 1982.
Stein, Stanley J., and Barbara H. Stein. *Silver, Trade, and War: Spain and America in the Making of Early Modern Europe*. Johns Hopkins University Press, 2000.
Strenski, Ivan. "The Religion in Globalization." *Journal of the American Academy of Religion* 72, no. 3 (2004): 631–52.
Sturniolo, Anthony C. "Influences of Western Philosophy and Educational Thought in China and Their Effects on the New Culture Movement." Master's thesis, State University of New York at Buffalo, 2016.
Sugihara, Kaoru. "The East Asian Path of Economic Development: A Long-Term Perspective." In *The Resurgence of East Asia: 500, 150 and 50 Year Perspective*, edited by Giovanni Arrighi, Takeshi Hamashita, and Mark Selden, 78–123. Routledge, 2003.
Suh, Kyung-Ho. *Ap'yŏnjŏnjaeng* [The Opium War]. Ilchokak, 2020.
Sullivan, Dylan, and Jason Hickel. "Capitalism and Extreme Poverty: A Global Analysis of Real Wages, Human Height, and Mortality Since the Long 16th Century." *World Development* 161 (January 2023). https://doi.org/10.1016/j.worlddev.2022.106026.
Suzuki, Tomoo. "Shanghai Silk-Reeling Industry During the Period of the 1911 Revolution." In *The 1911 Revolution in China: Interpretive Essays*, edited by Eto Shinkichi and Harold Z, Schiffrin, 49–59. University of Tokyo Press, 1984.
Sweezy, Paul. "A Critique." In *The Transition from Feudalism to Capitalism*, edited by R. H. Hilton, 33–67. Verso, (1976) 1992.
Tao, De-Chen 陶德臣. "Lun qing dai cha ye mao yi de she hui ying xian" 论清代茶叶贸易的社会影响 [The social influence of the tea trade in the Qing dynasty]. *Shixuiyuekan* 史学月刊 5 (2002): 90–95.
Teng, Emma Jinhua. *Taiwan's Imagined Geography: Chinese Colonial Travel Writing and Pictures, 1683–1895*. Harvard University Press, 2004.

Teng, S. Y., and John K. Fairbank. *China's Response to the West: A Documentary Survey, 1839-1923*: Harvard University Press, (1954 1979.
Terent'yev, M. A. *Russia and England in Central Asia. Volume 2*. Routledge, 1876.
The Gentry and People. *Death Blow to Corrupt Doctrines: A Plain Statement of Facts*. Shanghai, 1870.
The Spectator: A Weekly Journal of News, Politics, Literature, and Science. Vol. 13, 1840.
Thilly, Peter. *The Opium Business: A History of Crime and Capitalism in Maritime China*. Stanford University Press, 2022.
Thomas, Stephen C. *Foreign Investment and China's Industrial Development, 1870-1911*. Westview, 1984.
Thompson, E. P. *The Making of The English Working Class*. Victor Gollancz, (1963) 1980.
Thompson, Ralph Wardlaw. *Griffith John: The Story of Fifty Years in China*. Religious Tract Society, 1906.
Tilly, Charles. *Big Structures, Large Processes, Huge Comparisons*. Russell Sage, 1984.
Tilly, Charles. *Coercion, Capital, and European States, AD 990-1990*. Basil Blackwell, 1990.
Tilly, Charles. *Roads from Past to Future*. Rowman and Littlefield, 1997.
Tilly, Charles. "War Making and State Making as Organized Crime." In *Bringing the State Back In*, edited by Peter Evans, Dietrich Rueschemeyer, and Theda Skocpol, 169–87. Cambridge University Press, 1985.
Tomich, Dale W. *Slavery in the Circuit of Sugar: Martinique and the World-Economy, 1830-1848*. 2nd ed. State University of New York Press, 2016.
Torgasheff, Boris P. *China as a Tea Producer*. Commercial Press, 1926.
Torr, Dona, ed. *Marx on China 1853-1860: Articles from the New York Daily Tribune*. Lawrence and Wishart, 1968.
Trocki, Carl A. *Opium, Empire and the Global Political Economy: A Study of the Asian Opium Trade 1750-1950*. Routledge, 1999.
Trotsky, Leon. *The History of the Russian Revolution*. Pluto, (1933) 1977.
Tsai, Shih-shan Henry. *China and the Overseas Chinese in the United States, 1868-1911*. University of Arkansas Press, 1983.
Tseng, Marquis [Zeng Jize]. "China: The Sleep and the Awakening." *Chinese Recorder* 18 (1887): 146–53.
Turner, Frederic Jackson. *The Frontier in American History*. Holt, Rinehart and Winston, 1962.
Urbansky, Sören. *Beyond the Steppe Frontier: A History of the Sino-Russian Border*. Princeton University Press, 2020.
Van, Tamar Rachel. "Cents and Sensibilities: Fairness and Free Trade in the Early 19th Century." *Diplomatic History* 42, no. 1 (2018): 72–89.
Van Dijk, Kees. *Pacific Strife: The Great Powers and Their Political and Economic Rivalries in Asia and the Western Pacific, 1870-1914*. Amsterdam University Press, 2015.
Varg, Paul A. *Missionaries, Chinese, and Diplomats: The American Protestant Missionary Movement in China, 1890-1952*. Princeton University Press, 1958.
Varma, Nitin. *Coolies of Capitalism: Assam Tea and the Making of Coolie Labour*. De Gruyter Oldenbourg, 2017.
Varma, Nitin. *Producing Tea Coolies? Work, Life, and Protest in the Colonial Tea Plantations of Assam, 1830s-1920s*. Humboldt-Universität, 2011.

Von Glahn, Richard. *The Economic History of China: From Antiquity to the Nineteenth Century.* Cambridge University Press, 2016.
Von Glahn, Richard. "Money Use in China and Changing Patterns of Global Trade in Monetary Metals, 1500–1800." In *Monetary History in Global Perspective, 1500–1808: B6 Proceedings, Twelfth International Economic History Congress,* edited by Clara Eugenia Nunex, 51–59. Universidad de Sevilla, 1998.
Vries, Peer. *State, Economy and the Great Divergence: Great Britain and China, 1680s–1850s.* Bloomsbury, 2015.
Wakeman, Frederic, Jr. "The Canton Trade and the Opium War." In *The Cambridge History of China,* vol. 10, pt. 1, *Late Ch'ing, 1800–1911,* edited by Denis Twitchett and John K. Fairbank, 163–212. Cambridge University Press, 1978.
Wakeman, Frederic, Jr. *The Fall of Imperial China.* Free Press, 1975.
Wakeman, Frederic, Jr. *The Great Enterprise,* vol. 1, *The Manchu Reconstruction of Imperial Order in Seventeenth-Century China.* University of California Press, 1985.
Wakeman, Frederic, Jr. "The Secret Societies of Kwangtung, 1800–1856." In *Popular Movements and Secret Societies in China 1840–1950,* edited by Jean Chesneaux, 29–47. Stanford University Press, 1972.
Wakeman, Frederic, Jr. *Strangers at the Gate: Social Disorder in South China, 1839–1861.* University of California Press, 1966.
Wakeman, Frederic, Jr., and Yeh Wen-hsin. Introduction to *Shanghai Sojourners,* edited by Frederic Wakeman and Wen-hsin Yeh, 1–14. University of California Press, 1992.
Waley, Arthur. *The Opium War Through Chinese Eyes.* Stanford University Press, 1958.
Waley-Cohen, Joanna. "Commemorating War in Eighteenth-Century China." *Modern Asian Studies* 30, no. 4 (1996): 869–99.
Waley-Cohen, Joanna. "The New Qing History." *Radical History Review* 88 (2004): 193–206.
Walker, Richard A. "Two Sources of Uneven Development Under Advanced Capitalism: Spatial Differentiation and Capital Mobility." *Review of Radical Political Economics* 10, no. 3 (1978): 28–37.
Walker, R. J. E. "Shao-Wu in Fuh-Kien: A Country Station." *Chinese Recorder and Missionary Journal* 9, no. 5 (1878): 343–52.
Wallerstein, Immanuel. "Antisystemic Movements: History and Dilemmas." In *Transforming the Revolution: Social Movements and the World-System,* edited by Samir Amin, Giovanni Arrighi, Andre Gunder Frank, and Immanuel Wallerstein, 13–53. Monthly Review, 1990.
Wallerstein, Immanuel. "Braudel on Capitalism, or Everything Upside Down." *Journal of Modern History* 63, no. 2 (1991): 354–61.
Wallerstein, Immanuel. "Class and Class Conflict in Africa." *Monthly Review* 26, no. 9 (1975): 34–42.
Wallerstein, Immanuel. "Class Conflict in the Capitalist World-Economy." In *The Capitalist World-Economy: Essays by Immanuel Wallerstein,* 283–93. Cambridge University Press, 1979.
Wallerstein, Immanuel. "Class-Formation in the Capitalist World-Economy." *Politics and Society* 5, no. 3 (1975): 367–75.
Wallerstein, Immanuel. "Dependence in an Interdependent World: The Limited Possibilities of Transformation Within the Capitalist World-Economy." In *The Capitalist World-Economy: Essays by Immanuel Wallerstein,* 66–94. Cambridge University Press, 1979.

Wallerstein, Immanuel. *European Universalism: The Rhetoric of Power*. New Press, 2006.
Wallerstein, Immanuel. "From Feudalism to Capitalism: Transition or Transitions?" In *The Capitalist World-Economy: Essays by Immanuel Wallerstein*, 138–51. Cambridge University Press, 1979.
Wallerstein, Immanuel. *Historical Capitalism with Capitalist Civilization*. Verso, 1983.
Wallerstein, Immanuel. "Incorporation of Indian Subcontinent into Capitalist World-Economy." *Economic and Political Weekly* 21, no. 4 (1986): 28–39.
Wallerstein, Immanuel. *The Modern World-System I: Capitalist Agriculture and the Origins of the European World-Economy in the Sixteenth Century*. Academic Press, 1974.
Wallerstein, Immanuel. *The Modern World-System III: The Second Era of Great Expansion of the Capitalist World-Economy, 1730s–1840s*. Academic Press, 1989.
Wallerstein, Immanuel. *The Modern World-System IV: Centrist Liberalism Triumphant, 1789–1914*. University of California Press, 2011.
Wallerstein, Immanuel. *The Politics of the World-Economy: The States, the Movements and the Civilizations*. Cambridge University Press, 1984.
Wallerstein, Immanuel. "The Present State of the Debate on World Inequality." In *The Capitalist World-Economy: Essays by Immanuel Wallerstein*, 49–65. Cambridge University Press, 1979.
Wallerstein, Immanuel. "Reflections on an Intellectual Adventure in Special Symposium on the Modern World-System, Vol. I–IV." *Contemporary Sociology* 41, no. 1 (2012): 6–9.
Wallerstein, Immanuel. "The Rise and Future Demise of the World Capitalist System: Concepts for Comparative Analysis." *Comparative Studies in Society and History* 16, no. 4 (1974): 387–415.
Wallerstein, Immanuel. *Unthinking Social Science: The Limits of Nineteenth-Century Paradigms*. 2nd ed. Temple University Press, 2001.
Wallerstein, Immanuel. "The West, Capitalism, and the Modern World-System." In *China and Historical Capitalism*, edited by Timothy Brook and Gregory Blue, 10–56. Cambridge University Press, 1999.
Wallerstein, Immanuel. *World-Systems Analysis: An Introduction*. Duke University Press, 2004.
Wallerstein, Immanuel. "World-Systems Analysis: Theoretical and Interpretative Issues." In *World Systems Analysis: Theory and Methodology*, by Terence K. Hopkins and Immanuel Wallerstein, 91–103. Sage, 1982.
Wallerstein, Immanuel. "World System Versus World-Systems: A Critique." *Critique of Anthropology* 11, no. 2 (1991): 189–94.
Wan, Ming. "The Monetarization of Silver in China: Ming China and Its Global Interactions." In *China's Development from a Global Perspective*, edited by M. D. Elizalde and J. Wang, 274–96. Cambridge Scholars Publishing, 2017.
Wang, Fang Zhong 王方中. *Zhong guo jin dai jing ji shi gao (1840 nian–1927 nian)* 中國近代經濟史稿 *(1840 年–1927 年)* [The economic history of modern China]. Beijing chubanshe, 1982.
Wang, Gunageu. "'Public' and 'Private' Overseas Trade in Chinese History." In *Sociétés et companies de commerce en orient at dans l'Océan Indien*, edited by M. Mollat, 215–25. SEVPEN, 1970.
Wang, Gungwu. "Merchants Without Empire: The Hokkien Sojourning Communities." In *The Rise of Merchant Empires: Long-Distance Trade in the Early Modern World, 1350–1750*, edited by in James D. Tracy, 400–421. Cambridge University Press, 1990.

Wang, Jianlang. *Unequal Treaties and China*. Silkroad Press, 2016.
Wang, Jingyu 汪敬虞. *Zhungguo Jindai Jingjishi 1895–1927* 中国近代经济史, 1895–1927 [Modern Chinese economic history, 1895–1927]. Renminchubanshe, 1998.
Wang Mingxing 王明星. *Hanguo jindai waijiao yu zhongguo 1861–1910* 韩国近代外交与中国, 1861–1910 [Modern Korean diplomacy and China, 1861–1910]. Zhongguo shehui kexue chubanshe, 1998.
Wang, Weijian 王维俭. "Pudandagu kou chuan bo shi jian yu xi fang guo ji fa chuan ru zhongguo," 普丹大沽口船舶事件和西方国际法传入中国 [Daguou's ship incident between Prussia-Denmark and China's acceptance of the West's international laws]. *Xueshuyanjiu* 学术研究 5 (1985): 84–90.
Wang, Wensheng. *White Lotus Rebels and South China Pirates*. Harvard University Press, 2014.
Wang, Xi. "Approaches to the Study of Modern Chinese History: External Versus Internal Causations." In *China's Quest for Modernization: A Historical Perspective*, edited by Frederic Wakeman Jr. and Wang Xi, 1–21. University of California Press, 1997.
Wang, Xiuyu. *China's Last Imperial Frontier: Late Qing Expansion in Sichuan's Tibetan Borderlands*. Lexington Books, 2011.
Wang, Yeh-chien. *Land Taxation in Imperial China, 1750–1911*. Harvard University Press, 1973.
Ward, J. R. "The Industrial Revolution and British Imperialism, 1750–1850." *Economic History Review* 47, no. 1 (1994): 44–65.
Warner, John. *Fragrant Harbor: Early Photographs of Hong Kong*. 3rd ed. John Warner, 1979.
Washbrook, David. "South Asia, the World System and World Capitalism." In *South Asia and World Capitalism*, edited by Sugata Bose, 40–84. Oxford University Press, 1990.
Weber, Max. *The City*. Edited by Don Martindale and Gertrud Neuwirth. Free Press, 1958.
Weber, Max. *Economy and Society*. Translated by Guenther Roth and Claus Wittich. University of California Press, (1922) 1978.
Weber, Max. *Economy and Society*. Volume 3. Translated by Guenther Roth and Claus Wittich. Bedminster Press, 1968.
Weber, Max. *From Max Weber*. Edited by H. H. Gerth and C. W. Mills. Oxford University Press, 1958.
Weber, Max. *Methodology of Social Sciences*. Edited by Edward A. Shils and Henry A. Finch. Free Press, 1949.
Weber, Max. *The Protestant Ethic and the Spirit of Capitalism*. Routledge, 2001.
Weber, Max. *The Religion of China: Confucianism and Taoism*. 1915. Edited by Hans H. Gerth. Free Press, 1951.
Wei, Betty Peh-t'I. *Shanghai: Crucible of Modern China*. Oxford University Press, 1987.
Wei, Yuan 魏源. "Guweitang Waiji" 古微堂外集. In *Weiyuan quanji* 魏源全集 [Complete works of Wei Yuan]. Vol. 12. Yuelu shushe, 2004.
Wei, Yuan 魏源. *Haiguo Tuzhi* 海國圖志 [Illustrated treatise on the maritime kingdoms]. Vol. 2, edited by Chen Hua 陈华 et al. Yuelu shushe chubanshe, 1998.
Weiss, Linda, and John M. Hobson. *States and Economic Development: A Comparative Historical Analysis*. Polity, 1995.
Wells, Richard Evan. "The Manchurian Bean: How the Soybean Shaped the Modern History of China's Northeast, 1862–1945." PhD diss., University of Wisconsin–Madison, 2018.

Westad, Odd Arne. *Restless Empire: China and the World Since 1750*. Basic Books, 2012.

Westminster Review. July 1873.

Westney, E. D. *Imitation and Innovation: The Transfer of Western Organizational Patterns to Meiji Japan*. Harvard University Press, 1987.

Wheaton, Henry. *Elements of International Law*. 8th ed. Edited by Richard Henry Dana Jr. Little, Brown, and Company, 1866.

White, Lynn, Jr. "What Accelerated Technological Progress in the Western Middle Ages?" In *Scientific Change*, edited by A. C. Crombie, 272–91. Basic Books, 1963.

Wickberg, Edgar. "Organization of Overseas Migration." In *Cosmopolitan Capitalists: Hong Kong and the Chinese Diaspora at the End of the 20th Century*, edited by Gary G. Hamilton, 35–55. University of Washington Press, 1999.

Willetts, William. "The Maritime Adventures of the Great Eunuch Ho." In *Papers on Early South-East Asian History*, edited by Colin Jack-Hinton, 25–42. Journal of Southeast Asian History, 1964.

Williams, Eric. *Capitalism and Slavery*. University of North Carolina Press, (1944) 1994.

Wilson, Sandra. "The Discourse of National Greatness in Japan 1890–1919." *Japanese Studies* 25, no. 1 (2005): 35–51.

Wolf, Eric R. *Europe and the People Without History*. University of California Press, 1982.

Wolf, Eric R. *Peasant Wars of the Twentieth Century*. University of Oklahoma Press, 1969.

Wong, J. W. *Anglo-Chinese Relations 1839–1860: A Calendar of Chinese Documents in the British Foreign Office Records*. Oxford University Press, 1983.

Wong, Roy Bin. "China and World History." *Late Imperial China* 6, no. 2 (1985): 1–11.

Wong, Roy Bin. *China Transformed*. Cornell University Press, 1997.

Woodside, Alexander. "The Centre and the Borderlands in Chinese Political Theory." In *The Chinese State at the Borders*, edited by Diana Lary, 11–28. University of British Columbia Press, 2007.

Wray, Leonard. *The Practical Sugar Planter: A Complete Account of the Cultivation and Manufacture of the Sugar Cane According to the Latest and Most Improved Processes*. Smith, Elder and Company, 1848.

Wright, Arnold. *Twentieth Century Impressions of Hongkong, Shanghai, and Other Treaty Ports*. Lloyd, 1908.

Wright, Mary C. "The Adaptability of Ch'ing Diplomacy: The Case of Korea." *Journal of Asian Studies* 17, no. 3 (1958): 363–81.

Wrigley, E. A. *Continuity, Chance, and Change: The Character of the Industrial Revolution in England*. Cambridge University Press, 1988.

Wrigley, E. A. "Urban Growth and Agricultural Change: England and the Continent in the Early Modern Period." *Journal of Interdisciplinary History* 15, no. 4 (1985): 683–728.

Wu Baosan 巫寶三, Feng Ze 馮澤, and Wu Chaolin 吳朝林. *Zhongguo jin dai jing ji si xiang yu jing ji zheng ce zi liao xuan ji, 1840–1864* 中国近代經濟思想与經濟政策資料選輯 [Selected writings on China's modern economic thinking and economic policies, 1840–1864]. Ke xue chu ban she, 1959.

Wu, Jie 吳傑. *Zhongguo jin dai guo min jing ji shi* 中国近代国民經濟史 [The national economy of modern China]. Renminchubanshe, 1958.

Wu, Juenong 吴觉农. *Zhongguo difangzhi chaye lishi ziliao xuanji* 中国地方志茶叶历史资料选辑 [Selection of historical materials on tea from Chinese local gazetteers]. Nongye chubanshe, 1990.

Wu, Li-Wei 吴莉苇. 18 shijiou renyan lide qingchao guojia xingzhi—cong <zhonghuadiguoquanzhi> dui xinan shaoshu minzhu de miaoshu tanqi 18世纪欧人眼里的清朝国家性质—从《中华帝国全志 》对西南少数民族的描述谈起 [European views of the nature of Qing government in the eighteenth century: Some notes on Du Halde's description of non-Han groups in Southwest China]. *Qingshiyanjiu* 清史研究, no. 2 (2007): 28–38.

Xiang, Lanxin. *The Origins of the Boxer War: A Multinational Study*. Routledge, 2003.

Xing, Fang. "The Role of Embryonic Capitalism in China." In *Chinese Capitalism, 1522–1840*, edited by Xu Dixin and Wu Chengming, 402–29. Macmillan, 2000.

Xu, Feng 徐峰 "Shangye yu jindaizhongguo chengshihuade qidong, 1840–1895 商业与近代中国城市化 的启动, 1840–1895) [Trade and the start of urbanization in modern China, 1840–1895]. *Beifangluncong* 北方论丛 2 (2008): 78–82.

Xu Jiyu 徐继畲. *Yinghuan zhilue* 瀛環志略 [A short account of the maritime circuit]. Vol. 9. 1848.

Xu, Yanghui 徐揚绘 and Yang Dongsheng 杨东胜. *Gusu fanhua tu* 姑苏繁华图 [A picture of the flourishing Suzhou City in the eighteenth century]. Tianjin Renmin meishu chubanshe, (1753) 2009.

Yamaguchi, Keiji. *Ilbon'gŭnseŭi Swaegukkwa Kaeguk* [Closed-door policies and the opening of Japan in modern times]. Translated by Kimhyŏnyŏng. Hyean, 2001.

Yamamura, Kozo. "Success Ill-Gotten? The Role of Meiji Militarism in Japan's Technological Progress," *Journal of Economic History* 37, no. 1 (1977): 113–35.

Yamamuro, Shin'ichi. *Manchuria Under Japanese Dominion*. Translated by Joshua A. Fogel. University of Pennsylvania Press, 2006.

Yan, Chongnian 阎崇年. *Nuerhachizhuan* 努尔哈赤传 [A bibliography of Nurhachi]. Beijing Chubanshe, 1983.

Yan, Zhongping, et al. 嚴中平 等著. *Zhongguo jindai jingjishi tongji zhliao xuanji* 中國近代經濟史統計資料選輯 [Selected statistics of modern Chinese economic history]. Kexuechubanshe, 1955.

Yang, Daqing. "Colonial Korea in Japan's Imperial Telecommunication Network." In *Colonial Modernity in Korea*, edited by Gi-Wook Shin and Michael Robinson, 161–88. Harvard University Press, 2000.

Yang, Laiqing, and Baofeng Sun. "20segi ch'o ch'ingdao ilbonin sahoeŭi hyŏngsŏnggwa pyŏnch'ŏn" [The formation and transformation of Japanese society in Qingdao in the early 20th century]. In *Ch'ingdao: Shingmindoshiesŏ Ch'ogukchŏktoshi-ro* [Qingdao: From colonial city to transnational city], edited by Koo Jiyoung, Kwon Kyung-Seon, and Choi Nack-Min, 157–77. Sŏnin, 2014.

Yang She Lian 杨余练 et al. *Qingdai dongbei shi* 清代东北史 [History of northeast China during the Qing dynasty]. Liaoning jiaoyu chubanshe, 1991.

Yang, Young Jin. "Durkheim and Weber: Two Approaches to the Study of Religion and Society." PhD diss., University of Chicago, 1986.

Yang, Zewei. "Western International Law and China's Confucianism in the Nineteenth Century: Collision and Integration." *Journal of the History of International Law* 13 (2011): 285–306.

Yang, Zhuo 楊焯. "Cong「yousi」dao「shuren」: "right" zai <wanguogongfa>zhongdefanyi" 從

「有司」到「庶人」:" right" 在《萬國公法》中的翻譯 [From the right of "the superior" to the right of the "general public": The translation of "right" in the Wanguogongfa]. *Bianyi luncong* 編譯論叢 7, no. 1 (2014): 213–34.

Yee, D. Cordell. "Traditional Chinese Cartography and the Myth of Westernization." In *Cartography in Traditional East and Southeast Asian Societies*, edited by John B. Harley and David Woodward, 170–222. University of Chicago Press, 1994.

Yeh, Catherine Vance. "Representing the City: Shanghai and Its Maps." In *Town and Country in China: Identity and Perception*, edited by David Faure and Tao Tao Liu, 166–202. Palgrave, 2002.

Yen, Ching-huang [Yan Qinghuang]. *Coolies and Mandarins: China's Protection of Overseas Chinese During the Late Ch'ing Period (1815-1911)*. Singapore University Press, 1985.

Yeung, Y. M., and David K. Y. Chu. *Fujian: A Coastal Province in Transition and Transformation*. Chinese University Press, 2000.

Yifenwenji 夷氛闻记 [The records of the barbarians' rise]. Vol. 4. Zhonghuashuju, 1959.

Yin, Zhiguang. "Heavenly Principles? The Translation of International Law in Nineteenth Century China and the Constitution of Universality." *European Journal of International Law* 27, no. 4 (2016): 1005–23.

Yip, Liping Wong. *From Wah Lee to Chew Keen: The Story of a Pioneer Chinese Family in North Cariboo*. Friesen Press, 2017.

Yoon, Hwytak. *Manjuguk: Shingminjijŏng sangsangi ingt'aehan pok'amminjokkukka* [Manchukuo: The sun of a new nation]. Hyean, 2013.

Yoshinobu, Shiba. *Chunggukdosisa* [History of Chinese cities]. Translated by Im Dahŭi and Sin T'aekap. *Sŏkyŏngmunhwasa, 2008.*

Yü, Ying-shih. *The Religious Ethic and Mercantile Spirit in Early Modern China*. Columbia University Press, 2021.

Yue, Bang. "Ch'amuyŏki chŏngnarae mich'in younghyang" [The tea trade's impacts on the Qing empire]. Master's thesis, Pusan University, 2013.

Yue, Meng. "Re-envisioning the Great Interior: Gardens and the Upper Class Between the Imperial and the 'Modern.'" *Modern Chinese Literature and Culture* 14, no. 1 (2002): 1–49.

Yun, Lisa. *The Coolie Speaks: Chinese Indentured Laborers and African Slaves of Cuba*. Temple University Press, 2008.

Yun, Lisa, and Ricardo Rene Laremont. "Chinese Coolies and African Slaves in Cuba, 1847–74." *Journal of Asian American Studies* 4, no. 2 (2001): 99–122.

Yun, Sang'u. "Beijing kŏnsensŏsŭ pip'an: Ramo wa Aligi ŭi nonŭi rŭl chungsim ŭro" [A critical review of the 'Beijing Consensus': Focusing on Ramo's and Arrighi's arguments]. *Yurasia yŏn'gu* 11, no. 4 (2014): 176–87.

Zarrow, Peter Gue. *After Empire: The Conceptual Transformation of the Chinese State, 1885–1924*. Stanford University Press, 2012.

Zevin, Robert B. "The Growth of Cotton Textile Production after 1815." In *The Reinterpretation of American Economic History*, edited by Robert W. Fogel and Stanley L. Engerman, 122–47. Harper and Row, 1971.

Zhan, Shaohua. *The Land Question in China: Agrarian Capitalism, Industrious Revolution, and East Asian Development*. Routledge, 2019.

Zhang Liheng 张礼恒. "Ping jiawu zhan zheng qian qing zheng fu de dui chao zhengce" 评甲午战争前清政府的对朝政策 [The Qing's policy on Korea before the First Sino-Japanese War]. *Anhui shixue* 安徽史学 [Anhui Historiography] 2 (1993): 51–54.

Zhang, Xianqing 张显清. "Wanming shehuibianqian yu zhongguo zaoqi jindaihua" 晚明社会变迁与中国早期近代化 [Social changes in the late Ming dynasty and China's early modernization]. *Hebei xuekan* 河北学刊 28, no. 1 (2008): 63–67.

Zhou, Yumin 周育民. *Wan Qing caizheng yu shehui bianqian* 晚清财政与社会变迁 [Financial and social changes in the late Qing]. Shanghai renmin chubanshe, 2000.

Zhou, Zhichu 周志初, Wan Qing caizheng jingji yanjiu 晚清财政經濟研究 [Research into fiscal policy and economy during the late Qing]. Qirushushe, 2002.

Zolberg, A. R. "Origins of the Modern World System: A Missing Link." *World Politics* 33, no. 2 (1981): 253–81.

Zuo, Zongtang 左宗棠. Zuo Wenxiang gong quan ji 左文襄公全集 [The collected works of Zuo Zongdang]. Edited by Yang shulin 楊書霖. Vol. 2, no. 19. Wenhaichubanshi, 1979.

Index

Note: Page numbers in *italic* refer to figures and appendix. References followed by "n" refer to notes.

abandoned people (*qimin*), 52
Acapulco, 48
Act of Settlement, 232
Adams, John Quincy, 166
Admiral Baudin and Indien, 208
Admiral Drury's occupation of Macao, 123
Admiral Perry's Black Ships, 221
Afghanistan, 294n11
African slaves, 83–84; trade, 84
age of partnership, 52
Ahow, 288n153
Aigun, Treaty of (*Aihuntiaoyue*), 144
Aisin Gioro Hala (the imperial family of the Qing regime), 119
Aizawa Yasushi, 221
Alaska, 165
Amherst Embassy, 103
Amity and Commerce, Treaty of, 318
Amoy, 41, 77, 97, 108, *242–44, 246–47*
Amur: river, 144, 170; region, 49, 145–46
ancien régime, 2–4, 19–20, 25, 40, 80, 93, 114, 133, 138, 156, 195, 213, 253n5, 329n30, 329n34–35, 340n80
Anglo-Japanese Alliance, 170, 189
Anglo-Japanese Friendship Treaty, 317n82
Anhakchu, 258n47
Anhui, 73, 79, 282n69

Annam, 51, 144, 306n144. *See* Vietnam
annexation of Hawaii, 165
Ansei Treaties, 221
Aral and Caspian Seas, 170
Arctic Ocean (*Beibingyang*), 144
Arrow Incident, 298n64, 318n82
Arthur, Chester A, 228
Arthur MacArthur, 166
"Asiatic mode" of production, 4
Assam, 57, 75, 90, 169; colonial, 233; Indian colony of, 233n69
Atlantic: frontier, 194; ocean world, 169; trade, 164
axial division of labor system, 25, 45, 46
Ayung, 288n53

Baltic Sea (*Boluodehai*), 144
baojia (household registrations), 272n46
barbarian/*yi*, 27
barbaric state, 223
barbarism, 197
Batavia, 15, 49, 51, *248*
Beiyang Army, 138
Beiyang Fleet, 137
Belgium *141*, 186, 320n99
Bengal, 64, 67, 103, 275n93
Bezaure, Comte de, 188

389

Biguanzishou (closed-door policies), 124–25, 221
black tea, 31, 73, 108, 282n69
Board of Foreign Affairs (*Waiwupu*), 142
Bo Gui, 208
Bombay, 104, 279n17
Boston, 164, 166
Boxer Protocol, 223, 333n88; Rebellion, 156, 189, 223–24; Uprising, 193, 206
Boxers, 193, 223, 333n88
Brazil, 85–86, 141, 188, 271n43
British-led opium trade, 50, 219, 298n64
British East India Company, ix, *58*, 64, 80, 103, 126, 269n21, 270n37, 273n67, 278n7, 282n69, 306n143, 318n82
British India, *71*, 75, 147, 279n17
British opium trade, 15. *See* British-led opium trade
British textiles, 64
Bu Dingbang, 288n153
Bunkyū Reforms, 221
Burma, 12, 118, 144–47, 306n144

Calcutta, India, 67
California, 88–90, 166, 314n31, 314n36
Cambodia, 51, 139
canal system, 96, 98, 290n181
Canton system, 57, 59, 103, 125, 127
caobian (straw weaving), 185
caoyun (tribute grain), 95
capitalist: development, 27, 82, 114, 115, 236, 257n30, 291n204, 338n44; integration, 29; mode of production, 16, 23–24, 33, 43–44, 48, 82, 115, 225, 232, 235, 278n6, 288n154; modernity, 4; space, 181–84, 219, 235–36, 239, 341n87; state, 3, 19, 230
Caribbean colonists, 194
Caribbean islands, 85
Carta Mercatoria, 140
cavalry, 123, 131. *See also* cavalrymen
cavalrymen, 155, 299n71
Central Asia, 13, 145, 161, 169–71, 177
Ceylon, ix, 57, *76*, 77, 233
Changchun, 189

Ch'angnyongho, 9
Chang Yen-mao, 238
cheap labor, 43, 46, 81–82, 85–86, 90, 286n129
cheap laborers, 85, 111
Chee Hsin Cement Company, 238
Chefoo Convention (*Yantaitiaoyue*), 147
Chen Baochen, 202
Chen Duxiu, 229
Chengdu, 100, 206
Chen Shu-Tang 320n100
Chien Lung, 90
China-Korea Treaty, 8, 60
China Imperial Maritime Customs, 73
China Merchants' Steam Navigation Company, 237
China's: Decline, 3, 7, 18–19, 156; junk trade, 269n21
China's imperial examination (*keju*), 199
China Steamship Company, 237
Chincha Islands of Peru, 84
Chinese Communist Party (CPC) 229, 324n142, 338n40, 341n88
Chinese coolie, 34, 46, 53, 82–86, 88–89, 110–11, 195, 203, 206–13, 225, *242–51*, 284n109, 285n116, 285n118, 293n230, 340n80
Chinese crimps, 86, 209, 287
Chinese Exclusion Act, 228
Chinese Maritime Customs Service, 17
Chinese silk, 39, 270n37
Chinese stagnation studies, xii
Chinese tea, xi, 46, 52, 57, *58*, 58–59, 64–65, 67, 75–78, 90, 105–7, 111, 148, 164–65, 233, 277n113, 282n69, 282n79; makers, 90; producers, 52, 75
Chonghou, 145
Chosŏn government, 258n47, 259n50
Chow Aaon, 288n153
Chuanbizhizhan (the second battle of Chuenpi), 304n118
Chungcheng Province, 259n50
Chun Mau Yung, 288n153
Chy Lung, 90

Cixi, Empress Dowager, 137, 198–99, 223, 329n32, 329n34, 333n88
closed-door policy, 124, 221
Cohong system, 92, 100
commercial capitalism, 41, 43
Company Law, 238
compradors, 11, 51, 81, 91–92, 111, 182, 184, 233–34, 236, 288n153–54, 288n156
Confucian: doctrine, 137, 196, 201, 332n79; elites, 120; ideological system, 194; ideology, 6, 39, 120–21, 194, 196, 223, 297n60, 336n15; orthodoxy, 203; practices, 120; principles, 137, 197, 228; values, 194, 198, 200–2, 213
Convention of Peking (*Beijingtiaoyue*), 145, 170
coolie: labor, 83–84, 90, 109–10; recruitment, 84, 207, 209, 287n135; ships, 84, 195, 210–13, *242–51*; traders, 88
core-periphery relationships, 227; structures, 13
core-semiperiphery-periphery dynamic, 24
coup de grace, 177
Crimean War, 220, 318
Cuba, 83–85, 109–10, 166, 207, 211–13, *243–46*, 248, 250, 286n124, 286n127, 286n130, 287n142, 294n11, 340n80
Cushing, Caleb, 166–67

Dagukouchuanboshijian, 151–52, 157
Dah Sun Mill, 238
Dalian, 182–84, 189, 226, 323n132, 324n146
Daoguang Emperor, 69, 128, 140, 259
daponggpao, 282n69
Daqinglüli (the Laws and Precedents of the Great Qing), 299n77
Dasheng cotton mill, 337n28
Dashishan (Australia), 131
Davis, John Frances, 128
Dayan Khan, 122, 298n67
de Goyer, Peter, 139
Deokheungho incident, 320
dependency theory, 41–43, 269n20

Dinghai, 57, 129, 132
Ding Richang, 305n130
disenchantment (*entzauberung*), 4
Donghak Peasant Revolution, 176
Duan Fang, 150
Dungan Revolt, 173
Dupont, Samuel F, 52–53
Dutch East India Company, 306n143
Dutch East Indies, 53
dynastic cycle, 40, 114, 268n12
dynasty-based approach, 15

East Africa, 46
East Asian dynamics, 29
East Asian region, 29–30, 60, 123, 161, 322n125
East India Company (EIC), 57–58, 64–65, 70, 80, 103, 126, 263n107, 269n21, 270n37, 273n67, 278n7, 282n69, 306n143, 318n82
Eastern Siberia, 49, 220
Eight Banners, 149, 311n187
Elements of International Law, 149–50
Ellies, Henry, 103
Elliot, Charles, 128, 301n89
Eluosi Wenguan (Russian College), 133
emancipation reform, 168
Emperor Daoguang, 69, 128–29, 140, 259n50; Guangxu, 31, 76, 186, 198–99, 329n33; Jiaqing, 68; Kangxi, 95–96, 131, 143, 271n45, 274n73, 299n77, 307n147, 309n164; Qianlong, 96, 144, 200, 261n75, 273n67, 289n173, 300n77, 306n143; Xianfeng, 329n32; Yongle, 95, 199; Yongzheng, 52, 254n9
Eurasia, 12–14, 21, 261n75, 275n89
Eurocentric bias, 50 *See also* Eurocentric idea
Eurocentric idea, 26, 49, 149, 272n55
European world-economy, 24, 29, 43, 51, 65, 272n55, 300n85
Europe's exceptionalism, 4
evangelism, 203, 205
exchange of preciosities, 49–50, 111

exploitation: of Chinese resources, 10; of nature, 79; of coolie, 210, 212; of the capitalist space economy, 236; of the peasantry, 334n117
export-oriented: commodity production, 218; crop, 34, 46, 72, 209, 219, 222; industries, 45; plantations, 85; sericulture, 39; soybean cultivation, 184; sugar cultivation, 86; tea cultivation, 52, 73, 80; tea industry, 31
external influences, 3, 7, 19, 47, 225, 231
external pressure, 2, 133, 172, 194, 268n12, 317n82
extraterritorial: jurisdiction rights, 155; privileges, 149; rights, 154

Fairbank, John K, 8, 93, 217, 331n67
Fang Dongshu, 200
Fanning (be fooled by), 175
Feng Guifen, 305n130
Ferry, Jules, 188
First Sino-Japanese War, 26, 60, 137–38, 171, 173, 176–77, 185, 189–90, 221, 224, 306n142, 319n97
Florida cession in 1819, 164
Folangxi (France), 131
Foochow Shipbuilding Institution, *134*
foreign aggression, 2
foreign intervention, 43, 138
Foreign Concessions in China, *154*
foreign language school, *158*
foreign maritime customs, 17
Fort Zelandia, 51
Foshan, 30, 109
Fourth Anglo-Dutch War, 57
Freycinet, Charles de, 188
Fujian, 49, 56, 73, 75, 77, 79, 85, 131, 206, 233, 282n69, 299n77, 305n142
Fujianxuzhi (The gazetteer of Fujian), 73
Fujita Yukoku, 221
Fukuzawa Yukichi, 173
fur: markets, 48; trade, 48
Fuzhou (Fuhchau), 73–74, 76–77, 97, 105, *134*, 136, 299n77, 304n128, 305n128, 337n32

Gansu, 123
Gapsin Coup, 176
Gelaohui (Elders Brothers Society), 331n54
General Rules for Merchants, 238
General Sherman incident in Korea, 319n95
gentlemen (*junzi*), 119, 201, 228–29
gentry militia, 38, 204, 214
geopolitical: competition, 13; dynamics, 14, 159, 309; order, 33
germination of capitalism, 231. *See* sprouts of capitalism
Ghent, Treaty of, 84
global: connected history, 5; dynamics, 2, 15, 21, 31; hegemony, 118, 160, 162, 294n14; history, 1, 18–19, 37, 49, 55, 60, 129; political economy, 7
Gold Rush, 88, 314n31
Gongchuanshuileitushuo, 304n127
Gongxinghao, 320n100
Goto Shinpei, 190
government-led industrialization, 172
government-supervision and merchant-operation (*Kuan tu shang pan*), 237–38, 340n80
Grand Council (*junjichu*), 196, 354n9
Grand Canal, 94–98, 112, 290n181–82
Grant, Ulyssess S, 319
great divergence, 1, 5–6, 8, 116, 121
Great Game, 170
Great Reforms under Alexander II, 167
green tea, 75, 90, 282n69
Gu Hongming, 306
Gutian, 206
Gu-gong-he-tong, 83
Guam, 166
Guan (government), 54
Guan Tong, 124
Guangdong, 30–31, 49, 69, *72*, 85, 103, 109, 128, 130, 200, 204, 208, 234, 254, 271n45, 285n119, 299n77, 336n15
Guangxi, 68–69, 109, 271n45, 336n15
Guangzhouwan, 185
Guizhou, 68

Gunboat diplomacy, 127, 154, 170, 319n95
Guo Songtao, 198

Haikou Quantu, 131
Hailam (Hainan), 85, *247*, 308n152
Haiti, 84, *246*
Haitian Revolution, 84
Hakka, 85, 109, 285n118
Hakodate, *247*, 317n82
Hamilton Fish, 319n95
Han Chinese, 12, 75, 130, 181–83, 214, 224, 323n128, 334n118
handicraft-based weaving industry, 64
Hankou, 74, 105–7, 112, 154, 187, 228, 289n162, 326n167
Hanlin Academy, 197, 306n144
Han Rivers (*Han Jiang*), 105
Hanyang, 106, 189
Hanyang Ironworks, 237
Havana, 88, 251
Hawaii, 86, 165, 315n40
Helan (Netherlands), 131
Henghua/Hokchia, 85
hereditary charisma, 119
Herrschaft, 142
hetonghe, 95
Heungseon Daewongun, 174
historical capitalism, 82, 217, 230
Hobukch'aep'yo, 259n48
Hojo, 175, 320n101
Hokchiu, 85
Hokkaido, 221
Hokkien, 85
hongmaoren (red-haired people), 273n67
Hong merchants, 59, *72*, 125, 127, 279n17, 301n94
Hong Yeong-sik, 321n114
House of Commons, 58, 86
Hu-Guang Railroad, 188–89
Hua-hsin Mill, 238
Huaian, 96
Huai Army, 138
Huang En-tong, 305n130
Huangqi (Germany), 131

Huangyu quanlan tu (the Kangxi Atlas), 309n164
Hubei, 105, 110, *135*, 286n125
Hubei Guangji Xingguo Coal Mine, *135*
Hugli, 104
Hui-tong-si-yi-guan, 139, 306n144
Huizhou merchant, 6, 96, 98
Hunan, 30–31, 109–10, 200, 331n54; merchants, 31
Hundred Days' reform, 329n33; *huolunche* (train), 186; *hushi zhuguo*, 139
Hyde, Hodge & Co, 207

Ilibu, 132
Iliyang, 130
Imo Incident, 176
impact-response approach, 8, 11, 19–20, 261n61, 317n75
Imperial Telegraph Administration, 237
incorporating comparison, 27–28, 31–32, 266n138, 268n1
incorporating dynamics, 22, 27, 30–32, 218–19, 222
indentured labor system, 88
Indian Ocean world, 54, 126
Indian subcontinent, 42, 47, 64, 103, 217, 220, 264n114
Indonesia, 46, 51, 139, *245*, *247*
Industrialization, 23, 138, 167, 169, 172, 183, 186, 224–25, 236–37, 278n6
informal imperialism, 9
instrumental Marxism, 262n102
interconnected histories, 8. See interlinked history
interlinked history, 34, 45, 46–47, 50
international division of labor system, 34, 49, 82, 110, 148, 184, 195, 210. See also axial division of labor
interstate competition; 7, 13–14, 116–18, 121, 297n55
Irish potatoes, 48
Isolationism, 174

Jaisohn, Philip, 321n114

Japan-owned First Bank, 9
Japanese colonization, 29, 219
Jardine Matheson and Company, 59, 101, 276n102
Jejeebhoy, Jamsetjee, 279n17
jen (humaneness), 201
Jiangnan, 95–96, 98, *134*, 136, 200, 254n9, 289n173, 293n226, 304n128
  Arsenal, 136, 304n128
Jiangsu, 20, 226, 299n77
Jiangxi, 110, 277n1, 282n69
Jiansheng, 199
Jianyangshan, 79
Jiaozhou Bay, 182, 184–85
jiaxiang (cangue), 68
joint-stock companies, 167, 234
junk trade, 42, 269n21, 275n94; ships, 132

Kaiping Coal Mines, 237–38; Mining Bureau, *135*
Kang Guangren, 199
Kanghwa Treaty, 174
Kangnamch'aep'yo, 259n48
Kang Youwei, 199
kaozheng, 196, 200
kaozheng xue, 200
Kashgar (Kashigaer), 144
Kashmir, 170
Keiō Reforms, 221
Keyzer, Jacob de, 139
Khun-ch'un (*Hunchun*), 146
Kiakhta, 105
Kiautschou Bay, 189
Kim Byŏnghak, 174
Kim Ok-gyun, 176
King Gojong, 174, 312n213, 319n95, 321n113–14
King of Silver, 48
Kobe, 318n82, 320n100
Kong Jixun, 204
koutou, 298
Kowloon Peninsula, 185
Kucheng Massacre, 206
Kuomintang (KMC), 229

Kyakhta, Treaty of, 144
Kyojuch'aep'yo, 259

labor-intensive: accumulation, 233; agricultural system, 120; guilds, 337; plantations, 90; transportation, 198, 325n162
labor-saving technology, 271
Lady Hughes incident, 123
Lanchou Official Mining Company, 238
Lanzhou Arsenal, *135*
laws on company registration, 238
Lee Chew, 90
legal imperialism, 155; imperium, 149
Lhasa, Treaty of, 171
Liang Qichao, 137, 199, 217, 302n105, 329n33
Liaocheng, 96
Liaotung Peninsula, 322n117
libu (the Ministry of Rites), 139
Li Dazhao, 229
lifanyuan, 139
Li Hongzao, 198
Li Hongzhang, 53, 137–38, 142, 150, 174–75, 182, 186–87, 189, 202, 222, 305n131, 306n146, 320n98, 320n105, 337n32
likin (transit dues), 76, 310n182
Lin Xu, 199
Linyin (Denmark), 131
Lin Zexu, 128–30
Li Shuchang, 305n130
Li Tangjie, 198
Liu Guangdi, 199
Liu Mingchuan, 186
Livadia, Treaty of, 145
local: elites, 2, 19, 119, 336n16; governance, 38–39
long-distance: overseas trade, 56; trade, 23, 49–50, 272n55; sea trade, 117; staple trade, 49–50
Lord Castlereagh, 140
Lord Palmerston, 140
Lord William Amherst, 124–25, 139, 259n50. *See* Amherst Embassy

Louisiana Purchase, 164
Louis XIII, 116
lower Yangtze: basin, 108, 218; River, 30
Low, Frederick, 319n95
Lue Gim Gong, 90
Lu Kun, 128
Lüshun, 182
Lu Xun, 229

Macau, 51
Machine Manufacture of Jiangnan, 134
Madras, 104
magic garden (*zaubergarten*), 4, 255n16
Ma Jianzhong, 197, 306n146
Malacca, 15
Malthusian trap, 1, 48, 256n22
Malwa, 67, 103
Manchu: Governance, 119; Government, 224, 271n45; regime, 196; identity, 12; origin, 12
Manchukuo, 183, 227, 322n124, 323n138, 324n142. *See also* puppet state
Manila galleon, 48, 110
Mao Zedong, 10, 231
maritime trade, 51, 53–54, 263n107, 274n73, 275n94
Martinique, 208
Marxism, 227, 262n102
Marx, Karl, 4–5, 10, 19, 23–24, 51, 67, 82, 238, 255n18, 255n20, 262n102, 266n138, 336n15
Masulipatnam, 103
May Fourth Movement, 229
McMichael, Philip, 28–31, 218, 266n136, 266n138, 268n1
Meiji Restoration, 220–21
mercantile capitalists, 90
Merchant-led capitalist economic system, 340n80
merchants without empire, 54
Messrs Tait & Co, 207
methodological internalism, 81, 257n31
Mexican-American War, 164
Minbei area, 73, 79, 275n89

Ming-Qing China (Ming–Qing continuum), 11–12
Ming dynasty, 3, 122, 222, 270n38, 277n1, 298n68, 302n105, 306n143
Ming Xu, 145
Ming Yi, 145
Ministry of Justice (*xingbu*), 68
Min River (*minjiang*), 73
Mok Shing, 288n153
Mongolian, 12, 122, 183, 261n75, 311n187
Monopolization, 1, 43, 116, 263n107
Mori Arinori, 175
Mount Niaoshi (*niaoshishan*), 73
Muraviev, Nikolai, 220
Muslim revolts, 145
Mutinies, 210
Myanmar, 139, 307n147

Nanjing (Nanking), 95, 100, 136, 229, 290n182; Arsenal, *134*
Nankeens, *70*
Nanking, Treaty of, 102, 140, 340n77
Nanning, 226
Napier, William John, 127–28
Nawab of Bengal, 64
Neo-Confucianism, 9
Nerchinsk, Treaty of, 118, 309n164
new Qing history, 11–12, 19, 21, 260n61
Nicholas I, 220
Ningbo, 68, 105, 184, 188, 273n67, 274n73, 282n69, 299n77

Old Summer Palace (*Yuanmingyuan*), 124
Open Door Policy, 167, 316n55
Opium: brokers, 80, 128; consumption, 67–68, 129, 225; cultivation, 66–68, 223; cultivators, 66; dens, 70, *72*, 128; market, 67, 279n17; production, 59, 224; prohibition, *72*, 131, 149; smoking, 67; smuggling, 67, 69–70, *72*, 103; wars (the First Opium War; the Second Opium War), 7, 26, 38, 43, 54, 60, 85, 99, 103, 115, 122–25, 131, 133, 138, 141, 143, 149, 156, 174, 214, 224, 236, 304n127, 334n118

Orientalism, 119, 152; in reverse (Reverse Orientalism), 119
Ottoman empire, 47, 117, 156
overseas Chinese businesses, 26, 236; workers, 53

Pacific Ocean, 162, 166, 169, 220, 269n21
Pacific powers, 26, 159–61, 168, 172, 177, 180–82, 184–87, 190–91, 219–20, 222, 226–27, 317n75, 329n34
Pan Shichung, 304n127
Paris Peace Conference, 229
Park Yeong-hyo, 321n114
path dependence, 232
patrimonial governance, 119–20
patrimonialism, 195
Pax Britannica, 191
"pax Manjurica," 196
Pearl Concubine, 199
Peking Treaty, 73
period of the sleeping giant, 3
peripheralization, 42–43, 264n114
periphery, 13, 24, 30, 42–44, 60, 193, 232, 235, 266n136, 283n88, 322n125
Perry Expedition, 165
Persian (or Parsi) traders, 67
Peru, 84–85, 89, 109–10, *141*, 211–13, *242–43*, *246–49*, 286n124, 287n142, 294n11, 340n80
Peter the Great, 168, 261n75
piglet (*zhuzai*), 83, 285n111
Poor Law, 232
porcelain, 48, 56–57, 64, 102, 166, 270n38
Port Arthur, 170, 185, 189
Port Era, Treaty, 108
Portsmouth, Treaty of, 183
precapitalist mode of production, 16, 24, 44
Prince Gong, 142, 145, 150, 197–98, 222, 329n32
proletariat, 80, 82, 213, 231
protection-providing enterprise, 43
Puerto Rico, 166
Punti, 109
puppet state, 183, 322n124, 323n138. See also Manchukuo

Putaoya (Portugal), 131

Qianlong nei fu yu tu, 144
Qi Junzao, 198
qimin (abandoned people), 52
Qing: bureaucracy, 137, 187, 214, 329n32, 335n13; dynasty, 6, 103, 139, 153, *181*, 235, 306n143, 321n114, 323n128; imperial family, 196; imperialism, 119; regime, 2, 6, 10, 13–14, 40, 43, 48, 52–54, 72, 92, 94–95, 119–24, 127–28, 131, 133, 136, 139, 143, 145–46, 149, 153–57, 170, 173–75, 180, 187–88, 195–96, 199, 214, 222–23, 230, 271n46, 273n62, 296n44, 299n77, 309n164, 317n75, 320n100, 324n142, 333n88, 335n118, 335n13, 336n16
Qing dai yitong ditu, 144
qingjiangpu, 95
qingyi, 198, 329n27, 329n30
Qi Shan, 129–30
Queen Min, 321n114; Victorica, 129, 307n152

racial conflicts, 214
railway: concession, 185–90; Beijing-Hankou, 187, 326n167; Guangzhou-Kowloon, 188; Shanghai-Ningbo, 188; the Chinese Eastern, 189; South Manchuria, 189–90, 229; Woosung, 188; Tianjin-Pukou, 188; Trans-Siberian, 148, 169 189, 220, 310n182
raw silk, 70, 270n37, 277n113
Reciprocity Treaty, 86
resistance movements, 35, 39, 104, 191, 193–95, 197, 203, 206–7, 210, 212–14, *215*, 227, 329n34, 330n34
Rev. J. E. Walker, 79
Rev. Justus Doolittle, 74
Revolt of the Three Feudatories, 119, 131
river networks, 94
Robert & Co, 207
Rodgers, John, 319n95
rump state, 113
Russian Cotton Spinning Company, 167
Russia's: eastward expansion, 168; expansion plan, 170; imperial sphere, 169; tea trade,

106, 310n182; territorial expansion 145, 148, 169–70, 177
Russo-Japanese War, 180, 183, 189, 221, 326n180
Ryukyu Kingdom, 219

Sakhalin, 221
salt trade, 96
Samarkand (*Samaerhan*), 144, 169
samurai, 172, 221
sanfanzhiluan (the Revolt of the Three Feudatories), 131
Sanyuanli Incident, 38, 204, 214, 268n5, 331n70
sea ban policy (*haijinzhengce*), 54, 299n77. See closed-door policies
seamless web of commercial interactions, 51
seasonal workers, 73
Sech'angyanghaeng, 9, 258n45
secret societies, 120, 296n50, 331n54, 331n70
Selden Map of China, 54, 274
Self–Strengthening Movement, 40, 133–38, 156, 304n127, 305n129, 305n131, 305n142, 329n34
sericulture, 39
Seven Years' War, 57
Seward, William, 166
shack people (*pengmin*), 74, 79, 281n55
Shanghai: City Council, 239; Concession, 100; Cotton Cloth Mill, 237; International Settlement, 99, *154*, 188
Shanghai jiqi zhibu ju, 235
Shantou, 53, 97, 109–10, *244–45*, 251
Shanxi traders, 148
Shaowu, 79
Shaoxing, 68
Shat fan-Kuei, ta fan-Kuei, 204
Sheng Xuanhuai, 288n156, 340n83
Shengyuan, 199
shijing (a classic poem), 297n60
Shimonoseki, Treaty of, 60, 176, 206, 313n5, 321n117
Shim Sanghak, 320n99
shi yi zhi changji yi zhi yi, 136
Showa Steel Works, 324n142

shuishi (water force), 131
Siam, 15, 51, *242*
Sichuan, 68, 110, *135*, 144, 206, 271n45
Sichuan Arsenal, *135*
sick man of Asia, 3
Sikkim-Tibet Convention, 147
silk: export, 39; industry, 39; market, 39
silk-reeling industry, 235
silver: mines, 31, 277n1, 283n88; outflow, 13, 64–66, 69–70, 128, 222, 336n15; standard, 48, 63; trade, 31, 48, 51, 63–65, 69
Simao , 226
Singapore, 53, 75, 90, 242–44
Sino-French War, 138, 187, 224, 305n142, 329n32, 329n34
Sino-Japanese Friendship and Trade Treaty, 173, 175
Sinocentrism, 9, 119
Six Boards (*liubu*), 199
slave labor, 46, 83
Smeird & Co, 207
Social Darwinism, 227
Society of the Divine Word, 206
Society of the Heaven and the Earth, 120
Songluoshan, 282
Song Xue, 200
South China Sea, 15, 54, 274n76
Southern Manchuria, 61, 190, 229
Southern Song, 113
sovereignty, 27, 138, 142–43, 152–53, 166, 223, 228
soybean: exports, 180; trade, 180
Spanish-American War, 166
Spanish merchants, 270n37
sprouts of capitalism (*zibenzhuyimengyalun*), 230
"state-resisting protests," 194
"state engaging-based protests," 194
Statute of Artificers, 232
Steamship Navigation Company, 135
Su-Leng-e, 69
Subei, 20
sugar plantations, 46, 83–84, 86, 91
Sulu, 139, *244*, 306n144
Sun I-yen, 2

Sun Yat-sen, 227, 335n118
Suqian, 96
Surat, 103
Suriname, 85–86
Suzerain-vassal relations, 174
suzerainty, 9, 171, 174
Suzhou, 94, 96, 98, *134*, *154*, 231, 290n174
Suzhou Foreign Artillery Bureau, 134
sweet potatoes, 48
"switchmen" (*Weichensteller*), 2
Syme, Muir, and Company, 207

Tahiti, 86
Taiping Rebellion, 6, 73, 104, 109, 224–25, 235, 325n160, 336n15
Tait & Co, 207
Taiwan, 15, 51, 60, 73, *74*, 108, 131, *135*, 144, 164, 277n113, 322n117
Taiyuan, 100
Taizhou, 68
Tamgŏlsaeng, 9, 51
Tamsui, 73
Tang Jingxing, 92
Tan Sitong, 199
Tan Tingxiang, 52–53
Taoyuan Plateau, 73
Tarbagatai, Treaty of, 145
Tashkent (*Tashigan*), 144, 169
tea: agriculture, 52, 75; consumption, 46, 52, 56–57, 65; exports, 46, 75–78, 80, 111, 233, 282n71; factories (*chachang*), 74, 75, 233; guilds, 106; industry, 31, 77–78, 164, 233, 282n79; pickers, 73; plantations, 75–76, 90, 233, 281n69; seller, 76; warehouses, 75, 106; workers, 73–75
tea-horse market, 123
tea-industry workers, 76
tea-silver trade, 65
Tennessee, 88
Teochiu, 85
Texas annexation, 164
Théophile Delcassé, 188
Thirteen Factory system, 103
Thirteenth-century world-system, 47

Thomas Francis Wade, 9
Thubten Gyatso, 171
Tianjin (Tientsin): Arsenal, *134*; Navy College, *135*; Telegraph General Administration, *135*; Massacre, 198, 328n24; Treaties of, 140
Tibet, 12, 118, 139, 146–47, 171, 260n70, 275n93, 317n75, 317n77, 317n78
Tilly, Charles, 3, 7, 116, 267n143
Tong King-Sing, 233–34, 238
Tongriamun, 320n101
Tongwenguan, 133, 136
Tonkin, 51, 187
ton'ya, 172
Torghuts, 14, 261
Tongsunt'ae, 9, 258n47, 259n49
Triads, 120
triangular India-China-Britain trade, 15
tributary relationship, 9, 127, 173–74, 176, 273n62, 277n113, 297n55; states, 121, 139, 173, 273n62, 297n58, 306n143; system, 25, 40, 121, 139, 155, 176–77, 190, 219, 273n62, 297n58, 306n143
Tripartite Intervention, 189
Tsiang Tingfu, 133
Tudor monarchs of England, 116
Tung Wah Hospital, 293n230
Tu Renshou, 197
Turner & Co, 207
Tusi, 146
Twenty-One Demands, 229
Tyler, John, 167

Underdevelopment, 5, 7, 10–11, 19, 26, 41–42, 52, 157, 231, 236, 256n22
unequal exchange, 43, 89, 184, 236, 269n25, 286n127; networks, 22; relationship, 26–27, 42, 149, 236, 277n113; trades, 44, 332n83
uneven geographical development, 236
"urban–rural split," 16
US hegemony, 162
US-China trade, 164, 166
US-Japan trade, 166

Vereenigde Oostindische Compagnie (VOC), 57, 270n38, 273n65, 275n94, 276n96, 276n104
Vietnam, 65, 131, 139, 144, 187, 277n113, 306n143, 307n147, 318n82
Vladivostok, 148, 189, 220, 310n182

wage labor(wage laborers), 83, 232
Wang Bingxie, 202
Wang Liu, 280n41
Wang Tao, 305n130
Wanguogongbao, 186
Wang Wenshao, 186, 197
Wanshan mountains, 75
Warring States period, 221
Weihaiwai, 185
Wei Yuan, 186, 200
Weng Tonghe, 197
Wenzhou, 68, 85, 308n152
Western Disturbance in the Shinmi Year, 174
West Indies, 83–84, *86*, 110
Wheaton, Henry, 148–52, 155
Witte, Sergei, 169, 189
Wo Ren, 137
Wuchang, 100, 106
wukoutongshangdachen, 141
Wusong, 208
Wuxi, 96
Wuyi Mountains, 73, 280n47, 282n69

Xiamen, 76–77, 105, 109–10, 132, *154*, 207, 274n73, 303n114
Xian, 100
xian (area), 75
xiang (countryside), 75
Xinjiang, 12, 13, 68, 118, 139, 144–46, 148, 170
Xu Jiyu, 186
Xu Run, 92
Xue Fucheng, 147, 186
Xunxing (imperial tour of inspection), 95
Xuzhou, 96
Yahang (Chinese traders or brokers), 273n67
Yan Botao, 132

Yan Fu, 228
Yang Fang, 130
Yangmingism, 200
Yang Rui, 199
Yang Shenxiu, 199
Yangtze River basin, 94; valley, 5; navy, *141*
Yang Yongyan, 204
Yangzhou, 96
Yantai, 226
Yanzhou, 68
yellow peril, 228
Yellow River, 95–96
Yiheyanghang (Jardine Matheson and Company), 59
Yili Zhong-Exinjiu jiehe tu (a map with the old and new borders of Ili between Qing China and Russia), 146
Yingjili (England), 131
Yingkou, 180–*81*, 182, 184, 226, 323n132, 324n146
Yinqi (a negative energy), 130
Yokohama, 318
Youhaifangerwuhaizhan (maintaining sea defense without sea battle), 303n106
Younghusband, Colonel Francis, 171, 317n77
Yuan dynasty, 123
Yuan Shikai, 174, 229, 321n105
Yunnan, 187
Yunnan Copper Mines, 135
Yu Qiaqing, 92
Yu Yue, 202

Zeng Guofan, 200, 222, 328n24
Zeng Jize, 150
Zhaijiao, 206
Zhan Tianyou, 133
Zhang Garden, 100
Zhang Xianqing, 3
Zhang Zhidong, 186, 198, 306n146, 337n32
Zhejiang province, 229, 234, 273n67, 282n69, 299n77
Zheng Bozhao, 288
Zheng Chenggong, 131

Zheng Guanying, 150
Zheng He, 302n105
Zheng Jing, 131
Zhou Xuexi, 288n156
Zhoushan, 130
Ziyiju (the popularly elected provincial councils), 223

zongfan (suzerain-vassal relations), 174
Zongligeguoshiwuyamenqingdang, *141*
Zongliyamen (a proto-foreign office), 133, 138–42, 151, 156–57, 175, 197–99, 213, 308n155, 312n201
Zunghar Mongols, 13
Zuo Zongtang, 77

www.ingramcontent.com/pod-product-compliance
Ingram Content Group UK Ltd.
Pitfield, Milton Keynes, MK11 3LW, UK
UKHW051851210426
5322IPUK00025B/659